Legal Theories

A Historical Introduction to Philosophy of Law

Paul Groarke

OXFORD

UNIVERSITY PRESS

OXFORD
UNIVERSITY PRESS

Oxford University Press is a department of the University of Oxford.
It furthers the University's objective of excellence in research, scholarship,
and education by publishing worldwide. Oxford is a registered trade mark of
Oxford University Press in the UK and in certain other countries.

Published in Canada by
Oxford University Press
8 Sampson Mews, Suite 204,
Don Mills, Ontario M3C 0H5 Canada

www.oupcanada.com

Copyright © Oxford University Press Canada 2013

The moral rights of the author have been asserted

Database right Oxford University Press (maker)

Library and Archives Canada Cataloguing in Publication

Groarke, Paul
Legal theories : a historical introduction to philosophy of law / Paul Groarke.

Includes index.
ISBN 978-0-19-543187-2

1. Law—Philosophy—Textbooks. 2. Law—Canada—Cases. I. Title.

K230.G76 2013   340'.1   C2012-906221-9

Cover image: Thomas Barwick/Getty Images

This book is printed on permanent (acid-free) paper ∞.

Printed and bound in the USA

1 2 3 4 — 16 15 14 13

Brief Contents

Contents

2 | The Christian Tradition   30

Thomas Aquinas   30

Reading

Discussion

3 | The Shift to Natural Rights and the Political Contract 51

Hugo Grotius and Samuel von Pufendorf 51

Readings

4 | Early Scientism: Law Is the Science of Judges and Places Limits on the King 74

Edward Coke, William Blackstone, and John Marshall 74

Readings

Discussion

5 | Law Is a Product of Utility or Pure Reason 97

Jeremy Bentham and Immanuel Kant 97

Readings

6 | Legal Positivism: The Political Order Takes Precedence 122

John Austin, Thomas Hill Green, and Albert Venn Dicey 122

Readings

From *The Province of Jurisprudence Determined*, by John Austin 123

From *Lectures on the Principles of Political Obligation*, by Thomas Hill Green 127

From *Introduction to the Study of the Law of the Constitution*, by Albert Venn Dicey 130

Discussion

7 | Modern Scientism: Formalism, Legal Skepticism, and Pragmatism   149

Christopher Columbus Langdell, Oliver Wendell Holmes, and Roscoe Pound   149

Readings

From *A Selection of Cases on the Law of Contracts*, by Christopher Columbus Langdell   149

From a "Book Notice" on Langdell's *A Selection of Cases on the Law of Contracts*, by Oliver Wendell Holmes   150

From "Mechanical Jurisprudence," by Roscoe Pound   152

Discussion

Langdell Believed that the Study of Law Should Be Based on the Scientific Method   158

    Formalism Is Based on Inductive as well as Deductive Principles   159

        The First Stage of the Formalist Analysis Is Inductive   159

        The Second and Third Stages Are Deductive   160

        Formalism Sees the Law as a Set of Logical Rules   160

    The Methodology of Formalism Can Be Applied to Statutory Law   160

        The Use of the Formalist Analysis in Statutory Interpretation Raises Questions with regard to Coherence and Political Authority   161

    Formalism Has Affinities with Legal Positivism   161

        The Formalists Shared the Positivists' Interest in Codification   161

        The Methodological Premises of Formalism Nevertheless Recall the Natural Law   162

        Formalism Prevents Us from Examining the Moral Views on which the Law Is Based   162

    Formalism Draws Attention to the Role of the Judiciary   162

        Formalism Fails to Recognize the Vagaries in the Determination of Facts   163

        Formalism Has Difficulty Explaining the Conflicting Rulings in the Caselaw   163

Holmes Argues that Formalism Fails to Capture the Role of Experience in the Common Law   164

    Holmes Rejects Langdell's Rationalism   164

8 | Constitutionalism: Legal Skepticism and the Doctrine of the Living Tree   172

Albert Venn Dicey, Oliver Wendell Holmes, and John Sankey   172

Readings

Discussion

9 | Legal Realism Adopts an External Perspective   200

Karl Llewellyn and Jerome Frank   200

Readings

From "A Realistic Jurisprudence—the Next Step," by Karl Llewellyn   200

From *Law and the Modern Mind*, by Jerome Frank   202

Discussion

Legal Realism Is an External Theory of Law, which Provides a Descriptive Account of the Legal Process   207

Justice Cardozo's Theory of the Judicial Role Provides Some of the Theoretical Background to Legal Realism   208

Cardozo's Theory Brings Political Considerations into the Process of Decision-Making   209

10 | Later Positivism: The Law Derives Its Authority from the State   226

Hans Kelsen and H.L.A Hart   226

Readings

Discussion

11 | The Hart–Fuller Debate and the Procedural Account of the Natural Law   250

H.L.A Hart and Lon L. Fuller   250

Readings

From *The Morality of Law*, by Lon L. Fuller   250

From "Positivism and the Separation of Law and Morals," by H.L.A. Hart   255

From "Positivism and Fidelity to Law—A Reply to Professor Hart," by Lon L. Fuller   257

Discussion

12 | Contemporary Liberal Theory: Dworkin's Critique of Hart's Positivism   275

13 | The New Realism: Critical Legal Studies, Feminism, and Postmodernism   300

Part II | Jurisprudence, Applied Philosophy, and Contemporary Developments 329

14 | Private Law: The Civil Law Is Based on the Rights of the Person 334

15 | Private Law: Liability Is Based on Legal Duties and the Principle of Cause   359

Readings

From *The Common Law,* by Oliver Wendell Holmes   359

From *Jordan House Ltd. v. Menow,* [1974] S.C.R. 239   362

From *Principles of Contract at Law and in Equity,* by Frederick Pollock   365

Discussion

16 | Public Law: A Crime Is a Public Wrong   387

Readings

Discussion

17 | Public Law: Punishment and Sentencing 416

18 | Public Law: The Constitutional Law Places Legal Limits on Political Government   448

Readings

Discussion

19 | Globalization: The International Law and the Doctrine of Sovereignty Are Changing   473

Preface

Perhaps the first concern in writing a textbook on the development of legal theory in the common law tradition is to clarify the meaning of the term "common law." Although the term is very general and inherently ambiguous, it has two principal uses. The first use refers to a kind of law, based on judicial decisions, that was developed in England after the Norman Conquest, when England was united under the control of a single King. The common law was essentially the law of the King, and later the state, though it originated in custom and tradition rather than the exercise of political authority. It was called "common law" because it applied wherever the King had authority and was therefore "common" throughout the country.

The significance of the common law comes out of its reliance on the rigorous application of the legal rules found in previous cases. As a result, the term also refers to a kind of law, originally based on tribal precedents, that searches through the reasoning in the caselaw, in order to find binding principles that determine how the case before the court should be adjudicated.

The term "common law" is also used, however, to refer to the entire system of English law, which naturally includes statutes and other forms of law. There is a fundamental distinction between the common law system and the civil system of law, which is usually traced to Roman law, and has provided the model of law in Germany and France. One of the fundamental differences between the two systems lies in the promulgative function of the common law judiciary, which has constructed large parts of the common law out of the decisions in individual cases. The differences go deeper, however, and the common law rests on the belief that the law should be decided on the basis of the facts that give rise to specific legal questions. This allows the law to evolve as the circumstances in the caselaw change, but leaves the system relatively unorganized. The civil system is based on the idea that the legal principles on which the legal system is based should be set out explicitly, beforehand, and then applied to the cases. The common law system is accordingly empirical rather than rational; the law is developed on the basis of the experience recorded in specific cases rather than on the basis of a grand logical scheme.

The law on which the common law is based comes out of a tangle of different traditions, which include the tribal law, the Church law, and fragments of the civil system of law (the "civilian" law) that became the basis of the European law. There is no doubt, however, that it is the mechanics of the common law system that distinguish it from the civil system. The original common law was based on a particular form of reasoning, within the bounds set by the facts of individual cases, which provided the rational machinery needed to answer the questions raised by specific cases. The logical nature of this form of reasoning guaranteed the consistency and the predictability of the common law system. These are probably the most important attributes in any legal system and provide order and justice across a wide range of cases.

The Common Law Contains a Wisdom Literature

The present textbook adopts a genealogical approach to the study of the law, which seems particularly appropriate in studying the common law tradition. The common law is itself a backward exercise in genealogy and has sources in the tribal law, which was based on the collective memory of the community. The people of northern Europe, like other tribal people around the world, found their law in the accounts of elders and the wisdom literature that entered into their narrative traditions. Legal matters were decided by custom and practice, and these decisions were based on a remarkably cogent concept of precedent. This idea that the law lies in the practices of the people still explains the fundamental idea that the common law is "found" rather than "made."

The customs of these northern peoples had the force of law. These customs provided the basis of the law that was applied by judges in individual cases. This law was elaborated and synthesized over time, since there were different customs in the regions of England. The common law was nevertheless based on the same respect for the legal rules that could be uncovered in the records of the past. It is for this reason that the common law tradition was generally rejected by those theorists associated with the eighteenth-century philosophical awakening described as the Enlightenment and the positivist tradition that came out of it. Positivism gave rise to modern science and was ultimately incorporated into the common law tradition, though largely by the actions of the legislature.

The social sciences, in particular, have had an enormous impact on contemporary legal theory and have raised legitimate questions with regard to the common law tradition. Although the genealogical approach that I have adopted does not reject the insights of the social sciences—indeed, I have spent enough time in criminology to call myself a "criminologist"—its foundations lie in the historical tradition. The present textbook follows the example of authors like Michel Foucault, who tried to trace the genealogy of significant ideas, concepts, and intellectual constructions through time. I do not believe that it is possible to grasp the meaning of fundamental common law concepts without tracing their intellectual pedigree back through the wisdom literature of the law to their historical origins. There is a sense in which this kind of task requires that these concepts be deconstructed, though the present textbook focusses on the provenance of such ideas rather than their current usage.

The approach that I have followed can also be described as a "wisdom" or "wisdom literature" analysis. This approach is based on the idea that the common law is properly understood as part of a long tradition that finds expression in the wise consensus recorded in the caselaw. There seems little doubt that this consensus has a moral and collective basis, though the legal system merely sets out the social parameters in which we are allowed to make our decisions.

There is an important issue here: the law may tell us that a certain form of conduct is wrong, but the fundamental purpose of the legal system is to resolve disputes. The common law originally did this by providing the victim of the offence with a right to a legal remedy. The availability of such a remedy inevitably sets limits on our conduct and reinforces the social consensus that tells us that certain kinds of conduct are wrong. In most cases, however, the residual view or value that the law falls back upon is already there. The law does not supply it.

It stands to reason that the study of the law and legal theory takes us into other areas of investigation. There is no reason to question the idea that the study of the law, like many other fields of study, raises psychological and sociological issues. It would seem obvious that a judicial decision tells us a good deal about the judge who wrote it, the judiciary in general, and the society or social groups to which judges belong. Although these kinds of insights take us outside the law itself, they may naturally yield insights into the caselaw and, indeed, into the nature of law and the legal order. There is no reason to exclude such insights from the theoretical tradition associated with the common law.

The heart of the common law tradition nevertheless lies in a substantial consensus, which finds expression in the application of settled principle to the situations presented by new cases. This body of principle can be traced back as far as the tribal law. Judges who consult precedents are applying the collective insights of the past to the facts that come before them. The mechanics of such an exercise are provided by a process of analogy that allows individual adjustments in the exact circumstances of each case.

One of the major strengths of the common law, in contrast to the civil system of law, and the strict use of statutes, is that it is flexible enough to accommodate the changes in human society without abandoning the fundamental insights of the past. In *Edwards v. A.G. of Canada* (the "Persons Case"), which is discussed in Chapter 8, John Sankey described a written constitution as a "living tree," capable of growth. In spite of the legislative restrictions placed on judges by the development of legal positivism, the capacity for growth that such a metaphor contemplates is evident in the entire common law tradition.

The evolution of the caselaw in the common law tradition can be attributed to the principle of narrow construction. This principle holds that the *ratio decidendi* of a decision—the legal principle on which the legal decision is based—applies to other cases only if those cases raise the same issue. As a result, judges in cases with slightly different facts—in legal language, cases that can be distinguished on the facts—may deviate from the ruling in the decision if they have a principled reason for doing so. As Oliver Wendell Holmes argued, this means that it is the material facts in a case that ultimately determine how it will be decided.

This emphasis on the facts of the case has given the common law an empirical character. The common law is nevertheless based on the application and development of principle and offers a rigorous means of resolving social disputes. The legal legitimacy of a particular decision comes from its logical pedigree, which provides a far more principled process for the resolution of conflict than does war or politics.

There is no doubt that the approach I have followed in the present textbook—like the common law—is based on a deep respect for the insights of the past. It is impossible, for example, to examine what we know of the tribal tradition without realizing that it provides a better vehicle for preserving social cohesion and harmony than do modern legal systems. It is no accident that Canadian criminal courts are starting to turn to sentencing circles and restorative justice in trying to address the dramatic *anomie* that stands behind so much contemporary crime. The caselaw clearly establishes that such practices sometimes succeed where more conventional sentencing practices have failed.

The fundamental goal of the present textbook was nevertheless to trace the genealogy of the theoretical tradition associated with the common law from its beginning to the present. The account of legal theory that the book presents is predominantly factual. I have tried to present the different theories that have arisen in the course of the common law from a fair-minded perspective, which recognizes both their strengths and their weaknesses. The idea is to provide instructors and students with an accurate view of the historical development of the common law and the theoretical discussion that has clustered around it.

Most of the readings in the first part of the book have become part of the standard syllabus in philosophy of law. There is a discernible canon in the academic literature, which includes figures like Jeremy Bentham and Immanuel Kant, in spite of the fact that their contributions to legal theory seem peripheral to their work in other areas. For some reason, the reading from Thomas Hill Green has been overlooked in the discipline, in spite of the fact that it provides the best *riposte* to John Austin's *The Province of Jurisprudence Determined* among his contemporaries.

The modern reality in legal theory stands in marked contrast to the original common law position, which was based on the natural law. Legal positivism and the natural rights tradition—as it is manifested in liberal theory—is that legal positivism and the natural rights tradition have become so predominant in legal theory that the current literature can be divided on the basis of those who subscribe to the fundamental liberal position and those who are uncomfortable with it. It is not clear that figures like H.L.A. Hart, Lon L. Fuller, or even Ronald Dworkin stray far from the liberal and positivist premise that the law has its source in the social contract. The more recent literature nevertheless presents a definite reaction to this narrowness in the theoretical tradition and includes a return to some kind of natural law tradition.

Legal Theories Has a Number of Sources

The present textbook also reflects my own experience as a teacher. There are many pedagogical approaches, but I have always found that the chronological approach provides the best introduction to a particular discipline. I think this is because theory always develops in a historical and social context, which is lost when a strict analytical approach is followed. The chronological approach inevitably illuminates the rationale behind each theory, revealing a genealogy of ideas that has been obscured by the passage of time.

It is rather surprising how easily we forget the reasons that a particular idea or theory came into prominence in the first place. One of the purposes of the present textbook is accordingly to reconnect the fundamental ideas in the law and legal theory with the reasons that contributed to their development. Such connections are particularly evident in the discussion of rights, punishment (of *peine forte et dure*), the development of the state, the evolution of international law, and even the belief that we take our legal identity from our existence as acute individuals rather than our membership in a family or a community.

There is a strong current of idealism in the Western philosophical tradition. This idealism has contributed to the belief that the mere examination of ideas, outside of the context in which they arose, is sufficient to reveal the truths that stand behind them. It follows that there may be a philosophical sense in which the present textbook is an attempt to reclaim the meaning that eludes such an analysis. Every age develops its own set of conceptual tools for the examination of the legal and philosophical issues that confront it. There is plenty of room for different opinions, and instructors and students must decide for themselves whether they find particular theories compelling.

Most of the present textbook is based on a series of lectures that I prepared for a course in philosophy some fifteen years ago, in an attempt to reconstruct the history of philosophy of law. I intuitively followed a chronological approach and quickly discovered that my students had difficulty with some of the standard readings in the area. It may come as no surprise that they found the excerpts from the *Summa Theologica* difficult, but they also struggled with the work of H.L.A. Hart. I would not have dared to give them anything from Hans Kelsen. In the end, I found myself explaining the readings rather than discussing philosophical issues. My original motivation in writing *Legal Theories* was accordingly to provide students with a convenient synopsis of the usual readings in the area, so that I could focus more directly on the issues that they raise.

The present textbook also reflects the fact that I completed my Ph.D. in philosophy after I had spent a decade as a lawyer in the courts. As someone with a background in practice, I discovered that some of the work in philosophy of law fails to grasp the legal basics of the common law. Another one of my motivations for writing *Legal Theories* was accordingly to bring the theoretical literature into line with the realities of legal practice. It is clear, to cite one example, that many academic authors do not appreciate the distinction that the courts draw between facts and law. As a result, a good part of the literature fails to understand the different roles assigned to trial and appellate judges.

I was also interested in concrete cases. Although the work of a theorist like Kelsen has its place in a historical review of legal theory, it seems hard to believe that such an abstract philosophy can ever capture the reality of the issues that arise in the legal tradition. The analytic approach, taken too far, leads into an arid discussion of technical issues that have very little bearing on what occurs within the legal system. This is particularly true in the common law tradition, which focusses on substantive issues. The technicalities in the caselaw are instrumental and pragmatic. My own view, which is undoubtedly a product of my experience as counsel, is that legal issues arise in historical and factual circumstances that contribute substantially to their resolution. In certain philosophical inquiries, at least, abstraction is the enemy of meaning.

The present textbook accordingly provides a historical survey of the major legal theories that have been employed to explain or critique the legal tradition associated with the common law. This naturally includes legal positivism, which overturns the original relationship between the legal and political orders, and traces the binding nature of the law to political authority. The original tradition nevertheless survived in the constitutional law. The book also provides an account of the working legal tradition. There are many errors in the current literature, which often misconstrues the historical tradition on which the common law is based. Some of these errors are discussed in the chapters dealing with rights and punishment; but there are technical problems, as well, in the current account of a criminal offence.

Legal Theories Is Divided into Three Parts

The present textbook is divided into three parts. Part I maps out a number of major historical developments in legal theory, from the tribal origins of the common law to the present. This part of the book covers two thousand years of law and attempts to fill a gap in the textbook literature, which does not explain the provenance of the law.

Many textbooks in philosophy of law consist of collections of readings from a canon of important philosophical and legal works. This approach presents a problem for many students who have difficulty with the writing of historical figures like Thomas Aquinas or John Austin, or even more contemporary authors like H.L.A. Hart. Each chapter of the present textbook accordingly contains readings from major figures followed by a narrative that discusses the general issues that the readings raise.

The readings are heavily edited to provide students with an accessible introduction to the original sources on which the philosophical tradition is based. The discussion sections in Part I provide both commentary on the readings and explanations of the wider issues that the readings raise. The focus in Part I is on exploring the most fundamental question in the philosophy of law: What makes certain rules, precepts, or principles "laws"?

Part II surveys the common law jurisprudence and applied philosophy. The distinction between these two areas of study has eroded, and the two fields are clearly merging. This part of the present textbook naturally emphasizes the nexus between theory and practice. Although I have divided these areas of study into their conventional departments, I have usually presented the material historically, since that presentation contributes to the students' understanding of the way in which the law developed.

The readings in Part II provide legal examples that supplement the wide-ranging discussions in each chapter. These discussions review some of the central concepts in our law, such as intention, causation, and the legal person. I have also reviewed the development of the notion of liability, and strict liability, as well as the historical idea that liability attached to an offending object. The discussion also ventures into the contemporary law and reviews current developments in areas like sentencing.

Part II takes its outline from the mechanics of the legal system. The common law contains private law, which discussed in chapters 14 and 15, and public law, which is discussed in chapters 16, 17, and 18. There are rights and liabilities, and, since rights attach historically to persons, the chapter on rights, Chapter 14, focusses on the person. Liabilities, the topic of Chapter 15, have historically been based on the idea that we have duties. This idea is still present in the law, particularly in the law of torts, which always bases liability on the breach of the defendant's duty to the plaintiff. This idea has been muddied by the introduction of the concept of rights to analyze and explain moral issues, outside the law, which has occasionally overwhelmed the traditional legal analysis.

Chapter 16 focusses on the criminal law. Chapter 17 deals with punishment, which comes out of *lex talionis* and the idea of retaliation. This is an important discussion because the modern concept of retribution does not recognize the metaphysical origins of the idea of retaliation. The contemporary concept of constitutional rights, which derives from the natural rights tradition and has been reconfigured as "human rights," provides the basis of Chapter 18. The final chapter examines the halting development of a global system of justice. As many authors and theorists have observed, there are conflicting trends in such a development, which has been associated with a forceful—and often threatening—re-assertion of the traditional doctrine of state sovereignty.

The third part of the present textbook is an online collection of additional readings that supplement the discussion in individual chapters. The additional readings for Chapter 9, for example, include further readings from the debate between Karl Llewellyn and Roscoe Pound on legal realism. The extra readings also include explanatory excerpts, such as the excerpt from Jean-Jacques Rousseau's "The Social Contract," in the additional online readings for Chapter 6. This reading provides a necessary footnote to Thomas Hill Green's response to John Austin's legal positivism. The extra readings extend the discussion well beyond the parameters of the individual chapters and give instructors additional material to draw from when creating assignments and exams.

Pedagogical Style

The present textbook is designed for students from a wide variety of backgrounds. The chapters are intentionally short and written in a lucid, cogent style. The readings are edited for clarity as well as length, which makes them relatively easy to access, freeing students to discuss the rich strata of issues productively in the classroom. Instructors may choose to focus on the discussions or on the readings. Many of the chapters in Part I deal with particular philosophers, in the order in which their works appeared. In my experience, students find it much easier to discuss particular authors before moving on to general theories.

The style of the book is explanatory. I have subscribed to the principle of charity and tried to present each theory or argument in the best possible light before considering the kinds of criticism that might be raised against it. As a matter of philosophy, the principle of charity is naturally supplemented by a belief in critical thinking, which holds that individual theories should not be accepted without scrutiny. This approach reflects the adversarial system in our courts, which allows each side its turn at argument.

The present textbook is intended primarily as a historical resource. I have tried to make material available to instructors and explain important positions, arguments, and issues without undermining the instructor's prerogative to decide exactly what material should be taught, and how. The idea is to give instructors as many choices as possible in developing their own curriculum. It is for instructors and students to decide which theories they find convincing and compelling.

The table of contents provides a propositional outline of the book, as well as a study guide for students. The discussions are supplemented by a few questions and a list of suggested readings at the end of each chapter. Since I have adopted a historical approach, I have tried, where I can, to suggest historical readings, some of which have been neglected in the current literature. It is impossible to provide an exhaustive list of possible readings, but the readings I have included offer a solid introduction to an extensive literature.

Legal Theories Reflects the Current Developments in the International Arena

The present textbook reflects the current resurgence of the idea that there is some binding natural or customary law—however it is constructed—that places binding constraints on the exercise of political power. This resurgence is evident in the process of globalization, in the appearance of a compulsory international law, and in the company of new theories and technologies that have extended the social life of humanity beyond the national and territorial confines of individual states. Legal positivism, which has long held sway in legal theory, rests on the existence of the state system, which traces the positive law to the political sources of authority within the state. This idea has recently been undermined by many theoretical developments, such as the argument—usually referred to as "pluralism"—that there are many other sources of law. There is also an increasing recognition that the theoretical immunity that states have enjoyed under the Westphalian system is more abstract than real. These developments naturally come at a time of increasing political, environmental, and economic instability.

The major development in legal theory in our time is clearly that the legal order has begun to reassert its ascendancy over the political order. There is no consensus on such a development, however, and the statist view, which finds expression in legal positivism, is still predominant. This is particularly true in the international realm, and the rhetorical statement that states are sovereign in some absolute sense persists. In spite of this, it has become more and more difficult to argue that there is a purely political realm, inside or outside the state, in which power can be exercised outside the restrictions of law. This is an important and positive development, though it has taken place without an institutional structure that is capable of dealing with the dire problems that the world confronts.

The law always seems to recognize the possibility of conflict. Although I have been unable to deal at length with legal institutions, no body of law is satisfactory unless it provides an effective mechanism for the resolution of disputes. One example will suffice. In investigating the ways of the Cheyenne, Karl Lewellyn and E. Adamson Hoebel discovered that the tribal law provides a nuanced and compelling means of dealing with conflict. This approach relies on custom rather than force and deserves its place alongside the increasingly complex mechanisms in the modern law.

Acknowledgements

I suspect that anyone who has argued a legal issue in a common law courtroom understands that a rigorous search of the precedents often provides a compelling answer to the most intractable questions. I have discovered this time and again, not merely in litigation, but also in my scholarship and research into the development of legal theory. What I learned from our predecessors has been augmented by the insights of my academic colleagues and students. Law is an art and craft, as much as anything else, and I have had many tutors, which include my professional peers, my secretaries over the years, and the support staff at the Human Rights Tribunal. Indeed, so many people have contributed to this book that it would be a mistake to try and list them. Many would be left out. I would nevertheless like to thank my brother Louis for contributing to the project and bringing it to the attention of Oxford University Press. I would also like to thank the reviewers— Tim Christie, at Fraser International College; Christopher Gray, at Concordia University; and Kira Tomsons, at Dalhousie University—who made a considerable contribution to the process. There were many times when I wondered if I would make it to the end of the project and I would like to thank the editorial staff at Oxford University Press for their patience and perseverance. I also wanted to mention Miranda Li's fastidious attention to detail in helping me proof the galleys for the book.

Part I | *Historical Theories of Law*

Part I introduces the reader to the major legal theories in the common law tradition. The theories put forward by Thomas Aquinas, Hugo Grotius, and Immanuel Kant form part of the general Western philosophical tradition and have come into the common law indirectly. They nevertheless have an important contribution to make in understanding the theoretical underpinning of the common law system. The rationalism of Kant, for example, contributed to the legal formalism that shaped the current law school curriculum and entered into the work of American theorists through the influence of German jurisprudents. The chapters in this part of the book focus on the work of the most influential thinkers in each school of thought.

It goes without saying that any abstract classification of theories is somewhat artificial. The chapters in Part I nevertheless make a pedagogical distinction between three kinds of legal theory: *natural law theory*, *legal positivism*, and *legal realism*. The purpose of this classification is to provide a simple means of comparing the theories set out by different thinkers. This does not mean that finer distinctions are neglected. The later chapters recognize the distinction, for example, between traditional natural law theories and the "naturalistic" theories that have replaced them. The latter theories are nevertheless classified as natural law theories, on the basis that they ultimately test the validity of the law on its moral or substantive content.

Natural Law Theory Has Its Origins in the Tribal Law

The book begins by examining the tribal law, which provides the original source of the common law tradition. This law contains a cosmological theory of law, based on the idea that there is a natural law. The conception of the natural law in this early law took on more overt religious overtones in the work of Thomas Aquinas, which is the focus of Chapter 2. Aquinas distinguishes between the positive law and the natural law, but he traces our fundamental obligation to obey the positive law to the moral obligations that the natural law imposes upon us. This kind of view has its roots in the tribal law, which traces the law to moral custom.

The idea in the Christian theory of the natural law that has assumed importance in Western legal theory is that the validity of a law is based on its substantive validity. Although this substantive validity may be determined in a variety of ways—by consulting religious sources, or the moral consensus in society, or reason—these differences do not change the basic framework of the theory. The important idea is that a law that contravenes an authoritative body of moral values and principles is invalid.

The Legal and Ethical Theories of the Natural Law Need to Be Distinguished

The term "natural law" rose to prominence in ethics rather than in legal theory. In the *Rhetoric*, for example, Aristotle writes about a "universal law":

> Universal law is the law of nature. For there really is, as everyone to some extent divines, a natural justice and injustice that is binding on all men, even on those who have no association or covenant with each other.[1]

This is a reference to a moral law, which contains a universal set of ethical rules.

Aristotle uses the example of Antigone, whose brother Polynices had rebelled against Thebes. When Polynices is killed, Creon, the King of Thebes, orders that his body be left to rot and be eaten by vultures. This treatment of the human body was considered highly sacrilegious in Greek society. Antigone accordingly defies Creon and buries her brother's body in accordance with the proper rites. This raises a question for the Greeks: has Antigone acted ethically in disobeying the law?

Aristotle argues that the natural law takes precedence over human law; thus Antigone has no moral obligation to obey an unjust decree. This is primarily an ethical argument. It is when we take this argument further and say that Creon's decree did not correspond with "the natural law," *and was therefore an invalid law*, that we have moved into legal theory. The legal theory of the natural law holds that an immoral positive law is not *legally* binding.

Legal Positivism Derives from the "Natural Rights" Tradition

The second legal theory in this book's classification of legal theories is legal positivism, which rejects the legal theory of the natural law. The legal positivists separated the question whether a positive law is valid from the question whether we are morally obliged to obey it. H.L.A. Hart, the most prominent legal positivist in recent years, for example, argued that there are formal social and political rules that determine what constitutes a law. If those rules have been followed, a law is valid, whatever its moral character. This position suggests that we are obliged, at least legally, to obey such laws. The significance of such a statement is open to discussion.

From a historical perspective, legal positivism comes out of the theory of natural rights, which is associated with the liberal tradition and was based on the idea that the natural law gave rise to personal rights. The theory of natural rights holds that there is a social contract under which the members of society have agreed to form a *polis*—some form of political association—in return for the peace and security that it provides. This contract gives the political branches of government the power to pass positive laws. The fundamental role of the judiciary is to apply and enforce the positive law.

The idea that the law is a product of the political process was a relatively late development in the history of the law. The original role of the government in the legal system was to administer and guarantee the law. The King had no legislative mandate, and the law came from local customs, which were binding because they expressed the beliefs of the people. The historical foundations of legal positivism can be found in the increasing authority of Parliament and other political institutions in the common law tradition.

Legal Realism Goes against Positivism

The third legal theory is legal realism, which rejects natural law theory and legal positivism. The essential idea in legal realism is that judges inevitably follow their own views and instincts in reaching their decisions. This idea originally came out of the social sciences, which suggested that the foundation of the law lies in behaviour rather than the natural order or the exercise of reason. It is simply what judges "do." The study of law and legal theory should accordingly investigate the deeper reasons that the judiciary interprets and applies the law in certain ways. This takes legal theory into sociology, politics, and the business of deconstructing the judiciary.

Legal positivism and legal realism reflect the differences in the legal traditions in England and the United States. The common law tradition in England was rigorous and relatively narrow, and the strength of the doctrine of parliamentary sovereignty favoured the development of positivism. The attitude of the early legal positivists was fostered by a certain suspicion of judges and by the belief that the political order should have ascendancy over the legal order. Jeremy Bentham and the utilitarians took the position that the chief role of the judiciary in interpreting legislation is to identify and follow the intentions of the legislature.

The American legal tradition took a different turn. This is in large part because the United States has a written constitution, which places legal constraints on the executive and legislative branches of government. These constraints gave rise to the practice of judicial review, which allows an applicant to challenge the constitutionality of federal or state legislation in the courts. This gave rise to an active judicial tradition, more in keeping with the American temperament, which gave judges a responsibility for developing policy. The positive side of such a tradition can be seen in the decisions of progressive judges, like

Benjamin Cardozo, who believed that judges have an obligation to develop the caselaw in a manner that reflects the moral and social changes in society.

There was a negative side to this tradition, however, which precipitated a crisis in legal theory. This crisis occurred when the appellate courts in the United States began striking down minimum-wage laws and other pieces of progressive legislation on the basis that they were unconstitutional. These decisions raised deep questions about the independence and impartiality of the judiciary, who were famously accused, by Oliver Wendell Holmes, of "taking sides" in social and political disputes.

Legal realism is usually traced to the work of Holmes, who was a dedicated skeptic. The early realists suggested that judges inevitably fall back on their own moral, social, and political predilections in deciding legal and constitutional issues. Although the realist movement eventually faltered, for failing to provide a theory of law that can actually be utilized in a courtroom, it continues to influence contemporary theory. It is realism, for example, that led Ronald Dworkin to investigate the extent to which judges can rely on moral or substantive beliefs in deciding what the law is in particular cases.

The influence of sociology and critical legal studies has taken the skeptical attack a step further, into epistemology. Some theorists have questioned whether the law has any definite order or meaning, and whether it can be objectively fixed. The postmodern movement has argued that any interpretation of the law is a personal and social construction, which can be deconstructed. Critical and feminist theorists have argued that legal realism raises questions about the privileging of certain interpretations of the law, which favour the existing distribution of power in society.

There Is a Normative and a Descriptive Side to the Theoretical Enterprise

Legal theory also has a normative and a descriptive side. The normative side of the theoretical exercise sets out what the law should be. It seems clear that there is a moral element in such a task. The descriptive side of the exercise, on the other hand, describes the operation of the system. This part of the theoretical task is fundamentally empirical.

The two sides of legal theory reflect a long-standing philosophical dispute as to the nature of the law. Greek philosophers in the fifth century were well aware that there was an antithesis between *nomos*—"that which is artificially contrived," a reference to custom or "convention"—and *physis*, or "nature."[2] These philosophers were keenly interested in the question whether the conventions of religion and society—and our notion of justice—originate in *nomos* or in *physis*.

It is interesting that the word "normative"—which, like the words "norm" and "normal," comes from *nomos*—has now migrated to the natural law side of the debate. Legal positivism retains some normative elements, since it holds that a valid law must meet certain requirements. These requirements are quite technical, however, and tell us little about the rectitude of a particular law. Legal positivism can accordingly be classified as a descriptive theory. Natural law theory, in contrast, is a normative theory. A statute becomes a valid law only if it meets a particular normative standard.

Both kinds of theories present problems. The observation in legal positivism that a particular law is valid does not tell us whether we have a moral obligation to follow the law. This is remarkably unhelpful, since the usual question in a legal context is whether we should obey the law. The problem in natural law theory, on the other hand, is that we must determine whether a human law is in accordance with the natural law—and whether it meets the normative requirement of a valid law—in order to determine whether it is legally binding. As John Austin observed, this makes it cumbersome, inefficient, and indeed artificial. The simplest way around these problems is probably to combine the most significant elements of both theories in a single theory.

The distinction between normative and descriptive theory also raises issues with regard to legal realism. Roscoe Pound, for example, criticized the realists for their failure to formulate a normative position. Pound's own theory of the law was based on a mix of sociology and a progressive social agenda. It accordingly had a normative thrust, though Pound rejected the religious and moral foundations of natural law theory and favoured legislative revisions of the law. He must therefore be classified as a legal positivist, who ultimately rests the authority of the law on its political sources and leaves fundamental normative issues in the keeping of the legislature.

Legal realism is a descriptive theory. The descriptive claim that it makes is much deeper than the claim in legal positivism, however, and poses profound questions as to whether the legal system has solid normative foundations. There are similar questions in the contemporary theoretical literature, which asks whether morality and law are socially constructed. The deeper concerns in both cases, as in so much of modern philosophy, are epistemological, and they raise the question whether we can "know" the law with any certainty. The significant feature of the natural law in this context is that it traces the law to moral values, which are—somehow—a product of *physis* and therefore certain.

Notes

1.   From *Rhetorica*, vol. 9 of *The Works of Aristotle*, trans. W. Rhys Roberts, ed. W.D. Ross (Oxford: Clarendon, 1924), 1.13.1373b.
2.   See W.K.C. Guthrie, *The Sophists* (Cambridge: Cambridge University, 1971), p. 55.

Further Reading

Sophocles, *Antigone*. Many translations of Sophocles' famous play are available, both online and in print.

Alan D. Cullison, "Morality and the Foundations of Legal Positivism," *Valpariso University Law Review* 20, no. 1 (Fall 1985): 61–70. Available at http://scholar.valpo.edu.

J.B. Crozier, "Legal Realism and a Science of Law," *American Journal of Jurisprudence* 29 (1984): 151–68. Available at http://heinonline.org.

Dennis J. Schmidt, "Translator's Introduction: In the Spirit of Bloch," in Ernst Bloch, *Natural Law and Human Dignity*, trans. Dennis J. Schmidt (Cambridge, MA: MIT, 1986), pp. vii–xxvi.

1 Tribes and the Origins of Law

Readings

- From *A First Book of Jurisprudence for Students of the Common Law*, by Frederick Pollock
- From "*Qaujimajatuqangit* and Social Problems in Modern Inuit Society," by Jarich Oosten and Frédéric Laugrand
- From "The Apache," by Edward S. Curtis
- From *Tribal Custom in Anglo-Saxon Law*, by Frederic Seebohm
- From *The Cheyenne Way*, by K.N. Llewellyn and E. Adamson Hoebel
- From *The Law of Primitive Man*, by E. Adamson Hoebel

This chapter introduces the concept of law and discusses its historical origins in tribal practices. It provides examples of the tribal law, which remains an active tradition, based on custom, that provides an alternative model of law to the political conception of law with which we are familiar. The chapter also discusses the customary law, the written law that came out of the tribal law and from which the common law developed.

In the first reading, Frederick Pollock, an English professor of jurisprudence, writes that the concept of law is much older than the state and provided the organizing principle of society before the advent of centralized government. It is notable that the older, more abstract meaning of the word "law" has now been lost in English. This loss can be attributed to the more recent concept of law in the common law tradition, which is fundamentally political and rests on the existence of the state.

As the readings demonstrate, the tribal law is consistent across many cultures, whether we are speaking of the traditional law among the Inuit, marriage and property laws among the Apache, the payment of *galanas* in medieval Welsh tribes, or the punishments among the Cheyenne. All of these examples deal with customs and laws that derive from social practices that developed before the emergence of the modern state and central government. In each case, the law is seen as part of a larger cosmological and metaphysical order, which preserves the natural state of things.

The clan and the community are central in the tribal law. In most cases, at least, it is the family or the clan rather than the individual that possesses legal personality in the tribal law. The law is there to govern the relations between families within the tribe. In the case of individuals, the legal process is designed to restore the individual to his or her place in the family and the community. This concern with the place of the individual in the community is reflected in banishment, the ultimate legal penalty in such societies, which deprives an individual of membership in society. These aspects of the tribal law raise deep questions with respect to the nature of law.

⚹ Readings ⚹

From Frederick Pollock, *A First Book of Jurisprudence for Students of the Common Law* (London: Macmillan, 1896).

In English we use the word "Law" in a concrete sense to mean any particular rule, having the nature of law in the abstract sense [i.e., having the nature of a compulsory or coercive rule], which is expressly prescribed by the supreme power in the State, or by some person or body having authority for that purpose.[1] . . .

Any such view, however, will be found hard to reconcile with the witness of history. For we find, if we look away from such elaborated systems as those of the later Roman Empire and of modern Western governments, that not only law, but law with a good deal of formality, has existed before the State had any adequate means of compelling its observance. . . . More than this, we find preserved among the antiquities of legal systems, and notably in archaic forms and solemnities, considerable traces of a time when the jurisdiction of courts arose only from the voluntary submission of the parties. . . .

In short the conception of law, many of its ideas, and much even of its form, are prior in history to the official intervention of the State, save in the last resort, to maintain law. True it is that in modern States law tends more and more to become identified with the will of the State as expressed by the authorities entrusted with the direction of the common power. But to regard law as merely that which the State wills or commands is eminently the mistake of a layman. . . . Law is enforced by the State because it is law; it is not law merely because the State enforces it.

Note

1.   Editor's note: Pollock goes on to observe that this ambiguity is "peculiar to English" and suggests that the two senses of the word "law" have become conflated in the common law tradition. Legislation (which is law in the "concrete" sense) has attained the status of law in the abstract sense.

From Jarich Oosten and Frédéric Laugrand, "*Qaujimajatuqangit* and Social Problems in Modern Inuit Society: An Elders Workshop on *Angakkuuniq*," *Études/Inuit/Studies* 26, no. 1 (2002): 17–44.

In 1954, Adamson Hoebel devoted the first chapter of *The Law of Primitive Man* to the Inuit and concluded that only "rudimentary law in a primitive anarchy" existed among the Inuit (see also Mowat 1953: 180). Geert Van den Steenhoven, who conducted fieldwork among the Inuit of the Keewatin district, gave systematic accounts of many cases of conflict (Steenhoven 1954, 1965) and concluded that the existence of some form of law among the Keewatin Inuit could not be demonstrated (Steenhoven 1962: 113). . . . [Yet] many scholars continued to search for some sort of legal system in Inuit societies which could be studied as an equivalent to the Western system of law (e.g., Rouland 1976, 1978, 1979). Other researchers opted for an alternative strategy either by studying a few social institutions or by focussing on "social control" (Hughes 1966; Rasing 1989, 1994).[1] These categories are useful in applying Western theoretical perspectives to Inuit society, but they do not help us understand Inuit perspectives. Inuit leaders and elders did not see themselves as agents of law and order or social control (Oosten et al., eds. 1999: 3).

Social norms and cosmic norms are difficult to separate in Inuit culture. Relations between the communities and the world around them are interdependent as was already perceived by Hoebel. The issue was again raised by Wim Raising in his study of *Order and Non-conformity in Iglulingmiut Social Process*. He concluded: "Iglulingmiut social norms, that is the norms that affected the interactions with other persons were tied in with the norms pertaining to their dealings with nature" (Rasing 1994: 269). Therefore, studies of Inuit social norms should not only take Inuit values into account (Briggs 1970, 1975, 1982), but also their worldview. . . . A social order that only aims at social control and does not involve the relationship to game and the spirits makes no sense to Inuit. In interviews with elders during the Nunavut Arctic College Oral Traditions Project,[2] it was repeatedly emphasized that transgressions were not so much sanctioned by the community as by spiritual "agencies" such as the weather or the game. Stingy people would catch less game. Sins would evoke bad weather. Transgressions would not only affect the offenders, but also their relatives and their descendants. . . .

The Translation of Legal Terms Is Often Culturally Imprecise

Maligaq, piqujaq, and *tirigususiit* refer to what had to be followed, done or not done, in Inuit culture.[3] Nowadays, these words are often used as equivalents to modern Western notions of "law." . . . Thus, "*piqujaq*" is translated as "Inuit customary law." This translation is useful in the context of the modern law system, but "customary law" is a Western concept that did not exist in Inuit society before the introduction of the Canadian system of law. The back translation of "*piqujaq*" is "which is asked to be done (by somebody)" and its implicit meaning is "which is asked by an authorized person to be done." Therrien (in Brice-Bennet et al. 1997: 253) explains that "*piqujaq*" "is used as a general concept pertaining to the obligation to respect rules imposed within Inuit society. These rules are orally transmitted and not codified. Only authorized persons have the right to make rules. Rules most often taught by parents concern offering help to the family or the elders, and respect due to animals." In this explanation we come much closer to the meaning of "*piqujaq*" than in the translation "customary law," but even here it is difficult to avoid terms such as "rules" and "authorized persons" that suggest a much more formalized structure than actually existed in Inuit society. Elders had much authority and were highly respected, but no one was under any obligation to follow their advice. The term "rule" suggests a general principle, which is always applied, whereas the term "*piqujaq*" emphasized the importance of the relation involved: people will comply with what people they respect ask from them. . . .

Elders, shamans, and campleaders all had their own responsibilities in preserving the peace and settling conflicts within the camps. The elders had great authority. As student Kim Kangok states in her essay for the second law course:[4] "The *Innatuqat* [elders] were known to have a powerful mind. So powerful that they were capable of changing one's future for good or bad." When they thought people were not behaving correctly they would counsel them, and their words carried great weight. The shamans were particularly important in cases of disease or when the relationship with the game was disrupted. As Aaju Peter states in her essay for this same second law course: "The *angakkuq* [essentially a shaman] was not there to judge a person, neither was he there to set the laws. He was there to find out who had broken the *tirigusiit* and get them to confess, but at the same time he held a lot of power since he could kill people with his *tuurngaq* [helping spirit]." Finally, the campleaders exercised considerable authority. In Aaju's words: "These great *angajuggaat* who got their status through their abilities as great hunters, or a combination of both ability and birthright, held a lot of power. In a world where you depend totally on game, you owe your life to persons who feed you." But if the campleaders went astray, the elders would not hesitate to counsel them (ibid.: 113). . . .

Angakkuuniq Is a Central Part of Inuit Law

The elders emphasized the necessity to broaden the notions of right, order, and law [to include *angakkuuniq* (shamanism),] as these do not only concern human beings but also animals and spirits. Thus animals are said to have *tarniit*, shades or souls, just like human beings. They can retaliate. Hunters have to respect animals and not abuse them. In the perspective of the elders, maintenance of social order requires that relationships with animals and spirits are preserved and maintained in the correct way. This belief was essential to the shamanic traditions.

The elders agreed that people should stop considering shamanism as a diabolical or an objectionable practice, and acknowledge that it has been very useful and might still be useful. They explained that it had been very powerful in the past and could still be used in desperate situations. Elders explained that while you can hide things in a confession to the priest, you can't do it to the *angakkuq*, because of his *gaumaniq* (enlightenment): "An *angakkuq* is capable of getting all wrongdoings out. That is very heavy, being an *angakkuq*." Thus, *angakkuit* [shamans] played an important role in discerning the causes of wrongdoings and setting out remedies to deal with them. . . .

The importance of shamanism for hunting was stressed. Shamans were important in preserving correct relations with game and could procure game. The elders thought *manilirijut* (providing game) was congruent with Christian prayer. . . .

In fact, many elders still practised *tirigusungniit* (abstaining from certain practices): no contact for the hunter with a menstruating woman; no eating of fish bones after a death, etc. These rules that were transmitted within families gave the elders a frame of reference in retaining the traditions of their parents or grandparents.

Notes

1.   Editor's note: This strategy reflects the contemporary view of the law.
2.   Editor's note: The authors here refer to a series of interviews, hosted by Nunavut Arctic College beginning in the mid-1990s, in which Inuit elders were invited to share their opinions about various issues affecting their communities.
3.   Editor's note: All three terms can be translated as "law," which refers to rules of behaviour in this context.
4.   Editor's note: The authors are referring to a course in Iqaluit, in which elders participated.

From Edward S. Curtis, "The Apache," in vol. 1 of *The North American Indian: Being a Series of Volumes Picturing and Describing the Indians of the United States and Alaska*, ed. Frederick Webb Hodge (New York: Johnson Reprint Corporation, [1907] 1970), pp. 3–52.

Among the Apache some of the younger generation are inclined to disregard tribal laws respecting marriage, but in former times they were rigidly enforced, marriage within the clan or the gens being regarded as incestuous. When asked what would happen if a man and a woman belonging to the same clan should marry, one old man answered that both would be quickly put to death. . . .

With the Apache, as with other tribes, the clan organization has an important bearing on property right. Regardless of what property either spouse may hold or own at the time of marriage, the other immediately becomes possessed of his or her moiety [half]. Should the wife die, her husband retains possession of the property held in common so long as he does not remarry, but what might be termed the legal ownership of the wife's half interest becomes vested in her clan. Should he attempt to dissipate the property the members of the deceased wife's clan would at once interfere. If the widower wishes to marry again and the woman of his choice belongs to the clan of his former wife, then he and the new wife become owners in common of all personal property held by him; but if the second wife belongs to a different clan from that of the former wife, then the husband must make actual transfer of half of the common property to the clanspeople of the deceased woman, who inherited the legal interest in it at their relative's death. The same tribal law applies in the case of a widow. . . .

With the breaking up of the clans, together with the rapid disintegration of ancient customs and laws, this property law is fast becoming forgotten; but so recently as 1906 such disputes as those mentioned [i.e., disputes regarding this division of property] occurred under both the Fort Apache and San Carlos agencies, creating no little ill-feeling. In one instance a man refused to deliver possession of half of his little herd of horses to his deceased wife's clanspeople when contemplating marriage with another woman, and appealed to the missionaries for aid. He was compelled to make the division, however, before he could remarry.

From Frederic Seebohm, *Tribal Custom in Anglo-Saxon Law: Being an Essay Supplemental to (1) "The English Village Community"; (2) "The Tribal System in Wales"* (New York: Longmans, Green, and Company, 1911).

If it [the murder] was of someone within the kindred, there was . . . nothing but execration and ignominious exile.

But if a tribesman of one kindred were killed by a tribesman of another kindred, then it was a serious matter of blood feud between the kindreds, or the payment of the blood fine. The tribal conscience demanded vengeance or composition [compensation].

It sometimes happened that the murderer had fled to a church for safety, taking his cattle with him. . . .

There he remained presumably till the kindred of the murdered tribesman, through negotiation and arrangement of the chiefs of the kindreds, had agreed to accept the payment of the *galanas* [the stipulated price for the death of a person who held the rank of the deceased], if it were the case of an *uchelwr* or full tribesman, of 126 cows. Six cows . . . were *saraad* [a payment for the injury to the deceased's honour] for the insult, and 120 cows *galanas* for the murder. The *saraad* was paid first—six cows or other cattle to the same value belonging to the murderer were driven from the herd in payment.

The murderer's life was then safe, and presumably he might return with his cattle to his place.

Within a fortnight, the tribesmen of the murderer's kindred met to apportion the payment of the rest. They came from *trefgordds* [tribal settlements] far and near, from the territories sometimes of various higher territorial chieftains within whose districts they had grazing rights.

The collected tribesmen having apportioned the payment, fortnight after fortnight installments must be paid till the whole number in value of 120 cows was completed.

But by whom was the payment to be made?

Forty cows must first be found by the murderer, his *father, mother, brothers,* and *sisters* with him. . . .

The murderer himself had to pay a third of the 40 cows if he had them. His father and mother between them paid the next third, and the brothers and sisters the remaining third, the sisters paying half what the brothers did. . . .

The remainder of the galanas, viz. 80 cows, fell on the kindred, to the seventh degree or fifth cousins. The paternal relations had to find two thirds of it and the maternal one third.

From K.N. Llewellyn and E. Adamson Hoebel, *The Cheyenne Way: Conflict and Case Law in Primitive Jurisprudence* (Norman: University of Oklahoma, 1941).

Cheyenne girls wore a chastity belt which was assumed upon puberty. It consisted of a thin rope placed about the waist, knotted in front over the abdomen, with the free ends passing down between the thighs to the back, thence down around the legs to the knees. It was worn always at night, as well as during the day when away from the home lodge.

Its respect was law. To disturb the rope, or to assault a girl, was a private delict of first magnitude. Unless the offender fled into temporary exile, he stood in danger of death at the hands of women relatives of the outraged girl.

As Dog stated it, the women's relatives, when informed by a girl of her misfortune, charged the lodge of the boy, and laying about right and left, destroyed whatever of his goods came to hand and killed his horses. If the father of the boy was at home, he came out of the lodge and stood to one side to let them at it. Even the parents could lose thereby. Dog avers he has seen this done. He probably refers to Lone Elk, who forty years ago untied a girl's rope, according to the testimony of Black Wolf. In this case the mother destroyed all the property of the boy's parents.

From E. Adamson Hoebel, *The Law of Primitive Man: A Study in Comparative Legal Dynamics* (Cambridge, MA: Harvard University, 1954).

The third basic [legal] postulate (*Life is hard*) and its corollary (*The unsupportability of unproductive members of society*) is expressed not in the form of legal injunctions but, on the contrary, in privilege [personal] rights. Infanticide, invalidicide, senilicide, and suicide are privileged acts: socially approved homicide. . . .

Weyer records a poignant example:

> A hunter living on the Diomede Islands related to the writer how he killed his own father, at the latter's request. The old Eskimo was failing, he could no longer contribute what he thought should be his share as a member of the group; so he asked his son, then a lad about twelve years old, to sharpen the big hunting knife. Then he indicated the vulnerable spot over his heart where his son should stab him. The boy plunged the knife deep, but the stroke failed to take effect. The old father suggested with dignity and resignation, "Try it a little higher, my son." The second stab was effective, and the patriarch passed into the realm of the ancestral shades.

Stabbing is but one form of Eskimo senilicide. Hanging, strangulation, blocking up in a snow house to freeze to death, and abandonment in the open wastes by a travelling group are all used by various Eskimos. . . .

Between suicide and senilicide and invalidicide stands suicide-with-assistance. . . . In East Greenland, a woman who led a blind neighbour to the local suicide cliff so that she could jump off to her end, virtuously told Holm how she had refused pay for her services. She was not a relative, but after all, she was a friend.

✦ Discussion ✦

The Concept of Law Has Changed Across History

As the reading from Frederick Pollock illustrates, the word "law" has an abstract and a concrete meaning. These meanings have been conflated in English. As a result, we now refer to legislation as "law," in both senses of the word. This usage implicitly suggests both that it is the role of the legislature to make law and that we are obliged to follow the laws that the legislature passes. As a result, the English common law holds that judges do not make law.

The tribal law out of which the common law developed had its origins in the moral customs of the people, however, rather than in legislation. These customs were binding in themselves and were "law" in the abstract sense. The idea that law is a product of the political system, in contrast, and that Parliament or Congress can change the law is a relatively late development in human history and has led to some extremes in theory, such as the idea that states exist above the law.

It is significant that the general outlines of tribal law are similar throughout the world. This body of law still operates in many societies and is an integral part of Aboriginal traditions. It is this body of law that gave rise to the abstract sense of the word "law," which recognizes that there are social customs and prescriptions that we are obliged to follow. Some of these prescriptions have a personal character and impose private duties on individuals, usually in the form of taboos. It is the cosmological significance of these early customs and prescriptions, however, that explains their binding nature. The failure to follow such customs has consequences, for the clan and the tribe, that extend beyond the social and physical world.

The Tribal Law Is Law in Pollock's Abstract Sense

The different senses of the word "law" are expressed in different words in other languages. Law in the abstract, Pollock tells us, is "*ius* in Latin, *droit* in French, *diritto* in Italian, *Recht* in German," while legislation is referred to as *lex* in Latin, *loi* in French, *legge* in Italian, and *Gesetz* in German.[1] The tribal custom out of which the customary law in England derived is law in the abstract sense. The failure to distinguish clearly between these senses of the word in English has rather remarkable philosophical consequences, since it makes it impossible linguistically to question whether a particular piece of legislation qualifies as "law" in the abstract sense. This difficulty can be attributed to the overwhelming influence of legal positivism in the English legal tradition, which holds that any law passed by Parliament is binding and must be obeyed.

This use of the term "law" in the context of legislation does not reflect the origins of the common law. Historically, laws existed, literally from time immemorial, long before the development of the formal political machinery that we now associate with the institutional process of making laws. As Pollock writes, law—and law in the strongest sense, as a specific, formalized rule of behaviour that must be obeyed—"has existed before the State had any adequate means of compelling its observance." It is not law, then, but the development of a formal mechanism to enforce the law that appears to have provided the impetus behind theories like legal positivism.

The Tribal Law Is Inherently Binding

The origins of the common law can be traced to pre-ancient societies—those societies that existed before recorded history. It is clear from the accounts that we have that these societies were essentially tribal.[2] It is also clear that social life within such societies was regulated by custom. The enforcement of these customs was relatively informal, and before the advent of the common law, it was families and clans who took it upon themselves to enforce the law.[3] This does not mean, however, that there was no law or that the law was vague or ill-defined.

The general view in early tribal societies was that the behaviour of people is governed by the law, which already exists. The idea that law can somehow be created by human institutions was foreign to early peoples. The tribal societies from which the common law developed had no police or centralized authority. Their customs were based on a wisdom tradition that rested on the memory and learning of elders.[4] This does not mean that the customs in these societies did not have binding force of law. Quite the contrary is true: in spite of their lack of formal institutional mechanisms, these societies were governed by law rather than by organized politics, and individuals were obliged to follow custom.

The historical supremacy of the law in these early societies has not been fully recognized in the modern literature. This omission may be a reflection of the degree to which politics and political theory have captured the modern imagination. It may also be a reflection of the centralization and concentration of political power. In either case, however, the development of legal theory in the common law tradition is based to a large extent on a historical shift away from societies governed by law to societies governed by politics.

The Tribal Law Is Cosmological

It is important, then, to say something about the tribal law and the theory behind it before discussing the common law. One of the problems that we encounter in considering the tribal theory of law is that tribal peoples consider it wrong to inquire too closely into the origins and meanings of the customs that take the form of law.[5] Some of the theoretical postulates in this body of law can nevertheless be inferred from our knowledge of such societies.

The law in modern Western societies is secular and rests on the existence of a centralized political authority. The law in tribal societies, in contrast, is a product of religious and metaphysical beliefs as well as the customs associated with those beliefs. It follows that there is no need for an external mechanism to enforce the tribal law.[6] This is because there is no conceptual separation between an individual's personal beliefs and the law. The law is internalized and exists in some sense psychologically, within the makeup of the individual.

These aspects of the tribal law distinguish it from the political conception of law that has supplanted it in the modern state. This law is often called "positive" law, a reference to the fact that it is made by humans. The tribal law is based on the belief, in contrast, that the law is grounded in the natural order of the universe, which must be respected. Actions that disrupt the natural and supernatural order lead to calamity. As a result, tribal people feel compelled to conform to the customs that find expression in the law.

The Sanctions for the Breach of the Tribal Law Extend into the Natural World

The compulsory character of the tribal law comes from the inclusion of natural and supernatural sanctions within the framework of the law. This is evident in the prescriptions in the tribal law that govern the relationship between people and animals. Such laws have strong significance among hunting peoples, and hunters are expected to respect the place of animals within the cosmological order. The traditional law of the Dunne-za (or "Beaver People") in western Canada, for example, are based on customs that are intended to maintain the correct relations between individual hunters and the animals they hunt. Animals were pleased by the hunter's respect for their bodies and noticed his generosity in distributing the meat.[7]

The modern, state-centred conception of the law is overwhelmingly secular, and we have difficulty with the spiritual aspect of the tribal law, which extends our social relationships into the dream world. Animals and people inhabit the same cosmological order, and animals will withdraw from people who have not respected their customary obligations. The traditional Dunne-za believe that a hunter enjoys a relationship with the animal he hunts in his dreams and that the proper maintenance of this relationship—through proper behaviour, the dream experience, and the use of "medicine"—is crucial to the survival of the tribe.

The cosmological nature of the tribal law means that our failure to adhere to moral and social rules has consequences in the natural and supernatural worlds. This can be seen in the role played by Inuit shamans in the traditional law, which was based on the idea that it was the disruption of the proper relations between things that led to misfortune. Even now, traditional Inuit believe that a hunter's failure to follow the restrictions in the traditional law will shorten that person's life or bring misfortune to his or her children.

The purpose of *angukkiq*—a kind of public inquisition and confession—is to repair the damage that a breach of the law has caused to the relations in the proper order of things.[8]

Religious and Legal Institutions Are Associated with Each Other in the Tribal Law

This connection between religious and legal institutions is apparent everywhere in the tribal law. As a result, an individual's social obligations are backed by natural and supernatural forces. This backing gives the law remarkable authority, since it has the force of the cosmos behind it. Although it would be naive to think that the tribal law subsists without some level of coercion, it is not possible to study this law without realizing that our own separation of law, religion, and culture may have inadvertently emptied the law of most of its force. The distinctive feature of the tribal law from a functional perspective is that it relies on internal rather than external mechanisms to uphold the law.

Among the Iroquois, for example, a sick person may still consult a fortune teller to determine whether he or she has failed to fulfill a legal obligation. As Annemarie Shimony writes,

> It is possible . . . though not frequent, that the fortune teller will merely see disease. . . . More typically, however, the fortune teller endowed with supernatural powers of diagnosis will perceive a cause which is less somatic in character. This might be neglect of a ritual obligation in either the social or religious spheres, in the traditional duties of the life cycle, or in the realm of the medicinal secret societies.[9]

The fortune teller may accordingly prescribe a set of songs or dances to repair the breach in the social, cultural, and religious order.

The Tribal Law Maintains Social Cohesion

Although the tribal law was a forerunner of our own system of law, this law still exists among native peoples and provides a compelling alternative to contemporary Western legal systems. Some of the essential doctrines in the common law—the doctrine of self-defence, for example—have their origins in this body of law. It is clear, moreover, that tribal law has its own strengths and is probably more successful in resolving social conflicts. This ability to resolve conflict should not surprise us: from a social perspective, at least, the purpose of the tribal law is to maintain the social harmony that is necessary to maintain cohesive relations between families and clans.

The social practices of tribes are based on the way of life of the members of the tribe rather than some form of majority rule. As a result, there is a level of personal commitment to the tribal law that is difficult to find in the law of the state. This commitment can be seen in Llewellyn and Hoebel's description of the punishment for sexual assault among the Cheyenne, which was accepted without rancor by the family of the man who had committed the assault. This kind of acceptance is based on the recognition that the family of the victim must be appeased, in order to maintain social harmony between the families involved in the dispute.

This concern with social harmony is apparent in the rights extended to victims in the tribal law, as well as the lack of moral denunciation. It is also clear that the tribal law is less concerned with the general regulation of public behaviour than our own law is, which has strong elements of social *control*.[10] Nor should the lack of a developed political system or the oral nature of the tribal law mislead us. The complexities in the tribal law relate to the exercise of judgement rather than to the substantive framework of the law and cannot be captured in a simple written code. It is clear, moreover, that the tribal law contains an extensive jurisprudence, which became part of the customary law and provided the original source of the common law.

The Tribal Law Governs the Relations between Families

Although the tribal law is based on cosmological beliefs, its primary purpose is to govern the social relations within the tribe. The logical antecedents of the tribal law can be found in the existence of families and clans, which together make up the tribe. This law has survived among many peoples. Most of the customs that made their way from the tribal law into the customary law governed the relations between families or clans within the larger organizational unit of the tribe. Thus the customary law can be seen as a precursor of our domestic law, which governs everyday life.

The term "tribal law" in this context does not refer to the law that governed the relations between tribes. The relations between tribes often took the form of war, which is usually seen as an activity outside the reach of law. There were at least some customs that regulated war, but these customs formed part of an early international law, rather than the tribal law. Tribes also recognized forms of peace-making and customs that facilitated trade, and they held general notions of honour and valour—all of which determined the correct conduct of war. War was useful, sociologically, in uniting the members of a tribe against a common enemy and providing an acceptable outlet for aggression.

There was a second source of law and legal administration within the tribe, which governed the relations inside the family and the clan. This was clan law, however, rather than tribal law. Clan law was enforced by the clan without the formal legal mechanisms that were developed to deal with the affairs between clans. An example of such enforcement is marriage within the clan, which violated the law forbidding endogamous unions and was therefore considered incestuous.[11] This prohibition remains active in many regions of the world and is generally punishable by death. The significant point in this context, however, is that the punishment—sometimes called "honour killing" because it is done to restore the family's honour—was carried out by the members of one's own family.[12]

It is nevertheless the law between families and clans that is primary in the tribal law. This is also the most significant aspect of the tribal law in terms of the later development of the common law. It is the relationship between families—sometimes called "kindreds"—that accordingly provides the immediate source of the early common law. The interesting legal fact is that it was the family that historically had legal status in tribal law and possessed a legal personality. This fact is evident in the case of marriage, which was seen as a contract between two families.

The Individual's Rights in Tribal Law Come From Membership in the Family

The legal status of the family does not deprive the individual of rights: on the contrary, as the example of suicide among the Inuit illustrates, it is membership in the family that gives individuals the authority to insist on their legal prerogatives. The significance of the legal personality of the family is probably clearest in those laws related to ownership. In the distant past, an individual might own private items, but property such as land was held in common among the members of a family or a clan.

The idea that the individual human being exists as a discrete legal entity, distinct from family and society, developed slowly over time.[13] There is no doubt that individuals enjoyed some form of rights in the tribal law. The idea of private ownership that we are familiar with developed later, however. As the readings illustrate, the distribution of marital property in tribal societies is a matter between families rather than individuals. Even in the Middle Ages, as land became seen increasingly as the property of a specific owner, this ownership came burdened with family obligations.

The Tribal Law Was Designed to Prevent Feuds

The law had become more and more complex with the introduction of the feudal system, which was hierarchical and provided the fundamental notion of allegiance that provided the foundation of the state. The fundamental purpose of the customary law, however, like the tribal law, was nevertheless to maintain the peace and the cohesiveness of the community. This desire for social cohesion found expression in the practice of compensation, which developed out of a desire to prevent feuds.

The term "feud" in this context refers to an unresolved, ongoing dispute between clans or kindreds. The difficulties that such disputes created in relatively fragile tribal societies—societies beset by the contingencies of climate or adverse circumstances like war—are easy to imagine. Feuds created deep ruptures between opposing kindreds and undermined the social harmony that was essential to maintaining cohesion among the members of the tribe.

Feuds Were Difficult to Control because They Were Based on Legal Obligations

The history of feuds in England and tribal Europe goes back beyond recorded history. The saga of *Beowulf*, which was recorded around the eighth century, is the story of a blood feud that was carried on within a strict set of customary obligations. These obligations persist in some areas of the world and have presented a major problem in Albania, for example, even though the state has denounced "blood feud" retaliation.[14] It is the obligatory nature of the feud that makes it so difficult to contain, since members of a family are required to avenge the family honour.[15] The prevalence of feuds among tribes has led some anthropologists to argue that the feud is actually a rudimentary legal mechanism, like a trial, and should not be seen as a simple outbreak of violence. This view is based on the common observation that the feud has been accepted as a legitimate way of resolving disputes in some societies.[16] The standard argument on the opposing side is that feuds rarely resolve the outstanding dispute and merely create additional conflict.[17]

The mechanics of the feud are often misunderstood. Individuals who participate in a feud are acting in accordance with their moral and legal obligations under the tribal antecedents of the law; they are not making an unfettered moral choice. This fact has led some theorists to conclude that feuds are most accurately seen as a *product* of early tribal law. This interpretation rests on an understanding of customary obligations, which have been replaced for the most part by our legal obligations to the state.

The Ultimate Tribal Sanction Was Banishment

The most severe legal sanction in tribal societies was banishment. This is because banishment represented the loss of one's membership in the clan and the tribe. Thus banishment was the loss of one's very existence. Really this was a kind of death, or something worse, since it seems that the exiled person—now no longer a "person"—would not be reconciled to his or her people in the afterlife. Émile Durkheim's notion of "anomie" may capture at least some of the emotional and psychological experience that accompanied banishment.

Those Who Lived Outside the Tribe Were Not Considered People

An individual's identity came from membership in a tribe. In modern terms, we might say that a member of an enemy tribe was not considered a human being. There were therefore few if any limits on the violence that a tribesman might visit upon his enemy. John C. Ewers, for example, describes the "inhuman" violence that tribes on the Canadian plains wreaked upon the members of enemy tribes:

> A Blackfoot [Siksika] warrior whose father, brother, or best friend had been killed by the tribe he was fighting was not content merely to take the scalp of a fallen enemy. He mutilated the body of his foe—cut off his hands, feet, and head, or even literally hacked him to pieces.[18]

In 1848, Canadian artist Paul Kane heard a report of a Blackfoot massacre of a party of Crees. Among "the slain was a pipe-stem carrier, whom they skinned and stuffed with grass; the figure was then placed in a trail which the Crees were accustomed to pass in their hunting excursions."[19]

It follows that there was a brutal side to tribal life. The moral magnitude of this kind of violence shrinks considerably, however, if we honestly confront the horrors of modern warfare, which include the use of nuclear weapons and chemical agents like napalm. The legal explanation, at least, is that a tribal enemy was not a legal person and was therefore not protected by the law. Indeed, he was less protected than the animals on which the hunters relied for sustenance, since there were many laws that required a hunter to treat an animal and its body with respect.

The Tribal Law Gave Rise to the Practice of Outlawry

The Blackfoot, like members of other tribes, saw themselves as humankind. Their enemies were accordingly the enemies of human society. This idea explains the origins of the "outlaw," who was seen as a predatory animal, like a wolf or a bear. John Reeves wrote, in 1787:

> WHEN a person was outlawed, everyone who knowingly fed, received, or harboured him, was subject to the same penalty as the outlaw himself; for which reason an outlaw had in earlier times been called "afriendlessman"; one who could not, by law, have a friend. An outlaw was said *caput gerere lupinum* [to have the head of a wolf] . . . and in the neighbourhood of the marshes of Wales, outlaws [seem to have been considered] literally as *capita lupini* [which meant that they could be killed as wild animals].[20]

This aspect of the tribal law carried over into the customary law. From there it made its way into the common law, which contained a cause of action under which a petitioner asked the courts to declare a particular individual an "outlaw."

Outlawry was a kind of conceptual banishment. The outlaw lost membership in society and was not entitled to enjoy the benefits of the law, since the purpose of the law is to govern the relations between the members of society. The outlaw was therefore civilly dead and could not enter into contracts or own property. This restriction on property ownership led to abuses, since the property of an outlaw reverted to the outlaw's lord, who had a vested interest in declaring his serfs outlaws.[21]

The Tribal Law Has Six Attributes

The main elements in the legal theory behind the tribal law are relatively easy to discern. The first conclusion we can draw is that the tribal law is cosmological. The philosophical idea behind this is that the natural order of things must be respected. The tribal law that governs our social behaviour—as well as family relations and the customs of the tribe—accordingly prescribes patterns of behaviour that conform to the order of the cosmos.

The second conclusion that we can draw is that the obligations under the tribal law are compulsory. People are required to follow the prescriptions in the law. This idea came into the customary law and then found its place in the common law, though it has been progressively weakened as the common law expanded and took on a policy function. The imperative nature of our concept of law clearly has its origins in these cosmological considerations and the metaphysics of law behind it.

The third conclusion is that the tribal law provided the essential structure of government before the introduction of centralized government. The development of an organized political system and the institutions of formal government came later. There are distinct advantages to the tribal system of government, since there is none of the opposition between the individual and the political institutions of government that characterizes modern democratic societies. It is true that some of this opposition is a product of the pluralistic nature of modern societies, which must maintain cohesion among individuals with differing religious, moral, and social beliefs.

The most social prominent fact in any comparison between life in tribes and life under the state is that individuals in a tribe are not subject to the same degree of social control. This social fact is apparent in many aspects of the social life of tribes. Although the Blackfeet, for example, often lived by raiding, they did so without formal government or the kind of formal military organization that we now associate with war. It was for individual warriors to decide for themselves whether they would participate in a raid and, if so, to what extent.

There is a philosophical argument that some of the freedom enjoyed by people in tribal societies is illusory, since the behaviour of the members of the tribe is still controlled by the customs of the tribe. This is a liberal criticism, which is based on the idea that a commitment to tribal customs restricts the personal choices, and intellectual and emotional freedom, of the individual. From a more functional perspective, however, the tribal system removes the fundamental irritant in the modern law, which comes from the fact that individuals often reject the legislation passed by the state.

This feature of the state system has no parallel in the tribal system of law. The two most obvious explanations for this difference seem to collapse into each other. The first reason is that the tribal law is based on consensus rather than majority rule. The second reason, which helps to explain the first, is that the customs of the people have been internalized by the members of the tribe. As a result, the need for the coercive mechanisms of the state (which may have reached their apex in the modern state, with its myriad of regulatory institutions) is very limited.

The fourth conclusion is that the civil purpose of the tribal law is to preserve harmony and peace. The tribal law achieves this goal by maintaining a harmonious relationship between the families and clans that make up the tribe. Reconciliation and the rights of victims therefore have a prominent place in this body of law, which is based on a system of self-help and the idea that something must be done to rectify the wrongful state of things. This idea manifests itself in practices like *infangthief*, which gave individuals the right to chase and kill a thief.

The fifth conclusion is that legal personality in the tribal law usually attaches to the family rather than the individual. This conclusion may reflect the arduous reality that individuals generally cannot survive without the help and support of others in tribal conditions. This aspect of the tribal law has profound implications for legal theory, since it runs directly against the modern assumption that society is legally composed of discrete individuals.

The sixth conclusion is related to the fifth. This final conclusion is that it is the individual's membership, first in the family and second in the tribe, that matters in the tribal law. The goal in tribal life is to be, in the profoundest sense, a member of the tribe. This means doing what a member of the tribe will do, according to the customs of the tribe and the tribal law. Thus the ultimate legal sanction is the loss of one's membership, originally in the tribe and later in society more generally. This idea made its way into the customary law and the common law under the institution of outlawry.

Anthropologists Have Debated Whether Tribal Law Is "Law"

Although people who live in tribes have a cogent concept of law, there is considerable confusion in the anthropological literature as to the exact status of the tribal law. This confusion has a philosophical source and can be attributed to the fact that anthropologists have tended to see the law, in positivist terms, as the product of the state. Many anthropologists have accordingly concluded that tribes have no law. The failure of such a position to account for the realities of the tribal view has led other anthropologists to disagree.

The resulting debate has often focussed on the traditional law of the Inuit. This law is of particular interest because the Inuit have historically lived in scattered settlements without a discernible social, legal, or political structure. Even the term "tribe" (like the term "Inuit") is problematic in this context, since the Aboriginal people in the Arctic were organized along family rather than tribal lines. The most that can be said is that there was an extremely loose collection of people in the North, related by kin, who shared common elements of an anthropological past.

It is nevertheless clear that the clan law that prevailed among the Inuit—and that manifests itself in extremely informal legal procedures—is the same kind of law that provides the basis of the tribal law. This testifies to the deeper origins of the concept of law, which existed among the Inuit in spite of the fact that they did not have a recognizable form of political government. The traditional law of the Inuit existed without any of the institutional machinery that has become such an essential part of Western legal systems.

It is the absence of a system of government among the Inuit that seems to have led the last generation of anthropologists to conclude that the Inuit had no law. Yet the concept of law on which these anthropologists relied is a legislative concept and has no place in the tribal scheme of conceptions. It is a historical mistake to think that the origins of law can be found in the political order and a formal system of government. This view nevertheless corresponds with the positivist conception of law that we find in the contemporary Western tradition.

Anthropologists Who Subscribe to a Political Conception of Law Have Argued that Tribal Law Is Not Law

The prevailing state-centred conception of law can be traced to the work of John Austin and H.L.A. Hart, which has had a profound influence on the use of the word "law" in ther domains. Thus anthropologists trying to discover whether tribal societies have "law" have often looked for evidence, however sparse, that these societies have the political machinery of government to pass law.[22] This is fundamentally problematic and is much like searching for the state where it does not exist.

The problem is that the law and tribes existed long before there was a state. The contemporary literature simply assumes, often unintentionally, that the state represents the only logical means of organizing human society. This is a constructed, ahistorical position, however, which fails to recognize that the state is a political invention. The tribal system existed before the state and provides an alternative form of social organization based on the concept of law rather than political government.

Other Anthropologists Have Argued that the Political Conception of Law Is Too Narrow

Some anthropologists have attempted to redefine the term "law" in a broader, less culturally specific manner. Leopold Pospíšil, author of *Anthropology of Law: A Comparative Theory*, himself refers to law as "one of the specialized and institutionalized forms" of "social control in general."[23] This definition comes out of the social sciences but neglects the moral and cosmological foundations of tribal law. There are hidden philosophical assumptions in the reduction of law to mere behaviour, however, and it is inappropriate to speak about the taboos in tribal law, for example, as if they were mere preferences. Such assumptions simply discard the claim to meaning in the cultural, religious, and metaphysical views of tribal peoples.

The more recent work in legal anthropology has nevertheless moved away from the positivist conception of law. Sally Falk Moore has written that there are now three distinct conceptions of law in the anthropological literature.[24] One is that law in "non-Western" societies is "an expression of basic, and often unique, cultural premises." This conception seems to finesse the philosophical issue, which is whether tribal law is law in the full sense of the word.

The second conception of law comes out of the sociological literature and has Marxist overtones. It holds that "law" is a means of social control that serves the interests of "the powerful" in society. This is a political conception of law, which is aligned with legal positivism and a legislative concept of law. One of the problems with such a view is that it neglects the views of those people who live in tribal societies and is foreign to their conceptions. Such a view inevitably minimizes the cosmological elements in the tribal law and treats tribal values as cultural artifacts, which have little authority.

Moore's third conception of law is more functional. This concept holds that we simply use the word "law" to identify the means that we use to minimize conflict in society and solve social problems. It is this view, Moore suggests, that is distinctly legal. Although this conception of law fails to tell us what the law is, it extends the concept of law well beyond the confines of positivism. This reflects the current tendency across a range of disciplines, which have embraced legal pluralism and recognized that there are many sources of law outside the state. These sources naturally include the tribal law.

The Tribal Law Developed Its Own Forms of Legal Redress

There is a related debate in the anthropological literature with respect to tribal forms of trial and dispute resolution. In *The Law of Primitive Man*, for example, E. Adamson Hoebel writes:

> Homicidal dispute, though prevalent, is made less frequent in many Eskimo groups by recourse to regulated combat—wrestling, buffeting, and butting. Buffeting is found among the central tribes along the Arctic Circle from Hudson Bay to Bering Straits. Wrestling occurs in Siberia, Alaska, Baffinland, and Northwest Greenland. Head-butting as a feature of the song duel occurs in West and East Greenland. All three forms are a type of wager by battle without the element of divine judgement.[25]

Hoebel describes these kinds of contests as "juridical forms," which leave the loser relatively unharmed, thus preserving his capacity to contribute physically to his people.

The question is whether these forms of trial and dispute resolution share in the characteristics of the legal process and, more fundamentally, what those characteristics might be. Before we reject such an idea, we should remember that these tribal forms of resolving dispute had counterparts in northern Europe, and in the early common law, which made use of trial by battle and trial by ordeal. It is clear, as many commentators have recognized, that the adversarial nature of the trial process in the common law, and the role of the common law judge, can be traced to tribal customs.

The Customary Law Was Based on the Tribal Law

The general origins of the common law tradition lie in the tribal law, which was well developed in Northern Europe. This body of law had many sources but came primarily from the customs of the Norse and the Teutonic tribes in England. These customs included elements of the ecclesiastical law, which came into the tribal law with the general conversion to Christianity. This body of law provided the foundations, at least, of the customary law, the collection of laws that made their way into the first written laws in England.

The Teutonic tribes came into England from the south and had a well-established system of traditional law. The Norse contributed a form of government that separated the legal and political process. It is said that the "Thing" (their general assembly) opened with a recitation of the law, which could not be changed. Their idea of a fixed law and an independent legal tradition laid the foundations for the later development of the constitutional law.[26] Thus it was often said that the Icelanders, for example, had no King "except the law."

The customary law in England is usually traced to King Ethelbert, who followed the general practice of the times publishing his "dooms." As Victor Windeyer, a celebrated judge and professor, writes:

> In the year of our Lord 600, or thereabouts, Ethelbert, King of Kent, set down
> in writing laws for his folk. These laws were called dooms. The word *doom* is,
> perhaps, best translated as "judgement." It survived in occasional use until the
> fourteenth century.[27]

The word "doom" expresses the common law idea that the law has its origins in the judgement of someone wise or powerful.[28]

Ethelbert's dooms are believed to be the first written laws in England. Windeyer writes:

> The distinction, which we make to-day between the legislator, who makes the
> law, and the judge, who interprets, declares, and applies it, was not known to our
> Anglo-Saxon ancestors.[29]

This is misleading, however, since the idea of legislation is a much later development, and Ethelbert's instruction to his counsellors to write down his dooms was not a legislative act.

Ethelbert's dooms simply record his account of the customs of the people, as they had been handed down from generation to generation. This idea of preserving the customs of the past is central to the common law tradition. Ethelbert was not making law, and the idea that the law could be changed came in centuries later, with the creation of Parliament. The customary law existed independently of any political institutions and was the chief source of social stability in changing circumstances. The King was obliged to respect the law and, after the general conversion to Christianity, he was under the threat of damnation if he failed to do so.

The fundamental purpose of Ethelbert's dooms was to provide some form of private compensation for those who had suffered a wrong. We have already seen that compensation developed as a legal alternative to feuds, and the two practices existed together for a considerable time. It is no surprise, then, that the same fundamental formula explains both practices. The introduction of compensation in the customary law—which is important in the development of a monetary economy—was based on the idea that wrongs had a price and that the payment of the price cancelled the original wrong.

This idea that a wrong was nullified by the payment of compensation provided the central idea in the customary law. There was an explicit *wergild* or "blood price" in the tribal laws of northern Europe, which set the value of a life according to a person's rank in society. And most of Ethelbert's dooms are made up of a tariff, which sets out specific compensations. Anyone who stole the property of a bishop, for example, had to pay the bishop elevenfold; for the property of a priest, ninefold payment was required. There is also a schedule of compensations for minor injuries: e.g., an ear, 12 shillings; an eye, 50; the chin-bone, 20; a front tooth, 6; a fingernail, 1; a big toe, 10.

The focus on compensation also explains the practice of paying *galanas* described by Frederic Seebohm. Since cattle were the most valuable possession that families owned, the payment of cattle reflects the fact that a relatively high price had to be paid for the killing of someone in another clan. The two payments required by the tribal law—*saraad* for the insult and *galanas* for the killing—seem to presage the division of liability into criminal and civil heads of liability. At the same time, it is a mistake to think that these payments were based on an assessment of blame. The obligation to pay these compensations was based on the fact that a member of a clan had died, rather than the evil intention or moral blameworthiness of the act that killed him.

Ethelbert was an Anglo-Saxon King and essentially an invader. The historical record at least suggests that he had the customary law written down in order to reassure the people that he would respect their native customs. The customary law that found its way into Ethelbert's dooms, and later into the common law, was tribal law. This law had local sources. The most prominent sources of the tribal law that made its way into the common law, however, can be found in the Norse and Teutonic law.

The Common Law Was a Product of the Customary Law

The common law itself, however, is a product of the Norman Conquest, a process that can be traced to the victory of William the Conqueror at the Battle of Hastings in 1066. Before the Norman Conquest, England was divided into a number of kingdoms that were autonomous in their internal affairs. William claimed all of England, but his authority over many regions of the country was limited, and he was forced to move carefully to assert control over the country. The new King had to respect the customary law and its tribal character, which was reflected in the concentration of legal and political power at the local level.

William the Conqueror is responsible for two efforts that ultimately unified the country. The first was the compilation of a list of all the property owners in England. This resulted in the publication of the *Domesday Book*, which provided William with a tax roll and placed all of the land in England under a single administration. The second effort, which is related to the first, was the development of a unified legal system and a corresponding body of law, which applied throughout the country. Although the formal establishment of such a system is usually attributed to Henry II (1154–1189), it was a gradual development over time.

The development of the common law was a product of the competition between local and national authorities. This competition was reflected in the constant assertion of the King's authority throughout the entire country. The political message in this development was clear: the King's law was "common" throughout the realm. The development of the law by the King's judges is discussed in Chapter 4. This development was based on the adoption of rules and principles from the customary law. This reliance on custom, and on precedent, is also evident in legal practices like trial by battle and the introduction of the jury system.

Notes

1. Pollock, *A First Book of Jurisprudence*, at p. 18.
2. There is an anthropological argument that some societies, like the Inuit, were even more rudimentary and functioned without tribes.
3. This is a general observation that goes far beyond the common law. See William Seagle, for example, *The History of Law* (New York: Tudor Publishing, 1946), where Seagle argues that the King's peace—and the emerging state—simply replaced "peace of the kindred." And see vol. 1 of Frederick Pollock and Frederic William Maitland, *The History of English Law before the Time of Edward I* (Cambridge: Cambridge University, 1895), at p. 7. Both sources are available in the *Legal Classics Library* at http://heinonline.org.
4. See Llewellyn and Hoebel, for example, *The Cheyenne Way*.
5. See the anecdote related by E. Adamson Hoebel in *The Law of Primitive Man: A Study in Comparative Legal Dynamics* (Cambridge, MA: Harvard University, 1954), at p. 69, where an Inuit man exclaims, in frustration: "We are content not to understand."
6. See the discussion in William A. Haviland, "Political Organization and the Maintenance of Order," in *Cultural Anthropology*, 10th ed. (Belmont, CA: Wadsworth, 2002), at p. 339, where Haviland discusses different kinds of "political systems." Social order and cohesion in tribes, which have no central government, is maintained by "beliefs and values deeply internalized in the minds of individuals." He argues that it is this internalization of norms, rather than some formal mechanism of external control, that provides the law with its legal force. The member of a tribe believes that he or she must follow the customs of the people—and accordingly does so.
7. See Robin Ridington, "Technology, World View, and Adaptive Strategy in a Northern Hunting Society," *Canadian Review of Sociology and Anthropology* 19, no. 4 (1982): 469–80; republished in David R. Miller et al., *The First Ones: Readings in Indian/Native Studies* (Piapot Reserve: Saskatchewan Indian Federated College, 1992), pp. 160–6.
8. See Mariano Aupilaarjuk et al., *Perspectives on Traditional Law* and *Cosmology and Shamanism*, as cited in the suggestions for further reading.
9. Annemarie Shimony, "Iroquois Witchcraft at Six Nations," in *Systems of North American Witchcraft and Sorcery*, ed. Deward E. Walker Jr. (Moscow: University of Idaho, 1970), pp. 239–65, at p. 241.
10. This is apparent in the development of constitutional rights that place limits on the more oppressive aspects of our own legal and political system. These rights have been rejected by Aboriginal authors, on the basis that they are based on a separation between the individual and the state that has no place in the tribal law. See the reading from Boldt and Long in Chapter 18.
11. "Endogamy" refers to marriage between individuals within the same clan. This refers to a social rather than a sexual prohibition, which has acquired different overtones in a modern context. The anthropological literature suggests that the customary rules requiring exogamy—marriage outside the clan—are universal. One of the more acclaimed pieces in the literature on this topic is Claude Levi-Strauss' *The Elementary Structures of Kinship* (Boston: Beacon, 1969). And see Roy Wagner, "Incest and Identity: A Critique and Theory on the Subject of Exogamy and Incest Prohibition," *Man* 7, no. 4 (December 1972): 601–13.
12. The punishment of death is nevertheless rare in tribal society. See Ralekvo Oberg, for example, "Crime and Punishment in Tlingit Society," *American Anthropologist* 36, no. 2 (April–June 1934): 145–56, at p. 146, where he writes that crimes like murder did not attract the death penalty. "A clan punished its members by death only when shame was brought to its honor. Crimes of this nature were incest, witchcraft, marriage with a slave, and prostitution." For a discussion of honour killing in Western societies, see Clementine van Eck, *Purified by Blood: Honour Killings amongst Turks in the Netherlands* (Amsterdam: Amsterdam University, 2003).

13. See the comment by Theodore Frank Thomas Plucknett in *A Concise History of the Common Law* (Union, NJ: Lawbook Exchange, 2001), at p. 8, regarding the introduction of the concept of the individual.

14. See Immigration and Refugee Board of Canada, *Albania: Statistics on Blood Feuds; State Protection and Support Services Available to Those Affected by Blood Feuds, Including Whether Individuals Have Been Prosecuted for Blood-Feud-Related Crimes (2007—September 2010)*, 15 October 2010, ALB103573.E, available at www.unhcr.org/refworld/docid/4dd10ee72.html. And see, for example, Michael L. Galaty, "Blood of Our Ancestors: Cultural Heritage Management in the Balkans," in *Contested Cultural Heritage: Religion, Nationalism, Erasure and Exclusion in a Global World*, ed. Helaine Silverman (New York: Springer, 2011), pp. 109–24.

15. Feuding takes place within the families and kindreds within a tribal society. Feuds can be distinguished from wars in a tribal context, as wars occur between tribes. This distinction is important in legal theory, since it was generally felt that no law exists in war, unless it is the law of nature. This analysis naturally falls short in the context of the development of societies that included different tribes, in which case the word might be applied to the conflicts that take place between different tribes.

16. This kind of idea found expression in institutions like trial by combat.

17. See the additional online reading by Pospíšil.

18. John C. Ewers, "Blackfoot Raiding for Horses and Scalps," in *Law and Warfare: Studies in the Anthropology of Conflict*, ed. Paul Bohannan (New York: Natural History, 1867), 327–44, at p. 339.

19. Paul Kane, *Wanderings of an Artist among the Indians of North America: From Canada to Vancouver's Island and Oregon through the Hudson's Bay Company's Territory and Back Again* (London: Longman, Brown, Green, Longmans, and Roberts, 1859), at p. 410.

20. John Reeves, vol. 2 of *History of the English Law, from the Time of the Saxons, to the End of the Reign of Philip and Mary*, 4 vols. (Dublin: Luke White, 1787). Available at http://heinonline.org. For a popular but nevertheless informative account of "outlawry," see the entry in *The Penny Cyclopedia for the Diffusion of Useful Knowledge*, as cited in the suggestions for further reading, which recounts the "fabulous" tale that the same bounty would be paid for the head of a wolf or an outlaw.

21. The sixth edition of *Bouvier's Law Dictionary*, published in 1856, puts it simply: "OUTLAW, Engl. law. One who is put out of the protection or aid of the law. 3 Bl. Com. 283, 4." "Bl. Com." is a reference to Sir William Blackstone's famous *Commentaries*, which are discussed in Chapter 4. *Bouvier's* is available at www.constitution.org/bouv/bouvier.htm.

22. See the discussion of "anthropological approaches," for example, in Edward van der Vliet, "Justice and Written Laws in the Formation of the Polis," in *The Law's Beginnings*, ed. F.J.M. Feldbrugge (Leiden: Martinus Nijhoff, 2003), pp. 23–43, where he describes the project of anthropologists like Pospíšil as a search for the distinction between law and mere custom in "stateless" societies.

23. Pospíšil's own theory of law is essentially political. He is looking for a political mechanism of government, even in the most unstructured human society. There is an important philosophical idea behind this, which is that the essential political framework of every human society may share the same fundamental attributes. This would be an important discovery, like discovering that all human languages ultimately rely on the same deep structure, which provides a universal grammar. That is a separate issue, however, which fails to recognize that law provided its own means of governance in these societies.

24. Sally Falk Moore, "Certainties Undone: Fifty Turbulent Years of Legal Anthropology, 1949–1999," in *The Journal of the Royal Anthropological Institute* 7, no. 1 (March 2001): 95–116.

25. Hoebel, *The Law of Primitive Man*, p. 92. It is probably an error to assume that there was no element of divine judgement in these forms of trial, since the Inuit, like other tribal people, did not reject the natural and supernatural worlds.

26. The word "law" itself comes from the Old Norse "*laga*," originally meaning "something laid or fixed."

27. W.J.V. Windeyer, "Before the Norman Conquest," in *Lectures on Legal History*, 2nd ed. (Sydney: Law Book Co. of Australia, 1957), at p. 20.

28. Thus the final day on which Christians believe that God will judge us all is called the "doomsday," the day when God "dooms."
29. Windeyer, "Before the Norman Conquest," op. cit.

Study Questions

1. Where does the obligation to obey tribal law come from?

2. How does the strength of tribal law lie in the fact that it is internalized by members of tribal societies?

3. It is often said that the law was originally brought in to prevent feuds. How did it accomplish this end?

4. Why did the outlaw have the head of a wolf? What are the philosophical implications of outlawry? In tribal law, marriage was historically a contract between two families. How is the modern conception of marriage different? What is the primary purpose of marriage in tribal societies?

5. Why was banishment the worst punishment in tribal law? (You might want to consider Tom Porter's "Banishment in the Constitutional Law of the Mohawk," included in the additional online readings for this chapter, listed in the Appendix.)

6. Why have legal anthropologists struggled with the question whether there was "law" in tribal society? (Consider the online additional reading from Leopold Pospíšil.)

7. What is the role of government in tribal law?

8. The tribal law is still intact in many societies and arguably provides a "communitarian" concept of law, based on the well-being of the community, which subordinates the rights of the individual to the interests of the family or clan. How is this significant?

Further Reading

Mariano Aupilaarjuk et al., *Perspectives on Traditional Law*, ed. Jarich Oosten, Frederic Laugrand, and Wim Rasing, vol. 2 of *Interviewing Inuit Elders* (Nunavut: Arctic College, 1999).

———, *Cosmology and Shamanism*, ed. Bernard Saladin D'Anglure, vol. 4 of *Interviewing Inuit Elders* (Nunavut: Arctic College, 2001).

Paul Bohannan, ed., *Law and Warfare: Studies in the Anthropology of Conflict* (Garden City: Natural History, 1967).

Charles Knight, "Outlawry," in *The Penny Cyclopedia for the Diffusion of Useful Knowledge*, vol. 17 (London: Charles Knight and Co., 1840), p. 69. Available at http://books.google.ca.

P.D. King, *Law and Society in the Visigothic Kingdom* (Cambridge: Cambridge University, 1972).

Ajay K. Mehrotra, "Law and the 'Other': Karl N. Llewellyn, Cultural Anthropology, and the Legacy of *The Cheyenne Way*," *Law & Social Inquiry: Journal of the American Bar Foundation* 26, no. 3 (2001): 741–55.

Sally Falk Moore, *Law and Anthropology: A Reader* (Madden, MA: Blackwell, 2006).

2 The Christian Tradition

Thomas Aquinas

Reading

- From *The Summa Theologica*, by Thomas Aquinas

This chapter explores the theory of the natural law, as set out by Thomas Aquinas (1225–1274) in the *Summa Theologica*. Aquinas' version of the natural law, one of the fundamental legal theories in the Western tradition, was disseminated through the teachings of the Church and provided the basis of the canon law. It accordingly provides part of the legal and intellectual background of the common law.

The *Summa* takes the form of an interrogation. It is organized into a series of questions, some of which raise the most fundamental issues in philosophy of law. These questions are followed first by a list of "objections" that answer the question in the negative, then by a statement setting out the contrary, and finally by an "answer" that sets out Aquinas' position, along with his replies to the list of objections. This structure reflects the role of the medieval philosopher, who was expected to be able to answer any and all objections to his position. The following excerpts provide an overview of some of Aquinas' theory of the natural law.

⚹ Reading ⚹

From St. Thomas Aquinas, *The Summa Theologica of St. Thomas Aquinas*, 2nd and rev. ed., trans. by the Fathers of the English Dominican Province (1920). Available at www. newadvent.org./summa. Online ed. © 2006 Kevin Knight.

Question 90. The Essence of Law

Article 1. Whether Law Is Something Pertaining to Reason?

I answer that, Law is a rule and measure of acts, whereby man is induced to act or is restrained from acting: for *lex* [law] is derived from *ligare* [to bind], because it binds one to act. Now the rule and measure of human acts is the reason, which is the first principle of human acts. . . .

Article 2. Whether the Law Is Always Something Directed to the Common Good?

I answer that . . . the last end of human life is bliss or happiness. . . . Consequently the law must needs regard principally the relationship to happiness. Moreover, since every part is ordained to the whole, as imperfect to perfect; and since one man is a part of the perfect community, the law must needs regard properly the relationship to universal happiness. Wherefore the Philosopher,[1] in the above definition of legal matters mentions both happiness and the body politic: for he says (Ethic. v, 1) that we call those legal matters "just, which are adapted to produce and preserve happiness and its parts for the body politic": since the state is a perfect community, as he says in Polit. i, 1.

Now in every genus, that which belongs to it chiefly is the principle of the others, and the others belong to that genus in subordination to that thing: thus fire, which is chief among hot things, is the cause of heat in mixed bodies, and these are said to be hot in so far as they have a share of fire. Consequently, since the law is chiefly ordained to the common good, any other precept in regard to some individual work, must needs be devoid of the nature of a law, save in so far as it regards the common good. Therefore every law is ordained to the common good. . . .

Article 3. Whether the Reason of Any Man Is Competent to Make Laws?

I answer that, a law, properly speaking, regards first and foremost the order to the common good. Now to order anything to the common good, belongs either to the whole people, or to someone who is the viceregent of the whole people. And therefore the making of a law belongs either to the whole people or to a public personage who has care of the whole people. . . .

Article 4. Whether Promulgation Is Essential to a Law?

I answer that . . . a law is imposed on others by way of a rule and measure. Now a rule or measure is imposed by being applied to those who are to be ruled and measured by it. Wherefore, in order that a law obtain the binding force which is proper to a law, it must needs be applied to the men who have to be ruled by it. Such application is made by its being notified to them by promulgation. Wherefore promulgation is necessary for the law to obtain its force.

Thus from the four preceding articles, the definition of law may be gathered; and it is nothing else than an ordinance of reason for the common good, made by him who has care of the community, and promulgated. . . .

Question 91. The Various Kinds of Law

Article 1. Whether There Is an Eternal Law?

I answer that . . . a law is nothing else but a dictate of practical reason emanating from the ruler who governs a perfect community. Now it is evident . . . that the whole community of the universe is governed by Divine Reason. Wherefore the very Idea of the government of things in God, the Ruler of the universe, has the nature of a law. And since the Divine Reason's conception of things is not subject to time but is eternal, according to Proverbs 8:23, therefore it is that this kind of law must be called eternal. . . .

Article 2. Whether There Is in Us a Natural Law?

I answer that . . . law, being a rule and measure, can be in a person in two ways: in one way, as in him that rules and measures; in another way, as in that which is ruled and measured . . . Wherefore, since all things subject to Divine providence are ruled and measured by the eternal law . . . it is evident that all things partake somewhat of the eternal law, in so far as, namely, from its being imprinted on them, they derive their respective inclinations to their proper acts and ends. Now among all others, the rational creature is subject to Divine providence in the most excellent way, in so far as it partakes of a share of providence, by being provident both for itself and for others. Wherefore it has a share of the Eternal Reason, whereby it has a natural inclination to its proper act and end: and this participation of the eternal law in the rational creature is called the natural law. . . . It is therefore evident that the natural law is nothing else than the rational creature's participation of the eternal law.

Article 3. Whether There Is a Human Law?

I answer that . . . a law is a dictate of the practical reason. Now it is to be observed that the same procedure takes place in the practical and in the speculative reason: for each proceeds from principles to conclusions. . . . Accordingly we conclude that just as, in the speculative reason, from naturally known indemonstrable principles, we draw the conclusions of the various sciences, the knowledge of which is not imparted to us by nature, but acquired by the efforts of reason, so too it is from the precepts of the natural law, as from general and indemonstrable principles, that the human reason needs to proceed to the more particular determination of certain matters. These particular determinations, devised by human reason, are called human laws, provided the other essential conditions of law be observed. . . .

Article 4. Whether There Was Any Need for a Divine Law?

I answer that, besides the natural and the human law it was necessary for the directing of human conduct to have a Divine law. And this for four reasons. First, because it is by law that man is directed how to perform his proper acts in view of his last end. . . . [And] since man is ordained to an end of eternal happiness . . . therefore it was necessary that, besides the natural and the human law, man should be directed to his end by a law given by God.

Secondly . . . it was necessary for man to be directed in his proper acts by a law given by God, for it is certain that such a law cannot err.

Thirdly, because man . . . is not competent to judge of interior movements, that are hidden, but only of exterior acts which appear: and yet for the perfection of virtue it is necessary for man to conduct himself aright in both kinds of acts. Consequently human law could not sufficiently curb and direct interior acts; and it was necessary for this purpose that a Divine law should supervene.

Fourthly, because, as Augustine says (De Lib. Arb. i, 5,6), human law cannot punish or forbid all evil deeds . . . In order, therefore, that no evil might remain unforbidden and unpunished, it was necessary for the Divine law to supervene, whereby all sins are forbidden. . . .

Question 94. The Natural Law

Article 2. Whether the Natural Law Contains Several Precepts, or Only One?

I answer that . . . the first principle of practical reason is one founded on the notion of good, viz. that "good is that which all things seek after." Hence this is the first precept of law, that "good is to be done and pursued, and evil is to be avoided." All other precepts of the natural law are based upon this: so that whatever the practical reason naturally apprehends as man's good (or evil) belongs to the precepts of the natural law as something to be done or avoided.

Since, however, good has the nature of an end, and evil, the nature of a contrary, hence it is that all those things to which man has a natural inclination, are naturally apprehended by reason as being good, and consequently as objects of pursuit, and their contraries as evil, and objects of avoidance. Wherefore according to the order of natural inclinations, is the order of the precepts of the natural law. Because in man there is first of all an inclination to good in accordance with the nature which he has in common with all substances: inasmuch as every substance seeks the preservation of its own being, according to its nature: and by reason of this inclination, whatever is a means of preserving human life, and of warding off its obstacles, belongs to the natural law. Secondly, there is in man an inclination to things that pertain to him more specially, according to that nature which he has in common with other animals: and in virtue of this inclination, those things are said to belong to the natural law, "which nature has taught to all animals" [Pandect. Just. I, tit. i], such as sexual intercourse, education of offspring, and so forth. Thirdly, there is in man an inclination to good, according to the nature of his reason, which nature is proper to him: thus man has a natural inclination to know the truth about God, and to live in society: and in this respect, whatever pertains to this inclination belongs to the natural law; for instance, to shun ignorance, to avoid offending those among whom one has to live, and other such things regarding the above inclination. . . .

Article 4. Whether the Natural Law Is the Same in All Men?

I answer that . . . the natural law, as to general principles, is the same for all, both as to rectitude and as to knowledge. . . . and yet in some few cases it may fail, both as to rectitude, by reason of certain obstacles . . . and as to knowledge, since in some the reason is perverted by passion, or evil habit, or an evil disposition of nature; thus formerly, theft, although it is expressly contrary to the natural law, was not considered wrong among the Germans, as Julius Caesar relates (De Bello Gall. vi). . . .

Question 95. Human Law

1. Its Utility

Article 1. Whether It Was Useful for Laws to Be Framed By Men?

Objection 1. It would seem that it was not useful for laws to be framed by men. Because the purpose of every law is that man be made good thereby. . . . But men are more to be induced to be good willingly by means of admonitions, than against their will, by means of laws. Therefore there was no need to frame laws. . . .

On the contrary, Isidore[2] says (Etym. v, 20): "Laws were made that in fear thereof human audacity might be held in check, that innocence might be safeguarded in the midst of wickedness, and that the dread of punishment might prevent the wicked from doing harm." But these things are most necessary to mankind. Therefore it was necessary that human laws should be made.

I answer that . . . man has a natural aptitude for virtue; but the perfection of virtue must be acquired by man by means of some kind of training. Thus we observe that man is helped by industry in his necessities, for instance, in food and clothing. Certain beginnings of these he has from nature, viz. his reason and his hands; but he has not the full complement, as other animals have, to whom nature has given sufficiency of clothing and food. Now it is difficult to see how man could suffice for himself in the matter of this training: since the perfection of virtue consists chiefly in withdrawing man from undue pleasures, to which above all man is inclined, and especially the young, who are more capable of being trained. Consequently a man needs to receive this training from another, whereby to arrive at the perfection of virtue. And as to those young people who are inclined to acts of virtue, by their good natural disposition, or by custom, or rather by the gift of God, paternal training suffices, which is by admonitions. But since some are found to be depraved, and prone to vice, and not easily amenable to words, it was necessary for such to be restrained from evil by force and fear, in order that, at least, they might desist from evil-doing, and leave others in peace, and that they themselves, by being habituated in this way, might be brought to do willingly what hitherto they did from fear, and thus become virtuous. Now this kind of training, which compels through fear of punishment, is the discipline of laws. Therefore in order that man might have peace and virtue, it was necessary for laws to be framed: for, as the Philosopher says (Polit. i, 2), "as man is the most noble of animals if he be perfect in virtue, so is he the lowest of all, if he be severed from law and righteousness"; because man can use his reason to devise means of satisfying his lusts and evil passions, which other animals are unable to do.

Reply to Objection 1. Men who are well disposed are led willingly to virtue by being admonished better than by coercion: but men who are evilly disposed are not led to virtue unless they are compelled. . . .

2. Its Origin

Article 2. Whether Every Human Law Is Derived from the Natural Law?

I answer that, as Augustine[3] says (De Lib. Arb. i, 5) "that which is not just seems to be no law at all": wherefore the force of a law depends on the extent of its justice. Now in human affairs a thing is said to be just, from being right, according to the rule of reason. But the first rule of reason is the law of nature. . . . Consequently every human law has just so much of the nature of law, as it is derived from the law of nature. But if in any point it deflects from the law of nature, it is no longer a law but a perversion of law. . . .

Notes

1. Editor's note: "The Philosopher" is Aristotle. "Ethic." refers to Aristotle's *Nicomachean Ethics*, and "Polit." refers to his *Politics*.
2. Editor's note: The reference is to St. Isidore of Seville (c. 560–636), scholar and archbishop. "Etym." refers to his *Etymologiae*, which discusses the general study of origins.
3. Editor's note: St. Augustine of Hippo (354–430), philosopher and bishop. "De Lib. Arb." refers to his *De libero arbitrio (literally, "Of the free will")*.

⇝ Discussion ⇜

The Idea of the Natural Law became Prominent under the Stoics

The theory of the natural law has a long history. The Greek Stoics, for example, gave the idea of the natural law a prominent place in ethics as early as the third century BCE. The Roman writer Cicero (106 BCE–43 BCE) speaks of this law as the law of God, "everlasting and unchangeable, extending to all nations and all times, with one common teacher and ruler of all."[1] In his treatise on laws, he applies the theory of a natural moral law to law itself. Those "who formulated wicked and unjust statutes for nations," he writes, "thereby breaking their promises and agreements, put into effect *anything but laws*. It may thus be clear that in the very definition of the term 'law' there inheres the idea and principle of choosing what is just and true."[2]

It Then Made Its Way into Christian Theology

The Stoics believed that the natural order was rational and therefore available to reason. After the conversion to Christianity, this idea of the natural law made its way into Christian theology and became a prominent part of the Church's teachings. In the fourth century CE, St. Augustine speaks more generally of the "eternal law," which comprises God's laws over the natural creation. He also, however, poses one of the most pivotal questions in philosophy of law: Has a soldier who refuses to slaughter the enemy in accordance with his orders disobeyed the law, or is this law unjust and therefore not *truly* a "law"? Augustine's answer to the question that he poses has come down to us in the form of a maxim: *lex iniusta non est lex* (an unjust law is not a law).

In *Summa Theologica*, which was written in the thirteenth century, Thomas Aquinas developed these ideas further. The influences on Aquinas' thought were varied. In spite of the fact that Aquinas was, philosophically at least, a student of Aristotle, he was also schooled in Latin, and he knew the Roman law. This body of law, and the general views of the Romans, which gave the idea of duty particular prominence, had considerable influence on the official Church. In addition, it is evident that Aquinas was familiar with the general legal conventions of the day. The *Summa* discusses institutional issues, such as the role of precedent, as well as abstract philosophical issues.

In spite of the historical transitions that affected Aquinas' thought, it is clear that much of the older conceptual apparatus of the law survived in the thinking of the times. The Germanic tribes, and the Visigoths in particular, had been successful in winning control of the Holy Roman Empire, the notional Christian empire that survived the fall of the Roman Empire. These tribes maintained their law, which was written down and widely propagated throughout Europe. There must have been considerable confusion. The general outlines of the law were nevertheless emerging, and the confusion may have been helpful, philosophically, in establishing a more abstract idea of the law and identifying the theoretical principles on which different codes were based.

From the perspective of philosophy, it is simplistic to think that our grasp of theories and concepts always advances and improves. It seems clear, for example, that there was a more distinct division between legal and political responsibilities in Aquinas' time than there has been in the modern era. Aquinas mentions the role of the judicial process in the removal of a tyrant, for example, and the medievals had a sophisticated grasp of the role of legal and political institutions, which has been lost in the general loss of religious beliefs.

The General Influence of Aquinas' Work Is a Product of Its Central Place in the Church's Teaching

The influence of Aquinas' philosophical work in the Western tradition is a product of the fact that his work was recognized as the source of Catholic doctrine. With the general conversion to Christianity in Europe, the teachings of the Church became the basis of education. The Church also had its own courts. It had the right to prosecute for heresy, and its inquisitorial system had enormous influence in the development of the civil system of trial in continental Europe. As a result of the influence of the Church, the theological and philosophical framework that Aquinas sets out in the *Summa Theologica* provided a fundamental part of the foundations of Western legal thought.

Aquinas' Influence on the Legal Tradition Is General Rather Than Specific

As we saw in Chapter 1, the beginnings of the common law can be traced to the victory of William the Conqueror at the Battle of Hastings in the eleventh century and the creation of a central government. The common law developed only gradually, over hundreds of years, and was based on the existing customary law and the tribal sources of that law. The slowness of this process reflects the fragility of the central government.

The common law nevertheless had a political message and asserted the King's authority throughout the whole of England. The King's law was accordingly "common" throughout the realm. It is the competition between the King's authority and the authority of the political actors at the local level that explains the fundamental evolution of the English legal system. It is clear that the law at the local level maintained much of its customary character. The attitude of the general population still reflected the past.

Aquinas' influence on the emerging legal tradition was relatively indirect and more theoretical than practical. The significance of his work came mainly from his synthesis of classical and ecclesiastical sources and the prominence accorded to his teachings by the Church. Aquinas was a professor at the University of Paris, and his work helped to shape the entire academic and ecclesiastical tradition. The legal side of this tradition still reflected the tribal law, however, which provided the backbone of the Old Testament.

There were a number of factors that affected this development. Tribal life had reasserted itself with the fall of the Roman Empire. It seems clear, moreover, that people like the Norse retained many of their original convictions when they converted to Christianity. There is also the fact that later practices tended to be modelled on the tribal antecedents. There seems little doubt that the tribal sense of the supernatural must have invested Christian beliefs with a similar cosmological force. There is also the fact that later practices tended to be modelled on the tribal antecedents. The idea of excommunication, for example, consisted of expelling an individual from the community of the Church. This practice follows the practice of outlawry.

Aquinas' Influence on the Common Law Is Tied to the Historical Origins of That Law

Aquinas' theory of the natural law that we find in the *Summa* is accordingly the culmination of a long historical tradition. Although the *Summa* provides a far more systematic analysis of the law than was previously available, it is based implicitly on the theoretical precedents in the tribal law. As we saw in Chapter 1, this law was based on the theory that the universe has some order, which must be respected. From this point, it seems only a small step to Aquinas' position outlined in the *Summa*, which holds that there is a natural logic in this natural order, to which we must conform if we are to meet our ethical and religious obligations.

There is an epistemological and even scientific push in Aquinas' theory, since the key to ethical behaviour in such a system is to determine the inherent logic of the natural order. It is apparent that this idea leaves the basic conceptual framework of the tribal law and accompanying process of adjudication intact, in spite of the increasing sophistication of the law. The idea that there is a natural law is based on the belief, rooted deep in tribal history, that the law is pre-existing and must therefore be "found" rather than made. "Found" is still the term we use in the common law courts.

The same idea has provided the historical mainstay of the common law tradition. The most fundamental contribution of the ecclesiastical natural law tradition to the common law, however, was probably the development of a moral notion of wrong.[3] This development can be attributed to the preoccupation with sin in the ecclesiastical law, which based liability on the individual's exercise of free will. The notion of fault that came out of the ecclesiastical law was pivotal in the development of the criminal law and in torts, which were called "civil wrongs," meaning wrongs between persons. These developments are discussed in more detail in Part II. Here it is enough to set out Aquinas' theory of the natural law, which provides an important part of the theoretical foundations of the Western legal tradition. Although this theory has an ethical as well as a legal side, the following discussion restricts itself to legal theory.[4]

Aquinas' Definition of Law Has Become the Classical Definition of Law

The conception of law in the *Summa* is based on the theory of the natural law. This conception is significant because it premises the validity of the human or "positive" law on the ethical validity of that law. Aquinas' definition of law has become the classical definition of law in the Western tradition. In his answer to Question 90 of the *Summa*, Aquinas writes:

> Thus from the four preceding articles, the definition of law may be gathered; and it is nothing else than an ordinance of reason for the common good, made by him who has care of the community, and promulgated.

These four conditions deserve further discussion.

Law Is an Ordinance of Reason

Aquinas begins by stipulating that the law must be rational. In saying this, he does not mean that the law must be reasonable in its prescriptions, though that may follow implicitly from his position. Rather, he means that the law must be rational and therefore intelligible—after all, we cannot obey a law that is incomprehensible, or contradicts itself, or commands us to perform the impossible. He is also arguing, more substantively, that a law must be rationally connected to the "good" at which it aims. This principle has become an integral part of the constitutional law. In *R. v. Oakes*, [1986] 1 S.C.R. 103, for example, the Supreme Court of Canada held that the measures contemplated by a particular piece of legislation must be "rationally connected" to the objective of that legislation. This provides part of the test that is used in determining whether a law that limits our rights under the *Canadian Charter of Rights and Freedoms* can be "demonstrably justified."[5]

Law Is for the Common Good

Aquinas holds that laws are "for the common benefit of the citizens." It follows that the law "must needs concern itself" with the "universal happiness," the happiness or beatitude of "the body politic." This requirement provides us with a convenient moral and social criterion that determines whether specific laws are valid or invalid. It is fundamental that Aquinas places the welfare of the community as a whole above that of the individual person.

Law Is Made By Him Who Has Care of the Community

Aquinas also holds that the law must proceed from someone who has the authority to govern society. Limiting the definition of law to those ordinances presented by someone with the authority to govern stresses the social and public nature of law. Since a private person generally has no authority to inflict penalties or demand obedience from other people, the ordinance of a private person does not have the character of law.

Law Must Be Promulgated, or Proclaimed

Then there is the requirement that the law be promulgated, or proclaimed. This requirement stresses the need to make the law public. In the requirement of promulgation, or proclamation, we find the importance of making the law public. The law is not binding unless it has been properly conveyed to those who are governed by it. There might seem to be an exception in the case of the natural law, but Aquinas believes that the natural law is written in our hearts and thus available to anyone who seeks it. This is promulgation enough. The legitimacy of the positive law rests on its promulgation. People cannot be expected to obey the set of laws passed by human governments unless they have the means of knowing it. This theme expresses itself throughout the history of the positive law and raises a basic question of fairness.

The ancient Chinese, and many other peoples, felt that it was necessary to post the laws for everyone to see. Shang Yang (c. 390 BCE–338 BCE) is said to have inscribed the laws on stone tablets and placed them in the marketplace. The Athenians inscribed their laws on wooden stands and placed them under *stoa*, public porches that functioned as places where official announcements would be posted. One of the philosophical observations that can be made in this context is that the positive law provides a means of communication between a government and the people.

Aquinas' requirement that the law be promulgated has a practical corollary in the legal concept of notice. As a general rule, a person cannot take legal action against another party without notifying that party of its intentions. This was true historically, even in unusual cases. In a famous sixteenth-century case, French jurist Bartholomé Chassenée argued that a legal case against rats—trials against animals were common at the time—could not proceed because the rats had not been properly summoned.[6]

The requirement that a law be promulgated by the proper authority has also become a formal feature of modern legislative systems. In Canada, a law or regulation does not come into force until the cabinet has approved it, theoretically in consultation with the Governor General. The consent of the "governor-in-council" is indicated in practical terms by the publication of the legislation in a federal or provincial gazette; without publication, the legislation has no force and effect. As we will see in later chapters, the legal positivists have argued that this kind of technical or descriptive requirement, which does not address the morality of the legislation, is sufficient to create a valid law.

Aquinas' Definition Has a Normative Character

Aquinas' definition of law provides a convenient basis on which to examine the natural law and legal positivist theories that have vied for pre-eminence in the Western theoretical tradition. Although the positivist tradition had ascendancy in the nineteenth century and much of the twentieth, the contemporary literature has reintroduced an ethical or normative component into our understanding of the law. This is in line with Aquinas' requirement that a law should promote the common good. It follows that a law that does not promote the common good is not a valid law.

Aquinas Distinguishes Four Kinds of Law

Aquinas makes a distinction between four *kinds* of law.

The Eternal Law

Aquinas describes the eternal law as "the exemplar of divine wisdom." This is the law of God, which organizes the whole order of things. Aquinas demonstrates the existence of such a law as follows: Since the law is "an ordinance of reason," and the universe is governed by divine reason, the dictates by which the universe is governed have "the nature of law." There is another side to this proposition, particularly in a medieval context, since the divine right of kings held that the authority to govern society derives from God. The divine reason and the eternal law was accordingly the source of all other laws.

The Natural Law

The natural law is the law by which rational creatures understand and participate in the eternal law. It is that part of the eternal law that is available to us through the faculty of reason. Because it is a part of the eternal law, the natural law is authoritative and objectively true.

The natural law is both the source of human morality and the source of our obligation to obey most laws. There are at least two sources of such an obligation, which is more complex than it might appear. One source can be found in the fact that some aspect of the natural law, which is compulsory, is inherent in these laws. The other, however, comes from the fact that we are morally obliged to follow a particular code or a legal system—whatever its origins—because the natural law directs us to obey it.

The Natural Law Derives From Our Inclination for Self-Preservation

The natural law is more general than the human law. Aquinas informs us that the first precept of the natural law, which contains the other precepts of the natural law, is simply that "good [i.e., moral good] is to be done and promoted, and evil is to be avoided." The other precepts of the natural law are ordered in accordance with our natural inclinations. They derive initially from

i)   our inclination for self-preservation;
ii)   our inclination to fulfill our animal nature; and
iii) our inclination to good, in the natural exercise of the faculty of reason.

Since the natural law phrases itself in terms of duties, these subsidiary precepts suggest that we have a positive duty to preserve ourselves, to fulfill our animal natures, and to promote the good.

It is the first of these three precepts that justifies the killing of another person in self-defence. It also explains the defence of necessity, which forms an integral part of our criminal law. There are difficulties, however. The second precept, which emphasizes the essential goodness of all creatures, has become controversial because there are situations where there is a fundamental disagreement as to what constitutes a part of our animal nature. This is typified by the debate over the moral status of homosexuality under the natural law. The Catholic Church, for example, has officially condemned homosexual inclinations as "unnatural."[7] Many commentators have argued, however, that homosexual inclinations are completely "natural." Nor is it possible to distinguish between homosexual and heterosexual inclinations, since not all heterosexual inclinations are related to procreation.[8]

The Emphasis in the Natural Law Is on Duty

The ethical theory of the natural law in the *Summa Theologica* is based on the concept of duty. This reflects the medieval view that the ethical character of our actions is based on our obligations and responsibilities. Thus, if the natural law says that we have a natural inclination to preserve ourselves, it follows that we have a duty to do so. This explains why suicide was considered wrong under the natural law, since a person who committed suicide had failed in his or her fundamental duty of self-preservation. Even a prisoner sentenced to execution had a duty to escape, if the opportunity presented itself.[9] This reasoning is the original source of the idea that attempted suicide and assisted suicide constitute criminal offences. The precepts of the natural law create a set of positive duties that determine our ethical obligations.

The idea that we have duties also has a corollary, however, in the idea of rights. If we have a duty to preserve our lives, it follows logically that we have a right to do so. This assertion seems to place obligations on other people, and on our government, in those situations where we cannot fulfill our duties without their assistance. There is some recognition of this principle in Aquinas, since he suggests that the wealthy must provide for the poor in times of deprivation. It is only later, however, when the idea of rights is coupled with a more political idea of personal freedom or autonomy, that the concept of natural rights becomes prominent in legal theory.[10]

Can the Natural Law Change?

In the final sections of Question 94, Aquinas deals with the question whether the natural law can be changed. In Article 5, he says that the natural law can be changed by addition, to deal with changes in our social life. Such changes might be necessary, for example, to deal with developments in medicine and genetics. The natural law can also be changed, however, by subtraction, when circumstances somehow intervene to prevent us from following it.

There is also the question whether the natural law is always accessible to reason. In Article 6, Aquinas writes that the abstract principles of the natural law, "can nowise be blotted out from men's hearts." They may nevertheless be blotted out in a particular case by the action of the passions "or by vicious customs and corrupt habits." Such customs or habits might include the sexual practices within a certain social group or the general business practices in a corrupt society.

The Positive Law

The human law, or the "positive law," refers to those laws recognized and enforced by human institutions. Since this law is valid only if it is in general accordance with the natural law, it derives its ultimate moral authority from the eternal law. We are therefore required to obey it by divine command, since it is part of the essential order of things. The term "positive," in this context, originally referred to a prescription that has been "formally laid down, imposed, or decreed."[11] We are "positively" obliged to follow the positive law, since it is backed up by the threat of human force. Although legal positivists often use the term "positive law" to refer to statutory law, Aquinas uses it to refer to all human law. In this sense, it includes the customs that find their way into the common law and other judicial pronouncements. It also includes fundamental religious and moral precepts.

Why Do We Need Positive Laws?

One of the philosophical questions that arise in this context is whether we need human laws. In the answer to Question 91, Aquinas writes that human laws are necessary because the natural law is usually too general to be applied directly to most human actions. The human law derives, Aquinas tells us, from the application of the precepts (i.e., the principles) of the natural law—and implicitly, the eternal law—to specific forms of human conduct. The "particular determinations" that find expression in the positive law are laws only if "the other essential conditions of law be observed."

We Have an Obligation to Obey a Positive Law that in Some Degree Departs From the Natural Law

This raises one of the central issues in philosophy of law, since Aquinas recognizes that a positive law may not be in keeping with the natural law. The consequences of such a failure are clear. Such laws may not be valid laws. Aquinas says that we are generally obliged to obey the positive law, even if it in some degree departs from the natural law. At the same time, a positive law that violates the natural law to such an extent that it requires us to act unjustly loses the character of law. We therefore have no legal obligation to obey it. This dynamic is particularly significant in a contemporary context because it seems to explain the operation of our constitutional law.

We also have a political obligation to obey the positive law, even when it fails to conform to the natural law. It is all a matter of degree. If a law seriously violates the natural law, we may find ourselves with conflicting moral and political obligations. The real focus of this analysis is civil disobedience. Aquinas' position raises the question: when are we obliged to obey the positive law? In the final passage of the reading, Aquinas cites Augustine as authority that an order "which is not just seems to be no law at all."

A Positive Law that Significantly Deviates From Reason Has the Nature of "Violence"

The natural law provides the necessary link between the law of God and the human law. In his answer to Question 93, Aquinas writes:

> Human law has the nature of law in so far as it partakes of right reason [because it is therefore in keeping with the natural law]; and it is clear that, in this respect, it is derived from the eternal law. But in so far as it deviates from reason, it is called an unjust law, and has the nature, not of law, but of violence.

This is presumably a matter of degree. A positive law that deviates significantly from reason and the natural law is no longer binding.

Aquinas' use of the word "violence" in this context is telling. Although the positive law derives its legitimacy from the natural law and is, in that sense, composed of moral rules, the defining character of this body of law comes from the fact that we are required by society to obey it. The difference between law and morality, in this context, is that the law is backed up by the threat of force. It follows that an unjust law is nothing more than the sheer application of force without justification. This gives an unjust law the character of "violence."

An Unjust Positive Law Is "a Perversion of Law"

In his answer to Question 95, Aquinas goes further. The force of a positive law, he states, depends on "the extent of its justice." Indeed, as Augustine says, something "which is not just seems to be no law at all." An unjust law, then, that "deflects" from the law of nature, "is no longer a law but a perversion of law."

On a psychological level, Aquinas is primarily observing that we do not feel compelled to obey an unjust law. It is the philosophical conclusion that he draws from such an observation, however, that has become crucial in the history of legal theory. Aquinas, like Augustine before him, takes the position that a positive law that is wrong according to the rule of reason does not have the true character of a law, presumably because it is not binding. Indeed it is the opposite of law, a kind of anti-law, since it directs and even forces us to act against the natural law. This proposition, which holds that an unjust positive law is not a true "law," has become the defining tenet in the legal theory of the natural law. The same proposition has also provided the essential point of departure for the legal positivists, who have rejected it.

The full significance of his comments is difficult to gauge, historically. It is hard to say how far Aquinas was willing to go in permitting the individual to disobey a law that he finds unjust. In the answer to Question 96, he suggests that such laws may be binding "in order to avoid scandal or disturbance, for which cause a man should even yield his right." Since the community has a general interest in maintaining the law, and since the general efficacy of human law is weakened whenever a law is disobeyed, Aquinas takes the position that we should disobey the law only when it is manifestly unjust.

Aquinas was nevertheless living in a time of increasing conflict between church and state, and his emphasis on the divine law is intended to preserve the Church's authority. In Article 4 of the answer to Question 96, he writes:

> laws may be unjust through being opposed to the Divine good: such are the laws of tyrants inducing to idolatry, or to anything else contrary to the Divine law: and laws of this kind must nowise be observed, because, as stated in Acts 5:29, "we ought to obey God rather than man."

There is accordingly no doubt that Aquinas felt there are many instances in which the individual is obliged to disobey the positive law.

Aquinas emphasizes that law must be for the common good, and his discussion of law is motivated by a concern for the welfare of the community. In spite of this, his theory of the natural law seems to place the decision whether a law is in keeping with the eternal law in the hands of the individual. In Question 96, Article 4, he speaks of "the court of conscience," which obliges an individual to obey or disobey the law. Thus, he seems to place the ultimate authority for deciding whether a positive law is binding within the individual.

This emphasis on the role of the individual's conscience in determining whether a positive law is binding raises the problem of individual interpretation. This has become a pressing issue in contemporary Western societies, which place a high priority on our freedom to make moral choices. As a result, individuals in these societies have a wide variety of moral views. This diversity of views naturally makes it much more likely that an individual will object to a particular law and refuse to obey it. Aquinas does not seem troubled by this issue, probably because he was living in a society in which there was a high level of agreement on moral issues. This was true legally, as well as religiously, since the Church had ecclesiastical courts, whose moral authority was beyond question. The ecclesiastical courts provided guidance on fundamental moral issues, and almost everyone accepted the same moral code.

The Divine Law

The fourth and final kind of law that Aquinas distinguishes is the divine law, which is made up of the part of the eternal law that is available only through revelation. The divine law is necessary philosophically because human reason is fallible. It is therefore possible for humans to disagree as to the application of the natural law in specific instances. There must also be a law to deal with internal wrongs—those wrongs that do not translate into external action and are therefore beyond the reach of the positive law. The primary feature of this law is that it is necessarily correct. Thus, in Aquinas' view of law, faith is above reason.

The Application of the Theory of the Natural Law Is Problematic

Natural Law Theory Has Difficulty Explaining how the Ethical Views in Society Change

One of the problems with Aquinas' theory in a contemporary context is that society has changed. The number of competing moral views in pluralistic societies often makes it difficult to find a consensus on specific moral issues. The tension between the individual and the larger community that this creates has become a major focus in contemporary legal, social, and political theory.

The medieval theory of the natural law eroded over time. Although the religious doctrine that there is a natural law survived the Protestant Reformation in the sixteenth century, the Protestant reformers rejected the idea that the pope and the Catholic Church had the authority to interpret its precepts. The theology of Protestantism emphasized grace rather than the natural law and subjected human nature to the discipline of a local church or congregation. The Calvinist theory of "total depravity," for example, states that we are depraved (morally corrupt) at birth, in every part of our being, and saved from damnation only by the grace of God.[12]

There were also advances in the physical sciences. Although these advances fit in well with the idea that there is a natural order to the universe, which can be discovered through the instrumentality of reason, the normative elements of the traditional theory of the natural law were lost in these developments. However powerful the natural sciences may be as a tool of inquiry, they do not tell us how we should act. The successes in the physical sciences also introduced a more pronounced idea that human reason is fallible, since science progresses by continually correcting itself. As a result, the view of the world that came out of the so-called "Enlightenment" lost much of the certainty that gave Aquinas' account of the natural law its authority.

There Is Wide Disagreement on Moral Issues

The problem of individual interpretation also presents difficulties for the proponents of the natural law, since it demonstrates that individual people may have different views of what the natural law requires. This helps to explain the shift away from the natural law in the nineteenth century with the development of legal positivism. This brought in a much starker separation between morality and law. Legal positivists avoided the problem of individual interpretation by resting our obligation to obey the positive law on our political obligations rather than its conformity with the natural law. There is almost no room for interpretation in such a system: people are simply obliged to obey the positive law, as long as it is properly passed and meets basic legal norms.

In recent decades, however the problem of individual interpretation has become a pressing philosophical issue. This can probably be attributed to the influence of the liberal tradition, which places enormous emphasis on the moral autonomy of the individual. The focus on freedom of thought and conscience in the contemporary ethical literature has brought out the fact that there is wide disagreement on controversial moral issues. It has also promoted the view that there are situations in which individuals should deliberately break the positive law, and commit civil disobedience, in order to protest against it. In the current view, at least, it follows that the question whether the positive law aligns with the natural law has many possible answers.

There Is Still Room for a Procedural Theory of the Natural Law

The moral theory of the natural law has two sides. The first is substantive and suggests that morality ultimately derives from the natural law, whether we trace this law to divine sources or not. The second is more procedural and concerns the manner in which we determine the morality of our actions and, more particularly, the law. This second side raises questions about the role of morality in determining the validity of specific laws. Although the contemporary view is that law has its origins in political authority, many theorists would accept that law derives much or most of its authority from the morality on which it is based.

This leaves plenty of room for the operation of a procedural theory of the natural law, even if we reject the argument that morality itself is based upon some kind of natural law. The study of anthropology and the social sciences has promoted a certain moral relativism, which suggests that there are many possible moralities. John Austin, whose work is discussed in Chapter 6, distinguished between a "positive" and a "critical" morality on this basis. The word "positive" in this context refers to moral beliefs and customs, like the positive law, which are made by human agency. The term "critical morality" refers to a set of moral beliefs that has been accepted as valid within a certain society.

The important observation is that any critical morality can operate as a provisional natural law for the purposes of the procedural theory of the natural law. In order to create a system of legal validity, we merely need to enshrine an ascertainable set of moral judgements in the normative framework that determines the validity and scope of the positive law. We might, for example, take a contractarian position, which holds that ethical obligations are a function of the agreements reached between individuals, or between individuals and society as a whole. As long as this ethical theory provides us with a set of verifiable normative standards, it will be sufficient to satisfy the procedural requirements, at least, of the legal theory that we have identified as the natural law.

The Constitutional Courts Have Taken Over the Legal Role of the Medieval Church

The procedural theory of the natural law has found expression, legally, in the constitutional law and the rights of the person. The increasing authority of this body of law in the common law tradition has renewed interest in the process of moral justification that provides the framework of the natural law. Statutory instruments like the *Canadian Charter of Rights and Freedoms* and its counterparts in the international arena hold that we are not obliged to obey laws that are out of keeping with their fundamental tenets. This body of constitutional and extra-constitutional tenets seems to serve much the same purpose as the natural law in determining which positive laws are morally binding.

The reasoning in constitutional courts bears many similarities to the dynamic that applies in determining whether the human law is in keeping with the eternal law. This observation inevitably takes us into questions of morality and value. The constitutional system solves the problem of individual interpretation by giving the courts the kind of role that the Church exercised in the past, in providing official guidance as to the binding nature of the positive law. Since the interpretation of the law provided by the courts is based on the moral consensus in society, individuals are legally obliged to respect such an interpretation.

The general nature of the provisions of a constitution, much like the precepts of the natural law, leaves many ambiguities and often makes it difficult to determine how the law applies in concrete situations. Indeed in Aquinas' view, there are many ways that the precepts of the natural law can be fulfilled. The modern view is clearly that the political branch of government has the authority to determine what the positive law should be, as long as it keeps within the boundaries of the constitution and the fundamental law. The question on such a determination is not whether the ordinary law can be derived from constitutional enactments, but whether it is in keeping with its provisions.

People within the Same Society Tend to Agree On the Contents of the Natural Law

There is nothing to prevent us from applying the theory of the natural law, in a loose way, to contemporary legal systems. The overriding problem that arises in this context is probably the most straightforward. What does the natural law tell us? One of the ways of answering this question is to try and identify the moral tenets that are common to the major religious and cultural traditions. In a secular society, however, in which many people reject the religious or theological tradition, we presumably need to find another means of determining these tenets.

There are two opposing views as to whether this is possible. The first view is that all human societies share certain moral norms. There is no society, for example, that would countenance a law that permits us to maim our children. The second, countervailing view holds that the moral beliefs in different societies diverge so widely that it is impossible to compose a list of moral precepts that apply in every society. Thus, there are societies that permit female circumcision or other practices that we find morally unacceptable. There are recent accounts, for example, that women have been stoned for committing adultery, even when the so-called "adultery" consists of rape.

The discussion of these issues comes more properly within the study of ethics than philosophy of law. The point in the present context is that there is no agreement as to how we can determine what the natural law contains. There is no doubt, however, that questions about the tenets of the natural law tend to be answered on the basis of our own experience. This experience varies in different societies. It may accordingly be possible to find enough of a moral consensus within a given society to establish that a certain interpretation of the natural law has been accepted in that society. This uniformity of opinion seems to provide the practical basis for the operation of the procedural theory of the natural law within the parameters of a specific society.

In point of fact, the courts regularly rely on this kind of moral consensus in deciding the issues that arise in the constitutional law. The interesting question is whether the current changes in communication and belief have begun to dissolve the ethical boundaries between different societies. If we are witnessing the emergence of a single global society, as many commentators have suggested, there is accordingly reason to believe that it may be possible to achieve the necessary consensus for a consistent interpretation of the natural law across state boundaries. Legally, this would provide the necessary basis for some kind of global constitutionalism, which gives international courts a common body of moral precepts that can be used in deciding the legal limits on the exercise of political power. In a contemporary context, we can find at least part of what we might call a "new natural law" in the rights of the person and in the *jus cogens*, that part of the international law that states are obliged to follow.

Notes

1. From *De legibus* II vol. 11, as quoted (and presumably translated) by Norman Kretzmann in "Lex Iniusta Non Est Lex: Laws on Trial in Aquinas' Court of Conscience," *American Journal of Jurisprudence* 33 (1988): 99–122, at p. 100.

2. ibid.

3. See James Fitzjames Stephen, for example, "Offences against Religion," in vol. 2 of *History of the Criminal Law of England* (London: Macmillan, 1883), at p. 436: "The result of this long history may be thus shortly summed up. The function of the ordinary ecclesiastical courts was to punish offences against religion and morals, in a word to punish sin as such. This function they discharged with little interruption till the year 1640, and during the latter part of the period they united with it the function, half political, half theological, of enforcing ecclesiastical conformity and suppressing writings and words opposed to the system established by law." Available at www.heinonline.org.

4. For a general discussion of ethics in this context, see Mark Murphy, "The Natural Law Tradition in Ethics," in *The Stanford Encyclopedia of Philosophy*, ed. Edward N. Zalta (Fall 2008). Available at http://plato.stanford.edu.

5. See *R. v. Oakes*, at para. 59.

6. Esther Cohen, *The Crossroads of Justice: Law and Culture in Late Medieval France* (Leiden, NL: E.J. Brill, 1993), p. 121.

7. See Robert Westerfelhaus, "A Significant Shift: A Pentadic Analysis of the Two Rhetorics of the Post-Vatican II Roman Catholic Church Regarding Homosexuality," *International Journal of Sexuality and Gender Studies*, 3, no. 4 (1998): 269–94. As Westerfelhaus suggests, the Church's attempt to accept homosexuals into the Church but condemn the homosexual impulse seems logically perilous. And see Derrick Sherwin Bailey, *Homosexuality and the Western Christian Tradition* (London: Longmans, Green, 1955). And see John Boswell's "The Church and the Homosexual: An Historical Perspective, 1979," available at www.fordham.edu/halsall/pwh/1979boswell.asp, where the author writes that it is a mistake to assume that homosexuality was considered "unnatural" or depraved in all periods of the Christian past: "As late as the eleventh and twelfth centuries, there appears to be no conflict between a Christian life and homosexuality. Gay life is everywhere in the art, poetry, music, history, etc. of the eleventh and twelfth centuries."

8. The arguments in the *Summa* are directed at "unnatural" copulations in general, and Aquinas seems to be concerned with the possible waste of semen in superfluous emission. (See the *Summa* II, ii, Question 154, Article 11). Yet Aquinas' position is more sophisticated than the discussion in the *Summa* might suggest, since he appears to recognize that homosexual inclinations are an ordinary part of the natural world. In the *Summa Contra Gentiles*, for example, he refers to "the natural inclination in man to preserve the species by the act of generation" but states that this act "need not be carried out by all men, but by some."

9. See Brian Tierney, for example, "Dominion of Self and Natural Rights Before Locke and After," in *Transformations in Medieval and Early-Modern Rights Discourse*, ed. Virpi Mäkinen and Petter Korkman (Dordrecht, NL: Springer, 2006), pp. 173–206, at p. 182: "The prisoner could not break free by force but if he were left in a cell unbound with the door unlocked, he could escape without injury and was obliged to do so in order to preserve his life."

10. Chapter 3 discusses this transition in more depth.

11. See the entry for "positive, *adj.* and *n.*," in the *Oxford English Dictionary*, available at www.oed.com.

12. This view favoured the development of secular authority in civil matters and gave the positive law a new prominence.

Study Questions

1. How did the natural law make its way into Christian teaching?

2. Where does our obligation to obey the human law come from, in the *Summa Theologica*? How does the concept of duty relate to this obligation?

3. What is the eternal law? What is the relationship between the eternal law and the natural law? What is the relationship between the eternal law and the human law?

4. What is the first precept of the natural law?

5. Why does Aquinas use the term "violence" to describe an unjust law?

6. Why does the natural law seem to provide the obvious basis for a law between different peoples, nations, and states?

7. How are we supposed to know whether our conduct contravenes the natural law?

8. Although legal positivism rejects the legal theory of the natural law, it may leave a role for the natural law in ethics. How so?

9. Do you agree that there is a natural law? Why, why not?

Further Reading

St. Thomas Aquinas, *On Law, Morality, and Politics*, 2nd ed., trans. Richard J. Regan, ed. William P. Baumgarth and Richard J. Regan (Indianapolis, MN: Hackett, 2002).

Anthony Battaglia, *Towards a Reformulation of Natural Law* (New York: Seabury, 1981).

Ernest Bloch, *Natural Law and Human Dignity*, trans. Dennis J. Schmidt (Cambridge: MIT, 1986).

John Finnis, *Aquinas: Moral, Political, and Legal Theory* (Oxford: Oxford University, 1998).

Ernest Fortin, "Augustine, Thomas Aquinas, and the Problem of Natural Law," *Mediaevalia* 4 (1978): 179–208.

Robert P. George, "Kelsen and Aquinas on 'The Natural Law Doctrine'," *Notre Dame Law Review* 75 (2000): 1625–46.

Jacques Maritain, *The Rights of Man and Natural Law*, trans. Doris C. Anson (New York: Charles Scribner's Sons, 1943).

Yves R. Simon, *The Tradition of Natural Law* (New York: Fordham University, [1965] 1992).

Leo Strauss, "On Natural Law," in *Studies in Platonic Political Philosophy*, ed. T.L. Pangle (Chicago: University of Chicago, 1983).

3 The Shift to Natural Rights and the Political Contract

Hugo Grotius and Samuel von Pufendorf

Readings

- From *De Jure Praedae Commentarius* (*Commentary on the Law of Prize and Booty*), by Hugo Grotius
- From *Elementorum Jurisprudentiae Universalis Libri Duo* (*The Elements of Universal Jurisprudence*), by Samuel von Pufendorf

The previous two chapters have discussed the place of tribal law and the natural law in the history of legal theory. The current chapter examines a third development, which took place some five hundred years after Aquinas wrote the *Summa*. This development takes us into the modern age. It concerns the historical shift from natural law theory to a theory of natural rights, which traces the origins of the law to a political contract. This shift had fundamental consequences in legal theory, since it rests the validity and legitimacy of the law on its political pedigree rather than its conformity with fundamental moral and religious principles.

The readings are from the work of two theorists whose work helped to provide the conceptual foundations of the current international order. Hugo Grotius (1583–1645) was a Dutch lawyer and jurist who set out a contractual model of the state system based on the sovereignty of the state and the existence of a set of international norms. Samuel von Pufendorf (1632–1694), another Protestant thinker, was a German philosopher and professor of law. Although Pufendorf consciously followed the example set out by Grotius, he based his own theory of international order on the primacy of the natural law rather than the agreement of states.

⚔ Readings ⚔

From Hugo Grotius, *De Jure Praedae Commentarius* [*Commentary on the Law of Prize and Booty*], vol. 1, trans. Gladys L. Williams and Walter H. Zeydel (Oxford: Clarendon, [1604] 1950).

Chapter II: Prolegomena, Including Nine Rules and Thirteen Laws

The Fundamentals of Law

WHERE should we begin, if not at the very beginning? Accordingly, let us give first place and pre-eminent authority to the following rule [Rule I]: *What God has shown to be His Will, that is law.* This axiom points directly to the cause of law . . .

It would seem, indeed, that the very term *ius* [law] is derived from *Iovis* [Jove] and that the same process of derivation holds good for *iurare* [to swear] and *iusiurandum* [an oath] or *Iovisiurandum* [an oath in the name of Jove]. . . .

Therefore, since God fashioned creation and willed its existence, every individual part thereof has received from Him certain natural properties whereby that existence may be preserved and each part may be guided for its own good, in conformity, one might say, with the fundamental law inherent in its origin. From this fact the old poets and philosophers have rightly deduced that love, whose primary force and action are directed to self-interest, is the first principle of the whole natural order. . . .

[F]rom this combination of concepts, two precepts of the law of nature emerge: first, [Law I] *It shall be permissible to defend* [*one's own*] *life and to shun that which threatens to prove injurious*; secondly, [Law II] *It shall be permissible to acquire for oneself, and to retain, those things which are useful for life.* The latter precept, indeed, we shall interpret with Cicero as an admission that each individual may, without violating the precepts of nature, prefer to see acquired for himself rather than for another, that which is important for the conduct of life. . . .

But God judged that there would be insufficient provision for the preservation of His works, if He commended to each individual's care only the safety of that particular individual, without also willing that one created being should have regard for the welfare of his fellow beings, in such a way that all might be linked in mutual harmony as if by an everlasting covenant. . . .

Many persons, indeed, have chosen to call that very accord the . . . PRIMARY LAW OF NATIONS; and Cicero has said that the principle informing this law is nothing more nor less than right reason derived from the will of the gods. In another passage, the same author declares that, "on any matter, the consensus of all nations should be regarded as a precept of the natural law." . . . Thus a second rule is derived from the first, namely [Rule II]: *What the common consent of mankind has shown to be the will of all, that is law. . . .*

Accordingly, from the First and Second Rules two laws arise, relating to the good of others, whereby the preceding laws, which relate to one's own good, are complemented and confined within just limits. One of the two laws in question runs as follows [Law III]: *Let no one inflict injury upon his fellow.* The other is the precept [Law IV]: *Let no one seize possession of that which has been taken into the possession of another. . . .*

For God created man "free and *sui iuris* [legally capable of making his own decisions]," so that the actions of each individual and the use of his possessions were made subject not to another's will but to his own. . . .

From the foregoing considerations the rule of good faith is derived [Rule III]: *What each individual has indicated to be his will, that is law with respect to him. . . .*

The Origins of the State

When it came to pass . . . that many persons [in the state of nature before the creation of the civil state] . . . either failed to meet their obligations or even assailed the fortunes and the very lives of others . . . the lesser social units began to gather individuals together into one locality, not with the intention of abolishing the [universal] society which links all men as a whole, but rather in order to fortify that universal society by a more dependable means of protection. . . . Accordingly, this smaller social unit, formed by a general agreement for the sake of the common good . . . is called a commonwealth [*Respublica*—i.e., a Republic]; and the individuals making up the commonwealth are called citizens [*cives*].

This system of organization has its origin in God the King, who rules the whole universe and to whom, indeed (so the philosophers declare) nothing achieved on earth is more acceptable than those associations and assemblies of men which are known as states [*civitates*]. . . .

Moreover, since it is the will involved that constitutes the measure of a good . . . it follows that the will of the whole group prevails in regard to the common good, and even in regard to the good of individuals, in so far as the latter is subordinate to the former. For the individual members of the group have themselves consented to this arrangement, and one of the various attributes of free will is the power to accommodate one's own will to that of another. The will of all, when applied to all, is called *lex* [statutory law]. This law . . . is approved by the common consent of all mankind, a point borne out by the words of Chrysippus:[1] "for *lex* is the guardian of those living beings who are by their natures adapted to civil life." In short, *lex* rests upon the mutual agreement and the will of individuals, and with this fact in mind, Demosthenes and Plato[2] sometimes refer to it as . . . "the common pact of the state."

Thus, on the basis of the earlier rules, the following additional rule has developed [Rule IV]: *Whatever the commonwealth has indicated to be its will, that is law [ius] in regard to the whole body of citizens.* This principle is the source of that branch of law described by the philosophers as [positive], or [conventional], or even [particular, domestic], and by the jurists as "municipal law." . . . Nor is it strange that laws of the kind in question should change with their cause—that is to say, in accordance with the human will—while natural precepts, based as they are upon a constant cause, remain constant in themselves; or that the former should vary in different localities, since the various communities differ, of course, in their conception of what is good. . . .

The Law of Nations

A supplementary observation should be introduced at this point, namely: that there exists a species of mixed law, compounded of the [primary] law of nations and municipal law [roughly, the international and domestic law],[3] and designated in correct and precise terminology as "THE SECONDARY LAW OF NATIONS." For just as the common good of private persons gave rise to the precepts above set forth, so also, owing to the existence of a common good of an international nature, the various peoples who had established states for themselves entered into agreements concerning that international good. From this circumstance another rule arose, a rule modelled on the fourth, which in turn had derived its basic principle from the second and third and, consequently, from the first. According to this Eighth Rule [Rule VIII], *Whatever all states have indicated to be their will, that is law in regard to all of them.* . . .

Among the other precepts of the law of nations—those binding upon the various peoples as if by force of contract—the most important is the one . . . which may be worded thus [Law XII]: *Neither the state nor any citizen thereof shall seek to enforce his own right against another state or its citizen, save by judicial procedure.* . . .

But a new difficulty presents itself at this point . . . . For citizens [are subject] to their respective states, and therefore, both in disputes with one another and in disputes with the state, they rightly submit to the judgement of the latter; whereas one state . . . is not in subjection but in contraposition to another state . . . . Truly, there is no greater sovereign power set over the power of the state and superior to it, since the state is a self-sufficient aggregation. . . .

Thus it was necessary to settle any controversy of this kind by resorting to some distinction, such as that incorporated in the following rule [Rule IX]: *In regard to judicial procedure, precedence shall be given to the state which is the defendant, or whose citizen is the defendant; but if the said state proves remiss in the discharge of its judicial duty, then that state shall be the judge, which is itself the plaintiff, or whose citizen is the plaintiff.* . . .

Notes

1.   Editor's note: Chrysippus of Soli (c. 280 BCE–c. 207 BCE), a renowned Greek Stoic, whose work has not survived but was frequently quoted by the ancients. Grotius is arguing a legal case and using Chrysippus and other authorities essentially as precedents. He cites Justinian's *Digest*, at I.iii.2 which deals with the origins of law. This work was published in the sixth century and was one of the founding documents in the Western legal tradition. The practice of citation in Grotius' time was approximate. Charles Henry Monro, *Digest of Justinian* (Cambridge: Cambridge University, 1904–9), at p. 19, translates the relevant passage as

"Law is the King of all things, both divine and human, it ought to be the controller, ruler, and commander of both the good and the bad, and thus to be a standard as to things just and unjust and" [director of] "beings political by nature, enjoining what ought to be done and forbidding what ought not to be done."

2.   Editor's note: Demosthenes (384 BCE–322 BCE) was a famous Greek orator. Grotius cites a passage in the same section of Justinian's *Digest*, which Monro translates as "The orator Demosthenes himself gives this definition [of law]: 'A law is . . . something which all men ought to obey for many reasons, and chiefly because every law is devised and given by God, but resolved on by intelligent men, a means of correcting offences both intentional and unintentional, a general agreement on the part of the community by which all those living therein ought to order their lives'." Plato (c. 424 BCE–c. 347 BCE), whose dialogues made Socrates (c. 469 BCE–399 BCE) so famous, was the author of the *Laws* and the *Republic*, and therefore a legal authority.

From Samuel Pufendorf, *Elementorum Jurisprudentiae Universalis Libri Duo* [*The Elements of Universal Jurisprudence*], vol. 2, trans. William Abbott Oldfather (Oxford: Clarendon, [1660] 1931).

Book I: Definition VIII

Right is an active moral power, belonging to a person to receive something from another as a matter of necessity.

Ambiguity of the Word

In addition to those meanings by which the word right (*jus*) is used for law . . . the most frequent use is to employ it for that moral quality by which we properly either command persons, or possess things, or by which things are owed to us. . . .

Perfect Right

Now right is either *perfect* or *imperfect*. He who has infringed upon the former does a wrong which gives the injured party in a human court of law ground for bringing action against the injurer. To this corresponds on the other side perfect obligation in him from whom that which is owed us is to come. Therefore, I am able to compel him, when he refuses to pay this debt voluntarily, either by directing action against him before a judge, or, where there is no place for that, by force. Rights of that kind, when they have not yet been deduced with sufficient clearness, or are disputed by him whom they regard, are commonly called pretensions. . . .

Imperfect Right

Now it is an imperfect right, which is called by some [i.e., by Grotius] an aptitude, when something is owed some one by another in such wise that, if he should deny it, he would, indeed, be acting unfairly, and yet the injured party would by no means be receiving a wrong which would furnish him with an action against the injurer; nor would he be able to assert for himself that right, except when necessity does not admit of any other means to secure his safety. . . . Thus, I am able neither to compel another to do me benefactions, nor to bring an action for ingratitude against another, although, in very truth, he is doing wrong who neglects an occasion for doing a benefaction to others, or does not return the favour as best he can in requital for benefactions received. . . .

Book I: Definition XIII

A law is a decree by which a superior binds one subject to him to direct his actions according to the command of the superior.

A Law Differs from a Word of Counsel

Now a law differs from a word of counsel, indeed, in the fact that through the latter, by means of reasons drawn from the facts of the case, a person endeavours to induce some one over whom he has no authority . . . to undertake or to give up some thing, without bringing any obligation to bear upon him, and in such a way that it is left to his own free choice whether he wish to heed the counsel, or not. . . .

A Law Differs from a Pact

Nor, in truth, are those sufficiently accurate who speak of laws as certain common agreements . . . since thereby they confuse a law with a pact. For assuredly, neither the positive divine laws nor the laws of nature can be said to have arisen from the agreement or consent of men. Nor are civil laws, properly speaking, pacts, even though they have their origin in a pact. For even if some multitude not bound to one another by supreme command should entirely agree with one another upon certain formulae for living together, still this would be in vain, if a supreme command had not yet been set up, through whose force the disobedient could be restrained by punishments. For this agreement would have no other force than that which, on the basis of the law of nature, inheres in pacts. . . .

A Law Differs from a Right

Now as the word *jus* (law) often means the same as *lex* (law), especially where it is used for a complex of laws, so we should be on our guard not to take it in the sense of law, when it denotes the authority to do something; for example, we are not to fancy, when it is said we have a right (*jus*) to this or that by a divine law (*lex*), that this has also been ordered by the divine law, and so we can rightly do it, even if it be forbidden by human laws. . . .

He Who Is about to Pass a Law for Some One Ought to Have Authority Over Him

Now in the one who is going to enact a law for another, it is first of all required that he should have such authority over him upon whom the law is to be enjoined, that he can force him to the observance of that law, by hanging a penalty over his head; for it is vain to order one to do that which can be neglected with impunity. And so no one is obligated by the laws of a person or a group which has no authority over him. And the faculty of enjoining something by way of a law or an order, implies superiority, just as the obligation of obedience convicts us of being inferior to the one who can give an order to us, at least where his command extends. . . .

The Object of Laws

The matter or the object of laws in genus is whatever may be done by those people for whom the laws are passed, at least at the time at which the laws are passed. . . . But in species natural laws have to do with those matters which so harmonize with the social nature of rational man, that, unless they are observed, violence is done in a certain fashion to nature herself, and an ordered and tranquil society cannot be preserved among men. Those things which are not determined by the laws of nature it is permissible to adjust by means of positive laws. . . .

Precisely What Coercive Force Is There in a Law?

Now just as it is required, in order to enjoin efficaciously an obligation upon a second person, that it be made clear to him what is to be done, and the fact that he will not go unpunished if he has not performed what is enjoined . . . so the same conditions are found to obtain also in a law, in that they define what must necessarily be done . . . and at the same time they indicate that evil threatens the one who neglects a precept or does a forbidden thing. . . .

Human Law

Every human law is civil. Now as to the subject-matter, some things manifestly harmonize with the very conditions of human nature as such, and flow from it; and some arise from the free choice alone of the legislator, as harmonizing especially with a definite status of men. Of these two classes the former are called natural, the latter positive. . . .

Disputes Concerning the Source of the Law of Nature

[T]hose who say that the law of nature is the dictate of right reason, which points out that there is a moral turpitude or a moral necessity about some act, derived from its agreement or disagreement with nature itself, and, consequently, that such an act is forbidden or enjoined by God as the author of this law, are correct enough on every point except that they do not define just what is the foundation of the congruence or the incongruence of those acts with rational nature. But this we conclude to be the fact, namely, that man was made by the Creator a social animal. For that this is properly the reason why that which is said to pertain to the law of nature so harmonizes with the nature of man, that, if the contrary should take place, it would seem as though violence, as it were, had been done to his nature. . . .

This much, indeed, is certain: Through the medium of the said precept, the law of nature obligates all persons whatsoever to obey the positive laws of their superiors, and therefore, those who neglect these laws are sinning against the very law of nature. But what prevents those positive laws from being called natural is that . . . the reason for obeying them is to be sought solely in the authority and will of the legislator. . . .

The Origin and Force of Civil Laws

Whatever laws, therefore, are enjoined by the supreme civil command for their subjects to observe, under the threat of inflicting punishment in a human court of law upon the violators of the same, are called *civil* laws. These, whether taken from the body of the law of nature, or from the body of positive law, or proceeding from the mere free choice of the rulers, obtain the whole effect which they exert in a civil court from the force of supreme power lending its authority to them. And, indeed, in all commonwealths, most features of the law of nature, at all events such as those without which peace in the society itself cannot stand, have the force of civil law, or have been included in the body of civil laws. . . . Now the reason why legislators have not assigned to all the precepts of the law of nature the force of civil law, is because they had primarily to attend to those matters without which the internal tranquillity of the commonwealth could not exist at all. . . . And so it is a true saying that utility is the mother of law, that is to say, the civil law as such (but not of natural law), or, in other words, that utility gave the reason for establishing law. For nothing but utility or public good decided to which natural laws, in this or that commonwealth, the effect of a civil law is to be assigned, and to which not. . . .

The Object of Civil Laws

The object of civil laws is, in general, all that which can be effectively enjoined by a supreme human authority. The inner acts of the mind, in regard to which laws are enacted in vain, are excluded therefrom, because, forsooth, it is beyond the power of other men to know whether obedience has been rendered the laws or not, so long as external acts do not reveal it. . . .

The Law of Nations

Something must be added now also on the subject of the *Law of Nations*, which, in the eyes of some men, is nothing other than the law of nature, in so far as different nations, not united with another by a supreme command, observe it, who must render one another the same duties in their fashion, as are prescribed for individuals by the law of nature. On this point there is no reason for our conducting any special discussion here, since what we recount on the subject of the law of nature and of the duties of individuals, can be readily applied to whole states and nations which have also coalesced into one moral person. Aside from this law, we are of the opinion that there is no law of nations, at least none which can properly be designated by such a name.

✦ Discussion ✦

The Theory of Natural Rights Has Shaped the International Order

The theory of natural rights found in the works of Hugo Grotius and Samuel von Pufendorf is important in the genealogy of legal thought because they provide the legal framework of our current system of international relations. Our system is commonly called the Westphalian system because it is based on the Peace of Westphalia (1648), a series of treaties that recognized the division of Europe into a collection of sovereign nation-states. The Peace was based on the principle that the rulers of Catholic and Protestant states would not interfere in each other's internal affairs. The Peace also removed the authority of the pope and the Holy Roman Empire, and it gave individual states the freedom to pursue their affairs independently of a central authority.

The Peace of Westphalia had two fundamental consequences in legal theory. Since states were sovereign under the Peace, the accepted view was that there were no sources of law outside the state. This idea, together with the centralization of power in the state and the increasing authority of the political branch of government, meant that those who held political authority within the state were theoretically supreme. In the common law, this notion found expression in the doctrine of parliamentary supremacy, which held that the will of Parliament could not be fettered. The House of Commons existed above the law and was not subject to legal constraints.

The second consequence was external. Although states had complete authority in their civil affairs, they had no authority outside their borders. There was therefore no source of positive law that could definitively regulate the affairs between states. The international order was accordingly based on the idea that states existed as individual persons in a state of nature and were free of the restraints of positive law. Although the natural law still applied in such a state, there was no external means of regulating the conduct of nation-states and this restriction had little force. States were left to interpret and apply the natural law for themselves.

Grotius and Pufendorf Give the Individual the Central Place in Their Theories of Law

There are two fundamental philosophical developments in the theory of natural rights. The first is the distinct emergence of the individual. The second, which is related to the first, is the emphasis on rights rather than duties. The origins of these two developments have been attributed to the Protestant Reformation, which must have been a significant influence. They were also a manifestation, however, of the increasing secularization of society. Nor was this all. There were social and economic developments, such as the growth of a money economy, which fostered an increased sense of the individual.

Philosophically, the conceptual framework in which Grotius and Pufendorf are working is fundamentally different from the conceptual framework in which Thomas Aquinas and earlier thinkers were working. Their world is composed of self-interested individuals who are at least implicitly in competition with each other.[1] This view of the world differs from the earlier view, which generally saw the world as a connected whole. The starting point for Grotius and Pufendorf in constructing a theory of law is personal and subjective rather than cosmological. The conception of law that they develop is based on a belief that the individual human person is discrete and free.

The Theory of Natural Rights Holds that the Individual Has Rights Rather Than Duties

The second philosophical development in the theory of natural rights concerns the duty of individuals to preserve their own being under the natural law. The argument of theorists like Grotius and Pufendorf is that this duty implicitly gives individuals the right to do whatever is necessary to preserve their being. This is the philosophical premise that explains the origins of human society and law in the broader theory of natural rights. The same premise later finds expression in the liberal or utilitarian theory of government, which receives its justification from the fact that it serves the interests and liberties of individuals. The historical irony is that this form of government appears to have subjected individuals to increasing levels of social control in the modern era.

The major difference between Grotius and Aquinas is that Aquinas does not conceive of individuals outside some form of community. The elements in the views of both thinkers nevertheless find their way into the common law tradition, which pays particular attention to the rights of the individual person. The moral freedom in the Reformation concept of the individual is apparent in the common law idea that the individual person has a right to do whatever is not prohibited. This idea is apparent in the freedom to contract.

The emphasis on individuals in the common law is counterbalanced by the general inclination of legal institutions to protect the collective interests of society. The theory of natural rights also explains the doctrine of parliamentary supremacy, however, which subordinates the role of the courts to the democratic institutions of government. The rights of the person in the constitutional law also guarantee the rights and freedoms of the individual, though this law has much deeper historical origins.

The influence of the theory of natural rights on the development of the international law is far more direct. In theory, at least, the lack of positive law in the international realm can be traced to the fact that states—the only individuals historically recognized in the international law—have chosen not to establish a government over their affairs. They are therefore in the state of nature, unlike the human individuals in society, who have consented to government. Philosophically, the historical relations between states can therefore be seen as the actions of individuals, free of the restraints of positive law.

The Theory of Natural Rights Was Based on the Natural Law

The history of legal theory follows a recognizable pattern. The common law had its earliest beginnings in the cosmological view in the tribal law, which was based on a kind of cosmological natural law. This view was eventually replaced by a theological conception of the natural law. The theories of Grotius and Pufendorf are also based on a conception of the natural law. The new concept of the natural law emphasizes individual rights, however, rather than duties. This idea of rights gives rise to a new theory of the positive law, based on the agreement and consent of individuals. It is not too much to say that this new focus on the individual is the door through which we enter the modern world.

The Theory of Natural Rights Is Based on a More Technical Approach to Theory

There are a number of new developments in philosophy that accompany these fundamental changes. We can see an increasing interest, for example, in technical issues and conceptual distinctions. There is a careful elaboration of abstract concepts like "law" and "right." The general tendency in this new tradition is to separate the law from its moral antecedents and trace its authority to the political institutions of government. This is the beginning of the legal positivist tradition, which is discussed in later chapters.

Pufendorf Takes a More Philosophical Approach than Grotius

There are differences in the approach adopted by Grotius and that adopted by Pufendorf. Although many of these differences are stylistic, Pufendorf's approach is more systematic. In *The Elements of Universal Jurisprudence*, he begins by defining basic concepts, such as "obligation" and "law," and then constructs a complete theory of law from first principles. The *Elements* accordingly provides a far more comprehensive theory of law.

There are some problems with such an approach. Pufendorf seems to conflate moral, legal, and political restrictions in such a way that the "law" in his theory is sometimes difficult to find. The law of nature provides personal and social guarantees. We are entitled to the necessities of life. Since human beings cannot survive without eating, the natural law has granted humans the right to utilize and consume "those things without which man is unable to preserve life." This includes the right to kill animals. The natural law guarantees the authority of the husband and forbids drunkenness, in order to preserve the social order and social harmony.

Grotius, on the other hand, often seems to be justifying conclusions that he has already formulated. This approach may reflect his career as a lawyer and successful diplomat, who had to defend positions that had already been adopted by those who gave him instructions. His work has a more pragmatic character than the work of Pufendorf, who was an academic. Grotius has also been criticized for taking the side of the ruler against the people, and he often justifies power. This feature of his writing led Jean-Jacques Rousseau to describe him in the novel *Émile* as nothing more than *"un enfant,"* a child, in the field of political theory, and what is more, *"un enfant de mauvaise foi."*[2]

These professional differences are reflected in the narratives of the two philosophers. Grotius' training as an attorney is evident in his tendency to rely on authority rather than rational argument. In the "Prolegomena" to *The Rights of Peace and War*, for example, he states that he will use the "witness" of philosophers, historians, poets, and even orators to demonstrate the existence of the natural law. Such statements reflect a legal rather than a philosophical style of argument, which rests on the consensus in the authorities.

Grotius and Pufendorf Have Different Concepts of Rights and Law

Grotius and Pufendorf also have different concepts of rights. The idea of freedom holds a prominent place in the concept that we find in Grotius' work. In *The Rights of War and Peace*, for example, Grotius states that the notion of right in war is "that which may be done without injustice with regard to an enemy."[3] This statement is significant because it does not impose substantive limits on the participants. Rights come first, in the Grotian theory, and have pre-eminence over duties. This feature of Grotius' work is characteristically liberal and comes into our conception of the rights of the person in the constitutional law.

Both Grotius and Pufendorf apply the word "right" to the acts of government. This usage gives the state the same conceptual freedom as the individual person. This idea has coercive implications for the individual. Indeed, aside from its traditional reference to justice, Grotius says, the word "right" has another sense, "according to which it signifies the same Thing as Law." This statement refers to the right of those in political office to pass laws that go beyond the requirements of justice and require that the rest of us obey them.

Pufendorf has a narrower conception of law. The Latin word *"jus,"* he writes, may mean "law" or "right," but in the latter sense refers to a "moral quality." Although earlier thinkers recognized that legal obligations cannot be reduced to simple moral obligations, Pufendorf's distinction goes further and begins to empty the concept of law of its moral considerations. This development moves us a significant step closer to the modern era and lays the foundations for a political conception of law, which holds that the positive law derives its authority solely from the fact that it is passed by the political branch of government.

Legal rights are "perfect," Pufendorf says, invoking a judicial term. The idea is that rights may be "perfected"—brought to full fruition by the order of a court or, notably, by the application of force. Imperfect rights are more in the nature of moral preferences. This distinction is important because it rests the significance of legal rights on their coercive force. Law is a command, which may be enforced. Imperfect rights are more in the nature of moral or cultural preferences, which have no legal sanction.

Pufendorf also distinguishes between law and "a pact." Both rest on agreement, in his view, but the obligations that arise out of an agreement take on the character of law only when there is a supreme power that punishes those who do not keep their obligations. This distinction is significant because it follows that the international law is composed of agreements that take the form of pacts rather than law. Indeed, Pufendorf accepts that there is nothing in the nature of positive law in the international arena, since there is no supreme power to enforce it.

The Natural Law Has Its Source in Reason Rather Than God

The rough outline of the natural law in Grotius and in Pufendorf remains much as it was in Aquinas. Still, Grotius and Pufendorf were Protestants, and their views reflect the changes in religious thought that took hold after the Reformation. These changes gave individuals the freedom to interpret the scripture and, by extension, the natural law. After the Reformation, the Catholic Church lost its paramount authority in spiritual matters and no longer had the authority to definitively determine the moral contents of this law.

The theory of natural rights accordingly places less reliance on received wisdom than does the earlier philosophical tradition. Grotius and Pufendorf rely more heavily on the role of the natural inclinations of human beings in discovering the law. They also subscribe to the idea that the natural law has a rational basis and can be discovered through the exercise of reason alone. Grotius makes it clear that God cannot change the nature of what is just—a moral act is inherently moral, by virtue of what it is—and remains unalterably so. In *The Rights of War and Peace*, he defines "natural right" as "the Rule and Dictate of Right Reason," and then adds, as an afterthought, that any act "is either forbid or commanded by God, the Author of Nature."[4]

The exclusive reliance on reason frees the natural law and morality from its divine sources. The new position presages the development of science in the Western tradition, which has often been called "positivism." The major significance of this position in the seventeenth century, however, was that it gave individuals the right to determine what is in accordance with the natural law for themselves. Grotius and Pufendorf see human society as a collection of individuals rather than families, clans, tribes, or ethnic or national groups.

The tribal view, as we have seen, is that the universe is an established order, with larger patterns, into which we must fundamentally fit. It would not be correct to say that the theory of natural rights rejects this view. It is rather that the theory sees individuals as conceptually independent, with the freedom to interpret the cosmological order as they see fit. This view opens up an area of personal freedom in which individuals can make their own moral decisions and insist on certain rights.

The Grotian view also recognizes on the psychological level that human beings are self-interested. Grotius elevates this observation, moreover, from a statement of fact to a normative judgement. The natural order is based on God's love, which is "directed to self-interest." From this, Grotius concludes that we are entitled first to defend ourselves, and second to provide for ourselves. Thus Grotius seems to assume—and here he differs from Pufendorf—that the state of nature is a state of war. For when he takes the position that we are entitled to provide for ourselves, he means that we have a right to do so even if it means taking goods from others.

The Political Contract Is Based on the Sovereignty of the Individual

It is the idea that the individual is a sovereign agent with natural rights that gave rise to the theory of the "social contract" in political theory. The term "political contract" seems to provide a better description of this contract, from a legal perspective, since the theory explains how the political branch of government obtained the authority to pass the positive law. The fundamental argument is nevertheless based on the existence of society: Grotius and Pufendorf, among others, argue that private individuals agreed to the formation of society, which required government. This was not a significant issue in Aquinas because he essentially believed that human society always existed.

The theory of natural rights accordingly divides the world into autonomous individuals who originally existed independently of each other. Like the English philosopher Thomas Hobbes, who lived during the same period, Grotius postulates a state of nature that existed before the creation of the political state. In theory at least, the individual persons who lived in the state of nature lived in freedom but without the benefit of positive law. This freedom gave them sovereignty over themselves. They accordingly enjoyed autonomy in their lives and were entitled to make their own decisions. This has become the defining feature in the liberal concept of the person.

There was no positive law in the state of nature. Although there was still the natural law to apply moral regulation, there was no mechanism to enforce it. It follows that the individuals in the state of nature lived in a state of perpetual fear and war. As a result, they entered into a social contract, under which they agreed to give up a portion of the freedom that they enjoyed in return for the peace and security that comes from the formation of government and the establishment of organized society.

The principal benefit of organized society under the social contract is the creation of a central government that has the power to enforce the positive law. This government is based on the consent of the governed, who can remove their consent if government fails to honour the contract. Historically, this idea of government replaces the medieval view that the King, for example, governs by divine right, on the express condition that he follows the natural law. This condition placed substantive moral limits on the ruler, a feature that the political contract often seems to lack.

The existence of the political contract raises important legal questions. The most obvious of these questions is simple enough: what are the essential terms of the contract? The discussion rarely goes beyond the legal question, which holds that the contract is binding only if we have received some benefit or advantage for entering into it. This position is problematic on a simple legal analysis because a party who enters into a contract is entitled to reject and even repudiate the contract if the other party fails to provide the promised consideration. It could be argued that the electoral process provides a democratic mechanism to deal with such issues. There is a more drastic remedy in the work of

John Locke, however, who took the position that the people have a right to rise up in revolt against rulers who do not meet their obligations under the contract.

The more fundamental problem with the political contract is nevertheless that it suggests that individual persons have somehow chosen to enter into the contract. This position naturally implies that individuals have a right to reject the contract and, more importantly, that the authority of the positive law rests ultimately on personal choice. This is not in keeping with the way the positive law operates in daily life. Although Grotius follows the lead of Aquinas, in arguing that the natural law obliges us to obey the positive law, even when we have rejected it, the position of Aquinas is based on the principle that the interests of the individual must be subordinated to the interests of the community. This is not clear in the theories of Grotius and Pufendorf.

The State and the Positive Law Are Based on the Consent of the People

The political contract also explains the origins of the state. The positive law within the state is referred to as the "civil" law because it deals with the relations between citizens— civilians—within the state. It is the existence of government—and, specifically, the political apparatus of government—that provides the mechanism necessary to make and enforce this body of law. Grotius, like Hobbes, argues that this enforcement requires the creation of a supreme authority that can command the members of society to obey the law and punish them if they fail to do so. It follows that our obligation to obey the civil law is based on the political contract and the raw exercise of power.

The major problem with this new scheme of law is that it is not sufficient to guarantee the moral efficacy of the law. As a result, Grotius and Pufendorf fall back on the natural law to justify the civil law. This is particularly true in the case of Pufendorf, who follows the Aristotelian convention in holding that the nature of human beings is essentially social. From this, he deduces as a matter of natural law that whatever is necessary to preserve social harmony is a proper subject of positive law. Laws that do not serve the "utility or public good," on the other hand, are illegitimate. The suggestion—which evokes our constitutional law—is that civil laws that conflict with the natural law are invalid.

Pufendorf also brings in certain criteria to determine when an individual is obliged to obey the positive law. Thus he suggests that a valid human law must respect certain conditions precedent, such as the need for specificity and notice. This suggestion opens up a role for the courts, in scrutinizing the law passed by the political branch of government, to determine whether the positive law is in keeping with the requirements of a valid law.

There are deeper issues here. If our only reason for obeying such a body of law is that we have consented to the political contract, on the basis that it serves our self-interest to do so, there will presumably be situations in which our self-interest lies in disobeying the law rather than honouring the contract. This problem is exacerbated in pluralistic societies where people have many conflicting loyalties and interests.

Grotius Has Been Acclaimed as the Father of the International Law

Grotius has been referred to as the father of the international law. Although this reverence is exaggerated, there is no doubt that Grotius' work contributed more to the development of the international law than that of any other thinker. This influence is partly due to the fact that he addressed the theoretical need of an international system of law at a critical moment in its inception.

Pufendorf was familiar with the work of Grotius. His own theory on the international law places particular reliance on the idea that states can be conceived of as moral persons and have many of the attributes of human persons. Like corporations, states enjoy some form of intellectual capacity and can follow the dictates of reason, in accordance with their nature. The Pufendorfian state system is accordingly based on the same foundations as the state. There are individuals who have the moral and volitional capacity to enter into contractual arrangements. Pufendorf's idea that societies can be seen as moral persons was taken further by Emer de Vattel (1714–1767), who combined it with elements of Grotius' theory to provide a "law of nations."[5]

Grotius and Pufendorf, like Vattel, then, conceive of states as individuals in a state of nature, with the kind of moral autonomy that characterizes human beings. This analogy often seems to fail, however. It is not clear, for example, that artificial persons like states and corporations have the inherent moral faculties that human individuals possess. Religious and altruistic factors do not have the same psychological hold on abstract entities. Nor is there a political contract in the international realm, or government. Although states have the capacity to enter into agreements, with varying degrees of commitment, they exist as persons in the state of nature, outside the positive law, and are subject only to an unenforceable natural law.

Grotius nevertheless argues that the application of the natural law in this international state of nature is sufficient to provide a system of norms to govern the conduct of states. Since the natural law is the same across different societies, and requires only the exercise of reason in order to be discovered, we should be able to assume that the individuals who hold political office in each state will reach the same fundamental conclusions as to what is in keeping with the natural law. It follows that there should be enough consensus and agreement, if not positive law, to provide a normative order in the international realm. The problem is naturally that there remains plenty of room for disagreement as to the moral character of specific state actions. This uncertainty has added a moral fluidity to the international system that makes it relatively easy for states to justify their pursuit of their own interests.

Grotius' Theory of the Open Seas Facilitated Capitalism

Grotius believed that states, like people, are driven by a desire to accumulate wealth. He accordingly endorsed the idea of open seas, which provided the basis for the law of the sea and facilitated the freedom of trade between different countries. This was a relatively new position. The control of the open sea was a matter of dispute in Grotius' time, and the claims of individual states to jurisdiction over the sea had led to many legal and military disputes.[6] This issue was exacerbated by the traditional view that a state's jurisdiction over a case came from the fact that the events giving rise to the case occurred within the territory of the state in question.

Grotius argued that the open sea was *res communes*, a place of common use, and owned by no one. Traffic on the sea was accordingly open to all and could not be subjected to legal interference from individual states. This theory is found in his celebrated *"Mare Liberum"* ("On the Freedom of the Seas"), one of the chapters in *The Rights of War and Peace*, but it derives from the *Commentary on the Law of Prize and Booty*, which can be traced to the facts of a particular case. These facts have been described by Martine Julia van Ittersum:

> In the early morning hours of February 25, 1603, the Dutch captain Jacob van Heemskerck attacked the Portuguese merchantman *Santa Catarina* in the Strait of Singapore and obtained its peaceful surrender by nightfall. His prize was a rich one indeed. When the carrack and its cargo were auctioned in Amsterdam in the autumn of 1604, the gross proceeds amounted to more than three million Dutch guilders—approximately three hundred thousand pounds sterling.[7]

The Portuguese argued that van Heemskerck had no authority to seize the ship. It followed that he had stolen its cargo.

The Dutch East India Company, on whose behalf van Heemskerck was acting, claimed that the ship was validly seized. Grotius appeared for the company in the Amsterdam Admiralty Court and argued that the Dutch were at war with Portugal. The *Santa Catarina* was therefore a legitimate prize—legal booty. Although the court found in favour of the company, the decision was widely criticized. One reason for the criticism was that the war in question had been declared after the ship had been seized. The company accordingly hired Grotius to write a pamphlet to defend its actions; this pamphlet became his *Commentary on the Law of Prize and Booty*.

The deeper issue between the Dutch and the Portuguese was that Portugal had tried to prevent the Netherlands from trading in the region. No nation, Grotius argued, had a right to control the open sea. The theory behind Grotius' concept of the open seas—and behind the international law more generally—was essentially that the open seas were not subject to positive law. Rather they remained in the state of nature, subject only to the natural law. Despite the more dubious aspects of the case, Grotius' argument played an important theoretical role in establishing the freedom of the seas.

The International Law Is Convention Rather Than Law

In spite of the success of Grotius' theory, there are deep philosophical problems with his concept of the international law. One problem is whether the natural law that applies in the international realm is properly considered law. The term "law" has historically been used to refer to binding prescriptions—that is, compulsory rules of behaviour that must be followed. Although we have no difficulty using such a term to describe the tribal law and the natural law, for religious, cosmological, and even social reasons, the most fundamental tenet in the Grotian theory is that states follow the international law by choice. Since individual states are sovereign, a state can be bound only if it chooses to be bound, by its own will. A sovereign state is not bound by the rules set by other states. As a result, the international law has historically been a matter of contract. States could agree to act in certain ways, and they were obliged to honour their agreements to avoid the spectre of war.

This lack of compulsory prescriptions is why international law is often referred to as "convention." The fundamental idea in this usage is that the international law is not inherently binding. The international law arises out of agreement, whether that agreement is a product of consensus (sometimes called "custom") or a result of formal treaties concluded between states. The normative assertion in this context is relatively weak and merely implies that states habitually act in a certain manner. This assertion goes beyond treaties—though treaties are often called "conventions"—and implies that states should conduct themselves in accordance with the general expectations of the community of states.

It is not possible to analyze the complexities involved in the practical application of these theories in the immediate context. The Grotian theory of the international law has nevertheless been pivotal in the development of a relatively complex body of convention to govern international relations, which has only recently begun to acquire the compulsory character of law. It is also important to appreciate that many philosophers and theorists, such as Immanuel Kant (1724–1804) and John Dewey (1859–1952), have recognized that the absence of government in the international sphere was a fundamental failure of the system. The reality is that, in many respects, the field of international relations has often borne the hallmarks of a lawless realm, in which individual states act as they will, subject only to the constraints of power.

The Reliance on Convention Has Made It Difficult to Enforce the International Law

The overriding theoretical problem with the Grotian theory of the international law—and where it has always seemed to fail—is the lack of a binding legal process to decide legal disputes in the international realm. Grotius relies on the natural law, but the natural law is open to interpretation, and states inevitably interpret the general moral principles that apply in the international realm, in accordance with their political interests. As a result of this lack of binding legal regulation in the international realm, the international order has historically been governed by politics rather than by law.

The success of Grotius' attempts to place moral constraints on the international order is questionable. There is ample evidence—as political realists have frequently argued—that the international law has merely served as a means of justifying the self-interested actions of powerful states.[8] Such theorists argue that the real currency in the international system is not law; it is power.[9] The system's reliance on the political mechanics of power makes it difficult to resolve conflicts in the international realm. Perhaps the best that can be said is that the international law, as it has developed under Grotius' theory, has provided a body of principle that allows us to determine the established means of conducting the affairs of states. The success of the current state system is decidedly mixed, however, and lacks the kind of robust legal system that can provide a meaningful, impartial adjudication of politically sensitive issues. The legal status of states, which are sovereign in the international law, logically collides with the idea that there is a compulsory law in the international sphere.

There are many issues here. In spite of Grotius' argument that there is a society of states and a law that governs it, the reality is that his idea of a society regulated by laws seems to serve a rhetorical rather than a legal purpose. Since the international legal system leaves states without a meaningful redress against other states, the only alternative left to a state is to impose its will on other states, often by oblique, subversive, or irregular means. This is as true in cases of justice as in cases of injustice.

The position that Grotius takes with regard to international relations has been compared to Thomas Hobbes' view in *Leviathan*, where he postulates that the state of nature was a state of "perpetuall warre."[10] Claire Cutler writes that the "Grotian tradition"

> has been distinguished from that based upon Hobbesian or realist assumptions, which deny that common values, rules, and institutions bind states together in a society and posit that international politics is a state of war and "an anarchy whose social elements are negligible."[11]

As Cutler acknowledges, however, Grotius bases his analysis on the view that wars are natural and necessary.[12] More importantly, Grotius' conception of sovereignty does not leave any room for the development of an effective system of law. The more pressing question, then, is whether the Grotian conception of natural law merely provides a theoretical facade that hides and ultimately legitimizes a perpetual state of war.

War Has Been Used as a Mechanism to Resolve Political Disputes in the International Realm

The justification of war is central to the Grotian scheme. War was a fixture in the moral and political life of seventeenth-century Europe, and it was impossible for a thinker who wanted to contribute to the development of international relations to simply outlaw war. The first book of *The Rights of War and Peace* accordingly derives the right to engage in war from the natural law. Grotius distinguishes between just and unjust wars, and he provides a compelling body of principle—based on moral consensus—that sets constraints on the right of nations to wage war. Grotius seems to recognize that there are laws of war, which limit the conduct of warring states.

Yet these constraints often seem more rhetorical than real. The problem with Grotius' use of the natural law in a secular environment—and this may be why he often seems open to an accusation of mendacity—is that the natural law has very little significance if there is no mechanism to enforce it. It is one thing to say that individual human beings must follow the natural law, when they are subject to the ordinary positive law backed up by the sanctions of society and government. It is another thing to say that states must do so, in an arena where there is no government and no such laws. Grotius makes the usual references to God, but these references seem empty in a secular setting.

Thus there is a view in the literature that war is an organizing principle in the Grotian theory of the international order. Inis Claude writes, for example, that the "sovereign right of states to go to war"

> stood essentially unchallenged in the eighteenth and nineteenth centuries. That fact tended to reinforce a deeply cynical and pessimistic view of international politics. The international system was, in principle as well as in reality, a war system; it was indifferent to the tragedy and the evil of war. Legally, it permitted war; morally, it condoned war.[13]

There is no means to resolve conflicts between states in such a system, other than to go to war.

The problems here are theoretical, however, and go beyond the history of war, which occurs theoretically in a political realm, outside the reach of law. The theory of natural rights seems inconsistent, in such a context, since it is predicated on the view that the state of nature is a place of inequality and war. In such a state, the theory holds, there are no practical means of preventing the powerful from oppressing the weak. Indeed, this is exactly why individual human beings have agreed to the political contract and the formation of civil government. But of course this raises the question, if the state of nature in the international realm is subject to all the vagaries of power, why is it that nation-states have no need for such a contract?

Pufendorf Bases the Law of Nations on Moral Obligations Rather Than Agreement

Pufendorf provides a competing and much more rigorous conception of the law of nations, based on a more traditional theory of the natural law. In *The Elements of Universal Jurisprudence*, he rejects the Grotian idea that the international law is based ultimately on choice and agreement. For him, the law of nations is a part of the natural law, and it is binding because it is morally obligatory. Thus he suggests that the sovereignty of states has its limits.

Most of the criticism of Pufendorf's thesis arises because the law governing the relations between states did not develop in the manner that Pufendorf foresaw. Such criticisms are practical rather than theoretical, however, and speak more to the fact that until recently the state system developed almost entirely along political lines. It is clear, moreover, that the trend in the contemporary world is to recognize that some parts of the international law—the fundamental law, for example—are inherently binding, ultimately for moral reasons, and do not derive their authority from the fact that states have consented to specific treaties or provisions. This view could be seen as a revival of Pufendorf's thesis.

Pufendorf also disagrees with Grotius on the subject of war. He takes exception to Hobbes' position in *Leviathan* and postulated that the state of nature is a state of peace.[14] He does not mean that war is never justified; nor does he place restrictions on the use of force. Pufendorf's view is rather that war is *prima facie* illegal. Thus states have a duty to do everything in their power to settle their differences before going to war.[15] This duty is apparently required by law, though it is not clear how such a law can be enforced.

In Pufendorf's view, war is permissible only when there is a just cause. This cause, he writes, must be indisputable. It is always preferable to settle the differences between states by other means, and a doubtful case should be submitted to arbitration. This proposal certainly provides a formal process for resolving disputes, but it should not be confused with an independent trial process, which does not depend upon the willingness of the parties to respect its outcome. Although Pufendorf went much further than Grotius did in denigrating war, his restrictions on the conduct of states are full of equivocations. Hans Wehberg concludes that Pufendorf's concessions "to the actual perversity of the human race were so great that in a certain sense they nullified his doctrine that the state as a moral person is bound to the laws of morality."[16]

The *Elements* deals with a number of practical issues that were significant at the time. Pufendorf's conception of the natural law upholds the freedom of the seas, but it also permits a conquering nation to restrict the freedom of trade in its colonies. There is a right of existence, however, and there are limits on any prohibition that might imperil the destruction of another country. Pufendorf also suggests that the citizens of a state may be liable for the debts of their fellow citizens and that the state itself is liable for foreign debts. Finally, he considers many of the standard questions regarding the nature and force of treaties, which bind the state and its legal successors.

Notes

1. The role of self-interest in Grotius' work has been disputed, but the arguments are not convincing. See Richard Tuck, "Grotius, Carneades and Hobbes," *Grotiana*, n.s., 4 (1983): 43–62. And see Benedict Kingsbury and Benjamin Straumann, "The State of Nature and Commercial Sociability in Early Modern International Legal Thought," *Grotiana*, n.s., 31 (2010): 22–43.

2. The conventional translation is "a child of bad faith." See Allan Bloom's translation of *Émile* (n.p.: Basic Books, 1979), at p. 422.

3. See Book 1, Chapter 1, of Grotius' *The Rights of War and Peace*, as cited in the suggestions for further reading.

4. ibid.

5. See Ben Holland, "The Moral Person of the State: Emer de Vattel and the Foundations of International Legal Order," *History of European Ideas* 37 (2011): 438–45, which includes a discussion of Pufendorf; and see Emer de Vattel, *The Law of Nations*, as cited in the suggestions for further reading.

6. Grotius was familiar with such disputes; for example, in 1613 he was sent to England to protest the English seizure of Dutch ships that had allegedly been "trespassing" on seas near Greenland that were claimed by England.

7. "Introduction," in Hugo Grotius, *Commentary on the Law of Prize and Booty*, ed. Martine Julia van Ittersum (Indianapolis: Liberty Fund, 2006). Available at http://oll.libertyfund.org.

8. This is a recurrent theme in political science and political theory. Jack Donnelly reviews "The Realist Tradition" in international relations in Chapter 1 of his *Realism and International Relations* (Cambridge: Cambridge University, 2000), pp. 6–42. Stephen D. Krasner's *Sovereignty: Organized Hypocrisy* (Princeton: Princeton University, 1999) provides a readable example of a contemporary work in such a genre.

9. See Gerry Simpson, *Great Powers and Outlaw States: Unequal Sovereigns in the International Order* (Cambridge: Cambridge University, 2004). The attempt by many authors to save the system from the criticism that it is based on power rather than law bears some similarities to the attempt by Ronald Dworkin to save the common law tradition from the skeptical assault mounted by legal realists (see Chapter 12). For more on this, see Allen Buchanan, *Justice, Legitimacy, and Self-Determination: Moral Foundations for International Law* (New York: Oxford, 2004); and see Anne-Marie Slaughter Burley, "International Law and International Relations Theory: A Dual Agenda," *The American Journal of International Law* 87, no. 2 (April 1993): 205–39.

10. See Thomas Hobbes, *Hobbes's Leviathan, Reprinted from the Edition of 1651 with an Essay by the Late W.G. Pogson Smith* (Oxford: Clarendon, 1909). Available at http://oll.libertyfund.org. Hobbes' position in *Leviathan* is discussed further in Chapter 17.

11. A. Claire Cutler, "The 'Grotian Tradition' in International Relations," *Review of International Studies* 17, no. 1 (January 1991): 41–65 at p. 41. The interior quotation is from M. Wight, "Western Values in International Relations," in *Diplomatic Investigations*, ed. H. Butterfield and M. Wight (Cambridge, MA: Harvard University, 1968), p. 92.

12. See ibid., p. 44: "In fact, Grotius begins with the assumption that war is inevitable and, indeed, 'is in perfect accord with first principles of nature,' for the aim of war is the 'preservation of life and limb'." The quotation from Grotius is taken from Book 1, Chapter 2, of *The Rights of War and Peace*.

13. Inis L. Claude Jr., "Just Wars: Doctrines and Institutions," *Political Science Quarterly* 95, no. 1 (Spring 1980): 83–96, at p. 89.

14. But see Fiammetta Palladini, "Pufendorf Disciple of Hobbes: The Nature of Man and the State of Nature: The Doctrine of *Socialitas*," *History of European Ideas* 34 (2008): 26–60, where she acknowledges the conventional view but argues that Pufendorf was a disciple of Hobbes, who was forced to disguise his views in order to escape accusations "of atheism and moral indifference."

15. This stipulation eventually made its way into Article 12 of the *Covenant of the League of Nations*, 28 April 1919.

16. Hans Wehberg, "Introduction," in *Elementorum Jurisprudentiae Universalis Libri Duo*, as cited in the suggestions for further reading.

Study Questions

1. Where does God fit into the theory of natural law put forward by Grotius and Pufendorf?

2. How do the theory of natural rights and the theory of the natural law treat the individual and the community?

3. How does the idea of a political contract come into Grotius' account of the domestic law?

4. There is a good argument that Grotius' concept of the international law is not law in the full sense of the word. Why?

5. If there is no "law" in the international sphere, on the Grotian view, what is there?

6. What is the legal status in Grotius' theory of the open seas?

7. What is the essential difference, philosophically, between the theory of the international law put forward by Grotius and the theory put forward by Pufendorf?

8. In the additional online reading from *The Elements of Universal Jurisprudence*, Pufendorf compares the so-called law of war to the practices of gladiators and dismisses the idea that they are "laws." Why?

Further Reading

Hugo Grotius, *The Rights of War and Peace*, ed. Richard Tuck (Indianapolis: Liberty Fund, [1724] 2005). Available at http://oll.libertyfund.org.

Jon Miller, "Hugo Grotius," in *The Stanford Encyclopedia of Philosophy*, ed. Edward N. Zalta (Summer 2009). Available at http://plato.stanford.edu.

Samuel Pufendorf, *De Jure Naturae et Gentium* [*On the Law of Nature and Nations*] (Oxford: Clarendon, [1660] 1934).

Kari Saastamoinen, "Liberty and Natural Rights in Pufendorf's Natural Law Theory," in *Transformations in Medieval and Early-Modern Rights Discourse*, ed. Virpi Mäkinen and Petter Korkman (Doredrecht, NL: Springer, 2006), pp. 225–56

James Brown Scott, "Introduction," in *De Jure Belli ac Pacis Libri Tres* [*On the Law of War and Peace*], by Hugo Grotius, trans. Francis W. Kelsey (Oxford: Clarendon, [1646] 1925).

D.F. Scheltens, "Grotius' Doctrine of the Social Contract," *Netherlands International Law Review*, 30 (1983): 43–60.

Richard Tuck, *Natural Rights: Their Origin and Development* (Cambridge: Cambridge University, 1979).

Emer de Vattel, *The Law of Nations; or, Principles of the Law of Nature, Applied to the Conduct and Affairs of Nations and Sovereigns*, trans. Joseph Chitty (Philadelphia: T. & J.W. Johnson & Co., 1883). Available at http://oll.libertyfund.org. The 1758 edition (Carnegie Institution: Washington, 1916) is available at http://heinonline.org.

Hans Wehberg, "Introduction," trans. by Edwin H. Zeydel, in vol. 2 of *Elementorum Jurisprudentiae Universalis Libri Duo* [*The Elements of Universal Jurisprudence*], by Samuel von Pufendorf, trans. William Abbott Oldfather (Oxford: Clarendon, [1672] 1931). Available at www.heinonline.org.

4 Early Scientism: Law Is the Science of Judges and Places Limits on the King

Edward Coke, William Blackstone, and John Marshall

Readings

- From *Dr. Bonham's Case* (1610), by Sir Edward Coke
- On the decision in *Case 1070: The City of London against Wood* (1701), 88 Eng. Rep 1592.
- From *Commentaries on the Laws of England*, by William Blackstone
- From *William Marbury v. James Madison* (1803), 5 U.S. 137

The following chapter reviews the legal theories that provide the foundation for the common law in the seventeenth and eighteenth centuries, when the common law took on the familiar outlines of the modern caselaw. This period extends from the time of Coke's *Reports* (written between 1579 and 1634) to the decision of the United States Supreme Court in *Marbury v. Madison* in 1803. This was an important and interesting time, philosophically, because the fundamental concept of law behind the caselaw changed during this period. The concept of the natural law, which provided the basic understanding of the law in Coke's time, was eventually superseded by the theory of natural rights, which provides the basis of the theory of the common law in William Blackstone's *Commentaries on the Laws of England*. There are nevertheless elements of both concepts of law in the contemporary law. Written constitutions were introduced in order to protect natural rights, but they also recognize that the legal order is ascendant and can be adduced through the exercise of reason. The constitutional law accordingly places legal limits on the authority of the political branch of government to pass positive laws.

The first three readings are from the English caselaw. The first reading is an excerpt from Coke's decision in *Dr. Bonham's Case* (1610), 77 Eng. Rep. 638, which places legal limits on the power of political institutions to pass law. The second reading is from the ruling in *London v. Wood* (1701), 88 Eng. Rep. 1592, which holds that the House of Commons has no power to pass laws that are contrary to reason and the natural law. The third reading is from Blackstone's influential but frequently misleading *Commentaries* (1765–9), which documents a historical change and rests the common law firmly on the concept of natural rights. The final reading is from the decision of the United States Supreme Court in *Marbury v. Madison* (1803), 5 U.S. 137, which is usually cited as the case that established the doctrine of judicial review. This doctrine holds that that the courts have the power to review the actions of the legislative and executive branches of government to determine whether they are in keeping with the constitution.

✬ Readings ✬

From Sir Edward Coke, *Dr. Bonham's Case*, from Part 8 of *The Reports*, in vol. 1 of *The Selected Writings and Speeches of Sir Edward Coke*, ed. Steve Sheppard (Indianapolis: Liberty Fund, [1826] 2003).[1]

Hilary Term, 7 James 1.
In the Court of Common Pleas.

Thomas Bonham, Doctor in Philosophy and Physick brought an action of false imprisonment against Henry Atkins, George Turner, Thomas Moundford, and John Argent, Doctors in Physick, and John Taylor, and William Bowden Yeomen, For that the Defendants, the 10 of *Novemb. anno 4 Jacobi*, did imprison him, and detain him in prison by the space of 7 days. The Defendants pleaded the Letters Patents of King Henry the 8 [and various statutes, which gave the College of Physicians the power to imprison those who were unlawfully practising medicine].

[And on] 7 *Novemb.* 1606. the said Thomas Bonham at their assembly came before the President and Censors, and they asked him if he would satisfy the College for his disobedience and contempt, an submit himself to be examined; and obey the censure of the College, who answered, That he had practised Physick and would practice Physick within *London*, asking no leave of the College, and that he would not submit himself to the President and Censors; and affirmed, that the President and censors had no authority over those who were Doctors in the University; For which cause, the said 4 Censors . . . did commit the Plaintiff to the prison of the Counter in London, *&c., without bail or mainprise. . . .*

As to the 2 points upon which the Chief Justice, Warburton and Daniel, gave judgement. 1. It was Resolved by them, That the said censors . . . have not power by the Letters Patents, and the Act to fine or imprison any for practising Physick within *London*, but only *pro delictis suis in non bene exequendo, &c. scil.* for ill and not good use and practise of Physick. . . . 2. The harm which accrueth by *non bene exequendo, &c.* doth concern the body of man; and, therefore, it is reasonable that the offender should be punished in his body, *scil.* by imprisonment; but he who practiceth Physick in *London* in a good manner, although he doth it without leave, yet it is not any prejudice to the body of man. . . .

The Censors, cannot be Judges, Ministers, and parties; Judges, to give sentence or judgement; Ministers, to make summons; and Parties, to have the moyety of the forfeiture [i.e., the benefit of the fine that they have levied] *quia aliquis non debet esse Judex in propria causa* [because no one ought to be a judge in his own cause] . . . and one cannot be Judge and Attorney for any of the parties, Dyer 3 E. 6. 65. 38 E. . . . *&c.* And it appeareth in our Books, that in many Cases, the Common Law doth controll Acts of Parliament, and sometimes shall adjudge them to be void: for when an Act of Parliament is against Common right and reason, or repugnant, or impossible to be performed, the Common Law will controll it, and adjudge such Act to be void. . . .

[Coke then cites a number of cases in support of his position.] The *Statute of Carlisle,* made *anno* 35 *E.* 1. enacteth, That [in] the Order of the *Cistercians* and *Augustines,* who have a Covent and Common Seal, that the Common Seal shall be in the keeping of the Prior, who is under the Abbot and others of the most grave of the house; and that any deed sealed with the Common Seal, which is not so in keeping, shall be void: and the opinion of the Court (*Anno 27 H.* 6 *Annuity* 41.) was that this Statute was void, for it is impertinent to be observed, for the Seal being in their keeping, the Abbot cannot seal any thing with it, and when it is in the Abbot's hands, it is out of their keeping.[2] . . .

Notes

1.   Editor's note: Dr. Bonham was a medical doctor at the University of Cambridge and took the position that the College of Physicians had no authority to discipline doctors practising at the university. The original report is in *The Reports of Sir Edward Coke, Knt.: in Thirteen Parts,* new ed. (London: Joseph Butterworth, 1826), which is available at http://heinonline.org.
2.   Editor's note: So that a deed (a legal instrument) is not valid unless it has been sealed by the abbot, the head of the order; but the abbot cannot seal it without taking the seal out of the keeping of the prior, which would void the deed. Thus the statute is contrary to reason.

From the decision in *Case 1070, The City of London against Wood* (1701), 88 Eng. Rep. 1592.

At the Sittings after Hilary Term.
In the Thirteenth of William the Third [1701]. At Guildhall, before Sir John Holt, Knt., Chief Justice. Sir Edward Ward, Knt., Chief Baron. Sir Henry Hatsell, Knt., Senior Baron. In the Court of King's Bench.

In an action brought in the Mayor's Court against Wood for four hundred pounds as a forfeiture . . . according to the Act of Common Council [a bylaw of the City of London] made in the seventh year of Charles the First, it appeared *the plaint* was levied in the Court of the Mayor and Aldermen on the fifteenth of November . . . and [eventually] sent down [to the Court of King's Bench] by *procedendo.* . . .

[Counsel argued] . . . whether the action be well brought in the Mayor's Court? . . .

Holt, Chief Justice. There are several points in this case. . . .

But the true great point is, that the Court is held before the mayor and aldermen, and the action brought in the names of the mayor and commonalty; and that very man, who is head of the city, and without whom the city has no ability or capacity to sue, is the very person before whom the action is brought; and this cannot be by the rules of any law whatever, for it is against all laws that the same person should be party and Judge in the same cause, for it is manifest contradiction; for the party is he that is to complain to the Judge, and the Judge is to hear the party; the party endeavours to have his will, the Judge determines against the will of the party,[1] and has authority to enforce him to obey his sentence: and can any man act against his own will, or enforce himself to obey? The Judge is agent, the party is patient, and the same person cannot be both agent and patient in the same thing. . . . it is manifest contradiction.

And what my Lord Coke says in *Dr. Bonham's Case* in his 8 Co. is far from any extravagancy, for it is a very reasonable and true saying, that if an Act of Parliament should ordain that the same person should be party and Judge, or, which is the same thing, Judge in his own cause, it would be a void Act of Parliament; for it is impossible that one should be Judge and party, for the Judge is to determine between party and party, or between the Government and the party; and an Act of Parliament can do no wrong, though it may do several things that look pretty odd; for it may discharge one from his allegiance to the Government he lives under, and restore him to the state of nature; but it cannot make one that lives under a Government Judge and party. An Act of Parliament may not make adultery lawful, that is, it cannot make it lawful for A. to lie with the wife of B. but it may make the wife of A. to be the wife of B. and dissolve her marriage with A.

Note

1. Editor's note: This is an old use of the word "against" to mean that the judge decides the case independently—i.e., not in simple conformity with the will of the party.

From William Blackstone, *Commentaries on the Laws of England*, facsimile ed., in 4 vols. (Buffalo, NY: William S. Hein, [1765–9] 1992).

Book the First. Of the Rights of Persons

Chapter the First. Of the Absolute Rights of Individuals

For the principal aim of Society is to protect individuals in the enjoyment of those absolute rights, which were vested in them by the immutable laws of nature; but which could not be preserved in peace without that mutual assistance and intercourse, which is gained by the institution of friendly and social communities. Hence it follows, that the first and primary end of human laws is to maintain and regulate these *absolute* rights of individuals. . . . Let us therefore proceed to examine how far all laws ought, and how far the laws of England actually do, take notice of these absolute rights, and provide for their lasting security. . . .

The rights themselves . . . consist in a number of private immunities . . . And these may be reduced to three principal or primary articles; the right of personal security, the right of personal liberty; and the right of private property. . . .

The Right of Personal Security

I. The right of personal security consists in a person's legal and uninterrupted enjoyment of his life, his limbs, his body, his health, and his reputation. . . .

The Right to Personal Liberty

II. Next to personal security, the law of England regards, asserts, and preserves the personal liberty of individuals. This personal liberty consists in the power of loco-motion, of changing situation, or removing one's person to whatsoever place one's own inclination may direct; without imprisonment or restraint, unless by due course of law. Concerning which we may make the same observations as upon the preceding article; that it is a right strictly natural; that the laws of England have never abridged it without sufficient cause; and, that in this kingdom it cannot ever be abridged at the mere discretion of the magistrate, without the explicit permission of the laws. . . .

Of great importance to the public is the preservation of this personal liberty: for if once it were left in the power of any, the highest, magistrate to imprison arbitrarily whomever he or his officers thought proper, (as in France it is daily practiced by the Crown) there would soon be an end of all other rights and immunities. . . .

III. The third absolute right, inherent in every Englishman, is that of property: which consists in the free use, enjoyment, and disposal of all his acquisitions, without any control or diminution, save only by the laws of the land. . . .

Subordinate Legal Rights

In the three preceding articles we have taken a short view of the principal absolute rights which appertain to every Englishman. But in vain would these rights be declared, ascertained, and protected by the dead letter of the laws, if the constitution had provided no other method to secure their actual enjoyment. It has therefore established certain other auxiliary subordinate rights of the subject, which serve principally as barriers to protect and maintain inviolate the three great and primary rights, of personal security, personal liberty, and private property. These are,

1. The constitution, powers, and privileges of Parliament. . . .
2. The limitation of the King's prerogative, by [legal] bounds so certain and notorious, that it is impossible he should exceed them without the consent of the people. . . . [The first auxiliary subordinate right] keeps the legislative power in due health and vigour, so as to make it improbable that laws should be enacted destructive of general liberty: . . . [the second auxiliary subordinate right] is a guard upon the executive power [i.e., the power of the King], by restraining it from acting either beyond or in contradiction to the laws, that are framed and established by [Parliament]. . . .
3. A third subordinate right of every Englishman is that of applying to the courts of justice for redress of injuries. Since the law is in England the supreme arbiter of every

man's life, liberty, and property, courts of justice must at all times be open to the subject, and the law be duly administered therein. The emphatical words of *Magna Carta*, spoken in the person of the King, who in judgement of law (says Sir Edward Coke) is ever present and repeating them in all his courts, are these; "*nulli vendemus* [We will not sell], *nulli negabimus* [We will not deny], *aut differemus rectum vel justitiam* [or delay right and justice]:[1] and therefore every subject," continues the same learned author ". . . may take his remedy by the courts of the law, and have justice and right for the injury done to him, freely without fail, fully without any denial, and speedily without delay." . . .

4. If there should happen any uncommon injury, or infringement of the rights beforementioned, which the ordinary court of law is too defective to reach, there still remains a fourth subordinate right appertaining to every individual, namely, the right of petitioning the King, or either house of Parliament, for the redress of grievances.

5. The fifth and last auxiliary right of the subject . . . is that of having arms for their defence, suitable to their condition and degree, and such as are allowed by law. Which is . . . indeed a public allowance, under due restriction, of the natural right of resistance and self-preservation, when the sanctions of society and laws are found insufficient to restrain the violence of oppression.

Note

1. Editor's note: The words are from section 40 of the *Magna Carta* of 1225. For the text of the *Magna Carta* and a technical commentary, see *Magna Carta: A Commentary on the Great Charter of King John*, with a "historical" introduction by William Sharp McKechnie (Glasgow: Maclehose, 1914). Available at http://oll.libertyfund.org.

From *William Marbury v. James Madison* (1803), 5 U.S. 137.

Editor's note: The case arose when the administration of President Thomas Jefferson refused to recognize the validity of the judicial "commissions" made by the previous President on his last day of office. As a result, Marbury applied to the Supreme Court for a writ ordering James Madison, the new secretary of state, to deliver the commission. In the first part of the decision, the Supreme Court held that Marbury was entitled to his appointment.

Mr. Chief Justice Marshall Delivered the Opinion of the Court

This brings us to the second inquiry; which is:

> If he has a right, and that right has been violated, do the laws of his country afford him a remedy?

The very essence of civil liberty certainly consists in the right of every individual to claim the protection of the laws whenever he receives an injury. One of the first duties of government is to afford that protection. In Great Britain, the King himself is sued in the respectful form of a petition, and he never fails to comply with the judgement of his court.

In the third volume of his *Commentaries*, page 23, Blackstone states two cases in which a remedy is afforded by mere operation of law.

"In all other cases," he says, "it is a general and indisputable rule that where there is a legal right, there is also a legal remedy by suit or action at law whenever that right is invaded." . . .

The Government of the United States has been emphatically termed a government of laws, and not of men. It will certainly cease to deserve this high appellation if the laws furnish no remedy for the violation of a vested legal right. . . .

It behooves us then to inquire whether there be in . . . [the] composition [of the case] any ingredient which shall exempt [it] from legal investigation or exclude the injured party from legal redress. . . .

[The court then rejects the idea that the loss of the commission can be described as "a loss without an injury," and goes on to consider the following question:] Is the act of delivering or withholding a commission to be considered as a mere political act belonging to the executive department alone, for the performance of which entire confidence is placed by our Constitution in the Supreme Executive, and for any misconduct respecting which the injured individual has no remedy?

That there may be such cases is not to be questioned; but that every act of duty to be performed in any of the great departments of government constitutes such a case is not to be admitted.

By the act concerning invalids, passed in June, 1794, the Secretary at War is ordered to place on the pension list all persons whose names are contained in a report previously made by him to Congress. If he should refuse to do so, would the wounded veteran be without remedy? Is it to be contended that where the law, in precise terms, directs the performance of an act in which an individual is interested, the law is incapable of securing obedience to its mandate? . . . Is it to be contended that the heads of departments are not amenable to the laws of their country?

Whatever the practice on particular occasions may be, the theory of this principle will certainly never be maintained. No act of the Legislature confers so extraordinary a privilege, nor can it derive countenance from the doctrines of the common law.[1] . . .

That the people have an original right to establish for their future government such principles as, in their opinion, shall most conduce to their own happiness is the basis on which the whole American fabric has been erected. The exercise of this original right is a very great exertion; nor can it nor ought it to be frequently repeated. The principles, therefore, so established are deemed fundamental. And as the authority from which they proceed is supreme, and can seldom act, they are designed to be permanent.

This original and supreme will organizes the government and assigns to different departments their respective powers. . . .

The powers of the Legislature are defined and limited; and that those limits may not be mistaken or forgotten, the Constitution is written. To what purpose are powers limited, and to what purpose is that limitation committed to writing; if these limits may at any time be passed by those intended to be restrained? . . .

The Constitution is either a superior, paramount law, unchangeable by ordinary means, or it is on a level with ordinary legislative acts, and, like other acts, is alterable when the legislature shall please to alter it. . . . Certainly all those who have framed written Constitutions contemplate them as forming the fundamental and paramount law of the nation, and consequently the theory of every such government must be that an act of the Legislature repugnant to the Constitution is void. This theory is essentially attached to a written Constitution, and is consequently to be considered by this Court as one of the fundamental principles of our society. . . .

It is emphatically the province and duty of the Judicial Department to say what the law is. Those who apply the rule to particular cases must, of necessity, expound and interpret that rule. If two laws conflict with each other, the Courts must decide on the operation of each. So, if a law be in opposition to the Constitution, if both the law and the Constitution apply to a particular case, so that the Court must either decide that case conformably to the law, disregarding the Constitution, or conformably to the Constitution, disregarding the law, the Court must determine which of these conflicting rules governs the case. This is of the very essence of judicial duty.

If, then, the Courts are to regard the Constitution, and the constitution is superior to any ordinary act of the Legislature, the Constitution, and not such ordinary act, must govern the case to which they both apply.

The Court Then Considers a Number of Examples

The Constitution declares that "no bill of attainder or *ex post facto* law shall be passed." If, however, such a bill should be passed and a person should be prosecuted under it, must the Court condemn to death those victims whom the Constitution endeavours to preserve?

"No person," says the Constitution, "shall be convicted of treason unless on the testimony of two witnesses to the same overt act, or on confession in open court."

Here the language of the Constitution is addressed especially to the Courts. It prescribes, directly for them, a rule of evidence not to be departed from. If the Legislature should change that rule, and declare one witness, or a confession out of court, sufficient for conviction, must the constitutional principle yield to the legislative act?

From these and many other selections which might be made, it is apparent that the framers of the Constitution contemplated that instrument as a rule for the government of courts, as well as of the Legislature. . . . It is also not entirely unworthy of observation that, in declaring what shall be the supreme law of the land, the Constitution itself is first mentioned, and not the laws of the United States generally, but those only which shall be made in pursuance of the Constitution, have that rank.

Thus, the particular phraseology of the Constitution of the United States confirms and strengthens the principle, supposed to be essential to all written Constitutions, that a law repugnant to the Constitution is void, and that courts, as well as other departments, are bound by that instrument.

Note

1.   Editor's note: Marshall then quotes Blackstone's *Commentaries*, where Blackstone says that "injuries to the rights of property can scarcely be committed by the Crown without the intervention of its officers," who are liable for the injury. See the excerpt from Blackstone, on the liability of the Crown, in the additional online readings for this chapter listed in the Appendix.

⤗ Discussion ⤙

The Sources of the Common Law Can Be Found in the Customary Law, which Was Rooted in the Tribal Law

The beginnings of the common law have already been sketched out in Chapter 1, which discussed the tribal law and the customary law. The tribal law can be described as pre-ancient law, since it goes back beyond ancient times, to a time before we possessed written historical records. Many of the traditions in this law persisted in the customary law, which provided the original source of the common law. As we have seen, these traditions were based on the existence of clans or families, the formalization of the feud, and an interest in expiation or atonement. The early legal process was designed to annul or cancel the wrong suffered by a private party. The kind of balancing that this process envisaged was a product of the cosmological views that found expression in the tribal law.

The customary law retained much of its tribal character and varied across Britain, which was divided into kingdoms. The fundamental role of the kings who ruled these early kingdoms was to see that the customary law was consistently enforced. The impartiality of the King probably served as a counterweight to the forces of village politics, which must have been oppressive. The customary law that had been preserved was essentially a schedule of payments for selected wrongs. These payments were blood money—money that was, in the words of the *Oxford English Dictionary*, "the price of blood." This money was paid to the victim and the kin of the victim to avoid acts of personal vengeance and feuds, though victims still had the right to take matters into their own hands.

There was also an independent legal tradition, however, which flourished in local courts. These courts derived their authority from the law itself rather than from any form of political government. The most significant feature of this early law, from our perspective, is that it derived its authority from the fact that it had been customarily applied. The certainty that this feature of the law provided was an important source of social stability and contained the raw power of those who held political office within fixed limits. The idea that the King could change the law was not merely foreign to the people of the time; it was anathema.

The other major source of law was Church law, which evolved separately from the Roman law and took its character from the civil system of law in Europe. It was the Church law, called "canon law," that contributed the moral element to our general conception of liability. The Church law, together with the local and the customary law, provided the main elements in the pre-common law. Over time, these sources of law slowly came together to form a single body of law.

The Common Law Has Its Origins in the Development of a Single System of Law

The beginning of the common law can be traced to the victory of William the Conqueror at the Battle of Hastings in 1066. The common law was essentially the King's law and was used by William and the kings who succeeded him to assert and maintain their control over the entire country.[1] This control was achieved only slowly, by the amalgamation of the local laws and legal customs throughout the country into a single body of law administered by the central government.

The *Domesday Book*, originally compiled in 1086 for the purposes of taxation, provided William the Conqueror with a list of every piece of land in England and the owners of that land.[2] Each entry in the *Domesday Book* was a legally binding judgement (a *dome*) and had the force of law. The publication of the book brought the country under a single legal administration for the purpose of deciding matters concerning land. There was also an attempt by the royal judges to consolidate the existing streams of law into a single, systematic body of law.

Henry of Bracton, a priest and a judge in the Court of King's Bench, wrote and edited *De legibus et consuetudinibus Angliae* (*On the Laws and Customs of England*) in the thirteenth century. Bracton's book was copied by hand and circulated in manuscript form among judges and lawyers over the next two hundred years. Bracton relied on classical legal sources and the canon law on substantive matters, but he gave judges the primary role in developing the law. This practice was based on the principle of precedent. The idea that the law should be developed on a case-by-case basis, in the context of the specific facts before the court, became the defining feature of the common law.[3] Bracton's work is significant in the genealogy of legal theory because it recognizes that there is a universal moral law, essentially the natural law, that is available through the exercise of reason. The law has its own, inherent authority and does not derive its authority from political sources.

The Magna Carta *Asserted the Authority of the Earlier Law over Political Government*

The early common law was based on the idea that the law was supreme. This idea is evident in the *Magna Carta* (the "Great Charter"), which King John was forced to sign in 1215. The significance of the *Magna Carta* lies in its assertion that the King and the emerging central government were subordinate to the laws of the land. This assertion is often seen as the source of the constitutional law, since it placed legal limits on those in political power. The constitutional law developed much later, however, as the political sources of authority in the central government acquired ascendancy in the system.

The *Magna Carta* was a product of a rebellion by the English barons, who resented the increasing authority of the central government.[4] The Charter endorses the right of *habeas corpus* and guarantees the legal rights of barons and freemen.[5] It also created a Grand Council, a consultative body that is usually seen as an institutional antecessor of Parliament. The Charter's significance in legal theory, however, lies in its assertion that the King and the central government had to respect the legal order. This idea, which placed legal limits on the exercise of political power, had its sources in the customary law.[6]

The *Magna Carta* was originally of somewhat dubious origin, and its gradual inclusion in the common law tradition was probably motivated by a desire to legitimize the restraints that it placed on the institutions of government. The authority of the Charter, however, comes from the general conception of law at the time. This concept surfaces in the references to the common law in the judicial decisions of Edward Coke and other judges, which include legal principles that would now be considered part of the constitutional law. The Charter recognizes explicitly that the legal order has ascendancy in the hierarchy of government.

The *Magna Carta* acquired its later status because it became an important political document in the struggles between the King and Parliament for supremacy within the emerging state. The House of Commons repeatedly fell back on the Charter to assert that there were legal limits on the prerogatives of the King. Indeed, by 1621, Parliament had passed no less than 32 bills confirming the *Magna Carta*.[7] These actions were principally intended to assert that there were legal limits on the authority of the King.

The idea that Parliament had the authority to place legal limits on the King was a relatively new idea, and the dynamic of such a process is the opposite of the legislative process that we are familiar with in modern times. The force and stature of the *Magna Carta* came from the authority of the customary law and the concept of law behind it, rather than from any act of Parliament. In point of fact, it was Parliament that borrowed from the authority of the *Magna Carta*, in passing it again, since the mere assertion that Parliament had the power to confirm and pass the law increased its authority. This kind of historical example suggests how Parliament eventually appropriated the supremacy that was enjoyed by the law and transferred it to the political order.[8]

The Original Common Law Was Found in the Written Judgements of the King's Judges

The term "common law" referred originally to the law found in the decisions made by the King's judges, who travelled regularly throughout the country. At the beginning, these judges represented the King in person and were given commissions to conduct his business. One of the standard commissions instructed them to determine whether prisoners were lawfully held. Trials were held at assizes (sittings of the court), where the visiting judge dealt with the cases that had accumulated since the last sitting of the court. A system of circuit courts was eventually developed, and this system continued the practice on a more regional level.

The royal judges were expected to respect local customs and apply these customs in their cases. These customs were supplemented by the statutes passed, first by individual kings, and later by Parliament. The concept of law in the customary law was still ascendant, however, even in the King's courts, and it provided a fundamental check on the powers of the King. This check became less significant as a new concept of law, based on natural rights, took hold and Parliament began to exercise its authority. It is nevertheless apparent that the older view that the King was subject to the common law persisted into the seventeenth century.

The respect for custom in the earlier tradition found expression in the doctrine of precedent. The common law was based on the principle of *stare decisis* (stand by the decision), under which the judges of the same court were obliged to follow each other's rulings. This principle reflects the idea in the natural law that the law can be discovered through the exercise of reason. Since the principle of *stare decisis*, which still governs the caselaw, applies only to the legal proposition that forms the *ratio decidendi* (the reason for the decision), it does not prevent judges from developing the law further.

The term *common law* is now used to describe the entire system of law that was built up from the decisions of Bracton, Coke, and the judges who followed them. Although Parliament eventually supplanted custom as the source of the law, the judiciary retained the authority to determine the contents of the law on the basis of the existing caselaw. This system migrated from England to Canada, the United States, and the other colonies of England. The legal tradition in the common law system places far more weight on the decisions of individual judges than does the tradition in the civil system of law, which is prominent in the rest of the world. Most of the law of contracts, real property, and torts in the common law system still derives from judicial decisions, though legislatures have often incorporated the principles and rulings in the caselaw in statutory codifications of the law. The common law judiciary has historically had a mediating role in the relations between the government and private individuals. This function can be traced to the original source of the common law in the customs of the people, independent of any government.

Coke Sees Law as the Science of Judges

There is a tradition of legal scientism in the common law tradition. This idea of scientism originates in the etymology of the word "science," which refers to the state of knowing and the production, essentially, of knowledge. Edward Coke (1552–1634), who became the Lord Chief Justice of England, and who wrote the decision in *Dr. Bonham's Case*, was probably the foremost proponent of the idea that law is a science in the earlier common law. This was before the idea of the social contract had taken firm hold in legal and political theory.

The ultimate source of the scientism in the common law tradition seems to be the theory of the natural law. As we saw in Chapter 3, the conception of the natural law changed at the time of the Protestant Reformation and was seen merely as a secular set of propositions that could be deduced through the exercise of reason. This commitment to the power of reason, which fed into the development of the natural sciences, led to the development of similar ideas in the legal arena.

Scientism Sees the Common Law as a Kind of Machine

Scientism suggests that the bulk of the law, at least, can be deduced from a set of fundamental moral and legal axioms. This suggestion gives judges the primary role in the development of the law and minimizes the role played by the legislature. Scientism also finds expression, however, in the set of rules developed by the courts to interpret and apply the statutes passed by the legislature. This body of rules provides a rational means of ascertaining the precise meaning of the words used in particular legislation.

The scientism in the common law tradition, however, focusses on the development of the substantive law by rational deduction from the rules and principles that have been established in the caselaw. Coke was an influential figure in this process for a number of reasons. One is that he published his reports, which contained a written explanation of the reasons for the decision that had been reached in particular cases. The legal principles on which Coke relied were followed by judges in subsequent cases, under the doctrine of precedent, and provided the basis for much of the common law.

The legal theory behind Coke's work is more important, however. Coke sees the common law more as a system of deduction, a rational machine, the rules of which are known only to those who have studied it. The focus of his scientism is accordingly on the rational methodology of the common law, which classifies relevant facts and then fits them into a sophisticated legal calculus in order to determine the proper outcome in specific cases. It is not too much to say that the law can be seen, on this view, as an epistemological machine that produces a just result in specific cases.

One of the neglected aspects of Coke's theory of the common law is that it rests the decision in each case on the judge's finding of facts. This is not a passive process. Thus, when Coke describes the common law as reason itself, in the first part of his *Institutes of the Laws of England*, he is referring to a logical act. The judge is a deducer, a person who applies the law to the facts and follows reason to its logical conclusion:

> And this is another strong argument in Law, *Nihil quod est contra rationem est licitum*. [Nothing that is against reason is lawful.] For reason is the life of the Law, nay the common Law it selfe is nothing else but reason, which is to be understood of an artificiall perfection of reason, gotten by long study, observation, and experience, and not of every mans naturall reason.[9]

The common law is something more than a simple storehouse of legal propositions, which are easily applied. It is a rational discipline, a form of analysis, that is reserved for those who have training in the law.

Coke saw the common law as a corporate enterprise, designed by many generations of judges. In the same section of the *Institutes*, Coke writes that the law of England has "by many successions of ages . . . been fined and refined by an infinite number of grave and learned men, and by long experience growne to such a perfection" that it can be described as "the perfection of reason." This comment reflects the conception of law found in the customary law, which rests the moral consensus in the community on the existence of a rationally verifiable law, which must be obeyed.

The Legal Order Is Ascendant and Places Limits on the King

The aspect of Coke's scientism that seems most significant in a modern context is the premise that the legal and political functions of the state must be separated. The law exists independently of the King and his government, and it does not derive its authority from political sources. It follows that the King cannot appoint judges, for example, at will. The common law, Coke writes, "doth disable some men to take any estate in some particular things." Thus, if the King appoints a man who "is unexpert, and hath no skill and science to exercise or execute the same" to a judicial position, the man is disabled by the law and cannot assume the position.[10]

Coke's legal theory relies heavily on the independence of the common law judges. In 1607, he tells us, he informed King James that he could not try a legal case, since legal cases "are not to be decided by naturall reason but by the artificiall reason and judgement of Law, which Law is an act which requires long study and experience, before that a man can attain to the cognizance of it."[11] The King cannot interfere with the law, he asserted, which is "the Golden metwand and measure to try the Causes of the Subjects." When King James objected that this means he is subject to the law, Coke supposedly quoted Bracton: *Quod Rex non debet esse sub homine, sed sub Deo et Lege* (the King ought not to be under any man, but under God and the Law).

Later, when the judges of the Court of King's Bench rejected the King's attempt to stay a case, Coke was summoned before the Privy Council to answer for his actions. There, he is supposed to have told the King that the law does not yield to the "private reason" of individual persons.[12] As a result of this comment, Coke was dismissed from his position as chief justice of the Court of King's Bench in 1616.[13] Afterward, he led the debate against the King's imprisonment of individuals who had refused to lend him money. In a famous speech to the House of Lords, he argued that the King did not have the legal authority to imprison without cause.

Coke's Ruling in Dr. Bonham's Case Heralded the Beginning of the Constitutional Law

Coke's ruling in *Dr. Bonham's Case* has been celebrated as a ruling that foreshadows the constitutional law.[14] Some of this significance comes from the importance that the ruling places on personal liberty. The case nevertheless has criminal overtones, since Dr. Bonham was imprisoned for practising without the permission of the College of Physicians. The substantive ruling in the case is simply that the same party cannot legally prosecute a case and decide it.

The broader significance of the case, however, lies in its holding that Parliament cannot pass a law that permits the same party to prosecute and decide a case. Coke's decision accordingly recognizes the ascendancy of the legal order over the political order. In Coke's view, Parliament, like the King, is under the law and subject to its authority. The common law "doth controll Acts of Parliament," at least in those situations where it runs against fundamental legal principles. This view has larger implications for the state and goes against the arguments of thinkers like Grotius, who argues that the state exists in some state of nature, outside the reach of the law.

The practical significance of Coke's assertion of legal supremacy should not be overstated. The important factor in *Dr. Bonham's Case* is nevertheless that the legal restrictions that Coke places on political institutions are moral and substantive. The decision holds, moreover, that the courts have the inherent authority to find a statute that does not meet those requirements "utterly void." This view recalls the idea, in Aquinas and others, that a positive law that clearly violates the natural law is invalid. It also foreshadows the ruling of Chief Justice Marshall in *Marbury v. Madison*.

Day v. Savadge Treats the Natural Law as a Kind of Constitutional Law

The same kind of question arose in *Day v. Savadge* (1614), where the Court of King's Bench held that the city of London could not "certify" a custom under a statute, since that would effectively allow the city to decide cases in which it was the defendant. The court held that "even an Act of Parliament, made against natural equity, as to make a man Judge in his own case, is void in itself, for *jura naturme sunt immutabilia*, and they are *leges legum*."[15] The laws of nature are immutable; they are laws of the law. In a modern context, this seems to describe the natural law as a kind of constitutional law, which governs the positive law passed by Parliament or the King.

London v. Wood Suggests that the Common Law Puts Limits on Parliament

The contest between legal and political institutions for ascendancy in the seventeenth century has been minimized, probably because it is less significant, historically, than the struggle between the King and Parliament for political power.[16] The original position in the common law was nevertheless that the law has inherent authority, which derives from custom and the natural law, rather than political institutions.

This concept of law survived in caselaw, well into the seventeenth century. The political conception of law that succeeded the older concept, which was based on natural rights and the social contract, ran into difficulty in those situations where the statutes passed by Parliament were illogical, made little sense, or could not be coherently applied. The court's remarks in *London v. Wood* reflect the inevitable frustration of the judiciary in dealing with such laws.

There is a technical and a substantive side to this frustration. On the technical side, the judicial irritation seems to suggest that there is ultimately a problem of definition in permitting the city to prosecute the case and decide it. The court appears to hold that a bylaw (which is likened to an Act of Parliament in the report) cannot name a party—here the mayor—as a party and a judge in his own case without rendering the usual use of these terms meaningless. A trial, by its very definition, requires separate parties—and in the idiom of the time, separate *wills*—to ensure that there is a logical possibility that the judge may decide against the party. The court holds that it is impossible for a litigant to act "against his own will."

On the substantive side, however, the issue is that it is arbitrary and unfair for a person to judge his or her own case. Parliament accordingly cannot legislate that the same person will be judge and party. This stipulation places ethical and legal limits on the exercise of the sovereign power. Like Coke, Chief Justice Holt resolves the question of ascendancy in favour of the law—in spite of the fact that an Act of Parliament "can do no wrong." This conclusion is difficult to explain, philosophically, if we accept the common understanding—presented in the legal theory of Grotius, Pufendorf, and many other authors—that the law obtains its authority only from the sovereign power and cannot logically restrict that power.

Holt's statement that Parliament "may do several things that look pretty odd" is a reference to the institution of outlawry, which Holt probably finds odd because Parliament is—in a similar sense—dissolving the contract that gives it its own authority. The argument on the substantive issues is only incidentally constitutional, since the issue does not concern the exact nature of the law in question. As the reference to adultery attests, the idea—which comes from the natural law—is that custom and moral reason determines what is lawful. When Parliament fails to respect the moral consensus in society in passing legislation, it seems that the legislation is void and unlawful.

The Conception of Law in Blackstone's *Commentaries* Is a Political Conception, Based on the Political Contract

William Blackstone (1723–1780) was a judge and a professor. His *Commentaries on the Laws of England* may well have been the most influential treatise on the common law. Blackstone's work seems to have been successful simply because it provided a convenient outline of a large and disorganized body of caselaw. Such disorder is one of the disadvantages of the common law, which—unlike its civil counterpart—has no obvious logical plan. Blackstone's writing is eminently readable and full of rhetorical flourishes. The *Commentaries* are significant in legal theory because he adopts a political conception of law, based on the idea of the political contract.

The Common Law Is Based on the Rights of the Individual

Blackstone's adoption of the theory of natural rights and the social contract in the context of his legal theory has two consequences. The first is that he bases the common law on the natural rights of the individual. Blackstone's conception of natural rights goes much further than the concept that we find in Grotius and Pufendorf: the human individual is born into the state of nature, with certain "absolute" rights, which the individual has traded for the protection of society. The purpose of society and the positive law, however, is to protect individuals and allow them to assert their personal interests. It is the general conception of law that we find in Blackstone that explains the liberal character of the later common law. This conception of law emphasizes acquisitive rights, for example, and gives fundamental tenets like freedom of contract a prominent place in the law. Indeed, there is a good argument that the focus on liberty becomes the defining feature of Blackstone's conception of the common law, which has often been expressed in the phrase "whatever is not prohibited is allowed."

The Power of Parliament Is Absolute

The second consequence of Blackstone's adoption of the political contract is that he believes in the supremacy of Parliament. This belief rests largely on the need to restrict the King, however, rather than a positive belief in the efficacy of democratic government, and it is another product of the theory of natural rights. Under the political contract, individuals have agreed to the formation of government in return for the peace and security that central government provides. In the new state, however, it is the authority of government that represents the major threat to personal liberties. The only way to protect individual freedom under the political contract is accordingly to limit the sovereign power. This means limiting the King.

The convention in England (and in the Commonwealth) is still that the law issues from the command of the King or Queen, who holds the sovereign power. In England, the Queen must approve the law; in the Commonwealth, legislation generally comes into force after it has received the assent of the Governor General, the Queen's representative. In theory, at least, Parliament merely advises the Queen. The same kind of dynamic lies behind the American system, under which it is the President who signs legislation into law. The historical origins of Parliament do not lie in the idea that Parliament makes law, though that has become its function. There are overlapping ideas in the theory of Parliament. One of these ideas is that the King should not make laws without the approval of the people.

The purpose of Blackstone's theory of the state is to limit the political power of the King. This concern is not new—in fact, it was the central focus of the medieval doctrine of the divine right of kings, which has been misconstrued in modern times. Under the doctrine of the divine right, and Coke's scientism, it is some form of natural law that places limits on the sovereign power. These kinds of theories became problematic under the political contract. This was partly because the natural law is open to individual interpretation, but more fundamentally because the social contract holds that the law is law because the sovereign power commands it. The real limits on the exercise of this authority are therefore political, rather than legal, and lie in the powers of an elected assembly. The law has its sources in the political order, which therefore has ascendancy over the legal order.

There are historical reasons Blackstone failed to see that his check on the arbitrary political power of the King was to provide Parliament with an equally arbitrary power. Principal among these reasons was the popular view that the power of Parliament was, as Blackstone writes, "absolute and without control." Blackstone refers specifically to *Dr. Bonham's Case* in the *Commentaries* and suggests—albeit with some equivocation in later editions of the work—that Coke is wrong. This judgement is a reflection of the increasing power of Parliament in Blackstone's time, though the idea that Parliament could—somehow—make the same person party and judge remained bad law.

The legal restraints that Blackstone places on the King are discretionary and procedural. Such restraints are nevertheless an integral part of the common law, which holds that the law applies equally to all. These restraints entered the American jurisprudence under the "due process" clause in the Fourteenth Amendment to the Constitution of the United States, though this was later given a substantive reading. In Canada and other Commonwealth countries, they formed part of the received law—that is, the law that these countries received from England—and generally arise by implication of the law. They are often included within the phrase "rule of law," though historically this phrase recalls the *Magna Carta* and the customary law. The substantive issue remains with Parliament, however, and in spite of exceptional cases the view in the English common law since the eighteenth century has been that there are no legal limits on the sovereign power.

Written Constitutions Were Introduced to Place Limits on the Exercise of Political Authority

One of the major problems with Blackstone's theory of the common law is that it seems to vest an unlimited, arbitrary power in the King and the political sources of government. This problem was addressed, first in the United States and later in Canada, by the introduction of written constitutions. The judicial decisions interpreting these constitutions have given rise to a distinct body of constitutional law, which is generally the prerogative of a supreme court. John Marshall (1755–1835) was the chief justice of the United States Supreme Court for 35 years and wrote many of the seminal decisions in that court. The importance of *Marbury v. Madison*, probably his most famous decision, is that it places legal limits on the exercise of political authority and at least implicitly returns us to the kind of scientism that we find in the earlier common law.

Marbury v. Madison *Institutes "Judicial Review"*

Although Blackstone gives the aggrieved individual very little recourse against the King, the rhetoric in the *Commentaries* favours the recognition of a constitutional law. In fact, Blackstone's emphasis on individual rights clearly finds expression in the Constitution of the United States. The judges who decided *Marbury v. Madison* departed from the concept of law in Blackstone, however, in holding that the constitution places legal limits on the exercise of political authority. This departure gave rise to the doctrine of judicial review, which gives judges the authority to determine whether the actions of the political and executive branches of government are in keeping with the constitution.

This new form of law—a "supreme" law—resembles the natural law in its operation, and it appears to take us back to the scientism that we find in Coke's decisions. This is complicated by the fact that a written constitution also serves a political purpose and sets out the terms of the political contract. The contractual analogy often falls short, however, since the constitutional inquiry is based on the common values in the community. This attribute of the constitutional law takes us back to the idea behind the customary law, which was based on the moral customs of the people rather than the kind of agreement contemplated by the contractual analogy.

Marshall's understanding of the constitutional law solves the problem of placing limits on the sovereign power by distinguishing between ordinary law, which is merely the command of government and the King, and another kind of law—we could call it "metalaw"— that determines whether the ordinary law and the exercise of political authority are in keeping with the general values of society. Whatever the powers of political actors, it is the courts that enforce the law, and in any system judges will have to decide whether to enforce laws that seem to go against the moral consensus in the community. This power to disallow the law brings in general constitutional concerns, which are inherent in the role played by the common law judiciary. It is significant in this context that the United States Supreme Court relies on the judicial oath at the end of its decision in *Marbury v. Madison*.

The facts in *Marbury v. Madison* arose out of the political crisis caused by President John Adams' desperate attempt to appoint "midnight judges" before he lost office. The crisis came to a head because the next administration—that of Thomas Jefferson—refused to honour the appointment of William Marbury as a justice of peace for the District of Columbia. There are obvious problems with the decision, and it would now be considered improper for Marshall to rule on the matter, since he had been responsible for the initial appointments. This is to say nothing about the fact that the appointments were unprincipled and at least morally illegitimate, since they had been made as part of a massive effort to keep Adams' opponents out of office.

The case nevertheless provides a lucid statement of the legal theory behind the American constitution, which in Marshall's view limits political authority. In point of fact, the court did not grant the application—thus avoiding a dangerous confrontation with the President and the secretary of state—and merely used the opportunity to assert the ascendancy of the written constitution. Although President Jefferson and other political figures criticized the decision, the major points in Marshall's decision seem decidedly uncontroversial from a legal perspective. As Marshall noted, of what significance is a supreme law if the courts cannot intervene to rectify an act of the political or executive branch of government that contravenes the supreme law?

The opinion in *Marbury v. Madison* reflects Alexander Hamilton's view in *The Federalist* (1788), which is that the "courts of justice" must have the power to "declare all acts contrary to the manifest tenor of the Constitution void."[17] This "constitutionalism" can be seen as a kind of moral or social scientism that relies on judges to determine whether the positive law is in keeping with the historical values of the people. In Marshall's formulation, at least, this type of scientism does not appear to deprive those in political authority of the power to formulate social policy and pursue a legitimate legislative agenda, though the history of the constitutional law demonstrates that judges may interfere with the legislative mandate.

The American literature in legal theory has often focussed on the potential for judges to overreach their own authority. This potential also raises the question whether the kind of neutral, rule-driven legal reasoning that Coke saw as the source of the common law—and that provides the basis of Marshall's constitutionalism—is as rational and neutral as these judges believed. Coke's position was certainly that the legal limits on the sovereign power were as much a product of observation and rational inquiry as were the natural and physical sciences. This analysis can be extended to the institutions of the state and even sovereignty itself. The state may be sovereign in the exercise of its powers. This does not give it the power to act irrationally, however, and sovereignty does not include the power to make odd numbers even, pass laws that contradict themselves, legalize murder, or legally deprive a person who has been imprisoned without cause of the right to legal redress.

In Hurtado v. California, *the United States Supreme Court Rejected Coke's Scientism*

Edward S. Corwin (1878–1963) argued that the American constitutional law can be traced to Coke's comments in *Dr. Bonham's Case*. Indeed, many legal theorists have seen the case as the source of the doctrine of judicial review. Coke's position is much broader, however, and holds simply that the King is under the law. There is no realm outside the law in which the King and the state have the freedom to act without constraints. Political power must accordingly be exercised within the limits set by the law. These limits are determined by the common law judiciary, who exercise their functions independently of the King. This independence plays an important role in the common law tradition.[18]

The argument against legal scientism is that the decisions in cases like *Dr. Bonham's Case*, *Day v. Savadge*, and *Wood v. London* are exceptions that do not reflect the view in the rest of the caselaw. In *Hurtado v. California* (1884), 110 U.S. 516 for example, a majority in the United States Supreme Court held that the *Magna Carta* and *Dr. Bonham's Case* did not place legal limits on Parliament:

> The concessions of *Magna Charta* were wrung from the King as guaranties against the oppressions and usurpations of his prerogative. It did not enter into the minds of the barons to provide security against their own body or in favour of the Commons by limiting the power of Parliament; so that bills of attainder,

ex post facto laws, laws declaring forfeitures of estates, and other arbitrary acts of legislation which occur so frequently in English history were never regarded as inconsistent with the law of the land, for, notwithstanding what was attributed to Lord Coke in *Bonham's Case*, 8 Rep. 115, 118a, the omnipotence of Parliament over the common law was absolute, even against common right and reason.

This passage is nevertheless inaccurate and does not reflect the state of the common law in Coke's time. The theory that Parliament is "omnipotent" is a later intrusion, which reflects the influence of Blackstone's *Commentaries* and captures the spirit of the caselaw at a later point in time.

There was nevertheless a dissent in *Hurtado*. Justice John Harlan found that the phrase "due process of the law" in the Constitution of the United States can be traced to both the *Magna Carta* and the English common law. The mistake in the thinking of the majority, he suggests, is a mixture of historical error and a failure to appreciate the full status of the early common law. If it did not enter into the minds of the barons to limit Parliament, it was because Parliament did not exist and posed no threat to their liberties.

The philosophical issue concerns the relationship between the legal and political orders. The issue is not so much whether the law provides a check on Parliament as whether it places limits on the sovereign power. The term "sovereign power" generally refers to the power of the state to act in its own interest and exercise authority, and it certainly includes the power to make laws. Since it was the King who held the political power within the state, it was the King who must be held in check. Indeed, up to the time of Blackstone, the purpose of Parliament, like the earlier law, was to place restraints on the exercise of power by the King.

It needs to be said, in conclusion, that Coke's theory of law sets limits only on the outer parameters of what the King and government can do. This underestimates the role of the common law in the seventeenth century, however, since there was relatively little government in the modern sense, and democratic institutions did not enjoy the authority that they now possess. It was therefore the law that provided the framework in which people lived their lives. One of the criticisms of such a system is accordingly that it favours the conservative interests in society and neglects the role of social policy in government. This kind of criticism does not take into account the fact that the common law was developed on a case-by-case basis, however, or that it accordingly evolved over time, in accordance with changing social norms.

Notes

1. Some historians have described the Anglo-Saxon King Edred (r. 946–55) as the first King of England, but it was William the Conqueror who united the country politically. For more on this history, see Francis Palgrave, *A History of the Anglo-Saxons* (London: Ward, Lock, c. 1800s), available in *World Constitutions Illustrated*, at http://heinonline.org.
2. The *Domesday Book* is available at www.domesdaybook.co.uk.

3. Bracton also published a notebook, which contained a compendium of over two thousand cases and provided the model for the case reports on which the common law tradition has been based.

4. For more on the historical events that led to the signing of the *Magna Carta*, see Richard Thomson's *An Historical Essay on the Magna Charta of King John* (London: John Major and Robert Jennings, 1829), at p. 1ff., available in the *Legal Classics Library*, at http://heinonline.org.

5. There has been a technical dispute as to whether the Charter guarantees *habeas corpus* (mostly because "*habeas corpus*" is a later term), but the idea behind the writ is certainly there.

6. The original *Magna Carta* was declared null and void by Pope Innocent III, essentially on the basis that it placed secular limits on the King. The pope took the position that the King was subject to the authority of the Church.

7. See vol. 3, part V of *The Selected Writings and Speeches of Sir Edward Coke*, cited *infra*.

8. The irony in this historical development is that Parliament was asserting that the King was not above the law. It took only the passage of time, however, for Parliament to find itself asserting that it was above the law.

9. Section 138 ("Frankalmoign") of Coke's *Commentary on Littleton*, vol. 2 of Sir Edward Coke, *The Selected Writings and Speeches of Sir Edward Coke*, ed. Steve Sheppard (Indianapolis: Liberty Fund, 2003), available at http://oll.libertyfund.org.

10. See Coke, op. cit.

11. *Prohibitions del Roy*, in vol. 1 of Coke, op. cit.

12. See Appendix 1.B ("*Commendams* and the King's Displeasure"), in vol. 3 of Coke, op. cit.

13. Although Coke appears to have attributed the loss of his position to his insistence on the independence of the judiciary, his disputes with other judges and courts make it clear that his tenure as chief justice was difficult.

14. For more on the significance of Coke's ruling in this case, see Theodore Plucknett, "*Bonham's Case* and Judicial Review," *Harvard Law Review* 40 (1926): 30; Thomas C. Grey, "Origins of the Unwritten Constitution: Fundamental Law in American Revolutionary Thought," *Stanford Law Review* 30 (1978): 843; and Joseph C. Cascarelli, "Is Judicial Review Grounded in and Limited by Natural Law?," *Cumberland Law Review* 30 (2000): 373, all of which are available at http://oll.libertyfund.org.

15. *Day v. Savadge*, [(1614) Hobart 85] 80 Eng. Rep. 235. Available at http://heinonline.org.

16. This struggle between law and politics accounts for at least a good part of the famous dispute between the Court of Chancery and the Court of King's Bench. See, for example, John P. Dawson, "Coke and Ellesmere Disinterred: The Attack on the Chancery in 1616," *Illinois Law Review* 36 (1941–2): 127–52. Mark Fortier, "Equity and Ideas: Coke, Ellesmere, and James I," *Renaissance Quarterly* 51, no. 4 (Winter 1998): 1255–81. For a lively account of the dispute, see vol. 2 of Samuel Rawlson Gardiner, *History of England from the Accession of James I to the Disgrace of Chief-Justice Coke 1603–1616* (London: Hurst and Blackett, 1863), p. 269ff. Available at http://books/google.ca.

17. Alexander Hamilton, "A View of the Constitution of the Judicial Department in Relation to the Tenure of Good Behaviour," in *The Federalist (The Gideon Edition)*, as cited in the suggestions for further reading.

18. See Gary L. MacDowell, "Coke, Corwin and the Constitution," as cited in the suggestions for further reading.

19. See *Prohibitions del Roy*, vol. 3 of Coke, op. cit.

Study Questions

1. Why was William the Conqueror's victory at the Battle of Hastings, and his claim to all of England, so significant in the history of the common law? What role did the *Domesday Book* play in the development of the common law?

2. Why would you say that Coke's scientism was based on a secular rather than a religious theory of the natural law?

3. Edward Coke takes the position that the science of the law goes beyond the exercise of "naturall reason." It follows, in *Prohibitions del Roy*, that the King cannot decide a legal case.[19] Why?

4. The constitutional law also holds that judges must be independent and impartial. It follows that people in political or executive office cannot decide legal cases. Why?

5. What were the facts in *London v. Wood*? What does the Court of King's Bench hold in the case?

6. The theory of the common law in Bracton and Coke is based on the idea that there are laws that are discernible through the exercise of reason. These laws must be obeyed. Blackstone has a different theory of the common law, which is based on natural rights and the existence of the state. Where does our obligation to obey the law come from in Blackstone's *Commentaries*?

7. The decision in *Marbury v. Madison* was based on the court's reading of the Constitution of the United States. It nevertheless takes us back to the *Magna Carta* and the customary law. How?

8. We now take the position that the statutes passed by the legislature are law. The *Magna Carta* was already law, however, when Parliament passed it in the seventeenth century. What does this tell us about the authority of Parliament in its early stages? What does it tell us about the concept of law? Why would Parliament pass a document that was already law?

Further Reading

Henry of Bracton, *On the Laws and Customs of England*, trans. Samuel E. Thorne (Cambridge, MA: Belknap, 1968). Available at http://heinonline.org.

Day v. Savadge, [(1614) Hobart 85] 80 Eng. Rep. 235. Available at http://heinonline.org.

Alexander Hamilton, *The Federalist (The Gideon Edition)*, no. 78, ed. George W. Carey and James McClellan (Indianapolis: Liberty Fund, [1788] 2001). Available at http://oll.libertyfund.org.

Gary L. MacDowell, "Coke, Corwin and the Constitution: The "Higher Law Background" Reconsidered," *The Review of Politics* 55, no. 3 (Summer 1993): 393–420.

Theodore Frank Thomas Plucknett, *A Concise History of the Common Law* (Union, NJ: Lawbook Exchange, 2001).

Ellis Sandoz, *The Roots of Liberty: Magna Carta, Ancient Constitution, and the Anglo-American Tradition of Rule of Law* (Indianapolis: Liberty Fund, 2008). Available at http://oll.libertyfund.org.

5 Law Is a Product of Utility or Pure Reason

Jeremy Bentham and Immanuel Kant

Readings

- From *Of Laws in General*, by Jeremy Bentham
- From *The Philosophy of Law: An Exposition of the Fundamental Principles of Jurisprudence as the Science of Right*, by Immanuel Kant

This chapter reviews the legal theories in two schools of thought. The first school is English utilitarianism; the second is German idealism. These two theories derive at least implicitly from the theory of natural rights, since they suggest that the law derives from a single source. If we can properly identify this source, we should be in a position to determine the outlines, at least, of a valid substantive law. The difference between legal utilitarianism and legal idealism is that utilitarianism replaced the moral and religious origins of the natural law with the principle of utility. Legal idealism, on the other hand, is based on the idea that the law can be derived from the exercise of "pure reason."

The readings are from Jeremy Bentham (1748–1832) and Immanuel Kant (1724–1804). Bentham was trained as a common law lawyer, but is known as a philosopher and social reformer. He is usually regarded, along with John Stuart Mill (1806–1873), as one of the founders of utilitarianism, which bases the morality of our actions on their usefulness, or "utility." The readings from Bentham deal with his definition of law and reveal his rather truculent attitude toward the common law. Bentham's legal theory is based on the Grotian model of the social and political contract, which traces law and legal authority to the political order. This theory is an early form of legal positivism, allied with the theory that John Austin set out, which is discussed in the next chapter.

Kant was a professor of philosophy who developed a comprehensive system of thought based on the laws of reason that govern the material and ethical worlds. This system of thought includes a science of right, which sets out "the principles of natural right" from which the positive law must be deduced. Although Kant sets out the general principles on which the law must be based rather than the law itself, his use of the term "science"—to indicate a rational machine for the production of knowledge—has its roots in the natural law and recalls the legal scientism in the work of Edward Coke.

❧ Readings ❧

From Jeremy Bentham, *Of Laws in General*, ed. H.L.A. Hart, in *The Collected Works of Jeremy Bentham*, gen. ed. H. Burns (London: Athlone, 1970).[1]

Chapter I. A Law Defined and Distinguished

A Law Defined as the Volition of a Sovereign

A law may be defined as an assemblage of signs declarative of a volition conceived or adopted by the *sovereign* in a state, concerning the conduct to be observed in a certain *case* by a certain person or class of persons, who in the case in question are or are supposed to be subject to his power: such volition trusting for its accomplishment to the expectation of certain events . . . the prospect of which it is intended should act as a motive upon those whose conduct is in question. . . .

This Definition Is More Extensive Than It Ought to Be to Correspond to the Phrases Legislation and Legislative Power

[I]t would naturally be expected that the signification given to the word *law* should be correspondent to that of its conjugates *legislation* and *legislative power*: for what, it will be said, is legislation but the act of making laws? or legislative power but the power of making them? that consequently the term *law* should be applied to every expression of will, the uttering of which was an act of legislation, an exertion of legislative power. . . .

(1) In the first place, according to the definition, the word *law* should be applicable to any [order, even] the most trivial order supposing it to be not illegal, which a man may have occasion to give for any of the most inconsiderable purposes of life: to any order which a master may have occasion to give to his servant, a parent to his child, or (where the request of the husband assumes the harsh form of a command) of a husband to his wife. Yet it would seem a strange catachresis to speak of the issuing of any such order as an act of legislation, or as an exercise of legislative power. . . .

(2) With equal propriety (according to the definition) would the word *law* be applicable to a temporary order issued by any magistrate who is spoken of as exercising thereby a branch of *executive* power, or as exercising the functions belonging to any department of *administration*. But the executive power is continually mentioned as distinct from the legislative: and the business of administration is as constantly opposed to that of legislation. Let the . . . Navy Board order such or such a ship to be fitted out, let the Board of Ordinance order such or such a train of artillery to be dispatched to such a destination—Who would ever speak of any of these orders as acts of legislative power, as acts of legislation?

(3) With equal propriety again would the word law according to the definition be applicable to any *judicial* order. . . . Yet the business of judicature is constantly looked upon as essentially distinct from the business of legislation and as constantly opposed to it: and the case is the same between the judicial and the legislative power. Even suppose the order to have been ever so general . . . still if issued in the course of a forensic contestation, the act of issuing it would not be looked upon in general as coming under the notion of an act of legislation, or as an exercise of legislative power. . . .

(4) Of course the term *law* would according to the definition be applicable to any order whatsoever coming directly from the sovereign. But it is not [so] in all cases. . . .

[W]here the sovereignty is in a single person and the party who is looked upon as principally affected by it is an individual, neither the word *law* nor any conjugate of it seems, in common speech at least, to be employed. When the King of France orders a man to quit the metropolis, or sends him to the Bastile, the power he exercises is not spoken of as a legislative power, not the act he performs as an act of legislation. . . .

(5) There are even cases in which although the command were in every point a general one . . . and although the party from whom it issued were a complex body, it might be a matter of dispute whether the command itself were according to common notion entitled to the appellation of a law. . . . In England the . . . magistrates who exercise the judicial power are allowed, many of them, to establish *ex mero motu* regulations of a durable nature [regulations that they make on their own initiative, which are called *Rules of Court*], regulations that are general in all points concerning the conduct of such parties as shall chance thereafter to be anyhow concerned in litigation. These regulations . . . are not usually characterized by that name [i.e., *law*]: they are sometimes called *orders*, sometimes by a compound sort of name *rules and orders* of the court from which they ensue. . . .

(6) . . . [T]he King is also allowed to establish of himself and *ex mero motu* a multitude of regulations; regulations which are to such a degree general that the conduct and the fate of large and numerous classes of individuals are regulated and determined by them, and which accordingly in point of duration, though limited by positive institution, are in their own nature susceptible of perpetuity. The articles of war for the government of the army and the instructions given to privateers may serve for examples. . . . At the same time the issuing of the commands referable to these heads would hardly without some reluctance be acknowledged as acts of legislation. . . .

(7) Some difficulty there may also be . . . with regard to various orders (general in point of extension or perpetual in point of duration or both) which are wont to be issued by various sets of magistrates, all of whom derive their authority originally, and many of them immediately, from the King. I am speaking of those [orders] for instance . . . which are issued by Justices of the Peace for the levying of rates in the counties for which they are commissioned. The unwillingness to employ in these cases the terms *law, act of legislation,* and *legislative power* will probably increase as the field of dominion becomes less extensive. No man ever made a difficulty about employing them in the case of Ireland, of the American provinces or other distant members of the empire: yet to many it might seem

odd to apply the same high sounding appellation to the powers acts and operations of a fraternity of weavers or tallow chandlers in a little town or parish. . . .

The Legislative Power Is Supreme

These discussions, local as they are, could scarcely be avoided on account of the influence which local establishments and local actions have on the idiom of the language. . . . In the present instance, from the confused ideas which men are wont to annex to the terms legislative power and executive power little can be collected but that the former it is thought is something superior to the latter; and where legislature and legislative power are mentioned without any epithet of addition, supreme legislature and supreme legislative power are commonly intended. . . .

Chapter XV. No Customary Law Complete

Having fixed the idea of a law . . . I perceived what anybody may perceive, that, in the case where the law is of the permanent kind, it was applicable only to a statute law: and that as to a customary law there was no such thing existing. . . .

Bentham Describes the Common Law System

The judges who perhaps at first did take and are still supposed or rather pretended to be supposed to take an account of every case that came before them never trouble their heads about the matter: the business is left to certain officers who are under them. These officers give what is called the history of the case, which history is termed by some such name as a *record.* This record being copied from precedents of the darkest antiquity . . . is in fact a partial and imperfect history of a different case that was determined upon some hundreds of years before: applied to the case in question it is in consequence, partly imperfect, partly false, partly irrelevant, and partly unintelligible. . . .

These documents such as they are are written in a form the most inconvenient *for* reading or consulting, of any that could have been devised: and being by many a wagon load too bulky for publication they are kept locked up in places where not one in ten thousand of those whose conduct is to be guided by them and whose fate depends on them can know how to find them: much less to make anything of them when found. . . .

These documents being become to such a degree useless, another set of documents come gradually into use under the appellation of *Reports.* . . . Here you have a little of the history of one court; there of another: sometimes the history of a court goes on pretty well for several years together: then comes a blank for twenty or thirty years during which all is darkness. . . . Sometimes you have the argument without the decision; sometimes the decision without the argument; sometimes the inferior decision of the inferior court without the superior which reverses it.

These reports are published by anybody that pleases, and by as many people as please. . . . If a lawyer who can get no practice happens to think of this method of making money: if the executor of a lawyer happens to find a manuscript among his papers; if either of these or any other such accident happens to throw a copy into the hands of a bookseller: the bookseller without being aware of it and without caring about it, becomes a legislator. . . .

Meantime out of these scattered atoms, be the collection of them ever so copious and exact, nothing is plain. . . . [And so] a set of general rules must be abstracted from them and worked up into the form of a treatise. A set of treatises accordingly start up: and here again the bookseller gets another share in the prerogative of legislation. It is plain these general rules can have no foundation in authority any further than as they are the necessary result of some particular assignable decisions: if they deviate but a hair's breadth from that standard, they become laws *suo jure* [in their own right] and the author if they are adopted and acceded to becomes *pro tanto* [to that extent] as much a legislator as the sovereign.

Accordingly the writer, while living, has no such independent authority. . . . But in proportion as he is more ancient, that is in proportion as the age he writes in is more barbarous, he stands a better and better chance of setting the law . . . The treatise is confused and barbarous: yet less so than the case; so much less, that out of pure weariness and despair the authority of the treatise is preferred. . . . First in point of original authority comes the record: then comes the report: last of all comes the treatise: the shadow of the shadow of a shade: and it is this shadow that is worshipped as the substance.

Note

1. Editor's note: *Of Laws in General* is a continuation of *An Introduction to the Principles of Morals and Legislation* (parts of which were apparently published in 1780 and 1781; though the full volume was not published until 1789) and was published posthumously. The *Introduction to the Principles of Morals and Legislation* is available at http://oll.libertyfund.org.

From Immanuel Kant, *The Philosophy of Law: An Exposition of the Fundamental Principles of Jurisprudence as the Science of Right*, trans. William Hastie (Edinburgh: T. & T. Clark, [1796] 1887).

Prolegomena to the Metaphysic of Morals

I. The Relation of the Faculties of the Human Mind to the Moral Laws

The Laws of Freedom as Moral, Juridical, and Ethical

The Laws of Freedom, as distinguished from the Laws of Nature, are *moral* Laws. So far as they refer only to external actions and their lawfulness, they are called *Juridical*; but if they also require that, as Laws, they shall themselves be the determining Principles of our actions, they are *Ethical*. The agreement of an action with Juridical Laws, is its *Legality*; the agreement of an action with Ethical Laws, is its *Morality*. . . .

II. The Idea and Necessity of a Metaphysic of Morals

The Laws of Nature Rational and also Empirical

It has been shown in *The Metaphysical Principles of the Science of Nature*,[1] that there must be Principles *a priori* for the Natural Science that has to deal with the objects of the external senses. And it was further shown that it is possible, and even necessary, to formulate a System of these Principles under the name of a "Metaphysical Science of Nature," as a preliminary to Experimental Physics. . . . [T]his latter Science, if care be taken to keep its generalizations free from error, may accept many propositions as universal on the evidence of experience . . . Thus Newton accepted the principle of the Equality of Action and Reaction as established by experience, and yet he extended it as a universal Law over the whole of material Nature. . . .

Moral Laws *a Priori* and Necessary

But it is otherwise with Moral Laws. These, in contradistinction to Natural laws are only valid *as* Laws, in so far as they can be rationally established *a priori* and comprehended as *necessary*. In fact, conceptions and judgements regarding ourselves and our conduct have no *moral* significance, if they contain only what may be learned from experience. . . .

If the Philosophy of Morals were nothing more than a Theory of Happiness (*Eudæmonism*), it would be absurd to search after Principles *a priori* as a foundation for it. For . . . [i]t is only Experience that can show what will bring us enjoyment. . . . All specious rationalizing *a priori*, in this connection, is nothing at bottom but carrying facts of Experience up to generalizations by induction (*secundum principia generalia non universalia*); and the generality thus attained is still so limited that numberless exceptions must be allowed to every individual in order that he may adapt the choice of his mode of life to his own particular inclinations and his capacity for pleasure. . . .

But it is quite otherwise with the Principles of Morality. They lay down Commands for every one without regard to his particular inclinations, and merely because and so far as he is free, and has a practical Reason. Instruction in the Laws of Morality is not drawn from observation of oneself or of our animal nature, nor from perception of the course of the world in regard to what happens, or how men act. But Reason commands [i.e. it is Reason that determines] how we *ought* to act, even although no example of such action were to be found; nor does Reason give any regard to the Advantage which may accrue to us by so acting, and which Experience could alone actually show. . . .

The Necessity of a Metaphysic of Morals

"Metaphysics" designates any System of Knowledge *a priori* that consists of pure Conceptions. Accordingly a Practical Philosophy not having Nature, but the Freedom of the Will for its object, will presuppose and require a Metaphysic of Morals. It is even a *Duty* to have such a Metaphysic; and every man does, indeed, possess it in himself, although commonly but in an obscure way. For how could any one believe that he has a source of universal Law in himself, without Principles *a priori*?

III. The Division of a Metaphysic of Morals

Two Elements Involved in All Legislation

All Legislation, whether relating to internal or external action, and whether prescribed *a priori* by mere Reason or laid down by the Will of another, involves two Elements:—1st, a Law which represents the action that ought to happen as necessary *objectively*, thus making the action a Duty; 2nd, a Motive which connects the principle determining the Will to this action with the Mental representation of the Law *subjectively*, so that the Law makes Duty the motive of the Action. . . .

Division of Duties into Juridical and Ethical

The Legislation which makes an Action a Duty, and this Duty at the same time a Motive, is *ethical*. That Legislation which . . . admits another Motive than the idea of Duty itself, is *juridical*. In respect of the latter, it is evident that the motives distinct from the idea of Duty, to which it may refer, must be drawn from the subjective (pathological) influences of Inclination and of Aversion, determining the voluntary activity, and especially from the latter: because it is a Legislation which has to be compulsory, and not merely a mode of attracting or persuading. The agreement or non-agreement of an action with the Law, without reference to its Motive, is its *Legality*; and that character of the action in which the idea of Duty arising from the Law, at the same time forms the Motive of the Action, is its *Morality*.

Duties specially in accord with a Juridical Legislation, can only be external Duties. For this mode of Legislation does not require that the idea of the Duty, which is internal, shall be of itself the determining Principle of the act of Will. . . .

Jurisprudence and Ethics Distinguished

From what has been said, it is evident that all Duties, merely because they are duties, belong to Ethics; and yet the Legislation upon which they are founded is not on that account in all cases contained in Ethics. . . . Thus Ethics commands that I must fulfill a promise entered into by Contract, although the other party might not be able to compel me to do so. It adopts the Law "*pacta sunt servanda*" ["pacts must be kept," a basic rule of civil law], and the Duty corresponding to it, from Jurisprudence or the Science of Right, by which they are established. It is not in Ethics, therefore, but in Jurisprudence, that the [compulsory] principle of the lies, that "promises made and accepted must be kept." . . . For were it not so, and were the Legislation itself not juridical, and consequently the Duty arising from it not specially a Duty of Right as distinguished from a Duty of Virtue, then Fidelity in the performance of acts, to which the individual may be bound by the terms of a Contract, would have to be classified with acts of Benevolence and the Obligation that underlies them, which cannot be correct. To keep one's promise is not properly a Duty of Virtue, but a Duty of Right; and the performance of it can be enforced by external Compulsion. . . .

The Science of Right

Private Right: The System of Those Laws Which Require No External Promulgation

The Rights of the Family as a Domestic Society: Conjugal Right (Husband and Wife) and the Natural Basis of Marriage

The domestic Relations are founded on Marriage, and Marriage is founded upon the natural Reciprocity or intercommunity (*commercium*) of the Sexes. This natural union of the sexes proceeds either according to the mere animal Nature (*vaga libido, venus vulgivaga, fornicatio*), or according to Law. The latter is Marriage (*matrimonium*), which is the Union of two Persons of different sex for life-long reciprocal possession of their sexual faculties. . . .

[This] is a Contract [made] necessary in its nature by the Law of Humanity. In other words, if a man and a woman have the will to enter on [into] reciprocal enjoyment in accordance with their sexual nature, they *must* necessarily marry each other; and this necessity is in accordance with the juridical Laws of Pure Reason.

The Rational Right of Marriage

For, this natural "*Commercium*" [intercommunity]—as a "*usus membrorum sexualium alterius*" [use of each other's sexual organs]—is an enjoyment for which the one person is given up to the other. In this relation the human individual makes himself a "*res*" [a thing, a piece of property], which is contrary to the Right of Humanity in his own Person. This, however, is only possible under the one condition, that . . . the other reciprocally [does the same]. . . . The Acquisition of a part of the human organism being, on account of its unity, at the same time the acquisition of the whole Person, it follows that the surrender and acceptation of, or by, one sex in relation to the other, is not only *permissible* under the condition of Marriage, but is further *only* really possible under that condition. But the Personal Right thus acquired is at the same time, *real in kind*; and this characteristic of it is established by the fact that if one of the married Persons run away or enter into the possession of another, the other is entitled, at any time, and incontestably, to bring such a one back to the former relation, as if that Person were a Thing.

Monogamy and Equality in Marriage

For the same reasons, the relation of the Married Persons to each other is a relation of equality [reciprocity] as regards the mutual possession of their Persons, as well as of their Goods. Consequently Marriage is only truly realized in Monogamy; for in the relation of Polygamy the Person who is given away on the one side, gains only a part of the one to whom that Person is given up, and therefore becomes a mere *res*.

Note

1.   Editor's note: This is a reference to Kant's *Metaphysische Anfangsgrÿnde der Naturwissenschaft*, usually translated as *Metaphysical Foundations of Natural Science*, which was published in 1786.

⤳ Discussion ⤝

Bentham Believes in the Science of Legislation

Bentham came from a wealthy background. He studied law and was called to the bar but devoted himself to legal theory rather than to practice. His career as a theorist was rambling and disorganized. He was rebellious and defiant by nature, and his temperament seems to have turned him instinctively against the authority institutionalized in the law. He also disdained the past, like other Enlightenment figures, and rejected the custom and precedent on which the common law was based. Bentham was attracted to the idea that law is a kind of social science and devoted most of his attention to the science of legislation. He studied the positive law at prodigious length, and his work offers many insights into the mechanics of a successful legal system.

Bentham's Philosophy of Law Is Based On the Supremacy of Political Authority

Bentham rejected the common law because it was "judge-made law" and therefore reflected the values of the judiciary rather than those of society. This kind of criticism has a political basis. Although Bentham's characterization is quite misleading, since it ignores the role of custom in the common law, it has made its way into the popular conception of the common law. The term "judge-made law" is a misnomer, however, particularly when it is applied to the early common law, since judges like Bracton, Coke, and Holt did not believe they were making law. The common law is based epistemologically on the idea that the law is found, not made. This idea provides one of its defining features. The deeper argument in Bentham is that the conception of law held by these and other judges was based on a set of moral values that made its way implicitly into the law. Bentham rejects this prescriptive notion of morality in favour of an empirical science—really, a science of morality—that bases the morality of our actions on their results.

There is accordingly a deep moral skepticism in Bentham's work, which leads him to favour the positive law over the common law. For Bentham, law is rightfully a product of the political system and government. It properly expresses the social and political policies of those who have been elected to political office and therefore have control of the apparatus of the state. This is a markedly different conception of law than we find in the earlier common law tradition and places Parliament firmly in the position to make law. It follows that the primary task in legal theory is to determine what policies should be pursued and implemented in legislation.

Although John Austin has usually been described as the founder of legal positivism, Bentham's conception of law is very similar to that of Austin. For both theorists, legislation is "law" in the full sense of the word and derives its binding force from the coercive powers of government. Like Austin, Bentham rejected the idea that the courts and the law have sources of authority outside the political order. It is rather ironic that Bentham's view was eventually adopted by the English judiciary, since it goes against the history of the common law, which was originally based on the idea that the law exists independently of the state. The source of this authority can be found in moral custom and the values and beliefs shared in common by the members of society.

Bentham Believes that Legislation Should Serve the Greatest Happiness

The major issue posed by Bentham's legal theory, then, is a question of policy. How do we decide which social and political policies should be put into law? The answer to this question can be found in Bentham's theory of ethics and policy, which is known as utilitarianism and holds that the rightfulness of any action is determined by its utility or usefulness. The utility of a particular action, in Bentham's view, is determined by its capacity to produce happiness and prevent unhappiness. Since happiness is the greatest good, it provides a reliable measure of the ethical and social value of any action. The principle of utility applies to all human actions and determines how we should act in our personal lives. It also applies, however, to the public and legislative actions of government.

In *An Introduction to the Principles of Morals and Legislation*, Bentham formulates a "greatest happiness principle."[1] This principle holds that "the greatest happiness of all those whose interest is in question" is the "only right and proper" end of the actions taken by "a functionary or set of functionaries exercising the powers of Government."[2] Since this principle is of little practical use without a means of quantifying the happiness and unhappiness promoted by different actions, Bentham also sets out a "felicific calculus" that determines the quantity of pleasure and pain produced by a particular act. This system of measurement considers the *intensity, duration, certainty, propinquity* or *remoteness, fecundity* (the likelihood that the result will produce further pleasure or pain), and *purity* of the pleasure or pain that any action will produce. Bentham notes that we must also calculate the number of persons to which the pleasure or pain extends.

The "Greatest Happiness" Is Based on the Happiness of the Individual

Bentham's legal utilitarianism rests on the same natural rights tradition that finds expression in philosophers like Grotius and Pufendorf and legal authors like Blackstone. Bentham believes that society is essentially composed of discrete, self-interested individuals whose primary motivation is to find their own happiness. This state of affairs is as it should be; it also reflects the psychological reality of our personal and social lives. Yet it raises a foundational issue in the natural rights tradition: If the individuals who have agreed to the political contract have done so only on the basis that it serves their self-interest, why should they follow the positive law in those situations where it does not serve their self-interest to do so? This question arises principally in ethics. It is nevertheless significant for our purposes because it suggests that we need some additional factor in legal theory to deal with such situations. This explains why legal theories in the natural rights tradition tend to rely so heavily on coercion to explain the binding nature of the positive law.

Bentham's theory runs into unusual difficulty in this context. Theorists such as Grotius and Pufendorf, like Aquinas, believe that there is a natural law, which ultimately obliges us to obey the restrictions imposed upon us by the positive law. Since the natural law is available to everyone, through a combination of our natural inclinations and the exercise of reason, it provides us all with a reason to obey the law. Bentham is unable to resolve the issue in this manner, since he rests utility on happiness and the pleasure on which he believes it is based. This position is problematic because happiness and pleasure are not open to the kind of rational analyses contemplated by the natural law. Indeed, most authors who have considered the question have agreed that there is an element of personal preference in pleasure that is not open to rational discovery.

Bentham's utilitarianism provides us with a rational scheme for the production of legislation. It does not, however, permit us to develop the positive law on a deductive rational basis. This observation holds whether we are speaking of the kind of substantive development that we find in the common law or the formal approach that we find in Kant. In order to make use of Bentham's felicific calculus, we need to determine the individual happiness that will be produced by competing legislative actions. This calculation is not a simple matter, since one of the major goals of such a system is to provide individuals with the freedom and autonomy to follow their own desires. In spite of his rejection of the common law, Bentham accordingly adopted Blackstone's position (he had heard Blackstone's lectures at Oxford) and implicitly based his theory of law on the rights and freedoms of the individual.

Later theorists, most notably Karl Marx, criticized the utilitarian conception of society because it treats the members of society as if they were abstract "atoms," essentially and irrevocably separated from each other. According to these critics, the "atomistic" view fails to capture the most fundamental fact of social life, which is premised on the idea that individuals in society are inextricably connected to one another. This kind of conceptual omission artificially separates the interests of the members of society and suggests that individuals must compete for happiness. It may be possible to correct such an omission, simply by postulating that the happiness of the individual depends on the happiness of other people, but this happiness is a matter of degree, and its definition is open to disagreement.

Under utilitarianism, the purpose of human society—like the purpose of legislation and the law—is to "maximize" utility and produce the greatest happiness. It is impossible to know whether society has achieved such a goal, however, without some measure of the total happiness in society. Some utilitarians have suggested that this happiness can be calculated as the average happiness of the members of society times the population. One of the problems with this idea is that this calculation leaves out the happiness enjoyed by groups. It also raises many technical problems. Who qualifies as an individual? Should we include the happiness of an infant, an illegal immigrant, or a person in prison in the total; and, if we do, should their happiness be considered equal to that of other people or discounted in some way?

It may or may not be possible to resolve these kinds of quantitative issues. Even if we accept that the goal of law and society is to maximize individual happiness, however, other questions arise. It is an open question, for example, whether a system of positive law that successfully maximizes individual happiness—so that the addition of each unit of individual happiness (or each unit of averaged happiness) reaches its maximum—will produce either the best society or a just community. As the ethical literature recognizes, there are many complicating factors. Should the happiness produced by opera, or drinking beer, or playing chess be scored the same? Should the happiness that people may obtain from making other people unhappy, or from illicit acts, be included?

The question of altruism also raises difficulties, since utilitarianism seems to force us to conclude that the value of self-sacrificing acts comes from the fact that they make us happy. The value of this happiness, moreover, needs to be calculated. There are related issues that arise in the institutions of government. Bentham seems to assume that the electoral process is sufficient, unto itself, and that Parliament will simply enact those laws that serve the greatest happiness. Yet if individuals should pursue their individual happiness, why should those in political office maximize the happiness of the community rather than their own happiness?

Bentham's reasoning introduces a fundamental change in the conception of law. The efficacy of legislation is determined by the results that it yields rather than by whether it aligns with a particular conception of right or can be rationally deduced from an accepted body of moral rules and principles. There is accordingly a sense in which the act of legislating literally resembles a social experiment, which can be tested only by trial and error. It seems to follow, as Roscoe Pound and early thinkers in sociology of law suggested, that the legislative process should logically include some form of empirical testing, which permits reconsideration and review. The science of legislation is an empirical science that, through trial and error, will ultimately produce a proper set of laws and the happiness that goes with it.

Utilitarianism Was Influential in the Development of an Economic View of Law and in Sentencing

Utilitarianism provided the philosophical framework for the development of a science of economics. It also fostered a kind of economic analysis, based on risk, that has received some attention in the American courts. The most significant application of the kind of quantitative approach that Bentham developed, however, is in the determination of the appropriate sentence for the commission of a crime or other offence.

In Chapter XIV of *An Introduction to the Principles of Morals and Legislation*, Bentham discusses the "proportion between punishments and offences." This is an area that lends itself to a formal and even mathematical analysis, particularly in the context of imprisonment. Bentham makes it clear that he favours such an analysis because it removes judicial discretion and leaves the determination of the sentence in the full control of the legislature. Although this now seems naive, Bentham's desire for precision has a scientific basis, and his concerns in this regard can be compared to the concerns of a physician prescribing medicine. His *Principles of Penal Law* contains one of the chief discussions of the rationale of punishment, the various types of punishment, and the purposes of imprisonment in the common law.

Since Bentham is primarily interested in reforming behaviour, one of the interesting features of this discussion is that he does not subscribe to the view that the sentence for an offence must always reflect the moral gravity of the offence. In spite of this anomaly, which has never had any resonance in the courts, the main elements in Bentham's theory of sentencing have made their way into the caselaw. Bentham opposed the simple idea of punishment, since the imposition of pain and the unhappiness that it caused was unethical under the principle of utility. Like other utilitarians, and the Italian philosopher Cesare Beccaria in particular, he accordingly argued that the idea of punishment should be replaced by the idea of correction. This calls for the development of a sentencing regime under which the judge sentencing an offender must determine the exact amount of suffering that would deter the offender from recommitting the offence.

Bentham's work bears witness to a number of dramatic changes in the theoretical framework of the law, including changes to the principles of sentencing. Legal utilitarianism has been remarkably successful in undermining the validity of retribution as a legitimate principle in sentencing, to the point that contemporary Western courts prohibit punishment for its own sake. In the criminal courts, at least, the idea of punishment has been replaced by a set of sentencing principles that are designed to change the behaviour of offenders and reintegrate them into the community. In the United States, courts have traditionally held that sentencing based on retribution offends the constitutional ban on cruel and unusual punishment. Bentham's discussion of sentencing, like his work on the model prison called the "Panopticon," which allowed a warden to "see-everywhere," was liberal and progressive. These philosophical traits have migrated to the criminal caselaw, which still focusses on the role of personal choice in the commission of crime and neglects larger social issues.

Ironically, as Michel Foucault has argued, Bentham's focus on freedom of choice provided the impetus for a prison system that is far more psychologically oppressive than earlier forms of punishment.[3] This is a reflection of the fact that Bentham's theoretical work favours the centralization of power and produces conforming behaviour by hiding and internalizing less socially acceptable impulses. The transfer of authority to political government under legal utilitarianism has produced a vast machinery of government that is far more coercive in regulating personal behaviour than was the customary system that it replaced.

Bentham Attacks the Positions Set Out in Blackstone's Commentaries

Bentham's first book, *A Fragment on Government* (1776), reflects his rebellious temper and his legal training. In this work, he criticizes Blackstone's *Commentaries on the Laws of England*, which provided the basis of the curriculum in law schools at the time. The major source of his dissatisfaction with the *Commentaries* is that it bases the common law on a rigorous principle of *stare decisis*, which requires judges to adhere strictly to the rulings in previous decisions. Bentham ridiculed the idea of precedent and argued that the only proper measure of law is whether it is socially useful.

The philosophical differences between Bentham's work and that of Blackstone are less significant than Bentham suggests, however. As we have seen, Blackstone subscribes to the "omnipotence" of Parliament, and the radical position that Bentham adopts merely reflects the increasing role of Parliament in government and the desire for social reform that swept England in his lifetime. Although Blackstone gives caselaw the predominant role in the law, the *Commentaries* are remarkably uncritical and simply do not recognize the constitutional rivalry between the legislature and the judiciary.

Bentham Describes "Natural Justice or Equity or Right Reason" as "the Phantom"

Although Bentham focuses on Blackstone's work, the real object of his critique is the idea of the natural law and the legal scientism that it gave rise to in the early common law. Bentham rejected the "natural equity" mentioned in a case like *London v. Wood* as a "phantom" and criticized the legal use of abstract "fictions" such as "right" and "possession," which obscure the real operation of the law.[4] Bentham also rejected the moral assumptions in the common law tradition. This rejection reflects the increasing secularization of society and his rejection of conventional religious views. There is a legal and evidentiary aspect to this position, since Bentham argues that the propriety of our actions can be determined only by an examination of their consequences. (This is in contrast to Kant, who believed that the moral and legal character of our actions exists *a priori*, as a function of their rational nature.)

Bentham's Rejection of the Natural Law Is Evident in His Work as a Social Reformer

Bentham's work is important in legal theory for detaching our concept of law from its original sources in custom and morality. Bentham believed that the common law must be subordinated to the science of legislation, which gives the legislature the primary role in determining the appropriate limits on human behaviour. His rejection of the moral assumptions in the common law freed him from prevailing views, and his positions on many of the social issues of his day have less in common with the prevailing attitudes of the eighteenth century than with contemporary beliefs. Bentham advocated a secret ballot, championed usury (the lending of money at interest, which had been considered a sin in Christianity), and supported the use of cadavers in medical schools. Since animals feel pain, and therefore unhappiness, he argued that their experience must be included in any calculation of the greatest happiness.

Bentham's Rhetorical Attack on the Common Law Does Not Acknowledge the Purpose of *Stare Decisis*

Some of Bentham's criticisms of the common law are justified. By the middle of the eighteenth century, the common law had become rigid and hopelessly entangled in the moral views of pre-industrial England. Whatever the merits of the common law, its rigour gave judges little leeway in their decisions, and it seemed increasingly arbitrary in the face of rapid social change. Bentham's attack on the common law is often exaggerated, however, and does not grapple seriously with the fundamentals of the common law system or recognize its merits.

Bentham wrote that his preference for legislation honoured the practical experience of ordinary people. He believed that the judiciary had used its privileged position, in the administration of the common law, to impose its moral views on the rest of society through the instrument of the law. Although it is an open question whether the common law judiciary respected its role in the system, Bentham's position misrepresents the origins of the common law, which was based on a customary law that rested on the values of the community. It also runs against the idea of *stare decisis*, the purpose of which is to make sure that similar cases are decided in the same way and prevent judges from imposing their personal views on the parties.

Bentham openly vilifies the judiciary and, like Blackstone, ignores the human frailties of those in political office. Although he recognizes that the members of Parliament need education in the science of legislation, he essentially assumes that the democratic process is sufficient to guarantee the efficacy of the legislative process. From a contemporary perspective, Bentham fails to deal with the sociology of power, which often defeats the public policy aspects of the political process. It seems rather obvious that the political process—like the common law—is full of pitfalls that may result in arbitrary laws.

For whatever reason, Bentham misses the fact that one of the chief merits of the common law system is that it limits the authority of judges. The whole purpose of precedent is to force judges to act in accordance with accepted rules and principles, rather than in accordance with their own inclinations. This is an essential part of Bentham's legal theory: Bentham champions the positive law and rejects the common law because he believes that the discretion of judges should be severely limited.

Bentham's real reason for rejecting the doctrine of precedent was that the doctrine stood in the way of legal and social reforms. This kind of argument is based on a misconception, however, since the principle of *stare decisis* is restricted to the *ratio decidendi* (the reason for the decision). This restriction is easily misunderstood, since the "reason" for a legal decision is restricted to the precise facts of the case, and a judge facing a different set of facts is free to develop the law in another direction. In point of fact, the doctrine of precedent gives the common law a flexibility that the statute law lacks, and it allows the common law to evolve in accordance with changes in social life.

The chief role of individual judges, at least at the trial level, is to determine the facts of particular cases. Bentham's failure to grasp the significance of this aspect of the legal process probably reflects the fact that he did not practise law. This aspect of the judicial role is significant because the policy argument for letting judges exercise discretion in individual cases is that they are the only persons who are familiar with the precise facts of individual cases. The legislature has relatively little knowledge of the judicial process and is not in a position to deal fairly with the differences between individual cases. The common law is based on the philosophical premise that the law must be decided in the context in which the facts arise rather than prescriptively, in the abstract, without regard to the empirical realities of the situation before the court.[5] The idea that the legislature is in a position to regulate the complexities that arise in a three-week trial, for example, with dozens of witnesses and thousands of documents seems naive.

One of the Legacies of Utilitarianism Was a Movement to Codify the Common Law

Bentham's rejection of the common law, and his preference for legislation, put him at the forefront of a movement to codify the common law. There was a scientific and a democratic idea behind this movement. Codification would take the law out of the keeping of the judiciary and allow it to be developed in accordance with the changing views of the populace.

The modern argument for codification is pre-eminently political: since the elected branch of government represents the people, it should logically decide the law.[6] This argument comes naturally out of the idea of the political contract. It nevertheless neglects the fact that the common law, like the constitutional law, had its origins in custom and moral consensus. This gives it an authority that the legislation passed by a democratic legislature does not possess.

The proper role of judicial and legislative institutions in deciding the law is open to debate. From an institutional perspective, it is plain that the movement for codification of the common law served the interests of the political branch of government and consolidated the power within the state. This was part of a long historical process that transferred the supremacy in government to the legislature. The democratic argument was naturally that the members of the legislature, unlike the members of the judiciary, are elected and therefore accountable to the people.

There are a number of criticisms of codification. One is that it politicizes the law. In an article on the attempt to codify the criminal law of evidence, for example, Barbara C. Salken writes:

> The Legislature, whose members must stand for election every two years, would be even more likely than the courts . . . to do what is perceived as politically popular—which generally coincides with the prosecution's point of view—rather than purely what best serves truth-finding and the ends of justice.[7]

This kind of argument is particularly compelling in procedural matters, which remain the natural preserve of the judiciary.

The paradoxical element in codification lies in the fact that the principles and rules that are to be codified must first be extracted out of the body of the existing law. Thus the process of codification is rooted in the judicial process. The theoretical argument for undertaking such a task is that it introduces "order and system into the mass of legal concepts" that can be found in the caselaw.[8] This process unifies the entire body of law in a coherent and related whole, prevents the deterioration of the substantive law into a series of isolated propositions, and unifies the entire body of law in a coherent and related whole. There is accordingly an argument that codification serves legal as well as political interests.

The utilitarians promoted the codification of the English common law in the 1800s. By that time, the caselaw in the criminal law, in particular, had become bewilderingly complex.[9] The political movement supporting codification culminated in the preparation of a draft criminal code by James Fitzjames Stephen, a student of Bentham's and the foremost authority on the criminal law in England. This led to the introduction of legislation in the House of Commons, in 1880, that would "compress" the entire criminal law into a single statute, but this legislation died on the order papers when the government that introduced it was defeated.[10] The British proposal nevertheless bore fruit in Canada, where Stephen's draft provided the basis for the *Criminal Code of Canada*, which was passed in 1892.[11]

There have been many attempts to codify other areas of the law. There is a general view that codification clarifies the outlines of the caselaw and reduces its fragmentation.[12] In Canada and the United States, many legislatures have enacted uniform or "model" statutes that codify the law relating to the sale of goods, insurance law, or the law of probate in order to maintain the consistency of the common law in different provinces and states. There is no doubt that this kind of systematization curbs some of the more adventuresome elements in the caselaw. This task has also been performed, however, by courts of final appeal, such as the Supreme Court of Canada and the United States Supreme Court. These courts regularly review different areas of the law, distill the fundamental principles in the law, and reformulate those principles, all in an orderly, systematic manner.[13]

One of the problems with codification is that it can be very difficult to amend legislation once it is passed. The statute books are full of outdated Acts and arcane provisions. In point of fact, one of the great strengths of the modern common law is that it allows the judiciary to continually develop the existing law. One of the historical examples of this capacity for evolution was the development of the law of automobiles, which was adapted, on a case by case basis, from the law that applied to carriages.

Kant's Theory of Law Is Based on Reason and the Concept of Duty

Bentham believed that the law was the product of an empirical science of legislation. Kant shared the same political conception of law, which originated in the political contract, but saw the science of legislation as a deductive science allied with logic. In the *Science of Right*,[14] he sets out the "immutable" principles of natural right, on which any legislation, he argues, must be based. These principles have an ethical source.

Like Bentham, then, Kant is primarily motivated by a desire for justice and freedom in human society. This focus on ethics distinguishes these theories from the tribal and customary theories of law, which seem to be motivated more by a desire for order in human society and the larger cosmos. Kant's conception of law is based on the "categorical imperative," which is an ethical rather than a legal principle.[15] This principle admits of no exceptions and requires that we act in a certain manner. There is a sense, at least, in which all of morality becomes the subject of law on his analysis.[16]

Kant also shares Bentham's desire for a rational or scientific methodology that provides unimpeachable answers to ethical and social questions. The legal theories in the work of these two enlightenment figures function, much like the law in Coke's work, as a kind of science or "artificial perfection of reason" that produces knowledge of what is right in any given circumstance. Kant essentially sets out a science of morality that requires us to act in a particular manner in any given set of circumstances. Compared to Kant's theory, Bentham's theory is more empirical and less dependent on formal logic. This is in keeping with the differences between the philosophical traditions in Germany and those in England.

The orientation of Bentham's and Kant's ethical views also differs. Bentham's utilitarianism leads him to propound a system of government and positive law that determines which social policies should be implemented by government. Kant's theory, on the other hand, creates a set of deontological propositions, based on duty, that determines how an individual person should act in any given circumstance. Thus the concept of law in Kant's theory seems "logically primitive." This term refers to a concept that expresses a meaning or proposition that is so basic that it cannot be explained further.

It could accordingly be said that Kant's ethical theory contemplates a comprehensive set of laws that provide an epistemological outline of the way we should behave. The concept of duty is nevertheless a subordinate concept in Kant's work, which focusses our attention on the central act of *willing*. Kant believes that it is the fact that we will ourselves to obey the law that makes our actions ethical. This perspective is part of the intellectual legacy of the Protestant Reformation and the Grotian model of law, which places so much emphasis on the autonomy and freedom of the individual. Thus, whereas Bentham was fundamentally interested in the personal experience of happiness, Kant separates happiness from morality and bases his general theory on one's duty to exercise one's will in conformity with the laws of reason.

Kant's General Philosophical Position Is that Our Minds Determine the Form of Our Experience

Kant's general philosophical position in his major philosophical work, the *Critique of Pure Reason*, is that our experience of being has a rational order—in fact, Kant argues, the rational order that gives meaning to our experience is a precondition of our experience. Concepts like time, space, and causality are mental attributes, properties of cognition, by which we construct our idea of the external world and the objects in it. It is therefore possible to have knowledge of the world that we perceive and experience simply by consulting the rational makeup of our perceptions. Kant carries this idea over into his concept of law, since he finds that the law is law by virtue of its rational properties and universal application rather than its substantive content. In Kant's view, there are physical laws—which determine the nature of the physical cosmos and govern non-rational beings—in much the same way that there are laws that determine how individual rational beings should exercise their will.

Kant describes the laws that govern rational beings as "normative." Although normative laws are laws in the full sense of the word, and obligatory, Kant does not actually demonstrate the logical necessity of these laws. Instead, he relies on the moral consensus in society and provides a social rather than a logical account of conventional morality. This approach is naturally in keeping with the common law, which has its origins in custom and moral consensus. As we will see in the following chapter, John Austin criticized Kant for setting out a rational approach but then falling back implicitly on the traditional theory of the natural law.

Kant's Concept of Law Supplies the Framework of His Ethical Theory and the Categorical Imperative

It is Kant's concept of law that supplies the framework for his ethical theory. At the same time, the form of his concept of law seems to derive from his moral theory—the idea of immoral laws seems foreign to his system. In the *Critique of Practical Reason* and the *Groundwork for the Metaphysics of Morals*, Kant postulates three "practical" ideas—God, freedom, and immortality—that are necessary presuppositions of moral conduct. These presuppositions, supplemented by reason, allow us to postulate a full system of laws that govern our conduct. It is the nature of these laws that gives rise to Kant's famous formulation of the categorical imperative. In the *Groundwork*, he writes that the ethical imperative is concerned with the "form" rather than the material or particular circumstances of the action.[17] His famous edict is: "Act only on that maxim by which you can at the same time will that it should become a universal law."[18]

It is the universal nature of an ethical maxim that makes it a moral law. Although the proposition that the law—to be law—must be the same in different cases, it is not clear that this takes us very far. Kant says that contracts are binding, for example, because contracts are always binding; this is a universal maxim. The maxim nevertheless seems unremarkable: surely it is little more than a statement that, indeed, contracts are binding. Although there is no reason to take issue with this formulation as an explanation of what we mean when we make such a statement, it is particularly unhelpful in legal practice, since the material issue in a courtroom is not in point of fact whether we should honour contracts but whether a particular agreement is a *valid* contract. The ruling that constitutes the right legal decision in a specific case would seem to turn on the facts before the court.

Kant's Legal Theory Holds that Law Is a Product of Pure Reason

Although Kant is a major figure in philosophy, his influence on the common law is relatively indirect. His idea of law is nevertheless of general significance and has had a lasting effect on jurisprudence. The law is a product of "pure reason" rather than empirical inquiry. At the very least, Kant established that it is possible to construct the outlines of a convincing legal theory, with very few assumptions, by the rigorous application of the principles of formal logic. In *The Science of Right*, for example, he deals with practical institutional and jurisprudential issues with a deductive rigour that is rare in philosophy of law.

Kant's Concept of Law Is Based on the Assertion that We Are Free

Kant's conception of law is based on the science of right. This development is significant in itself, given the singular importance of rights in the contemporary discussion of law. It is nevertheless paradoxical, since the concept of right presupposes that we have some choice in what we do. The notion of law, on the other hand, refers to a binding prescription that must be followed.

The explanation for this foundational paradox in Kant's concept of law lies in the fact that the individual, rather than society, is primary in Kant's theory of law. As a result, the authority of government cannot rest—as it does in Aquinas' work—on the mere fact of its existence. The positive law must be justified. The fundamental justification in Kant's theory of law accordingly lies in the idea that the private freedom of individuals requires the positive law.

The central metaphysical tenet of Kant's philosophy of law is accordingly that we have free will. The origins of society and the positive law, on Kant's view, can be traced to the free choice of individuals to form government and abide by law. The notion of right that comes out of the political contract also rests, however, on the proposition that it is only the existence of a condition of individual freedom that gives us the capacity to make meaningful decisions. It is the law—however counterintuitive this may initially seem—that creates the possibility of living in a free and "rightful" condition. The most obvious illustration of this thesis in practice is found in that part of the civil law that allows us to enter into legal relationships with other people.

Kant's Philosophy of Law Borrows Elements from the Grotian Natural Law

The philosophical foundations of Kant's concept of law derives historically (if not directly) from the deductive and contractual aspects of the Grotian model of the natural law. There are two essential ideas here. The first is that individuals are free. This idea is in keeping with Kant's moral theory, which places the highest value on personal autonomy, and the idea that society exists only because individuals have freely, through the political contract, agreed to the formation of government.

The second idea is that the law exists *a priori* to experience. This idea stands in opposition to Bentham's ethical and legal theory, which is usually described as "consequentialist." It also differs from the conception of law in the common law tradition, which is distinctly empirical, since it always issues from a particular set of facts. Kant holds that the law can be ascertained by pure reason, and it could be said that his theory subscribes to a kind of logical natural law, with most of its substantive content removed. This position, however, raises linguistic and epistemological issues. It is not clear that logical propositions, for example, have meaning outside their reference to empirical facts.

The Positive Law Is Based on the Idea that We Are Entitled to Enjoy Our Freedom Equally

It is the first idea that explains why the positive law is necessary in Kant's theory. In a characteristic logical move, which may seem counter-intuitive and even contradictory, Kant argues that the positive law is necessary because it guarantees our personal freedom.[19] It does so by mitigating and regulating the conflict between separate wills and by requiring individuals to respect the freedoms and rights of others. This view suggests that the law can create a "rightful condition" in which all of us can enjoy our personal freedom equally. It is this idea of equality of freedom that provides the justification for the coercive powers of the Kantian state. The state is not entitled, however, to use force in order to positively promote or implement a social policy—at least in the sense that the government cannot logically compel people to behave in certain ways, if that act interferes with the exercise of personal freedom that the government is there to guarantee.

Some of Kant's ideas have parallels in the common law. He postulates, for example, that individuals own their own bodies—and while the term "ownership" seems awkward, the common law certainly recognizes that individuals have an inviolable right to make decisions that concern the integrity of their own bodies. Kant postulates that there is a mutual transfer of some part of this notional ownership in the case of marriage, which recalls the common law action for "loss of consortium," but it is the equality in the Kantian conception of marriage that stands out. This concern with equality is a hallmark of liberal democracies; it is also central in the contemporary positive law, both inside and outside the common law tradition.

Kant also argues that it is not possible to have a system of positive law without public institutions and a system of impartial courts to apply the law consistently. This need for public institutions is demonstrated by the need to enforce the obligations required to maintain the right to personal property. Kant explains the possession of private property as a right that by its essential nature places obligations on other people. These obligations may be as simple as the obligation not to interfere with other people's enjoyment of the things they own. These obligations must be enforced through government and public institutions, which have authority over the people who possess such obligations.

The Political Contract Has a Kind of Constitutional Status

There are competing tendencies in Kant's theory of the law. On the one hand, his conception that there is a necessary and rightful condition in which we can enjoy our liberties places constitutional limits on the exercise of political power. Such limitations are also apparent in Kant's notion of the "original contract," which holds that the positive law is valid only if it is consistent with the contract. Legislation must be such that the people would have willed it themselves, individually and collectively.

These requirements of legal validity place conceptual limits on the sovereign power, which many philosophers in the tradition of the social contract have failed to do. Thus the political realm is at least notionally under the rule of law. There is a sense in which the principles of natural right, like the original contract, function as an immutable legal check on the authority of political government. The independence and rigour of Kant's logic evokes not merely the natural law, but the cosmological law behind it.

On the other hand, Kant's general position, to quote Ernst-Jan Wit, "is characterized by a strong suspicion of any form of civil disobedience."[20] Some authors have gone much further. Don Becker, for example, writes that

> Kant's absolute prohibition against rebellion and resistance, while holding a theory of illegitimate legislation, is evident. . . . Kant both recognizes that there are things beyond the legitimate authority of the state, and asserts that the people cannot use coercion in response to such transgressions. The absolute nature of this prohibition is stated unequivocally: "it is the people's duty to endure even the most intolerable abuse of supreme authority."[21]

It is clear of course that Kant has ontological as well as logical reasons for discouraging civil disobedience, since we cannot depose of the sovereign without breaking the categorical imperative, which requires that we always obey the law.

From a contemporary philosophical perspective, Kant's refusal to permit breaches of the positive law seems to identify him as a legal positivist who accepts the authority of the political sources of the positive law. There seems to be no doubt that he accepts the full exercise of the state's coercive powers in enforcing the positive law. This position is complicated, however, and even trumped, by the constitutional aspects of his theory and the fact that the positive law must conform to the principles of law—the principles of natural right—that he sets out in the *Science of Right*. The actual applicability of Kant's position in a legal system may be debated, since the restrictions on the state apply as much to the judiciary as to those in political office, and there is very little room for discretion in such a system. It is nevertheless significant that Kant's theory logically maintains the historical ascendancy of law over politics.

Kant's Theory of Law Lends Credence to the Idea of Codification

Kant's theory of law also lends itself to the idea of codification, since Kant holds that it is possible to construct an entire theory of law from reason alone, without the knowledge that we gain from individual cases. As we will see in Chapter 7, Oliver Wendell Holmes argued that this goes against the empirical foundations of the common law, which is based on experience. One of the difficulties with the kind of deductive legislative process that Kant envisages is that it is extremely difficult to anticipate all of the moral and social considerations that may arise in difficult cases.

The movement for codification in the eighteenth century made little headway in England, in spite of the efforts of the utilitarians. The movement was successful in Europe, however, where it fit more readily into the prevailing legal and philosophical traditions. These traditions were abstract and rationalistic, and they implicitly supported Kant's idea that a system of law could be deduced from metaphysical principles and applied, prescriptively, to human experience.

Roscoe Pound describes Kant's approach as a "method of deduction from predetermined conceptions" that "arrived at certain propositions as to human nature, and deduced a system from them."[22] Although this system bears some resemblance to the natural law, the substantive premises of Kant's theory are much sparser, and the religious and cultural neutrality of his ideas are remarkably appealing in a contemporary context. This sort of neutrality leaves a significant degree of legislative discretion in passing particular laws.

Kant Proposes a Congress of Nations and Holds that Nations Have a Duty to Leave the State of Nature

Kant's discussion of the rights of nations is also significant. He begins, like Grotius, by treating states as natural individuals that live in the "condition of natural freedom," or state of nature. This starting-point leads Kant to conclude that nations are *"consequently in a state of continual war."* There is no difference, in Kant's formulation, between nations and human individuals. It follows that the only way nations can bring the ongoing war to an end is by entering into an international political contract and creating an international government with the power to pass and enforce a positive law of nations. Kant accordingly argues for the creation of a federation of nations—essentially a world government—by which nations could bring themselves out of the state of nature.

Kant proposes a permanent "congress of nations" that has been compared with the United Nations. The existence of a congress is insufficient, however, on Kant's analysis, if it merely facilitates some measure of dialogue between nations. As we have seen, historically, with the League of Nations and the United Nations, consultative bodies that provide a forum for political negotiations between nations do not have the authority to take the international realm out of the Grotian state of nature. The formation of a government with the authority to make or enforce law, on the natural rights analysis, would require a source of supreme political authority with the ability to exercise authority over individual nations.

A Kantian government of nations would come with its own problems and create a fearsome concentration of power. Kant's discussion is nevertheless illuminating. Kant is unusually forthright in recognizing that the existence of states in a purely political realm, outside the reach of compulsory law, is tantamount to anarchy. There seems, moreover, to be no logical escape from such a development in the broader confines of his ethical and legal theory. The law exists *a priori*, for Kant, and presumably places positive obligations on nations, which have a duty to exercise their individual wills in a manner that is consonant with the law. It may accordingly be argued that states have a duty to pass out of the state of nature and enter into a legal state.

Notes

1. See Jeremy Bentham, *An Introduction to the Principles of Morals and Legislation*, in *The Works of Jeremy Bentham*, vol. 1 (Edinburgh: William Tait, 1843). Available at http://oll.libertyfund.org.

2. ibid.

3. Michel Foucault, *Discipline and Punish: The Birth of the Prison*, trans. Alan Sheridan (New York: Pantheon, 1977).

4. See *Of Laws in General*, as cited in the readings, p. 192.

5. There is an interesting contradiction here between Bentham's position in ethics, which is consequentialist, and his belief in a prescriptive legislative scheme.

6. A standard argument is that codification makes the law accessible to the public. "The average man," in the words of Letourneau and Cohen, cited *infra*, at p. 185, "if he so desires, can find and read the law that governs him." This is a rather naive view, which fails to take account of the realities of legislation. It is hard to believe that anyone who bothers to read a legislative codification will find its meaning accessible to an ordinary person.

7. Barbara C. Salken, "To Codify or Not to Codify—That Is the Question: A Study of New York's Efforts to Enact an Evidence Code," *Brooklyn Law Review* 58, no. 3 (1992): 641–704, at p. 696.

8. Gilles Letourneau and Stanley A. Cohen, "Codification and Law Reform: Some Lessons from the Canadian Experience," *Statute Law Review* 10, no. 3 (1989): 183–99, at p. 185.

9. See Brown's comment, in "Abortive Attempts to Codify English Criminal Law," as cited *infra*, at p. 2: "In early Stuart days there were between 60 and 70 volumes of reports which recorded the facts and judgements of several hundred cases. By 1877 there were about 1,400 volumes and the number of cases reported was well in excess of 100,000. Embedded in this mass from the outset was the criminal law."

10. For a historical account of these events, see Desmond H. Brown, "Abortive Attempts to Codify English Criminal Law," *Parliamentary History* 11, no. 1 (1992): 1–39. And see Lindsay Farmer, "Reconstructing the English Codification Debate: The Criminal Law Commissioners, 1833–45," *Law and History Review* 18, no. 2 (Summer 2000): 397–425, and Sanford H. Kadish "Codifiers of the Criminal Law: Wechsler's Predecessors," *Columbia Law Review* 78 (1978): 1098–144.

11. See Graham Parker, "The Origins of the Canadian Criminal Code," in vol. 1 of *Essays in the History of Canadian Law*, ed. David H. Flaherty (Toronto: Osgoode Society, 1981), pp. 249–80. Also see J.H. Batten, "Common Law, Its Elimination from the Code," *University of Toronto Faculty of Law Review* 15 (1957): 7–12. And see Joseph Sedgwick, "The New Criminal Code: Comments and Criticisms," *Canadian Bar Review* 33, (1955): 63–73.

12. See, for example, Aubrey L. Diamond, "Codification of the Law of Contract," *The Modern Law Review* 31, no. 4 (July 1968): 361–85.

13. The publication of definitive texts or learned treatises plays a similar role in the common law and regularly reformulates the entire body of existing rules. Two examples of such treatises are John Henry Wigmore's exhaustive *Wigmore on Evidence: Evidence in Trials at Common Law* and P.S. Atiyah's *Sale of Goods*, now available in its twelfth edition, under the authorship of John Adams and Hector L. MacQueen, and rechristened *Atiyah's Sale of Goods* (Harlow: Longman/Pearson, 2010).

14. This is the more common title used for Kant's work that was published as *The Philosophy of Law: An Exposition of the Fundamental Principles of Jurisprudence as the Science of Right*, as cited in the readings.

15. See Wolfgang Gaston Friedmann, *Legal Theory*, 5th ed. (London: Stevens, 1967), at p. 159: "This is what Kant's *Categorical Imperative* says: 'Act in such a way that the maxim of your action could be the maxim of a general action.'"

16. See Friedmann, ibid.: "It must be emphasized that Kant's legal philosophy is entirely a theory of what the law ought to be. A discrepancy between the law that is and the law that ought to be is not discussed. His is the legal philosophy of the philosopher, not the lawyer."

17.   Kant, *Groundwork for the Metaphysics of Morals*, as cited in the suggestions for further reading, 2.22.217.

18.   ibid., 2.25.222.

19.   Kant's argument recalls the idea of "liberty" that found expression in the *Magna Carta*, which was based on the existence of the customary law.

20.   See Ernst-Jan C. Wit, "Kant and the Limits of Civil Obedience," *Kant-Studien* 90, no. 3 (1999): 285–305, at p. 285.

21.   Don Becker, "Kant's Moral and Political Philosophy," in *The Age of German Idealism*, ed. Robert C. Solomon and Kathleen M. Higgins (London: Routledge, 1993), pp. 68–102, at p. 98. The interior quote is from Kant's *Metaphysics of Morals*.

22.   See Roscoe Pound, "Mechanical Jurisprudence," *Columbia Law Review* 8 (1908): 605–23. Note that a part of Pound's article is included as a reading in Chapter 7.

Study Questions

1.   Why are we obliged to obey the law in utilitarianism? Why are we obliged to obey the law in the theory of law proposed by Immanuel Kant?

2.   What are the advantages and disadvantages of codifying the common law? Is a complete codification possible?

3.   How does Bentham's view of legislation and the legal process reflect his training as a lawyer? How might his view have changed if he had actually *practised* law?

4.   Both Bentham and Kant seem to be looking for an intellectual mechanism that produces the outlines, at least, of an ideal body of law. The same might be said, however, of the judges and sages who recorded the customary law. Which approach do you prefer? Why?

5.   How would you describe the relationship between the moral law and the human law in Kant's theory of law?

6.   What is the role of "pure" reason in Kant's theory of law? Is there any possibility of error in its exercise?

7.   Why must the partners to a marriage be equal, logically, in Kant's theory of law?

Further Reading

Jeremy Bentham, *An Introduction to the Principles of Morals and Legislation*, ed. J.H. Burns and H.L.A. Hart (London: Athlone, [1789] 1970).

Elie Halévy, *The Growth of Philosophical Radicalism*, trans. M. Morris (Boston: Beacon, 1955).

H.L.A. Hart, "Natural Rights: Bentham and John Stuart Mill," in *Essays on Bentham: Studies in Jurisprudence and Political Theory* (Oxford: Clarendon, 1982).

Immanuel Kant, *Groundwork for the Metaphysics of Morals*, trans. Arnulf Zweig, ed. Thomas Hill and Arnulf Zweig (Oxford: Oxford University, 2002).

———, *Perpetual Peace: A Philosophical Sketch* (Indiana: Hackett Publishing Company, 1795).

Gerald Postema, *Bentham and the Common Law Tradition* (Oxford: Clarendon, 1986).

Arthur Ripstein, *Force and Freedom: Kant's Legal and Political Philosophy* (Cambridge, MA: Harvard University, 2009).

6 Legal Positivism: The Political Order Takes Precedence

John Austin, Thomas Hill Green, and Albert Venn Dicey

Readings

- From *The Province of Jurisprudence Determined*, by John Austin
- From *Lectures on the Principles of Political Obligation*, by Thomas Hill Green
- From *Introduction to the Study of the Law of the Constitution*, by Albert Venn Dicey

The following chapter examines early legal positivism, the most influential legal theory in the common law tradition. In the early nineteenth century, with the development of a strong, centralized state, it was widely agreed that the law derived its authority from political sources. As a result, the controversy between the theory of the natural law and the theory of natural rights died away, and the focus of legal theory shifted to the institutional rather than the theoretical sources of the law. The two questions posed by the early legal positivists reflected the increasingly analytic nature of the Western philosophical tradition, which focussed on technical rather than foundational issues. The first question arose out of the desire to distinguish legal propositions from other propositions: what is it, these theorists asked, that makes a particular utterance a "law"? Their answer was essentially that the law is compulsory. The second question came out of the answer to the first: what is it, they asked, that makes the law compulsory? Although there is nothing new in the idea that the character of the law derives from its compulsory nature, the legal positivists are significant because they argued that this compulsion is quintessentially political. This view has many unintended consequences, since it empties the concept of the law of its moral implications and suggests that directions that do not originate in the political order cannot be considered law.

John Austin (1790–1859), the most prominent figure in the early positivist tradition, argued that law is the command of the sovereign. Thomas Hill Green (1836–1882) argued, as a riposte to Austin, that the law can be traced to the common good. Green's view moderates the absolutism in Austin's theory, which appears to reduce the law to the exercise of raw political power and contains echoes of the customary sources of the common law. The emergence of early legal positivism was a reflection of the ascendancy of the political order, which by the time of the legal positivists had been utterly entrenched in the English common law. This aspect of the English common law found expression in the work of Albert Venn Dicey (1835–1922), a constitutional scholar, who argued that the English constitution was based on the sovereignty of Parliament, a doctrine commonly known as "parliamentary supremacy."

⚔ Readings ⚓

From John Austin, *The Province of Jurisprudence Determined* (London: John Murray, 1832).

Lecture I: The Nature of Law

[T]he term *law* embraces the following objects: Laws set by *God* to his human creatures, and laws set by *men* to men.

The whole or a portion of the laws set by God to men, is frequently styled *the law of nature*, or *natural law*. . . .

Laws Set by Men to Men

The laws or rules set by men to men, are of two leading or principal classes. . . .

1. Positive Laws

Of the laws or rules set by men to men, some are established by *political* superiors, sovereign and subject: by persons exercising supreme and subordinate *government*, in independent nations, or independent political societies. The aggregate of the rules thus established, or some . . . portion of that aggregate, is the appropriate matter of jurisprudence . . . But, as contradistinguished to *natural* law, or the law *of nature* (meaning, by those expressions, the law of God), the aggregate of the rules, established by political superiors, is frequently styled *positive* law. . . .

2. Innominate Laws

Though *some* of the laws or rules, which are set by men to men, are established by political superiors, *others* are *not* established by political superiors, or are *not* established by political superiors, in that capacity or character. Of human laws belonging to this second class, *some* are laws, properly so called. . . . [For such laws, however,] current or established language has no collective name.

There Are Two Classes of Laws Improperly Styled Laws

1. Positive Moral Rules

[T]he aggregate of the human laws, which are *improperly* styled *laws*, is not unfrequently denoted by one of the following expressions: "*moral* rules," "the *moral* law," "the law set or prescribed by *general* or *public* opinion." . . . [These so-called laws] may be named commodiously *positive morality*. The name *morality* severs them from *positive law*: whilst the epithet *positive* disjoins them from the *law of God*. . . .

2. Metaphorical or Figurative Laws

But in numerous cases wherein it is applied improperly, the applications of the term *law* rest upon a slender analogy, and are merely metaphorical or figurative. Such is the case when we talk of *laws* observed by the lower animals; of *laws* regulating the growth or decay of vegetables; of *laws* determining the movements of inanimate bodies or masses. . . .

A Law Is a Command

Every law or rule (taken with the largest signification which can be given to the term *properly*) is a *command*. . . .

Accordingly, I shall endeavour . . . to analyze the meaning of "*command*." . . .

If you express or intimate a wish that I shall do or forbear from some act, and if you will visit me with an evil in case I comply not with your wish, the *expression* or *intimation* of your wish is a *command*. A command is distinguished from other significations of desire, not by the style in which the desire is signified, but by the power and the purpose of the party commanding to inflict an evil or pain in case the desire be disregarded. . . .

Being liable to evil from you if I comply not with a wish which you signify, I am *bound* or *obliged* by your command, or I lie under a *duty* to obey it. If, in spite of that evil in prospect, I comply not with the wish which you signify, I am said to disobey your command, or to violate the duty which it imposes.

Command and duty are, therefore, correlative terms. . . .

The evil which will probably be incurred in case a command be disobeyed, or (to use an equivalent expression) in case a duty be broken, is frequently called a *sanction*. . . . Considered as thus abstracted from the command and the duty which it enforces, the evil to be incurred by disobedience is frequently styled a *punishment*. . . .

By some celebrated writers (by Locke, Bentham, and, I think, Paley), the term *sanction*, or *enforcement of obedience*, is applied to . . . reward as well as to punishment. But, with all my habitual veneration for the names of Locke and Bentham, I think that this extension of the term is pregnant with confusion and perplexity. . . .

If *you* expressed a desire that *I* should render a service, and if you proffered a reward as the motive or inducement to render it, *you* would scarcely be said to *command* the service, nor should *I*, in ordinary language, be *obliged* to render it. . . .

It appears, then, . . . that the ideas or notions comprehended by the term *command* are the following.

1. A wish or desire conceived by a rational being, and that another rational being shall do or forbear.
2. An evil to proceed from the former, and to be incurred by the latter, in case the latter comply not with the wish.
3. An expression or intimation of the wish by words or other signs. . . .

Commands Are General or Particular

Commands are of two species. Some are *laws* or *rules*. The others have not acquired an appropriate name, nor does language afford an expression which will mark them briefly and precisely. I must, therefore, note them, as well as I can, by the ambiguous and inexpressive name of "*occasional* or *particular* commands." . . .

[T]he distinction between laws and particular commands may, I think, be stated in the following manner. By every command, the party to whom it is directed is obliged to do or to forbear. Now where it obliges *generally* to acts or forbearances of a *class*, a command is a law or rule. But where it obliges to a *specific* act or forbearance . . . a command is occasional or particular. . . .

If you command your servant to go on a given errand . . . or to rise at such an hour on such a morning . . . the command is occasional or particular. . . . But if you command him . . . to rise at that hour *always*, or to rise at that hour *till further orders*, it may be said . . . that you lay down a *rule* [i.e., a law] for the guidance of your servant's conduct. . . .

To conclude with an example . . . which shows the importance of the distinction most conspicuously, *judicial commands* are commonly occasional or particular, although the commands, which they are calculated to enforce, are commonly laws or rules. For instance, the lawgiver commands that thieves shall be hanged. A specific theft and a specified thief being given, the judge commands that the thief shall be hanged, agreeably to the command of the lawgiver. . . . The command of the lawgiver is, therefore, a law or rule. But the command of the judge is occasional or particular. . . .

The Positive Law Is General in a Twofold Manner

To frame a system of duties for every individual of the community, were simply impossible. . . . Most of the laws established by political superiors, are, therefore, *general* in a twofold manner: as enjoining or forbidding generally acts of kinds or sorts; and as binding the whole community, or, at least, whole classes of its members. . . .

Customary Law

I think it will appear . . . that customary law is *imperative*, in the proper signification of the term; and that all judge-made law is the creature of the sovereign or state. . . . A subordinate or subject judge is merely a minister. . . .The rules which he makes derive their legal force from authority given by the state, an authority which the state may confer expressly, but which it commonly imparts in the way of acquiescence. . . .

Considered as rules of positive morality, customary laws arise from the consent of the governed, and not from the position or establishment of political superiors. But, considered as moral rules turned into positive laws, customary laws are established by the state: established by the state directly, when the customs are promulgated in its statutes; established by the state circuitously, when the customs are adopted by its tribunals. . . .

Lecture V: The Nature of the Positive Law

Every positive law . . . is set by a sovereign person, or a sovereign body of persons, to a member or members of the independent political society wherein that person or body is sovereign or supreme. Or (changing the expression) it is set by a monarch, or sovereign number, to a person or persons in a state of subjection to its author. . . .

Laws properly so called are a species of *commands*. But, being a *command*, every law properly so called flows from a *determinate* source, or emanates from . . . a *determinate* rational being, or a determinate body or aggregate of rational beings. . . . [E]very positive law . . . is a direct or circuitous command of a monarch or sovereign number in the character of political superior: that is to say, a direct or circuitous command of a monarch or sovereign number to a person or persons in a state of subjection to its author.

Lecture VI: The Nature of Sovereignty

The superiority which is styled sovereignty . . . is distinguished from other superiority, and from other society, by the following marks or characters. 1. The *bulk* of the given society are in a *habit* of obedience or submission to a *determinate* and *common* superior. . . . 2. That certain individual, or that certain body of individuals, is *not* in a habit of obedience to a determinate human superior. . . .

To that determinate superior, the other members of the society are *subject*. . . . The mutual relation which subsists between that superior and them, may be styled *the relation of sovereign and subject*, or *the relation of sovereignty and subjection*. Hence it follows, that it is only through an ellipsis, or an abridged form of expression, that the *society* is styled *independent*. The party truly independent . . . is not the society, but the sovereign portion of the society: that certain member of the society, or that certain body of its members, to whose commands, expressed or intimated, the generality or bulk of its members render habitual obedience. . . .

By "an independent political society," or "an independent and sovereign nation," we mean a political society consisting of a sovereign and subjects, as opposed to a political society which is merely subordinate: that is to say, which is merely a limb or member of another political society. . . .

[C]onsidered in respect of one another, independent political societies live, it is commonly said, in a state of nature. And considered as entire communities, and as connected by mutual intercourse, independent political societies form, it is commonly said, a natural society. These expressions, however, are not perfectly apposite. . . .

Society formed by the intercourse of independent political societies, is the province of international law, or of the law obtaining between nations. . . . Speaking with greater precision, international law, or the law obtaining between nations, regards the conduct of sovereigns considered as related to one another.

And hence it inevitably follows, that the law obtaining between nations is not positive law: for every positive law is set by a given sovereign to a person or persons in a state of subjection to its author. As I have already intimated, the law obtaining between nations is law (improperly so called) set by general opinion. The duties which it imposes are enforced by moral sanctions: by fear on the part of nations, or by fear on the part of sovereigns, of provoking general hostility, and incurring its probable evils, in case they shall violate maxims generally received and respected. . . .

In order that a given society may form a society political and independent, the positive and negative marks which I have mentioned above must unite. The *generality* or *bulk* of its members must be in a *habit* of obedience to a *certain* and *common* superior: whilst that certain person, or certain body of persons, must *not* be habitually obedient to a certain person or body. . . .

The definition or general notion of independent political society, is therefore vague or uncertain. Applying it to specific or particular cases, we should often encounter the difficulties which I have laboured to explain.

For example: When did the revolted colony, which is now the Mexican nation, ascend from the condition of an insurgent province to that of an independent community? When did the body of colonists, who affected sovereignty in Mexico, change the character of rebel leaders for that of a supreme government? Or (adopting the current language about governments *de jure* and *de facto*) when did the body of colonists, who affected sovereignty in Mexico, become sovereign *in fact*? And . . . when did international law authorize neutral nations to admit the independence of Mexico with the sovereignty of the Mexican government? . . .

[T]he questions suggested above are equivalent to this: When had the inhabitants of Mexico obeyed that body [the body that exercised the powers of the Mexican government] so generally, and when had that general obedience become so frequent and lasting, that the inhabitants of Mexico were independent of Spain in practice, and were likely to remain permanently in that state of practical independence?

At that juncture exactly . . . neutral nations were authorized, by the morality which obtains between nations, to admit the independence of Mexico with the sovereignty of the Mexican government.

From Thomas Hill Green, *Lectures on the Principles of Political Obligation* (London: Longmans, Green, 1941).

Sovereignty and the General Will[1]

83. [John] Austin's doctrine seems diametrically opposite to one which finds the sovereign in . . . [Jean-Jacques Rousseau's] *"volonté générale"* [general will] because (a) it only recognises sovereignty in a *determinate* person or persons, and (b) it considers the essence

of sovereignty to lie in the power, on the part of such determinate persons, to put compulsion without limit on subjects, to make them do exactly as it pleases. . . .

84. The two views thus seem mutually exclusive, but perhaps it may be by taking each as complementary to the other that we shall gain the truest view of sovereignty as it actually exists. In those states of society in which obedience is habitually rendered by the bulk of society to some determinate superior . . . the obedience is so rendered because this determinate superior is regarded as expressing or embodying what may properly be called the general will. . . .

As [Henry Sumner] Maine says (*Early History of Institutions* p. 359), "the vast mass of influences, which we may call for shortness moral, perpetually shapes, limits, or forbids the actual direction of the forces of society by its sovereign." Thus . . . it may fairly be held that the ostensible sovereign—the determinate person or persons to whom we can point and say that with him or them lies the ultimate power of exacting habitual obedience from the people—is only able to exercise this power in virtue of an assent on the part of the people, nor is this assent reducible to the fear of the sovereign felt by each individual. It is rather a common desire for certain ends—specially the "*pax vitæque securitas*" [the secure and peaceful life]—to which the observance of law or established usage contributes, and in most cases implies no conscious reference on the part of those whom it influences to any supreme coercive power at all. . . .

85. If, then, those who adopt the Austinian definition of a sovereign mean no more than that in a thoroughly developed state there must be some determinate person or persons, with whom, in the last resort, lies the recognised power of imposing laws and enforcing their observance, over whom no legal control can be exercised . . . they are doubtless right. . . .

86. But the Austinians . . . are apt to suppose that the sovereign, with the coercive power (i.e. the power of operating on the fears of the subjects) which it exercises, is the real determinant of the habitual obedience of the people. . . . [However,] this is not the case. . . . [I]t can no longer be said to reside in a determinate person or persons, but in that impalpable congeries of the hopes and fears of a people, bound together by common interests and sympathy, which we call the general will.

Despotism

87. It may be objected that this view of the general will, as that on which habitual obedience to the sovereign really depends, is at best only applicable to "self-governing" communities, not to those under a despotic sovereign. The answer [to such an objection] is that it is applicable in all forms of society where a sovereign in the sense above defined . . . really exists, but that there are many where there cannot fairly be said to be any such sovereign at all. . . .

88. Maine has pointed out (*Early History of Institutions*, Lecture XIII) that the great despotic empires of ancient times . . . were in the main tax-collecting institutions. They exercise[d] coercive force over their subjects of the most violent kind for certain purposes

at certain times, but they [did] not impose laws as distinct from "particular and occasional commands," nor [did] they judicially administer or enforce a customary law. . . .

89. The same account is applicable to most cases of foreign dominion over a people with any organized common life of their own. The foreign power is not sovereign in the sense of being a maker or maintainer of laws. . . . The subject people inherits laws, written or unwritten, and maintains them for itself, a certain shelter from violence being afforded by the foreign power. . . .

True Sovereignty

90. It is otherwise where the foreign power is really a law-making and law-maintaining one, and is sovereign in that proper sense, as was the Roman Empire. But just so far as the Roman Empire was of this sovereign, i.e. law-making and law-maintaining, character, it derived its permanence, its hold on the "habitual obedience" of its subjects, from the support of the general will. As the empire superseded customary or written laws of conquered countries, it conferred rights of Roman citizenship, a much more perfect system of protection in action and acquisition [i.e., legal protection] than the conquered people had generally possessed before. Hence, while nothing could be further removed from what Rousseau would have counted liberty than the life of the citizens of the Roman Empire, for they had nothing to do with making the laws which they obeyed, yet probably there was never any political system more firmly grounded on the good-will of the subjects, none in the maintenance of which the subjects felt a stronger interest.

The Middle Function

The British power in India exercises a middle function between that of the Roman Empire and that of the mere tax-collecting and recruit-raising empire. . . . It leaves the customary law of the people mostly untouched. But if only to a very small extent a law-making power, it is emphatically a law maintaining one. It regulates the whole judicial administration of the country, but applies its power generally only to enforce the customary law which it finds in existence. For this reason an "habitual obedience" may fairly be said to be rendered by the Indian people to the English government . . . but the "habitual obedience" is so rendered only because the English government presents itself to the people, not merely as a tax-collector, but as the maintainer of a customary law, which, on the whole, is the expression of the general will. . . .

Political Obedience and the Common Good

91. The essential thing in political society is a power which guarantees men rights, i.e. a certain freedom of action and acquisition . . ., impartially or according to a general will or law. . . . It is the power of guaranteeing rights, as defined above, which the old writers

on sovereignty and civil government supposed to be established by covenant of all with all [i.e., by the idea of a social contract, by which they were], translating the common interest which men have in the maintenance of such a power into an imaginary historical act by which they instituted it. It was this power that they had chiefly in view when they spoke of sovereignty. . . .

92. [W]hen the power by which rights are guaranteed is sovereign (as it is desirable that it should be) in the special sense of being maintained by a person or persons, and wielding coercive force not liable to control by any other human force, it is not this coercive force that is the important thing about it, or that determines the habitual obedience essential to the real maintenance of rights. That which determines this habitual obedience is a power residing in the common will and reason of men, i.e. in the will and reason of men as determined by social relations, as interested in each other, as acting together for common ends. . . .

93. Thus . . . [t]he sovereign should be regarded, not in abstraction as the wielder of coercive force, but in connection with the whole complex of institutions or political society. It is as their sustainer, and thus as the agent of the general will, that the sovereign power must be presented to the minds of the people if it is to command habitual loyal obedience; and obedience will scarcely be habitual unless it is loyal, not forced. . . .

98. The truth which underlies this proposition is that an interest in common good is the ground of political society, in the sense that without it no body of people would recognize any authority as having a claim on their common obedience. It is so far as a government represents to them a common good that the subjects are conscious that they ought to obey it, i.e. that obedience to it is a means to an end desirable in itself or absolutely.

Note

1. Editor's note: In this section of his lecture, Green tries to reconcile Austin's concept of sovereignty with Jean-Jacques Rousseau's (1712–1778) idea that the law is the expression of the *volonté générale* (the general will), which represents the collective will of the state. An excerpt from Rousseau's *The Social Contract* is included in the additional online readings listed in the Appendix.

From Albert Venn Dicey, *Introduction to the Study of the Law of the Constitution*, 6th ed. (London: Macmillan, [1885] 1902).

The Nature of Parliamentary Sovereignty

The principle of Parliamentary sovereignty means neither more nor less than this, namely, that Parliament . . . has, under the English constitution, the right to make or unmake any law whatever; and, further, that no person or body is recognized by the law of England as having a right to override or set aside the legislation of Parliament.

A law may, for our present purpose, be defined as "any rule which will be enforced by the Courts." The principle then of Parliamentary sovereignty may, looked at from its positive side, be thus described: Any Act of Parliament, or any part of an Act of Parliament, which makes a new law, or repeals or modifies an existing law, will be obeyed by the Courts. . . .

Some apparent exceptions to this rule no doubt suggest themselves. But these apparent exceptions . . . are resolvable into cases in which Parliament either directly or indirectly sanctions subordinate legislation. . . .

The Unlimited Legislative Authority of Parliament

This supreme legislative authority of Parliament is shown historically in a large number of instances. . . . But there is no single statute which is more significant either as to the theory or as to the practical working of the constitution than the *Septennial Act* . . . . In 1716 the duration of Parliament was under an Act of 1694 [the *Triennial Act*] limited to three years. . . . The King and the Ministry were convinced (and with reason) that an appeal to the electors, many of whom were Jacobites, might be perilous not only to the Ministry but to the tranquillity of the state. The Parliament then sitting, therefore, was induced by the Ministry to pass the *Septennial Act* by which the legal duration of Parliament was extended from three to seven years, and the powers of the then existing House of Commons were in effect prolonged for four years beyond the time for which the House was elected. . . .

The peculiarity of the Act was not that it changed the legal duration of Parliament or repealed the *Triennial Act*; the mere passing of a *Septennial Act* in 1716 was not and would never have been thought to be anything more startling or open to graver censure than the passing of a *Triennial Act* in 1694. What was startling was that an existing Parliament of its own authority prolonged its own legal existence. . . . That Act proves to demonstration that in a legal point of view Parliament is neither the agent of the electors nor in any sense a trustee for its constituents. It is legally the sovereign legislative power in the state. . . .

Austin's Theory of Sovereignty

Sovereignty, like many of Austin's conceptions, is a generalization drawn in the main from English law. . . . In England we are accustomed to the existence of a supreme legislative body, i.e. a body which can make or unmake every law; and which, therefore, cannot be bound by any law. This is, from a legal point of view, the true conception of a sovereign, and the ease with which the theory of absolute sovereignty has been accepted by English jurists is due to the peculiar history of English constitutional law. So far, therefore, from its being true that the sovereignty of Parliament is a deduction from abstract theories of jurisprudence, a critic would come nearer the truth who asserted that Austin's theory of sovereignty is suggested by the position of the English Parliament, just as Austin's analysis of the term "law" is at bottom an analysis of a typical law, namely, an English criminal statute.

It should, however, be carefully noted that the term "sovereignty" . . . is a merely legal conception, and means simply the power of law-making unrestricted by any legal limit. If the term "sovereignty" be thus used, the sovereign power under the English constitution is clearly Parliament. But the word "sovereignty" is sometimes employed in a political rather than in a strictly legal sense. That body is "politically" sovereign or supreme in a state the will of which is ultimately obeyed by the citizens of the state. In this sense of the word the electors of Great Britain may be said to be . . . the body in which sovereign power is vested. . . . But this is a political, not a legal fact. . . . The judges know nothing about any will of the people except in so far as that will is expressed by an Act of Parliament, and would never suffer the validity of a statute to be questioned on the ground of its having been passed or being kept alive in opposition to the wishes of the electors.

⤖ Discussion ⤖

Austin Is the Seminal Figure in English Positivism

John Austin practised briefly as a lawyer and lectured in jurisprudence. The book for which he is principally remembered, *The Province of Jurisprudence Determined*, is widely regarded as the seminal work in legal positivism. Although many of the elements of positivism can be found in the work of Jeremy Bentham, and even earlier, in the work of Thomas Hobbes, it is Austin who sets out the theory in a clear, comprehensive manner.

Austin described legal positivism as "analytical jurisprudence," a term that is still commonly used in a legal context. In a broader philosophical context, however, Austin's theory is better known as "legal positivism," a nomenclature that draws our attention to the human role in the production and recognition of the law. The laws recognized by the courts, like the laws recognized by the sciences, are made. They are rationally constructed and open to change and revision. The primary significance of these ideas, from a legal perspective, is that they place the authorship of the law in the hands of the legislature and the state.

Legal positivism became part of the legal dogma accepted by the English courts in the nineteenth and twentieth centuries. Judges accepted that it is the responsibility of the political branch of government and the legislature in particular to make the law. The English law holds that judges do not make law. The task of the judiciary is merely to interpret the law, in accordance with the intentions of Parliament.

This view naturally runs into difficulties in situations where the law does not exist in the form of legislation, either because it is a product of the older common law or because it consists of rules or principles invented by the courts. Every court has "Rules of Court" that set deadlines for the filing of pleadings, require the disclosure documents, and deal with issues like costs. These rules are problematic, under legal positivism, since they have the compulsory character of law but do not derive from a political source.

Legal positivism in other common law countries is moderated by the differences in their systems of government. The courts in Canada and the United States, for example, have subscribed to a less rigorous form of legal positivism. This difference in judicial attitudes probably reflects the fact that Canada and the United States, unlike England, have written constitutions that maintain the historical supremacy of the law. It is the constitution that is supreme in Canada and the United States, and, since the powers of the legislature are legally limited, it is the courts rather than the legislature that has supervision of the system.

The general rule in the modern common law is nevertheless that judges do not make law. This kind of statement is easily misunderstood, since the common law has never given judges the authority to make law. Like the tribal law and the customary law before it, the common law is found, not made, and is a product of custom and practice rather than a legislative act. The proverbial statement that the common law is judge-made law, in the sense that it was invented by the judiciary, is a blatant misconception, which serves the idea in Bentham and the early legal positivists that, indeed, the law is made. The early legal positivists take this position further, theoretically, and assert that the law is made exclusively by the legislature.

Austin's Definition of Law Is Political

The conception of law in legal positivism is quintessentially political. Austin and other early legal positivists tried to restrict the term "law" (which in this context refers to orders or directions enforced by the courts) to those orders or directions that can be traced to a valid political source. For Austin, this source is found in the sovereign power of the state, which comes into existence through the political contract. This is complicated by a division of powers in England: although the sovereign power is held by the King or Queen, he or she exercises it legislatively only in accordance with the wishes of Parliament. The statute law in England is accordingly written by Parliament, but does not become law until it is issued by the King or Queen.

Austin has this arrangement in mind when he writes that a law "may be said to be a rule laid down for the guidance of an intelligent being by an intelligent being having power over him." Austin's definition has at least two significant components. First, Austin speaks of "rules," a concept that has become a central feature of modern legal positivism. Second, he speaks of "an intelligent being" having power over another intelligent being. This bare statement is descriptive rather than normative—it bases the authority of the law on the mere existence of the sovereign power, regardless of its moral character.

Austin's reference to "intelligent" beings indicates that a law must meet certain rational standards. This goes beyond the intelligibility of the law and includes a requirement, for example, that the positive law be proclaimed, since it is not possible to guide the conduct of "an intelligent being" without informing that being, in a meaningful way, of how he should act. This requirement remains descriptive, however, and does not place substantive limits on the positive law.

Among legal theories, legal positivism is usually seen as a rival to natural law theory. As we have seen, Aquinas and other natural law theorists argue that law is directed to "the common good" and that a law is valid only if it satisfies the fundamental requirements of justice. For Aquinas, this concept of justice is normative and limits the substantive content of the positive law. Austin's concerns are far more functional. Legal positivism rests the validity of the positive law on whether it meets a variety of descriptive standards, such as whether it is logically coherent and comprehensible rather than whether it is rationally connected to some public good. "The existence of law is one thing," Austin writes, "its merit or demerit is another."

Austin is a realist in political theory, and one of his major arguments in *The Province of Jurisprudence Determined* is simply that legal positivism captures the reality of the legal system more accurately than does the theory of the natural law.

> Now, to say that human laws which conflict with the Divine law are not binding, that is to say, are not laws, is to talk stark nonsense. The most pernicious laws, and therefore those which are most opposed to the will of God, have been and are continually enforced as laws by judicial tribunals.[1]

This aspect of legal positivism recalls the position adopted by many of the sophists in ancient Greece, who argued that law and justice are what those in a position of power over us have deemed it to be.[2]

Austin Distinguishes between Morality, Law, and Convention

Austin does not question the existence of a natural law or the idea that such a law derives from God. His objection to natural law theory is rather that we have no reliable way of ascertaining the natural law and cannot resolve the differences of opinion that arise with regard to it. It is therefore made up of moral rather than legal injunctions and cannot be considered law in the strict sense of the word.

Austin restricts the use of the word "law" in a legal context to the positive law. The popular use of the term is misleading, he suggests, because it fails to distinguish between positive law and positive morality. Positive law is composed of laws "established by *political* superiors" exercising the powers of government. It is the fact that these laws emanate from a political source—and ultimately from the sovereign, who has the power to enforce them—that makes them laws. Positive morality is composed of conventions, social rules that are "set and enforced by mere opinion." These rules include a wide variety of social customs, such as "the laws of etiquette" or "the law set by fashion."

The Ruler's Exercise of the Sovereign Power Is Governed by Convention

One of the major conceptual problems with legal positivism is that it frees the persons who hold the sovereign power from legal constraints. Since the positive law is the command of the King and Parliament, which together constitute the ruler, the King and Parliament exist above the law. By definition, the King cannot act illegally and is accordingly immune from legal actions. As we have seen, this is a departure from Henry of Bracton and Edward Coke, both of whom held that the King was subject to the law. The view in the early common law had wasted away by the time of Blackstone, in the face of the increasing authority of Parliament, and was eventually superseded by the doctrine of parliamentary supremacy. This doctrine finds its philosophical vindication in legal positivism.

The theoretical solution to the problem that the sovereign power is legally unregulated can be found in the development of the common law. Although the King and Parliament exist above the law, in some purely political realm, they are still subject to convention. The Austinian rationale behind such an idea is that conventions are made up of tenets that form part of a positive morality, which the sovereign accepts as fundamentally binding. Since the sovereign accepts this positive morality, there is no need to order the sovereign to follow it.[3]

This conception of positive morality provides a convenient explanation of the common law position that many of the rules that form part of the constitution exist only as conventions. One example is the requirement that the Prime Minister must have the support of a majority of the members of Parliament. Another is the requirement that the Governor General must accept the Prime Minister's advice in the appointment of ministers. These conventions are followed because they represent the way in which the relevant political actors have customarily and habitually acted. They create constitutional norms rather than laws, and there is no law that requires the relevant actors to follow them.

There are many other conventions in the English legal tradition. In his *Study of the Law of the Constitution*, Albert Venn Dicey refers to the rule that a statute does not become law until the King has consented to it. This reflects Austin's idea that a law is a command of the sovereign and must therefore be issued from the King. Dicey writes that this rule has given rise to the convention that the King will consent to any bill of legislation passed by both Houses of Parliament.[4] This convention is a political rule—if the King refuses to consent to a bill, the courts cannot order him to do so, since the sovereign is above the law.

There are similar practices in other common law countries. The same rule has been constitutionally entrenched in article 1, section 7 of the Constitution of the United States, which stipulates that a bill passed by Congress must be signed by the President. It accordingly does not become law until the President has consented to it. The Constitution of the United States nevertheless replaces the political convention with a law that can be enforced by the courts.

The Canadian Constitution Includes Conventions

The Supreme Court of Canada recognized the role played by political conventions in the Canadian constitution in the *Patriation Reference*, [1981] 1 S.C.R. 753.[5] In the majority decision, the court states that constitutional conventions are "rules," rather than laws, that maintain the constitutional order in accordance with the views that prevail in society. The court then quotes Canada's most noted constitutional scholar, Peter Hogg, who writes that a "convention is a rule which is regarded as obligatory *by the officials to whom it applies*."[6] As a result, the court writes, "the conventional rules of the Constitution present one striking peculiarity. In contradistinction to the laws of the Constitution, they are not enforced by the courts."

From the perspective of legal theory, the unenforceability of these political conventions means that there is no real recourse when the person who holds the sovereign power chooses not to follow them. This issue arose in 2008, when Canada's Governor General prorogued Parliament at the request of Prime Minister Stephen Harper, in spite of the fact that he had clearly lost the confidence of Parliament, without giving the leader of the opposition the opportunity to form a majority government.[7] Austin's position makes it difficult to deal with this kind of issue, since the political realm is ascendant and exists outside the rule of law.[8]

The International Law Is Convention

Convention also plays a role in the international arena. Austin's restriction of the term "law" to positive law means that the law cannot exist without a ruler and a government. This requires a political contract and a sovereign power, which do not exist in the international realm. It follows that the only source of positive law lies in the centralization of authority in the state, which gives rise to the ruler's legislative power. The state, however, like the ruler, exists above this source of law. One of the chief criticisms of legal positivism is that these problems do not arise in earlier legal theories, which trace the law to custom or some set of religious or cosmological views that do not rely on the existence of government.

Legal positivism nevertheless fits well with the Grotian concept of the international law, which holds that states exist in the state of nature and are subject only to the natural law. Since Austin dispenses with the natural law, his theory moves nation-states into a realm beyond the reach of even the vestiges of law. This does not mean that the international realm is entirely unregulated. It is rather that it is regulated by the sovereign will of individual states, acting in accordance with their own interests, and by politics instead of law. The rules of conduct in the international arena are accordingly based on the existence of established norms, which reflect the way that states customarily and habitually act in the international realm. As a result, the so-called international law is convention and has not, historically, been enforced by the courts unless it is adopted and ratified by the state.

Law Is a Command from a Political Superior

Austin's concept of law is based on the existence of a person or body that has the power to demand obedience from the rest of society. Austin states that positive law exists when

1. The *bulk* of the given society are in a *habit* of obedience or submission to a *determinate* and *common* superior, [and]
2. That certain individual, or that certain body of individuals, is *not* in the habit of obedience to a determinate human superior.

Every law or rule, Austin writes, can be construed as the command of this political superior. Laws are "a species of command."

Austin's concept of a "command" is predicated on the idea that a person who disobeys a command will be punished. This is problematic because it suggests that laws cannot confer rewards. If Austin's concept of a command is accurate, how can we explain those laws that permit us to apply for a driver's licence, for example, or obtain employment insurance? There are also laws—which H.L.A. Hart draws to our attention, and which Immanuel Kant contemplates—that allow us to determine the legal relations that we enjoy with other people. The statutes that regulate wills and contracts, for example, are permissive: they enable us to govern our personal affairs in a manner that will be enforced by the courts, but they do not prescribe a course of action, and they do not take the form of a command.

Austin's idea of a "command" nevertheless brings his concept of law into line with Kant's concept, since it is the fact that a command gives rise to a duty that creates legal obligations. It is equally clear that the idea of a command fits implicitly into Kant's theory of law. Like Austin, Kant traces "juridical" or legal obligations to the compulsory nature of the law, which is a product of the coercive powers of the state. This element of coercion seems to be an essential positive claim. The greater the punishment and "the greater the chance of incurring it," Austin writes, the greater the legal obligation.

Austin's Legal Theory Has Difficulty Explaining the Customary Law

Austin acknowledges that his theory has difficulty explaining the customary law. This is troubling because the common law comes from the customary law. The courts still rely on customs in specific cases: a court may consult the practices in a particular trade, for example, in determining whether a contract has been breached. This reliance on custom goes against Austin's theory, since these practices derive from the people who have followed them rather than from the command of a sovereign.

The larger problem lies in Austin's argument that the law derives exclusively from political sources. This position leaves no role for the judiciary in deciding what rules and principles make up the law. In order to maintain his thesis, Austin is forced to fall back on the argument that Parliament has given the judiciary the authority to act as its agent in such circumstances. This argument inverts the history of the law, which existed long before central government, and has no historical basis. The best that can be said is that the common law has given the legislature the authority to overrule the decisions of the judiciary.

Austin's Legal Theory Does Not Explain the Writs against the Crown

Austin's theory also runs into difficulty explaining the constitutional aspects of the common law. If the law is the command of the sovereign, how is it that the courts can issue prerogative writs (sometimes called "extraordinary writs") like *habeas corpus* ("have the body") and *quo warranto* ("on what authority") against the Crown? Although the prerogative writs were originally used to move cases into the King's courts, they became significant because they were used to provide redress against the actions of public officials. The writ of *habeas corpus*, for example, gave a judge in the superior courts the authority to command the sheriff to deliver the "body" of a prisoner to the court, so that the judge could determine if the prisoner was lawfully imprisoned.

The logic of *habeas corpus* goes against Austin's theory. The sheriff was a royal official who represented the King in his corporate capacity, as the head of state. The judge who issued a writ was accordingly issuing it against the Crown and the state, and against the exercise of the King's authority. Although Blackstone was willing to resort to virtually any stratagem to maintain the ascendancy of the King, it is difficult to argue that the judge was acting on the command of the Crown and the state in ordering it to comply with the order. This is particularly clear in those cases where the sheriff was ordered to release the prisoner. The obvious explanation for the operation of the writs is that the courts have independent sources of authority, outside the political sources of the positive law, which give them the authority to countermand the King's command.

The writ of *quo warranto* was used, in a similar fashion, to determine if the actions of an administrative or political official were within the scope of his legal authority. Although Justice Martland suggests, in the *Patriation Reference*, that a writ of *quo warranto* may not lie against a minister of the Crown, the prerogative writs demonstrate that political authority must be exercised in accordance with the law. In the case of *habeas corpus*, for example, the prisoner must be released if the imprisonment was carried out unlawfully, even if the prisoner's detention serves the public interest. Logically, this suggests that the legal restrictions on the power of the Crown are paramount and pre-exist any exercise of the Crown's political authority.

Laws Are General Commands

Although Austin writes that laws are "a species of command," not all commands are laws. Commands can be general or particular, but laws are inherently general. Austin's example is the export of grain: a general prohibition against the export of grain would be a law, but a temporary order to stop the export of grain to meet a specific scarcity would not be a law. This distinction is nevertheless difficult to sustain in practice.

The House of Commons occasionally passes laws that deal with specific matters. One of the more common examples is "back-to-work" legislation, which orders striking workers—such as longshoremen or grain handlers—to return to their jobs. Still, an Austinian might argue that back-to-work legislation is only a specific application of some more general injunction or command, since the passage of such legislation is based on the idea that the same legislation would be appropriate and necessary in similar situations.

There is some support for Austin's position in the common principle that statutes should be given a general application. This clearly prevents the law from being applied in an arbitrary or capricious manner and introduces a normative element into his descriptive argument. The general stipulation prevents a tyrant from claiming that his personal whims—directed against particular people and their particular actions—have the authority of laws.

This kind of restriction is related to "the rule of law," a constitutional principle that guarantees that the law will be applied equally, in accordance with recognized legal rules and principles. The real difficulty in the application of Austin's restriction on the sovereign, however, is that it is only effective if the courts have the authority to determine whether the sovereign's commands constitute valid laws. In spite of Austin's argument that a law's validity depends upon its political provenance rather than its moral character, a law that is inherently unequal is apparently invalid.

Austin Fails to Acknowledge that General Laws May Be Used to Target Specific Groups

Austin's restriction of the law to general commands is also problematic because it fails to capture the way in which general laws may be used to target specific individuals or groups. This kind of unfairness often takes place at the administrative level. For example, if a municipal council is upset that members of the Communist Party are selling their newspaper on street corners, it might pass a bylaw prohibiting the sale of pamphlets and other literature without a licence. The new law would meet Austin's criterion, since it is a general rule that, on the face of it, applies equally to everyone. But of course the motive of the councillors would be to prevent the specific acts of a specific group of people.

A similar situation arose in *Roncarelli v. Duplessis*, [1959] S.C.R. 121, where the municipal authorities had charged Jehovah's Witnesses who were selling *The Watch Tower* and *Awake* on the street corners of Montreal. It was evident that the authorities had used the bylaw prohibiting the sale of such goods without a licence for the purpose of targeting the Witnesses. This situation ultimately led the province to revoke the liquor licence of a restaurant owner, Roncarelli, who had paid the bail for 375 Witnesses who had been charged under the bylaw.

The Supreme Court found against the province. Justice Rand held, for the majority, that "action dictated by and according to the arbitrary likes, dislikes and irrelevant purposes of public officers" undermines the rule of law, which constitutes an essential part of "our constitutional structure."[9] The case illustrates that Austin's definition of the law as a general command is too simple, since a general law can be applied selectively. In order to catch these issues, it is necessary to move from a formal analysis of the law to the exercise of discretion that lies underneath it.

It Is Compulsion that Provides the Reason to Obey the Law

There is a practical reason that morality is a significant part of the customary law, since a legal system cannot function successfully unless individuals have a reason to obey the law. When a legal system is based on a prevailing moral code, the resulting sense of shared morality naturally provides people with a motivation to obey the law. The converse is also true, however. When a legal system is based on the freedom of the individual to hold divergent moral beliefs, there must be another means of providing individuals with the impetus to obey the law.

Austin's positivism meets this need by postulating that the legal system is based on coercion. The primary reason that we have for obeying the law in early legal positivism is that we will be punished if we disobey. As Austin writes, the binding force of the law derives from the physical "superiority" of those in political power.

[T]he term *superiority* signifies *might*: the power of affecting others with evil or pain, and of forcing them, through fear of that evil, to fashion their conduct to one's wishes. . . . For superiority is the power of enforcing compliance with a wish.

There is no hiding the fact that the primary component of this conception of law is the use of force.[10]

One of the advantages of Austin's theory is that it gives people with conflicting moral views an incentive to follow the law. The need for such an incentive is one of the chief difficulties facing a legal system in a modern, pluralistic state, which lacks the moral consensus that we find in earlier societies. The logical way out of such a difficulty is to separate morality from law and base our duty to obey the law on some other form of obligation. This separation is often called "the separation thesis," and it is an important step in philosophy of law. This thesis is nevertheless more convincing when the separation is expressed in looser terms, since there are many situations in which the moral consensus in society is sufficient to provide individuals with the necessary motivation to follow certain laws. Most criminal offences, for example, are widely regarded as wrong.

The starkness of Austin's legal positivism is a product of a highly self-conscious, rigorous logical approach to the problems that arise in legal theory. This approach comes from the Kantian and analytic traditions.[11] There is plenty of room, however, for a mitigated legal positivism, which maintains the fundamental separation between law and morality, but also holds that the immorality of a law may undermine its legality in egregious cases.

The real problem with Austin's theory is that it does not contain a viable mechanism for dealing with such an issue. If the only test of the validity of the positive law is whether the state has the power to compel our obedience, it is clear that the courts are obliged to enforce the laws of a government like the Third Reich. The only alternative available to an individual who faces an unjust law is accordingly to disobey it. The fact that such governments are extremely coercive, moreover, seems only to augment the validity of their laws, since it increases our obligation to obey the law.

Section 15 of the *Criminal Code*

The Austinian idea that the mere exercise of power is sufficient to create binding law finds some support in the criminal law. The defence in section 15 of the *Criminal Code of Canada* could easily be called the legal positivist defence, since it is premised on the assertion that the binding nature of the law does not depend upon its morality. The section codifies the common law principle that individuals cannot be convicted of an offence for their obedience to the law "made by persons in *de facto* possession of the sovereign power." The use of the term *"de facto"* ("in fact") indicates that the mere possession of political authority, even illegitimately or unlawfully, is sufficient to create a valid legal obligation. As a result, an accused who obeys an unjust law has obeyed a valid law and cannot be charged with a breach of the law.

The place of section 15 in the common law has been questioned over time, and the *Criminal Code* now contains a number of exceptions to the section. The defence afforded by the principle of *de facto* law does not extend to the offences of torture, war crimes, or crimes against humanity. The application of these exceptions is more in keeping with the natural law theory and suggests that egregiously immoral laws have no legal force.

Green Provides a Communitarian Account in Response to Austin's Legal Positivism

Thomas Hill Green is now a neglected figure in philosophy of law and is generally seen as a political rather than a legal theorist.[12] His *Lectures on the Principles of Political Obligation* was nevertheless a celebrated work in its time, and it probably provided the most significant response to Austin.

Although Green is mostly remembered as a British idealist who believed in an all-comprehending consciousness, this belief gave rise to a strong communitarian element in his work. His theory of law is based on the fundamental primacy of the community, in spite of its emphasis on the role of individual rights.[13] Indeed, the broader significance of Green's work in legal, social, and political theory seems to lie in his reconciliation of a liberal and communitarian perspective. His belief in individual rights is reflected in his progressive political views: he advocated that the vote, for example, should be extended to those who did not own real property, well in advance of the major political figures of his time.

Green did not reject Austin's position entirely, and he accepts many of the aspects of the theory that deal with the role of the legislature. The major difference between Green and Austin lies in their conception of "the people." Austin traces the sovereign power to the ruler, who the people habitually obey; Green, under the influence of Jean-Jacques Rousseau, traces it to the people themselves.[14] Green relies heavily on the work of Henry Sumner Maine (1822–1888), a famous legal historian, in defending his position. Maine dismissed Austin and his school as "analytical jurists" and championed the historical approach.

Early legal positivism was a product of the "Enlightenment," a period in which many thinkers rejected the established tradition in favour of reason and scientific enquiry. The thought that the law could be "made" through scientific investigation, reflection, and the conscious development of policy was a relatively new and exciting idea. These historical influences led Austin and Bentham, for example, to question the authority of the past, which played such a significant role in the common law tradition. They also led to a new trend in legal theory, which takes legal theory into a more academic enterprise, well outside the precincts of legal practice.[15]

Green's legal theory also reflects the influence of the Enlightenment. Unlike Austin and Bentham, however, Green is an idealist. This idealism leads him into a kind of social ontology, premised on the existence of the community. He accordingly argues that the sources of law lie in the existence of the community rather than the individual. The political contract is therefore less important than the customs of the people in the provenance of the law. In spite of the many technical issues that Green's idealism raises, his ontological position resembles the position advanced by many feminists, since he suggests that it is the presence of society that gives rise to the existence of the individual. It follows that society, customs, and the law pre-exist the individual in some sense and have sources outside the political contract.

Green was not a historical jurist. It was rather that he found evidence that substantiated his theory, which held that the law is an expression of the consciousness of the community, in the work of the historical school. He accordingly takes the side of the historical school in arguing that the law has its origins in custom.

There Is a Methodological Side to the Dispute between Green and Austin

The influence of early legal positivism on legal practice is still apparent in the methodology of the common law. Rather than adopt Green's position, which aligns itself with the earlier legal tradition, the modern common law has adopted the views set out and promoted by the positivists. The general approach by the judiciary to the interpretation of the law is premised on the replacement of the customary sources of the law with political sources. These sources lie in the institutional machinery of government and the legislative process, which determine what the ruler commands. It follows that the judiciary is obliged to consult the will of Parliament in resolving any issues that arise in applying the law. This changes the role of the judiciary, which was originally to enquire into custom, practice, and belief in search of the applicable law. The new role is merely to apply and interpret the law in accordance with the intentions of the legislature.

The positivist view of the judicial role has entrenched itself in the orthodoxy of the common law. The changes that this view contemplates have never completely taken hold, however, since large areas of the common law are still governed by the caselaw. As a result, the law in these areas has evolved on a case-by-case basis, in accordance with the traditional common law approach. In spite of this, legal positivism has been remarkably successful—outside the constitutional law, at least—in suggesting that the mere exercise of logic and deductive reason is sufficient to determine the law. The formal and rather technical approach that this view has engendered usually leaves the substantive issues in the law to the legislature or the precedents. These methodological developments were clearly buttressed by historical trends, which included the introduction of popular democracy and increased the authority of the legislature.

Green's Communitarian Account Raises Three Pivotal Questions

Green's account draws our attention to three questions that arise in the context of early legal positivism. First, *if law is the command of the sovereign, who is the sovereign?* Second, and most troubling, *who rules the ruler?* Third, *what rights does the individual have against the ruler?* A convincing account of legal positivism must provide a satisfactory answer to all three questions.

Who Is the Sovereign?

Green believes that sovereignty ultimately lies in the people rather than the King or Parliament. His position accordingly raises the question: who, on the legal positivist account, is the sovereign? Modern democracies are multifarious and complex, and political power does not exist in a single office or person. It is accordingly not clear that the sovereign power can be confined to a single official or institution, whether it is the Queen, the Prime Minister, or Parliament as a whole.

On the positivist account, the sovereign appears to be the person who holds the sovereign power and exercises the authority of the state. The general political literature often speaks of the executive, legislative, and judicial branches of government. This characterization implicitly suggests that all three branches share the sovereign power. From a technical perspective, this seems to rob Austin's theory of the simplicity that makes it so attractive, at least in a constitutional system based on the division of powers, and raises concerns about the transparency of the law.

Who Rules the Ruler?

Green phrases the second question more directly: *If law is the command of the sovereign, who exists above the law, who rules the ruler?*[16] If it is the legislature rather than the King that is sovereign, the most obvious problem with Austin's theory is that the members of the legislature may or may not share the beliefs, customs, and aspirations of the people. What is there in legal positivism, then, to correct the legislature if it fails to act in accordance with the wishes of the people?

The obvious answer to such a question in a democratic system is that the electorate may defeat the governing party in the legislature in the next election. The political process at least theoretically gives the people an opportunity to remove a party of a politician who does not respect the beliefs, values, and customs of society as a whole. The net result of the shift to a political conception of law in legal positivism is nevertheless the creation of a sovereignty of political institutions, which often act in their own interest rather than in the interest of the people as a whole.

The most troubling issue in legal positivism is its implicit authoritarianism. This is a direct consequence of the supremacy of political authority. Austin's legal positivism is not restricted to democratic governments, and his theory makes it abundantly clear that a tyrant's command gives rise to valid legal obligations. The consequences of such a statement may be open to debate, but the positivist position gives those who exercise raw political power enormous licence. The most striking feature of Austin and Bentham's theory is that it places very few checks on the exercise of political power.

These new ideas were momentous. From a grand historical perspective, it could even be said that the ascendancy of political authority in legal positivism—and the idea that law is merely the command of the sovereign—is a wrenching development in legal theory. This is because—in one bold theoretical stroke—it frees the political order from legal constraints. The legal response to such a move lies primarily in the development of a separate body of constitutional law, which limits the actions of government. This is not a part of Austin's theory, however, which raises the political order unequivocally above the legal order.

This kind of criticism comes with a necessary qualification. It is not that legal positivism has no answer to the problem of the tyrant's command but that its answer lies in the political realm. The electoral and political process provides some form of accountability, but this does not ease the tyranny of majorities, and democratic governments have often oppressed moral and cultural minorities or acted in defiance of the popular will. It may be salutary to remember that Adolf Hitler came to power through the electoral process.

What Rights Does the Individual Have against the Ruler?

The third question—*What rights does the individual have against the ruler?*—arises out of Austin's failure to guarantee the independence of the legal order, which is completely subordinated to the political order. If the government—in its myriad of functions—wrongs an individual person, what is the remedy? The law and the legal system cannot logically be used against the sovereign, unless it has other sources of authority. In fairness to Austin, this is a long-standing issue in the common law, which originally arose out of the idea that the common law is the law of the King and therefore cannot be used against him. As we have seen, William Blackstone argued that the English King cannot wrong his subjects, though he left some room for discretionary remedies, particularly against the King's officials. The common law has historically awarded the Crown a prerogative that rendered it immune from lawsuits. This immunity has eroded over time, but is still a feature of the common law, particularly in jurisdictions like England, where there is no written constitution.

Green criticizes this aspect of Austin's theory and argues vigorously for a concept of individual rights. Although this has all the appearances of a constitutional law, which guarantees the rights of the person, the derivation of these rights lies in society. From Green's perspective, it is the legal tradition as a whole—as the embodiment of custom— that contains the general will and keeps the exercise of political power under popular control. Green's conception of law is interesting because it protects the interests of both individuals and society from the arbitrary exercise of the sovereign power. This protection includes the provision of individual rights, which include substantive guarantees. Austin does not address these issues.

Green's Concept of the Common Good May Also Serve as a Legal Standard

Although Green is aware of the historical role of the law in placing moral and policy limits on the exercise of political power, his own theory remains pre-eminently political. Indeed, Green's theory seems to converge with legal positivism in those cases where those in political authority respect the common good. There is an important issue, however, that arises when those who hold the sovereign power do not respect the common good. That issue is whether Green's concept of the common good—which is fundamentally political— holds enough substantive content to provide a legal standard that might be applied by the courts. This would place at least some limits on the sovereign and the legislature and require that the positive law be interpreted in accordance with the public interest.

There are some references in the constitutional law that would support an affirmative answer to such a question. Section 91 of Canada's *British North America Act, 1867*, for example, seems to place legal constraints on the Crown:

> 91. It shall be lawful for the Queen, by and with the Advice and Consent of the Senate and House of Commons, to make laws for the Peace, Order, and good Government of Canada.

This is naturally a provision from a written constitution. It nevertheless suggests that the rule of law and the legal order guarantee the common good.

Dicey's Doctrine of Absolute Sovereignty Can Be Seen as the Legal Arm of Positivism

Albert Venn Dicey was an influential professor of law at Oxford University. The primary significance of his *Introduction to the Study of the Law of the Constitution* in the context of the current chapter is that it demonstrates how the theoretical elements in early legal positivism made their way into general legal thinking.[17] The doctrine of absolute sovereignty in Dicey's work can be seen as the legal expression of legal positivism. Although Austin's theory naturally reflects his knowledge of the English common law, his approach is ahistorical and reflects political realities rather than the history of the law.

There is nevertheless a real connection between early legal positivism and one aspect of the historical English tradition. This connection is political rather than legal and lies in the idea that the authority of the King of England (and therefore the central government) was absolute. This feature of the political system did not disappear with the advent of democracy and was merely transferred—practically and theoretically—to the Houses of Parliament. Like the legal positivists, Dicey models his argument on the idea that the sovereign is absolute. It is true that he tries to alleviate the effects this creates by insisting on the independence of the English courts; but in spite of this, his discussion of the English constitution reads like an intellectual capitulation that simply subordinates the legal order to the political order.

Dicey does not even acknowledge the possibility that the legal order might have ascendancy. In Chapter IV of his *Introduction to the Study of the Law of the Constitution*, for example, he states that two features have characterized the political institutions of England since the Norman Conquest. One is "the omnipotence or undisputed supremacy throughout the whole country of the central government." This characterization is really a historical error, since the significance of the *Magna Carta*, to cite the most obvious example, lies precisely in the fact that it disputed the supremacy of the central government.

Dicey's account of the common law is tendentious and reflects some of the same intellectual forces that led theorists like Bentham and Austin to reject the earlier tradition.

There were other innovations, like the use of juries in criminal trials, which provide clear evidence that the people rejected the authority of the central government. The survival of the legal maxim that a man's home is his castle placed legal limits on the powers of the King and his officials, and it harkened back to a time without central government. Dicey fails to recognize that the early common law was both a product of local customs and a check on the authority of the King.

The second feature that has characterized the political institutions of England, in Dicey's estimation, is the rule of law. This might seem to place significant constraints on the exercise of political power. Dicey's idea of the rule of law is a procedural doctrine rather than a substantive doctrine, however, and places no obvious restraints on the law-making function of Parliament. This narrow version of the doctrine holds, for example, that no one is above the law. These are procedural restrictions, however, which require only that the law be applied equally. They do not place constraints on the content of the law.

The problem, again, is that Dicey's view is more polemical than he acknowledges and runs against the idea of the natural law that surfaces in cases like *London v. Wood*. Dicey's formulation of the rule of law nevertheless entered into the English common law, and the Canadian law as well, where it remained until the passage of the *Canadian Charter of Rights and Freedoms*. There was a vigorous debate in the United States as to the nature of the due process clause in the American constitution, which was ultimately resolved in favour of a substantive notion of due process.

Notes

1. John Austin, *The Province of Jurisprudence Determined*, as cited in the suggestions for further reading, at p. 158.
2. This is the topic of the famous argument between Thrasymachus and Socrates in Book I of Plato's *Republic*.
3. See Roger Cotterrell, for example, in *The Politics of Jurisprudence* (Philadelphia: University of Pennsylvania, 1992), at p. 74, where he writes: "Austin asserted that much of constitutional "law" must, in fact, be merely positive morality for this reason."
4. Dicey states that the King "cannot" veto a bill that has been properly passed, but this phrases the convention as a law, which must be obeyed. The idea in the common law is rather that he always chooses to consent.
5. See *Resolution to Amend the Constitution of Canada*, [1981] 1 S.C.R. 753.
6. Peter W. Hogg, *Constitutional Law of Canada* (Toronto: Carswell, 1977), p. 9.
7. See Andrew Heard, for example, "The Governor General's Suspension of Parliament: Duty Done or a Perilous Precedent," in Peter H. Russell and Lorne Sossin, eds., *Parliamentary Democracy in Crisis* (Toronto: University of Toronto, 2009), pp. 47–62.
8. At p. 783, the majority quotes C.R. Munro, "Laws and Conventions Distinguished," *Law Quarterly Review* 91 (1975), at p. 228: "The validity of conventions cannot be the subject of proceedings in a court of law. Reparation for breach of such rules will not be effected by any legal sanction. There are no cases which contradict these propositions. In fact, the idea of a court enforcing a mere convention is so strange that the question hardly arises."
9. It is interesting that the provincial government had argued that Roncarelli's actions had essentially frustrated the bylaw and rendered it ineffective. He was therefore interfering with the rule of law and was deemed to be morally unfit to hold a liquor licence.

10. This has led some commentators to argue that there is a strong strain of realism in Austin's work. See Timothy Binkely, for example, "The Consistency of Positivist and Realist Views of Law," *Personalist* 51 (January 1970): 85–98. And see Roger Cotterrell's discussion of Austin's theory of law in *The Politics of Jurisprudence*, op. cit., at p. 74, where he states: "Austin's theory is not a theory of the Rule of Law: of government subject to law. It is a theory of the 'rule of men': of government using law as an instrument of power. Such a view may be considered realistic or merely cynical. But it is, in its broad outlines, essentially coherent."

11. See the comment by Dan Priel, in "Jurisprudence between Science and the Humanities," Warwick School of Law Research Paper No. 2010/07 (8 March 2010), at p. 18, where he says that we see in Austin's work "the birth of what has come to be known as 'analytic jurisprudence', the analysis of fundamental legal concepts." Available at http://ssrn.com.

12. There is a certain irony in this, since the ultimate effect of legal positivism was to subordinate the legal analysis to politics. For a general discussion of Green's work, see Colin Tyler, "Some of the Recent Scholarship on Thomas Hill Green," *European Journal of Political Theory* 5, no. 13 (2006): 213–21; David O. Brink, *Perfectionism and the Common Good: Themes in the Philosophy of T.H. Green* (Oxford: Clarendon, 2003); Denys P. Leighton, *The Greenian Moment: T.H. Green, Religion and Political Argument in Victorian Britain* (Exeter: Imprint Academic, 2004); and Ben Wempe, *T.H. Green's Theory of Positive Freedom: From Metaphysics to Political Theory* (Exeter: Imprint Academic, 2004). For a brief historical account of Green's influence, see Melvin Richter, "T.H. Green and His Audience: Liberalism as a Surrogate Faith," *The Review of Politics* 18, no. 4 (October 1956): 444–72.

13. See Avital Simhony, "Rights that Bind: T.H. Green on Rights and Community," in Maria Dimova-Cookson and William J. Mander, eds., *T.H. Green: Ethics, Metaphysics, and Political Philosophy* (Oxford: Clarendon, 2006), pp. 236–62.

14. Dicey makes a similar point in a more institutional context and suggests that the two are the same thing in a democracy. As a result, he sees Parliament as sovereign in place of the King.

15. One of the interesting developments in this regard is the emergence of the idea that it might be possible to construct a general theory of law, which explains the general features and deeper structure of any legal system. This provided the impetus for the development of the abstract models of law that we find in later positivists like Hans Kelsen and H.L.A. Hart. See Mauro Barberis, "Universal Legal Concepts? A Criticism of 'General' Legal Theory," *Ratio Juris* 9, no. 1 (March 1996): 1–14.

16. From a theoretical perspective, legal positivism is inherently more authoritarian than the natural law tradition, which historically placed legal and moral limits on the sovereign.

17. Green and Dicey have both been seen as prominent liberal thinkers. For a discussion of their differing views, see Martin Loughlin, "The Functionalist Style in Public Law," *University of Toronto Law Journal* 55, no. 3 (Summer 2005): 361–403.

Study Questions

1. What is the source of our legal obligations in early legal positivism? What is it exactly that makes a direction or orders a law on Austin's formulation?

2. What is the source of our legal obligations in Green's theory of law? What is it that makes a direction or orders a law on Green's formulation?

3. Why does legal positivism often seem to fit modern societies better than the natural law, from a moral perspective? What has changed since the Middle Ages?

4. Suppose the public rejects the laws that make the possession of marijuana an offence. Does it matter in Austin's theory? What is the public's recourse?

5. Who rules the ruler in Austin's theory of law? Is there a satisfactory answer to this question?

6. Why is Green's view of the law "communitarian"? How does his use of Rousseau's idea of the general will match up with the view in the customary law?

7. Why does Green's discussion of the "common good" recall Aquinas' theory of law? How does Green's theory fit into the tradition of the natural law?

8. Dicey's theory of Parliamentary sovereignty seems exaggerated. After all, how far can the doctrine of Parliamentary sovereignty be extended? Does Parliament or the legislature have the power to remove the offence of theft or murder from the criminal law?

Further Reading

John Austin, *Lectures on Jurisprudence*, 5th ed. (London: John Murray, [1863] 1885).

———, *The Province of Jurisprudence Determined*, ed. W.E. Rumble (Cambridge: Cambridge University, 1995).

Kenneth R. Hoover, "Liberalism and the Idealist Philosophy of Thomas Hill Green," *The Western Political Quarterly* 26, no. 3 (September 1973): 550–65.

John Stuart Mill, "Austin on Jurisprudence," in *Dissertations and Discussions*, vol. 4 (New York: Henry Holt, 1874).

W.L. Morison, *John Austin* (Stanford, CA: Stanford University, 1982).

Resolution to Amend the Constitution of Canada, [1981] 1 S.C.R. 753. Available at www.canlii.org.

H.W.R. Wade, "The Basis of Legal Sovereignty," *Cambridge Law Journal* 13 (1955): 172–97.

7 Modern Scientism: Formalism, Legal Skepticism, and Pragmatism

Christopher Columbus Langdell, Oliver Wendell Holmes, and Roscoe Pound

Readings

- From *A Selection of Cases on the Law of Contracts*, by Christopher Columbus Langdell
- From a "Book Notice" on Langdell's *A Selection of Cases on the Law of Contracts*, by Oliver Wendell Holmes
- From "Mechanical Jurisprudence," by Roscoe Pound

A new "scientism" based on the work in the natural sciences emerged in the teaching of Christopher Columbus Langdell (1826–1906), the Harvard professor who developed the "case method" of teaching. The major philosophical problem with such a pedagogy is that it fails to explain how the law changes. Oliver Wendell Holmes (1841–1935) argues that Langdell's methodology reduces the law to a set of logical propositions; as such, it does not account for the role of human experience in the development of the law. Roscoe Pound (1870–1964), who followed Langdell as a professor of law and dean at Harvard, makes a similar argument against a "mechanical jurisprudence." Pound argues, instead, for a "sociological jurisprudence" that subordinates the law to its larger social purpose. The theories set out by Holmes and Pound were influenced by the philosophical movement known as "pragmatism" and align themselves with communitarianism.

❧ Readings ❧

From Christopher Columbus Langdell, *A Selection of Cases on the Law of Contracts* (Boston: Little, Brown, 1871).

I entered upon the duties of my present position [as Professor of Law], a year and a half ago, with a settled conviction that law could only be taught or learned effectively by means of cases in some form.... Now, however, ... I was expected to take a large class of pupils, meet them regularly from day to day, and give them systematic instruction in such branches of law as had been assigned to me....

Only one mode occurred to me which seemed to hold out any reasonable prospect of success; and that was, to make a series of cases, carefully selected from the books of reports, the subject alike of study and instruction. . . . I was [then] led to inquire into the feasibility of preparing and publishing such a selection of cases as would be adapted to my purpose as a teacher. The most important element in that inquiry was the great and rapidly increasing number of reported cases in every department of law. In view of this fact, was there any satisfactory principle upon which such a selection could be made? It seemed to me that there was.

Law, considered as a science, consists of certain principles or doctrines. To have such a mastery of these as to be able to apply them with constant facility and certainty to the ever-tangled skein of human affairs, is what constitutes a true lawyer; and hence to acquire that mastery should be the business of every earnest student of law. Each of these doctrines has arrived at its present state by slow degrees; in other words, it is a growth, extending in many cases through centuries. This growth is to be traced in the main through a series of cases; and much the shortest and best, if not the only way of mastering the doctrine effectually is by studying the cases in which it is embodied. But the cases which are useful and necessary for this purpose at the present day bear an exceedingly small proportion to all that have been reported. . . .

Moreover, the number of fundamental legal doctrines is much less than is commonly supposed . . . If these doctrines could be so classified and arranged that each should be found in its proper place, and nowhere else, they would cease to be formidable from their number. It seemed to me, therefore, to be possible to take such a branch of the law as Contracts, for example, and . . . select, classify, and arrange all the cases which had contributed in any important degree to the growth, development, or establishment of any of its essential doctrines; and that such a work could not fail to be of material service to all who desire to study that branch of law systematically and in its original sources.

It is upon this principle that the present volume has been prepared.

From Oliver Wendell Holmes, "Book Notices: *A Selection of Cases on the Law of Contracts, with a Summary of the Topics Covered by the Cases* (*A Summary of the Law of Contracts*) by C.C. Langdell (1879)" in *The American Law Review* 14 (1880): 233–5.[1]

It is hard to know where to begin in dealing with this extraordinary production—equally extraordinary in its merits and its limitations. No man competent to judge can read a page of it without at once recognizing the hand of a great master. Every line is compact[ed] of ingenious and original thought. . . . It may be said without exaggeration that there cannot be found in the legal literature of this country, such a *tour de force* of patient and profound intellect working out original theory through a mass of detail, and evolving consistency out of what seemed a chaos of conflicting atoms.

Mr. Langdell Is a Legal Theologian

But in this word "consistency" we touch what some of us at least must deem the weak point in Mr. Langdell's habit of mind. Mr. Langdell's ideal in the law, the end of all his striving, is the *elegantia juris*, or *logical* integrity of the system as a system. He is, perhaps, the greatest living legal theologian. But as a theologian he is less concerned with his postulates than to show that the conclusions from them hang together. A single phrase will illustrate what is meant.

> "It has been claimed that the purposes of substantial justice and the interests of contracting parties as understood by themselves will be best served by holding etc., . . . and cases have been put to show that the contrary view would produce not only unjust but absurd results. *The true answer to this argument is that it is irrelevant*; but" etc. (pp. 995, 996, pl. 15).

The reader will perceive that the language is only incidental, but it reveals a mode of thought which becomes conspicuous to a careful student.

Mr. Langdell Could Be Called a Hegelian in Disguise

If Mr. Langdell could be suspected of ever having troubled himself about Hegel, we might call him a Hegelian in disguise, so entirely is he interested in the formal connection of things, or logic, as distinguished from the feelings which make the content of logic, and which have actually shaped the substance of the law. The life of the law has not been logic: it has been experience. The seed of every new growth within its sphere has been a felt necessity. The form of continuity has been kept up by reasonings purporting to reduce everything to a logical sequence; but . . . [t]he important phenomenon is . . . the justice and reasonableness of a decision, not its consistency with previously held views.

No one will ever have a truly philosophic mastery over the law who does not habitually consider the forces outside of it which have made it what it is. . . . As a branch of anthropology, law is an object of science; the theory of legislation is a scientific study; but the effort to reduce the concrete details of an existing system to the merely logical consequence of simple postulates is always in danger of becoming unscientific, and of leading to a misapprehension of the nature of the problem and the data.

Note

1.   Editor's note: Christopher Columbus Langdell. *A Selection of Cases on the Law of Contracts*, 2nd ed. (Boston: Little, Brown, & Co., 1879).

From Roscoe Pound, "Mechanical Jurisprudence," *Columbia Law Review* 8 (1908): 605–23.[1]

The Modern Demand for Full, Equal, and Exact Justice Has Made the Law Scientific

What is scientific law? What constitutes science in the administration of justice? Sir Frederick Pollock gives us the clue when he defines the reasons that compel law to take on this scientific character as three: the demand for full justice, that is for solutions that go to the root of controversies; the demand for equal justice, that is a like adjustment of like relations under like conditions; and the demand for exact justice, that is for a justice whose operations, within reasonable limits, may be predicted in advance of action. In other words, the marks of a scientific law are conformity to reason, uniformity, and certainty.

Scientific Law Is a Means to an End

Scientific law is a reasoned body of principles for the administration of justice, and its antithesis is a system of enforcing magisterial caprice, however honest, and however much disguised under the name of justice or equity or natural law. But this scientific character of law is a means—a means toward the end of law, which is the administration of justice. . . .

Law is not scientific for the sake of science. Being scientific as a means toward an end, it must be judged by the results it achieves, not by the niceties of its internal structure; it must be valued by the extent to which it meets its end, not by the beauty of its logical processes or the strictness with which its rules proceed from the dogmas it takes for its foundation.

The Danger in a Scientific Legal System Is that Jurisprudence May Become Artificial or Mechanical

Two dangers have to be guarded against in a scientific legal system, one of them in the direction of the effect of its scientific and artificial character upon the public, the other in the direction of its effect upon the courts and the legal profession. With respect to the first danger, it is well to remember that law must not become too scientific for the people to appreciate its workings. Law has the practical function of adjusting everyday relations so as to meet current ideas of fair play. It must not become so completely artificial that the public is led to regard it as wholly arbitrary. . . . When Lord Esher said, "the law of England is not a science," he meant to protest against a pseudo-science of technical rules existing for their own sake and subserving supposed ends of science, while defeating justice. . . .

In the other direction, the effect of a scientific legal system upon the courts and upon the legal profession is more subtle and far-reaching. . . . Perfection of scientific system and exposition tends to cut off individual initiative in the future, to stifle independent consideration of new problems and of new phases of old problems, and to impose the ideas of one generation upon another. This is so in all departments of learning. One of the obstacles to advance in every science is the domination of the ghosts of departed masters. Their sound methods are forgotten, while their unsound conclusions are held for gospel. Legal science is not exempt from this tendency. Legal systems have their periods in which science degenerates, in which system decays into technicality, in which a scientific jurisprudence becomes a mechanical jurisprudence.

Roman law in its decadence furnishes a striking example. The Valentinian "law of citations" made a selection of jurisconsults of the past and allowed their writings only to be cited. It declared them, with the exception of Papinian, equal in authority. It confined the judge, when questions of law were in issue, to the purely mechanical task of counting and of determining the numerical preponderance of authority. Principles were no longer resorted to in order to make rules to fit cases. The rules were at hand in a fixed and final form, and cases were to be fitted to the rules. The classical jurisprudence of principles had developed, by the very weight of its authority, a jurisprudence of rules; and it is in the nature of rules to operate mechanically. . . .

The Idea of Science as a System of Deductions from *A Priori* Conceptions Is Obsolete

I have referred to mechanical jurisprudence as scientific because those who administer it believe it such. But in truth it is not science at all. We no longer hold anything scientific merely because it exhibits a rigid scheme of deductions from *a priori* conceptions. In the philosophy of today, theories are "instruments, not answers to enigmas, in which we can rest." The idea of science as a system of deductions has become obsolete, and the revolution which has taken place in other sciences in this regard must take place and is taking place in jurisprudence also.

This revolution in science at large was achieved in the middle of the nineteenth century. In the first half of that century, [the] scientific method in every department of learning was dominated by the classical German philosophy. Men conceived that by dialectics and deduction from controlling conceptions they could construe the whole content of knowledge. Even in the natural sciences this belief prevailed and had long dictated theories of nature and of natural phenomena. Linnaeus, for instance, lays down a proposition, *omne vivum ex ovo* [all life is from an egg], and from this fundamental conception deduces a theory of homologies between animal and vegetable organs. He deemed no study of the organisms and the organs themselves necessary to reach or to sustain these conclusions. Yet, today, study of the organisms themselves has overthrown his fundamental proposition. . . .

Legal Institutions Must Be Based on Their Utility

We [no longer] base institutions upon deduction from assumed principles of human nature; we require them to exhibit practical utility, and we rest them upon a foundation of policy and established adaptation to human needs. It has been asserted that to no small extent the old mode of procedure was borrowed from the law [i.e., the natural law]. . . . We have, then, the same task in jurisprudence that has been achieved in philosophy, in the natural sciences and in politics. We have to rid ourselves of this sort of legality and to attain a pragmatic, a sociological legal science. . . .

Sociological Jurisprudence Is a Pragmatic Movement

The sociological movement in jurisprudence is a movement for pragmatism as a philosophy of law; for the adjustment of principles and doctrines to the human conditions they are to govern rather than to assumed first principles; for putting the human factor in the central place and relegating logic to its true position as an instrument. . . .

[Rudolf von] Ihering [Jhering][2] was the pioneer in the work of superseding [a] jurisprudence of conceptions (*Begriffsjurisprudenz*) by a jurisprudence of results *Wirklichkeitsjurisprudenz*). He insisted that we should begin at the other end; that the first question should be, how will a rule or a decision operate in practice? . . .

In the Civil Law, the doctrine as to mistake in the formation of a contract affords an example of the working of the two methods. [Friedrich Carl von] Savigny[3] treated the subject according to the jurisprudence of conceptions. He worked out historically and analytically the conception of a contract and deduced therefrom the rules to govern cases of mistake. It followed, from his conception, that if *A* telegraphed *B* to *buy* shares and the telegram as delivered to *B* read *sell*, there was no contract between *A* and *B*, and hence no liability of *A* to *B*; and for a time it was so held. But this and some of the other resulting rules were so far from just in their practical operation that, following the lead of Ihering, they have been abandoned and the ordinary understanding of businessmen has been given effect. . . .

The Development of the Law by "Juristic Speculation" and Judicial Decision Is Based on a Jurisprudence of Ends

In periods of legal development through juristic speculation[4] and judicial decision, we have a jurisprudence of ends in fact, even if in form it is a jurisprudence of conceptions. . . . The development of equity in England was attained by a method of seeking results in concrete causes. The liberalizing of English law through the law merchant was brought about by substituting business practice for juridical conceptions.

The development of the common law in America was a period of growth because the doctrine that the common law was received only so far as applicable led the courts . . . to study the conditions of application as well as the conceptions and their logical consequences. Whenever such a period has come to an end, when its work has been done and its legal theories have come to maturity, the jurisprudence of conceptions tends to decay. Conceptions are fixed. The premises are no longer to be examined. Everything is reduced to simple deduction from them. Principles cease to have importance. The law becomes a body of rules. This is the condition against which sociologists now protest, and protest rightly.

The Development of the Law by Legislation Is Based on a Jurisprudence of Rules

A period of legislative activity supervenes to supply, first new rules, then new premises, and finally a systematic body of principles as a fresh start for juristic development. But such periods hitherto have not been periods of growth. Usually legislative activity has not gone beyond the introduction of new rules or of new premises, and the chief result has been a summing up of the juristic accomplishment of the past in improved form. . . .

And in the first and second stages of a period of legislation the mechanical character of legal science is aggravated by the imperative theory, which is a concomitant of legislative activity. Austin's proposition that law is [a] command [is] so complete that even the unwritten law must be given this character. . . . [W]hen law is felt to be positive, to be the command of the law-maker, a tendency to enact rules as such becomes manifest. . . .

Before the analytical school, which revived the imperative theory to meet the facts of an age of legislation, had become established, historical jurists led a revolt. But their jurisprudence is a jurisprudence of conceptions. . . . The philosophical jurists have protested also and have appealed from purely legal considerations to considerations of reason and of natural law.[5] But theirs, too, is a jurisprudence of conceptions, and their method, of itself, offers no relief. . . .

In Europe, it is obvious that the different schools are coming together in a new sociological school that is to dominate juristic thought. Instead of seeking for an ideal universal law by metaphysical methods, the idea of all schools is to turn "the community of fact of mankind into a community of law in accord with the reasonable ordering of active life." Hence they hold that "the less arbitrary the character of a rule and the more clearly it conforms to the nature of things, the more nearly does it approach to the norm of a perfect law." . . .

That our caselaw at its maturity has acquired the sterility of a fully developed system, may be shown by abundant examples of its failure to respond to vital needs of present-day life. Its inadequacy to deal with employers' liability; . . . its inability to hold promoters to their duty and to protect the interests of those who invest in corporate enterprises against mismanagement and breach of trust; its failure to work out a scheme of responsibility that will hold legal entities . . . to their duty to the public—all these failures . . . speak for themselves. . . .

The Low Point of Mechanical Jurisprudence Is Reached When Conceptions Become the End of the Juristic Search

The nadir of mechanical jurisprudence is reached when conceptions are used, not as premises from which to reason, but as ultimate solutions. So used, they cease to be conceptions and become empty words. [William] James has called attention to a like vice in philosophical thought:

> Metaphysics has usually followed a very primitive kind of quest. . . . [T]he universe has always appeared to the natural mind as a kind of enigma of which the key must be sought in the shape of some illuminating or power-bringing word or name. That word names the universe's *principle*, and to possess it is after a fashion to possess the universe itself. "God," "Matter," "Reason," "the Absolute," "Energy," are so many solving names. You can rest when you have them. You are at the end of your metaphysical quest.[6]

Current decisions and discussions are full of such solving words: estoppel, malice, privity, implied, intention of the testator, vested and contingent—when we arrive at these we are assumed to be at the end of our juristic search. . . .

The Solution Is a New Legislative Restatement of the Common Law

With legislative law-making in the grip of the imperative theory and its arbitrary results, and judicial decision [i.e., the common law] in the grip of a jurisprudence of conceptions and its equally arbitrary results, whither are we to turn? Judicial law-making cannot serve us. . . . No court could hold such hearings as those had by legislative committees upon measures for the protection of operatives, described by Mrs Kelley,[7] or that recently had before the Interstate Commerce Commission as to uniform bills of lading. We must soon have a new starting-point that only legislation can afford. That we may put the socio-logical, the pragmatic theory behind legislation, is demonstrated every day. Legislative reference bureaus, the Comparative Law Bureau, the Conferences of Commissioners on Uniform State Laws, . . . such conferences as the one held recently with respect to the Sherman Anti-trust Law, bar association discussions of reforms in procedure—all these are furnishing abundant material for legislation of the best type. . . .

Hence common-law lawyers will some day abandon their traditional attitude toward legislation; will welcome legislation and will make it what it should be. The part played by jurists in the best days of Roman legislation, and the part they have taken in modern Continental legislation, should convince us, if need be, that juristic principles may be recognized and juristic speculation may be put into effect quite as well by legislation as by judicial decision.

Herein is a noble task for the legal scholars of America. To test the conceptions worked out in the common law by the requirements of the new juristic theory, to lay sure founda-tions for the ultimate legislative restatement of the law, from which judicial decisions shall start afresh—this is as great an opportunity as has fallen to the jurists of any age.

Notes

1. Editor's note: This paper was delivered at a meeting of the North Dakota Bar Association at Valley City, North Dakota, on 25 September 1908 and published in the *Columbia Law Review* later that year.
2. Editor's note: Rudolf von Jhering (1918–1892) was a famous German jurist and professor of Roman law. He developed a system of "natural jurisprudence," similar to utilitarianism in its goals but based on the development of a jurisprudence rather than legislation, which reconciles self-interest with the larger social interest. Jhering believed that the purpose of law must always be considered in applying it. See Rudolf von Jhering, *Law as a Means to an End*, 2nd ed., trans. Isaac Husik (New York: [Boston Book Co., 1913] A.M. Kelley, 1968).
3. Editor's note: Friedrich Carl von Savigny (1779–1861) was a distinguished German jurist and professor of Roman law who belonged to the "historical school" of interpretation. He argued vigorously against codification because it neglected the history of the positive law.
4. Editor's note: Pound popularized the term "jurist" in the American and common law tradition. The term is taken from the civil law system and, in Pound at least, suggests that academics and legal commentators

have a role to play in developing and reforming the law. See Eugen Ehrlich, "The Function of Juristic Science," in *Fundamental Principles of the Sociology of Law* (Cambridge, MA: Harvard University, 1936), 341–65.

5. Editor's note: This is a reference to the school of Jhering.

6. Editor's note: William James, "Lecture II: What Pragmatism Means," in *Pragmatism: A New Name for Some Old Ways of Thinking* (New York: Longmans, Green, 1907).

7. Editor's note: A reference to Florence Kelley, *Some Ethical Gains through Legislation* (New York: Macmillan, 1910), at p. 56, where Kelley writes of the efforts of glassworkers in promoting "statutory prohibition of night work for children" and observes that "their efforts have here and there been foiled by a weak brother proving open to the persuasions of the employers and ready to appear before legislative committees on behalf of the farther work of children in the same old way."

⇾ Discussion ⇽

The success of positivism—particularly the positivist belief that scientific inquiry creates knowledge—in the eighteenth and nineteenth centuries led to a general attempt to construct a new science of law. This attempt was based initially on a deep belief that reason, as Kant suggested, was the arbiter of truth. This new faith in reason, often called "rationalism," made its way legally into analytical jurisprudence. It also provided the epistemological foundations of the social sciences. This rationalism, which has older antecedents in the natural law and the common law tradition, gave rise to a school of thought called "formalism."

Christopher Columbus Langdell is usually classified as a formalist. He held that the methods of the natural sciences could be used to construct a complete jurisprudence out of existing cases. This idea was based on the use of a kind of formal logic to draw out and develop the legal propositions in the existing body of cases. Langdell is famous for his part in applying such a method to the law of contracts, and to the civil law more generally. Formalism also bore fruit, however, in the development of the rules of statutory construction. The most conspicuous attribute of such an approach in legal theory is that it removes most of the moral and policy elements in the process of interpretation. This raises a theoretical question whether a system of logical inference is sufficient, on its own, to develop a workable body of caselaw.

Formalism has retained its vitality in contracts. There was a strong reaction against formalism in legal theory, however, in the twentieth century.[1] Oliver Wendell Holmes and Roscoe Pound, like many other theorists, wanted to establish a science of law—but a science of law based on human experience and behaviour, rather than the study of the existing caselaw.[2]

The major problem with formalism's use of the existing caselaw is that it rests on a relatively rigid set of substantive values, which may not reflect the current thinking in society. A caselaw that is continually confronting new situations in the development of technology, science, and morals must accordingly develop substantively, in order to deal adequately with such situations. Since Holmes was a skeptic, he rejected the idea that there were definite moral values and was willing to accept a shifting standard of morality. This view is reflected in the political process and the statutory law, which should accordingly be given some deference.

The great advantage of Holmes' legal skepticism is that it is flexible enough as a theory to permit substantive changes in the foundations of the law. Although Pound's "sociological jurisprudence" is based on a more empirical and less substantive approach to the study of law, it addresses the same need for evolving legal standards. Pound was a pragmatist who believed that the legal system could not deal successfully with fundamental changes in society without some means of cross reference, which constantly investigates the current exigencies of the human condition. The same idea surfaces in Holmes, who believed that the strength of the caselaw system lies in its empirical, rather than its rational, foundations. Both of these suggest that the positive law cannot exist as a self-contained formal system, without some external grounding.

Langdell's Formalism Holds that the Study of Law Should Follow the Tradition of the Natural Sciences

Formalism has a pedagogical side. Langdell is famous for being the professor who developed the "case method" of teaching the law of contracts.[3] This body of law is a product of an extensive caselaw—indeed, it has been argued that Langdell and other systematizers, such as Frederick Pollock, actually created the law of contracts out of a disorganized and somewhat random aggregation of cases. Formalism was accordingly a tool that allowed theorists to slowly assemble the logical skeleton of an entire area of the law, which had been built up on an impressionistic basis, from a relatively loose collection of legal principles.[4]

The caselaw method is well known. Langdell required that his students study a selection of cases. They were expected to be able to state the facts of a specific case in class, identify the legal issue in the case, and provide the *ratio decidendi*—the reason behind the decision. The *ratio* was to be expressed in the form of a legal proposition, which then provided a piece of the logical skeleton of the larger body of contract law. This style of teaching has also been called the "Socratic method" because it is based on a process of question and answer that evokes the form of inquiry Socrates used in Ancient Greece.

Langdell became prominent, in spite of his lack of published work, because he played such a significant role in the development of the curriculum at the Harvard Law School. One of the more practical criticisms of Langdell and his approach is that he intentionally divorced the study of law from legal practice. There were competing views at the time as to how lawyers should be trained, and many members of the profession had merely apprenticed to those who were already in the practice. Langdell went a different way and consciously separated the study of law from its practice. This raises obvious institutional and methodological issues: should those who teach the law, for example, have some experience in practice? Or is the study of law a separate discipline?

It is the rather fragmentary legal theory that Langdell developed to explain his pedagogy that became known as "formalism." Langdell saw this study of law as a science in the tradition of the natural sciences.[5] This approach has antecedents in the empiricism of the English intellectual tradition, and it is interesting that Francis Bacon (1561–1626), a judge and rival of Edward Coke, is better known as the person who invented the scientific method.

Formalism is also associated with the development of the social sciences. Arthur E. Sutherland writes that Langdell's "gospel"

> was the application of the method of the natural sciences to the science of society. To him [the] proper study of the law, like the study of chemistry, physics, zoology, and botany, consisted in the careful observation and recording of many specific instances, and then from these instances derivation of general conclusions that the qualities of the phenomena or specimens observed would hold constant for other instances of the same classes.[6]

Langdell accordingly believed that the study of law rests on an examination of the decisions in individual cases. The real subject of study in the Langdell's theory, however, seems to be the legal propositions on which these decisions rest. There is accordingly an argument that it is these propositions, rather than the cases that contain them, that become the specimens the legal scientist studies. Langdell seems to have seen scientific inquiry primarily as an exercise in taxonomy: cases and legal propositions can be classified according to their essential characteristics and placed in categories and sub-categories, in much the same way that a botanist might classify different kinds of plants. This scheme is based on the approach that Carl Linnaeus followed in his scientific work and contributes to the recognition of distinct bodies of caselaw, like contracts and negligence.

Formalism Is Based on Inductive as well as Deductive Principles

Formalism has been characterized as a kind of deductivism. This characterization reflects the way that the law is developed and elaborated in formalist theory. It is nevertheless possible to distinguish between the scientific and the judicial aspects of the theory. The more scientific aspects of formalism are empirical and inductive rather than deductive, and they consist of abstracting principles or propositions from specific cases. It is the judicial task that is deductive.

The First Stage of Formalist Analysis Is Inductive

From a philosophical perspective, it seems possible to divide the formalistic enterprise into three stages of analysis. The first stage is inductive. Langdell's ratiocination—a kind of reverse deduction—traces the logic of the judgements in decided cases backward, to the general principles on which the decisions are based. This part of the process is fundamental and distinguishes Langdell's method from the methods of judges like Henry of Bracton and Edward Coke, who generally believed that the natural law supplied first principles.

The Second and Third Stages Are Deductive

The second and third stages of the formalist analysis are deductive. These parts of the process are more in keeping with the legal scientism promoted by Bracton and Coke. The second stage consists of deducing more specific principles of law from the application of the most basic principles, on which there is general agreement, to the sets of facts that arise in individual cases. There is accordingly an assumption in formalism—reminiscent of Kant—that it is possible to deduce an entire system of law from basic principles.

The third stage of the formalist analysis is related to the second, but it uses the deductive method to determine how the case in question should be decided. The rough idea is that the facts of the case provide the substantive premise in a conditional proposition. For example, if a contract has been made for an illegal purpose such as the sale of illicit drugs, it is void *ab initio*. If we know that the real purpose of a particular contract is to sell drugs, we can accordingly deduce that the contract in question is void. The propositional character of this analysis reflects the logical interests in legal positivism.

Formalism Sees the Law as a Set of Logical Rules

It seems more apt to compare the third and final stage of the formalist analysis with logic mathematics rather than the natural sciences. The ultimate purpose of Langdell's method is to create a body of rules, based on a set of fundamental axioms, that can be used to solve the problems presented by individual cases. The essential judicial task is accordingly to find the proper rule and apply it to the facts of the case. This is a relatively mechanical task: when the rule is applied, it automatically determines the proper disposition of the case. This process suggests that there is a necessary outcome in any given case and a correct answer to the legal problem that the case poses.

The Methodology of Formalism Can Be Applied to Statutory Law

Formalism is associated with legal positivism. Although Langdell studied the caselaw, his methodology is also significant in the interpretation of statutes. This addresses one of the fundamental problems of positivism, which is that the meaning of statutory provisions is often unclear. The formalist methodology can accordingly be used to determine the principles on which statutes are based.

A judge faced with the task of applying a certain piece of legislation to the facts before him faces many of the same problems that arise in the context of ordinary speech. Language is polysemous—it has a variety of meanings—and even in casual conversation it can be surprisingly difficult to determine the exact meaning of a statement. This lack of clarity presents considerable difficulties, particularly when we are trying to understand a document, such as a statute, that expresses the will of a body of people.

The Use of the Formalist Analysis in Statutory Interpretation Raises Questions

The interpretation of statutes in this context raises its own set of problems. The common law rests on the general premise that the law exists as a single whole. The principle of coherence assumes that the entire body of the common law has an integrated rational framework that is open to analysis. It follows that the statute law, as well as the caselaw, is logically consistent and can be interpreted as a coherent whole. The reality is that the legislation enacted by different governments diverges considerably. One of the major criticisms of the legal positivists is that they failed to acknowledge the more adventitious aspects of the statutory law.

There is a neglected issue here, which the formalist analysis brings to the forefront. Even if the legislature passes inconsistent statutes—or statutes that are based on inconsistent principles—the principle of coherence requires that the statutes be interpreted in a manner that is logically consistent. Since the courts can do so only by disregarding the intentions of Parliament, this calls into question the ascendancy of the legislature. It is an interesting question whether formalism, if it is a form of positivism, allows the legislature to pass inconsistent laws and "command" the courts to apply them.

Formalism Has Affinities with Legal Positivism

There is a sense in which the normative elements in formalism rest on a descriptive foundation, since formalism does not subject the existing law to any moral scrutiny. Indeed the word "formalism" suggests that the law can be deduced—as Kant and the analytical jurisprudents argued—through the formal operation of logic. This idea seems to place the formalists firmly within the positivist camp in legal theory. It is not clear, however, that the first principles on which the formalist analysis relies are free of moral values, or that it is possible to enter the second stage of the analysis and develop further principles without relying at least implicitly on a variety of substantive principles.

The formalist analysis is nevertheless in keeping with the history of the common law and, as a practical matter, it has to be acknowledged that it still captures the deductive aspects of the judicial task. The purpose of the original caselaw in the common law tradition was to produce a set of rules, which would be applied consistently in different cases. This feature of the tradition, which has formalist elements, naturally prevented judges from applying the law in accordance with their own inclinations, and it protected the integrity of the legal system as a whole. Indeed this is one of the foundations of the system.

The Formalists Shared the Positivists' Interest in Codification

The affinity between formalism and legal positivism is apparent in the formalists' interest in cataloguing the legal rules and principles embedded in the caselaw. This classification of legal rules and principles can be seen as a kind of codification, though it is carried out without legislative sanction. The benefits of such a process are apparent: formalism clarified many areas of the law that were originally developed on a relatively *ad hoc*, case-by-case basis, and it created a system of torts and contracts. One of the chief merits of such a process is that it makes the legal system more predictable and provides order and certainty in social life.

There are practical reasons that codification seems to meet the needs of formalism. Since formalism is based on the idea that there are rules that logically determine the right outcome in any case, the efficiency of the system depends upon the ability of judges to find the relevant rules. There is accordingly a need for an exhaustive compilation of rules, set out in a manner that will help judges find the precise rule that applies to the specific facts of a case. The most prominent example of such a compendium may be John Henry Wigmore's *Treatise on the Anglo-American System of Evidence in Trials at Common Law* (first published in 1904 and now commonly known as *Wigmore on Evidence*), which remains one of the most authoritative sources in the area.

The Methodological Premises of Formalism Recalls the Natural Law

Formalism does not rely on the natural law. The affinities between formalism and the system of the natural law are nevertheless obvious—once we have a set of first principles, or axioms, it seems clear that the first principles will ultimately determine both the rules and principles that make up the law and the results in particular cases.

There is a philosophical gap in the work of formalists, however, which does not address two key ontological questions. How do these first principles come into existence, and how do we explain their authority? The most likely answer is that the truth or validity of these first principles is self-evident—perhaps because they have been used in cases—and derives from some consensus in society. If this is the position of the formalists, however, it becomes difficult to distinguish these first principles from some form of natural law.

Formalism Prevents Us from Examining the Moral Views on which the Law Is Based

One of the simplest arguments against formalism is that judges are at least occasionally forced to fall back on substantive values and beliefs in deciding the law. This is evident in notions like due process, fairness, equity, fundamental justice, and the common law requirements of natural justice. All of these notions require an exercise of judgement, which is clearly predicated on the moral consensus in society at any given point in time. This consensus is clearly grounded in ethical beliefs and values that lie outside the positive law. Although the legal positivists accused the judiciary of imposing their moral views on society, and were therefore attracted to the logical and descriptive character of formalism, it follows that one of the major problems of formalism is that it hides the moral and social considerations that decide the law and determine its validity.

Formalism Draws Attention to the Role of the Judiciary

One of the reasons formalism sets the stage for the contemporary discussion in legal theory is that it draws our attention to the role of judges in the legal system. The initial reason the role of judges became such a prominent issue is that Jeremy Bentham rejected the common law on the basis that it allowed the judiciary to impose their views on the rest of society. The irony, of course, is that the purpose of doctrines like precedent and *stare decisis*, which Bentham rejected, was to prevent judges from deciding cases on the basis of their individual views.

The logical and descriptive character of formalism responds implicitly to these kinds of concerns, since it severely restricts the discretionary powers of the judiciary. There is, in addition, no real place in formalism for judges to exercise their moral judgement in deciding particular cases. At the same time, formalism reinvigorates Edward Coke's idea that the law is the "peculiar science" of judges, which can be gained only by a long and exhausting study of the cases. This is in spite of the fact that the judicial task in deciding a particular case consists of a relatively mechanical—if occasionally abstruse—application of legal rules to the facts of the case.

Formalism Fails to Deal With the Vagaries in the Determination of Facts

Another criticism of formalism is that it neglects the vagaries in the trial process. From a courtroom perspective, formalism misrepresents the judicial role, since it fails to recognize that the initial and primary role of trial judges in the common law is to decide the facts of the case. It is only after these judges have made findings of fact that they turn to the law and apply the law to the facts. As the legal realists argued, in criticizing formalism, the problem is that different judges may make different findings of fact on the same evidence. As a result, there is no simple way of determining what legal rules will apply to a given case. Formalism glosses over this kind of issue and fails to recognize that judges can easily determine the outcome in a case, intentionally or otherwise, by making the appropriate findings of fact.

Formalism Does Not Explain the Conflicting Rulings in the Caselaw

There are similar issues in the application and interpretation of the law. Any lawyer who practises in the appellate courts encounters situations in which there are conflicting lines of cases. The Ontario Court of Appeal may go one way; the Nova Scotia Court of Appeal may go another. In point of fact, this kind of disagreement on the application of legal principles is one of the major factors that the Supreme Court considers in deciding whether it will hear an appeal in a particular case. It follows that there is no judicial consensus on the legal propositions that make up the law, and formalism fails to recognize that judicial controversy is an ordinary part of the legal process.

The presence of conflicting rulings is significant because it suggests that there is a level of ambiguity in the law that the formalists failed to acknowledge. In many cases, moreover, there is no obvious way to reconcile the differences of opinion among the judiciary without turning to some substantive source of authority outside the positive law.[7] We can appeal a decision, but that simply substitutes the judgement of the judges on the Supreme Court for the judgement of their counterparts on the lower courts and does not solve the problem.

Holmes Argues that the Common Law Is Based on Experience

Oliver Wendell Holmes served on the United States Supreme Court from 1902 to 1932. He was one of the most famous judges on the court, and he is best known for his belief that the judiciary should exercise restraint in striking down progressive social legislation on constitutional grounds. This position was a product of Holmes' moral skepticism rather than a reflection of his personal views. Holmes also contributed to our understanding of the history of the common law.

Since Holmes was a skeptic, he rejected the idea that moral values could be fixed. He accordingly rejected the natural law. He developed a more refined judicial position than Bentham or Austin did, however, and, since the United States has a written constitution, he was willing to divide sovereignty between the legal and political institutions of the state. Holmes rejected formalism on the basis that the foundations of the common law lie in experience rather than the exercise of pure reason. There is a judicial side to this development, since Holmes felt that judges can develop the law only in the context of the facts that arise in particular cases. It is the empiricism of the common law tradition that stands out.

Holmes Rejects Langdell's Rationalism

In his review of *A Summary of the Law of Contracts*, the second book in Langdell's treatise on the law of contracts, Holmes describes Langdell as a legal theologian. This kind of description is a criticism, as it suggests that Langdell treats the law as a given and does not question its premises. This approach is insufficient, in Holmes' estimation, to explain the development of the common law because many of the premises on which the law and the legal system are based have changed.

Holmes associates the rationalism in Langdell and philosophers like Kant with idealism. Langdell is a "Hegelian"—a reference to Georg Wilhelm Friedrich Hegel (1770–1831)— because he seems to share Hegel's view that what exists is a single idea. This single idea, which includes everything, is unfolding rationally, through a logical process. Whatever exists in such a process, including the law, exists as an instantiation of reason. It follows that reason is sufficient in itself to disclose the full meaning and pattern of law and morality.

Holmes is a skeptic, but he is also a realist who believes that things exist outside of their instantiation in ideas. He accordingly rejects the logical idealism that he associates with Langdell's formalism. Thus, in "The Path of Law," Holmes refers to formalism as the fallacy "that the only force at work in the development of the law is logic." He accepts, "in the broadest sense," that law is "a logical development, like everything else." But this statement, he writes, should not be distorted:

> The danger of which I speak is not the admission that the principles governing other phenomena also govern the law, but the notion that a given system, ours, for instance, can be worked out like mathematics from some general axioms of conduct.[8]

This is a rejection of the natural law as well as formalism. From Holmes' perspective, the idea that the entire law can be deduced logically, from the existing caselaw, cannot explain the substantive development of the law.

Holmes Argues that Formalism Fails to Explain the Substantive Aspects of the Law

There are some similarities between Holmes and Langdell. Like Langdell, Holmes saw the law as a kind of science. His own view of science was overwhelmingly empirical, however, and Holmes wanted a legal theory that provided an accurate account of the way in which the law actually operates. Like Roscoe Pound, Holmes formulated a theory of law that reflects the emergence of the social sciences. Holmes essentially asserted that law is whatever decisions judges reach, in the cases that come before them. This reduces the law to the behaviour of judges.

Holmes accordingly argued that the proper subject of the study of law is the experience that makes up the decisions of the courts. This idea is another extension of the view, in Langdell's work, that social phenomena can be studied in the same way as the physical world. The problem for Holmes is that formalism focusses exclusively on the deductive content of written decisions and fails to capture what occurs in the courtroom. It is psychology and sociology, rather than written rules, that determines how a judge will decide a case.

Formalism Does Not Permit Substantive Changes in the Law

Holmes believed that the substantive "axioms of conduct" on which the law is based evolve and change over time. Formalism is defective because it fails to recognize these changes. It is unable to go beyond the first stage of the formalist analysis, in capturing the development of the law. This is a backward-looking function, moreover, that merely identifies the operative principles in the precedents and expands them, in an ever-more-sophisticated elaboration of the substantive premises that already exist in the caselaw. It follows that formalism traps the law in a set of substantive values that cannot be changed.

The epistemological issues that arise in this context go beyond philosophy of law. It does not seem possible to test the substantive validity of a legal proposition by means of formal logic, without some external criteria that determines whether the proposition is in keeping with a chosen set of moral, cultural, or religious beliefs. The laws of physics, to use a different example, derive their authority from their correlation with what actually occurs in an objectively existing physical world.

Holmes' criticism of formalism runs along the same lines. The problem with Langdell's theory is that it treats the law as a self-contained system and fails to recognize that the substantive validity of a proposition or a ruling depends on its correspondence with some set of values or beliefs. It is evident that the natural law and the constitutional law function in exactly this way and provide an external set of precepts that can be used to authenticate the ordinary law. The analogy with physics is particularly apt in the case of Holmes and Pound, since they both argue that the merit and validity of the law depends on whether it corresponds—in some meaningful way—with the empirical realities of contemporary life.

Holmes' Empiricism Offers a Solution to the Problem of Novel Cases

Holmes' empiricism—a skeptical empiricism—provides the kind of external reference that is missing from the formalist system. This feature of Holmes' legal theory is important because it allows for changes in the substantive foundations of the law. This raises the problem of novel cases.

Formalism cannot explain new developments in the law. If there are novel cases, which cannot be decided on the basis of the existing law, it seems clear that judges must develop new rules and principles to deal with them. It is true that there is room to adapt and reformulate the existing rules, even in formalism, but the philosophical question is whether this room is sufficient to accommodate major changes in our moral views. Can we abolish slavery, or give animals the rights of human persons, without changing the substantive framework within which the law exists?

There is a related question, which is equally pressing. If there are cases that call for substantive changes in the framework of the law, where do judges—or the members of the legislature—find these rules and principles? Do they find them in their own moral views, in the moral consensus in society, or in some set of political or legal tenets?

Holmes' position is that formalism does not have the theoretical resources to deal with novel cases. This issue became important because Holmes and his contemporaries lived in a time of radical moral, social and technological change, in which the common law often seemed outmoded. Since Holmes was a skeptic, he had no difficulty with the fact that our moral views are continually shifting, as the circumstances in which we live evolve and change. He accordingly argued that the results of the decision in a case must be consulted in determining whether the decision is correct. His position in this regard resembles the position set out by Roscoe Pound.

Holmes' position is nevertheless much vaguer than the position adopted by Pound. Although it is not clear what is involved in Holmes' idea that the results of a decision must be empirically justified, it is evident he believes that experience of ordinary life often provides a sufficient basis for us to determine whether a judicial decision is a just decision. The results of a legal case must coincide with our sense of social justice. This means that judges may occasionally have to step outside the confines of the formalist approach and consult the changing standards and conventions in society in deciding their cases.

Holmes Believed that Economics Provided the Necessary Means for Testing the Results of Judicial Decisions

Holmes' philosophy of law would clearly be incomplete without a means of testing the empirical results of a decision, in order to determine whether the decision serves the public interest and the common good. This philosophical need, in conjunction with Holmes' willingness to countenance changes in the law, left him open to many influences. Foremost among these influences was economic theory. Holmes argued that the new science of economics provided the necessary mechanism for determining whether the results of court decisions were empirically sound.

Holmes had little confidence in the views of his judicial colleagues and was suspicious of personal opinions. Economics appealed to him because it provided a highly object-ive, scientific means of measuring the efficiency and efficacy of legal rulings. Holmes' prominence in legal circles earned him a place in the development of a "sociological jurisprudence" and in legal realism; but his real legacy lies in the economic school of legal theory.[9] This school holds—in the utilitarian manner—that the law should maxi-mize the public good and minimize social costs. One of the more theoretical issues raised by such a school is whether these factors should be measured on an individual or a collective basis.

Pound's Legal Pragmatism Supports a Jurisprudence Based on Results

Nathan Roscoe Pound, the son of a judge, was called to the bar in 1890. He was an unusual figure in law, since he received a Ph.D. in botany from the University of Nebraska in 1899. He was accordingly interested, like Langdell, in the application of the scientific method—which was often described as the "empirical method"—to the development of the law. In his earlier work, Pound was influenced by social Darwinism, which holds that society evolves in the same way that natural species evolve. This school of thought recalls the work of Émile Durkheim (1858–1917), who suggested that societies, like biological organ-isms, can be viewed as healthy or ill.

After giving up his botanical studies, Pound became a professor of law and served as the dean of the Harvard Law School from 1916 to 1936. He was a prolific academic, known for his prodigious reading in a variety of languages and legal traditions, and he published hundreds of papers before his death in 1964. Pound shared Holmes' empiri-cism and rejected the idea that the natural law was sufficient to explain the development of the common law. He believed that the law must reflect the gradual evolution of society. Yet it was Pound's earlier work in sociological jurisprudence that was his most influential contribution to the development of legal theory.

The Pragmatists Believed that the Law Should Progress as the Experimental Sciences Progress

Pound was heavily influenced by pragmatism—sometimes called "American pragmatism"—a nineteenth- and twentieth-century school of philosophy that drew heavily on the experimental method. The most famous pragmatists were William James (1842–1910), Charles Sanders Pierce (1839–1914), and John Dewey (1859–1952), who became famous for their work in fields as wide-ranging as psychology, linguistics, and educational theory. The pragmatists wanted to develop an epistemological theory that explained the advances in science. Philosophers like Dewey were also interested in social and political theory, however, and reasoned that the same epistemology could be used in other areas.

The Pragmatists Were Fallibilists and Believed that the Law Must Be Tested

There were at least two epistemological premises that carried over into Pound's work and legal pragmatism more generally. The first is that any assertion is a matter of belief and is therefore potentially wrong. This philosophical view is called fallibilism and has its antecedents in the Greek skeptics, who held that any claim to truth is inherently uncertain. If we accept fallibilism, the search for metaphysical certainty—and this means the search for knowledge, or true belief—is a mistake. Certainty is not possible; but more importantly, we do not need certainty in our endeavours, which become perfectible as a result.

Pragmatists like Pierce took the position that the indeterminacy of our beliefs does not prevent us from relying upon them. Unlike the skeptics, the pragmatists believed that uncertainty opens up the possibility of correction. Science progresses by means of a continual process of revision and correction. Such a process is a fundamental part of the legal theories of Pound and of Holmes.

The important observation here is that this scientific epistemology dramatically changes how we view the law. The pragmatic approach treats propositions—and in the context of legal theory, this means legal rules—essentially as hypotheses. Like scientific hypotheses, these legal hypotheses are subject to continual scrutiny and development. There is an idea in this that the law can be empirically validated or invalidated. Holmes and Pound were willing to accept the common law and the legal past as a convenient starting point, but only on the basis that it meets the needs of the present. This approach gives rise to the idea, in Pound's work and in the work of other modern figures, that the law should be subject to a process of empirical confirmation. As the reading from Pound's "Mechanical Jurisprudence" illustrates, this demand for confirmation seems to take us out of the legal system and into the political process.

The Pragmatists Also Believed that the Meaning and the Validity of the Law Are Found in Its Results

The second epistemological premise that finds its way into Pound's theory and legal pragmatism more generally is the belief that the meaning and the truth of an assertion are found in its practical consequences. This assertion leads to the understanding that a logic based on the earlier law is insufficient. If logic is to be retained as an instrument of law, Dewey writes,

> it must be a logic *relative to consequences rather than to antecedents*, a logic or prediction of probabilities rather than one of deduction of certainties. For the purposes of a logic of inquiry into probable consequences, general principles can only be tools justified by the work they do. They are means of intellectual survey, analysis, and insight into the factors of the situation to be dealt with. Like other tools they must be modified when they are applied to new conditions and new results have to be achieved.[10]

The general principles of the law need to be revised constantly to ensure that the results they produce are in keeping with the changes in society.

Sociological Jurisprudence Focusses on the Community as a Whole

The philosophical differences between Pound and positivists like Jeremy Bentham are more ethical and political than legal. Pound takes a communitarian rather than a strict liberal position and sometimes seems to see society as a kind of social experiment. Society is primary in his thinking: the well-being of the community is an end in itself rather than a means of advancing the self-interest of individuals. This seems to separate Pound and Holmes, and it provide a link to the work of Thomas Hill Green and the customary origins of the common law.[11]

Pound's interest in society explains his "sociological" emphasis, which leads to a view of the law as a form of social control. This view has now acquired more sinister overtones. In addition, while the details of his general theoretical system are relatively vague, it is significant that Pound introduced the concept of interests, as a counterpart to the concept of rights, and distinguished between individual, public, and social interests. It is the object of law to maintain a balance between these competing interests and keep the community together.

The pragmatists may have overstated their position. It is not clear that our most basic moral beliefs—the belief that it is wrong to inflict pain on other people gratuitously, for example—evolve over time. Pound's rhetoric was exaggerated, however, and he did not reject "the taught legal tradition" or formalism altogether. He believed that judges were obliged to follow definite legal rules, in order to maintain the coherence of the legal system and guarantee a consistent result in individual cases. It accordingly seems that he endorsed a *shifting* formalism, which maintains the logical integrity of the law while allowing its substantive foundations to evolve and change. Although these rules might change, Pound's view of the judiciary—much like Holmes'—still reflects the original common law view that judges must ultimately fall back on the moral consensus in society in interpreting and developing the law.

Notes

1. Formalism was rejected by many judges in general and by Benjamin Cardozo, whose theory of the judicial role is discussed in Chapter 9, in particular. In *The Nature of the Judicial Process*, cited in the suggestions for further reading, at p. 66ff., Cardozo writes that "the demon of formalism tempts the intellect with the lure of scientific order." Cardozo adopts a utilitarian and pragmatic stance, arguing that the "welfare of society" should determine "how far existing rules are to be extended or restricted." The formalist approach has nevertheless renewed itself over recent decades. See Curtis Bridgeman, for example, "Why Contracts Scholars Should Read Legal Philosophy: Positivism, Formalism, and the Specification of Rules in Contract Law," *Cardozo Law Review* 29, no. 4 (2008): 1443–85.
2. For a historical discussion of these developments, see Thomas C. Grey, "Judicial Review and Legal Pragmatism," *Wake Forest Law Review* 38 (2003): 473–511. And see the references to formalism in Morton J. Horwitz, *The Transformation of American Law 1870–1960: The Crisis of Legal Orthodoxy* (New York: Oxford University, 1992).

3.   See David A. Garvin, for example, "Making the Case: Professional Education for the World of Practice," *Harvard Magazine* (November–December 2011). Available at http://harvardmagazine.com. Also see Paul D. Carrington, "Hail Langdell!," *Law and Social Inquiry* 20, no. 3 (Summer 1995): 691–760. For a more critical discussion, see Myron Moskovitz, "Beyond the Case Method: It's Time to Teach with Problems," *Journal of Legal Education* 42 (1992): 241–70.

4.   See Grant Gilmore, *The Death of Contract*, 2nd ed., ed. K.L. Collins (Columbus: Ohio State University, [1974] 1995).

5.   See Marcia Speziale, "Langdell's Concept of Law as Science: The Beginning of Anti-Formalism in American Legal Thought," *Vermont Law Review* 5 (1980): 1–38.

6.   Arthur E. Sutherland, *The Law at Harvard: A History of Ideas and Men, 1817–1967* (Cambridge, MA: Belknap, 1967), p. 176.

7.   The formalists implicitly adopted the positivist conception of law. If we adopt a theory like the natural law, there is no simple distinction between legal and moral sources of authority, and the law includes moral principles. So there is no need to go—conceptually—outside the law to find substantive values.

8.   See Holmes, "The Path of Law," *Harvard Law Review* 10 (1896–7): 457–78, at p. 462.

9.   The most well-known figure in such a movement is Richard A. Posner, whose *Economic Analysis of Law* (Boston: Little, Brown, 1973), now published in many editions, provides the major source of theory in the area.

10.   John Dewey, "Logical Method and Law," as cited in the suggestions for further reading, at p. 139.

11.   Pound nevertheless argued against the historical school of jurisprudence, which rested its conception of law on the primacy of the community and custom, on the basis that it prevented the kind of empirical and legislative review that Pound favoured. See Lewis A. Grossman, "'From Savigny through Sir Henry Maine': Roscoe Pound's Flawed Portrait of James Coolidge Carter's Historical Jurisprudence," Washington College of Law Research Paper No. 2009–21, available at www.ssrn.com.

Study Questions

1.   Why does Holmes describe Langdell as a "theologian"?

2.   Suppose you are a formalist. You will rely on logic to develop the law, but where will you get the premises on which the caselaw is based? From the natural law? From the exercise of pure reason, as Kant suggested?

3.   Langdell's deeper interests seem to lie in the logic employed in individual decisions. Does this recall the theory of law in Aquinas, Bentham, or Kant? Why?

4.   Although legal skepticism is a descriptive rather than a normative theory, it has a normative element. Where does our obligation to obey the law come from in skepticism?

5.   Where does our obligation to obey the law come from in sociological jurisprudence? Is social policy sufficient to create an obligation to obey the law?

6.   Which is more like the scientism that we find in the work of Edward Coke: Langdell's formalism or Pound's sociological jurisprudence? Why?

7.   How does a pragmatic jurisprudence differ from a formalist jurisprudence?

8.   Why do pragmatism and sociological jurisprudence seem to take us into a political conception of law?

Further Reading

Benjamin N. Cardozo, *The Nature of the Judicial Process* (New Haven, CT: Yale University, 1921). Available at http://xroads.virginia.edu/~hyper/CARDOZO/CarNat.html.

Roger Cotterrell, *The Politics of Jurisprudence: A Critical Introduction to Legal Philosophy* (Philadelphia: University of Pennsylvania, 1989).

John Dewey, "Logical Method and Law," in *Philosophy and Civilization* (New York: Minton Balch, 1931), pp. 126–40.

Oliver Wendell Holmes, "Law in Science and Science in Law," *Harvard Law Review* 12, no. 7 (1899): 443–63.

Roscoe Pound, "Sociology of Law and Sociological Jurisprudence," *The University of Toronto Law Journal* 5, no. 1 (1943): 1–20.

8 Constitutionalism: Legal Skepticism and the Doctrine of the Living Tree

Albert Venn Dicey, Oliver Wendell Holmes, and John Sankey

Readings

- From *Introduction to the Study of the Law of the Constitution*, by Albert Venn Dicey
- From "The Path of the Law," by Oliver Wendell Holmes
- From *Edwards v. A.G. of Canada*, [1930] A.C. 124 (P.C.)

The following chapter deals with the constitutional role of the courts. In the first reading, Albert Venn Dicey sets out the constitutional framework of a federal system. The next readings set out the theories that emerged in two federal systems: one in the United States, the other in Canada. In "The Path of the Law," Oliver Wendell Holmes, who later became a judge on the United States Supreme Court, suggests that American judges have used the constitutional law to restrain the efforts of state legislatures to introduce progressive social legislation. Holmes was a legal skeptic who was suspicious of the natural law and believed that judges were obliged to distance themselves from their moral and political views. John Sankey (1866–1948) was a lord justice of appeal and member of the Judicial Committee of the Privy Council in England. In *Edwards v. A.G. of Canada* (commonly referred to as the "Persons Case"), he describes a written constitution as "a living tree capable of growth and expansion within its natural limits" and holds that judges should give constitutional statutes a liberal interpretation.

❈ Readings ❖

From Albert Venn Dicey, *Introduction to the Study of the Law of the Constitution*, 6th ed. (London: Macmillan, [1885] 1902).

Chapter III: Parliamentary Sovereignty and Federalism

My present aim is to illustrate the nature of Parliamentary sovereignty as it exists in England, by a comparison with the system of government known as Federalism as it exists in several parts of the civilized world, and especially in the United States of America. . . .

The Constitution of the United States . . . holds a very peculiar relation towards the institutions of England. In the principle of the distribution of powers which determines its form, the Constitution of the United States is the exact opposite of the English constitution, the very essence of which is, as I hope I have now made clear, the unlimited authority of Parliament. . . .

The principle, in short, which gives its form to our system of government is . . . "unitarianism," or the habitual exercise of supreme legislative authority by one central power, which in the particular case is the British Parliament. The principle which, on the other hand, shapes every part of the American polity, is that distribution of limited, executive, legislative, and judicial authority among bodies each co-ordinate with and independent of the other which, we shall in a moment see, is essential to the federal form of government. . . .

Federalism Requires Two Conditions

A federal state requires for its formation two conditions. There must exist, in the first place, a body of countries such as the Cantons of Switzerland, the Colonies of America, or the Provinces of Canada, so closely connected by locality, by history, by race, or the like, as to be capable of bearing, in the eyes of their inhabitants, an impress of common nationality. . . .

A second condition absolutely essential to the founding of a federal system is the existence of a very peculiar state of sentiment among the inhabitants of the countries which it is proposed to unite. They must desire union, and must not desire unity. If there be no desire to unite, there is clearly no basis for federalism. . . . If, on the other hand, there be a desire for unity, the wish will naturally find its satisfaction, not under a federal, but under a unitarian constitution [like the English constitution]. . . . We may perhaps go a little further, and say, that a federal government will hardly be formed unless many of the inhabitants of the separate States feel stronger allegiance to their own State than to the federal state represented by the common government. . . .

Federalism Rests on a Division of Powers

A federal state is a political contrivance intended to reconcile national unity and power with the maintenance of "state rights." The end aimed at fixes the essential character of federalism. For the method by which Federalism attempts to reconcile the apparently inconsistent claims of national sovereignty and of state sovereignty consists of the formation of a constitution under which the ordinary powers of sovereignty are elaborately divided between the common or national government and the separate states. The details of this division vary under every different federal constitution, but the general principle on which it should rest is obvious. Whatever concerns the nation as a whole should be placed under the control of the national government. All matters which are not primarily of common interest should remain in the hands of the several States. . . .

From the notion that national unity can be reconciled with state independence by a division of powers under a common constitution between the nation on the one hand

and the individual States on the other, flow the three leading characteristics of completely developed federalism—the supremacy of the Constitution—the distribution among bodies with limited and co-ordinate authority of the different powers of government—the authority of the Courts to act as interpreters of the Constitution.

The Written Constitution Is the Supreme Law

A federal state derives its existence from the Constitution, just as a corporation derives its existence from the grant by which it is created. Hence, every power, executive, legislative, or judicial, whether it belong to the nation or to the individual States, is subordinate to and controlled by the Constitution. . . . This doctrine of the supremacy of the Constitution is familiar to every American, but in England even trained lawyers find a difficulty in following it out to its legitimate consequences. The difficulty arises from the fact that under the English constitution no principle is recognized which bears any real resemblance to the doctrine (essential to federalism) that the Constitution constitutes the "supreme law of the land."

   In England we have laws which may be called fundamental or constitutional because they deal with important principles . . . but with us there is no such thing as a supreme law, or law which tests the validity of other laws. There are indeed important statutes, such as the Act embodying the Treaty of Union with Scotland, with which it would be political madness to tamper gratuitously; there are utterly unimportant statutes, such, for example, as the Dentists Act, 1878, which may be repealed or modified at the pleasure or caprice of Parliament; but neither the Act of Union with Scotland nor the Dentists Act, 1878, has more claim than the other to be considered a supreme law. Each embodies the will of the sovereign legislative power; each can be legally altered or repealed by Parliament; neither tests the validity of the other. Should the Dentists Act, 1878, unfortunately contravene the terms of the Act of Union, the Act of Union would be *pro tanto* [to that extent] repealed,[1] but no judge would dream of maintaining that the Dentists Act, 1878, was thereby rendered invalid or unconstitutional. The one fundamental dogma of English constitutional law is the absolute legislative sovereignty or despotism of the King in Parliament. . . .

The Canadian Constitution Is Modelled on That of the United States

Turn for a moment to the Canadian Dominion. The preamble to the British North America Act, 1867, asserts with diplomatic inaccuracy that the Provinces of the present Dominion have expressed their desire to be united into one Dominion "with a constitution similar in principle to that of the United Kingdom." If preambles were intended to express anything like the whole truth, for the word "Kingdom" ought to have been substituted "States," since it is clear that the Constitution of the Dominion is in its essential features modelled on that of the Union. This is indeed denied, but in my judgement without adequate grounds, by competent Canadian critics.[2]

The differences between the institutions of the United States and of the Dominion are of course both considerable and noteworthy. But no one can study the provisions of the British North America Act, 1867, without seeing that its authors had the American constitution constantly before their eyes, and that if Canada were an independent country it would be a Confederacy governed under a constitution very similar to that of the United States. The Constitution is the law of the land; it cannot be changed . . . either by the Dominion Parliament or by the Provincial Parliaments. . . .

Throughout the Dominion, therefore, the Constitution is in the strictest sense the immutable law of the land. Under this law again, you have, as you would expect, the distribution of powers among bodies of co-ordinate authority; though undoubtedly the powers bestowed on the Dominion Government and Parliament are greater when compared with the powers reserved to the Provinces than are the powers which the Constitution of the United States gives to the federal government. In nothing is this more noticeable than in the authority given to the Dominion Government to disallow Provincial Acts.

This right was possibly given with a view to obviate altogether the necessity for invoking the law Courts as interpreters of the Constitution; the founders of the Confederation appear in fact to have believed that "the care taken to define the respective powers of the several legislative bodies in the Dominion would prevent any troublesome or dangerous conflict of authority arising between the central and local governments." The futility however of a hope grounded on a misconception of the nature of federalism is proved by the existence of two thick volumes of reports filled with cases on the constitutionality of legislative enactments, and by a long list of decisions as to the respective powers possessed by the Dominion and by the Provincial Parliaments—judgements given by the true Supreme Court of the Dominion, namely, the Judicial Committee of the Privy Council.[3] In Canada, as in the United States, the Courts inevitably become the interpreters of the Constitution.

Notes

1.   Editor's note: Under the English common law and the doctrine of parliamentary sovereignty, Parliament has the power to repeal any Act. If Parliament passes an Act (such as the *Dentists Act*) that is inconsistent with an earlier Act, it is accordingly assumed that Parliament intended to repeal the inconsistent provisions.

2.   Dicey's note: If we look at the federal character of the Constitution of the Dominion, we must inevitably regard it as a copy, though by no means a servile copy, of the Constitution of the United States. . . . If, on the other hand, we compare the Canadian Executive with the American Executive, we perceive at once that Canadian government is modelled on the system of Parliamentary cabinet government as it exists in England, and does not in any wise imitate the Presidential government of America.

3.   Editor's note: When Dicey's *Introduction to the Study of the Law of the Constitution* was published, it was still possible to appeal a decision of the Supreme Court of Canada to the Privy Council, which was therefore the "court of last resort" for Canada.

From Oliver Wendell Holmes, "The Path of the Law," *Harvard Law Review* 10, no. 8 (1896–7): 457–78.

The Object of the Study of Law Is Prediction

When we study law we are not studying a mystery but a well-known profession. We are studying what we shall want in order to appear before judges, or to advise people in such a way as to keep them out of court. The reason why . . . people will pay lawyers to argue for them or to advise them, is that in societies like ours the command of the public force is entrusted to the judges in certain cases, and the whole power of the state will be put forth, if necessary, to carry out their judgements and decrees. People want to know under what circumstances and how far they will run the risk of coming against what is so much stronger than themselves, and hence it becomes a business to find out when this danger is to be feared. The object of our study, then, is prediction, the prediction of the incidence of the public force through the instrumentality of the courts. . . .

It Is the Bad Man Who Knows the Law

You can see very plainly that a bad man has as much reason as a good one for wishing to avoid an encounter with the public force. . . . A man who cares nothing for an ethical rule which is believed and practised by his neighbours is likely nevertheless to care a good deal to avoid being made to pay money, and will want to keep out of jail if he can. . . . If you want to know the law and nothing else, you must look at it as a bad man, who cares only for the material consequences which such knowledge enables him to predict, not as a good one, who finds his reasons for conduct, whether inside the law or outside of it, in the vaguer sanctions of conscience. . . .

The Moral Fallacy Holds that the Moral Phraseology in the Law Is Used in a Moral Sense

The law is full of phraseology drawn from morals, and by the mere force of language continually invites us to pass from one domain to the other without perceiving it. . . . Take the fundamental question, What constitutes the law? You will find some text writers telling you that it is something different from what is decided by the courts of Massachusetts or England, that it is a system of reason, that it is a deduction from principles of ethics or admitted axioms or what not, which may or may not coincide with the decisions. But if we take the view of our friend the bad man we shall find that he does not care two straws for the axioms or deductions, but that he does want to know what the Massachusetts or English courts are likely to do in fact. I am much of his mind. . . .

Nowhere is the confusion between legal and moral ideas more manifest than in the law of contract. Among other things, here again the so-called primary rights and duties are invested with a mystic significance beyond what can be assigned and explained. The duty to keep a contract at common law means a prediction that you must pay damages if you do not keep it, and nothing else. . . .

For my own part, I often doubt whether it would not be a gain if every word of moral significance could be banished from the law altogether, and other words adopted which should convey legal ideas uncolored by anything outside the law. We should lose the fossil records of a good deal of history and the majesty got from ethical associations, but by ridding ourselves of an unnecessary confusion we should gain very much in the clearness of our thought.

The Logical Fallacy Holds that the Law Is Developed on the Basis of Logic Rather than Policy

The next thing which I wish to consider is what are the forces which determine its [the law's] content and . . . growth. . . . It is [here] that a second fallacy comes in, which I think it important to expose. The fallacy to which I refer is the notion that the only force at work in the development of the law is logic. . . .

This mode of thinking is entirely natural. The training of lawyers is a training in logic. The processes of analogy, discrimination, and deduction are those in which they are most at home. The language of judicial decisions is mainly the language of logic. . . . [But behind] the logical form lies a judgement as to the relative worth and importance of competing legislative grounds, often an inarticulate and unconscious judgement, it is true, and yet the very root and nerve of the whole proceeding. . . .

Why does a judge instruct a jury that an employer is not liable to an employee for an injury received in the course of his employment unless he is negligent, and why do the jury generally find for the plaintiff if the case is allowed to go to them? It is because the traditional policy of our law is to confine liability to cases where a prudent man might have foreseen the injury, or at least the danger, while the inclination of a very large part of the community is to make certain classes of persons ensure the safety of those with whom they deal. . . .

There is a concealed, half conscious battle on the question of legislative policy, and if anyone thinks that it can be settled deductively, or once for all, I only can say that I think he is theoretically wrong. . . . I think that the judges themselves have failed adequately to recognize their duty of weighing considerations of social advantage. The duty is inevitable, and the result of the often proclaimed judicial aversion to deal with such considerations is simply to leave the very ground and foundation of judgements inarticulate, and often unconscious. . . . When socialism first began to be talked about, the comfortable classes of the community were a good deal frightened. I suspect that this fear has influenced judicial action both here and in England, yet it is certain that it is not a conscious factor in the decisions to which I refer.

I think that something similar has led people who no longer hope to control the legislatures to look to the courts as expounders of the Constitutions, and that in some courts new principles have been discovered outside the bodies of those instruments, which may be generalized into an acceptance of the economic doctrines which prevailed about fifty years ago, and a wholesale prohibition of what a tribunal of lawyers does not think about right. . . .

The Study of Law in the Future Will Include Statistics and Economics

The rational study of law is still to a large extent the study of history. History must be a part of the study, because without it we cannot know the precise scope of rules which it is our business to know. It is part of the rational study, because it is the first step toward an enlightened skepticism, that is, toward a deliberate reconsideration of the worth of those rules. When you get the dragon out of his cave on to the plain and in the daylight, you can count his teeth and claws, and see just what is his strength. But to get him out is only the first step. The next is either to kill him, or to tame him and make him a useful animal.

For the rational study of the law the black letter man may be the man of the present, but the man of the future is the man of statistics and the master of economics. It is revolting to have no better reason for a rule of law than that so it was laid down in the time of Henry IV. . . . I am thinking of the technical rule as to trespass *ab initio*, as it is called, which I attempted to explain in a recent Massachusetts case.[1] . . .

Far more fundamental questions still await a better answer than that we do as our fathers have done. What have we better than a blind guess to show that the criminal law in its present form does more good than harm? . . . A modern school of Continental criminologists plumes itself on the formula, first suggested, it is said, by Gall, that we must consider the criminal rather than the crime.[2] The formula does not carry us very far, but the inquiries which have been started look toward an answer of my questions based on science for the first time. If the typical criminal is a degenerate, bound to swindle or to murder by as deep seated an organic necessity as that which makes the rattlesnake bite, it is idle to talk of deterring him by the classical method of imprisonment. . . . If, on the other hand, crime, like normal human conduct, is mainly a matter of imitation, punishment fairly may be expected to help to keep it out of fashion. . . .

I look forward to a time when the part played by history in the explanation of dogma shall be very small, and instead of ingenious research we shall spend our energy on a study of the ends sought to be attained and the reasons for desiring them. As a step toward that ideal it seems to me that every lawyer ought to seek an understanding of economics. . . .

The Study of Law Should Also Include Jurisprudence

There is another study [i.e., jurisprudence] which sometimes is undervalued by the practical minded, for which I wish to say a good word. . . . Jurisprudence, as I look at it, is simply law in its most generalized part . . . [its] broadest rules and most fundamental conceptions. . . . If a man goes into law it pays to be a master of it, and to be a master of it means to look straight through all the dramatic incidents and to discern the true basis for prophecy.

Therefore, it is well to have an accurate notion of what you mean by law, by a right, by a duty, by malice, intent, and negligence, by ownership, by possession, and so forth. . . .

Notes

1.   Holmes' note: *Commonwealth v. Rubin*, 165 Mass. 453.
2.   Editor's note: Franz Joseph Gall (1758–1828) developed the science of phrenology, which held that the human psychology can be determined by the shape of a person's skull. Phrenology was based on the idea that the criminal traits—personality traits, for example—had their origins in the physical characteristics of the brain.

From *Edwards v. A.G. of Canada*, [1930] A.C. 124 (P.C.).[1]

The judgement of their Lordships was delivered by Lord Sankey, Lord Chancellor:
By sec. 24 of the British North America Act, 1867, it is provided that:

> The Governor General shall from time to time, in the Queen's name, by instrument under the Great Seal of Canada, summon qualified persons to the Senate. . . .

The question at issue in this appeal is whether the words "qualified persons" in that section include a woman, and consequently whether women are eligible to be summoned to and become members of the Senate of Canada. . . .

The Historical Evidence: Under the Common Law, Women are Incapable of Exercising Public Functions

The exclusion of women from all public offices is a relic of days more barbarous than ours, but it must be remembered that the necessity of the times often forced on man customs which in later years were not necessary. Such exclusion is probably due to the fact that the deliberative assemblies of the early tribes were attended by men under arms, and women did not bear arms. "*Nihil autem neque publicae neque privatae rei, nisi armati, agunt:*" [they do not conduct public nor private business without arms] *Tacitus Germania*, Ch. 13. Yet the tribes did not despise the advice of women: "*Inesse quin etiam sanctum et providum putant, nec aut consilia earum aspernantur aut responsa neglegunt:*" [in fact they believe that there is something holy and provident in women, and do not reject their advice or neglect their answers] *Germania*, Ch. 8.

The likelihood of attack rendered such a proceeding unavoidable, and . . . [this] exclusion of women found its way into the opinions of the Roman jurists, Ulpian (AD 211) laying it down: "*Feminae ab omnibus officiis civilibus vel publicis remotae sunt:*" [women are excluded from every civil and public office] Dig. 1.16.195. . . . In England no woman under the degree of a Queen or a Regent, married or unmarried, could take part in the government of the state. A woman was under a legal incapacity to be elected to serve in Parliament. . . .

No doubt in the course of centuries there may be found cases of exceptional women and exceptional instances, but as Lord Esher said in *De Souza v. Cobden*, [1891] 1 Q.B. 687, at 691, 60 L.J.Q.B. 533:

> By the Common Law of England women are not in general deemed capable of exercising public functions . . .

[S]upposing in an Act of Parliament several centuries ago it had been enacted that any person should be entitled to be elected to a particular office it would have been understood that the word only referred to males, but the cause of this was not because the word "person" could not include females but because at common law a woman was incapable of serving a public office. . . .

The appeal to history . . . in this particular matter is not conclusive. . . . [T]heir Lordships do not think it right to apply rigidly to Canada of to-day the decisions and the reasonings therefor which commended themselves, probably rightly, to those who had to apply the law in different circumstances, in different centuries to countries in different stages of development. . . .

The "Internal Evidence" in Canada's Constitution Is Inconclusive and the Constitution Should be Given a "Large and Liberal" Interpretation

Canada had its difficulties both at home and with the mother country, but soon discovered that union was strength. Delegates from the three maritime provinces met in Charlottetown on 1 September 1864 to discuss proposals for a maritime union. A delegation from the coalition government of that day proceeded to Charlottetown and placed before the maritime delegates their schemes for a union embracing the Canadian provinces. As a result the Quebec conference assembled on 10 October continued in session till 28 October and framed a number of resolutions. These resolutions as revised by the delegates from the different provinces in London in 1866 were based upon a consideration of the rights of others and expressed in a compromise which will remain a lasting monument to the political genius of Canadian statesmen. Upon those resolutions the British North America Act of 1867 was framed and passed by the Imperial Legislature. . . .

The British North America Act planted in Canada a living tree capable of growth and expansion within its natural limits. The object of the Act was to grant a Constitution to Canada. Like all written constitutions it has been subject to development through usage and convention. . . . Their Lordships do not conceive it to be the duty of this Board . . . to cut down the provisions of the Act by a narrow and technical construction, but rather to give it a large and liberal interpretation so that the Dominion to a great extent, but within certain fixed limits, may be mistress in her own house, as the provinces to a great extent, but within certain fixed limits, are mistresses in theirs. . . .

It is in sec. 11 that the word "persons" . . . occurs for the first time. It provides that the persons who are members of the Privy Council shall be . . . summoned by the Governor-General. The word "person" as above mentioned may include members of both sexes, and to those who ask why the word should include females, the obvious answer is why should it not. . . .

Secs 21–36 deal with the creation, constitution, and powers of the Senate. . . . Sec. 24 provides that the Governor-General shall summon qualified persons to the Senate. As already pointed out, "persons" is not confined to members of the male sex, but what effect does the adjective "qualified" before the word "persons" have? In their Lordships' view it refers back to the previous section, which contains the qualifications of a senator. . . .

Subsec. 3 of sec. 23 provided that the qualification of a senator shall be that he is legally and equitably seized of a freehold for his own use and benefit of lands and tenements of a certain value. This section gave some trouble to Mr. Justice Duff who says that subsection points to the exclusion of married women [and would have been expressed in a different way if the presence of married women had been contemplated]. A married woman can possess the property qualification required by this subsection. Apart from statute a married woman could be equitably seized of free hold property for her own use . . . and by an Act respecting certain separate rights of property of married women, Consolidated Statutes of Upper Canada, ch. 73, sec. 1, it was provided: Every woman who has married since the 4th May, 1859, or who marries after this Act takes effect, without any marriage contract or settlement, shall and may, notwithstanding her coverture, have, hold and enjoy all her real and personal property . . . in as full and ample a manner as if she continued sole and unmarried. . . .[2]

Their Lordships think that this difficulty is removed by a consideration of the rights of a woman under the Married Women's Property Acts. . . .

Looking at the sections which deal with the Senate as a whole (secs 21–36) their Lordships are unable to say that there is anything in those sections themselves upon which the Court could come to a definite conclusion that women are to be excluded from the Senate. . . .

Are there any other sections in the Act which shed light upon the meaning of the word "persons"? Their Lordships think that there are. . . . [I]n sec. 133 [for example] it is provided that either the English or the French language may be used by any person or in any pleadings in or issuing from any Court of Canada. . . . The word "person" there must include females as it can hardly have been supposed that a man might use either the English or the French language but a woman might not. . . .

A heavy burden lies on an appellant who seeks to set aside a unanimous judgement of the Supreme Court . . . but having regard

1. to the object of the Act, viz., to provide a constitution for Canada, a responsible and developing state;
2. that the word "person" is ambiguous and may include members of either sex;
3. that there are sections in the Act above referred to which show that in some cases the word "person" must include females; . . .

their Lordships have come to the conclusion that the word "persons" in sec. 24 includes members both of the male and female sex and that, therefore, the question propounded by the Governor-General must be answered in the affirmative and that women are eligible to be summoned to and become members of the Senate of Canada. . . .

Notes

1.   Editor's note: 'P.C.' is the accepted acronym for the Judicial Committee of the Privy Council.
2.   Editor's note: A married woman could not own real property under common law. Justice Lyman Poore Duff (1865–1955), one of Canada's most influential judges, served on the Supreme Court of Canada from 1906–1944 and was named Chief Justice of Canada in 1933.

✦ Discussion ✦

Dicey Describes the Federal System of Government, which Restores the Ascendancy of the Legal Order

The theory of the common law branched into two streams with the emergence of federalism, which is crucial to the development of the constitutional law. Federalism is based on the division of political powers between a central or "federal" government, in most cases, and provinces or states. This division of powers requires a written constitution, which gives the courts the authority to decide which level of government has the authority to legislate with regard to matters like taxation, health and welfare, schooling, and transportation. In Canada, this division of powers is exclusive—provincial governments are generally not permitted to pass laws with regard to matters that come under federal jurisdiction. Examples include foreign affairs and the substantive criminal law, which in Canada come within the jurisdiction of the federal government.

The American constitution goes further than a division of powers, since it includes an implied and explicit bill of rights; this kind of constitutional development occurred much later in Canada. In spite of the differences between the American and Canadian constitutions, both constitutions create a federal state, based on a supreme law that limits the political authority of government. From a historical perspective, this supreme law recalls the natural law and restores the ascendancy of the legal order over the political order.

The constitutional law in a confederation provides the fundamental framework of government and sets out the parameters within which political power can be legally exercised. This limitation on political power gives the role of the judiciary a new poignancy, in Canada and in the United States, since it is the judiciary that has the final say in the interpretation of these limits. The English constitution is usually described as "unitarian" and does not give the courts the same role in deciding the limits within which Parliament exercises its powers.

The English common law is still based on the supremacy of Parliament, though this has slowly been eroded by the recognition that individuals have basic human rights, which place legal limits on the powers of government. Dicey's explanation of the English law is a simplification, which does not recognize that the common law originally placed limits on the exercise of the sovereign power, whether it was exercised by the King or Parliament. There are instances, moreover, in which the English courts exercise authority over those in political power, independently of Parliament and outside the positive law. One example is *habeas corpus*. These attributes of the English common law go against the positivist idea that the law derives its authority from the exercise of the sovereign power, which therefore exists outside the reach of the courts.

Holmes Stakes Out an American Position

The American and Canadian courts (which were still answerable to the British courts) took different positions, historically, on the role of the courts in federalism. The American position was set out by Oliver Wendell Holmes, who by the end of his career had become the most celebrated judge on the United States Supreme Court. Holmes was known for his constitutional decisions and is best remembered for setting out the test for freedom of speech in *Schenck v. United States* (1919), 249 U.S. 47. This test holds that Congress may limit freedom of speech only when it poses "a clear and present danger" to the state. This does not mean that Holmes rejected the idea that the legislature can curtail our freedom speech: "the most stringent protection of free speech," he wrote, "would not protect a man falsely shouting fire in a theater and causing a panic."

It is an interesting question whether Holmes was a legal positivist. The development of positivism in the United States was checked by the American constitution, which naturally made it very difficult to argue that the President or Congress was supreme, or that the sovereignty of Congress was unlimited. The doctrine of parliamentary supremacy could not be imported into the United States and Canada without modifications, in spite of the fact that the Canadian courts often stated that the procedural elements of the doctrine continued to apply in Canada. Both systems are clearly based on the supremacy of a written constitution, which in Holmes' case, guaranteed the rights of the individual.

The American and Canadian law nevertheless has had its positivist side, and Holmes subscribed, like his British counterparts, to the idea that substantive issues should generally be left to the legislature. This kind of statement comes with reservations, since Holmes' position was obviously restricted by the rights recognized by the American constitution, which was ultimately rooted in the natural law, and which placed moral limits on the political sources of authority within the state. Holmes accordingly adopted a qualified positivism, which called on judges to exercise "judicial restraint" in exercising their constitutional authority.

Holmes took the position that the constitution should not be used to obstruct the legitimate work of the legislature. In *Lochner v. New York* (1905), 198 U.S. 45, another famous decision, Holmes held that state legislatures had the power to pass and implement social legislation, as long as such legislation did not offend the "due process" clause in the American constitution. Holmes believed that the positive morality of society is constantly evolving, and that the law must evolve with it, without taking sides in economic or political controversies. This view put him in regular conflict with his judicial colleagues, who often held that legislatures were obliged to respect the substantive views enshrined in the constitution.

Holmes Was a Skeptic but Recognized that the Law Has a Moral Foundation

Holmes was a considered skeptic.[1] He did not believe that "knowledge"—which is usually described in philosophy as "justified true belief"—can ever be attained, since this requires a level of certainty that is not available to anyone in the human condition. We can never be certain that our beliefs are true. Like the Greek skeptics, who asserted that all views—including their own—are matters of opinion, Holmes refused to commit himself to definite views.

Since Holmes, like many of his contemporaries, believed that law should be an empirical science, it is notable that the skeptical assertion applies to sensory and empirical impressions as well as religious, political, and philosophical beliefs: Emily may think it is raining outside—she may think that she feels the drops on her forehead—but the skeptic will probably say that there is still an element of uncertainty in her experience, and she does not "know" it is raining. There are reasons to believe that her view is the right one; but we all know that our senses can be mistaken: people have visual or auditory hallucinations, dreams can be confused with waking states, and there is always the possibility of error.

Holmes seems to have adopted the same fundamental position as the Greek skeptics, who believed that the real source of unhappiness is our desire for certainty, which is unattainable. The skeptic avoids dogmatic positions, which cannot be sustained, and in doing so achieves *ataraxia*, or quietude. For the skeptic, the philosophical quest ends not with the knowledge that there is a God or some definite truth but with the suspension of belief. It is an interesting question whether Holmes' training as a lawyer and a judge entered into such a view, since lawyers in the common law tradition are trained to take either side of a case and judges are expected to suspend their judgement during argument.

There is another side to the skeptical position, however, which is associated with the scientific epistemology constructed by the pragmatists. In point of fact, the Western scientific tradition is usually seen as a reaction to skepticism. In his *Meditations*, René Descartes saw doubt as a tool of inquiry and argued that reason was sufficient to refute the skeptical position. It is significant that Descartes was important in the development of the scientific tradition, and he influenced thinkers in the rational and empirical traditions who were also searching for a mechanism or procedure that produced knowledge. The pragmatists responded to the skeptical challenge in a more positive manner, however, and saw the failure to achieve certainty as a positive element in their scientific epistemology, since it provided an engine, essentially, that could be used to produce a more and more accurate idea of reality. The epistemological position behind this view is called "fallibilism," which holds that any set of intellectual propositions is subject to error and is always capable of correction.

The fallibilism of the pragmatists carried over into legal theory, along with their progressive idea of knowledge, and made its way into the work of Holmes and Roscoe Pound. There was a general attempt among legal theorists and jurisprudents, in the late nineteenth and early twentieth centuries, to place the law on a scientific footing. The difference between a science of law and the natural sciences, however, is that the law has a moral rather than a physical foundation, which reflects the values, beliefs, and conventions in society. Holmes believed that this moral foundation continually shifted, and he denounced the idea of the natural law as a "relentless effort to give human values a more than human significance."[2] Our belief as to what is right or wrong is always subject to revision, in Holmes' judgement, and moral judgements are relative to the society or culture in which we live.

Holmes' Positivism Is Mitigated by His Constitutionalism

Holmes adopts a mitigated positivism, which recognizes that the origins of the common law are found in the historical tradition. There is, moreover, a direct connection between law and morality. "The law," he writes, "is the witness and external deposit of our moral life. Its history is the history of the moral development of the race. . . . [T]he law, if not a part of morality, is limited by it."[3] The law is binding because it rests on the moral consensus in society.

Holmes nevertheless adopts the positivist position in arguing that there is no simple equivalence between law and morality. The immorality of the positive law does not prevent the courts from enforcing the law. "No one will deny," he writes, "that wrong statutes can be and are enforced, and we should not all agree as to which were the wrong ones."[4] If the courts enforce a bad law—an immoral law—it is no less a law.

The positivist separation between law and morality comes to the surface of Holmes' work in his idea that the law exists independently of any rational or moral justification that we find in the caselaw. The real impact of his skepticism is that the law is—in some conceptual sense—cut free from its substantive roots, which are no longer beyond question. "If you want to know the law and nothing else," Holmes writes, "you must look at it as a bad man, who cares only for the material consequences which such knowledge enables him to predict." The concept of law in Holmes' work accordingly migrates from the ruling made by a judge to the consequences of a legal decision. This is a momentous move away from the substantive rationalism in the early common law to a scientific examination of results.

Holmes' theory of the law is nevertheless mitigated by a desire to maintain the efficacy and legitimacy of the law, which loses its binding character if it fails to reflect the prevailing views in society. This evokes the kinds of concerns that surface much later in legal theory, in the work of Lon L. Fuller (see Chapter 11). He is also a constitutionalist, since he was a judge, and naturally agreed, with his judicial peers, that a law that violates the American constitution is invalid. This brings elements of the natural law into his work. There is some point, at least, where a positive law diverges so significantly from the substantive standards enshrined in the constitution that the law is of no force and effect. The difference between Holmes and his judicial contemporaries is that he believed these substantive standards are continually shifting.

Holmes Takes the General Position that the Law Should Be Studied from an Internal and an External Perspective

The simplest way to explain the different currents in Holmes legal skepticism is to recognize that he examines the common law from two different perspectives. The first is an internal perspective, which is essentially the perspective of a practitioner or a judge. A lawyer arguing a difficult case in a court must provide compelling legal reasons—reasons that are recognized as valid within the judicial system—to convince the presiding judge to rule in a particular manner. These reasons might include an appeal to the rulings in other cases, to logic and consistency, to the prevailing views in society, or to the substantive values enshrined in the provisions of the constitution. Holmes recognizes the validity of all these sources of authority, from an internal perspective within the legal system.

It is the second perspective, which is external and descriptive, that is significant in Holmes' work, however. This perspective comes out of the same scientific interests that manifest themselves in formalism and sociological jurisprudence. Although Holmes was a lawyer and a judge, and was therefore familiar with the justifications for legal decisions that were accepted within the legal system, he also believed that the legal system should be studied from an external and ultimately empirical perspective. This external perspective is a part of the new scientism, which reflects the emergence of the social sciences. Strictly speaking, the law is what the courts do rather than the set of rules that they enforce. In this view, the law loses its obvious source of validity and must be justified in some objective—and ultimately more scientific—way. It is not enough that the law has its origins in our customs and beliefs.

Holmes' use of the metaphor of the bad man is possible only because his skepticism has already detached him from the substantive justifications in the caselaw. By introducing this metaphor, however, Holmes takes the essential theoretical step from an internal to an external perspective. This step detaches the law from its internal sources and gives it an objective existence. The empirical consequences of legal decisions may then be studied in their own right, independently of the process of justification that brought them into being. It is this perspective that Holmes is articulating when he describes rights and duties as "prophecies." A "legal duty so called is nothing but a prediction that if a man does or omits certain things he will be made to suffer in this or that way by a judgement of the court."[5] This kind of reasoning discounts the internal, explanatory element in the judicial process and suggests that legal decisions must be externally justified.

The External Perspective Gives Rise to Two Lines of Inquiry

There are aspects of the internal and external perspectives in Holmes' legal theory. It is his introduction of an external perspective, however, that is distinctive. In the final analysis, Holmes is primarily interested in the results of a legal ruling rather than its internal logic. This gives rise to two separate lines of inquiry. The first is factual and descriptive: if law is what the courts do, and we want to know the law, we need to investigate the behaviour of judges. This inquiry leads into legal realism and brings psychology, the social sciences, and politics into the legal analysis. The second line of inquiry is normative and leads into legal skepticism, which sets out the way that judges should interpret the constitution.

Holmes' Descriptive Inquiry Leads Into Legal Realism

There is enough legal realism in Holmes to hold that the study of law should include a study of the motivations behind judges' decisions. As he writes:

> You can always imply a condition in a contract. But why do you imply it? It is because of some belief as to the practice of the community or of a class, or because of some opinion as to policy, or, in short, because of some attitude of yours upon a matter not capable of exact quantitative measurement, and therefore not capable of founding exact logical conclusions.[6]

It is the psychological side of the process that seems notable in the development of legal theory.

This naturally brings politics into the judicial process and implicitly raises questions as to legitimacy of judicial decisions. Socialism, Holmes notes, has "frightened" the "comfortable classes of the community" and thus become an invisible factor in many judicial decisions. Holmes' concern is not so much with the conservative bias of the courts.[7] It is rather that he believes theorists and jurisprudents should candidly acknowledge the significance of these kinds of factors and open the judicial process to a full examination.

Holmes' Normative Inquiry Leads Into Legal Skepticism

The normative component in Holmes' views is found in legal skepticism, which supplies his constitutional theory. This skepticism has a weaker and a stronger thesis. The stronger thesis—which applies to Holmes—is that judges should be moral skeptics. The weaker thesis is that judges must distance themselves from their personal opinions and base their decisions on the prevailing moral consensus in society. There are internal and external elements at work in such a theory. A judge deciding a constitutional case must meet the internal criteria within the legal system for a valid legal decision. The empirical and scientific aspects of Holmes theory push him further, however, and suggest that the judiciary should also consider external criteria.

Legal Skepticism Was a Product of the Contest between the Courts and the Legislature

Legal skepticism was a product of the historical rivalry between legal and political institutions in the United States. This rivalry broke through the surface of the American jurisprudence during Holmes' tenure on the Supreme Court. It was part of larger changes in society, which gave government a much larger role in social policy. Although Bentham—in his inflammatory way—accused the judiciary of imposing its views on the rest of society, it was rather that Parliament had entered into the business of social change and pushed the older order aside.

There are a number of reasons the rivalry between legal and political institutions became such a prominent issue in the United States. Some of these reasons are economic and concern the rise of capitalism. Some of them concern the conservative political views of individual judges. The major source of the contest between legal and political institutions, however, lies in the fact that the American constitution gives the legal order ascendancy over the political order. The constitutional law, moreover, reflected the historical distrust of the centralized authority of the state, which found expression in the *Magna Carta* long before the emergence of democratic institutions. The legal order was rooted in the past; the politics of the day looked to the future.

In *Lochner* (1905) and *Adkins* (1923), Holmes Argued that Judges Should Suspend Their Political Views

The constitutional aspects of this dispute can be seen in Holmes' dissent in *Lochner v. New York* (1905), 198 U.S. 45. The antecedents of the decision are recounted by Catherine Drinker Bowen:

> New York State had passed a law prohibiting more than ten hours work per day in bakeries. A man named Lochner who owned a bakery in Utica broke the law twice and was fined for it. Lochner appealed on the grounds that the ten-hour law was class legislation, favouring workers. It denied, said Lochner's counsel, "equal protection of the laws."[8]

The argument was that the legislature was taking sides in a dispute between an employer and his employees.

The majority in the United States Supreme Court took the position that the legislation restricted the owner's freedom of contract and had therefore violated the constitution.

> Justice Peckham wrote the majority opinion, and on April 5, 1905, announced it in Court. The ten-hour law, he declared, was a "meddlesome interference"; the spread of such laws in the various states was deplorable.[9]

Holmes dissented on the basis that states have a constitutional right "to make their own social experiments."[10]

Holmes began his brief dissent by stating that the majority in the court had decided the case "upon an economic theory which a large part of the country does not entertain." Rather than express an opinion as to whether he agreed with such a theory, Holmes took the position that the majority had no right "to embody their opinions in law."[11] After listing a number of decisions that upheld laws that constrained the liberty of contract, Holmes wrote:

> Some of these laws embody convictions or prejudices which judges are likely to share. Some may not. But a constitution is not intended to embody a particular economic theory, whether of paternalism and the organic relation of the citizen to the State or of *laissez faire*. It is made for people of fundamentally differing views, and the accident of our finding certain opinions natural and familiar or novel and even shocking ought not to conclude our judgment upon the question whether statutes embodying them conflict with the Constitution of the United States.[12]

A law should be held unconstitutional only if "a rational and fair" person would necessarily reach the conclusion that it cannot be justified under the constitution.

Similarly, in *Adkins v. Children's Hospital* (1923), 261 U.S. 525, the United States Supreme Court held that federal legislation that gave a labour board the power to set a minimum wage for women was unconstitutional.[13] The decision of the majority rests, again, on its assertion that the constitution protects the "equality" of contracting individuals. The state accordingly has no power to restrain "the individual freedom of action contemplated by the Constitution." Holmes became known as "the great dissenter" for his dissents in these kinds of cases.[14]

The problem with the position of the majority is that it reduces the equality protected by the constitution to a formal equality, which does not capture the reality of the relationship between the parties.[15] It follows that the legal concepts used by the court—concepts like "equality" and "freedom of contract"—are merely abstract ideas that preserve the imbalance of power that exists between the parties. The troubling question is whether the judiciary in a case like *Adkins* was actually taking the side of the wealthy and powerful in society and protecting inequalities—in the name of equality.

Legal Skepticism Permits Changes in the Substantive Grounding of the Law

The fundamental argument for legal skepticism is that it leaves room for social change. Holmes believed that a workable constitutional theory—one that did not set the courts and legislatures against each other—must permit changes in the substantive grounding of the law. Although the common law was based on the moral consensus in society, this consensus came under increasing pressure as a result of the profound changes in society in the eighteenth and nineteenth centuries. These changes appear to have been a product of the Industrial Revolution and the emergence of capitalism, which created competing classes and interests in society.

Historically and philosophically, legal skepticism is a response to the epistemological crisis that came out of the Protestant Reformation and the Enlightenment. This crisis has its religious origins in the fact that the Reformation permitted different interpretations of the natural law. This openness to interpretation is apparent in Grotius' work, and it made its way into the theory of natural rights and the liberal tradition, which gave rise to a strong sense of individualism and made it increasingly difficult to find agreement on substantive issues.

The moral, social, and political upheavals during Holmes' life made it apparent that any viable legal theory must be able to accommodate a variety of moral and social views. This is a complex matter, which raises ethical issues. For one thing, it is often the import of our moral views that changes rather than the views themselves. It is evident, for example, that the American slave-owners who insisted that legislation outlawing slavery contravened their property rights under the United States Constitution were Christians who held substantially the same beliefs as contemporary Christians.[16] It is the interpretation of these beliefs that has changed.

Judges Have an Obligation to Bring the Law into Conformity with the Current Consensus in Society

Holmes has been criticized on the basis that the skepticism in his work leads to a kind of moral relativism, so much so that a comparison has been drawn between Holmes and Adolf Hitler.[17] There are limits to Holmes' skepticism, however, and it does not prevent him from accepting that we should accept the moral judgements of society at large. It is therefore the beliefs of the community that the judiciary should fall back on in deciding the law, even if those beliefs go against judges' personal opinions.

In "The Path of Law," Holmes writes that it is the special responsibility of the judiciary to continually bring the law "into conformity with the current standards of morality." A judicial decision

> can do no more than embody the preference of a given body [of people] in a given time and place. We do not realize how large a part of our law is open to reconsideration upon a slight change in the habit of the public mind.[18]

The enlightened judge continually reinterprets the existing body of jurisprudence in the light of changing social values.

This kind of moderated skepticism goes beyond the constitutional law and is now an ordinary part of the judicial role. A Catholic judge who does not believe in divorce may be expected to apply the *Divorce Act*; a judge who believes in euthanasia may have to try an accused for "assisted suicide"; a judge who does not believe in the government's policy on immigration may have to determine the legal issues that arise out of it. In each of these cases, we expect the judiciary to set aside personal beliefs. The same rule applies to juries. A jury trying a case of obscenity is instructed to apply the standards of "the contemporary Canadian community"—the members of a jury cannot simply fall back on their personal beliefs or the beliefs of a particular segment of the community.[19]

It seems clear that legal skepticism usually favours the legislature rather than the judiciary in deciding substantive issues, since it is the legislature that responds directly to the changing views of society. There is a good discussion of this issue in *Furman v. Georgia* (1972), 408 U.S. 238, where the United States Supreme Court found that the death penalty was "cruel and unusual punishment." The deeper issue, however, was whether it was for the courts or the legislature to decide the issue. The Holmesian position is that the judiciary should intervene constitutionally only when the legislature has gone demonstrably beyond the rational limits of its mandate.

Judges Have an Obligation to Set Out the Moral and Social Purpose of the Law

The external perspective in Holmes' work goes beyond mere skepticism, however. Although Holmes believes that the law should express the current consensus in society, he also predicts that empirical methods will be available in the future to test the efficacy of the law. Judges should see the law as a science and rely on the scientific method to validate it. This idea recalls the "jurisprudence of ends" envisaged by Roscoe Pound. The law is a kind of social experiment, with operational hypotheses, which are verified or falsified by the empirical results that it provides.

The immediate consequence of such an approach is that it brings the policy aspects of the law to the surface of the legal discussion. As Holmes says, in the reading:

> I think that the judges themselves have failed adequately to recognize their duty of weighing considerations of social advantage. The duty is inevitable, and the result of the often proclaimed judicial aversion to deal with such considerations is simply to leave the very ground and foundation of judgements inarticulate, and often unconscious.

Judges should follow a more scientific approach. They are obliged to set out the purpose of the law and then examine the results it produces, to see if the rule or provision in question achieves its purpose.

Legal skepticism accordingly extends the legal analysis into the purpose or objective of legal rules. This means that the purpose of legislation must be rationally justified. As Holmes writes,

> a body of law is more rational and more civilized when every rule it contains is referred articulately and definitely to an end which it subserves, and when the grounds for desiring that end are stated or are ready to be stated in words.[20]

There must be a rational connection between the purpose of a law or statute and the means by which it endeavours to carry out that purpose.

On a practical level, the process of rational justification requires that judges consider the reason for a legal rule, and the means by which it accomplishes its purpose, before applying it in difficult cases. For Holmes, it is the science of economics that captures the empirical and rational sides of such a process and determines whether a particular policy is sound. One of the important aspects of economics in this context is that it is predictive and tells us what results we can expect if certain policies are implemented.

The idea that the purpose of a law must be rationally justified has become a fundamental part of the constitutional law. This idea of justification has also become prominent under section 1 of the *Canadian Charter of Rights and Freedoms*, which places "reasonable limits" on individual rights and freedoms guaranteed under the enactment. In *R. v. Oakes*, [1986] 1 S.C.R. 103, the Supreme Court of Canada held that a legislative provision cannot be justified under this section unless the means that it employs are "rationally connected" to a valid objective. This kind of inquiry takes the courts into the kind of analysis that Holmes espouses in "The Path of the Law."

Sankey Deals With the Problem of Substantive Change through a Historic Compromise

There are differences in the way that the Canadian and the American courts have dealt with the problem of substantive change. This is a reflection of the different constitutional traditions in the United States and in Canada. Holmes' legal skepticism was a reaction to the ideological stance adopted by many American judges, who frequently used the constitution to defeat social legislation. It is the political aspects of the judicial task that seem to come to the forefront in the American caselaw.

The Canadian judicial tradition, like the tradition in most Commonwealth countries, was historically based on the common law tradition in England. The style of adjudication in England has often been described as "plain fact" adjudication.[21] This style of adjudication holds that it is the legislature that makes the law.[22] Since England does not have a written constitution, English judges had relatively few opportunities to place overt legal limits on the exercise of political power.

The historical character of the constitutional law in Canada reflects the influence of the English judicial tradition. The *British North America Act*—Canada's original constitution, which was proclaimed in 1867—was an Act of the British House of Commons rather than an indigenous declaration or manifesto. It follows that the Canadian constitution, from an English perspective, was an English statute, to be interpreted in accordance with the English law. In addition, there is the fact that the Privy Council in London was the court of last resort for Canada until 1949. As a result, it was English judges, trained in English law, who originally had the final say in the interpretation of the Canadian constitution.

There is also the fact that the *BNA Act* does not contain a bill of rights. As a result, the Canadian constitution did not place the same kind of limits on the exercise of political authority as the American constitution did. The provisions in the Act that attracted the most litigation dealt with the division of powers between the federal and provincial governments. As a result, the early constitutional law concerned itself primarily with the question whether the federal or provincial governments had the power to pass a particular law, rather than with the limits on parliamentary government. There were also differences in the attitude toward government in Canada and the United States. The "Dominion" of Canada was a creation of the English Crown and Parliament. The United States was formed in the legal discontinuity—the breach in the legal order—created by the American Revolution, which rescinded the authority of the Crown and Parliament.

These differences are crucial. The *BNA Act*, unlike the American constitution, presupposes the fact of government and a concomitant legal and political order. This is reflected in the retention of the monarchy and the recognition, in the preamble to the *BNA Act* that the provinces of the Dominion of Canada desired "a Constitution similar in Principle to that of the United Kingdom." It has accordingly been said that the Canadian tradition, like the British tradition, is based on a fundamental respect for authority.[23]

All of these factors placed implicit constraints on the Canadian judiciary, which was less inclined to overturn legislation on constitutional grounds than the American judiciary was. The institutional and sociological factors that account for the differences in the attitudes of the two judiciaries have not been properly investigated. One issue that demands attention is the historical process of appointing judges in the two countries, along with the ideological factors that go into such a process.

For all of these reasons, the Canadian judiciary has historically been a black letter judiciary and was reluctant to go against the common law.[24] This may have changed somewhat with the entrenchment of the *Canadian Charter of Rights and Freedoms* in the constitution.[25] The decision of John Sankey and the Privy Council in *Edwards v. A.G. of Canada*, [1930] A.C. 124 (P.C.), nevertheless illustrates the conservative character of the Supreme Court of Canada at the time. After all, the decision of the Privy Council overturned the decision of the Supreme Court, which had held that the Governor General had no power to appoint women to the Senate.[26]

The Privy Council Held that the BNA Act Should Be Given a Large and Liberal Interpretation

The Privy Council overruled the Supreme Court of Canada on the basis that the *BNA Act* should be interpreted in a manner that befits its constitutional status:

> Their Lordships do not conceive it to be the duty of this Board . . . to cut down the provisions of the Act by a narrow and technical construction, but rather to give it a large and liberal interpretation.

The Privy Council accepted the position adopted by counsel in *St. Catherine's Milling and Lumber Co. v. Reg.* (1888) 14 App. Cas. 46 (P.C.), an earlier case in which the lawyers had argued that the *BNA Act* should be "interpreted in a large, liberal, and comprehensive spirit," in light of "the magnitude of the subjects with which it purports to deal."[27]

This is a progressive interpretation, but one that is well within the ordinary rules of statutory construction. In theory, at least, it means that the judiciary is charged with interpreting a statute in accordance with the wishes of a legislative body rather than applying its own views. As the Privy Council observes, however, the rules of statutory construction vary in the case of different kinds of statutes. Penal statutes, and statutes dealing with taxation, are interpreted strictly, in order to narrow the scope of any personal liability.[28] Constitutional statutes, and statutes that confer rights and privileges, on the other hand, are interpreted broadly, in order to extend their effect. In both cases, the rules of construction favour personal liberty.

This reading of the rules of construction has been seen, in Canada, as part of an implied bill of rights in the English constitutional tradition, which places inherent restrictions on the legislature. This interpretation derives from the liberal orientation of the common law tradition. The constitutional tradition in England was primarily a procedural tradition, however, and placed few substantive constraints on the legislature. This is in distinct contrast to the American tradition and the United States Constitution, which gives the courts a substantive mandate. In the last thirty years, the *Canadian Charter of Rights and Freedoms* has given the Canadian courts a similar mandate and contributed an American flavour to the contemporary law.

The Constitution Must Nevertheless Contain Fixed Limits

It follows that there are two principal elements in the constitutional mandate set down by John Sankey and the Privy Council in *Edwards v. A.G. of Canada*. The progressive element recognizes that the courts are obliged to respect the continuing social and moral development of Canadian society. The more conservative element recognizes that the courts are obliged to pay close attention to the intentions of the written constitution.

Although the Canadian judiciary, as Dicey argues, has historically had oversight of the political branches of government, it did not have the kind of overt moral prerogative that a bill of rights imports into a constitutional framework. Thus, the Canadian courts generally left moral and social issues to the legislature, and the record of the Canadian courts in matters like punishment, the internment of "enemy aliens," and the exercise of personal freedoms before the entrenchment of the *Canadian Charter of Rights and Freedoms* is relatively restrained. On the other hand, the Canadian courts generally refrained from interfering with the passage of the kind of social legislation that caused such controversy in the United States.

The theory set out in *Edwards v. A.G. of Canada* can be called the Canada thesis. This thesis is central to the development of the constitutional law in Canada, which fostered the "purposive" interpretation of constitutional and quasi-constitutional legislation in

Canada.[29] The position that the Privy Council adopts is a progressive position, but one that subordinates the policy elements in any interpretation of the constitution to the purpose and structure of the existing document. This approach seems to meet Holmes' call for judicial restraint and keeps the judiciary's constitutional mandate within intelligible bounds. The compromise that this envisages seems typically Canadian.

The Canada Thesis Holds that the Constitution Is a Living Tree

The Canada thesis holds that a written constitution is a "living tree," capable of growth within certain fixed limits. This doctrine allows for incremental changes in the substantive grounding of the law, as long as they occur within the broader intentions of the original document.

The Canada thesis allows the constitutional law and the legal system as a whole to evolve in a principled way. The interesting feature of the doctrine of the living tree, however, is that it recognizes that the substantive framework of the law—which functions much like the natural law—may develop over time. This takes legal theory well beyond the confines of formalism and legal positivism and recognizes that the values and customs of a community may change. This approach may explain why the rivalry that developed in the United States—between judges who favour the progressive evolution of the constitution and those who favour "strict construction"—was far less visible in Canada.[30]

The doctrine of the living tree highlights the differences between ordinary and constitutional legislation. Since the provisions of a written constitution set out general rather than specific principles for a legal system, the phraseology of the constitutional law is relatively empty, from a substantive perspective. This makes the judicial interpretation of the law the central feature in the constitutional arena and leaves it open to continual elaboration.[31] This leaves room for the social and moral views of the community to develop.

The Canada thesis and the doctrine of the living tree have been expanded by the judiciary in recent years. In *Reference re Secession of Quebec*, [1998] 2 S.C.R. 217, for example, the Supreme Court of Canada held, at paragraph 50:

> Our Constitution has an internal architecture, or what the majority of this Court in *OPSEU v. Ontario (Attorney General)*, [1987] 2 S.C.R. 2, at p. 57, called a "basic constitutional structure." . . . As we recently emphasized in the *Provincial Judges Reference*, certain underlying principles infuse our Constitution and breathe life into it.

This internal conceptual architecture includes the rule of law, the principle of federalism, the democratic principle, and a fundamental respect for minorities.

The court in the *Secession Reference* held that these architectural principles assist the judiciary in interpreting the text of the constitution and help to determine "the scope of rights and obligations" and "the role of our political institutions."

Equally important, observance of and respect for these principles is essential to the ongoing process of constitutional development and evolution of our Constitution as a "living tree," to invoke the famous description in *Edwards v. Attorney-General for Canada*, [1930] A.C. 124 (P.C.), at p. 136. As this Court indicated in *New Brunswick Broadcasting Co. v. Nova Scotia (Speaker of the House of Assembly)*, [1993] 1 S.C.R. 319, Canadians have long recognized the existence and importance of unwritten constitutional principles in our system of government.

It follows that any attempt to interpret the provisions of the written constitution outside the context provided by such a conceptual structure is incomplete.

The Constitutional Law of Canada Has Allowed Legislatures to Enact Progressive Social Legislation

Holmes' solution to the problem presented by the conservatism of the judiciary is generally to give the legislature the lead in passing social legislation. This deference toward the legislature was far less controversial in Canada than it was in the United States, since the supremacy of Parliament in such matters went largely unchallenged. Sankey nevertheless goes further than Holmes does and essentially instructs the Canadian judiciary to adopt a progressive stance in interpreting the constitution. It is interesting that the Canadian law retained its conservative character, in spite of this, and was based firmly on the English common law tradition. As a result, the historical posture of the Canadian judiciary has been progressive and communitarian in interpreting the constitution, but remarkably restrained in dealing with legislation. This combination of traits has historically given Canadian legislatures the constitutional permission that they need to enact progressive social legislation.[32]

Notes

1. For an introduction to skepticism, see Leo Groarke, "Ancient Skepticism," in *The Stanford Encyclopedia of Philosophy*, ed. Edward N. Zalta (Spring 2009). Available at http://plato.stanford.edu.
2. Mark DeWolfe Howe, "The Positivism of Mr. Justice Holmes," as cited in the suggestions for further reading.
3. Oliver Wendell Holmes, "The Path of the Law," as cited in the readings, pp. 459–60.
4. ibid., p. 460.
5. ibid., p. 458.
6. ibid., p. 466.
7. Holmes' skepticism is apparent in the fact that he did not follow a consistent ideology on the bench. Although he was known for his more liberal decisions, he has been criticized for his conservative judgement in *Buck v. Bell* (1927), 274 U.S. 200, in which he upheld compulsory sterilization and infamously stated: "three generations of imbeciles are enough." It is apparent that Holmes' penchant for literary flourishes occasionally misfired.
8. Catherine Drinker Bowen, *Yankee from Olympus* (Boston: Little, Brown & Co., 1944), pp. 373–4.
9. ibid., p. 374.
10. ibid., p. 373.

11. *Lochner v. New York*, p. 75.

12. ibid., p. 76.

13. An excerpt from *Adkins v. Children's Hospital* is included in the additional online readings for this chapter listed in the Appendix.

14. See G. Edward White, for example, *Justice Oliver Wendell Holmes: Law and the Inner Self* (New York: Oxford University, 1993), at p. 368: "In 1929 a comment in the *Oregon Law Review*, precipitated by Holmes eighty-eighth birthday, demonstrated that the image of Holmes as 'liberal' was firmly in place. 'Justice Holmes,' the comment noted, 'has been a great dissenter, but to his credit let it be said that this is perhaps due to the fact that he has been a great liberal. He has sturdily resisted the tendency of the Supreme Court of the United States to translate its own conceptions of social policy into the laws of the state.'" It should be kept in mind that the phrase "great dissenter" has been applied to many other judges, such as Justice John Marshall Harlan (1833–1911), who preceded Holmes on the United States Supreme Court and from whom Holmes may have inherited the description.

15. This is still a theme in feminist theory. See the discussion of Catharine MacKinnon's theory of "substantive" equality in Chapter 13.

16. It is worth reviewing *Dred Scott v. John F.A. Sandford* (1856), 60 U.S. 393, the decision in which the United States Supreme Court upheld slavery, because it illustrates the profound changes in the moral foundations of the law. Holmes fought in the civil war and lived through these changes.

17. See Ben W. Palmer, "Hobbes, Holmes, and Hitler," as cited in the suggestions for further reading.

18. "The Path of the Law," as cited in the readings, p. 466.

19. See *R. v. Wagner* (1985), 43 C.R. (3d) 318 (Alta. QB) and *R. v. Kiverago* (1973), 11 C.C.C. (2d) 463 (Ont. C.A.).

20. "The Path of the Law," as cited in the readings, at p. 469.

21. The term "plain fact" has been loaded with more philosophical baggage than it can comfortably hold. This can be attributed to Ronald Dworkin and David Dyzenhaus, who have used the term to describe both a certain kind of legal positivism and a judicial tradition that restricts the role of judges to the application of the law passed by the legislature. See David Dyzenhaus, *Hard Cases in Wicked Legal Systems: Pathologies of Legality*, 2nd ed. (Oxford: Oxford University, 2010) and Ronald Dworkin, *Law's Empire* (Cambridge, MA: Harvard University, 1986).

22. In a recent parliamentary paper on judicial appointments, for example, the Lord Chancellor of Britain states: "While the legislature passes laws and the executive implements them, the judiciary interprets them in cases of dispute. The judiciary's primary role is to interpret and apply the law that Parliament has laid down." Section 1.10, "The Governance of Britain: Judicial Appointments" (October 2007). Available at www.justice.gov.uk/consultations/docs/cp2507.pdf. The following section admits, rather begrudgingly: "The judges also have a crucial role in developing the common law. However, because Parliament is sovereign, Parliament may always legislate to change or override the common law position."

23. This is an intellectual commonplace. See, for example, Michael E. Manley-Casimir, Wanda M. Cassidy, and Suzanne de Castell, "The Charter of Rights and Legal Literacy," in *Canada and Citizenship Education*, ed. Keith A. McLeod (Toronto: Canadian Education Association, 1989), pp. 83–100, at p. 87: "The link to Britain and the English Common Law tradition is much stronger in Canada than in the United States. . . . Whereas in the United States the dominant emphasis seems to be the preservation of individual freedom in a society of equal citizens, in Canada the dominant emphasis seems to be the preservation of social order in a more elitist and traditional society. There is greater respect in Canada for traditional authority, greater acceptance of elitism, of hierarchical differentiation, of administrative authority. Greater respect for authority in Canada may be due to the historical experience of living under monarchical authority."

24. Although Holmes, like many contemporary commentators, seems to use "black letter" disparagingly, the term is commonly used to refer to uncontested or well-established legal doctrine, which is based on the plain meaning or literal interpretation of rules.

25. See Charles D. Gonthier, "Sustainable Development and the Law," *McGill Journal of Sustainable Development Law and Policy* 1 (2005): 11–18, at 13: "The rule of law is fundamental to an ordered society. Black letter law serves to create a certain level of determinacy and predictability in the outcome of legal disputes. But an ordered society requires commitment to others; otherwise order will not prevail for very long. A society that does not succeed in meeting the needs of a significant segment of its population is a society doomed to instability, no matter how many black letter laws it has. There can be no proper application of the law in such a context. Thus, as a complement to the rule of law, there is the spirit of the law. The spirit of the law is not concerned so much with setting down rules. Rather, it reflects the values which a society draws upon in its development of legal rules."

26. There is an extensive discussion of the personal, social, and political background to the decision in *Edwards v. A.G. of Canada* in Robert J. Sharpe and Patricia I. McMahon, *The Persons Case: The Origins and Legacy of the Fight for Legal Personhood* (Toronto: University of Toronto, 2007).

27. *St. Catherine's Milling and Lumber Co. v. Reg.* (1888) 14 App. Cas. 46 (P.C.), p. 50.

28. See *R. v. Richardson*, for example, 2003 NBQB 36 (CanLII), at para. 24, where the court adopts the statement in E.G. Ewaschuk, *Criminal Pleadings and Practice in Canada*, 2nd ed. (Aurora, ON: Canada Law Book, 1987–present), para. 33: 1030: "In construing a statute imposing criminal or other penalties, or affecting the liberty or security of a person, a court may interpret the statute in such a way as to resolve any *reasonable ambiguity* in favour of the person subject to conviction or penalty." The court then continues: "As a practical consequence, if there is an ambiguity in the use of a word, a criminal court will use the meaning that restricts the scope of the criminal law to the smallest number of cases."

29. See *Charlebois v. Mowat*, 2001 NBCA 117 (CanLII), for example, at para. 20, where the Court of Appeal holds: "The jurisprudence on the interpretation of rights and freedoms in Canadian constitutional law shows that the Supreme Court of Canada has on several occasions articulated general principles designed to guide our courts in the interpretation of constitutional rights. Generally speaking, the Supreme Court can be said to advocate a large, liberal, dynamic and purposive interpretation of constitutional rights." And see *Re Manitoba Language Rights*, [1985] 1 S.C.R. 721, where the Supreme Court of Canada, at para. 65, holds: "This Court cannot take a narrow and literal approach to constitutional interpretation. The jurisprudence of the Court evidences a willingness to supplement textual analysis with historical, contextual, and purposive interpretation in order to ascertain the intent of the makers of our Constitution."

30. It will be interesting to see if this kind of relative peace survives the political tensions that the *Canadian Charter of Rights and Freedoms* has introduced into the jurisprudence.

31. It is true that the same might be said, to a lesser extent, of the entire common law tradition, which is remarkably supple in its use of language.

32. The stance of the Canadian courts might be compared with the stance adopted by American judges like Justice Benjamin Cardozo, which was also progressive but more judicially assertive. See note 1, in Chapter 7, which concerns Cardozo.

Study Questions

1. Dicey writes that federalism requires a division of political power between the federal government and provincial or state governments. Why does this arrangement restore the ascendancy of the legal order and guarantee the supremacy of the courts?

2. Although Holmes writes that the law is "the history of the moral development of the race," he is also a moral skeptic. Would you classify Holmes as a legal positivist? Or is he someone who believes that the validity of the legal order ultimately rests on its correspondence with the moral law?

3. What is the "moral fallacy" that Holmes finds in legal theory? What is the "logical fallacy"?

4. Legal skepticism and the Canada thesis are a response to a problem that probably arises in the development of any body of law. What is the problem?

5. The decision of the Privy Council in *Edwards v. A.G. of Canada* holds that women are "persons" within the meaning of the relevant provision in the *BNA Act*. What exactly was the basis of this finding?

6. What is the essential moral and philosophical difference between legal skepticism and the doctrine of the living tree?

7. In *Edwards v. A.G. of Canada*, the Privy Council holds that a constitution must be given a "large and liberal interpretation." Some American commentators have taken the opposite position, however, and proposed a theory of "strict construction," under which the judiciary is required to interpret the constitution in accordance with the intentions of its original founders. Which position do you take, and why?

Further Reading

Bowers v. Hardwick (1968), 478 U.S. 186 and *Lawrence v. Texas* (2003), 539 U.S. 558. Both available at http://supreme.justia.com. In *Bowers*, the United States Supreme Court held that the Constitution of the United States "does not confer a fundamental right upon homosexuals to engage in sodomy." This decision was reversed in *Lawrence*. Taken together, these cases appear to illustrate the Holmesian view that the common law necessarily evolves as moral attitudes change.

Buck v. Bell (1927), 274 U.S. 200. This famous case has raised issues as to Holmes' legal skepticism.

Samuel V. LaSelva, *Moral Foundations of Canadian Federalism: Paradoxes, Achievements, and Tragedies of Nationhood* (Montreal: McGill-Queen's, 1996).

Mark DeWolfe Howe, "The Positivism of Mr. Justice Holmes," *Harvard Law Review* 64 (1951): 529–46.

Ben W. Palmer, "Hobbes, Holmes, and Hitler," *American Bar Association Journal* 31 (1945): 569.

R. v. Wagner (1985), 43 C.R. (3d) (Alta. QB). This case examined the meaning of "obscenity," based on a community-standards test.

Robert J. Sharpe and Patricia I. McMahon, *The Persons Case: The Origins and Legacy of the Fight for Legal Personhood* (Toronto: University of Toronto, 2007).

9 Legal Realism Adopts an External Perspective

Karl Llewellyn and Jerome Frank

Readings

- From "A Realistic Jurisprudence—the Next Step," by Karl Llewellyn
- From *Law and the Modern Mind*, by Jerome Frank

Legal skepticism and pragmatism gave rise to legal realism. Karl Llewellyn (1893–1962), a professor at Columbia University, advocated a study of law based on the behaviour of judges and the individuals affected by judicial decisions. This approach treats the law as a social science. Legal realism has two main branches. The sociological branch emanates from the work of Roscoe Pound and Llewellyn, and it gave rise to sociology of law and critical legal studies. The psychological branch emerges conspicuously in the work of Jerome Frank (1889–1957), an appellate judge, who investigated the psychological dimensions of the judicial process.

⚔ Readings ⚕

From Karl N. Llewellyn, "A Realistic Jurisprudence— the Next Step," *Columbia Law Review* 30, no. 4 (April 1930): 431–65.

The Behaviour Analysis

I should like to begin by distinguishing real "rules" and rights from paper rules and rights. The former are conceived in terms of behaviour; they are but other names, convenient shorthand symbols, for the remedies, the actions of the courts. They are descriptive, not prescriptive, except in so far as [it] may occasionally be implied that courts *ought to* continue in their practices.

"Real rules," then, if I had my way with words, would by legal scientists be called the practices of the courts, and not "rules" at all. And statements of "rights" would be statements of likelihood that in a given situation a certain type of court action loomed in the offing. Factual terms. No more. This use of "rights," at least, has already considerable standing among the followers of Hohfeld.[1] . . .

"Paper rules" are what have been treated, traditionally, as rules of law: the accepted *doctrine* of [a given] time and place—what the books there say "the law" is. The "real rules" and rights—"what the courts will do in a given case, and nothing more pretentious"—are then predictions. They are, I repeat, on the level of isness and not of oughtness; they seek earnestly to go no whit, in their suggestion, beyond the remedy actually available. . . . [T]heir intent and effort is [merely] to describe. And one can borrow for them Max Weber's magnificent formulation in terms of probability: a right (or practice, or "real rule") exists *to the extent that* a likelihood exists that *A* can induce a court to squeeze, out of *B*, *A*'s damages. . . .

The measure of a "rule," the measure of a right, becomes what can be done about the situation. . . . Facts, in the world of isness, to be compared directly with other facts, also in the world of isness.

A reversion, do you say, to the crude and outmoded thinking of rules in terms of remedies only, to confining legal thinking to the vagaries of tradition-bound procedure [i.e., the thinking of the early common law, which was based the availability of specific remedies]? Not quite. . . . Gone is the ancient assumption that law is because law is; there has come since, and remains, the inquiry into the purpose of what courts are doing. . . . Here value judgements re-enter the picture, and should. Observing particular, concrete facts of conduct and of expectation which suggest the presence of "an interest," one arrives at his value conclusion that something in those facts calls for protection at the hands of state officials. . . .

In conclusion, . . . I have argued that the trend of the most fruitful thinking about law has run steadily toward regarding law as an engine (a heterogeneous multitude of engines) having purposes, not values in itself; and that the clearer visualization of the problems involved moves toward ever-decreasing emphasis on words, and ever-increasing emphasis on observable behaviour. . . . Indeed that the focus of study, the point of reference for all things legal has been shifting, and should now be consciously shifted to the area of contact, of interaction, between official regulatory behaviour and the behaviour of those affecting or affected by official regulatory behaviour; and that the rules and precepts and principles which have hitherto tended to keep the limelight should be . . . [replaced by] rules with real behaviour correspondences. . . .

Included in the field of law under such an approach is everything currently included, and a vast deal more. At the very heart, I suspect, is the behaviour of judges, peculiarly, that part of their behaviour which marks them as judges—those practices which establish the continuity of their office with their predecessors and successors. . . . Close around it on the one hand lies the behaviour of other government officials. On the other, the sets of accepted formulae which judges recite, seek light from, try to follow. Distinguishing here the formulae with close behaviour-correspondences from others; those of frequent application from those of infrequent.

Close around these again, lie various persons' ideas of what the law is; and especially their views of what it or some part of it ought to accomplish. . . . Farther from the centre lies legal and social philosophy. . . . As to the overlapping of the field as thus sketched with that of other social sciences, I should be sorry if no overlapping were observable. The social sciences are not staked out like real estate. Even in law the sanctions for harmless trespass are not heavy.

Note

1. Editor's note: Wesley Newcomb Hohfeld (1979–1918). This seems to interpret Hohfeld's work, since it is the technical abstraction of Hohfeld's discussion of rights that stands out. Still, Hohfeld's work is in the analytic tradition, and his attempt to map out the logical or conceptual structure of our legal rights is descriptive rather than normative. See Wesley Newcomb Hohfeld, "Some Fundamental Legal Conceptions as Applied in Judicial Reasoning," *Yale Law Journal* 23 (Nov. 1913): 16: 28–59.

From Jerome Frank, *Law and the Modern Mind* (London: Stevens & Sons, [1930] 1949).

Part 1

Chapter II: A Partial Explanation

That religion shows the effects of the childish desire to recapture a father-controlled world has been often observed. But the effect on the law of this childish desire has escaped attention. And yet it is obvious enough: To the child the father is the Infallible Judge, the Maker of definite rules of conduct. He knows precisely what is right and what is wrong and, as head of the family, sits in judgement and punishes misdeeds. The Law . . . inevitably becomes a partial substitute for the Father-as-Infallible-Judge. That is, the desire persists in grown men to recapture, through a rediscovery of a father, a childish, completely controllable universe, and that desire seeks satisfaction in a partial, unconscious, anthropomorphizing of Law . . .

Chapter IV: Judicial Law-Making

The Reigning View Is that Judges Do Not Make Law

The conventional view [of the law] may be summarized thus:

> Law is a complete body of rules existing from time immemorial and unchangeable except to the limited extent that legislatures have changed the rules by enacted statutes. . . .

When a former decision is overruled, we must not say that the rule announced in the earlier decision was once the law and has now been changed by the later decision. We must view the earlier decision as laying down an erroneous rule. . . .

The Minority View Is that Judges Make Law

There is a contrary minority view, which any dispassionate observer must accept as obviously the correct view:

"No intelligent lawyer would in this day pretend that the decisions of the courts do not add to and alter the law," says [Frederick] Pollock, a distinguished English jurist. "Judge-made law is real law," writes [Arthur Venn] Dicey, another famous legal commentator, "though made under the form of, and often described by judges no less than jurists, as the mere interpretation of law. . . . Nine-tenths, at least, of the law of contract, and the whole, or nearly the whole, of the law of torts are not to be discovered in any volume of the statutes. . . . Whole branches, not of ancient but of very modern law, have been built up, developed or created by action of the courts."

Judges, then, do make and change law. The minority view is patently correct; the opposing arguments will not bear analysis.

It Is the Desire for a Father-Fixed Universe that Explains the View that the Law Does Not Change

What, then, explains the belief so tenaciously held that the judiciary does not ever change the law or that, when it does, it is acting improperly? . . . We revert to our thesis: The essence of the basic legal myth or illusion is that law can be entirely predictable. Back of this illusion is the childish desire to have a fixed father-controlled universe, free of chance and error due to human fallibility. In early stages of legal development this desire was more intense than now and there was what Sir Henry Maine has called "a superstitious disrelish of change" which went to the extent of making men oppose any modification of existing law even by statutory legislation.

The Problem If Judges Make Law Is that They Do So Retroactively

We have partially overcome the superstitious antipathy to legal change so far as the change results from the action of legislative bodies, and no little part of the law is modified each year by statutes enacted by state legislatures and by Congress.

But such statutory legislation, while it may alter the law, does so, ordinarily, only prospectively. It is the usual practice—to some extent it is required by constitutional prohibitions—that changes embodied in statutes enacted by legislative bodies should not be retroactive but should apply only to future conduct. . . . Consequently, absolute certainty and predictability are apparently not endangered by alterations of law made or adopted by legislatures.

But if it is once recognized that a judge, in the course of deciding a case, can for the first time create the law applicable to that case, or can alter the rules which were supposed to exist before the case was decided, then it will also have to be recognized that the rights and obligations of the parties to that case may be decided retroactively. A change thus made by a judge, when passing upon a case, is a change in the law made with respect to past events—events which occurred before the law came into existence. . . .

If, therefore, one has a powerful need to believe in the possibility of anything like exact legal predictability, he will find judicial law-making intolerable and seek to deny its existence.

Hence the myth that the judges have no power to change existing law or make new law: it is a direct outgrowth of a subjective need for believing in a stable, approximately unalterable legal world—in effect, a child's world.

This remark might be challenged on the ground that the desire to avoid legal retroactivity is not "subjective" but practical, because, it may be said, men cannot and will not engage in affairs without having in mind the pertinent law. Yet reflection reveals the fact that the supposed *practical* importance of avoiding legal retroactivity and uncertainty is much overrated, since most men act without regard to the legal consequences of their conduct, and, therefore, do not act in reliance upon any given pre-existing law:

> "Practically," says John Chipman Gray, "in its application to actual affairs, for most of the laity, the law, except for a few crude notions of the equity involved in some of its general principles, is all *ex post facto*. When a man marries, or enters into a partnership, or buys a piece of land, or engages in any other transactions, he has the vaguest possible idea of the law governing the situation, and with our complicated system of Jurisprudence, it is impossible it should be otherwise. . . ."

The no judge-made law doctrine, it seems, is not, fundamentally, a response to practical needs. It appears rather to be due to a hunger and a craving for a non-existent and unattainable legal finality. . . .

The Dangers of Denial Lie in the Accusation that the System Is Dishonest

But what of it? What harm in this myth? No harm, if the denial of judicial law-making were a mere pleasantry, in the category of what Austin and Morris Cohen refer to as polite or euphemistic fictions; that is, statements contrary to fact, but known by all to be such and comparable to the fibs of daily social intercourse. But the denial of the fact of judge-made law is no mere fib. . . . It leads, sooner or later, to a distrust of the judges, a disrespect for their opinions. For now and again the public becomes aware that in some actual cases the judges have made or changed the law. Then follow accusations of dishonesty, of corruption, of usurpation of authority, of revolutionary violation of the judicial oath of office, and the like. And it is difficult to reply to such accusations when the judges themselves deny that they have power to make law and yet go on (unavoidably and unmistakably) making it. . . .

Chapter XII: The Judging Process and the Judge's Personality

The process of judging, so the psychologists tell us, seldom begins with a premise from which a conclusion is subsequently worked out. Judging begins rather the other way around—with a conclusion more or less vaguely formed; a man ordinarily starts with such a conclusion and afterwards tries to find premises which will substantiate it. . . .

Tulin's Study

Professor [Leon A.] Tulin has made a study which prettily illustrates that fact. While driving at a reckless rate of speed, a man runs over another, causing severe injuries. The driver of the car is drunk at the time. He is indicted for the statutory crime of "assault with intent to kill." The question arises whether his act constitutes that crime or merely the lesser statutory crime of "reckless driving." The courts of several states have held one way, and the courts of several other states have held the other. The first group maintain that a conviction for assault with intent to kill cannot be sustained in the absence of proof of an actual purpose to inflict death. In the second group of states the courts have said that it was sufficient to constitute such a crime if there was a reckless disregard of the lives of others. . . .

With what, then, appears to be the same facts before them, these two groups of courts seem to have been sharply divided in their reasoning and in the conclusions at which they have arrived. But upon closer examination it has been revealed by Tulin that, in actual effect, the results arrived at in all these states have been more or less the same. In Georgia, which may be taken as representative of the second group of states, the penalty provided by the statute for reckless driving is far less than that provided, for instance, in Iowa, which is in the first group of states. . . . In order to make it possible for the Georgia courts to give a reckless driver virtually the same punishment for the same offense as can be given by an Iowa judge, it is necessary in Georgia to construe the statutory crime of assault with intent to kill so that it will include reckless driving while drunk. . . .

In other words, the courts in these cases began with the results they desired to accomplish: they wanted to give what they considered to be adequate punishment to drunken drivers: their conclusions determined their reasoning.

But the conception that judges work back from conclusions to principles is so heretical that it seldom finds expression. Daily, judges, in connection with their decisions, deliver so-called opinions in which they purport to set forth the bases of their conclusions. . . . They picture the judge applying rules and principles to the facts, that is, taking some rule or principle (usually derived from opinions in earlier cases) as his major premise, employing the facts of the case as the minor premise, and then coming to his judgement by processes of pure reasoning.

Judge Hutcheson Argues that Judicial Decisions Are Based on "Hunching"

Now and again some judge, more clear-witted and outspoken than his fellows, describes (when off the bench) his methods in more homely terms. Recently Judge Hutcheson[1] essayed such an honest report. He tells us that after canvassing all the available material at his command and duly cogitating on it, he gives his imagination play,

> and brooding over the cause, waits for the feeling, the hunch, that intuitive flash of understanding that makes the jump-spark connection between question and decision and at the point where the path is darkest for the judicial fact, sets its light along the way. . . .

Judge Hutcheson adds:

> I must premise that I speak now of the judgement or decision, the solution itself, as opposed to the apologia for that decision. . . . The judge really decides by feeling and not by judgement, by hunching and not by ratiocination, such ratiocination appearing only in the opinion. . . .

We may accept this as an approximately correct description of how all judges do their thinking. But see the consequences. If the law consists of the decisions of the judges and if those decisions are based on the judge's hunches, then the way in which the judge gets his hunches is the key to the judicial process. Whatever produces the judge's hunches makes the law.

The "Hunch-Producers" Include the Political and Moral Prejudices of the Judge

What, then, are the hunch-producers? What are the stimuli which make a judge feel that he should try to justify one conclusion rather than another? The rules and principles of law are one class of such stimuli. But there are many others . . . To the infrequent extent that these other stimuli have been considered at all, they have been usually referred to as "the political, economic, and moral prejudices" of the judge. . . .

But are not those categories—political, economic, and moral biases—too gross, too crude, too wide? Since judges are not a distinct race and since their judging processes must be substantially of a like kind with those of other men, an analysis of the way in which judges reach their conclusions will be aided by answering the question, What are the hidden factors in the inferences and opinions of ordinary men?

The answer surely is that those factors are multitudinous and complicated, depending often on peculiarly individual traits of the persons whose inferences and opinions are to be explained. . . . So the judge's sympathies and antipathies are likely to be active with respect to the persons of the witness, the attorneys, and the parties to the suit. His own past may have created plus or minus reactions to women, or blonde women, or men with beards, or Southerners, or Italians, or Englishmen, or plumbers, or ministers, or college graduates, or Democrats. A certain twang or cough or gesture may painful start up memories painful or pleasant in the main. Those memories of the judge . . . may affect the judge's initial hearing of, or subsequent recollection of, what the witness said, or the weight or credibility which the judge will attach to the witness's testimony. . . .

Jurisprudence Should Include the Study of the Judicial Personality

The peculiar traits, disposition, biases, and habits of the particular judge will, then, often determine what he decides to be the law. In this respect judges do not differ from other mortals: "In every case of actual thinking," says F.C.S. Schiller, "the whole of a man's personality enters into and colours it in every part." To know the judge's hunch-producers which make the law we must know thoroughly [and therefore study] that complicated congeries we loosely call the judge's personality.

If the personality of the judge is the pivotal factor in law administration, then law may vary with the personality of the judge who happens to pass upon any given case. How much variation there is, as we pass from judge to judge, is not, as matters now stand, discoverable, because of the method of reporting cases and the verbal contrivances used by the judges which conceal judicial disharmony. We have little statistical material in this field. . . .

Schroeder, one of the few lawyers who has thought deeply and courageously about this problem . . . believes that "every choice of conclusion, argument, precedent, phrase, or word," in a judge's opinion, "is expressive of an unconscious, a dominant personal motive of the judge. Every such choice is a fragment of autobiography because it reveals not only the present conscious motive, but also the still potent, past and immature experimental causes, which determined the unconscious impulses submerged in, but controlling the avowed motive. . . . Every opinion thus amounts to a confession."

Note

1. Editor's note: Joseph C. Hutcheson Jr. (1879–1974) was a trial and appellate judge in Texas, whose theory of judicial decision-making is found in "The Judgement Intuitive: The Function of the 'Hunch' in Judicial Decisions," *Cornell Law Quarterly* 14 (1929): 274–8.

✦ Discussion ✦

Legal Realism Is an External Theory of Law

In the last chapter, we distinguished between internal and external theories of law. An internal theory of law explains how the legal process works to those working within the system. Such explanations are convincing only if we accept the internal principles within the system. Formalism can be seen as an internal theory, since the formalists— who were really setting out a theory of jurisprudence—argued that a valid legal decision must be deduced logically from the rules of the system. Legal realism, in contrast, is an external theory, which examines the empirical functioning of the system from a perspective outside the system.

Legal realism was initially allied with the social sciences, which supplied the realists with the idea that legal decisions could be studied and classified psychologically and sociologically, as an empirical form of behaviour, in the same way that the behaviour of animals or plants might be studied. Oliver Wendell Holmes' description of the law as a prediction of what judges do in particular cases was pivotal in this regard. Legal realism undermines the idea that there is a definite set of legal or moral principles, like the natural law, from which we can deduce legal rules and argues that the social and psychological provenance of the law needs investigation.

There are at least three theorists that deserve particular mention in the development of legal realism: Roscoe Pound, Karl Llewellyn (who introduced the term "realism"), and Jerome Frank. We have already considered Pound, whose legal pragmatism was influential in promoting the empirical study of the law. This empirical approach led to a more descriptive study of law and the social and psychological considerations that determine how judges make their decisions. Pound later turned against the realists, on the basis that they had neglected the primary question in legal theory. That question was normative: how, Pound asked, should the judiciary reach their decisions?

Justice Cardozo's Normative Realism Provides Some Historical Background to Legal Realism

Legal realism has its historical roots in the same constitutional controversies that led Oliver Wendell Holmes to develop the theory of legal skepticism. Holmes was only one of many theorists, however, who influenced the movement. Benjamin Cardozo (1870–1938), a justice on the New York State Court of Appeals and later the United States Supreme Court, developed a theory of the judicial role that helped to provide the theoretical foundations of legal realism.[1] In 1921, Cardozo gave the Storrs Lectures at Yale University, which were later published as *The Nature of the Judicial Process*. In these lectures, Cardozo argued that the general nature of common law concepts like "reasonable care" or "undue influence" left enough room for individual judges to justify whatever outcome they preferred in the case before them.[2]

Cardozo's theory naturally brought the personal views of the judiciary to the fore. Some judges, he wrote, favoured plaintiffs and the "weaker" members of society; others favoured defendants. It is clear, moreover, that these tendencies in the caselaw were exacerbated by the many attempts to defeat progressive legislation on constitutional grounds. We have already seen how Holmes argued, in response, that legislatures should be allowed to develop social policy; but judges like Cardozo suggested that the real problem was that the common law was ill-equipped to deal with modern social problems. It followed that the judiciary should be allowed to reconstruct the common law on more progressive lines and develop policy of their own.

The new theory can be described as normative realism. Although Cardozo's theory claims, descriptively, that judges develop the law in accordance with their own beliefs, his theory suggests that the role of the legislature and the judiciary overlap. It follows that judges should act like elected representatives, adjusting and changing the law so that it conforms with the moral and social realities of contemporary life. Cardozo accordingly refers to the judge as a "legislator" in *The Nature of the Judicial Process* and describes aspects of the judicial process as "legislative."

Cardozo rejects the idea that "the rule of adherence to precedent ought to be abandoned altogether." He nevertheless treats the doctrine of *stare decisis* more as a convenient guideline than an obligatory rule. He notes that the rule has been relaxed in the United States and quotes Wheeler, J., in *Dwy v. Connecticut Co.*, (1915) 89 Conn. 74, at p. 99, where Wheeler states that "rules of law which grew up in a remote generation" and "serve another generation badly" should be replaced with rules that reflect the current judgement of society. This is a task for the judiciary and should not be left to the legislature.

Cardozo's Theory Brings Political Considerations into the Process of Decision-Making

Cardozo was a progressive judge, who was famous for his decisions in negligence. These decisions extended the notion of "foreseeability" beyond the parties immediately affected by a tortious act. Cardozo nevertheless recognized that there had to be a common standard in the jurisprudence, to prevent judges from simply following their own predilections. This standard could be found, he suggested, in the general welfare of society.[3]

The real significance of Cardozo's theory, however, is that it obliges the judiciary to consider social issues in applying settled rules of law. This obligation inevitably requires that judges examine the empirical results of their decisions. It is not enough to merely follow the internal rules within the legal system, in order to determine how a case should be decided. Cardozo accordingly rejects formalism. Judges must consult the moral and social values in society and determine whether the consequences of a decision correspond with the prevailing views. This position is significant because it ultimately brings political considerations into the process of determining the law.

Cardozo uses a famous example to illustrate how moral and social issues come into the common law process. In *Riggs v. Palmer* (1889), 115 N.Y. 506, 22 N.E. 188, a man who murdered his grandfather was a beneficiary in his grandfather's will. The Court of Appeals was accordingly asked to determine whether the man could inherit. The case was difficult because one set of precedents held that the courts must respect the explicit intentions of the testator, the person who made the will. The murderer was therefore entitled to his inheritance.[4]

There was another set of precedents, however, from equity, which stated that no one should benefit from committing a wrong. As a result, the murderer was not entitled to inherit. Cardozo argues that either of these competing answers could be justified on the caselaw. It seems to follow—and this is the decisive theoretical move—that the judges deciding such a case must turn to their personal views and the larger public interest in deciding the case.

Cardozo's reasoning is based on the idea that there are "hard cases," which cannot be decided under the existing legal rules.[5] These cases must accordingly be decided on the basis of the judge's determination of whether the external results of the decision are desirable. It follows that these cases cannot be decided without the exercise of some moral or political judgement, which brings a judge's beliefs into the legal analysis. These cases cannot be decided without an analysis of the external results of the decision and a determination whether those results are desirable. The existence of hard cases is inherently contentious. The example that Cardozo uses is not entirely clear, since the conflicting principles in *Riggs v. Palmer* are from different areas of the law. If one takes the position that equity takes priority, for example, the case is relatively simple and the paradox that

Cardozo relies upon simply disappears.[6] In spite of this, Cardozo's argument that the judiciary had an obligation to make these kinds of policy decisions provided a crucial premise in the development of legal realism.

Some of the deeper issues raised by a case like *Riggs v. Palmer* concern the conflict between legal forms of reasoning, which are based on a rigorous application of legal principle, and a political line of reasoning based on results. Cardozo argues, at least, that there are cases in which formalism and the rigorous application of the internal legal rules within the system produce an unacceptable moral or social result. In such cases, judges are not merely entitled to fall back on prevailing moral, social, or political views; they are obliged to do so. This brings the substantive values and judgements of the judiciary into the legal process.

Realism Was Also a Response to the Reliance on Formalism in the Law Schools

Legal realism is an academic theory that took root in universities and responded to the heavy reliance on formalism in the American law schools. It accordingly led to academic struggles, which manifested themselves in the debate between Pound and Llewellyn in the pages of the *Harvard Law Review*.[7] The academic origins of legal realism distinguish it from formalism, which still provides many of the routine doctrines used by judges in the courts. Realism heralded a new and more academic study of the judicial process, which has many theoretical elements but provided an external rather than an internal theory of the common law.

Legal Realism Tries to Capture the Reality of the Judicial Process

The term "realism" has many meanings in philosophy and was originally used to describe the argument that metaphysical entities exist. It has also been used to describe the view that political decisions are often designed to preserve the existing distribution of power in society. The term was originally used in legal theory to criticize theories like the natural law and legal positivism, which—in the view of the realists—were blind to "legal realities." In a later edition of *Law and the Modern Mind*, Jerome Frank suggested that the term "constructive skepticism" would be more appropriate than "legal realism." The skepticism that Frank refers to is not the skepticism that Holmes set out; Frank's "skepticism" is an attitude rather than a theory, which questions the idea that legal decisions are based on legal principles or rational deduction.

The legal realists rejected formalism and the idea that the law is composed of a set of logical rules. Realism is nevertheless part of the legal positivist tradition, which rejects the idea that the validity of the positive law depends on whether it corresponds with an objective moral code. Rather than take such a position themselves, the realists took a theoretical stance, outside the law, that essentially held that individual judges have a critical morality—a set of deep-seated substantive beliefs that differs from the beliefs held by the average person—that determines their reading of the law.

The realists accordingly saw legal decisions as an expression of the larger social and political factors that determine the substantive beliefs held by individual judges. There is no objective standard of morality or reason that decides what the content of the law will be or determines its validity. The legal reasons that judges provide to justify their rulings—and that provide an adequate justification, within the system—fail to capture the true workings of the system. These workings are best uncovered by examining the empirical effects of such rulings in the real world, outside the system.

Legal realism, like legal pragmatism and Holmes' later skepticism, takes the position that the empirical results of specific legal rulings should be studied. This idea is a manifestation of a deeper philosophical undercurrent in legal positivism, which is significant historically because it raised the question whether the law can be determined with any certainty. From this perspective, realism can be seen as the culmination of the epistemological crisis that undermined natural law theory after the Protestant Reformation. In spite of Llewellyn's reluctance to acknowledge the idea, legal realism is based on the idea that the law is essentially indeterminate and is therefore open to individual interpretation. The realists accordingly stressed the uncertainty of the trial process.

Law Consists of the Specific Decisions of the Court

Jerome Frank wrote in *Courts on Trial* that he had no interest in the "silly word battle" that results from trying to provide a strict definition of the word "law."[8] The primary argument in legal realism is not that the word "law" has a particular meaning; it is that subjective factors will always intervene in the judicial process and affect the outcome of particular cases. As a result, the conventional idea that the common law consists of a defined body of formal rules and principles fails to capture the way in which the judiciary decides cases.

Frank takes Holmes' position and argues that the law consists of the specific decisions of the courts:

> For any particular lay person, the law, with respect to any particular set of facts, is a decision of a court with respect to those facts so far as that decision affects that particular person. Until a court has passed on those facts no law on that subject is yet in existence.

It is the decision in each case rather than the legislation or the judicial principles on which the decision has been based that constitutes the "law." In this conception, a legal system is the rather arbitrary totality of the individual decisions of the courts. This idea is problematic because it suggests that the law has no unified or systematic structure.

The Realist Conception Runs against the Idea That Judges Do Not Make Law

This conception of law runs against the historical theory of adjudication in the later common law, which holds that that judges do not make law. This position may have arisen originally in the customary law, which was based on the idea that judges found the law in the customs of the people. The notion that judges merely follow the law, which is found elsewhere, was carried over into the doctrine of *stare decisis*, which holds that judges are bound by the precedents. This notion appears to have gone through a political conversion and reappeared in the positivist doctrine of parliamentary supremacy, which holds that it is the special prerogative of the political branch to make law.

Frank is reacting to the positivist position, which had become the orthodoxy in the English law. The positivists hold that judges "are not to make or change the law but to apply it. The law, ready-made, pre-exists the judicial decisions."[9] Frank argues that this theory is not in keeping with the reality of practice, since judicial decisions are often over-ruled. This changes the law.

> If the judges in any case come to a "wrong" result and give forth a decision which is discordant with their own or anyone else's rules, their decision is nonetheless law.[10]

The law is made up of judicial decisions, which are binding whether they are wrong or right.

One of the more obvious criticisms of Frank's argument is that it is highly artificial and fails to acknowledge the ordinary meaning of the word "law." Frank's position is nevertheless explained by his adoption of the external perspective, which focusses on the results of a decision rather than the internal process that produces it. From this perspective, the defining feature of the law is that it has empirical consequences outside the legal system. These consequences naturally change when a judicial decision is changed or overturned. Frank's position stands in contrast to the position adopted by the formalists, who believed that the law is made up of the logical rules that have been accepted as binding within the system. From the perspective of the formalists, nothing has changed within the legal system when the court of appeal overturns a judge's decision. It is merely that the judge has misapplied the rules. The law accordingly remains as it was, and the internal architecture of the system remains intact.

There are two separate situations that need to be dealt with in this context. The first concerns the interpretation of legislation, which naturally "pre-exists" judicial decisions and fits easily into the formalist framework. The natural response to Frank in this context is accordingly that changes in the judicial interpretation of legislation are exactly that: changes in interpretation. They are not substantive changes in the law. It follows that the law does not change when there is a new ruling from an appellate court; the law is found in the legislation, which remains exactly as it was before the ruling takes effect.

The second situation concerns the common law proper, which is a product of judicial decisions. There are still many areas of the common law, such as torts and contracts, that are made up principally of the caselaw. It follows, in a certain descriptive sense, that the judiciary has "made" this law. The word "made" has a strong and a weak sense, however. The fact that judges have "made" the common law, in the sense that they have written it down and created the caselaw that contains it, does not mean that they have "made" it in a substantive sense. As we have seen, the common law developed out of custom and popular belief and was never considered the product of the personal views of the judiciary.

There is accordingly a new idea in realism, which is that judges "make" law in the strong sense—they create it. This is a recurring theme in the contemporary legal theory, particularly in the United States. The real innovation in realism is accordingly its rejection of the idea that judges "find" the law, whether it is in custom or the statutes. This innovation is explained, in both cases, by its replacement of an internal perspective with an external perspective. If we look only at the rational process within the law, by which the judge arrives at his decision, it is clear that he finds his answer to the legal question posed by a case internally, within the system. This is incidental to the "real" effect of the decision, which lies in its empirical consequences.

Frank argues that the common law tradition rejects the idea that judges make law because it would mean that the judiciary is applying the law retroactively. This kind of criticism has analytic sources, and Frank takes the substance of his argument from the work of John Chipman Gray (1839–1915), a distinguished lawyer and professor of law, who published a series of lectures under the title *The Nature and Sources of the Law* in 1909.[11] Since judicial decisions usually apply to circumstances that arose in the past, Frank argues, a judge who changes the law, or makes a new law, is applying rules that did not exist at the time those circumstances arose. This is unfair.

The argument against retroactivity seems misplaced. The principle of notice, which holds that no one can be expected to obey a law that is not yet in force, is a political rule, which applies to the positive law proclaimed by those who hold political authority. It has little relevance to the common law, which is based on the historical consensus in the community. Frank's criticism applies only if judges are making law, in the strong sense, rather than relying on the existing custom and practice.

The Realists Rejected the Idea that the Law Is Composed of Legislation or Common Law Rules

The realists' introduction of an external concept of law was problematic for a number of reasons. If the law is made up of judicial decisions, as they manifest themselves—empirically—outside the legal system, why do we describe the legal rules within the system as laws? A lawyer arguing a case might say: "The law is clear. A contract is not binding without consideration." What does the term "law" refer to in such a statement, if the rule that a binding contract requires consideration is not a law? Are lawyers and judges simply mistaken?

The linguistic issue that this raises is a legacy of legal positivism. John Austin described the law as a "command." As a result, compulsion came to be seen as the defining attribute of the law, and generations of theorists attempted to isolate exactly what it was in a judicial decision that made it binding. Although the positivists traced the binding nature of the positive law to its origins in political power and the political sources of authority, the realists believed that the law received its binding nature from the power of the judiciary to enforce its decisions externally, outside the system. The internal rules within the legal system merely provide the machinery out of which the judiciary made these decisions.

Frank accordingly negotiates his way around the linguistic issue in *Law and the Modern Mind* by distinguishing between law and the sources of the law. He borrows this distinction from Gray's *The Nature and Sources of the Law*, which argues that "the law" consists only of the rules that the judiciary have actually used in deciding cases. The "sources" of the law, in contrast, can be found in statutes, judicial precedents, and public policy.[12] It follows that legislation is no longer law, on the realist view, and merely provides an internal resource, within the system. Theorists like Gray, Frank writes, "scoff at the idea that law-making occurs anywhere except in the courtroom."[13]

Frank takes the distinction between law and sources of the law much further than Gray, however, and argues that the legal rules on which judges rely are also "sources" of the law. Holmes is right, Frank states; it is the bad man who understands what the law is, and the bad man has no interest in the rules applied in the courts. The bad man is interested only in the decisions of the judiciary:

> Holmes' description of law can be stated as a revision of Gray's definition, thus: Law is made up not of rules for decision laid down by the courts but of the decisions themselves. All such decisions are law. The fact that courts render these decisions make them law.[14]

There is "no mysterious entity" called "the law," apart from the decisions of the court. It is the mere fact that the decisions of judges are enforced, Frank argues, that makes them law.

The new concept of law in realism revises the role of the common law judiciary. Rather than apply the law found in precedents, or legislation, the judge becomes a "law-maker" and implicitly acquires a legislative mandate. This introduces a political component into the task of the judiciary and imports the substantive and political beliefs of the judiciary into the internal architecture of the system. These changes have a profound effect on the legal system. The introduction of political elements into the judicial role is compounded by the loss of binding internal criteria within the legal system, which determine whether a judge's decision is correct. Although Frank takes the position that a judge seized with a case has a duty to look at the relevant statutes and precedents, these sources of the law function more as guidelines and protocols than as laws. Judges who are familiar with the internal rules of the system learn to use—and unconsciously manipulate—the rules in order to produce the result that they prefer. It follows that it is the psychology of the judge and the sociology of the process that determine the ultimate disposition of a case.

From a historical perspective, realism is remarkably permissive. It allows judges to follow their own inclinations, even as it frees them from the logical and substantive constraints in the existing law. Although realism was first presented as a descriptive theory, there are many descriptive problems with the theory. The idea, for example, that a law that forbids us to drive over the speed limit is consultative goes against our ordinary understanding of the situation. The legal rules regarding the proper disposition of a case, or the requirements of pleadings, appear at least to function as compulsory rules.[15] Frank's views may be a reflection of his experience as an appellate judge, since appellate judges have more latitude in interpreting and applying the law than do trial judges. The general conduct of the common law judiciary is nevertheless governed by an abundance of technical rules and principles that appear to determine their actions in particular cases.

Frank's Realism Suggests that the Law Cannot Be Codified

There are many difficulties with realism. The realists nevertheless drew attention to the psychological aspects of the judicial role, which had been neglected in earlier theory. There is no doubt that this is explained, to some extent, by the heightened political sensibilities in the American caselaw, which saw conservative and progressive judges diverge markedly from each other in their interpretation of the common law. The realists' interest in the psychological and political aspects of the legal process was not always critical, however. Frank argued that the strict legal positivism in Bentham and Austin was simply blind to the intricacies of the legal and evidentiary process, which rest on the exercise of judicial discretion.

In *Courts on Trial*, Frank accordingly rejects the idea of codification and criticizes the idea that it is possible to construct an exhaustive list of laws:

> No code can anticipate every possible set of facts. Moreover, when social conditions change and social attitudes alter, many portions of any code act as an intolerable straitjacket. Resort is necessarily had to judicial interpretations. These interpretations, or "glosses" as they are sometimes called, take the place of the letter of the code. Judge-made glosses possess all the uncertainties of judge-made rules. Indeed, some persons have suggested that elaborate codes increase judicial legislation.[16]

These comments seem to echo the opinions of Cardozo and Wheeler. Frank's point is not merely that judges make law—it is that this is a necessary and inevitable part of the legal process, which must leave the "law" to the judiciary.

Llewellyn's Theory Represents the Sociological Branch of Legal Realism

Legal realism has two major branches—a branch that takes the study of law into sociology and another that takes the study of law into psychology. The sociological branch of realism took much of its impetus from Roscoe Pound's idea of a "sociological jurisprudence" and found expression in the work of Karl Llewellyn. This branch of realism is a reaction primarily to formalism, which failed to account for the external and empirical consequences of judicial decisions.

Pound Rejected Llewellyn's Realism because It Does Not Answer the Normative Questions in Legal Theory

Llewellyn eventually became the spokesman for a generation of realists, who questioned the orthodox view of the common law. He accordingly quarrelled with Pound, who represented an older and less radical view, which acknowledged the fundamental legitimacy of both the legal and the political process. Pound separated from Llewellyn and the realists on the basis that the primary study of law—and the curriculum of the law schools—must remain normative. This aspect of the "science of law," Pound argued, distinguishes it from physics, astronomy, and the natural sciences. Pound also argued that the realists exaggerated the "alogical or non-rational element in judicial action."

Llewellyn responded to Pound—albeit though with characteristic equivocation—by listing a number of "points of departure." The realists, he wrote, believed that there must be a "'temporary' divorce of Is and Ought" in the study of law. They firmly believed that society and the law are "in flux" and that judges inevitably make law. They regarded "traditional legal rules and concepts" with suspicion and did not believe that legal rules are "*the* heavily operative factor in producing court decisions."[17] The positivist view that judges only apply and interpret the law is erroneous.

The deeper argument between Pound and Llewellyn was whether an internal or external view should be adopted in studying the law. Although Pound believed that the law must be studied, empirically, as a science, his later view appears to have been based on the idea that judicial practice, within the system, rests on the internal perspective. From a disciplinary perspective, the realists were really drawing the outlines of a new study of the law, which found its way into sociology of law and the "law and society" movement. This development led, for example, to a "pure sociology" of law, which intentionally restricts itself to the study of the external social attributes of law.[18]

The real challenge mounted by the realists is to find a way to bring the external perspective into the traditional methodology of the common law. Any system is based on axioms, which are taken for granted by those working within the system. At the same time, these axioms are subject to change, particularly on the basis of the insights provided by an external study of the law. One of the few legacies of realism in practice is that it supported the role of experts in the trial process, who are in a position to bring scientific research into the evidentiary process. Unlike ordinary witnesses, experts are also entitled to express an opinion on the empirical issues before the court.

Llewellyn's Theory of Law Is Based on Social Groups

Llewellyn's theory of law did not have a lasting influence, probably because it contains so little normative content. Legal realism generally holds that the law consists of the behaviour of individual judges in specific cases. This seems to undermine the idea that there is an integrated system of law, which somehow functions as a coherent, logical whole. It is notable, however, that the function of the law in Llewellyn's theory is to preserve the existence of social groups.[19] It does this by providing what Llewellyn calls a "reasonable" solution to the disputes that arise within and between groups. The central function of the legal system is accordingly to provide a process of adjudication that can resolve social conflict.

Llewellyn also argued, on a more metaphysical level, that the law represents a human "quest" for justice. His argument in this regard has transcendental overtones and suggests that justice takes certain recognizable patterns across cultures. As we saw in Chapter 1, Llewellyn co-authored *The Cheyenne Way*, which studies the use of traditional legal process to resolve a number of individual cases. Although Llewellyn's argument is abstract and structural, there are affinities between the position he adopts and the natural law, which manifests itself in the same kinds of outcomes in different cultures and societies.

Llewellyn's Realism Suggests that Politics Plays an Important Role in the Judicial Process

Legal realism is problematic because it raises questions with regard to the impartiality of the legal process. Llewellyn acknowledges this issue in *The Common Law Tradition*, where he responds directly to the concern that the written reasons provided by many judges have become little more than rationalizations that justify a result in keeping with the political views of the presiding judge.[20] This raises ethical and professional issues; but it also introduces an element of uncertainty and even capriciousness into the caselaw. This uncertainty undermines the integrity of the legal system and erodes the legal legitimacy of the courts, which become participants in a political struggle for power.

From the perspective of legal practice, legal realism tends to exaggerate the uncertainty of the common law. In spite of this, Llewellyn ultimately concludes that there is a high degree of "reckonability" in the caselaw.[21] The common law is knowable. This conclusion is based on a "cluster of factors," which include the common training of legal officials and the use of recognized forms of argument and pleading. Although Llewellyn's view is similar to Pound's, in this context, Llewellyn distinguishes between a "formal" and a "grand" style of legal reasoning. The formal style is internal and logical, and related to formalism. The grand style allows judges to consider larger external and political factors in reaching their decisions. This opens up many ways in which political influences can infiltrate the decision-making process.

Llewellyn, like Frank, accepts that judges are obliged to review precedent and follow the logic of the existing legal rules in deciding particular cases. He nevertheless believes that it is the policy considerations that arise in applying the law that control the legal process. It is the normative idea in such an argument that is significant. Llewellyn's theory changes the judicial role: judges are the true authors of the law, in a personal and a substantive sense, and have a right to bring their subjective moral and political views into the decision-making process.

Llewellyn's theory changes the provenance of the common law. The original theory of decision-making in the earlier common law was driven by rules and principles, which take their authority from the fact that they are derived from a common set of substantive beliefs. The supremacy of the law in the customary law and the early common law was based on the moral ascendancy of these beliefs. Indeed, it is clear that the independence of the judiciary and the legitimacy of the common law rested historically on the deductive nature of such an approach. The logical rigour of the process was designed to prevent political and personal considerations from affecting the outcome in a case.

The reasoning behind such a position seems simple enough. A judge who has a duty to follow the law, rigorously, will have fewer opportunities to impose his will upon the legal process. Bentham and Austin replaced the historical idea with a political conception of law, which traces the authority of the positive law to its source in the legislative branch of government. In theory, at least, this change in the sources of the law did not change the nature of the judicial role, since judges were obliged to rigorously follow the intention of Parliament, much as they were obliged to follow precedent.

The historical reality is that the judicial role changed in America, for a variety of legal and social reasons, as judges took on the task of adjusting the common law to fit the demands of an industrial society. Legal realism is significant because it recognized that the political views of the judiciary played a major role in this shift in the provenance of the law. It follows that the origins of these views—which are usually seen as a product of sociological factors—need to be investigated and studied.

The descriptive approach in realism accordingly led to a study of the role of these political factors in the judicial process.[22] This led to a movement called "judicial behaviouralism" (or, alternatively, "judicial behaviourism"), which still uses the quantitative methods employed in the social sciences to study the correlation between the social and political background of judges and their decisions.[23]

Frank's Theory Represents the Psychological Branch of Legal Realism

Jerome Frank's major contribution to legal theory consists of his relatively early examination of the role played by psychology. His work suggests that it is the emotional and psychological factors in the judicial process that make it difficult to predict the decisions in future cases. Frank rejected formalism on the basis that the judicial process cannot be reduced to a simple, mechanical use of logical propositions. Psychological realism is based on the empirical argument that the decisions of individual judges are based on a "human factor" outside the rules and principles that make up the formal law.

Frank's Realism Recognizes the Problems that Arise in Deciding the Facts of a Case

Frank's position changed over time. In his later work, he characterized himself as a "fact skeptic" who believed that the findings of fact in a particular case will depend to a lesser or greater extent on the personality of the judge. This draws attention to the importance of the fact-finding process in the legal system. It is simply a mistake to think—as formalism implies—that a judge's task is merely to determine the legal rules that apply to the facts before the court. A trial judge's primary responsibility is to decide the facts of the case.

From a practical perspective, the trial judge's obligation to find the facts of the case is probably the most significant part of the trial process, since it is not possible to appeal a decision on a question of fact. As Frank recognizes, there are many ways in which the psychology of the judge may enter into this process through the evaluation of evidence. A judge's decision that the testimony of a single witness is credible—or not credible—may easily determine the verdict in a case.

It is nevertheless clear that Frank exaggerates this aspect of the evidentiary process, which—like so many other facets of the law—is often uneventful. Many of the situations that come before the courts are entirely predictable. Lawyers have their own diagnostic tools, like other professionals, and trial lawyers recognize that the events that come before the courts often assume a recognizable pattern, which is covered by the caselaw. Although it is a commonplace among trial lawyers that anything can happen in a courtroom, it is equally clear that the existing caselaw often determines the outcome of a case.

The Findings of Fact May Also Determine the Legal Issues in the Case

Frank's declaration that he was a "fact skeptic" rather than a "rule skeptic" may also reflect his experience as an appellate judge. This is because the fundamental function of a court of appeal is to determine whether the judges on the trial courts have applied the law correctly to the facts in the cases that come before them. It is accordingly the responsibility of the appellate courts to correct the legal errors made by the courts below them. The facts are decided by the trial judge, however, who decides them for the court of appeal as well as for himself.

The reality is significantly more complicated, since it is the facts that determine which rules and principles of law come into play in deciding a case. As a result, trial judges learn to craft their findings of fact in ways that predetermine what rules or principles the appellate courts will apply to the case and guarantee a particular result. Trial lawyers often refer to this as "cooking the facts." This is part of the venerable art of "appeal proofing," by which experienced trial judges immunize their verdicts from any attack in the appellate courts. Perhaps the most important observation, however, is that this "cooking" often appears to happen on a psychological level, as Frank suggests, without bad faith on the part of a judge.

Legal realism is important because it acknowledges these possibilities. It is nevertheless very difficult to quantify the extent of this kind of manipulation in the legal system. There are many cases in which judges appear to be sincerely following the general rules laid down by the appellate courts in reaching their decisions. Judges in the common law often say that they disagree with a particular rule but are bound to apply it. Most of the procedural and evidentiary issues that come before the courts are governed by a comprehensive set of well-litigated rules. One example is the rule in *R. v. Kienapple*, [1975] 1 S.C.R. 729, which prevents judges from entering multiple convictions for the same set of facts. The application of this relatively mechanical rule is governed by an extensive caselaw.

Frank's Theory Sets Out a Psychological Model of Judicial Decision-Making

Frank sets out a psychological theory of judicial decision-making, which replaces at least some of the rational aspects of the process with more intuitive judgements. The process of judging, he writes, actually begins with a conclusion, which manifests itself as a psychological experience rather than a logical deduction.[24] The origins of the law can therefore be found in the psychological process that creates this experience rather than in the judge's decision, which merely provides the formal justification for the conclusion within the system.

This provides a valuable model of what is actually happening when a judge decides a case. As Judge Hutcheson puts it:

> the judge really decides by feeling and not by judgement, by hunching and not by ratiocination, such ratiocination appearing only in the opinion.[25]

As Hessel Yntema, a legal scholar renowned for his work in comparative law, states

> Of the many things which have been said of the mystery of the judicial process, the most salient is that decision is reached after an emotive experience in which principles and logic play a secondary part.[26]

It follows that the law is a product of the personal experience of the judge.

Frank and Hutcheson both suggest that judges writing decisions are engaged in the act of justifying their feelings as to the proper course of action in the case. The question then becomes: where do these feelings come from? Frank acknowledges that one class of "hunch-producers" is found in the rules and principles of law that apply to the facts of the case. Another class, however, which has rarely been considered, is "'the political, economic, and moral prejudices' of the judge." There is naturally an empirical question as to the extent that these influences determine the decision in particular cases. The mere existence of these influences, however, demonstrates that the legal process cannot be reduced to a logical process.

Frank's Theory Raises the Problem of Incommensurables

One of the problems with Frank's theory of judicial decision-making is that it is difficult to express "hunching" in rational terms. Frank openly argues that judges do not follow the caselaw: "What the courts in fact do is to manipulate the language of former decisions." The problem does not lie in judges so much as it lies in the idea that the common law can be reduced to a rational process that is amenable to logical analysis. In point of fact, judicial decisions should be seen and examined as a kind of psychological phenomena, which can be understood only in the psychological context of the case:

> The rules a judge announces when publishing his decision are . . . intelligible only if one can relive the judge's unique experience while he was trying the case—which, of course, cannot be done.[27]

It follows that judicial decisions are inherently subjective and closed to rational analysis.

This issue raises the problem of incommensurables, which arises in many other contexts. There are figures in other fields who at least implicitly disagree with Frank: T.S. Eliot, for example, argued that the whole aim of poetry is to recreate the sensibility and experience of the poet.[28] The same kind of issue arises in philosophy of mathematics, where most of us are inclined to think that a mathematician who works through one of Euclid's proofs has gone through the same experience as Euclid. Even if Frank is right in saying that the original experience of the trial judge cannot be conveyed to others, it is not clear that another judge has to relive the original judge's experience in order to follow and enforce that judge's ruling on the law.

Many theorists and jurisprudents argue, against Frank, that judicial decisions must ultimately be justified on rational grounds, which satisfy the internal requirements of the legal system. In *The Judicial Decision*, Richard Wasserstrom argues that Frank confuses the process of *discovery* (in which the judge receives a hunch) with the process of *justification*.[29] It is the second, more explicitly logical task—rather than the emotional or psychological state that precedes it—that determines the efficacy and validity of a decision. This internal focus nevertheless leaves the psychological and political factors in the original decision open to question, however, and does not refute Frank's suggestion that much of the justification offered by judges is a kind of rationalization.

Frank's Theory Sees the Judge as an Arbitrator

Frank's rejection of the idea that rational analysis is sufficient to explain the law has other consequences. In *Law and the Modern Mind*, for example, he argues that a judge is more of a mediator than a logician.

> *The judge, at his best, is an arbitrator*, a "sound man" who strives to do justice to the parties by exercising a wise discretion with reference to the peculiar circumstances of the case.[30]

This view gives judges more discretion than they have under formalism, which limits the role of judges to the application of legal rules. The "arbitral function," Frank nevertheless asserts, "is the central fact in the administration of justice."[31] This idea provides a normative side to psychological realism and clearly suggests that it is the parties' psychological experience of the feelings consonant with justice that determines whether the case has been successfully resolved.

But the Historical Role of a Judge and that of an Arbitrator Are Fundamentally Different

There are problems with Frank's view of the judicial function, which is not in keeping with the history of the common law. Most jurisdictions have an arbitration act, which provides for the binding arbitration of contested issues, and there is caselaw that distinguishes between the role of an arbitrator and the role of a judge. The source of an arbitrator's authority comes from the parties who have agreed to the arbitration. The historical authority of a judge, in contrast, comes from the community. It does not derive from the consent of the parties.

Frank emphasizes the importance of fairness in the arbitral process, and his criticism of the orthodox legal view is more in keeping with equity than with the common law. Equity was based not on strict legal rules and precedents but on a set of principles that placed particular emphasis on the conduct of the parties. These principles gave judges in the Court of Chancery (which dispensed equitable remedies) more discretion in the decision-making process than their counterparts in the common law courts. Equity and law were eventually merged in a single system of courts, however, administered by the same judges. It is now said that equity mitigates "the rigour of the common law," since it allows judges to take the fairness of the parties' conduct into account in applying legal rules.

Frank's view also seems relevant in the context of juries. Under the common law, the members of a jury are considered judges of the facts. They make the findings of fact in a jury trial and decide the verdict in the case. The "judge" who sits with them is the judge of the law and decides any legal issues that arise in the course of the trial. At the end of the case, the trial judge also instructs the jury as to the law that applies to the facts of the case. In spite of these instructions, the members of a jury rarely have a significant grasp of the law. As a result, juries have a tendency to function in the arbitral manner that Frank is describing. They are interested in fairness and make decisions on the basis of their fundamental sense of right and wrong rather than a strict application of legal rules.

Frank's emphasis on the arbitral role of the judiciary reflects the subjective focus in realism. The chief problem with his idea that a judge's primary responsibility is to satisfy the parties to a legal dispute is that it leaves out the community. This is a serious omission, since it is the substantive consensus in society that historically provided the source of a judge's authority. This omission is apparent in the fact that both parties in a case often feel that the judge's decision is unfair. This is frequently because there is a social context in which the decision is made, which brings the larger interests of the community into the trial process. There is no doubt that one of the subjective focusses of legal realism is that it tends to neglect these interests and implicitly disconnects the judiciary from the original sources of its authority.

Notes

1.   Cardozo was one of the most respected judges of his generation. This is evident in his appointment to the position on the United States Supreme Court that was left vacant when Oliver Wendell Holmes retired.

2.   Benjamin N. Cardozo, *The Nature of the Judicial Process* (New Haven, CT: Yale University, 1921). Available at http://xroads.virginia.edu/~hyper/CARDOZO/CarNat.html.

3. The same idea surfaces in Roscoe Pound's "sociological jurisprudence." The progressive standard that Cardozo envisages has some affinities with the "large and liberal" standard endorsed by John Sankey in *Edwards v. A.G. of Canada*, but it extends that kind of standard well beyond the constitutional law, into the ordinary common law.

4. The murderer (the defendant) was sixteen years old at the time of the murder and had apparently poisoned his grandfather because the grandfather "had manifested some intention" to change the will and remove the grandson as the "residuary" beneficiary. He had been convicted of second-degree murder and was serving his time in the state reformatory at the time of the appeal.

5. Ronald Dworkin has relied upon this notion in developing his own legal theory.

6. The Court of Appeals was divided on the question of inheritance. In point of fact, the dissenting judges argued that the case did not arise in equity and could not be decided on equitable principles. So the second line of precedents did not apply. The real issue was whether the judges had the authority to go beyond the relevant statutes, and the case illustrates how Bentham's attempt to limit the discretion of the judiciary creates difficulties in the caselaw.

7. Karl Llewellyn, "Some Realism about Realism—Responding to Dean Pound," *Harvard Law Review* 40 (1930–1): 1222–64, and Roscoe Pound, "The Call for a Realist Jurisprudence," *Harvard Law Review* 44 (1930–1): 697–711. Available at http://heinonline.org.

8. See Jerome Frank, *Courts on Trial: Myth and Reality in American Justice* (Princeton, NJ: Princeton University, 1949), p. 66ff.: "Some nineteen years ago, I published a book in which I was foolish enough to attempt my own definition of 'law,' one which, as it stressed trial-court decisions, did highlight the uncertain elements of litigation. I found myself in the middle of a fierce terminological quarrel with other law-definers. . . . Since then, I have, whenever possible, avoided the use of the word 'Law.' I have instead (as in this book) stated directly—without any intervening definition of that vague and troublesome word—just what I was talking about, namely, what courts and lawyers do, and should do, or the entire province of the 'administration of justice.'"

9. Frank, *Law and the Modern Mind*, as cited in the readings, p. 32.

10. ibid., p. 125.

11. See John Chipman Gray, *The Nature and Sources of the Law* (The Carpentier Lectures 1908–1909) (New York: Columbia University, 1909), at p. 97.

12. ibid., pp. 191–247.

13. Frank, *Law and the Modern Mind*, p. 133.

14. ibid., p. 134.

15. But see Frank, ibid., p. 127, where Frank writes that rules "will not directly decide any other cases in any given way, nor authoritatively compel the judges to decide those other cases in any given way; nor make it possible for lawyers to bring it about that the judges will decide any other cases in any given way."

16. Frank, *Courts on Trial*, op. cit., p. 290.

17. Llewellyn, "Some Realism about Realism," op. cit.

18. The most notorious example of this is Donald Black's *The Behavior of Law*, which is cited in the suggestions for further reading.

19. See Karl Llewellyn, "The Normative, the Legal, and the Law-Jobs: The Problem of Juristic Method," *Yale Law Journal* 49, no. 8 (June 1940): 1355–400.

20. Karl Llewellyn, *The Common Law Tradition: Deciding Appeals* (Boston: Little, Brown, 1960).

21. Like Justice Cardozo, Llewellyn exaggerates the conflict between different canons of construction. He implies, for example, that the principle that obliges judges to give effect to the "plain" reading of a statute conflicts with the principle that "literal" interpretations should be avoided if they lead to mischievous results. There is no real conflict between the two principles, however, and the dichotomy simply disappears when one recognizes that the second principle merely qualifies the first.

22. See, for example, Martin Shapiro, *Law and Politics in the Supreme Court*, as cited in the suggestions for further reading.

23. For an introduction to the study of the influence of judges' backgrounds on their decisions, see the symposium in the *Harvard Law Review* 79, no. 8 (June 1966): 1551.

24. It is interesting that this is in keeping with the general training of lawyers, since lawyers have no choice but to argue that a case should be decided in favour of their client.

25. Hutcheson, quoted in Frank's *Law and the Modern Mind*, as cited in the readings, p. 285.

26. Hessel E. Yntema, "The Hornbook Method and the Conflict of Laws," *Yale Law Journal* 37, no. 4 (February 1928): 468–83.

27. Frank, *Law and the Modern Mind*, as cited in the readings, p. 150.

28. This view comes out of symbolism. See T.S. Eliot, *On Poetry and Poets* (New York: Farrar, Straus, Cudahy, 1957). And see Jerome Frank's comparison of law and music in Chapter 21 of *Courts on Trial*, op. cit., pp. 292–309.

29. Richard A. Wasserstrom, *The Judicial Decision: Towards a Theory of Legal Justification* (Stanford, CA: Stanford University, 1961).

30. Frank, *Law and the Modern Mind*, p. 168.

31. ibid., p. 169.

Study Questions

1. Pound criticizes legal realism as a descriptive theory. This raises a difficult and important question. Where does our obligation to obey the law come from in legal realism? If you were a realist judge, how would you decide a case?

2. Do you think there *is* an obligation to obey the law? Why or why not?

3. Llewellyn suggests that the law has a sociological function, since it serves the larger needs of groups. What does "justice" consist of on his analysis?

4. Frank believes that the desire for certainty in the law comes from a psychological desire for a strong father figure. What do you think of this line of reasoning?

5. We could just as easily say that legal realism is a manifestation of a psychological rebellion against authority. What do you think? Why are the realists taking a realist position?

6. Do you prefer Llewellyn's version of realism or Frank's? Why? Which theory seems to provide a more accurate account of what happens in the courts?

7. Frank says that a judge is an arbitrator. But there are problems with this view. Many legal experts would disagree, however, and say a judge is more than an arbitrator. Why? What does the concept of arbitration leave out?

8. How does the theory of legal realism apply to juries? Does it have an impact on the selection of jurors?

Further Reading

Donald Black, *The Behavior of Law* (New York: Academic, 1976).

William Fisher, M.J Horowitz, and T.A Reed, eds., *American Legal Realism* (New York: Oxford University, 1993).

Lon L. Fuller, "American Legal Realism," *University of Pennsylvania Law Review* 82 (1934): 429–62.

Joel B. Grossman et al., "A Symposium: Social Science Approaches to the Judicial Process," *Harvard Law Review* 79, no. 8 (June 1966): 1551–628. Available at http://heinonline.org.

Joseph C. Hutcheson Jr., "The Judgement Intuitive: The Function of the "Hunch" in Judicial Decisions," *Cornell Law Quarterly* 14 (1929): 274–8. Available at http://heinonline.org.

Brian Leiter, "American Legal Realism," in *The Blackwell Guide to Philosophy of Law and Legal Theory*, ed. Martin P. Golding and William A. Edmundson (Malden, MA: Blackwell, 2005).

Glendon Schubert, *Judicial Behavior: A Reader in Theory and Research* (Chicago: Rand McNally, 1964).

Martin Shapiro, *Law and Politics in the Supreme Court* (New York: Free, 1964).

10 Later Positivism: The Law Derives Its Authority from the State

Hans Kelsen and H.L.A. Hart

Readings

- From *Pure Theory of Law*, by Hans Kelsen
- From *The Concept of Law*, by H.L.A. Hart
- From "Positivism and the Separation of Law and Morals," by H.L.A. Hart

The following chapter reviews later positivism, which rests on a stark separation of our legal and moral obligations. Hans Kelsen (1881–1973) sets out a "pure" theory of law, based on the idea that legal norms have no substantive content and can be derived only from other legal norms. Kelsen was less influential than H.L.A. Hart (1907–1992), who held the chair of jurisprudence at Oxford University and remains the most prominent legal philosopher in the contemporary canon. Hart's major work, *The Concept of Law*, sets out a liberal and positivist theory of law based on the liberal common law tradition. It also provides an analytic model of the legal system that sets out the conceptual structure of the positive law. The theories of Hart and Kelsen are based firmly on a political conception of law.

⚔ Readings ⚔

From Hans Kelsen, *Pure Theory of Law*, trans. Max Knight (Berkeley: University of California, 1967).

The "Pure" Theory

The Pure Theory of Law is a theory of positive law. It is a theory of positive law in general, not of a specific legal order. . . . [It] is called a "pure" theory of law, because it only describes the law and attempts to eliminate from the object of this description everything that is not strictly law: Its aim is to free the science of law from alien elements. . . .

The Act and Its Legal Meaning

[T]he question arises whether the science of law is a natural or a social phenomenon. But the clean delimitation between nature and society is not easy . . . For if you analyze any body of facts interpreted as "legal" or somehow tied up with law, such as a parliamentary decision, an administrative act, a judgement, a contract, or a crime, two elements are distinguishable: one, an act or series of acts—a happening occurring at a certain time and in a certain place, perceived by our senses . . . ; two, the legal meaning of this act, that is, the meaning conferred upon the act by the law. For example: People assemble in a large room, make speeches, some raise their hands, others do not—this is the external happening. Its meaning is that a statute is being passed, that law is created. . . .

The Norm

The Norm as a Scheme of Interpretation

The external fact whose objective meaning is a legal or illegal act is always an event that can be perceived by the senses (because it occurs in time and space) and therefore a natural phenomenon determined by causality. However, this event as such, as an element of nature, is not an object of legal cognition. What turns this event into a legal or illegal act is not its physical existence, determined by the laws of causality prevailing in nature, but the objective meaning resulting from its interpretation. The specifically legal meaning of this act is derived from a "norm" whose content refers to the act; this norm confers legal meaning to the act, so that it may be interpreted according to this norm. The norm functions as a scheme of interpretation. . . .

Norm and Norm Creation

Those norms, then, which have the character of legal norms and which make certain acts legal or illegal are the objects of the science of law. The legal order which is the object of this cognition is a normative order of human behaviour—a system of norms regulating human behaviour. By "norm" we mean that something *ought* to be or *ought* to happen, especially that a human being ought to behave in a specific way. . . .

The word "ought" is used here in a broader than the usual sense. According to customary usage, "ought" corresponds only to a command, while "may" corresponds to a permission, and "can" to an authorization. But in the present work the word "ought" is used to express the normative meaning of an act directed toward the behaviour of others; this "ought" includes "may" and "can." . . . "Norm" is the meaning of an act by which a certain behaviour is commanded, permitted, or authorized. . . .

The *Grundnorm*

The reason for the validity of a norm can only be the validity of another norm. A norm which represents the reason for the validity of another norm is figuratively spoken of as a higher norm in relation to a lower norm.

It looks as if one could give as a reason for the validity of a norm the circumstance that it was established by an authority, human or divine; for example, the statement: "The reason for the validity of the Ten Commandments is that God Jehovah issued them on Mount Sinai"; or: "Men ought to love their enemies, because Jesus, Son of God, issued this command in his Sermon on the Mount." But in both cases the reason for the validity is not that God or his son issued a certain norm at a certain time in a certain place, but the tacitly presupposed norm that one ought to obey the commands of God or his son.[1] . . .

The norm which represents the reason for the validity of another norm is called, as we have said, the "higher" norm. But the search for the reason of a norm's validity cannot go on indefinitely like the search for the cause of an effect. It must end with a norm which, as the last and highest, is presupposed. It must be *presupposed*, because it cannot be "posited," that is to say: created, by an authority whose competence would have to rest on a still higher norm.

This final norm's validity cannot be derived from a higher norm, the reason for its validity cannot be questioned. Such a presupposed highest norm is referred to in this book as basic norm ["*Grundnorm*"]. All norms whose validity can be traced back to one and the same basic norm constitute a system of norms, a normative order. . . . The fact that a certain norm belongs to a certain order is based on the circumstance that its last reason of validity is the basic norm of this order. . . .

Note

1.   Editor's note: This is a response to Austin's theory that law is a command.

From H.L.A. Hart, *The Concept of Law*, 2nd ed. (Oxford: Clarendon, 1994).

The Concept of Obligation: The Gunman Situation

Let us recall the gunman situation. *A* orders *B* to hand over his money and threatens to shoot him if he does not comply. According to the theory of coercive orders [the theory found in Austin] this situation illustrates the notion of obligation or duty in general. Legal obligation is to be found in this situation writ large; *A* must be the sovereign habitually obeyed and the orders must be general, prescribing courses of conduct not single actions.

The plausibility of the claim that the gunman situation displays the meaning of obligation lies in the fact that it is certainly one in which we would say that *B*, if he obeyed, was "obliged" to hand over his money. It is, however, equally certain that we should misdescribe the situation if we said, on these facts, that *B* "had an obligation" or a "duty" to hand over the money. . . .

[The] statement that a person was obliged to obey someone is, in the main, a psychological one referring to the beliefs and motives with which an action was done. . . . [But] facts of this sort, i.e. facts about beliefs and motives, are *not necessary* for the truth of a statement that a person had an obligation to do something. Thus the statement that a person had an obligation, e.g. to tell the truth or report for military service, remains true even if he believed (reasonably or unreasonably) that he would never be found out and had nothing to fear from disobedience. . . .

Some theorists, Austin among them, seeing perhaps the general irrelevance of the person's beliefs, fears, and motives to the question whether he had an obligation to do something, have defined this notion not in terms of these subjective facts, but in terms of the chance or likelihood that the person having the obligation will suffer a punishment or "evil" at the hands of others in the event of disobedience. This, in effect, treats statements of obligation not as psychological statements but as predictions or assessments of chances of incurring punishment or "evil." . . .

The fundamental objection is that the predictive interpretation obscures the fact that, where rules exist, deviations from them are not merely grounds for a prediction that hostile reactions will follow or that a court will apply sanctions to those who break them, but are also a reason or justification for such reaction and for applying the sanctions.[1] . . .

To understand the general idea of obligation . . . we must turn to a different social situation which, unlike the gunman situation, includes the existence of social rules . . . . Rules of etiquette or correct speech are certainly rules: they are more than convergent habits or regularities of behaviour; they are taught and efforts are made to maintain them; they are used in criticizing our own and other people's behaviour in the characteristic normative vocabulary. "You ought to take your hat off," "It is wrong to say 'you was.'" But to use in connection with rules of this kind the words "obligation" or "duty" would be misleading and not merely stylistically odd. It would misdescribe a social situation; for though the line separating rules of obligation from others is at points a vague one, yet the main rationale of the distinction is fairly clear.

Rules are conceived and spoken of as imposing obligations when the general demand for conformity is insistent and the social pressure brought to bear upon those who deviate or threaten to deviate is great. Such rules may be wholly customary in origin: there may be no centrally organized system of punishments for breach of the rules; the social pressure may . . . be limited to verbal manifestations of disapproval or of appeals to the individuals' respect for the rule violated; it may depend heavily on the operation of feelings of shame, remorse, and guilt. . . . Conversely, when physical sanctions are prominent or usual among the forms of pressure, even though these are neither closely defined nor administered by officials but are left to the community at large, we shall be inclined to classify the rules as a primitive or rudimentary form of law.[2] . . .

Characteristically, rules so obviously essential as those which restrict the free use of violence are thought of in terms of obligation. So too rules which require honesty or truth or require the keeping of promises, or specify what is to be done by one who performs a distinctive role or function in the social group are thought of in terms of either "obligation" or perhaps more often "duty." . . .

The Internal and External Points of View

[I]t is possible to be concerned with the rules, either merely as an observer who does not himself accept them, or as a member of the group which accepts and uses them as guides to conduct. We may call these respectively the "external" and the "internal points of view." . . .

The external point of view may very nearly reproduce the way in which the rules function in the lives of certain members of the group, namely those who reject its rules and are only concerned with them when and because they judge that unpleasant consequences are likely to follow violation. . . . What the external point of view, which limits itself to the observable regularities of behaviour, cannot reproduce is the way in which the rules function as rules in the lives of those who normally are the majority of society.[3] These are the officials, lawyers, or private persons who use them, in one situation after another, as guides to the conduct of social life, as the basis for claims, demands, admissions, criticism, or punishment, viz., in all the familiar transactions of life according to rules. For them the violation of a rule is not merely a basis for the prediction that a hostile reaction will follow but a *reason* for hostility.[4] . . .

Primary Rules

[T]here are many studies of primitive communities which . . . depict in detail the life of a society where the only means of social control is that general attitude of the group towards its own standard modes of behaviour. . . . [W]e shall refer to such a social structure as one of primary rules of obligation. . . .

Three Defects of a System Based on Primary Rules

It is plain that only a small community closely knit by ties of kinship, common sentiment, and belief, and placed in a stable environment, could live successfully by such a regime of unofficial rules. In any other conditions such a simple form of social control must prove defective and will require supplementation in different ways.

1. In the first place, the rules by which the group lives will not form a system, but will simply be a set of separate standards, without any identifying or common mark . . . Hence if doubts arise as to what the rules are or as to the precise scope of some given rule, there will be no procedure for settling this doubt. . . . This defect in the simple social structure of primary rules we may call its *uncertainty*.

2. A second defect is the *static* character of the rules. The only mode of change in the rules known to such a society will be the slow process of growth, whereby courses of conduct once thought optional become first habitual or usual, and then obligatory, and the converse process of decay. . . . There will be no means, in such a society, of deliberately adapting the rules to changing circumstances, either by eliminating old rules or introducing new ones. . . .

3. The third defect of this simple form of social life is the inefficiency of the diffuse
    social pressure by which the rules are maintained. . . . It is obvious that the waste of
    time involved in the group's unorganized efforts to catch and punish offenders, and
    the smouldering vendettas which may result from self-help in the absence of an offi-
    cial monopoly of "sanctions," may be serious.[5] . . .

The remedy for each of these three main defects in this simplest form of social structure consists in supplementing the *primary* rules of obligation with *secondary* rules which
are rules of a different kind. The introduction of the remedy for each defect might, in
itself, be considered a step from the pre-legal into the legal world . . . [in which] law may
most illuminatingly be characterized as a union of primary rules of obligation with such
secondary rules. . . .

Secondary Rules

[The secondary rules] may all be said to be on a different level from the primary rules, for
they are all *about* such rules. . . . They specify the ways in which the primary rules may
be conclusively ascertained, introduced, eliminated, varied, and the fact of their violation
conclusively determined.

1. The Rule of Recognition

The simplest form of remedy for the *uncertainty* of the regime of primary rules is the
introduction of what we shall call a "rule of recognition." . . .The existence of such a rule
of recognition may take any of a huge variety of forms, simple or complex. It may, as in the
early law of many societies, be no more than that an authoritative list or text of the rules
is to be found in a written document or carved on some public monument. . . . This is not
itself the crucial step, though it is a very important one: what is crucial is the acknowledgement of reference to the writing or inscription as *authoritative*, i.e. as the *proper* way
of disposing of doubts as to the existence of the rule. . . .

   In a developed legal system the rules of recognition are of course more complex; instead
of identifying rules exclusively by reference to a text or list they do so by reference to some
general characteristic possessed by the primary rules. This may be the fact of their having been enacted by a specific body, or their long customary practice, or their relation to
judicial decisions. . . .

2. Rules of Change

The remedy for the *static* quality of the regime of primary rules consists in the introduction of what we shall call "rules of change." The simplest form of such a rule is that which
empowers an individual or body of persons to introduce new primary rules for the conduct of the life of the group, or of some class within it, and to eliminate old rules. . . .

3. Rules of Adjudication

The third supplement to the simple regime of primary rules, intended to remedy the *ineffi-ciency* of its diffused social pressure, consists of secondary rules empowering individuals to make authoritative determinations of the question whether, on a particular occasion, a primary rule has been broken. The minimal form of adjudication consists in such deter-minations, and we shall call the secondary rules which confer the power to make them "rules of adjudication." Besides identifying the individuals who are to adjudicate, such rules will also define the procedure to be followed. . . . Again these rules, like the other secondary rules, define a group of important legal concepts: in this case the concepts of judge or court, jurisdiction, and judgement. . . .

If we stand back and consider the structure which has resulted from the combina-tion of primary rules of obligation with the secondary rules of recognition, change, and adjudication, it is plain that we have here not only the heart of a legal system, but a most powerful tool for the analysis of much that has puzzled both the jurist and the political theorist.

Notes

1. Editor's note: Hart is referring to the theory put forward by Oliver Wendell Holmes in "The Path of Law" and arguing that theories based on an external perspective cannot capture the legal process.
2. Editor's note: Hart's analysis has been used by anthropologists in examining tribal systems law.
3. Editor's note: This is the perspective of Holmes' "bad man." Hart is criticizing the legal realists for adopt-ing the point of view used in the social sciences.
4. Editor's note: As Hart notes, at a later point in his discussion, at p. 105: "[This] becomes immediately apparent when we consider how the judge's own statement that a particular rule is valid functions in judicial decision; for, though here too, in making such a statement, the judge presupposes but does not state the general efficacy of the system, he plainly is not concerned to predict his own or others' official action. His statement that a rule is valid is an internal statement recognizing that the rule satisfies the tests for identifying what is to count as law in his court, and constitutes not a prophecy of but part of the *reason* for his decision."
5. Editor's note: And of course this reflects the origins of the common law, which was developed as a means for resolving disputes without resorting to feuds.

From H.L.A. Hart, "Positivism and the Separation of Law and Morals," *Harvard Law Review* 71 (1957): 593–629.

The Core and Penumbra of Meaning

The insight of this school [the school of legal realism] may be presented in the following example. A legal rule forbids you to take a vehicle into the public park. Plainly this for-bids an automobile, but what about bicycles, roller skates, toy automobiles? What about airplanes? Are these, as we say, to be called "vehicles" for the purpose of the rule or not?

If we are to communicate with each other at all, and if, as in the most elementary form of law, we are to express our intentions that a certain type of behaviour be regulated by rules, then the general words we use—like "vehicle" in the case I consider—must have some standard instance in which no doubts are felt about its application.[1] There must be a core of settled meaning, but there will be, as well, a penumbra of debatable cases in which words are neither obviously applicable nor obviously ruled out. . . .

Formalism

The misconception of the judicial process which ignores the problems of the penumbra and which views the process as consisting pre-eminently in deductive reasoning is often stigmatized as the error of "formalism" or "literalism." . . . It would be easy to show that Austin was guiltless of this error; . . . he thought that in the penumbral situation judges must necessarily legislate. . . .

But we are concerned with "formalism" as a vice not of jurists but of judges. What precisely is it for a judge to commit this error, to be a "formalist," "automatic," a "slot machine"? Curiously enough . . . we have only descriptions which cannot mean what they appear to say: it is said that in the formalist error courts make an excessive use of logic, take a thing to "a dryly logical extreme," or make an excessive use of analytical methods. . . . But logic does not prescribe interpretation of terms . . . Logic only tells you hypothetically that *if* you give a certain term a certain interpretation then a certain conclusion follows. . . .

So this reference to logic and to logical extremes is a misnomer for something else, which must be this. A judge has to apply a rule to a concrete case—perhaps the rule that one may not take a stolen "vehicle" across state lines, and in this case an airplane has been taken. He either does not see or pretends not to see that the general terms of this rule are susceptible of different interpretations. . . . Instead of choosing in the light of social aims, the judge . . . takes the meaning . . . of a standard case and then arbitrarily identifies certain features in it—for example, in the case of a vehicle, (1) normally used on land, (2) capable of carrying a human person, (3) capable of being self-propelled—and treats these three as always necessary and always sufficient conditions for the use in all contexts of the word "vehicle," irrespective of the social consequences of giving it this interpretation. . . .

Decisions made in a fashion as blind as this would scarcely deserve the name of decisions; we might as well toss a penny in applying a rule of law. But it is at least doubtful whether any judicial decisions (even in England)[2] have been quite as automatic as this. Rather, either the interpretations stigmatized as automatic have resulted from the conviction that it is fairer in a criminal statute to take a meaning which would jump to the mind of the ordinary man at the cost even of defeating other values, and this itself is a social policy (though possibly a bad one); or much more frequently, what is stigmatized as "mechanical" and "automatic" is a determined choice made indeed in the light of a social aim but of a conservative social aim. Certainly many of the Supreme Court decisions at the turn of the century which have been so stigmatized represent clear choices in the penumbral area to give effect to a policy of a conservative type. . . .

The Meaning of "Ought"

We must, I think, beware of thinking in a too simple-minded fashion about the word "ought".[3] . . .The word "ought" merely reflects the presence of some standard of criticism; one of these standards is a moral standard but not all standards are moral. We say to our neighbour, "You ought not to lie," and that may certainly be a moral judgement, but we should remember that the baffled poisoner may say, "I ought to have given her a second dose."

The point here is that intelligent decisions which we oppose to mechanical or formal decisions are not necessarily identical with decisions defensible on moral grounds. We may say of many a decision: "Yes, that is right; that is as it ought to be," and we may mean only that some accepted purpose or policy has been thereby advanced; we may not mean to endorse the moral propriety of the policy or the decision. . . .

Of course, it is good to be occupied with the penumbra. Its problems are rightly the daily diet of the law schools. But to be occupied with the penumbra is one thing, to be preoccupied with it another. And preoccupation with the penumbra is, if I may so, as rich a source of confusion in the American legal tradition as formalism in the English.

Notes

1. Editor's note: In this instance, the rule can be deductively applied.
2. Editor's note: This is an example of British humour.
3. Editor's note: Hart is referring to the idea that judges should make decisions on the basis of what the law "ought" to be.

✧ Discussion ✧

Kelsen Sets Out a "Pure" Theory of Law

Hans Kelsen is described in the *Stanford Encyclopedia of Philosophy* as a "formidable Austrian jurist and philosopher."[1] His major philosophical work, *Reine Rechtslehre*, has been published in English under the title *Pure Theory of Law.*[2] As the title suggests, Kelsen's theory attempts to remove all of the non-legal elements that make their way into the legal system from the concept of law. These elements include the moral, sociological, and psychological sources of the law. The defining properties of law, he suggests, are quintessentially legal and cannot be found in the forces and conditions that manifest themselves in specific laws.

Kelsen Is a Kantian and Sets Out an Epistemological Theory of Law

Kelsen's theory of law has its philosophical roots in idealism. His account of the law is usually described as Kantian, since he believed that the law takes its legal character exclusively from its formal properties. Like Kant, Kelsen argues that the defining features of the law exist independently of its content and can therefore be determined *a priori*, as a matter of deductive logic. As a result, Kelsen's attempt to determine what constitutes a valid law becomes an epistemological rather than an empirical inquiry. Philosophically, the hard legal positivism that we see in *A Pure Theory of Law* bears many resemblances to logical positivism, which developed a highly analytical language to guarantee the certainty and verifiability of empirical claims.[3]

The hard character of Kelsen's positivism derives from its reliance on a narrow logical analysis, which keeps other elements out of his description of the law. Kelsen adopts a formal approach because, in his mind, it separates the legal character of the law from its extraneous content. There is a technical sense in which this analysis succeeds, and Kelsen's theory contains a careful examination of the way in which the law operates. His crucial premise, however, is problematic. Kelsen's view that the law cannot be reduced to morality, politics, or the sciences of human behaviour is little more than an assumption. He accordingly removes the substantive features of the law from his conception of the law, simply by philosophical fiat, and reconfigures the legal system as an empty vehicle of social control.

Law Is a Normative Science and Is Based on a Hierarchy of "Oughts"

Like so many theorists, Kelsen sees the study of law as a kind of science. He divides the field of sciences into descriptive sciences and normative sciences like law, ethics, and aesthetics. The division between these sciences is based on a hard distinction between "is" and "ought." This kind of distinction can be traced to David Hume (1711–1776), who famously reasoned, in his *Treatise of Human Nature*, that it is not possible to derive an "ought" from an "is." Inquiries in these different kinds of sciences must therefore be separate from each other. The normative sciences, unlike the descriptive sciences, are based on a hierarchy of norms.

It may be convenient to think of Kelsen's theory as a procedural theory of law. For the legal positivists, the fundamental model of law is always the statutory law, which is law because it has met certain procedural requirements. The procedural account does not explain the legal character of much of the common law, however, which derives from its substantive origins. A "pure" procedural theory also fails to account for the fact that the substantive content of the statutory law is subject to many moral, legal, and constitutional restraints. It is not clear that Kelsen's idea of a legal ought, which is purely formal and therefore empty of substantive content, can be maintained in practice.

The Central Aim of Kelsen's Theory Is to Identify Valid Legal Norms

Kelsen's focus on the formal attributes of the law is stark and exclusive. He rejects the natural law because it treats the law as a descriptive science, with an empirical subject matter that is open to objective investigation. He rejects utilitarianism on the same basis. Like Kant, Kelsen believed that it is possible to construct the rational outline, at least, of a complete body of positive law that exists as a single coherent whole. Unlike Kant, however, he saw this rational outline as a normative but formal structure, which has no particular content. The attempt to construct this outline of the law is significant because in theory it provides us with a formal model of any system of positive law.

The motivating principle behind the theory that Kelsen develops is that the law exists independently of its substantive elements. As a result, the central distinction in his model of law is between formal and substantive oughts. Since legal "oughts" exist only legally and formally, they can be derived only from other legal oughts. It follows that it is the process of deduction—albeit a relatively loose deduction—that provides the fundamental mechanism used by the legislature or the judiciary in creating law. The law is essentially deductive, as the formalists suggested, and the validity of a legal norm is established by its pedigree, which can be traced back to more general legal norms within the system.

Every Legal Norm Can Be Traced to the Base Norm, the Grundnorm

Kelsen's model of the law captures the formal aspects of the legal process as well as the common law idea that the law is a rational science, which rests the validity of legal rules on their logical pedigree. The process of deduction cannot go on forever, however, in an infinite regress. Kelsen accordingly reasons that there must be a base norm, the *grundnorm*, from which all other norms can be derived.[4]

This is easily misconstrued. It may be tempting to see a written constitution as the prototype of the *grundnorm*—in spite of its many provisions, the Canadian or American constitution could be seen as the single, if complex, rule on which the entire system rests. The *grundnorm* is not a legal norm, however; it is the premise on which norms are based, and it functions like an axiom in a system of mathematics, which exists outside the internal mechanics of the system. The *grundnorm* is therefore not the constitution, but the rule or principle—or habit—that holds that the constitution should be followed.

Kelsen's Positivist Conception of Law Is Political and Statist

Kelsen's idea of law is firmly rooted in the positivist tradition. Kelsen's model of law is coercive and the integrity of the system he envisages is maintained by force. A law requires a sanction. From a sociological perspective, Kelsen's thinking has elements of behaviourism and emphasizes social control. His reliance on "norms" rather than rules nevertheless brings in a more graduated notion of compulsion that explains some of the uncertainty in the legal system.

Like other positivists, Kelsen has a political conception of law. His model of the law is based on the idea of statutory law and gives the legislature the leading role in the legal system. He nevertheless leaves a place for the constitutional law, which gives the judiciary the final say in determining what constitutes a valid law. This is augmented by his reference to norms, rather than rules, since he recognizes that the derivation of a legal norm from another legal norm is open to a variety of logical possibilities. As a result, the derivation of legal norms is as much a political act as it is a legal act, in spite of the fact that substantive values have no place in his formal theory. This aspect of Kelsen's theory fits remarkably well with the position adopted by theorists like Benjamin Cardozo and Karl Llewellyn, who believed that judges had an active role in developing public policy.

Kelsen's positivism is also apparent in his reliance on centralized government. This reliance is a product of his assumption that there is a single source of law, which gives the legal order its authority. The reasons behind such an assumption are foundational, since Kelsen is trying to construct a unified, logically coherent model of the law. As a result, his project is inherently monistic and assumes that there is one, integrated system of law, which finds expression in the existence of the state. It is true that the conception of the state in *Pure Theory of Law* is remarkably vague and often seems to refer simply to the legal order.[5] The legal order has origins outside itself, however, in the existence of a central government, which has a monopoly on the power to pass laws. This kind of assumption is too simple, however, and more recent theorists have drawn our attention to the fact that many sources of law, such as religious traditions and trading practices, exist outside the state.

Kelsen Gives Us a Grand Unified Theory, but the Abstraction of His Theory Makes It Difficult to Apply

Kelsen's theory is significant because it theoretically provides us with a logical model of any body of positivist law. Like Kant, he constructs a grand unified theory, which explains the purpose and function of everything in the system. From an operational perspective, the logical skeleton that he sets out contains a complete set of plans or blueprints for a system of social control.

The abstraction of Kelsen's theory makes it difficult to apply, however, and it is not clear that the legal system can ever be completely explained in logical terms. The idea that laws are binding only because they have met the formal requirements of Kelsen's legal norms is artificial at best. Indeed, if legal obligations are an empty product of coercion, as Kelsen suggests, this may simply raise the question whether the limits that such obligations place on our conduct are meaningful.

Hart Tries to Save Legal Positivism from the Criticisms that Have Been Raised against It

Herbert Lionel Adolphus Hart remains the most influential figure in contemporary legal positivism. In his celebrated book *The Concept of Law*, Hart disputes Austin's argument that law is a command on the basis that there is "much, even in the simplest legal system, that is distorted if presented as a command."[6] He nevertheless wants to preserve the basic features of the positivism set out by Jeremy Bentham and John Austin and provide a purely descriptive account of the law. Although Hart accepts that moral principles can constitute an integral part of a legal system, he rejects the idea that the validity of a law is determined by its morality.

Hart Acknowledges that the Legal Realists Have Drawn Our Attention to the Open Texture of the Law

Hart argues that the law is made up of legal rules and rejects legal realism, which he describes as "rule skepticism." He nevertheless acknowledges that the legal realists have "made us acutely conscious" of the open-ended nature of legal reasoning. Consider, for example, a law that makes the presence of a "vehicle" in a public park illegal. "Plainly this forbids an automobile," Hart writes, "but what about bicycles, roller skates, toy automobiles? What about airplanes?" Since the law does not expressly stipulate what vehicles are prohibited, it is the judiciary who must determine the precise meaning of the term in any cases where the application of the law is disputed. As Hart writes, "laws are incurably incomplete."[7]

Hart Argues that the Law Is Open-Textured Only in the Penumbra

Hart takes the traditional positivist position. Although the fundamental role of the judiciary is to apply the law, they must also interpret it.

> There must be a core of settled meaning, but there will be, as well, a penumbra of debatable cases in which words are neither obviously applicable nor obviously ruled out. These cases will each have some features in common with the standard case; they will lack others or be accompanied by features not present in the standard case.[8]

It follows that Benjamin Cardozo and the realists are right, but only with regard to legitimate questions of interpretation. Judges have the discretion to consider social policy in deciding questions that arise in the penumbra of meaning.

The existence of the penumbra raises at least two issues. The first is theoretical: if the questions that arise in the penumbra are open-ended, formalism simply does not have the resources to decide them.

> If a penumbra of uncertainty must surround all legal rules, then their application to specific cases in the penumbral area cannot be a matter of logical deduction, and so deductive reasoning . . . cannot serve as a model for what judges, or indeed anyone, should do in bringing particular cases under general rules.[9]

The philosophical issue here is whether there are "new" cases that cannot be decided on the basis of the existing rules.

Hart nevertheless exaggerates the extent of the discretion that judges exercise in the penumbra. The example that he gives is extremely limited and merely raises a question of interpretation, which is not the kind of issue that concerned the legal realists, since there are many legal rules that govern how a judge should interpret the words and phrases in a statute. It is a mistake to think that a judge deciding the meaning of a word like "vehicle" in a legislative provision—a word that has been extensively litigated—is following his own inclinations. Hart nevertheless agrees with the realists that formalism does not provide a satisfactory account of what occurs in penumbral cases.

The second issue is more applied. Although Hart limits the role of policy in the judicial role, he recognizes the political element that led Oliver Wendell Holmes to criticize the constitutional decisions of so many of his fellow judges. The kind of formalist position that is "stigmatized as 'mechanical' and 'automatic,'" Hart suggests,

> is a determined choice made indeed in the light of a social aim but of a conserva-
> tive social aim. Certainly many of the Supreme Court decisions at the turn of the
> century which have been so stigmatized represent clear choices . . . to give effect
> to a policy of a conservative type.[10]

Hart accordingly acknowledges that there is a political element in the judicial process.

Hart Remains a Firm Positivist

The significance of the penumbra is easily overstated. Hart remains a firm positivist and rejects the realist argument that it is judges who make the law. There is a "hard core of set-tled meaning" in statutes and precedents that can be described as law "in some centrally important sense."[11] The realists are wrong in referring to these components of the law as "sources of the law," and it is the legislature, not the judiciary, that retains the leading role in the system. The law exists in some hard propositional sense, outside the behaviour of judges, and determines the decisions in individual cases.

The deeper issue between Hart and the legal realists concerns the role of the judiciary in the legal process. Although Hart accepts that the courts have the final authority in deciding what the law "is," judges are bound by legal rules and standards, which they are obliged to follow. The realists fail to distinguish between a legal system in which the judi-ciary makes the law and a system in which they interpret it.[12] The problem, Hart writes, in "Positivism and the Separation of Law and Morals," is that this opens "*all* questions . . . to reconsideration in light of social policy."[13]

Hart's conception of law, like Austin's, is political. The power to make laws vests in the state, and Hart subscribes to the doctrine of parliamentary supremacy. Although it is the sovereign who nominally exercises the sovereign power, she does so on the advice of Parliament, which has the sole authority to make laws. The primary role of the judiciary is accordingly to apply rules that have their origin outside the courts, in the will of the sovereign. The precedents in the caselaw are binding because they establish legal rules that have been implicitly accepted by Parliament and the sovereign, who may overturn them. In Hart's view, the decisions in most cases, at least, are determined by "the hard core of settled meaning" in the statutes and the precedents. The kinds of questions that arise in the penumbra of meaning are peripheral in this context.

Hart's theory of law gives philosophical expression to the traditional position in the English common law. The fundamental task of the judiciary is to apply the law in accordance with the intentions of Parliament, without resort to moral criteria. A law is valid as long as it has been properly passed and meets the procedural and descriptive requirements of valid legislation. A judge who finds the "hard core" of a particular law morally offensive has no choice—at least no legally valid choice—but to enforce it. There may come a point where a judge feels obliged to resign his office, for moral or political reasons, but that raises a separate set of issues.

Hart Nevertheless Believes that the Account of Obligation in Austin's Positivism Is Inadequate

Hart nevertheless believes that the problem with Austin's positivism does not provide an adequate account of obligation. This is crucial, since Hart believes that the law is normative in some essential sense and creates an "ought." Like Kelsen, he wants to construct a grand theory of law that identifies the fundamental features of the law in any legal system. He accordingly disconnects our legal obligations from their moral and cultural antecedents. This kind of approach fits in well with the secular nature of contemporary Western society, which is remarkably pluralistic.

There is another reason that Hart separates our moral and legal obligations, however. A convincing legal theory, he writes, must account for the laws in our system that confer private or public powers:

> Such laws do not impose duties or obligations. Instead, they provide individuals with facilities for realizing their wishes, by conferring legal powers upon them to create, by certain specified procedures and subject to certain conditions, structures of rights and duties within the coercive framework of the law.[14]

The fundamental purpose of the civil law is to regulate the relations between private persons. This aspect of our legal obligations is primarily left to individuals, however, who have the power to make their own contracts and wills, and to dispose of their property as they see fit. It follows that these laws give us the freedom to choose the moral and social obligations that we will accept as legally binding.

Hart sees those laws that protect our legal autonomy—and it must be said, our legal dignity—as an integral part of the liberal tradition that manifests itself in the English common law. Austin's theory fails to recognize this part of the common law tradition. The power that the law confers on individuals to enter into such binding relationships is only "obscured" by the idea that the law can be formulated as "a matter of orders backed by threats."[15] In "Positivism and the Separation of Law and Morals," Hart argues that the command theory has difficulty explaining the existence of rights.

The Poisoner and the Gunman Illustrate Different Normative Standards

Like Kelsen, Hart argues that there are different kinds of normative standards. Moral and legal "oughts" can be distinguished from each other:

The word "ought" merely reflects the presence of some standard of criticism; one of these standards is a moral standard but not all standards are moral. We say to our neighbour, "You ought not to lie," and that may certainly be a moral judgement, but we should remember that the baffled poisoner may say, "I ought to have given her a second dose."[16]

It follows that the word "ought" may be used to indicate that a particular course of action serves to advance some "purpose or policy," whatever its moral character.

Hart uses the example of the gunman to illustrate these two senses of obligation. A person who is ordered to hand over his money to the gunman is "obliged" to hand his money to the gunman, but he is not "obligated" to do so. Hart argues that the problem with Austin's legal positivism is that it seems to put the courts in the position of the gunman. The only concern of the person who is "obliged" to follow the law is that he will—like Holmes' bad man—suffer consequences if he does not obey.

Hart's positivism does not rely exclusively on coercion. It is "crucial," Hart writes, "to see that in individual cases the statement that a person has an obligation under some rule and the prediction that he is likely to suffer for disobedience may diverge."[17] This brings in an internal standard:

> Most of the obscurities and distortions surrounding legal concepts arise from the fact that they essentially involve reference to what we have called the internal point of view: the view of those who do not merely record and predict behaviour conforming to rules, but *use* the rules as standards for the appraisal of their own and others' behaviour.[18]

The question is whether the community at large—and in particular, its courts, its administrators, and its police—accepts and internalizes a law that determines the law's validity.

We Cannot Say that a Person Is "Obligated" to Do Something Unless Three Conditions Have Been Met

Hart argues that we cannot say a person is "obligated" to do something unless three conditions have been met. The first is that there is a social "rule of obligation" that requires the person to act in a certain way. The second is that there is insistent or serious pressure from the other members of society to conform to such a rule. The distinction between social and legal obligations is that a breach of a legal obligation attracts a formal sanction, which may be physical. The third condition is that the rule is accepted in society as a reason for placing pressure on other people. This final condition is the central point in Hart's analysis and distinguishes between the external and the internal point of view.

The Problem with Austin's Positivism Is that It Fails to Take the Internal Point of View into Account

Hart writes that Austin's theory fails to recognize the distinction between an internal and an external point of view. The external observer, who does not accept the rules of society, may be able to predict whether "a deviation from the group's normal behaviour will meet with hostile reaction or punishment." This is nothing more than a prediction, however, and cannot reproduce

> the way in which the rules function as rules in the lives of those who normally are the majority of society. . . . For them the violation of a rule is not merely a basis for the prediction that a hostile reaction will follow but a *reason* for hostility.[19]

The real target of this analysis is the legal realists, rather than Austin, and it is no accident that the external perspective is based entirely on the observation of behaviour.

Hart's explanation seems to cast the internal perspective in a psychological light. A person brought up in a religious tradition that has internalized monogamy will believe that someone who has two wives should be punished. There is therefore no need to justify the punishment within the system.

It is not always clear that our psychological commitment to such laws exists independently of our moral and social commitments, however, and if those who "feel" that someone should be punished for bigamy do so because they believe it is morally wrong, Hart's separation between legal and moral obligations seems to dissipate. Hart seems to respond to this criticism by arguing that there is a difference between internalizing a law—and recognizing that we have an obligation to obey it—and the psychological feeling that we are obliged to do so. "Hence there is no contradiction in saying of some hardened swindler . . . that he had an obligation to pay the rent but felt no pressure to pay."

The decisive question that Hart's concept of obligation raises is whether we feel—and whether other people feel—that we are "obligated" to follow a certain law. This is not a moral obligation, but a legal obligation, which justifies the state's use of coercion to enforce it. It is nevertheless difficult to keep these obligations apart, since most of us would agree that we have a moral obligation to follow the law, even when we disagree with it. There is therefore an argument that our moral obligations seep into our legal obligations and give them their psychological force.

Hart also fails to acknowledge that the views of those who enact and administer the law may be out of keeping with the views of ordinary people. As a result, ordinary people may not adopt an internal attitude toward a law, in spite of the fact that the individuals working within the system have done so. This is obviously problematic, since it means that ordinary people may not feel any kind of compulsion to obey a law. Perhaps the law that makes the possession of marijuana an offence is an example. This kind of discrepancy may nevertheless provide a significant test of legal validity, since it suggests that laws that have not been widely internalized may not be valid laws.

Hart's Theory of Law Is Based on the Political Contract

Hart's theory provides considerable insight into legal positivism and the political conception of law. Unlike the commands that Austin postulates, Hart's legal rules have a social character, which gives them a normative—and a psychological—force that the arbitrary commands of a sovereign cannot possess. Hart's theory appears to be based on a parliamentary system, since he seems to assume that the rules that the sovereign enforces have already received the implicit endorsement of society at large. This gives them legitimacy and goes some distance, at least, in explaining why ordinary people have internalized them.

Hart's positivism is decidedly liberal and rests on the idea that there is a social and political contract. As we have seen in earlier chapters, this contract is based on the idea that the individuals in the state of nature personally consented to the formation of political government in order to obtain the benefits of civil society. It is the fact of this consent that gives government the authority to enact and enforce the positive law, within the terms of the original contract. This is significant in the context of Hart's positivism because it is the act of entering into the political contract that gives rise to the internal perspective. Once we have accepted the contract, we have accepted its most fundamental term: that the government has the right to the use of force.

Hart Defines a Legal System as a Union of Primary and Secondary Rules

Hart has two fundamental goals in *The Concept of Law*. The first is to explain what the law is; the second is to provide the basic plans of the legal system, which sets out the institutional structure of the system. This goes beyond Kelsen, who is more concerned with the analytical structure of the law. In *The Concept of Law*, Hart distinguishes between primary and secondary rules. Primary rules are those "rules of obligation" that provide the basic "social structure" of society. They consist of basic commands, which concern actions, and inform us what behaviour is appropriate in a given situation. At the very least, these rules of obligation restrict "the free use of violence, theft, and deception." These rules create internal obligations.

The primary rules of obligation also explain the operation of those aspects of the civil law that seem foreign to the command theory. The "power conferring" laws that allow individuals to make contracts, enact wills, and marry give them the ability to "vary their initial positions" under the primary rules.[20] Hart suggests that the legal choices made by individuals share the same legal character as the collective decisions made when setting legal rules for the community. It follows that the legislative function is not restricted to public bodies.

Secondary Rules Determine the Validity and Scope of Primary Rules

The primary rules set out a code of conduct, which determines whether our conduct in any given case is lawful or unlawful. Such rules are rarely sufficient, however, to govern a society:

It is plain that only a small community closely knit by ties of kinship, common sentiment, and belief, and placed in a stable environment, could live successfully by such a regime of unofficial rules.

A social structure that is based solely on primary rules will have three major defects: 1) it will be *uncertain* which rules are primary rules; 2) it will be *static*, since there will be no rules to change the primary rules; and 3) it will be *inefficient*, since there will be no means of adjudicating the inevitable disagreements as to whether a primary rule has been violated.

It follows that a "system" of rules requires a second set of rules to resolve these defects. Secondary rules accordingly provide a means of determining what the law is, whether it has been changed, and how it should be interpreted. It is the secondary rules that seem pivotal, from a theoretical perspective, since they decide the validity of the primary rules of obligation.

In order to meet the defects of a unitary social structure, we need three kinds of secondary rules.

1.   We need a "rule of recognition," which will identify whether a particular rule is a primary rule. This is akin to deciding whether a particular rule is a valid primary rule. This rule introduces "the idea of a legal system"; it is "the germ of the idea of legal validity."
2.   We need "rules of change," which permit society to change the primary rules. "The simplest form of such a rule," Hart writes, "is that which empowers an individual or body of persons to introduce new primary rules for the conduct of the life of the group, or of some class within it, and to eliminate old rules."
3.   We need "rules of adjudication" to determine how to interpret the primary rules and the scope of their application. These rules identify who has the power to enforce the primary rules, and they determine how disputes about the application of the primary rules will be settled. They define "the concepts of judge or court, jurisdiction, and judgement."[21]

These kinds of secondary rules constitute "the heart of a legal system." A developed legal system will nevertheless contain other kinds of secondary rules, which specify matters like the means of recovery in a civil suit and the authority of public officers.

The principal task of a judge in Hart's system is to decide whether the primary rules have been broken. It is the secondary rules, however, that determine whether the decisions of the judiciary are properly rendered and are valid within the system. The judge deciding a case has the discretion to go beyond these rules and consider social policy in the area of the penumbra. It is not entirely clear whether Hart believes that judges can take overt political considerations into account in such an analysis, or whether he believes that they must restrict themselves to the public policy concerns that find expression in the legal rules and standards that have been accepted in the system.

Hart's model of the legal system is designed to give judges some flexibility in their inter-pretation of positive law without imperilling the stability of the system. The idea that there is a core and a penumbra of meaning guarantees predictability, but it also gives judges some flexibility in the application of the law. Since the secondary rules provide the conceptual framework in which the judiciary makes their decisions, they are internal and explain the subjective rather than the objective nature of the judicial process. As Hart explains it, they do not merely indicate that a judge will act in a particular manner. They provide a reason for him to do so.

It Is the Rule of Recognition that Keeps the System in Place

Hart recognizes that the reasoning he employs could create an infinite regress. Since the kind of problems that arise with respect to the interpretation of the primary rules may also arise with respect to the interpretation of the secondary rules, someone could argue that we need a set of tertiary rules to interpret the secondary rules. Hart prevents this kind of proliferation by postulating that every secondary rule can be traced back to a rule of recognition. The rule of recognition is not a literal rule, however, but a complex set of standards found in the constitution, legal precedents, and statutes, all taken together. These standards are ranked in order of their ascendancy within the system.

Hart was familiar with Kelsen's conception of the *grundnorm*, and the two ideas share some similarities, though Hart does not set out the attributes of the rule of recognition in any detail. It is nevertheless the rule of recognition that provides the ultimate test of legal validity. Like a mathematical axiom, it exists outside the system that it validates: "The assertion," Hart writes, "that it exists can only be an external statement of fact."[22] Since the state is the source of the Hartian law, it seems clear that the rule of recognition is essentially political. In England, at least, it might conceivably be expressed in the doctrine that Parliament is supreme.

It is not entirely clear that the rule of recognition is free from legal scrutiny, however. In dealing with the same kind of foundational issues, H.W.R. Wade, for example, wrote that the legal system is based on the deeper premise that the judiciary will apply and enforce the law. Wade called this "the rule of judicial obedience" and described it as the "ultimate political fact" on which the system rests.[23] This fact is in the moral keeping of the judiciary, however, and is subject to legal review. This suggests that the external political premises on which the system rests can be legally challenged.[24] This suggestion seems more in keeping with natural law theory, however, which locates the source of legal authority outside the state, in moral norms.

The *Reference* Cases in Canada Deal With the Legal Side of These Issues

There are historical events such as the American Revolution (1775–83) and the Bolshevik Revolution (1917) in which the entire premises of the legal system change. This is interest-ing from a Kelsenian or Hartian perspective, since it means that the *grundnorm* or rule of recognition has also changed. In order to decide whether a particular law is valid after a revolution, it would follow that we have to determine whether it can be logically deduced from—or is at least consistent with—the new *grundnorm* or rule of recognition. This determination apparently depends on whether the law can be validly derived from the new source of political power.

The problems that arise in this kind of context have been at least implicitly considered by the Supreme Court of Canada. In *Reference re Resolution to Amend the Constitution of Canada*, [1981] 1 S.C.R. 753, the court was asked whether the federal government had the authority to request that the Parliament of the United Kingdom surrender its legislative authority over the Canadian constitution without the consent of the provinces. In *Reference re Secession of Quebec*, [1998] 2 S.C.R. 217, the same court considered the right of Quebec to secede.

In the first case, the Supreme Court held that the actions of the federal government were governed by constitutional convention rather than by law. These conventions are interesting because they function solely on the basis that they describe the way that the relevant parties traditionally act and cannot be enforced by the courts. Their existence is accordingly a political fact that exists outside the legal system. This idea is in keeping with the positivist view that changes to the rule of recognition take place in a political realm, outside the reach of the law. In the *Secession Reference*—in contradistinction to the earlier case—a later bench of judges held that the political actors who negotiate secession do so within a binding legal framework. This framework obliges them to respect fundamental principles like the rule of law. The second decision accordingly suggests that changes in the rule of recognition are subject to legal review.

There Are Fundamental Criticisms of Hart's Theory

Hart's legal positivism has been remarkably influential. This is probably because it provides a theory that explains the modern state system. There are, however, fundamental criticisms of his work.

Hart Fails to Establish the Existence of Discrete Legal Obligations

As we have already seen, one of the major difficulties with Hart's theory is that it fails to establish the existence of discrete legal obligations. The examples of the gunman and the poisoner certainly establish that the meaning of words like "ought" and "oblige" is relative to the circumstances in which they are used.[25] There are many issues here, however. Hart seems to be arguing that we may have a positive obligation to do something, in the absence of both moral obligations and coercion. This is not clear. Hart also fails to acknowledge the logical possibilities in ordinary language. We can say that a certain law "obliges" us to act immorally, for example, but this may simply mean that our moral obligation to obey the law is outweighed, in such a case, by the immorality of its provisions. It does not necessarily mean that our obligation to obey the law is a legal obligation that exists separately from our moral obligations. Even if Hart is right in his analysis, his argument does not take us very far, since the discrete legal obligations that Hart postulates are relatively weak and merely force us to enter into an ethical inquiry in deciding whether to obey questionable laws.

Hart Fails to Account for the Constitutional Law

There are other criticisms. Hart's restriction of policy considerations to the penumbra runs into obvious difficulty in the context of the constitutional law. There is no real question about this, since judges deciding constitutional questions with regard to the "hard settled meaning" of statutes often rely on moral, social, and political views—albeit very generalized moral and political views—in determining the law.[26] Hart's failure to grasp this feature of the common law tradition probably reflects the lack of a constitutional tradition in the English jurisprudence.

Hart also misses, however, the response to the legal realists in the English common law. This response can be found in the writing of eminent judges like Matthew Hale (1609–1676), James Fitzjames Stephen (1829–1894), and Patrick Devlin (1905–1992).[27] All of these judges clearly believed that judges are not entitled to rely on their personal beliefs in deciding their cases. They may nevertheless rely on moral or social views, if those views express the moral consensus in society. Hart's neglect of this judicial position may be based on his liberal stance, which individualizes our views, and simply fails to acknowledge the possibility of such a consensus.

Hart Fails to Recognize the Historical Origins of the Law

Hart's discussion of "pre-legal" societies is also problematic. His division between societies with primary rules and more developed societies, with primary and secondary rules, may be helpful analytically. His understanding of "pre-legal" societies, however, is misleading and ahistorical. There is a philosophical error, moreover, at the root of his misunderstanding: it is clear that, in speaking of "pre-legal" societies, Hart is referring to societies without formal legal institutions and simply assumes that these societies do not possess a legal system. This is a positivist fallacy and deprives tribal societies, for example, of their legal traditions.

This criticism is significant because Hart is trying to construct a grand theory of law. There is a second issue, however. As Hart acknowledges, one of the distinguishing features of the law in pre-industrial societies is that it is internalized.[28] This changed dramatically with the introduction of the machinery of the state and democratic government, which gave governments the authority to make law. Legal positivism neglects the fact that the acute need for coercion in the political conception of law arises precisely from the fact that the law in such a system is a product of the external apparatus of government and often fails to reflect the internal views of the members of society.

Notes

1. Andrei Marmor, "The Pure Theory of Law," *The Stanford Encyclopedia of Philosophy*, ed. Edward N. Zalta (Fall 2010). Available at http://plato.stanford.edu.

2. Hans Kelsen, *Pure Theory of Law*, trans. Max Knight (Berkeley: University of California, 1967). This text is a translation of the second edition of *Reine Rechtslehre* (Vienna: Verlag Franz Deuticke, [1943] 1960).

3. The strictest proponent of such a view in the field of jurisprudence was Wesley Newcomb Hohfeld (1879–1918), whose analysis of fundamental legal concepts is remarkably abstract. See Jonathan Gorman,

"The Truth of Legal Analysis," in *Jurisprudence or Legal Science*, ed. Sean Coyle and George Pavlakos (Oxford: Hart Publishing, 2005), pp. 33–50, at p. 44, for a comment on Hohfeld's approach. And see Hohfeld's *Fundamental Legal Conceptions, as Applied in Judicial Reasoning and Other Legal Essays*, ed. Walter Wheeler Cook (New Haven, CT: Yale University, 1919).

4. The idea of a norm here is propositional. One of the questions that might be asked in this context is why does the system have to rest on a single proposition? Why not two, or three?

5. See Hans Kelsen, "The Pure Theory of Law and Analytical Jurisprudence," *Harvard Law Review* 55 (1941–42): 44–79, at p. 64f: "Law and state are usually held to be two distinct entities. But if it be recognized that the state is by its very nature an ordering of human behaviour, that the essential characteristic of this order, coercion, is at the same time the essential element of the law, this traditional dualism can no longer be maintained. By subsuming the concept of the state under the concept of a coercive order which can only be the legal order, by giving up a concept of the state distinct in principle from the concept of law, the pure theory of law realizes a tendency inherent in the doctrine of Austin."

6. Hart, "Positivism and the Separation of Law and Morals," as cited in the readings, p. 602.

7. ibid., p. 614.

8. ibid., pp. 607–8.

9. ibid.

10. ibid., p. 611.

11. Quoting Hart, ibid., p. 614.

12. See Hart, *The Concept of Law*, as cited in the readings, at p. 141: "there remains a distinction between a constitution which, after setting up a system of courts, provides that the law shall be whatever the Supreme Court thinks fit, and the actual constitution of the United States—or for that matter the constitution of any modern State."

13. Hart, "Positivism and the Separation of Law and Morals," as cited in the readings, at p. 604.

14. Hart, *The Concept of Law*, as cited in the readings, p. 27.

15. Hart nevertheless agrees with Austin that these laws are law because the coercive mechanisms of the state are available to enforce them.

16. Hart, "Positivism and the Separation of Law and Morals," as cited in the readings, p. 613.

17. Hart, *The Concept of Law*, as cited in the readings, p. 85.

18. ibid., p. 98.

19. ibid., p. 90.

20. Though it is historically plain that the power to enter into agreements is not conferred by the law—it is merely that the law recognizes and enforces certain agreements.

21. Hart, *The Concept of Law*, as cited in the readings, pp. 94–7.

22. ibid., p. 107.

23. See H.W.R. Wade, "The Basis of Legal Sovereignty," *Cambridge Law Journal* 13, no. 2 (November 1955): 172–97, at p. 188ff.

24. There are at least a few historical situations in which this kind of principle seems to have expressed itself in the actions of a court. Perhaps the most recent example was the unsuccessful attempt by the President of Pakistan, General Pervez Musharraf, to suspend Iftikhar Muhammad Chaudhry, the chief justice of the Supreme Court, in 2007.

25. It is significant that the person confronted by the gunman has a moral obligation—under the natural law, at least—to obey the gunman and preserve his own being. It follows that the statement that he is "obliged" to hand his money over is not entirely free of moral implications.

26. This explains the further development of Hart's positivism by W.J. Waluchow, for example, in *Inclusive Legal Positivism*, as cited in the suggestions for further reading.

27. Stephen and Devlin are mentioned in Chapter 16.

28. One of the recurring statements in the tribal literature is that individuals are not separated from their beliefs—or the law that enshrines those beliefs. This of course explains why the constitutional law does not have the same resonance in a tribal context. See Menno Boldt and J. Anthony Long, "Tribal Philosophies and the Canadian Charter of Rights and Freedoms," excerpts from which are included in the readings for Chapter 18.

Study Questions

1. Why does Kelsen describe his theory as a "pure" theory of law?

2. Kelsen says he is setting out a normative theory of law. But it is not "normative" in the usual sense of the word, since it empties the law of moral obligations. What is left, then, to make it normative?

3. Hart based his concept of a rule of recognition on Kelsen's concept of the *grundnorm*. What gives a legal rule the status of a rule of recognition or a *grundnorm*? Can you give examples?

4. What is a primary rule? What is a secondary rule?

5. Why does Hart reject formalism?

6. Does the "penumbra" of meaning bring moral or political factors into the legal analysis?

7. Why does Hart believe that Austin's formulation of legal positivism is deficient?

8. How does Hart respond to the legal realists?

9. The overriding philosophical question that comes out of the work of Kelsen and Hart is whether we can separate moral obligations from legal obligations. What do you think? Can we?

Further Reading

David Gray Carlson, "The Collapse of Positivist Jurisprudence into Legal Realism after Dworkin," (working paper no. 289, Benjamin N. Cardozo School of Law, Jacob Burns Institute for Advanced Legal Studies, February 2010). Available at http://papers.ssrn.com.

John Gardner, "Legal Positivism: 5½ Myths," *American Journal of Jurisprudence* 46 (2001): 199. Available at http://heinonline.org.

Robert P. George, ed., *The Autonomy of Law: Essays on Legal Positivism* (Oxford: Clarendon, 1996).

Hans Kelsen, *General Theory of Law and State*, trans. A. Wedberg (Cambridge, MA: Harvard University, 1946).

Joseph Raz, "The Purity of the Pure Theory," in *Normativity and Norms: Critical Perspectives on Kelsenian Themes*, ed. Stanley L. Paulson and B.L. Paulson (Oxford: Clarendon, 1998).

E.H. Taylor, "H.L.A. Hart's Concept of Law in the Perspective of American Legal Realism," *Modern Law Review* 35 (1972): 606–20.

Richard Tur and William Twining, eds., *Essays on Kelsen* (Oxford: Clarendon, 1986).

W.J. Waluchow, *Inclusive Legal Positivism* (Oxford: Clarendon, 1994).

11 The Hart–Fuller Debate and the Procedural Account of the Natural Law

H.L.A. Hart and Lon L. Fuller

Readings

- From *The Morality of Law,* by Lon L. Fuller
- From "Positivism and the Separation of Law and Morals," by H.L.A. Hart
- From "Positivism and Fidelity to Law—A Reply to Professor Hart," by Lon L. Fuller

The following chapter focusses on the work of Lon L. Fuller (1902–1978), who criticized legal positivism for upholding the validity of immoral laws. This criticism led to a famous debate in the *Harvard Law Review* between Fuller and H.L.A. Hart on the validity of the laws of the Third Reich, the Nazi state. Fuller developed his position further in *The Morality of Law,* which sets out a "procedural" theory of the natural law. In spite of its moral implications, Fuller's theory retains the central feature of legal positivism, since it rests the validity of the law on procedural rather than substantive criteria and leaves questions with regard to the content of the law in the political realm.

⚔ Readings ⚕

From Lon L. Fuller, *The Morality of Law* (New Haven, CT: Yale University, 1964).

Chapter 2: The Morality that Makes Law Possible

Eight Factors that Promote the Morality of Law

[There] are eight kinds of legal excellence toward which a system of rules may strive. . . .

The Generality of Law

The first desideratum[1] of a system for subjecting human conduct to the governance of rules is an obvious one: there must be rules. This may be stated as the requirement of generality. . . .

In the analysis presented in these lectures the requirement of generality rests on the truism that to subject human conduct to the control of rules, there must be rules. . . .

Promulgation

Turning now to the promulgation of laws, this is an ancient and recurring problem, going back at least as far as the Secession of the Plebs in Rome.[2] . . .

Even if only one man in a hundred takes the pains to inform himself concerning, say, the laws applicable to the practice of his calling, this is enough to justify the trouble taken to make the laws generally available. . . . Furthermore, in many activities men observe the law, not because they know it directly, but because they follow the pattern set by others whom they know to be better informed than themselves. In this way knowledge of the law by a few often influences indirectly the actions of many. The laws should also be given adequate publication so that they may be subject to public criticism. . . .

Retroactive Laws

If . . . we are to appraise retroactive laws intelligently, we must place them in the context of a system of rules that are generally prospective. Curiously, in this context situations can arise in which granting retroactive effect to legal rules not only becomes tolerable, but may actually be essential to advance the cause of legality. . . .

Suppose a statute declares that after its effective date no marriage shall be valid unless a special stamp, provided by the state, is affixed to the marriage certificate by the person performing the ceremony. A breakdown of the state printing office results in the stamps' not being available when the statute goes into effect.

Though the statute is duly promulgated, it is little publicized, and the method by which it would ordinarily become known, by word of mouth among those who perform marriages, fails because the stamps are not distributed. Many marriages take place between persons who know nothing of the law, and often before a minister who also knows nothing of it. This occurs after the legislature has adjourned. When it is called back into session, the legislature enacts a statute conferring validity on marriages which by the terms of the previous statute were declared void. Though taken by itself, the retrospective effect of the second statute impairs the principle of legality, it alleviates the effect of a previous failure to realize two other desiderata of legality: that the laws should be made known to those affected by them and that they should be capable of being obeyed. . . .

The easiest case is that of the statute which purports to make criminal an act that was perfectly legal when it was committed. Constitutional provisions prohibiting *ex post facto* laws are chiefly directed against such statutes. The principle *nulla poena sine lege* [no punishment without law; i.e., without the existence of a prior law] is one generally respected by civilized nations. The reason the retrospective criminal statute is so universally condemned does not arise merely from the fact that in criminal litigation the stakes are high. It arises also—and chiefly—because of all branches of law, the criminal law is most obviously and directly concerned with shaping and controlling human conduct. It is the retroactive criminal statute that calls most directly to mind the brutal absurdity of commanding a man today to do something yesterday. . . .

The Clarity of Laws

The desideratum of clarity represents one of the most essential ingredients of legality. . . . To put a high value on legislative clarity is not to condemn out of hand rules that make legal consequences depend on standards such as "good faith" and "due care." Sometimes the best way to achieve clarity is to take advantage of, and to incorporate into the law, common sense standards of judgement that have grown up in the ordinary life lived outside legislative halls. After all, this is something we inevitably do in using ordinary language itself as a vehicle for conveying legislative intent. Nor can we ever, as Aristotle long ago observed, be more exact than the nature of the subject matter with which we are dealing admits.

Contradictions in the Laws

It is rather obvious that avoiding inadvertent contradictions in the law may demand a good deal of painstaking care on the part of the legislator. . . . At one time in canonical law there was a principle according to which any promise made under oath was binding and another principle according to which certain kinds of promises, such as those extorted or usurious, imposed no obligation. What should the courts do then in the case of a usurious promise under oath? The solution was to order the promisor to render performance to the promisee and then immediately to compel the promisee to return what he had just received. There may even have been a certain symbolic value in this curious procedure. By first enforcing the contract the court would dramatize the rule that men are bound by promises under oath, and then by undoing its decree, the court would remind the promisee of what his overreaching had cost him. . . .

It has been suggested that instead of speaking of "contradictions" in legal and moral argument we ought to speak of "incompatibilities," of things that do not go together or do not go together well. Another term, a great favorite in the history of the common law, is useful here. This is the word "repugnant." It is especially apt because what we call contradictory laws are laws that fight each other, though without necessarily killing one another off as contradictory statements are assumed to do in logic. . . .

Laws Requiring the Impossible

The principle that the law should not demand the impossible of the subject may be pressed toward a quixotic extreme in which it ends by demanding the impossible of the legislator. It is sometimes assumed that no form of legal liability can be justified unless it rests either on 1) an intent to do a harmful act, or 2) some fault or neglect. If a man is held accountable for a condition of affairs for which he was not to blame . . . then he [i.e., the law] has ascribed to him responsibility for an occurrence that lay beyond his powers. . . .

With respect to the proof of fault, for example, the law faces an insoluble dilemma. If we apply to a particular defendant an objective standard—traditionally that of "the reasonable man"—we obviously run the risk of imposing on him requirements he is incapable of meeting, for his education and native capacities may not bring this standard within his reach. If we take the opposite course and attempt to ask whether the man before us, with all his individual limitations and quirks, fell short of what he ought to have achieved, we enter upon a hazardous inquiry in which all capacity for objective judgement may be lost. . . .

Constancy of the Law through Time

It is interesting to note that [James] Madison, when he sought to defend the provisions in the Constitution prohibiting *ex post facto* laws . . . used language more apt for describing the evil of frequent change than that resulting from retroactive laws:

> The sober people of America are weary of the fluctuating policy which has directed the public councils. They have seen with regret and indignation that . . . one legislative interference [in their affairs] is but the first link of a long chain of repetitions.[3]

The affinity between the problems raised by too frequent or sudden changes in the law and those raised by retrospective legislation receives recognition in the decisions of the Supreme Court. . . .

Congruence between Official Action and Declared Rule

We arrive finally at the most complex of all the desiderata that make up the internal morality of the law: congruence between official action and the law. This congruence may be destroyed or impaired in a great variety of ways: mistaken interpretation, inaccessibility of the law, lack of insight into what is required to maintain the integrity of a legal system, bribery, prejudice, indifference, stupidity, and the drive toward personal power. . . .

In this country it is chiefly to the judiciary that is entrusted the task of preventing a discrepancy between the law as declared and as actually administered. This allocation of function has the advantage of placing the responsibility in practiced hands, subjecting its discharge to public scrutiny, and dramatizing the integrity of the law. There are, however, serious disadvantages in any system that looks solely to the courts as a bulwark against the lawless administration of the law. It makes the correction of abuses dependent upon the willingness and financial ability of the affected party to take his case to litigation. It has proved relatively ineffective in controlling lawless conduct by the police, this evil being in fact compounded by the tendency of lower courts to identify their mission with that of maintaining the morale of the police force. . . .

Chapter 3: The Concept of Law

There Is a Procedural Natural Law

The purpose of the present chapter is to put the analysis presented in my second chapter into its proper relation with prevailing theories of and about law. . . . Proceeding with that exposition, then, the first task is to relate what I have called the internal morality of the law to the ages-old tradition of natural law. Do the principles expounded in my second chapter represent some variety of natural law? The answer is an emphatic, though qualified, yes.

What I have tried to do is to discern and articulate the natural laws of a particular kind of human undertaking, which I have described as "the enterprise of subjecting human conduct to the governance of rules." These natural laws . . . are not "higher" laws;[4] if any metaphor of elevation is appropriate they should be called "lower" laws. They are like the natural laws of carpentry, or at least those laws respected by a carpenter who wants the house he builds to remain standing and serve the purpose of those who live in it. . . .

[T]hese natural laws . . . have nothing to say on such topics as polygamy, the study of Marx, the worship of God, the progressive income tax, or the subjugation of women. If the question be raised whether any of these subjects, or others like them, should be taken as objects of legislation, that question relates to what I have called the external morality of law. . . . [T]he internal morality of law is in this sense a procedural version of natural law, though to avoid misunderstanding the word "procedural" should be assigned a special and expanded sense so that it would include, for example, a substantive accord between official action and enacted law. . . .

With writers of all philosophic persuasions it is, I believe, true to say that when they deal with problems of legal morality it is generally in a casual and incidental way. . . . [T]here is one significant exception. This lies in a literature that arose in England during the seventeenth century, a century of remonstrances, impeachments, plots, and civil war, a period during which existing institutions underwent a fundamental re-examination. It is to this period that scholars trace the "natural law foundations" of the American Constitution. Its literature . . . was intensely and almost entirely concerned with problems I have regarded as those of the internal morality of law. It spoke of repugnancies, of laws impossible to be obeyed, of parliaments walking contrary to their own laws before they have repealed them. . . . But the most famous pronouncement to come down from that great period is that of Coke in *Dr. Bonham's Case*. . . .

In the course of Coke's judgement upholding Bonham's cause, this famous passage appears:

> The censors [of the Royal College] cannot be judges, ministers, and parties. . . . And it appears in our books, that in many cases, the common law will controul Acts of Parliament, and sometimes adjudge them to be utterly void: for when an Act of Parliament is against common right and reason, or repugnant, or impossible to be performed, the common law will controul it, and adjudge such Act to be void.[5]

Today this pronouncement is often regarded as the quintessence of the natural law point of view. Yet notice how heavily it emphasizes procedures and institutional practices.

Notes

1. Editor's note: Something that is wanted or required.
2. Editor's note: The plebs, or plebeians, constituted "the general citizenry in ancient Rome" (*Britannica Online*). The legal rights of the plebeians were severely restricted by the fact that the decisions of the patrician courts were rendered according to secret laws. In 449 BCE, the plebeians left the city (which could not function without their labours) in order to force the patricians to pass a written code of law. This withdrawal, which has been compared to a general strike, was called a *secessio* (literally, "a withdrawal") or secession.
3. Fuller's note: *The Federalist* 44.
4. Editor's note: They are not laws that derive from God or any other religious source.
5. Fuller's note: 8 Rep. 111a (1610).

From H.L.A. Hart, "Positivism and the Separation of Law and Morals," *Harvard Law Review* 71 (1957): 593–629.

The Grudge Informer

The third criticism of the separation of law and morals . . . consists of the testimony of those who have descended into Hell, and, like Ulysses or Dante, brought back a message for human beings. Only in this case the Hell was not beneath or beyond earth, but on it; it was a Hell created on earth by men for other men.

This appeal comes from those German thinkers who lived through the Nazi regime and reflected upon its evil manifestations in the legal system. One of these thinkers, Gustav Radbruch[1] . . . concluded from the ease with which the Nazi regime had exploited subservience to mere law—or expressed, as he thought, in the "positivist" slogan "law as law" (*Gesetz als Gesetz*)—and from the failure of the German legal profession to protest against the enormities which they were required to perpetuate in the name of law, that "positivism" (meaning here the insistence on the separation of law as it is from law as it ought to be) had powerfully contributed to the horrors. His considered reflections led him to the doctrine that the fundamental principles of humanitarian morality were part of the very concept of *Recht* or Legality and that no positive enactment or statute, however clearly it was expressed and however clearly it conformed with the formal criteria of validity of a given legal system, could be valid if it contravened basic principles of morality. . . .

After the war Radbruch's conception of law as containing in itself the essential moral principle of humanitarianism was applied in practice by German courts in certain cases in which local war criminals, spies, and informers under the Nazi regime were punished. The special importance of these cases is that the persons accused of these crimes claimed that what they had done was not illegal under the laws of the regime in force at the time these actions were performed. . . .

Let me cite briefly one of these cases. In 1944 a woman, wishing to be rid of her husband, denounced him to the authorities for insulting remarks he had made about Hitler while home on leave from the German army. The wife was under no legal duty to report his acts, though what he had said was apparently in violation of statutes making it illegal to make statements detrimental to the government of the Third Reich or to impair by any means the military defence of the German people.

The husband was arrested and sentenced to death, apparently pursuant to these statutes, though he was not executed but was sent to the front. In 1949 the wife was prosecuted in a West German court for an offence which we would describe as illegally depriving a person of his freedom (*rechtswidrige Freiheitsberaubung*). This was punishable as a crime under the German Criminal Code of 1871 which had remained in force continuously since its enactment. The wife pleaded that her husband's imprisonment was pursuant to the Nazi statutes and hence that she had committed no crime.

The court of appeal to which the case ultimately came held that the wife was guilty of procuring the deprivation of her husband's liberty by denouncing him to the German courts, even though he had been sentenced by a court for having violated a statute, since, to quote the words of the court, the statute "was contrary to the sound conscience and sense of justice of all decent human beings." This reasoning was followed in many cases which have been hailed as a triumph of the doctrines of natural law and as signalling the overthrow of positivism.

The unqualified satisfaction with this result seems to me to be hysteria. Many of us might applaud the objective—that of punishing a woman for an outrageously immoral act—but this was secured only by declaring a statute established since 1934 not to have the force of law, and at least the wisdom of this course must be doubted.

There were, of course, two other choices. One was to let the woman go unpunished; one can sympathize with and endorse the view that this might have been a bad thing to do. The other was to face the fact that if the woman were to be punished it must be pursuant to the introduction of a frankly retrospective law and with a full consciousness of what was sacrificed in securing her punishment in this way. Odious as retrospective criminal legislation and punishment may be, to have pursued it openly in this case would at least have had the merits of candour.

Note

1.   Editor's note: Gustav Radbruch (1878–1949) was a German professor of criminal law and legal philosophy who argued—against Hans Kelsen and others—that a law that is intolerable under the principle of justice is invalid. See Frank Haldemann "Gustav Radbruch vs. Hans Kelsen: A Debate on Nazi Law," *Ratio Juris* 18, no. 2 (June 2005): 162–78.

From Lon L. Fuller, "Positivism and Fidelity to Law— A Reply to Professor Hart," *Harvard Law Review* 71, no. 4 (1957): 630–72.

Throughout their period of control the Nazis took generous advantage of a device not wholly unknown to American legislatures, the retroactive statute curing past legal irregularities. The most dramatic use of the curative powers of such a statute occurred on July 3, 1934, after the "Roehm purge." When this intraparty shooting affair was over and more than seventy Nazis had been—one can hardly avoid saying—"rubbed out," Hitler returned to Berlin and procured from his cabinet a law ratifying and confirming the measures taken between June 30, and July 1, 1934, without mentioning the names of those who were now considered to have been lawfully executed. . . .

A general increase in the resort to statutes curative of past legal irregularities represents a deterioration in that form of legal morality without which law itself cannot exist. The threat of such statutes hangs over the whole legal system, and robs every law on the books of some of its significance. . . .

During the Nazi regime there were [also] repeated rumors of "secret laws." In the article criticized by Professor Hart, Radbruch mentions a report that the wholesale killings in concentration camps were made "lawful" by a secret enactment. Now surely there can be no greater legal monstrosity than a secret statute. . . .

But the most important affronts to the morality of law by Hitler's government took no such subtle forms as those exemplified in the bizarre outcroppings I have just discussed. In the first place, when legal forms became inconvenient, it was always possible for the Nazis to bypass them entirely and "to act through the party in the streets." There was no one who dared bring them to account for whatever outrages might thus be committed. In the second place, the Nazi-dominated courts were always ready to disregard any statute, even those enacted by the Nazis themselves, if this suited their convenience or if they feared that a lawyer-like interpretation might incur displeasure "above." . . .

The Grudge Informer

Let us turn . . . to the actual case discussed by Professor Hart. In 1944 a German soldier paid a short visit to his wife while under travel orders on a reassignment. During the single day he was home, he conveyed privately to his wife something of his opinion of the Hitler government. He expressed disapproval of . . . Hitler and other leading personalities of the Nazi party. He also said it was too bad Hitler had not met his end in the assassination attempt that had occurred on July 20 of that year.

Shortly after his departure, his wife, who during his long absence on military duty "had turned to other men" and who wished to get rid of him, reported his remarks to the local leader of the Nazi party, observing that "a man who would say a thing like that does not deserve to live." . . .

After the collapse of the Nazi regime, the wife was brought to trial for having procured the imprisonment of her husband.[1] Her defence rested on the ground that her husband's statements to her about Hitler and the Nazis constituted a crime under the laws then in force. Accordingly, when she informed on her husband she was simply bringing a criminal to justice. . . .

This defence rested on two statutes, one passed in 1934, the other in 1938. . . . I reproduce below a translation of the only pertinent section [in the 1938 act]:

> The following persons are guilty of destroying the national power of resistance and shall be punished by death: Whoever publicly solicits or incites a refusal to fulfill the obligations of service in the armed forces of Germany, or in armed forces allied with Germany, or who otherwise publicly seeks to injure or destroy the will of the German people or an allied people to assert themselves stalwartly against their enemies.

It is almost inconceivable that a court of present-day Germany would hold the husband's remarks to his wife . . . to be a violation of the final catchall provision of this statute. . . .

Let us turn now to the other statute upon which Professor Hart relies in assuming that the husband's utterance was unlawful. This is the act of 1934, the relevant portions of which are translated below:

1. Whoever publicly makes spiteful or provocative statements directed against . . . the leading personalities of the nation or of the National Socialist German Workers' Party, . . . of such a nature as to undermine the people's confidence in their political leadership, shall be punished by imprisonment.
2. Malicious utterances not made in public shall be treated in the same manner as public utterances when the person making them realized or should have realized they would reach the public. . . .

I should like to ask the reader whether he can actually share Professor Hart's indignation that, in the perplexities of the postwar reconstruction, the German courts saw fit to declare this thing not a law. . . .

He [Hart] would have preferred a retroactive statute. Curiously, this was also the preference of Radbruch. But unlike Professor Hart, the German courts and Gustav Radbruch were living participants in a situation of drastic emergency. The informer problem was a pressing one, and if legal institutions were to be rehabilitated in Germany it would not do to allow the people to begin taking the law into their own hands, as might have occurred while the courts were waiting for a statute. . . .

To me there is nothing shocking in saying that a dictatorship which clothes itself with a tinsel of legal form can so far depart from the morality of order, from the inner morality of law itself, that it ceases to be a legal system. When a system calling itself law is predicated upon a general disregard by judges of the terms of the laws they purport to enforce, when this system habitually cures its legal irregularities, even the grossest, by retroactive statutes, when it has only to resort to forays of terror in the streets, which no one dares challenge, in order to escape even those scant restraints imposed by the pretence of legality—when all these things have become true of a dictatorship, it is not hard for me, at least, to deny to it the name of law.

Note

1. Editor's note: It seems clear that the woman had at least attempted to procure his death and could have been charged with some form of homicide.

⟿ Discussion ⟻

Fuller Sets Out a Procedural Theory of the Natural Law

Lon Luvois Fuller was a professor of law at Harvard. He is significant because he argued, against the legal positivists, that there is a moral element in the law. He nevertheless retains many elements of positivism and does not place substantive constraints on the law. Fuller's focus is on the system as a whole, and the operation of the law, rather than specific laws. He argues that it is not possible to maintain a coherent legal system without imposing on the law procedural restrictions, which contain moral content. The substantive issues raised by individual laws remain in the custody of the legislature.

Fuller's Work Draws Attention to the Question: When Are We Obliged to Obey the Law?

Fuller's work reflects a historical shift in the focus of legal theory. He seems less interested in the question "what is a valid law?" than in the question "when should we obey the law?" This change in focus is a result of the questions that arose, after the Second World War, with respect to the legal system under the Third Reich. This is the system that Fuller is struggling to deal with, in proposing his modified theory of the natural law.

Fuller's position is that the legal system under the Third Reich degenerated to such an extent that the system's legitimacy came into question. As he writes,

> In situations like these there can be no simple principle by which to test the citizen's obligation of fidelity to law, any more than there can be such a principle for testing his right to engage in a general revolution. One thing is, however, clear. A mere respect for constituted authority must not be confused with fidelity to law.[1]

Under Adolf Hitler, the German legal system deteriorated to such an extent that the German people were no longer obliged to obey the law.

Fuller is arguing against the positivism that we find in the work of John Austin. He is also arguing, however, that Hart's and Kelsen's reformulation of positivist doctrine leaves us in the same position as the earlier version of the theory. There are contrary impulses here, however. In spite of his arguments against a simple positivism, Fuller maintains the essential positivist position. It is clear that he is trying to develop a theory that maintains the separation thesis, which separates the question whether a particular law is valid from the question whether a law conforms to a particular moral code. At the same time, unlike Hart and Kelsen, he believes that the immoral laws enforced by the Third Reich were not binding on the people.

Fuller Argues that Legal Positivism Has a Moral Element

Fuller makes two arguments. The first is that moral considerations enter into the positivist formulation of law. Fuller argues for a broader use of the term "morality." The second is that moral considerations arise in the context of the "internal morality" of the law. In both cases, the most significant philosophical issue may be whether Fuller's use of the term "morality" is accurate.

Fuller's first argument is that morality enters into the secondary rules in Hart's model of a legal system. The "fundamental rules that furnish the framework within which the making of law takes place," Fuller argues, appear to be moral rules rather than rules of law.[2] These rules derive their "efficacy" from the fact that they are generally accepted in society. This "in turn rests ultimately on a perception that they are right and necessary." It follows that these laws are a "merger" of law and morality.

The *Grundnorm* Is a Substantive Principle

Fuller complains that Kelsen and Hart do not address this criticism of legal positivism adequately. It is not possible to create a legal system without some moral grounding.

> The solution for this problem in Kelsen's theory is instructive. . . . Kelsen realizes that . . . [i]n any legal system there must be some fundamental rule that points unambiguously to the source from which laws must come in order to be laws. This rule Kelsen called "the basic norm." In his own words, "the basic norm is not valid because it has been created in a certain way, but its validity is assumed by virtue of its content. It is valid, then, like a norm of natural law."[3]

It follows that the *grundnorm* and Hart's rule of recognition have substantive force.

Fuller's reference to the natural law is not entirely apt, however, since the natural law is made up of a universal body of moral law that is accessible to the human persons in any society. This feature of the natural law distinguishes it from the *grundnorm* and from

Hart's rule of recognition, which are more in the nature of sociological norms and, thus, apply only in distinct societies. The significant feature of these postulates is that they are principles on which everyone in a particular society can agree. It is open to debate whether this feature—in itself—gives them a substantive character.

Fuller's Second Argument Is that the Legal System Has an "Internal Morality"

Fuller then turns to his second argument. There is a similar moral consensus, he argues, as to the internal requirements of a system of law. He is clearly right, moreover, in suggesting that this consensus shares the most significant feature of the natural law, since it crosses over the cultural and moral differences between societies.

Fuller tells a "parable" of a King, Rex, who fails—eight times over—to reform his kingdom's legal system. These eight ways illustrate the formal, or "procedural," ways in which any system of law may cease to function. The significance of this is that a system of law that ceases to function cannot be followed and therefore begins to lose its normative force.

The Parable of Rex Reveals Eight Ways in which a Legal System May Fail

Fuller begins by arguing that a legal system may fail in three ways:

1. It lacks rules—that is to say, it is based on specific decisions made on a case-by-case, *ad hoc* basis. This argument upholds the positivist conception of law as a system of rules.
2. It fails to communicate the rules to the persons to whom they are directed. This argument is implicit in most concepts of positive law and is in keeping with Aquinas' definition of law as an ordinance "made by him who has care of the community, and promulgated."
3. It uses retroactive rules. These rules are problematic because a) they cannot provide a guide to the conduct of those to whom they are directed, and b) they decrease the stability of a system of law by undermining the authority of its rules.

It is not clear, however, that this takes Fuller's position beyond the position set out by the legal positivists, who have no difficulty with the idea that the law must meet fundamental procedural requirements.

Fuller then argues that a legal system may fail because its formulation of individual legal rules is inadequate. The system may contain

1. incomprehensible rules;
2. contradictory rules, which are impossible to obey;
3. rules requiring conduct that is beyond the capacity of those to whom they are directed;
4. rules that are subject to constant change; and, finally,
5. rules that are not administered in the way they are "announced."

The general principle under such a list seems clear enough. Any formal attribute of the system that makes it impossible to govern one's conduct in accordance with the law will contribute to its failure.

This raises the question whether a legal system burdened with the deficiencies that Fuller sets can be said to exist in any meaningful sense. This kind of question can be distinguished from any question as to a legal system's validity.

> A total failure in one of these eight directions does not simply result in a bad system of law; it results in something that is not properly called a legal system at all.[4]

Although Fuller's concern is with the system of law, rather than with specific laws, it seems clear that a law that fails to meet these requirements cannot be considered a law.

A Viable Legal System Must Satisfy Eight Requirements

It may be more helpful to consider the positive requirements of a legal system. In Fuller's view, such a system requires

1.   general rules that are
2.   properly promulgated,
3.   prospective,
4.   comprehensible,
5.   logically consistent,
6.   feasible,
7.   reasonably certain, and
8.   administered as they are announced.

Laws must be general, rational, and fair. A legal system must be logically sound. If proper notice has been given, however, and it is possible to obey the law, we are apparently obliged to follow it.

Fuller speaks of the eight requirements that he lists as "the internal morality of the law," a concept that is related to the "ages-old tradition of natural law." The natural law is substantive, however. The requirements that Fuller puts forth do not seem to form part of a higher law, like the natural law, in its religious or secular formulation. Fuller nevertheless makes a distinction between the "internal" morality of the law and the "external" morality of the law. This distinction seems counterintuitive, since it places the content of the law somehow outside of it, as if the law exists quintessentially as an empty formal or logical structure. Still, Fuller argues that the requirements he sets out have no bearing on the "external" morality of the law, which is expressed in the views that make their way into legal provisions dealing with issues like abortion, capital punishment, and indeterminate detention.

Fuller's Requirements Are Descriptive

There is considerable confusion in Fuller's theory, since he classifies his requirements as normative requirements. Fuller's theory is not a normative theory, however, and is more appropriately classified as a descriptive theory, since it basically lists the formal character-istics of a functional legal system. This kind of inquiry is recognizably scientific. Rather than study the individual specimens provided by specific cases, Fuller studies systems of law. The legal system under the Third Reich provides him with a classic example of a legal system that had ceased to function as a recognizable legal system.

Fuller's theory can be compared with natural law theory, which provides the classical example of a normative theory of law. Natural law theory has traditionally held that an immoral law is invalid. Aquinas states that an unjust law "has the nature, not of law, but of violence." We are therefore not obliged to obey unjust laws. The morality that concerns Aquinas is substantive: it usually exists in the fact that the law directs us to act in a man-ner that contravenes the ethical order. Although Fuller certainly suggests that the legal system of the Third Reich substituted power and the rule violence for law, and that the legal regime under the Third Reich ceased to function in any meaningful sense, he does not argue that the Nazi laws were immoral in a substantive sense and therefore invalid.

Fuller's argument is directed against legal positivism, which holds that it is the power of the state that guarantees the positive law and makes this law compulsory. It follows that the immorality of the state, or those who control the apparatus of the state, does not undermine the normative validity of the law. It is not clear, however, that Fuller is arguing that the laws of the Third Reich were invalid. His concern is with the political interference of the government in the legal system, and with the corresponding uncertainty in the legal process, rather than with the morality of specific laws. It might be possible to describe the entire legal system of the Third Reich as "immoral"—and even to make the argument that it is the immorality of the system that deprived it of the formal attributes of a healthy legal system. This is another kind of argument, however.

Fuller is arguing at cross-purposes. There is no reason to believe that Austin—or any of the legal positivists—is arguing that an incomprehensible law, for example, is a valid law. There accordingly seems to be a philosophical problem with Fuller's use of the term "morality." It may be immoral to enforce a contradictory or incomprehensible law, and the motive behind such a law may be immoral, but we do not normally dismiss a law that cannot be understood because it is "immoral." We rather tend to hold that such a law does not constitute a law. The same kind of observation can be made with respect to Fuller's other examples: the fact that laws are not published, for example, does not necessarily make the laws immoral. It is the failure to publish them that is immoral. The same kind of statement can be made in the context of retroactive legislation.[5]

The same kinds of questions arise with respect to the judiciary's obligation to admin-ister legal rules as they are "announced" by the political arm of government. Although the integrity of the legal system suffers when laws are not administered as intended, the law is far more dynamic than Fuller acknowledges, and the rigour of harsh laws may be mitigated by the judiciary's refusal to enforce them as the government intended. The obvious example of this can be found in the Bloody Code, the criminal law passed by the English Parliament in the eighteenth century, which was extremely punitive—so much so that William Blackstone wrote that a hundred and sixty offences carried the penalty of "instant death." The criminal law became extremely technical as a result, as judges and jurors took advantage of any of the means available to them to reduce the carnage produced by such laws. The suggestion that this was "immoral" is out of place, and clearly wrong, in spite of our general assumption that the law should be applied, in accordance with its intentions. It follows that Fuller's use of the word "morality" breaks down in these kinds of circumstance.

Fuller Describes His Theory as "Procedural"

It is evident that Fuller's conception of law is political. In his view, it is for the legislature to decide the substantive content of specific laws. He accordingly describes the natural laws that he is relying upon as procedural, rather than substantive:

> The term "procedural" is ... broadly appropriate as indicating that we are concerned, not with the substantive aims of legal rules, but with the ways in which a system of rules for governing human conduct must be constructed and administered.[6]

This description maintains the separation thesis and focusses on the need to maintain a coherent system.

There Is a Judicial Side to the Procedural Argument

Fuller focusses on the legislative requirements of a valid legal system. It seems clear, however, that his view imposes similar restrictions on the judicial process. If judges do not apply the rules in the system consistently and comprehensibly, in a manner that respects the coherence and integrity of the system, the system will plainly fail.

The judicial side of the procedural argument can be found in the common law jurisprudence. The most obvious example of this, in the English law, is probably the doctrine of natural justice. This doctrine has three main branches. The first is that individuals are entitled to know the substance of the case that has been raised against them. The second is that individuals have the right to respond to the allegations that have been made against them. And finally, individuals have the right to know the reasons for the decision in their case.

These rules have been gradually broadened and now include a standard of fairness. The kinds of concerns that Fuller identifies also trigger constitutional provisions. The Canadian courts have incorporated the same standard into their interpretation of Section 7 of the *Canadian Charter of Rights and Freedoms*, which guarantees the right not to be deprived of life, liberty, and security of the person, "except in accordance with the principles of fundamental justice." The "due process" clause in the fifth and fourteenth amendments to the Constitution of the United States provides similar protections.

It Seems More Accurate to Describe Fuller's Theory as a Coherence Theory

Fuller's account is more abstract than these legal accounts, however. His argument is not that a valid legal system must contain identified rules. It is rather that the rules that it contains must be applied consistently, in accordance with the intentions behind them. It accordingly seems more accurate to describe Fuller's theory as a coherence theory, which holds that a legal system begins to lose its normative force when external forces enter the system, without regard for its formal and logical integrity. At some point in the process of disintegration, a system that operates inconsistently or illogically no longer binds us.

It is by no means clear that the coherence of a legal system is enough to guarantee the substantive fairness of the legal process, however. The reality is that procedural safeguards like the rules of natural justice or due process have their own substantive component. This fact has been explicitly recognized by the American courts. As soon as we begin to define procedural terms—and give them meaningful content—it seems plain that we begin to enter into a moral inquiry. If we say that statutes must be passed by a majority or begin to specify how a statute must be promulgated, we inevitably enter into an arena of right and wrong. It accordingly becomes difficult to separate the procedural and substantive requirements of a valid legal system.

Fuller is arguably taking a positivist position, in spite of the analogy that he makes with the theory of the natural law. This connection to positivism is borne out by his definition of the law. The law, he writes, "is the enterprise of subjecting human conduct to the governance of rules." This view is in keeping with Austin's conception of law as "a rule laid down for the guidance of an intelligent being." The purpose of the law is social control. Both theorists take the position that a legal system cannot be composed of *ad hoc* decisions made by a person in authority.

There is nothing in Fuller's rules that prevents a legal positivist from applying them to Austin's conception of law. There must be rules, and Austin holds that they must be general rules, which ensure "the rule of law." There is nothing in legal positivism that requires us to accept secret or retroactive laws, or laws that are applied inconsistently and in contravention of their plain meaning. The kinds of procedural safeguards that Fuller sets out do not prevent the legislature from passing immoral laws.

The Major Advantage of Fuller's Theory Is that It Places Rational Limits on the Exercise of Power

The major advantage of Fuller's theory is not that it invalidates immoral laws. The reality is that it validates such laws, as long as they meet his procedural requirements. The advantage of Fuller's theory is that it places rational limits on the exercise of political authority. In point of fact, there are echoes of formalism in Fuller's theory, since formalism holds primarily that the law exists as a logical and coherent body of principle.

But Fuller's Theory Does Not Deal With the Substance of Immoral Laws

The procedural theory nevertheless seems to neglect many of the moral issues that arise in the context of specific laws. It seems plain that the laws of the Third Reich, under which Jews and other minorities were interned, remain valid laws under the procedural theory as long as they are administered in accordance with Fuller's eight requirements. The problem with such laws cannot be addressed by a theory that concerns itself solely with issues relating to the coherence of the system.

The same issues have arisen in the case of the apartheid laws of South Africa. David Dyzenhaus describes such laws, and the legal regime that contained them, as "wicked."[7] This kind of terminology identifies a substantive rather than a procedural deficiency, which cannot be corrected by the equal and consistent application of the law. It is the content of a discriminatory law—a law that deprives a minority of the right to participate in a political system, for example—that is offensive. The fact that such a law is applied inconsistently may raise additional issues of unfairness, but has no bearing on the substantive issue.

Fuller Also Neglects the Fact that a Successful Legal System May Produce Immoral Laws

Although Fuller's theory may be able to deal with an immoral regime like the Third Reich, it neglects the fact that a successful legal system may produce immoral laws. An example might be the Jim Crow laws, which required that black people leave American municipalities by sunset, or laws enforcing segregation.[8] The moral issue that these laws raise is whether we are obliged to obey such laws. The legal issue is whether they are valid laws. Fuller does not speak to either of these issues. He appears to believe that as long as the legal system maintains its internal coherence, we are obliged to follow the law. We can probably infer from many of his comments that the law must also be politically legitimate, an additional condition that puts him in much the same position as the positivists. Although Fuller acknowledges that a revolution might be justified in the instance of the Nazi state, it is the political system, rather than the legal system, that must be overthrown.

The Grudge Informer Case Illustrates the Shortcomings of Legal Positivism

The case of the grudge informer has acquired a central place in the debate between legal positivists and other theorists. Fuller believes that the case demonstrates the failure of legal positivism to place meaningful constraints on wicked laws. The case also helps to clarify the principles that come into play, however, in applying Hart's and Fuller's theories to concrete cases. In addition, it forces us to consider the differences between different legal theories and the positions adopted by the courts.

There are a number of reservations that should be made at the outset. Legal constraints on the criticism of a war-time leader are not unusual and, as Hart points out, many aspects of the German law remained the same under the Third Reich.[9] Thus, the laws of contract and marriage remained largely as they were, and the argument that such laws were rendered invalid by the regime's abuses in other areas is not convincing.

Hart Takes the Position that the Law Prohibiting Criticism of Hitler Was a Valid Law

Hart focusses on the laws passed by the Third Reich rather than the legal system. Although Hart's position is that the laws prohibiting insulting remarks about Hitler were not invalid because they were depraved or wicked, this is open to question. If we adopt Hart's analysis in *The Concept of Law*, and the informer laws were valid, we are forced to say that the husband of the grudge informer had an "obligation" to refrain from speaking candidly to his wife. This is a dubious statement, even in a technical sense, since it goes against the much deeper historical assumption in the law that spouses may share each other's thoughts. The later positivists naturally want to separate legal obligations from other kinds of obligations, but this seems contrived, in the case of the grudge informer. The best that we can say, convincingly, in the case is that the husband is in much the same position as the man who is "obliged" to obey the gunman, without feeling "obligated" to do so.

It follows that there is at least some doubt as to whether the grudge informer law created the kind of obligation that Hart contemplates in *The Concept of Law*, at least in the precise circumstances of the case.[10] Hart also argues, however, that legal rules create obligations because they have been internalized, both by those who administer the system and by the general public. This is not clear in the case of the grudge informer. Although judges enforced the laws prohibiting any criticism of Hitler, there are reasons to believe, as Fuller suggests, that judges applied these laws out of fear for their own safety. Nor is it clear that the public accepted the laws as a "reason" for punishment within the system. Indeed, the prosecutions for criticism of the *Fuhrer* suggest that the laws were not internalized, as Hart assumes, and were therefore erratic and inconsistent in their application.

It follows that we run into difficulties when we try to apply Hart's theory to the grudge informer case. This still leaves Hart's general position intact, at least in some cases. There are clearly historical situations in which the bulk of society adopts "an internal point of view" with respect to immoral laws, particularly in the instance of minorities. There have been many discriminatory and even genocidal laws that have received the approval of a democratic majority.[11] If these laws have been passed in accordance with Hart's secondary rules, it seems he would have no choice but to conclude that they are valid laws.[12] Hart is cognizant of the fact that this makes legal positivism morally unattractive, but he ultimately argues that the unattractiveness of the theory does not detract from the reality of Austin's insight that the binding force of the positive law comes from the use of force. If the political system changes, and the immorality of previous laws becomes apparent, the best we can do is invalidate those laws—retrospectively, in spite of Fuller's argument against retrospective laws—and frankly acknowledge that there are cases in which people may be punished for ostensibly following laws that were valid at the time of their actions.

Fuller Takes the Position that the German Legal System Had Stopped Functioning in Any Meaningful Sense

Fuller's response is that the law prohibiting criticism of Hitler was not a law in any meaningful sense of the term. As the German legal system disintegrated, it changed from a set of rules that were internally adopted to a set of external rules that existed as the arbitrary directives of a military and political authority. In Hartian terms, the Nazi government took on the character of the gunman. The only reason that citizens had for obeying the law was that they would be punished for disobeying it.

Fuller's argument is based on the political contract.

> As the sociologist Simmel has observed, there is a kind of reciprocity between government and the citizen with respect to the observance of rules. Government says to the citizen in effect, "These are the rules we expect you to follow. If you follow them, you have our assurance that they are the rules that will be applied to your conduct."[13]

The duties of both sides under the contract are grounded in each other. When the government breaches its fundamental duty under the contract, the contract accordingly ceases to be binding, and citizens no longer have a duty to obey the law.

Fuller's Theory Does Not Address the Underlying Substantive Issues

Fuller does not deal directly with the trial of the grudge informer. On the procedural theory, however, the informer could legitimately be punished because the law under which she reported her husband was not a law that she had any obligation to follow. In an ethical sense, at least, it is not clear that this statement is very different from the statement that the informer law was an invalid law, though Fuller's reason for saying this is that the legal system had deteriorated to the point where at least some of the laws of the Third Reich were no longer binding. The grudge informer was accordingly a free agent, who made use of the mechanisms that were in place at the time to have her husband killed. These mechanisms must be discounted as political rather than legal mechanisms, which thus had no legal hold on her. It follows that she could not claim to be following the law in any meaningful sense of the word.

Fuller's position is closer to Hart's position than he acknowledges, since it focusses exclusively on the procedural failures of the legal system and does not address the moral issues raised by the law. The procedural theory does not place any substantive limits on the legislative or executive authority of government. Indeed, from an ethical perspective, Fuller's theory is remarkably timid and places the sovereign power, which gives rise to the positive law, outside the reach of legal constraints. This may reflect a certain political realism, since it may simply be unrealistic to expect the judiciary under a regime like the Third Reich to place substantive limits on the authority of the state.

The procedural focus in Fuller's theory nevertheless seems to bypass the fundamental legal issue that arises under the Nazi legal system. That issue concerns the contents of the regime's oppressive laws. The law that made it a capital crime to criticize Hitler is only one example of such a law: in his article "The Grudge Informer Revisited,"[14] David Dyzenhaus has described it as a "terror law," since the purpose of the law was to silence the public by instilling fear. The informer laws also placed criminal restrictions on private conduct that was well within the ordinary parameters of our behaviour. Fuller does not ask the obvious question, which is whether the Nazi state had the authority to pass such laws.

The Legal Analysis of the Grudge Informer Case Raises Different Issues

The legal question raised by the grudge informer case is whether the prosecution proved that the accused committed the offence of deprivation of liberty. This question raises different issues than does the theoretical analysis in Fuller and Hart. For one thing, the debate between Hart and Fuller as to the validity and status of Nazi law was apparently based on an erroneous account of the original case. This came to light in an article by H.O. Pappe, published in the *Modern Law Review*, which draws our attention to a second case with similar facts.[15] In his article "The Grudge Informer Revisited," David Dyzenhaus has reviewed the reasoning in a number of similar cases.[16]

Pappe and Dyzenhaus Demonstrate that the Post-War German Courts Believed the Informer Laws Were Valid

One fact that comes to light in this review of the caselaw by Pappe and Dyzenhaus is that the Court of Appeal in the original grudge informer case did not rely on the natural law. Although the court held that the laws prohibiting criticism of Hitler were "grossly unfair," it found that the laws in question were valid laws. The accused was convicted on the basis that she had used valid laws and the legal process—here "a passive instrument"—to achieve immoral and indeed criminal ends. The crime was one "of indirect perpetration."

Dyzenhaus dismisses this argument, which requires "that the court-martial judge be regarded as akin to a dog set on someone by its owner."[17] The court's analysis, in his view, fails to recognize the independence of the judiciary. The description nevertheless seems apt, and it reflects the formalism of the German legal process, and indeed positivism, which sees the legal process as a kind of logical machine and requires that judges apply the law neutrally to the facts of the case. If the informer laws were valid, and the elements of an offence were made out, it is not clear that the judge had any discretion to alter the result.

In the second case mentioned by Pappe, the Federal Supreme Court held that the original conviction was erroneous because the conversation between the accused and his wife had not been made in public.[18] There is a suggestion, at least, that matrimonial conversations were either inadmissible or implicitly exempt from the laws prohibiting criticism. The court held, in addition, that the death penalty was a grossly disproportionate sentence and at least implicitly unconstitutional. It follows, in spite of the ostensible legality of the process, that the accused woman had used illegal means to obtain the death or imprisonment of her husband.

A Common Law Analysis of the Case Merely Requires Proof of *Mens Rea* and *Actus Reus*

Some of the issues in the theoretical discussion of the grudge informer case seem spurious in the context of the legal analysis. The fundamental positivist argument against convicting the grudge informer is that such a conviction essentially changes the law under which she originally acted and convicts her for acting lawfully. This naturally seems wrong, since it changes the law retroactively, and no one can have notice of retroactive changes. Fuller essentially sidesteps this issue, since he does not accept that the legal system under the Third Reich had any binding effect on citizens. As a result, we cannot say—in any meaningful sense—that the grudge informer was acting in accordance with the law when she reported her husband or that the law has somehow changed.

The prominence of the issue of retroactivity in the theoretical discussion can be attributed to the reliance of modern legal theorists on a political conception of the law, which assumes that the law is a product of legislation. This kind of assertion is remarkable in the context of the criminal law, chiefly because it is erroneous. The reality is that crimes like murder (which came out of the law of "*mudrum*" in the customary law) have their origins in moral custom and the religious tradition.[19]

The common law holds that proof of a crime requires proof of *actus reus* and *mens rea*, a guilty act and a guilty mind. The argument regarding retroactivity seems to assume that the grudge informer could not be convicted of an offence unless she had been given notice of whatever law had made her actions criminal. This assumption is based on a misunderstanding of the moral element in *mens rea*, however, which is not related to the legislative details of an offence. The historical issue in the criminal courts was whether the accused committed a public wrong, with "malice aforethought." This merely requires proof of blameworthiness, which generally lies in the fact that the accused knew he was doing something wrong.

This issue is further simplified by the presumption that ordinary people understand what is regarded as wrong in their society. As a result, there is no need to agonize over the question whether an accused who breaks into a home at night or carries a loaded gun knows that his actions are wrong. People know they should not rob or arrange the death of their spouses, and they do not need to be informed that these kinds of actions attract penal sanctions. The argument with respect to retroactivity applies plausibly only to laws of political origin—laws like the law prohibiting criticism of Hitler—that cannot be foreseen in the ordinary exercise of our moral faculties.

The German courts that convicted grudge informers were undoubtedly relying on these factors. The real legal issue in the grudge informer case concerns voluntariness, which has historically been seen as an aspect of the *actus reus* of an offence.[20] This raises a possible defence. The significant issue is not whether a particular law was valid, however.

The common law recognizes the existence of *de facto* as well as *de jure* laws, and the legal validity of the informer laws is not the decisive factor. This is apparent in section 15 of the *Criminal Code of Canada*, which recognizes that obedience to *de facto* law is a defence to a criminal charge.

The defence of obedience to law is based on the positivist idea that a person following the law is under some form of threat or compulsion, which negates the voluntariness of the act.[21] The grudge informer cases do not fit comfortably under section 15, however, since the distinguishing feature of these cases is that the accused chose to use the criminal process, freely and wilfully, for improper purposes.[22] There was accordingly no compulsion.

The simplest argument for conviction may be that the *actus reus* of the offence of deprivation of liberty, properly construed, includes a mental element. This kind of construction is an ordinary feature of the criminal law. Section 88 of the *Criminal Code of Canada*, for example, makes it an offence to carry a weapon for "a purpose dangerous to the public peace." On this reading, the grudge informer's offence did not consist of testifying against her husband. It consisted of testifying against him for the explicit purpose of depriving him of his liberty.

It is notable, in this context, that the use of the criminal process for private or improper purposes in the common law is considered an abuse of process.[23] This is a bar to prosecution, however, rather than an offence. There are also questions of proportionality. It may be offensive if a wife reports her husband to the police for capital murder, or turns in the murder weapon, merely because she wants to see him executed. This does not mean that she has committed an offence. It is worth asking whether the grudge informer would have been convicted if the penalty for criticizing Hitler was relatively minor and her husband was sentenced to five days in jail.

Hart and Fuller Also Fail to Separate the Questions of Political and Legal Legitimacy

The theoretical analysis of the grudge informer case in the literature also fails to canvass other approaches to the question of validity. The validity of a legal system normally rests on its legitimacy. It may also be argued, however, that a valid statutory law must be legally and politically legitimate. It could then be said that the law prohibiting criticism of Hitler was politically legitimate, since it issued properly from a person or body with the appropriate political authority, in accordance with positivist criteria. It is legally legitimate, however, only if it meets the minimum legal standards, whether they lie in the substantive tradition of the natural law or the procedural view put forward by Fuller.

The problem with Fuller's view is the same as the problem with legal positivism. Both theories fail to capture the second requirement of a valid law. This does not necessarily prevent the state from enforcing an invalid law. The grudge informer case provides us with an example of a situation in which the deficiencies in the political analysis simply make it impossible to access the issue of legal legitimacy. The application of an invalid law in such circumstances is nevertheless a political rather than a legal act.

The Deeper Theoretical Issue Concerns the Inherent Limits of a Political Conception of Law

The major theoretical issue that manifests itself in the example of the grudge informer is that there were no real substantive limits on the political power exercised by the Third Reich. The law prohibiting criticism of Hitler accordingly demonstrates the deficiencies of a political conception of law, which is not subject to the kinds of legal, constitutional, and moral constraints found in substantive theories like the natural law. Although Hart's discussion in *The Concept of Law* is sophisticated enough to raise issues with regard to the Nazi laws, it is difficult to see how either Hart's positivism or Fuller's procedural theory addresses the substantive defects that deprived the legal regime.

The irony is that this kind of issue arises on both sides of the debate, since the conviction of the accused is open to similar criticism. If Dyzenhaus is right in asserting that the postwar German courts were determined to convict the accused, their reasoning seems incidental to the convictions.[24] Hart makes the same point, in describing "the unqualified satisfaction" that met the convictions as "hysteria." The question that this poses in legal theory is whether the conviction of the grudge informer merely satisfied the political impulses of the time and provided the right result, or whether it was a justifiable legal verdict, derived logically from the application of settled principles to established facts.

Notes

1. Fuller, *The Morality of Law*, as cited in the readings, at p. 41.
2. Fuller, "Positivism and Fidelity to Law," as cited in the readings, at p. 639.
3. ibid., at p. 641.
4. Fuller, *The Morality of Law*, p. 38.
5. In point of fact, the common law distinguishes between legislation that confers a benefit and legislation that imposes a punishment. A benefit may be conferred retroactively.
6. Fuller, *The Morality of Law*, p. 97.
7. See David Dyzenhaus, *Hard Cases in Wicked Legal Systems: Pathologies of Legality*, 2nd ed. (Oxford: Oxford University, 2010).
8. For a discussion of the legal aspects of these laws, see Michael J. Klarman, *From Jim Crow to Civil Rights: The Supreme Court and the Struggle for Racial Equality* (Oxford: Oxford University, 2004).
9. Many countries also have laws of *lese-majesty*. The difference is that these laws are there to protect the dignity of the state rather than to keep a particular person or party in power. See section 49 of the *Criminal Code of Canada*, for example, which makes it an offence to wilfully do an act "with intent to alarm Her Majesty."
10. It seems clear that Hart feels the law can be justified in other situations, since public criticism of political authority may be legitimately dangerous in wartime.
11. There are good reasons to believe that the laws in Canada and the United States interning the Japanese in the Second World War—which the Canadian government has officially apologized for—were overwhelmingly accepted by the majority of citizens. They were accordingly politically legitimate.
12. It could also be argued, however, that many of the laws in the Third Reich did not meet the secondary rules of the system and were therefore invalid. This would take us into the kind of position that Fuller sets out: it would follow that the judiciary simply enforced invalid laws and was afraid to question them.

13. Fuller's note: *The Sociology of Georg Simmel* (1950), trans. Wolff, §4, "Interaction in the Idea of 'Law,'" pp. 186–89; see also Chapter 4, "Subordination under a Principle," pp. 250–67. Fuller, *The Morality of Law*, pp. 39–40.

14. This article is noted in the suggestions for further reading.

15. See H.O. Pappe, "On the Validity of Judicial Decisions in the Nazi Era," as cited in the suggestions for further reading.

16. See David Dyzenhaus, "The Grudge Informer Case Revisited," as cited in the suggestions for further reading.

17. Dyzenhaus, ibid., at p. 1009.

18. The accounts of the case make it clear that the spouse was, in the language of the common law, a competent but not compellable witness. The wife accordingly made a conscious decision to testify against her husband, in spite of the fact that she was not obliged to do so. This seems to be the most salient feature of the entire case.

19. One might ask oneself, is murder an offence because Parliament or Congress has made it so? And, if this is the case, does Parliament or Congress have the authority to pass legislation "legalizing" murder?

20. See the discussion in Chapter 16, and see *R. v. Parks*, [1992] 2 S.C.R. 871. The idea in the common law is that an accused who has involuntarily committed an act has not "acted" in any meaningful sense.

21. So the defence contemplated by section 15 is more a defence in the nature of duress than a statutory exception.

22. In the second case, the wife was explicitly advised by the trial judge that she had no obligation to testify against her husband. See Dyzenhaus, op. cit.

23. The common law courts will not allow a private party to use the criminal process for private purposes, such as the collection of a debt. See *Ontario (Ministry of Labour) v. 3 for 1 Pizza & Wings Inc.*, 2006 ONCJ 143 (CanLII), for example, at para. 67, as cited in the suggestions for further reading.

24. See Dyzenhaus, "The Grudge Informer Case Revisited," op. cit., at p. 1009, where he writes: "It is clear from the court's reasoning that it was determined to reach a conclusion that the woman was guilty."

Study Questions

1. What is the "procedural" natural law? How does it differ from the historical conception of the natural law in Aquinas' work? Is the term "natural law" even appropriate in this context? Why, why not?

2. There is an argument that Fuller's argument doesn't go far enough. Suppose an apartheid law in South Africa meets the procedural requirements of the natural law. Is it a valid law?

3. Most of us would agree that there is a point at which an immoral government becomes illegitimate. The more difficult issue, however, arises when a legitimate government passes unjust laws. Is there any real difference between Hart and Fuller in such cases?

4. Do you agree with the statement that Fuller remains a legal positivist, in spite of his reliance on the natural law? Why, why not?

5. Consider section 15 of the *Criminal Code of Canada*, which is included in the additional online readings listed in the Appendix. Would the grudge informer have a defence in Canada?

6. Would you convict the grudge informer? Why, why not?

7.   Hart seems to take the same position that Austin took in *The Province of Jurisprudence Determined*: a law is valid as long as it is the command of the sovereign. This is determined by whether it meets the requirements of the political process. What should we do, then, when we are faced with a valid but unjust law, like the laws under the Third Reich?

Further Reading

David Dyzenhaus, "The Grudge Informer Case Revisited," *New York Law Review* 82, no. 4 (October 2008): 1000–34.

Lon L. Fuller, *The Principles of Social Order: Selected Essays of Lon L. Fuller*, ed. Kenneth I. Winston (Durham, NC: Duke University, 1981).

Frank Haldemann, "Gustav Radbruch vs. Hans Kelsen: A Debate on Nazi Law," *Ratio Juris* 18, no. 2 (June 2005): 162–78.

Neil MacCormick, "Natural Law and the Separation of Law and Morals," in Robert P. George, ed., *Natural Law Theory*, (Oxford: Clarendon, 1992), 105–133.

Ontario (Ministry of Labour) v. 3 for 1 Pizza & Wings Inc., 2006 ONCJ 143 (CanLII).

H.O. Pappe, "On the Validity of Judicial Decisions in the Nazi Era," *Modern Law Review* 23 (1960): 260–74.

Stanley L. Paulson, "Lon L. Fuller, Gustav Radbruch, and the 'Positivist' Theses," *Law & Philosophy* 13 (1994): 313.

12 Contemporary Liberal Theory: Dworkin's Critique of Hart's Positivism

Readings

- From "The Model of Rules," by Ronald Dworkin
- From *The Concept of Law*, by H.L.A. Hart

American philosopher Ronald Dworkin succeeded H.L.A. Hart in the Chair of Jurisprudence at Oxford University in 1969. His early work includes a critique of Hart's conception of rules. It also questions the larger philosophical assumptions in Hart's work and takes issue with the positivist dichotomy between law and morality. Although Hart and Dworkin are both liberals and implicitly accept the notion of a social contract, Dworkin's legal theory reflects the American constitutional tradition. His view of the judicial role contains elements of the natural law and gives the "political morality" of the judiciary a legitimate role in the legal process.

❖ Readings ❖

From Ronald Dworkin, "The Model of Rules," *University of Chicago Law Review* 35 (1967–8): 14–47.[1]

Positivism Holds that the Law Is Made up of Rules

Positivism has a few central and organizing propositions as its skeleton. . . . These key tenets may be stated as follows:

a. The law of a community is a set of special rules used by the community directly or indirectly for the purpose of determining which behaviour will be punished or coerced by the public power. These special rules can be identified and distinguished by specific criteria, by tests having to do not with their content but with their *pedigree* or the manner in which they were adopted or developed. . . .

b. The set of these valid legal rules is exhaustive of "the law," so that if someone's case is not clearly covered by such a rule . . . then that case cannot be decided by "applying the law." It must be decided by some official, like a judge, "exercising his discretion," which means reaching beyond the law for some other sort of standard to guide him in manufacturing a fresh legal rule or supplementing an old one.

c.   To say that someone has a "legal obligation" is to say that his case falls under a valid legal rule that requires him to do or to forbear from doing something. . . . In the absence of such a valid legal rule there is no legal obligation; it follows that when the judge decides an issue by exercising his discretion, he is not enforcing a legal obligation as to that issue.

This is only the skeleton of positivism. The flesh is arranged differently by different positivists, and some even tinker with the bones. Different versions differ chiefly in their description of the fundamental test of pedigree a rule must meet to count as a rule of law. . . .

Rules, Principles, and Policies

I want to make a general attack on positivism, and I shall use H.L.A. Hart's version as a target, when a particular target is needed. My strategy will be organized around the fact that when lawyers reason or dispute about legal rights and obligations, particularly in those hard cases when our problems with these concepts seem most acute, they make use of standards that do not function as rules, but operate differently as principles, policies, and other sorts of standards. Positivism, I shall argue, is a model of and for a system of rules, and its central notion of a single fundamental test for law forces us to miss the important roles of these standards that are not rules.

I just spoke of "principles, policies, and other sorts of standards." Most often I shall use the term "principle" generically, to refer to the whole set of these standards other than rules; occasionally, however, I shall be more precise, and distinguish between principles and policies. . . . I call a "policy" that kind of standard that sets out a goal to be reached, generally an improvement in some economic, political, or social feature of the community (though some goals are negative, in that they stipulate that some present feature is to be protected from adverse change). I call a "principle" a standard that is to be observed, not because it will advance or secure an economic, political, or social situation deemed desirable, but because it is a requirement of justice or fairness or some other dimension of morality. Thus the standard that automobile accidents are to be decreased is a policy, and the standard that no man may profit by his own wrong a principle. . . .

Riggs v. Palmer: *A Murderer Cannot Inherit*

My immediate purpose, however, is to distinguish principles in the generic sense from rules, and I shall start by collecting some examples of the former. The examples I offer are chosen haphazardly; almost any case in a law school casebook would provide examples that would serve as well.

In 1889 a New York court, in the famous case of *Riggs v. Palmer* [(1889), 115 N.Y. 506, 22 N.E. 188], had to decide whether an heir named in the will of his grandfather could inherit under that will, even though he had murdered his grandfather to do so. The court began its reasoning with this admission: "It is quite true that statutes regulating the making, proof, and effect of wills, and the devolution of property, if literally construed, and if their force and effect can in no way and under no circumstances be controlled or modified, give this property to the murderer." But the court continued to note that "all laws as well as all contracts may be controlled in their operation and effect by general, fundamental maxims of the common law. No one shall be permitted to profit by his own fraud, or to take advantage of his own wrong, or to found any claim upon his own iniquity, or to acquire property by his own crime." The murderer did not receive his inheritance.

Henningsen v. Bloomfield Motors, Inc.: *The Courts Will Not Allow Themselves to Be Used as Instruments of Inequity*

In 1960, a New Jersey court was faced, in *Henningsen v. Bloomfield Motors, Inc.* [(1960), 32 N.J. 558, 161 A.2d 69], with the important question of whether (or how much) an automobile manufacturer may limit his liability in case the automobile is defective. *Henningsen* had bought a car, and signed a contract which said that the manufacturer's liability for defects was limited to "making good" defective parts—"this warranty being expressly in lieu of all other warranties, obligations, or liabilities." *Henningsen* argued that, at least in the circumstances of his case, the manufacturer ought not to be protected by this limitation, and ought to be liable for the medical and other expenses of persons injured in a crash. He was not able to point to any statute, or to any established rule of law, that prevented the manufacturer from standing on the contract. The court nevertheless agreed with *Henningsen*. At various points in the court's argument the following appeals to standards are made: (a) "We must keep in mind the general principle that, in the absence of fraud, one who does not choose to read a contract before signing it cannot later relieve himself of its burdens." (b) "In applying that principle, the basic tenet of freedom of competent parties to contract is a factor of importance." (c) "Freedom of contract is not such an immutable doctrine as to admit of no qualification in the area in which we are concerned." (d) "In a society such as ours, where the automobile is a common and necessary adjunct of daily life, and where its use is so fraught with danger to the driver, passengers and the public, the manufacturer is under a special obligation in connection with the construction, promotion and sale of his cars. Consequently, the courts must examine purchase agreements closely to see if consumer and public interests are treated fairly." (e) "[I]s there any principle which is more familiar or more firmly embedded in the history of Anglo-American law than the basic doctrine that the courts will not permit themselves to be used as instruments of inequity and injustice?" . . .

Principles Differ from Rules, which Are "All-or-Nothing"

The standards set out in these quotations are not the sort we think of as legal rules. They seem very different from propositions like "The maximum legal speed on the turnpike is sixty miles an hour" or "A will is invalid unless signed by three witnesses." They are different because they are legal principles rather than legal rules.

The difference between legal principles and legal rules is a logical distinction. Both sets of standards point to particular decisions about legal obligation in particular circumstances, but they differ in the character of the direction they give. Rules are applicable in an all-or-nothing fashion. If the facts a rule stipulates are given, then either the rule is valid, in which case the answer it supplies must be accepted, or it is not, in which case it contributes nothing to the decision.

This all-or-nothing is seen most plainly if we look at the way rules operate, not in law, but in some enterprise they dominate—a game, for example. In baseball a rule provides that if the batter has had three strikes, he is out. An official cannot consistently acknowledge that this is an accurate statement of a baseball rule, and decide that a batter who has had three strikes is not out. Of course, a rule may have exceptions (the batter who has taken three strikes is not out if the catcher drops the third strike). However, an accurate statement of the rule would take this exception into account, and any that did not would be incomplete. . . .

If we take baseball rules as a model, we find that rules of law, like the rule that a will is invalid unless signed by three witnesses, fit the model well. If the requirement of three witnesses is a valid legal rule, then it cannot be that a will has been signed by only two witnesses and is valid. The rule might have exceptions, but if it does then it is inaccurate and incomplete to state the rule so simply, without enumerating the exceptions. In theory, at least, the exceptions could all be listed, and the more of them that are, the more complete is the statement of the rule.

Principles Can Be Weighed

But this is not the way the sample principles in the quotations operate. Even those which look most like rules do not set out legal consequences that follow automatically when the conditions provided are met. . . . A principle like "No man may profit from his own wrong" does not even purport to set out conditions that make its application necessary. Rather, it states a reason that argues in one direction, but does not necessitate a particular decision. . . . All that is meant, when we say that a particular principle is a principle of our law, is that the principle is one which officials must take into account, if it is relevant, as a consideration inclining in one direction or another. . . .

This first difference between rules and principles entails another. Principles have a dimension that rules do not—the dimension of weight or importance. When principles intersect (the policy of protecting automobile consumers intersecting with principles of freedom of contract, for example), one who must resolve the conflict has to take into account the relative weight of each. This cannot be, of course, an exact measurement, and the judgement that a particular principle or policy is more important than another will often be a controversial one. . . .

Rules do not have this dimension. . . . [O]ne legal rule may be more important than another because it has a greater or more important role in regulating behaviour. But we cannot say that one rule is more important than another within the system of rules, so that when two rules conflict one supersedes the other by virtue of its greater weight. If two rules conflict, one of them cannot be a valid rule. The decision as to which is valid, and which must be abandoned or recast, must be made by appealing to considerations beyond the rules themselves. . . .

It is not always clear from the form of a standard whether it is a rule or a principle. . . . The First Amendment to the United States Constitution contains the provision that Congress shall not abridge freedom of speech. Is this a rule, so that if a particular law does abridge freedom of speech, it follows that it is unconstitutional? Those who claim that the First Amendment is "an absolute" say that it must be taken in this way, that is, as a rule. Or does it merely state a principle, so that when an abridgement of speech is discovered, it is unconstitutional unless the context presents some other policy or principle which in the circumstances is weighty enough to permit the abridgement? That is the position of those who argue for what is called the "clear and present danger" test or some other form of "balancing." . . .

Judges Rely on Principles in Changing Legal Rules

Once we identify legal principles as separate sorts of standards, different from legal rules, we are suddenly aware of them all around us. Law teachers teach them, law books cite them, legal historians celebrate them. But they seem most energetically at work, carrying most weight, in difficult lawsuits like *Riggs* and *Henningsen*. In cases like these, principles play an essential part in arguments supporting judgements about particular legal rights and obligations. After the case is decided, we may say that the case stands for a particular rule (e.g., the rule that one who murders is not eligible to take under the will of his victim). But the rule does not exist before the case is decided; the court cites principles as its justification for adopting and applying a new rule. In *Riggs*, the court cited the principle that no man may profit from his own wrong as a background standard against which to read the statute of wills and in this way justified a new interpretation of that statute. In *Henningsen*, the court cited a variety of intersecting principles and policies as authority for a new rule respecting manufacturer's liability for automobile defects.

An analysis of the concept of legal obligation must therefore account for the important role of principles in reaching particular decisions of law. There are two very different tacks we might take.

a. We might treat legal principles the way we treat legal rules and say that some principles are binding as law and must be taken into account by judges and lawyers who make decisions of legal obligation. If we took this tack, we should say that in the United States, at least, the "law" includes principles as well as rules.

b.   We might, on the other hand, deny that principles can be binding the way some rules are. We would say, instead, that in cases like *Riggs* or *Henningsen* the judge reaches beyond the rules that he is bound to apply (reaches, that is, beyond the "law") for extra-legal principles he is free to follow if he wishes. . . .

If we take the first tack, we are still free to argue that because such judges are applying binding legal standards they are enforcing legal rights and obligations. But if we take the second, we are out of court on that issue, and we must acknowledge that the murderer's family in *Riggs* and the manufacturer in *Henningsen* were deprived of their property by an act of judicial discretion applied *ex post facto*. . . .

Positivism Holds that the Courts Have Discretion in the Strong Sense and Are Not Bound by Principles

Sometimes we use "discretion" in a weak sense, simply to say that for some reason the standards an official must apply cannot be applied mechanically but demand the use of judgement. . . . Sometimes we use the term in a different weak sense, to say only that some official has final authority to make a decision and cannot be reviewed or reversed by any other official. . . . I call both of these senses weak to distinguish them from a stronger sense. We use "discretion" sometimes not merely to say that an official must use judgement in applying the standards set him by authority, or that no one will review that exercise of judgement, but to say that on some issue he is simply not bound by standards set by the authority in question. . . . Hart, for example, says that when the judge's discretion is in play, we can no longer speak of his being bound by standards, but must speak rather of what standards he "characteristically uses." . . .

It therefore seems that positivists, at least sometimes, take their doctrine in the third, strong sense of discretion. In that sense it does bear on our treatment of principles; indeed, in that sense it is nothing less than a restatement of our second approach. It is the same thing to say that when a judge runs out of rules he has discretion, in the sense that he is not bound by any standards from the authority of law, as to say that the legal standards judges cite other than rules are not binding on them.

Positivists Could Argue that Principles Are Not Binding

So we must examine the doctrine of judicial discretion in the strong sense. . . . Do the principles judges cite in cases like *Riggs* or *Henningsen* control their decisions, as the sergeant's orders to take the most experienced men or the referee's duty to choose the more aggressive fighter control the decisions of these officials? What arguments could a positivist supply to show that they do not?

1.   A positivist might argue that principles cannot be binding or obligatory. That would be a mistake. It is always a question, of course, whether any particular principle is *in*

fact binding upon some legal official. But there is nothing in the logical character of a principle that renders it incapable of binding him. . . .

2. A positivist might argue that even though some principles are binding, in the sense that the judge must take them into account, they cannot determine a particular result. . . . [This is not convincing.] If a judge believes that principles he is bound to recognize point in one direction and that principles pointing in the other direction, if any, are not of equal weight, then he must decide accordingly. . . .

These are the most obvious of the arguments a positivist might use for the doctrine of discretion in the strong sense, and for the second approach to principles. . . .

Rules Are Binding because Principles Prevent Judges from Changing Them

[T]he higher courts not infrequently reject established rules. . . . If courts had discretion to change established rules, then these rules would not be binding upon them, and so would not be law on the positivists' model. . . .

When, then, is a judge permitted to change an existing rule of law? Principles figure in the answer in two ways. First, it is necessary, though not sufficient, that the judge find that the change would advance some policy or serve some principle, which policy or principle thus justifies the change. . . .

Second, any judge who proposes to change existing doctrine must take account of some important standards that argue against departures from established doctrine, and these standards are also for the most part principles. They include the doctrine of "legislative supremacy," a set of principles and policies that require the courts to pay a qualified deference to the acts of the legislature. They also include the doctrine of precedent, another set of principles and policies reflecting the equities and efficiencies of consistency. . . . . .

Consider, therefore, what someone implies who says that a particular rule is binding. He may imply that the rule is affirmatively supported by principles the court is not free to disregard, and which are collectively more weighty than other principles that argue for a change. If not, he implies that any change would be condemned by a combination of conservative principles of legislative supremacy and precedent that the court is not free to ignore. . . . Either of these implications, of course, treats a body of principles and policies as law in the sense that rules are; it treats them as standards binding upon the officials of a community, controlling their decisions of legal right and obligation.

Note

1. Editor's note: This article was later incorporated as Chapter 2 in Dworkin's *Taking Rights Seriously* (Cambridge, MA: Harvard University, 1977).

From H.L.A. Hart, *The Concept of Law*, 2nd ed., ed. Penelope A. Bulloch and Joseph Raz (Oxford: Clarendon, 1994).

Postscript: A Reply to Professor Dworkin's Criticism of My Theory[1]

The General Orientation of My Theory Is Descriptive and General, Not "Interpretive"

My aim in this book [*The Concept of Law*] was to provide a theory of what law is which is both general and descriptive. It is *general* in the sense that it is not tied to any particular legal system or legal culture, but seeks to give an explanatory and clarifying account of law as a complex social and political institution with a rule-governed (and in that sense "normative") aspect. This institution, in spite of many variations in different cultures and in different times, has taken the same general form and structure. . . . My account is *descriptive* in that it is morally neutral and has no justificatory aims. . . .

The central task of [Dworkin's] legal theory . . . is termed by Dworkin "interpretive" and is partly evaluative, since it consists in the identification of the principles which both best "fit" or cohere with the settled law and legal practices of a legal system and also provide the best moral justification for them, thus showing the law "in its best light." . . .

Dworkin appears to rule out general and descriptive legal theory as misguided or at best simply useless. . . . His central objection seems to be that legal theory must take account of an internal perspective on the law which is the viewpoint of an insider or participant in a legal system, and no adequate account of this internal perspective can be provided by a descriptive theory whose viewpoint is not that of a participant but that of an external observer. But there is in fact nothing in the project of a descriptive jurisprudence as exemplified in my book to preclude a non-participant external observer from describing the ways in which participants view the law from such an internal point of view. . . .

My Theory Cannot Be Described as "Plain-Fact Positivism"

Dworkin misrepresents my form of legal positivism. He treats my doctrine of the rule of recognition as requiring that the criteria which it provides for the identification of law must consist only of historical facts [such as the fact that a statute was passed by Parliament] and so is an example of "plain-fact positivism."

But though my main examples of the criteria provided by the rule of recognition are matters of what Dworkin has called "pedigree," concerned only with the manner in which laws are adopted or created by legal institutions and not with their content, I expressly state . . . that in some systems of law, as in the United States, the ultimate criteria of legal validity might explicitly incorporate besides pedigree, principles of justice or substantive moral values, and these may form the content of legal constitutional restraints. . . .

But secondly and more importantly, whereas Dworkin's interpretive legal theory in all its forms rests on the presupposition that the point or purpose of law and legal practice is to justify coercion, it certainly is not and never has been my view that law has this as its point or purpose. . . . In fact I think it quite vain to seek any more specific purpose which law as such serves beyond providing guides to human conduct and standards of criticism of such conduct. This will not of course serve to distinguish laws from other rules or principles with the same general aims; the distinctive features of law are the provision it makes by secondary rules for the identification, change, and enforcement of its standards and the general claim it makes to priority over other standards. . . .

My Theory Is a "Soft Positivism"—It Allows for a Penumbra of Uncertainty

[Dworkin] ignores my explicit acknowledgement that the rule of recognition may incorporate as criteria of legal validity conformity with moral principles or substantive values; so my doctrine is what has been called "soft positivism" and not, as in Dworkin's version of it, "plain-fact" positivism. . . . Dworkin's most fundamental criticism is that there is a deep inconsistency between soft positivism . . . and the general positivist "picture" of law as essentially concerned to provide reliable public standards of conduct which can be identified with certainty as matters of plain fact. . . .

This criticism of soft positivism seems to me to exaggerate . . . the uncertainty which will result if the criteria of legal validity include conformity with specific moral principles or values. . . . [T]he exclusion of all uncertainty at whatever costs in other values is not a goal which I have ever envisaged for the rule of recognition. . . . A margin of uncertainty should be tolerated, and indeed welcomed in the case of many legal rules, so that an informed judicial decision can be made when the composition of an unforeseen case is known and the issues at stake in its decision can be identified and so rationally settled. . . .

My view advanced in this book is that legal rules and principles identified in general terms by the criteria provided by the rule of recognition often have what I call frequently "open texture," so that when the question is whether a given rule applies to a particular case the law fails to determine an answer either way and so proves partially indeterminate. . . . [T]he law in such cases is fundamentally incomplete: it provides no answer to the questions at issue in such cases. They [these cases] are legally unregulated and in order to reach a decision in such cases the courts must exercise the restricted law-making function which I call "discretion." Dworkin rejects the idea that the law may be incomplete in this way. . . .

Rules and Principles

For long the best known of Dworkin's criticisms of this book was that it mistakenly represents law as consisting solely of "all-or-nothing" rules, and ignores a different kind of legal standard, namely legal principles, which play an important and distinctive part in legal reasoning and adjudication. . . .

[L]aw for Dworkin comprises both all-or-nothing rules and non-conclusive principles, and he does not think that this difference between them is a matter of degree. But I do not think that Dworkin's position can be coherent. His earliest examples imply that rules may come into conflict with principles and that a principle will sometimes win in competition with a rule and sometimes lose. The cases he cites includes *Riggs v. Palmer*, in which the principle that a man may not be permitted to profit from his own wrongdoing was held notwithstanding the clear language of the statutory rules governing the effect of a will to preclude a murderer inheriting under his victim's will. This is an example of a principle winning in competition with a rule, but the existence of such competition surely shows that rules do not have an all-or-nothing character, since they are liable to be brought into such conflict with principles which may outweigh them. Even if we describe such cases (as Dworkin at times suggests) not as conflicts between rules and principles, but as a conflict between the principle explaining and justifying the rule under consideration and some other principle, the sharp contrast between all-or-nothing rules and non-conclusive principles disappears; for on this view a rule will fail to determine a result in a case to which it is applicable according to its terms if its justifying principle is outweighed by another. The same is true if (as Dworkin also suggests) we think of a principle as providing a reason for a new interpretation of some clearly formulated legal rule.[2]

This incoherence in the claim that a legal system consists both of all-or-nothing rules and non-conclusive principles may be cured if we admit that the distinction is a matter of degree. Certainly a reasonable contrast can be made between near-conclusive rules, the satisfaction of whose conditions of application suffices to determine the legal result except in a few instances . . . and generally non-conclusive principles which merely point towards a decision but may very frequently fail to determine it.

Notes

1.   Editor's note: Hart was in the process of writing this postscript when he died in 1992.
2.   Editor's note: In other words, Dworkin's sharp contrast disappears as soon as we examine problematic cases, since these cases show that the rule in question is not an "all-or-nothing" rule.

✢ Discussion ✢

Dworkin Begins His Critique of Hart by Setting Out Three Positivist Claims

Ronald Dworkin's "Model of Rules" is the most well-known critique of legal positivism in the contemporary literature. It begins by arguing that Hart's model of the legal system rests on three central claims. The first is that law is a set of rules. These rules can be identified by "their *pedigree* or the manner in which they were adopted or developed." There is a rule of recognition that allows us to distinguish legal rules from other social rules.

The second claim is that this set of legal rules is exhaustive. The law is made up exclusively of rules. This claim is misleading, however. It is not clear that Hart is taking this position, since he recognizes that there will be cases in the penumbra of meaning that are not covered by the existing rules. Dworkin assumes that this does not change the makeup of the law, probably because judges in the penumbra have the discretion to make new rules, which then become a part of the existing law. It therefore does not matter whether a case falls in the "core" or penumbra of meaning: in either instance, the essential task of a judge is to apply legal rules to the facts of the case. These rules constitute "the law."

Dworkin's interpretation of Hart's theory is nevertheless strained. Although Hart does not address the matter explicitly, his concept of a legal rule is a product of the doctrine of precedent, which maintains the consistency of the caselaw. This doctrine holds that cases that raise the same issue must be decided in the same way. It follows that when judges decide cases, they are not making unique decisions; they are applying a rule—a logical generalization that exists outside any individual case—that determines the decision in all of the relevant cases. Indeed, as a simple matter of logic, it is impossible to decide a case in the common law without first recognizing a "rule," in each and every case, that requires that all such cases must be decided in a particular way. There is nothing contentious in the suggestion that the set of these rules can be described as "the law." Such an assertion means very little, in itself, and says very little about the process by which judges reach their decisions, or the factors that come into play, in establishing such rules.

There is another problem, however. Dworkin also draws a hard dichotomy between legal rules and the moral and political standards on which judges rely in the penumbra. This dichotomy is simplistic, since it suggests that Hart's description of the law as a set of legal rules leaves principles and other standards out of his analysis. There is no reason to believe that this was Hart's intention, and the interpretation ignores the obvious fact that Hart was aware of the role that such standards play in the judicial process. As Hart suggests, Dworkin fails to consider the makeup of rules, which are complex enough to include many other kinds of standards and propositions. If judges in the penumbra are entitled to rely on these artifacts, and they represent the decisive factors in many legal decisions, why shouldn't they be considered part of the law?

Dworkin's second claim is more convincing in the context of formalism. If we take a strict formalist position, which holds that judicial reasoning is deductive, the law is apparently made up of a set of legal rules that can be deduced. It follows that there is no obvious way of deciding novel cases. Although it might still be argued that judges can infer new rules from the existing set of rules, Dworkin takes the position that there will be situations where this approach is insufficient.

The third claim is that our legal rights and obligations derive exclusively from this set of rules.[1] Dworkin argues that this means the positivists have to fall back on some form of legal realism in order to explain how judges decide cases that have not been anticipated in the rules. This realism takes judges outside the system of rules—and therefore outside the law—in making their decisions. This suggestion lies at the heart of Dworkin's critique of Hart's positivism.

Dworkin raises a number of issues in the context of the third claim. One is the familiar criticism that a judge who exercises the kind of discretion that realism contemplates is making and applying the law retroactively. This is fundamentally unfair.

The more basic issue is that this exercise of discretion allows judges to impose their personal views on the parties before them. It is clear, of course, that Hart is responding to this kind of concern when he limits the role of policy in the judicial process to "the problems of the penumbra." Dworkin argues, however, that Hart's conception of penumbra leaves too much out of the analysis and fails to recognize the role played by principles and other standards in the legal process.

Dworkin believes that Hart's theory fails to capture the richness of the common law. As Dworkin writes, in the reading,

> when lawyers reason or dispute about legal rights and obligations, particularly in those hard cases when our problems with these concepts seem most acute, they make use of standards that do not function as rules, but operate differently as principles, policies, and other sorts of standards.

The question is whether a judge who relies on these kinds of standards is working within the law.

Hart does not address Dworkin's question directly, though he suggests that Dworkin's hard distinction between rules and principles is simplistic and breaks down in practice. It nevertheless seems clear that judicial reasoning is always driven by the moral and social values that find expression in the law. Both theorists tend to neglect the fact that the law is full of rules of construction and interpretative principles, which place many limits on a judge in choosing between different interpretations of the law. These rules and principles exist inside a larger body of beliefs that reflects prevailing moral and social views. It is accordingly misleading to say that they are being applied on a subjective or *ex post facto* basis.

Dworkin Then Argues that Positivism Is Based on Two Misconceptions

Dworkin also raises two fundamental criticisms of legal positivism, which are directed more specifically at John Austin. One is that government in a modern society is divided between different institutions. This means that power is shared by more than one person. As a result, there is no one who fits the description of Austin's sovereign.

Much of Dworkin's critique of legal rules can be traced to the differences between the English and the American legal systems and to the different conceptions of the judicial role in the two systems. Austin's hard positivism is a reflection of the unitary nature of the

English political system, and the English doctrine of parliamentary sovereignty, which leaves less room for judges to develop policy. Although Hart's "soft" positivism makes concessions to the American system, it still fails to account for the division of sovereignty in the United States, the idea of limited government, and the broad constitutional role of the American courts. This gives principles and policies a more prominent role in the legal system.

The second criticism is that our legal obligations do not depend upon the use of physical force. Dworkin acknowledges that the social component that Hart introduces into positivism solves some of the problems in Austin's theory. The validity of a law in Hart's theory does not depend upon the fact that it is backed up by the raw existence of some absolute power. The state is not a gunman. The law is binding because it has been internalized by officials in the legal system and therefore creates recognized obligations. This is expressed legally and constitutionally in the rule of recognition, which derives its authority from the fact that it reflects a political consensus in society. Dworkin argues that the rule of recognition is not enough, however, to explain the role of moral and political principles in the legal system.

Dworkin's Theory Brings Moral Values into the Body of the Law

There are competing tendencies in Dworkin's work. He is a liberal theorist, who is developing a legal theory that respects the autonomy of the individual and is therefore neutral in its values. His response to the positivists is nevertheless notable, primarily because it rejects the positivists' "separation thesis," which separates our legal obligations from our moral obligations and brings moral values into the body of the law. These values enter the law through the application of principles and policies, which are more general than rules, and which introduce accepted standards of fairness, justice, and morality into the decision-making process. Dworkin is accordingly a mitigated liberal, who emphasizes the role of collective values and beliefs in the legal system.

Dworkin's theory of law has affinities with the theory of the natural law because it implicitly suggests that we need some set of standards outside the positive law to decide the issues that arise with regard to our legal rights and obligations. These issues include the determination of whether a law is a valid law. In point of fact, Dworkin's position goes significantly further, since his suggestion is that we cannot even determine what the positive law is, without such a set of standards. This idea is reminiscent of Aquinas' belief that the human law "partakes" of the natural law.

Moral Values Enter the Law through Principles and Policies

Dworkin argues that the law is more than a set of rules. The law is a set of "standards" that include rules, principles, and policies. A principle is a standard that sets out "a requirement of justice or fairness or some other dimension of morality." A policy is "that kind of standard that sets out a goal to be reached." "Thus the standard that automobile accidents are to be decreased is a policy, and the standard that no man may profit by his own wrong a principle." The inclusion of policies and principles under the general rubric of "legal standards" brings moral and social beliefs back into the judicial process.

The decisions in *Riggs v. Palmer* and *Henningsen v. Bloomfield Motors, Inc.* illustrate the use of principles in the judicial process. In the former case, a young man had murdered his grandfather because he was named as the heir in his grandfather's will. The court refused to let him inherit the property on the basis of the equitable principle that no one should be entitled "to acquire property by his own crime." In the latter case, the court ruled that an automobile is an inherently dangerous product. This ruling creates a special duty of care, which prevents a manufacturer of automobiles from placing limits on its liability for a defective product. The courts in these cases based their decisions on principles rather than rules; this demonstrates that principles constitute an integral part of the law.

Rules Are "All-or-Nothing"; Principles "Argue in One Direction"

Dworkin draws a logical dichotomy between rules and principles. Rules "are applicable in an all-or-nothing fashion":

> either the rule is valid, in which case the answer it supplies must be accepted, or
> it is not, in which case it contributes nothing to the decision.

Unlike principles, rules dictate a particular course of action.

Principles and rules operate differently from one another. There is nothing to prevent legal principles from conflicting with one another, and a judge is often required to "weigh" competing principles and determine which principle deserves priority in the case before the court. This determination does not affect the validity of the rejected principle, which may take precedence in another case. Rules do not function in this way: "If two rules conflict, one of them cannot be a valid rule."

Dworkin's idea of rules comes out of formalism and the deductive nature of the early common law. This deductivism has its advantages. Since legal rules operate in a mechanical way, they make it relatively easy to predict the results in particular cases. They accordingly increase the certainty of the system and contribute to the basic tenet of order that gives the law its purpose.

A System Based on Rules Is More Predictable but Less Flexible

The mechanical nature of rules increases the predictability of a legal system. A system based on rules is less flexible, however, and reduces the ability of judges to adjust their decisions to meet the exigencies of individual cases. This has advantages and disadvantages, and a system based on rules is less vulnerable to the realist critique. Dworkin fails to acknowledge that the fundamental purpose of rules is to prevent judges from imposing their personal views on the parties who come before them.

Principles add an element of uncertainty to the law, but they give judges more latitude in making their decisions. As Dworkin writes:

A principle like "no man may profit from his own wrong" does not even purport to set out conditions that make its application necessary. Rather, it states a reason that argues in one direction, but does not necessitate a particular decision.

The differences between rules and principles can be seen in the development of the formal system of principles in the common law. This system of principles was called "Equity," and was developed by the Court of Chancery in England to alleviate the harsh application of the strict rules of the common law. The principles that make up the system of equity have a distinct moral character, and they may decide a case, but they do not contain the substantive content that we ascribe to rules.[2] They are more commonly seen as rules of conduct that ensure fair dealing. Two of equity's maxims are "he who seeks equity must do equity" and "one who comes into equity must come with clean hands."

Principles Are Particularly Prominent in the Constitutional Law

Principles are particularly important in the constitutional realm, which calls for a difficult balancing between public, private, and policy interests. Dworkin uses the guarantee of freedom of speech in the First Amendment to the Constitution of the United States to demonstrate the role played by principles in the law.

A few legal theorists have argued that freedom of speech, for example, is an "absolute" right.[3] This argument treats the First Amendment as a rule, which automatically invalidates a law that infringes it. The United States Supreme Court has rejected such an approach, however, and held that the government has the right to abridge freedom of speech when it presents a "clear and present danger" to public order. Dworkin argues that the court's position treats freedom of speech as a principle, in which case a principle of greater weight—such as an immediate need to preserve the republic—may override it.

There are rules that function "substantially" as principles. The example that Dworkin gives is section 1 of the *Sherman Act* in this regard, which prohibits the restraint of trade. This section has been construed by the United States Supreme Court as prohibiting "unreasonable" restraints of trade. The word "unreasonable" is open to interpretation and requires that a judge weigh the competing elements in the case before the court. The section accordingly functions "logically as a rule," but it is subject to the same kind of contextual considerations that enter into the application of principles.[4]

Section 1 of the *Canadian Charter of Rights and Freedoms* provides a more complex example of a set of principles that restrict the operation of rules:

> 1. The *Canadian Charter of Rights and Freedoms* guarantees the rights and freedoms set out in it subject only to such reasonable limits prescribed by law as can be demonstrably justified in a free and democratic society.

It follows that the provision of rights and freedoms in the *Charter* is not absolute: the extension of a right or freedom is subject to the limits that the principles in section 1 have placed upon it.

The guarantee of freedom of expression in section 2(b) of the *Charter*, which reads as follows, does not contain any reservations.

> 2. Everyone has the following fundamental freedoms:
> (b) freedom of thought, belief, opinion, and expression, including freedom of the press and other media of communication.

There is a sense in which section 2(b) has the absolute character of a rule. When the subsection is read in concert with section 1, however, it is clear that it comes into operation only in the context of a whole cohort of principles, values, and considerations that determine whether a person is entitled to a remedy in any given situation.

Nor does the process end there. In *R. v. Oakes*, [1986] 1 S.C.R. 103, the Supreme Court of Canada held that the objective (in Dworkin's terminology, the "policy") served by any law that violates the *Charter* must be important enough to justify curtailing our fundamental rights and freedoms. It follows that the principles that qualify our constitutional protections are subject to their own qualifications. The tendency to consult a wide variety of policy factors in deciding constitutional cases goes against the positivist attempt to reduce the judicial task to a mechanical application of legislation and the existing caselaw. The positivist reduction accordingly leaves out too much: the thrust of Dworkin's larger argument is that the extent of our constitutional rights and freedoms can be determined only in a larger and more nuanced context that rules provide.

The Major Issue for Dworkin Is Whether Judges Are Bound by Legal Principles

Dworkin's theory of law is based on the prominence of principles. In "The Model of Rules," he writes:

> Once we identify legal principles as separate sorts of standards, different from legal rules, we are suddenly aware of them all around us.

The natural inquiry then becomes: how do principles fit into our concept of law? Are they part of the law, and therefore binding on the judiciary?

If principles are binding, the law is something more than a system of rules. It is clear, moreover, that this would bring morality back into the law, since it is difficult to distinguish between many legal and moral principles. If we accept that principles are "extralegal principles," however, we seem to open up an area of decision-making that is free of legal restrictions.

Dworkin's deeper concern is that Hart's conception of the penumbra takes us into realism, since judges acting in the penumbra are acting outside the legal rules. If judges in the penumbra are relying on principles, which are not binding, there is accordingly a question whether they are subject to constraints. This question is quite artificial, since it simplifies Hart's position and goes against the realities of the common law. Dworkin nevertheless argues that the answer to such a question lies in judicial discretion.[5] If we want to test Hart's theory, and determine whether principles are binding, we need to determine how much discretion judges actually enjoy in the penumbra.

The Term "Discretion" Has a Weaker Sense and a Stronger Sense

Dworkin argues that the term "discretion" has different senses. We can use it in a weak sense to indicate either that the principles in question cannot be applied mechanically or that the person with the discretion has the authority to make a final decision. "It's the referee's call," someone might say, to indicate that the referee is the only person who has the right to determine whether a soccer player committed a foul.

The word "discretion" also has a stronger sense, however. In this sense, Dworkin writes, we use the word:

> not merely to say that an official must use judgement in applying the standards set him by authority, or that no one will review that exercise of judgement, but to say that on some issue he is simply not bound by standards set by the authority in question.

Dworkin argues that the positivists give judges discretion in the strong sense.

Dworkin's concern is principally with the penumbra. In the penumbra, at least, judges are free to choose the standard that they feel is appropriate. This freedom does not give judges the licence to ignore issues like fairness. They are still expected to act rationally, fairly, and effectively, whatever standards they choose. In spite of this, judges have free rein to choose the principles on which they will rely, in creating new legal rules.

Like so many of the positions that Dworkin attributes to Hart and the positivists, this idea of the positivist penumbra is an exaggeration, a "straw man" set up mainly for the purpose of knocking it down. Although the legal realists argued that judges fall back on their own views in interpreting the law, no one has seriously suggested that judges can follow whatever principles they like in deciding cases.

Principles Are Binding in Some Sense

Dworkin nevertheless draws our attention to a significant aspect of the judicial task. His discussion of cases like *Riggs v. Palmer* and *Henningsen* demonstrates that judges do not have discretion in the strong sense. The language that the judiciary uses in these kinds of cases suggests that they feel obliged to follow established legal principles when there are no explicit rules to govern their actions. It is accordingly clear, merely from a reading of the caselaw, that the judicial exercise of discretion is more in keeping with the weak senses of the word.

There is plenty of evidence in the caselaw that principles like freedom of contract or the right to personal autonomy place rational restrictions on the decision-making process.

Dworkin nevertheless considers a number of arguments that a positivist might make in asserting that judges are not bound by principles. To begin with, Dworkin writes, a positivist might accept that legal principles are binding but argue that they cannot determine the outcome of a specific case. This interpretation of the law simply runs counter, Dworkin argues, to the decisions in cases like *Riggs v. Palmer* and *Henningsen*.

Another objection is that principles are inherently controversial and simply cannot bind the judiciary in the same way as rules. Dworkin takes the position that this objection merely complicates their function. This objection also seems to miss the fact that the most distinguishing feature of legal principles is that they are widely accepted in society and, as a result, they are anything but controversial. Does anyone take issue with the general principle that no one should be allowed to retain the legal title to property that was obtained by the commission of a crime?

This is a critical point. It is the application of principles in the context of specific cases, rather than the principles themselves, that attracts notoriety. This is illustrated by the decision in *R. v. Morgentaler* [1988] 1 S.C.R. 30, where the Supreme Court of Canada held that the provisions of the *Criminal Code* creating offence of "procuring a miscarriage" were unconstitutionally broad. Justice Wilson based her decision on the principle that a woman has "a right to liberty" under section 7 of the *Charter*. There is nothing controversial in such a proposition. It is the extent of such a principle, and its precise application in individual cases, that gives rise to controversy.

Indeed, Rules Are Changed When Principles Require It

Dworkin's position is that principles bind the judiciary. In point of fact, Dworkin argues, it is evident that the courts occasionally alter or overturn established legal rules. When we examine what judges do in such circumstances, we discover that the existing rules are altered when the change would advance a policy or principle that is of greater weight than the other principles that militate in favour of the *status quo*. It follows that legal rules derive their authority from principles.

A good illustration of Dworkin's thesis can be found in the case of *Woods v. Lancet* [1951], 303 N.Y. 349, where the infant plaintiff was born with an injury that it had suffered before birth as a result of his mother's fall. The defendant contested the case on the basis that a child *en ventre sa mere* was not a legal person. The infant was accordingly suing for injuries that it suffered before it legally came into being.

The Appellate Division of the New York Supreme Court overturned the decision of the lower courts that the infant had no standing to sue. In doing so, it held:

> No right is more inherent, more sacrosanct, than that of an individual in his possession and enjoyment of his life, his limbs, and his body.

The decision in *Woods* accordingly changed the rule that applied to the case on the basis of a statement of principle.

This discovery in the caselaw demonstrates that there is a contradiction in the argument that judges have discretion in a strong sense. If the positivists are right, and judges have the freedom to choose whether to follow legal principles, they have *carte blanche* to change the existing legal rules. This clearly misstates the positivist position: it nevertheless follows that legal rules cannot be binding unless principles are binding. We can therefore conclude that judges in the penumbra are subject to the constraints placed upon them by principles. They are not free actors. We accordingly need a theory of law that is much richer than positivism to explain the way in which judges reach their decisions.

Furthermore, Principles Exist Independently of the Rule of Recognition

The important point is that Hart's model of the legal system does not seem to have the resources to provide an adequate explanation of the role of principles in the law. Hart's fundamental response is simply that he did not address the issue in *The Concept of Law*. Dworkin nevertheless suggests that there is room for an argument that principles form part of Hart's rule of recognition, which determines which social rules qualify as "law" in the legal system. This would explain why they bind the judiciary.

The set of legal principles in the common law is too complex, however, to be included in a standard as simple as a rule of recognition.

> We argue for a particular principle by grappling with a whole set of shifting, developing, and interacting standards (themselves principles rather than rules) about institutional responsibility, statutory interpretation, the persuasive force of various sorts of precedent, the relation of all these to contemporary moral practices, and hosts of other such standards. We could not bolt all of these together into a single "rule," even a complex one, and if we could the result would bear little relation to Hart's picture of a rule of recognition.[6]

If legal principles are "law," the law accordingly has sources outside the rule of recognition.

This raises a question as to how principles enter the law. It is significant in this context that Hart actually makes an exception to the rule of recognition in the instance of custom, on the basis that it obtains its legal force from the fact that the members of society consider it binding. Although Dworkin argues against this exception in the instance of principles, on the basis that it would place a large body of law outside the scope of the rule of recognition, his own move is far more dramatic, since his recognition that the law includes principles brings moral and social legal values into the main body of the law.

Dworkin concludes that we must reject the first two of the three claims that the positivists have made. The law is not made up of legal rules. The legal rules that the law contains are not exhaustive. There is no rule of recognition that can capture the inherent complexity of the law and identify the rules that make up the Hartian concept of law. This leaves us with the third claim, which concerns the concept of legal rights and obligations. This claim is also problematic, since it is evident that some account of principles is necessary to explain our rights and obligations. By Dworkin's own analysis, it follows that these obligations are indeterminate.

Dworkin's Real Target Is Legal Realism

The real target of Dworkin's arguments, in spite of his focus on Hart, is legal realism. This is because it is the legal realists who claim that judges have discretion in the strong sense. Dworkin's argument against Hart is based on his contention that Hart adopts the same position as the realists in penumbral cases.

Dworkin's position is that legal realism does not provide a convincing explanation of the judicial process. This is the central thesis in Dworkin's argument, which points to the inadequacy of Hart's conception of the penumbra. The law is richer than Hart suggests. There is little in the caselaw that would support the contention that judges are exercising personal choices when they change legal rules or develop new ones. In point of fact, judges seem to be going back to principles that have been accepted by society at large, and that provide the moral consensus or value judgements on which existing rules of law have been premised.

The importance of Dworkin's theory of principles lies in its explanation of the way in which social and moral beliefs work their way into the common law caselaw. It is clear that principles provide an essential mechanism, which opens up the law to the evolving standards in society. This mechanism provides the means whereby the values of equality, autonomy, and equity are brought to bear on the development of legal rules. The use of legal principles, which cross over legal and ethical boundaries, also brings procedural requirements like notice and fairness into the law. Moreover, the fact that principles are continually in flux, and can be weighed against each other, allows judges to continually adjust the law to match the changing consensus in society.

Hart and Dworkin Both Neglect the Process of Finding Facts

It is nevertheless notable that theorists like Dworkin tend to neglect the realities of the legal process. From a practical perspective, rules and principles have different functions. As Dworkin suggests, rules appear to provide the logical machinery for reaching an actual decision in a case. This explains their imperative character, which is a necessary part of the logical machinery employed in the courts, since judges ultimately have to make decisions. The suggestion that cases are decided on the basis of principles goes against Dworkin's own characterization of principles, since principles do not dictate a particular result. Most legal principles are abstract statements of belief that remind us of the explanatory factors that govern the legal process.

From the perspective of practice, however, it is a mistake to think that the common law is driven by rules or principles rather than the process of finding facts. The initial task of a trial judge is to find the facts of the case, and it is the facts that determine which rules and principles apply to the case. The truth is that Hart's and Dworkin's conception of the judicial process tends to break down in practice, since the evidence before the court is paramount. Both theorists treat legal rules and principles as if they exist as abstractions, outside the facts of individual cases. Although many rules and principles are of general application, one of the fundamental tenets of the common law is that it is misleading to use them independently of the factual context in which they are applied.

This raises an issue with respect to "hard cases," which provide an essential ingredient in Dworkin's theory of the judicial role, since they concern situations in which the existing legal rules provide different answers to the question before the court. The reality is that rules or principles that are logically inconsistent or divergent, once again, exist within a larger context that usually explains away the logical inconsistencies. The reduction of the common law to a simple storehouse of propositions, which apply abstractly, on the basis of their merit outside the specific facts of individual cases, is artificial. The facts of a case provide many implicit qualifications on the application of rules and principles, which do not register in a simple statement of the rules and principles. These complexities tend to be lost in a restricted logical approach that cannot in itself capture the significance of legal rulings.

Hart Argues That His Theory Is Descriptive Rather Than Normative

Dworkin's critique of Hart is problematic for a number of reasons. As the second reading illustrates, Hart felt that Dworkin has misconstrued his theory. Dworkin sets out a theory of jurisprudence that describes the process of adjudication. This endeavour is "a radically different enterprise" than his own work, which provides an institutional model of the legal system.[7] Hart's theory is "descriptive" and "general." Dworkin's is normative: his primary interest is how judges, in particular, should interpret and apply the law.

The Descriptive Nature of Hart's Theory Is Reflected in His View of the Judicial Role

There is a clear difference, however, between Hart's and Dworkin's views of the judicial role. The essential task of a judge in Hart's theory is descriptive. A judge determines what the law is and applies it. Dworkin's reliance on principles reflects his belief that the normative elements in judicial decisions are more significant than Hart acknowledges. Judges have a fundamental role to play in determining what the law should be.

This difference in emphasis reflects the difference between the English and American common law traditions. Principles add a political element to judicial reasoning and are particularly important in the constitutional law. This helps to explain why a legal system based on a written constitution is more likely to produce an active judicial tradition. There is no doubt that the introduction of the *Canadian Charter of Rights and Freedoms* has made the positivist account and the model of rules less compelling in Canada.

The vagueness and complexity of legal principles increases the ability of judges to impose their personal views on the law. There are many examples on both sides of the political spectrum. Some of these examples arise in the ordinary law but raise recognizable constitutional issues. In *Re Noble and Wolf* [1949] O.R. 503, for example, the Ontario Court of Appeal upheld a restriction on the sale of resort property to "any person of the Jewish, Hebrew, Semitic, Negro, or Coloured race or blood." In doing so, it overruled the earlier decision of the Ontario High Court in *Re Drummond Wren* [1945] O.R. 78, which upheld restrictive covenants.

The decision in *Re Noble and Wolf* is based on the freedom of private parties to enter into contracts. The words of Chief Justice Robertson appear to express the views of a certain class in the community:

> To magnify this innocent and modest effort to establish and maintain a place suitable for a pleasant summer residence into an enterprise that offends against some public policy requires a stronger imagination than I possess.

The concurring judge bases his decision on the principle that the "sanctity of contract is a matter of public policy which we should strive to maintain."

The question that the legal realists raise is whether freedom of contract simply provides a rational justification for a decision that preserves the existing social realities. There are legal arguments against the position adopted by Chief Justice Robertson: if the legal system is based on the equality of persons, for example, there is an argument that contracts must respect the fundamental equality of persons. The case nevertheless demonstrates that there is nothing in the nature of principles that prevents them from being used to advance the social or political views held by those within a particular class or group in society.

This is the kind of argument that appears in the work of Jeremy Bentham, who argued that the power of judges to decide the law should be severely restricted. This does not necessarily solve the problem, however, and may simply substitute the prejudices of the legislature—and those who control it—for the prejudices of the judiciary. As we have seen, it was the constitutional crisis in the American caselaw that led the legal realists to argue that the judiciary favours the interests of the capitalist classes over the interests of ordinary people. It follows that the heavy reliance on principles may introduce an unanticipated political agenda into the caselaw. This tendency is naturally exacerbated in those legal traditions that give judges more freedom.

Dworkin's Concept of Principles Is Part of a Larger Attempt to Provide a Working Model of the Constitutional Law

The prominence of principles in Dworkin's legal theory appears to be part of an effort, in his larger work, to develop a working model of the constitutional law. This effort is a response to the challenge set by the legal realists. Dworkin argues that the decisions of judges cannot be reduced to their psychological or sociological antecedents or divorced from the process of rational justification that provides the basis of the common law analysis. In Dworkin's theory, the law has a rational structure that preserves and advances the values of society as a whole. It follows that sincere judges will carry out their responsibilities in accordance with the values and beliefs on which the rational structure of the law is based.

There is no doubt that the common law was originally based on the kind of moral and legal consensus that Dworkin envisages. There are, however, two fundamental questions that arise in this context. One concerns Dworkin's use of the term "political morality," which suggests that judges apply political rather than legal standards. Whether, and to what degree, these standards are political is open to question.

The second fundamental question is whether Dworkin makes the mistake that he criticizes the realists for making. This question raises itself because Dworkin suggests that judges have no choice but to fall back on their personal moral and political views in deciding hard cases. This suggestion seems to go against the argument that judges are proxies for the rest of society in making their decisions. Dworkin appears to take the position that there are lacunae in the law, which require judges to exercise their preferences on policy issues, in the manner of Benjamin Cardozo or other American judges. This goes against the original common law position, which was certainly that the law was a product of a consensus in society.

The normative side of Dworkin's position is nevertheless troubling, since it suggests that judges should follow their personal inclinations in creating new legal rules. This takes us into an assertive realism, which can be separated from the simple psychological realism that we find in many theorists. There is a real difference between saying that judges' personal political views will inevitably enter into their decisions in specific cases and saying that these political views form a legitimate part of the body of rules and principles that we describe as law.

There are other issues here. The common law tradition holds that judges must be independent and impartial. This requires that judges suspend their personal beliefs and make their decisions on the merits of the case. Dworkin himself distinguishes between authentic judicial decision-making and results-based reasoning, in which the rational justification of the decision merely justifies a particular conclusion. There is nothing absolute in such an idea, which merely requires that judges retain enough objectivity to decide the issues that arise between the competing parties fairly.

Dworkin argues for an "activist" interpretation of the constitution, which gives progressive judges the prerogative to consider objectives in the penumbra. The constitution does not refer to a specific "conception" of rights. It refers merely to "concepts," much broader notions, which are open to extension in individual cases. Although an ethical standard like fairness, for example, is familiar to each of us, our conception of how it should be defined, or what it consists of, varies from person to person. We accordingly need someone to determine the particular conception of a right or a freedom that applies in an individual case.

Dworkin bases his discussion of constitutional rights on one of the central philosophical principles in John Stuart Mill's discussion of liberty. In *Taking Rights Seriously*, for example, Dworkin writes,

> The constitutional theory on which our government rests is not a simple majoritarian theory. The *Constitution*, and particularly the *Bill of Rights*, is designed to protect individual citizens and groups against certain decisions that a majority of citizens might want to make, even when that majority acts in what it takes to be the general or common interest.[8]

An individual exercising a constitutional right is often exercising it against the wishes of the majority. It follows that "decisions about rights against the majority are not issues that in fairness ought to be left to the majority."[9]

Dworkin accordingly takes the position that the courts provide a better forum for the determination of our constitutional rights. This takes us much closer to the roots of the common law, which was based on the moral and social consensus that found expression in the customary law. This substantive consensus was diluted by the historical development of central government, which gave rise to both the modern state and the democratic system. Mill suggests that the transfer of sovereignty to democratic government created its own kind of tyranny, which fails to respect the rights of the individual. Dworkin finds the remedy to such a problem in an active constitutional tradition, which expresses the current consensus in society and keeps the political apparatus of government within its proper limits.

Dworkin's theory of the constitution brings principles into the legal discussion, since it requires that the courts fall back on broad moral concepts in determining the extent of our constitutional rights.

> Constitutional law can make no genuine advance until it isolates the problem of rights against the state and makes that problem part of its own agenda. That argues for a fusion of constitutional law and moral theory, a connection that, incredibly, has yet to take place.[10]

In the end, Dworkin's position evokes the natural law, which holds that law ultimately derives its authority from its moral justification.

Notes

1. The statement that the law is made up "exclusively" of legal rules is misleading in the same way that the statement that a novel is made up exclusively of sentences is misleading. In one sense, this assertion may be clearly correct, but in another sense it is clearly wrong, since sentences contain words, phrases, and many other forms of speech.

2. On the history of equity, see William Searle Holdsworth, "The Early History of Equity," *Michigan Law Review* 13 (1914–15): 293–301 and George Burton Adams, "The Origin of English Equity," *Columbia Law Review* 16, no. 2 (1916): 87–98.

3. See Alexander Meiklejohn, *Free Speech and Its Relation to Self-Government* (New York: Harper Brothers Publishers, 1948).

4. See Ronald Dworkin, "The Model of Rules," as cited in the readings, at p. 28.

5. The suggestion that Dworkin makes in this regard goes against the realities of the common law, with which Hart, as a practising lawyer, was familiar.

6. Dworkin, "The Model of Rules," p. 41.

7. See the postscript to Hart, *The Concept of Law*, as cited in the readings, p. 240ff.

8. See "Constitutional Cases," Chapter 5 of Ronald Dworkin, *Taking Rights Seriously* (Cambridge, MA: Harvard University, 1978), pp. 131–49. And see Ronald Dworkin, *Freedom's Law: The Moral Reading of the American Constitution*, as cited in the suggestions for further reading. And see Ian Harris, "Professor Dworkin, the American Constitution and a Third Way," *Cambridge Law Journal* 57, no. 2 (July 1998): 284–300.

9. Dworkin, *Taking Rights Seriously*, op. cit., p. 142.

10. ibid., p. 149.

Study Questions

1. What was the ruling of the court in *Henningsen v. Bloomfield Motors, Inc.*? Do you agree with the decision? Why, why not?

2. How does Dworkin distinguish between a rule and a principle? Why are values associated with principles?

3. How does discretion enter into Dworkin's concept of a principle?

4. Why does Hart reject Dworkin's distinction between a rule and a principle? What does this tell us about Hart's legal positivism?

5. Dworkin argues that Hart's positivism is based on the idea that the law is a closed system of rules. Is this fair? What about the penumbra of meaning?

6. Do you agree with the statement that Dworkin is responding to legal realism? Why, why not?

7. What role does the process of finding facts play in the debate between Dworkin and Hart?

Further Reading

M. Cohen, ed., *Ronald Dworkin and Contemporary Jurisprudence* (Lanham, MD: Rowman and Littlefield, 1984).

Ronald Dworkin, *Freedom's Law: The Moral Reading of the American Constitution* (Cambridge, MA: Harvard University, 1996).

———, *Law's Empire* (Cambridge, MA: Harvard University, 1986).

———, "'Natural' Law Revisited," *University of Florida Law Review* 34 (1982): 165–88.

Stanley Fish, "Still Wrong after All These Years," *Law and Philosophy* 6, no. 3 (1987): 401–18.

Stephen Guest, *Ronald Dworkin* (Stanford, CA: Stanford University, 1992).

Ian Shapiro, *The Evolution of Rights in Liberal Theory* (Cambridge: Cambridge University, 1986).

Scott J. Shapiro, "The 'Hart–Dworkin' Debate: A Short Guide for the Perplexed" (working paper no. 77, Public Law and Legal Theory Working Paper Series, March 2007). Available at http://papers.ssrn.com.

13 The New Realism: Critical Legal Studies, Feminism, and Postmodernism

Readings

- From *A Guide to Critical Legal Studies*, by Mark Kelman
- From "Critical Legal Studies: A Political History," by Mark Tushnet
- From "Liberal Jurisprudence and Abstracted Visions of Human Nature: A Feminist Critique of Rawls' *Theory of Justice*," by Mari J. Matsuda
- From "New Directions in Feminist Theory," by Margaret L. Anderson

The following chapter reviews several alternative strands in the theoretical literature. Although critical legal studies, feminism, and the theories associated with the postmodern movement have different sources, they have all criticized legal positivism and the liberal tradition for its failure to address the external moral, social, and political realities that find expression in the legal system. Like legal realism, these dissenting theories challenge the role of the law in the general distribution of power in society. This work brings the inequities hidden in the traditional analysis of the law and the political system to the surface of the discussion.

⚔ Readings ⚔

From Mark Kelman, *A Guide to Critical Legal Studies* (Cambridge, MA: Harvard University, 1987).

The invitation to the first annual Conference on Critical Legal Studies in 1977 gave little hint as to what the organizers thought "critical legal studies" (CLS) was or might become. In a sense I suppose this was perfectly natural, since only those organizers long associated with the empiricist, generally politically reformist Law and Society movement had done much of their work yet. It seems that the organizers were simply seeking to *locate* those people working either at law schools or in closely related academic settings (legal sociology, legal anthropology) with a certain vaguely perceived, general political or cultural predisposition. . . .

In terms of the cultural politics of the law schools, the people the organizers were seeking were those appalled by the routine Socratic discussions of appellate court decisions, repelled by their sterility and thorough disconnection from actual social life (their mainstream fellow teachers seemed barely to care or notice whether either arguments or case results had any impact on actual practice);[1] repelled by the supposition that neutral and apolitical *legal* reasoning could resolve charged controversies; impatient with the idea that people freed by Rigour from a stereotypically feminized or infantilized pre-professional sentimentality must ultimately share some sober centrist ideals. . . .

By . . . the fall of 1984, there had been nine large national meetings of this once tiny Conference; innumerable "summer camps" and workshops where newcomers and founders alike argued obsessively over the usual issues that have puzzled those on the academic left since the cruder Marxisms have gone out of vogue; a popular book, *The Politics of Law*, published collaboratively with the National Lawyers Guild . . . ; an increasingly lengthy underground bibliography of CLS work . . . ; and a hefty symposium on the movement in the *Stanford Law Review*. Yet it was still a fair question whether anyone knew what "critical legal studies" meant. . . .

Critical Legal Studies Was a Reaction against Liberal Theory

The essential picture I propose is that of a movement attempting to identify the crucial structural characteristics of mainstream legal thought as examples of something called "liberalism." While some CLS writers try to define what they mean by liberalism at considerable length . . . more often "liberalism" is little more than a very loose term for the dominant postfeudal beliefs held across all but the left and right fringes of the political spectrum. . . .

The descriptive portrait of mainstream liberal thought that I present is a picture of a system of thought that is simultaneously beset by internal *contradiction* (not by "competing concerns" artfully balanced until a wise equilibrium is reached, but by irreducible, irremediable, irresolvable conflict) and by systematic *repression* of the presence of these contradictions. I will argue that a standard four-part critical method has been used again and again, whether consciously or not.

Critical Legal Studies Identified Three Oppositions in Liberal Thought

First, the Critics attempted to identify . . . three central contradictions in liberal thought . . . : (1) the contradiction between a commitment to mechanically applicable rules as the appropriate form for resolving disputes (thought to be associated in complex ways with the political tradition of self-reliance and individualism) and a commitment to situation-sensitive, *ad hoc* standards (thought to correspond to a commitment to sharing and altruism); (2) the contradiction between a commitment to the traditional liberal notion that values or desires are arbitrary, subjective, individual, and individuating while facts or reason are objective and universal *and* a commitment to the ideal that we can "know" social and ethical truths objectively . . . ; and (3) the contradiction between a commitment to an intentionalistic discourse, in which human action is seen as the product of a self-determining individual will, and determinist discourse, in which the activity of nominal subjects . . . is simply deemed the expected outcome of existing structures.

Liberal Theory Privileges Individualism and the Rule of Law

Second, the Critics tried to demonstrate that each of the contradictions is utterly pervasive in legal controversy, even in cases where [legal] practice is [well] settled. . . . These impulses are ready to destabilize settled practice should we ever be forced to articulate or ground that practice. . . . .

Third, Critics have attempted to show that mainstream thought invariably treats one term in each set of contradictory impulses as *privileged* in three distinct senses. The privileged term is presumptively entitled as a normative matter to govern disputes; it is simply assumed, as a descriptive matter, to govern the bulk of situations; and most subtly, but perhaps most significantly, departures from the purportedly dominant norm, even if they are obviously frequent, are treated as *exceptional*, [and] in need of special justification. . . .

In essence, my argument is that liberal legal discourse most strongly purports to be committed to and to exceptionalize departures from both individualism and the Rule of Law. It is also committed to the idea that subjective value choices are the only arbiter of the good, at least in the abstract sense that the general theory of law and the state is one in which the state seeks not to further particular life plans but to facilitate people's fulfilling diverse plans. . . .

Fourth, the Critics note that, closely examined, the "privileged" impulses describe the program of a remarkably right-wing, quasi-libertarian order. . . . Thus, I do not believe that I, or other CLS practitioners, have by any means been attacking straw men, even when the positions we analyze, in their purest forms, are not the mainstream positions but somewhat more extreme ones. . . . CLS authors have [exposed, for example,] the politically conservative institutional biases of Law and Economics scholars . . . [and] their suppositions about the beneficence of private property or competitive markets.

Note

1.   Editor's note: Kelman is referring to the "case-study method," which was developed by Christopher Columbus Langdell and is discussed in Chapter 7.

From Mark Tushnet, "Critical Legal Studies: A Political History," *Yale Law Journal* 100, no. 5 (March 1991): 1515–44.

Critical Legal Studies (CLS) Is a "Political Location"

From the inside there is something awkward in talking about critical legal studies as a "movement" or "school." . . . The most plausible explanation . . . is that critical legal studies is [more properly described as] a political location for a group of people on the left who share the project of supporting and extending the domain of the left in the legal academy. . . .

At present one might describe the political location of critical legal studies as occupied by certain feminists ("fem-crits"), certain theorists concerned with the role of race in law (critical race theorists), a group influenced by recent developments in literary theory (postmodernists), a group of cultural radicals, and a group that stresses the role of the economic structure in setting the conditions for legal decisions (political economists). Even on this description of the location, however, there do seem to be some common elements to that which is found there. . . . And, in general, there does seem to be a sufficient degree of commitment to three propositions about law: that it is in some interesting sense indeterminate; that it can be understood in some interesting way by paying attention to the context in which legal decisions are made; and that in some interesting sense law is politics. . . .

The Investigation of Paired Oppositions and an Informal Sociology of Law: The Law Is Indeterminate

The origins of critical legal studies as a political location are relatively easy to identify. In early 1976 David Trubek returned from a trip to Cambridge and told me that he had spoken with Duncan Kennedy. They had agreed that there were a number of people doing academic studies of law that seemed to have certain common themes, and that it might be useful to gather these people, and a few others, to see whether that perception was accurate. . . .

One characteristic of the work to which Kennedy and Trubek referred was the identification, in numerous substantive areas of law, of paired oppositions and standard arguments deploying sets of claims from one side of those oppositions against sets drawn from the other side. Deriving from the work of the legal realists, this technique led, in the first instance, to the development of the "indeterminacy" argument. As it was derived from the analysis of paired oppositions, the indeterminacy argument held that within the standard resources of legal argument were the materials for reaching sharply contrasting results in particular instances. Those results, it appeared, were exactly what people arguing directly over moral or political goals were seeking. . . . [And] adherents of CLS continue to hold to the general perception that there is no interesting difference between legal discourse and ordinary moral and political discourse.

As we saw it, the legal realist versions of this technique had led some of the realists to offer a relatively informal descriptive and normative sociology of law. Descriptively, the existence of a community of lawyers, sharing what Llewellyn called a "situation sense," eliminated the possibility that contradictory results, available as a matter of theory, would actually be realized in practice. Normatively, the values of that community, or some other community into which it could be transformed, justified the choices among possible results at which the legal system arrived.

The law and society tradition, with which Trubek and I were particularly sympathetic, had attempted to provide a more systematic basis for the realists' informal sociology of law.[1] Some in that tradition, however, were more skeptical of the normative acceptability of the results found acceptable by the community of lawyers. . . . [This critique of legal realism] drew upon the work of [Max] Weber[2] and [Karl] Marx . . . [and] was reinforced by [a number of competing elements, such as] the cultural-radical strand of CLS, which presented the experience of law as oppressive and alienating rather than as a normatively attractive solution to problems of social coordination. . . .

The indeterminacy argument and the critique of social theory [ultimately] led CLS to a different understanding of the proposition that law is politics. We saw law as a form of human activity in which political conflicts were worked out in ways that contributed to the stability of the social order ("legitimation") in part by constituting personality and social institutions in ways that came to seem natural. The legitimating and constitutive operation of law occurred on all levels. . . .

In the end, adherents of CLS argue that the entire notion of "the rule of law" and associated distinctions between objectivity and subjectivity incorporated a partial, and therefore political, definition of rational behaviour. . . .

More important than these difficulties, however, were what we took to be the implications of the analysis of indeterminacy for social theory itself. Classical social theory had not paid much attention to questions of law, yet legal terms—in particular, "ownership of private property"—played a large role in the fundamental structure of Marxist . . . social thought. . . . [T]he indeterminacy thesis threatened the social theory that legal realists had relied on to resolve the normative and descriptive difficulties exposed by their analysis of law. . . .

[F]ew people associated with CLS at the outset thought that each element in the program was as important as the others, and many who agreed with some parts of the program were uncomfortable with others. The family resemblance among the works that initially identified themselves with CLS was their political orientation on the left. . . .For CLS as a political location, what mattered was not getting the intellectual line right. . . . What mattered was keeping the location available to people who needed it. . . .

Future Prospects: Determiniles

The CLS critique of legalism has . . . reached a point where it may be difficult to develop substantial political energy from its continuation. The point may be made by imagining that we have developed a measure of the determinacy of a set of legal rules, the "determinile." A completely determinate legal system would measure one hundred determiniles, while a completely indeterminate one would measure zero. CLS adherents at present defend the position that the proper measure of legal systems is probably between five and fifteen; that is, no system is completely indeterminate, but the level of determinacy is relatively low.

Mainstream legal theorists at present defend the position that the proper measure of well-functioning legal systems like that of the United States is somewhere between forty and sixty; that is, such systems have a substantial amount of indeterminacy, but not nearly as much as the CLS position claims. The positions differ, as is suggested by the existence of a gap between the "most determinate" version of the CLS position and the "least determinate" one of the mainstream position. In addition, among CLS adherents there is disagreement about the primary reason for the degree of determinacy that there is: power relations associated with gender differences, race differences, and class differences are all candidates of some. Yet at this point we are simply arguing over a mere detail, the question of degree. . . .

The assimilation of CLS into the academy appears to have led to a general acceptance of a weak version of the position that law is politics, all the way down. . . . At present, most of the force of the strong form—the "all the way down" part—is being carried by feminist and minority scholarship, not all of which is associated with CLS. . . . [The] radical program associated with critical legal studies [also] seem[s] disconnected from the mission of the law school. People associated with CLS have a different sense of where the real political action is, and have started to develop forms of legal theorizing and legal practice that orient themselves toward mobilizing communities for more than incremental change. . . .

The legal academy has accepted our scholarship in a weakened form, and has thereby given us the sense that we are doing work that meets its criteria of merit. Yet in providing us with that degree of legitimacy, the academy simultaneously defuses the political explosiveness of the positions we thought we were taking: it reinforces its definition of merit and gives us a stake in the maintenance of the system as it is. . . .

Notes

1. Editor's note: The law and society movement is an interdisciplinary movement based on the idea that the law must be studied in the social context in which it arises and functions. The movement originally came out of the historical school of jurisprudence, and later out of sociology of law; it argues that the internal perspective adopted within the legal system cannot capture the phenomenon of law. See Susan S. Silbey, "Law and Society Movement," in vol. 2 of *Legal Systems of the World: A Political, Social and Cultural Encyclopedia*, ed. Herbert M. Kritzer (Santa Barbara: ABC CLIO), pp. 860–3.
2. Editor's note: Max Weber (1864–1920) is one of the seminal figures in the sociological tradition. His work has also been influential in economics and political theory.

From Mari J. Matsuda, "Liberal Jurisprudence and Abstracted Visions of Human Nature: A Feminist Critique of Rawls' *Theory of Justice*," *New Mexico Law Review* 613, no. 16 (1986): 613–30.[1]

Rawls' "Original Position" Is an Abstraction

The central abstraction in [Rawls'] theory is called the original position. Imagine, Rawls suggests, a group of people deciding what kind of political structure they would like to live under. Rawls places these people in an imaginary spot behind what he calls the "veil of ignorance." Behind the veil, these people do not know who they will be when they emerge in the "real world." They do not know whether they will be rich or poor, male or female, black or white, talented or untalented, swift or slow.[2]

Not knowing their future status, Rawls argues, these people will decide upon two principles—the liberty principle and the difference principle. . . . The liberty principle . . . [guarantees] the full range of individual liberties—free speech, freedom of religion, freedom of conscience, freedom of the person, and equal political rights. The difference principle will compensate for the lost worth of liberty that arises from "the inability to take advantage of one's rights and opportunities as a result of poverty and ignorance, and a lack of means generally."[3] . . .

Rawls suggests that without an agreed starting place, without a common way of looking at the world, we could never conclude that one theory of justice is preferable to another. Thus he abstracts out as much as possible, ostensibly to avoid skewing the outcome. . . . [The problem is that the abstraction is] weighted to derive a theory consistent with the liberal tradition, and alternative conceptions of the nature of humankind are ignored. . . .

Legal History Has Refused to Acknowledge the Context in which Women and Individuals Live

[F]eminist theory . . . is characterized by some basic tenets. First is the charge . . . that traditional scholarly discourse largely ignores the lives and voices of women. Second is the charge . . . [that] intuition, experience, and emotion [are seen] as the inferior antitheses of logic, reason, and science . . .

From these critiques of mainstream scholarship, feminists have derived [the insight] . . . that the personal is political. By this it is meant that what happens in the daily lives of real people has political content in the same way as . . . the structure of economic systems and governments. That is, who makes breakfast, who gets a paycheck, who gets whistled at in the street—all the experiences of daily life—are a part of the distribution of wealth and power in society. . . .

The refusal to acknowledge context—to acknowledge the actual lives of the human beings affected by a particular abstract principle—has meant time and again that women's well-grounded, experiential knowledge is subordinated to someone else's abstract presumptions.

Legal history is rife with examples. The abstract principle that women . . . belong in a separate sphere, protected and cared for by men, supported the rule preventing married women from owning property. In their life experience, however, many women went uncared for, and were required to provide for themselves through their own resources. Women's experiential reality confronted the male-created abstraction of women's privileged sphere. . . .

Similarly, women who are currently told that strict enforcement of the legal guarantee of equal pay for equal work has created an abstract condition called "equality" look at their own experience as underpaid workers, and then redefine "equality" as equal pay for work of equal value.[4] This is not to suggest that the abstraction of "equality" lacks instrumental value to feminists. Rather, for women, the pursuit of equal rights as an abstract goal was developed around the struggle for tangible manifestations of equality in their daily lives:

the vote, the ownership of property, and pay equity. This connection to the concrete has made women particularly conscious of the ever-looming paradoxes and abuses inherent in the equality principle.

Time and again women have found that their own experiences are more valuable truth-seeking tools than the abstractions of others. . . . [T]alk with other women about women's experience . . . has taught distrust of theory built without the foundation of contextual understanding. . . .

Rawls' Assumptions about Human Nature

This section explains some of the major assumptions that are worked into the original position. I will propose feminist counter-assumptions, and ask whether it is logical for Rawls to choose one set of assumptions over another. . . .

Rawls assumes self-interest and mutual disinterest. They will be concerned for others only under two circumstances. First, they may end up with a conception of the good that includes altruism as a plan for life: They may be saints or heroes. Second, they may come to see that there is personal advantage in assisting others to maximize their talents. . . .

Rawls admits that persons in the original position "have a certain psychology." . . . They know that there will be scarcity of goods and advantages. They know that they will prefer larger shares of these. They know that conflict is inherent in social life and that cooperation is preferable only to the extent that cooperation is mutually rewarding. . . .

Persons in the original position, viewing the world of human possibilities as Rawls does, and knowing nothing of their own place in that world, would quite likely choose the [principles of liberty and difference]. . . . In a world where everyone looks after themselves, and where mutual concern is merely an extension of self-interest, people are wise to place primary value on liberty. . . .

The problem with the general facts let into the original position is that they are not facts at all. . . . A rudimentary knowledge of history and anthropology tells us that the potentialities of the human personality are far from fixed in the twentieth century Western liberal conception. . . .

The list of possibilities that Rawls ignores and abstracts out of consideration is equally instructive. . . . Feminist theory suggests that we can achieve identity of interest on the real-life side of the veil. In that world, people would not be moved solely by self-interest, but also by feelings of love, intimacy, and care for others. They would be in a perpetual state of mutual concern. Rawls begins to consider this possibility when he discusses families and social unions, but his dominant idea is that it is personally advantageous for individuals to join social unions. . . .

This leaves the problem of distribution of such Rawlsian goods as self-respect and excellences. . . . The whole concept of self-respect presumes that others will try to interfere with our plans. Self-respect is defined by Rawls as being left alone to pursue one's own ends. . . . This ignores the possibility that we can take collective pleasure in knowing that there is some rare and fine advantage that only a few can have, and that we can all celebrate when those few are chosen. Sports fans might understand this.

It seems that what really hurts, and this Rawls seeks to avoid, is when those rare and fine advantages are distributed not by grace, but by arbitrary privilege. If this is the real problem, then perhaps justice requires elimination of class differences.

Notes

1. Editor's note: Most of the contemporary work in legal theory has a liberal slant and a positivist slant. The idea of a social contract, which is so central in the natural rights tradition, was reinvigorated by the publication of John Rawls' *A Theory of Justice* (Cambridge, MA: Belknap, 1971), in which Rawls argues that neutral, freely contracting individuals would choose a political system based on liberal democratic principles. This naturally assumes that the law derives its authority from political sources.

2. Editor's note: The veil is meant to prevent them from choosing a political system on the basis of their self-interest.

3. Editor's note: Rawls argues that the difference principle requires some redistribution of resources to compensate those who are unable to take advantage of the principle of liberty. This is the crucial step in his theory.

4. Editor's note: In other words, the "legal guarantee" of equality is based on an abstract idea of equality, which fails to question the assumption that male work has a higher value than does female work. It follows that the resulting equality is a formal or logical equality, which does not correspond with the substantive reality behind the terms.

From Margaret L. Anderson, "New Directions in Feminist Theory," in *Thinking about Women: Sociological Perspectives on Sex and Gender* (Boston: Allyn and Bacon, 1997), pp. 370–81.

Current developments in feminist theory stem from the fundamental recognition that knowledge is socially constructed and, therefore, must be seen in the context of the social relations in which knowledge production occurs. In this regard, feminist epistemology is one of the new modes of feminist thought. . . .

One major area of discussion in feminist epistemology is the social construction of science, a particularly important subject because of the deep and central ways that scientific knowledge shapes Western ways of knowing. . . . According to standard arguments about sociological research, rigorous observation and the use of the scientific method eliminate observer bias, but feminists argue that the observer is not a neutral party. Because knowledge is socially produced, the particular experiences and attitudes that observers bring to their work influence what they study, how they study it, and what they conclude about it. . . .

Dorothy Smith (1990) and Nancy Hartsock (1983) note that all research is done from a particular standpoint or location in the social system.[1] . . . [Smith] explains this idea by using an example from the German philosopher Hegel. Suppose we want to comprehend the world of a master and a slave. Both of them live in the same world, but their experience within that world is quite different. The master takes the slave's labour (in fact, the slave's very existence) for granted. . . . The slave, on the other hand, conforms to the master's will; his or her labour is an object of the master's consciousness. . . . If the master were describing the world they both inhabit, his account would be less objective because the structures of that world are invisible to him. The slave's description of the world, on the other hand, would include the master, plus the fact of his or her own labour and its transformation to the status of an object. As a result, the slave is more objective because his or her account is both more complete and more directly related to the empirical events within the relationship and the world in which it is located. . . .

Standpoint theory assumes that systems of privilege are least visible to those who benefit the most from them and who, at the same time, control the resources that define dominant belief systems. Whites, for example, are more likely to deny that racism exists; people of colour both see the assaults racism produces and understand the nuances of racism in everyday life. Similarly, men can more easily deny the presence of patriarchy than can women, even when women do not fully grasp the workings of sexist oppression. It takes the standpoint of oppressed groups to see and recognize systems of race, class, and gender privilege. . . .

Feminism and Postmodernism

Feminist standpoint theory and the epistemological assumptions on which it rests grow from, and have contributed to, a theoretical framework known as postmodernism. Postmodernism is a form of contemporary social theory that explains all knowledge as stemming from the specific historical period and the conditions in which it is produced, and that interprets society not as an objective thing but as a fluid and illusive construction of alternative meaning systems. . . .

Postmodernism has arisen primarily from the field of literary criticism and also from the critiques of science symbolized by feminist standpoint theory. . . . Because the focusses of postmodernism are on alternative discourses and meaning systems, not goals, choices, behaviour, and attitudes, emphasis is placed on what are called *texts*—whether those be actual literary texts like books or conversations, media images, and other cultural forms. The concept of a text in postmodernist theory is thus more than the literal text; it refers to the contested meaning systems that appear in all of social reality. A conversation between two people or the nightly news is considered a text. . . . The major method used in postmodernism is to examine texts as socially constructed objects. This has resulted in a new field of study, known as *cultural studies*. . . .

For feminists, postmodernism has had much appeal because of some commonly shared assumptions in both feminist and postmodernist theory. One of the basic premises of feminist thought is that gender is socially constructed . . . This critical attitude makes postmodernism appealing to feminists because feminism and postmodernism are fundamentally skeptical about existing knowledge. Each also recognizes the embedment of social assumptions in such things as language, cultural images, and the ideas of a given period. Because feminists see how ideas and images have been used to oppress women, they want to criticize these discourses, not take them for granted. . . .

Another basic insight of postmodernism and a reason for its attractiveness to feminists is that postmodernists think there is nothing essentially male or female; rather, there are socially constructed categories that emerge from specific cultural and historical contexts, not from anything fundamental about male or female biology. Postmodernists even challenge the idea that there are real biological categories to begin with, since they understand "male" and "female" only as constructed through human definition. . . .

A good way to explain this point is to use the metaphor of a coat rack, suggested by Linda Nicholson, a postmodernist feminist thinker. The coat rack metaphor assumes that the body is a rack upon which differing cultural artifacts are hung. In other words, the idea is that there is some constancy to nature but that culture elaborates this basic difference into different societal forms (Nicholson, 1994).[2] Postmodernists question whether the coat rack itself is anything other than a cultural construction. . . .

A third premise for the connection between feminism and postmodernism is the insight of both on the social construction of language. Postmodernist theorists understand language as not just a technical device for describing something "out there." Rather, they see language itself as actually constituting the thing it allegedly describes (Agger, 1991).[3] Postmodernist analyses of language rest on the idea that language, like other forms of knowledge, is not pure; instead, language reflects the social categories and practices that characterize a given time and cultural period. For example, calling someone a *man* or a *woman*, just like calling someone *White* or *Black*, has a specific socially constituted meaning that makes no sense outside of its cultural time and place. . . .

Feminist Theory and Sexuality

The influence of postmodernist theory has been especially strong in new feminist scholarship on sexuality. In part because feminists have wanted to break down taken-for-granted categories of sexual differentiation, postmodernist thought is consistent with the value placed on the fluidity of sexual categories. Postmodernist feminist theorists have thus found subjects like cross dressing, transvestism, and the crossing of sexual categories represented in some new forms of gay and lesbian studies to be fascinating and to provide new theoretical constructs for all feminist thought. . . .

One of the arguments, from a postmodernist perspective, is that categories like *homosexual* and *heterosexual* have . . . been constructed through particular scientific discourses—namely, the work of sexologists and others who have labelled sexual behaviours in dichotomous categories; furthermore, these "discourses" have assumed an authoritative stance, with systems of power enforcing these labels. To postmodernists, sexual power is embodied in various aspects of social life (popular culture, scientific writings, literary texts, and daily conversations, to name a few); these "texts" establish sexual boundaries that regulate sexual behaviour and identities. . . .

Not all new feminist studies of sexuality use a postmodernist framework. . . . Many feminists are, indeed, critical of the postmodernist approach to sexuality, arguing that it does not provide a political perspective that challenges the real structural basis of sexual oppression (Kitzinger and Wilkinson, 1994).[4] In their criticisms, feminists are arguing that structural systems of heterosexual privilege and power are real and cannot be reduced to texts, discourses, and performance. . . .

Feminism and the Analysis of Race, Class, and Gender

Feminist theory is itself incomplete without an analysis of the intersections of race, class, and gender in society. To date, this has been one of the greatest limitations of feminist theory, and it stems from the fact that much of feminist theory has been constructed from the particular experiences of White, middle-class women. . . .

Given the inadequacies in existing categories of feminist theory, it has taken the independent development of feminist theory by women of colour to produce new analyses, grounded in the experiences of women of colour, that provide new starting points for feminist thought and action. The experience of women of colour, most usually Black women, has been typically described as *double jeopardy*—a term meant to suggest the cumulative effect of experiencing both race and gender exploitation. Although this phrase is descriptively valuable, it is analytically limited, suggesting that the racism that women of colour experience is simply added to sexism, when, in fact, race, class, and gender are systems of oppression experienced simultaneously, not additively, by women of colour (Combahee River Collective, 1982; Andersen and Collins, 1995).[5]

Conceptualizing feminist theory from the experience of women of colour requires analyses that interpret race, class, and gender as intersecting and interlocking systems of oppression; moreover, it requires shifting the starting point for the development of feminist thinking. Centring knowledge in the experiences of those who have traditionally been excluded causes us to question all of the assumptions made in studying not only people of colour, but dominant groups as well. This approach is more likely to give us a rich account of the experience of oppressed groups . . .

For example, Patricia Hill Collins writes that if we want to know the thoughts and lives of African American women as intellectuals, we have to revise our way of thinking about who is an intellectual. African American women have historically been denied access to formal education; they have not had the privilege of finding publishers and public platforms for their ideas. To recover the work of African American women intellectuals, we must look to new sources and find intellectual thought in the everyday activities of Black women. As she writes, "Reclaiming the Black female intellectual tradition also involves searching for its expression in alternative institutional locations and among women who are not commonly perceived as intellectuals" (1990: 14).[6]

Notes

1. Editor's note: The references are to Dorothy E. Smith, *The Conceptual Practices of Power: A Feminist Sociology* (Boston: Northeastern University, 1990) and Nancy Hartsock, "The Feminist Standpoint: Developing the Ground for a Specifically Feminist Historical Materialism," in *Money, Sex and Power*, ed. Nancy Hartsock (New York: Longman, 1983), pp. 231–51.
2. Editor's note: The reference is to Linda E. Nicholson, ed., *Feminism and Postmodernism* (New York: Routledge, 1990).
3. Editor's note: The reference is to Ben Agger, "Critical Theory, Poststructuralism, Postmodernism: Their Sociological Relevance," in vol. 17 of *Annual Review of Sociology*, ed. W. Richard Scott and Judith Blake (Palo Alto: Annual Reviews, 1991).
4. Editor's note: The reference is to Celia A. Kitzinger and Sue Wilkinson, "Virgins and Queers: Rehabilitating Heterosexuality?," *Gender & Society* 8, no. 3 (September 1994): 444–62.
5. Editor's note: The references are to Combahee River Collective, "A Black Feminist Statement," in *But Some of Us Are Brave*, ed. Gloria T. Hull, Patricia Bell Scott, and Barbara Smith (Old Westbury, NY: Feminist, 1982) and Margaret L. Anderson and Patricia Hill Collins, *Race, Class and Gender: An Anthology*, 2nd ed. (Belmont, CA: Wadsworth, 1995).
6. Editor's note: The reference is to Patricia Hill Collins, *Black Feminist Theory: Knowledge, Consciousness and the Politics of Empowerment* (Boston, MA: Unwin Hyman, 1990).

✦ Discussion ✦

The following chapter canvasses the contemporary theoretical literature. Since it is impossible to do so comprehensively in a historical survey, the chapter simply identifies some of the major trends in the current literature. This literature has two sides: the first side essentially continues in the liberal and legal positivist tradition, which comes out of the idea of a social contract. This side of the literature includes theories like law and economics, which adopts an economic approach but maintains the fundamental premises of positivism. The second, alternative side critiques positivism. There are also other approaches to the study of law—such as the approach endorsed by the law and society movement—that possess a critical edge but do not offer a firm theoretical position.

This chapter focusses on the alternative theories in the literature, since it is the alternative account that presents new positions. These theories have their roots in legal realism. The current literature goes further than legal realism, however, and rejects positivism on the basis that it is biased in its stance and incapable of delivering justice. Two developments in this literature stand out. One is critical legal studies, which is important because it represents the point of departure at which the alternative view first defined itself. The other is feminist theory, which has become a potent force in the universities.

These two sets of theories are seminal. Although critical legal studies is often dismissed as a spent force in philosophy of law, it developed the critical stance that characterizes the alternative theories. These theories include sociological and Marxist theories; critical theories like critical feminist theory, critical race theory, and critical discourse analysis;

structuralism and poststructuralism; critical cultural studies and postmodern theories of law; and at least some of the work in phenomenology of law.[1] The critical stance questions the internal explanations of the law and generally looks outside the legal system for the external reasons that explain the development of the law. These reasons can be found in the personal and political views of the judiciary, for example, or in the sociology of power.

There are difficulties with both sets of theories. One is that the alternative literature is extremely fragmented. This is particularly true of feminist theory. If the post-feminists and liberal feminists are included in feminist theory, it is clear that there are conflicting tendencies within the tradition. This may be the inevitable result of the fact that more recent feminists have rejected the essentialism that gave the early literature its character and attempted to define a distinct female view.

The abstraction of the alternative theories is also problematic, since the existing literature also fails to provide a convincing working theory of the law. Although many theorists who adopt a critical stance have dismissed the historical tradition in legal theory as a kind of apologetics, which serves entrenched interests, there remains little in the alternative literature that rivals the explanatory success of historical theories of law like natural law theory and legal positivism. There is also a subjective strain in much of the alternative literature that works against the formulation of a general theory. This subjective influence is evident in the epistemological side of these developments, which calls into question the idea that law is a proper subject of knowledge rather than opinion or belief.

Critical Legal Studies Is an Academic Movement Rather Than a Theory

Critical legal studies emerged in the 1970s as an academic movement rather than a theory. This movement was a reaction by academics to an orthodoxy based on the conventional pedagogy in the law schools, which was based on formalism and analytical jurisprudence. The legal curriculum accepted the legal system and the existing law uncritically, without questioning the fundamental tenets of legal positivism. There was also a reaction to the liberal orientation of the later common law, which favoured a conception of individual rights that neglected larger interests.

There is now a discernible divide in the theoretical literature, which sets critical theorists against those who have tried to provide a philosophical account of the existing legal system, like H.L.A. Hart and Ronald Dworkin. There is a definite perception in the critical literature that the legal system provides the machinery of social control, which maintains the existing order. There is also a prominent view that the rational elements in the caselaw hide and transmute unpalatable political realities. Although critical legal studies has had relatively little impact on legal practice and the methodology of the common law, it has had a marked effect on judicial attitudes and made judges far more aware of the political implications of their decisions.

Critical Legal Studies Critiques the Use of the Law to Maintain Power

There is a political side to critical legal studies, which sees law as a political enterprise and often enters into the field of political theory. In terms of conventional politics, the movement quickly aligned itself with a left-wing critique of the existing social order. This critique holds that the inequities in the distribution of wealth and power in society find their way into the political system and the law. Some of this is a product of the thinking of judges, who use the language of the common law, often unconsciously, to satisfy the needs and interests of those in power.

The political side of critical theory has focussed on the failure of positivism and the liberal tradition to guarantee the impartiality or fairness of the legal system. There is also a neglected critique of legislative democracy and the political conception of law that it entails. Some of this critique can be traced to the inherent tendency of democratic systems to produce conflict between a majority and minorities. There are Marxist elements in the critique, however, and the level of conflict is exacerbated by the competitive nature of capitalism and the ability of those with wealth and power to manipulate the democratic process. This conflict inevitably makes its way into the legal process, which then becomes a second front in the struggle between competing political interests. There is no escaping the fact that critical theory has a subversive edge, since it raises questions about our allegiance to the law, which was based historically on the belief that the law is a product of a substantive consensus in society and therefore binds everyone.

Critical Legal Studies Has Its Philosophical Roots in Skepticism

It is what critical studies says about the philosophical tradition, however, that seems more significant from the perspective of legal theory. Mark Kelman writes that many "progressive" academics felt a general dissatisfaction with the narrowness of positivism and the liberal tradition. This narrowness is a product, historically, of the analytic tradition in philosophy, which holds that rational deduction is sufficient to resolve ethical and legal issues. The analytic position, which is aligned with positivism, is based on the political contract and neglects the substantive premises of the system.

The roots of critical legal studies are in skepticism and legal realism. The skepticism in critical legal studies goes deeper than realism, however, and throws the entire structure of the political system and government into question. Critical legal studies tends to reject the conventional rationales for the enactment of specific laws, on the basis that the deeper purpose of the law is to maintain the distribution of power in society.

There is also an epistemological skepticism in the critical studies movement. The obvious criticism of this skepticism is that it does not provide a positive foundation for further enquiries, since it rejects the idea that anything can be known with certainty. All in all, it comes as no surprise that critical legal studies has been more successful in questioning the liberal and positivist assumptions in the common law tradition than in providing a convincing legal theory of its own.

Critical Legal Studies Argues that There Are Antinomies in Liberal Theory

Critical legal studies purportedly questions the liberal assumptions in Kant, Bentham, and the more recent liberal tradition, which includes Hart and Dworkin. There is some confusion in this approach, however, since liberalism is a general philosophical position that comes out of the natural rights tradition, and the critical literature does not provide a cogent précis of the central legal tenets of liberalism. In one sense, this is understandable, since liberal theory sets out a political rather than a legal theory and rests on a relatively simple assumption that the authority of the law can be traced to its positivist origins in the political order. As a result, the law is merely the instrument of politics. It is notable, and perhaps ironic, that critical legal studies has failed to question the political conception of law at the heart of such a position.

In spite of the failure of critical legal studies to set out the liberal position precisely, Kelman writes that critical legal studies has drawn our attention to three fundamental contradictions in liberal thought: a contradiction between the logical and empirical elements in the legal tradition; a contradiction between a subjective and an objective point of view; and a contradiction between individual choice and determinism. It is not clear that these are "contradictions" in the ordinary sense of the word, however, and it seems more accurate to use Kant's term and call them "antinomies."

There is no doubt that Kelman's antinomies capture some of the competing interests that enter into the caselaw. It is not clear, however, that he has isolated the most fundamental tensions in the common law. The abstraction of the critical formulation is noticeable, and it seems much plainer to say, for example, that there is a tension in the later common law between the prerogatives of the individual and the interests of the community. This is expressed in legal principles like eminent domain, which gives the state the right to expropriate land. There is a much deeper, historical tension between the rights of individuals, which came from membership in society, and the controlling interests of the state. The critical view is nevertheless clear: the skepticism in critical theory expresses itself in the idea that these kinds of antinomies are incapable of resolution within the legal system, which ultimately privileges one set of interests over the other.[2]

The three antinomies that Kelman sets out can be seen, to some extent, as an expression of the competition between an internal and an external point of view. The implicit position in critical legal studies is that the external point of view is not available within formalism or legal positivism. As a result, legal reasoning fails to deal with the social or economic realities behind legal conflicts. This gives rise to a discrepancy between practice and reality that the law is unable to resolve.

The critical view migrated into the work of feminists, who have held that the ordinary process of adjudication perpetuates or hides social inequalities. The legal process preserves the injustices in the system and prevents the system from resolving the conflicts expressed in these competing interests. One of the purposes of critical theory is simply to bring this to the surface of the discussion.

Tushnet Argues that the Law Is Politics "All the Way Down"

It may be skepticism in critical legal studies that has led it to embrace ambiguities in the law. Tushnet certainly argues that law has the logical and intellectual tools to justify opposing conclusions. It is therefore possible for judges to find legal justifications to support the moral and political conclusions that they favour. Tushnet's view takes us further than legal realism, since it suggests that judges can legitimately decide cases on the basis of their moral and political views. Although this normative brand of realism brings the personal opinions of judges—along with the sociological and psychological influences that affect their decisions—into the legal analysis, critical legal studies has never clarified the ethical limits of such intrusions.

The fundamental observation is that critical legal studies, like legal positivism, subscribes to a political conception of law. The difference is that the critical theory rejects the idea that the law is a simple product of the legislative process and gives the judiciary a much larger role in its determination. The law is, again, a second front in politics, and it must be judged on the correctness and efficacy of its political consequences outside the legal system. This kind of view abandons the pretension that the common law courts are a neutral forum for the impartial resolution of conflicts on the basis of principles that have been accepted on all sides.

Law is politics "all the way down," and the significance of legal reasoning lies in the fact that it justifies a certain policy result. This position has migrated into the work of feminists and many theorists working in sociology of law who argue that the meaning of legal decisions lies in their effect on the distribution of power in society. This can be judged only by an examination of their consequences on the lives of those individuals who are traditionally powerless in society. There is a sense, at least, in which the law is a repressive force, since it prevents social change. This argument takes us into the struggle for social justice, rather than legal theory, and calls for political action.

Tushnet's Conception of Law Is Intensely Adversarial

The political conception of law in critical legal studies holds that the law is open to individual interpretation. The relativity that this introduces into the legal system makes it an intensely adversarial system, in which the political views of different actors in the system vie for priority. The suggestion in critical studies is that this struggle below the surface of the law merely reveals the deeper tensions that are hidden by the legal discourse. This is a central theoretical issue because liberal theory and legal positivism assume that the law is morally and culturally neutral.

The position in critical legal studies seems to suggest that an ideal legal system needs a common set of positive values, which overrides political interests. In such a system, of course, it is necessary to determine where those values should come from, and which values take precedence over others. The most likely source in a pluralistic society is a broad substantive consensus across religious, ethical, and cultural traditions. It is interesting that in many ways this position takes us back to the development of the common law, which emerged slowly, out of a synthesis of competing moral customs.

Critical Legal Studies Emphasizes the Indeterminacy of the Legal System

The skepticism that infuses critical legal studies highlights the indeterminacy of the law. This is more significant than it might appear, since the common law places a high value on the certainty of the system. One of the objectives of *stare decisis* is to provide finality in the resolution of disputes. The idea that the certainty of the legal system can be measured is intriguing but difficult to test in practice. Although Tushnet seems to suggest that the consistency of the decision in the legal system should be empirically measured, his views are more theoretical than scientific. The theoretical challenge is to design the conceptual framework of the legal system in a way that delivers a consistent set of results in individual cases.

There are clear differences between the models of the legal system that we find in the most prominent legal theories. It is evident that Hart, for example, believed that the legal system has a high level of determinacy, with relatively few penumbral cases. Dworkin, by contrast, gives penumbral and indeterminate cases a major role in the system. Some part of this difference can be attributed to the differences between the legal traditions in England and those in the United States. Critical legal studies, on the other hand, often seems to attribute the uncertainty that Hart associated with the penumbra of meaning to the entire system. One of the problems with the model of the legal system that we find in critical theory is that it seems to leave the system at the mercy of the same unregulated political forces that it critiques.

Critical Legal Studies Has Fostered an Interest in Phenomenology of Law

The skepticism in critical legal studies also goes against the idea that it is possible to find an objective legal standard, the methodological side of the movement has focussed on the subjective aspects of judicial decision-making. This focus leads into phenomenology, a branch of philosophy that essentially argues that existence is made up of the phenomena of consciousness.[3] The study of law, on this view, is a study of the structures of consciousness that make up legal experience. What is it in our experience of the norms that make up the law, legal phenomenologists have asked, that supplies their obligatory or compulsory character?

Duncan Kennedy has argued that Hart's theory of law has neglected the phenomenological "work" of legal interpretation.[4] If a case comes within the scope of a legal rule, and lies within its core of meaning, the rule, automatically, produces the same result. It is still necessary to establish, however, that the case falls within the scope of the rule. The crucial phenomenological task is accordingly to persuade the judge that the case falls—or does not fall—within the core of meaning that attaches to the relevant rule. There is a philosophical question whether the answer to this question is a product of the "work" done by lawyers, for example, in re-constructing the case to fit within the relevant norm or something inherent in the rule and the facts of the case.

Critical Legal Studies Has Also Fostered an Interest in Rhetoric

The skepticism in critical legal studies has also fostered the idea that law is a branch of rhetoric, the art or science of persuasion. This idea is buttressed by the belief that law and justice are matters of opinion. James Boyd White has suggested that the legal system essentially becomes a machine, on this understanding, that provides the coercive mechanism of social control.[5] It is inevitable that the law loses most of its moral authority in such a rendering and becomes an instrument of the regulatory choices made by those in political power. This view sees the law and the legal system merely as the machinery of social control.

The rhetorical view is problematic because it leaves us without a means of resolving difficult moral issues within the legal system. As a result, it is clear that judges cannot deal with the substantive issues that arise in such a system without moving conceptually outside the system and entering into the political struggle between those who have set the rules and those who dispute them. This politicized view seems to force the judiciary to take sides in the political conflicts that find their way into the courts.

Feminist Legal Theory Is Allied with Legal Realism but Has a Critical Edge

Like critical legal studies, feminist theory has often assumed the character of a movement rather than a school of thought.[6] As a result, the character of the earlier literature reflects the ethical and political activism that brought feminism into the public domain. At a later stage, when feminists examined judicial reasoning, they found it highly rhetorical and generally concluded that it was designed to justify policy results that supported the existing social order. The recent developments in feminist theory are more aligned with sociology than with philosophy and deconstruct concepts like gender and race. The newer work also questions some aspects of the earlier literature.

The First Wave of Feminism Manifested Itself in Activism

These three distinct developments in the feminist literature correspond roughly to three "waves" of feminism.[7] The first wave has to be attributed to a hard sense of inequality and the recognition that the law has not traditionally treated men and women equally. This recognition led to a historical struggle to improve the position of women in society and to obtain for women basic rights such as the right to vote. It follows that legal feminism came out of a belief that the inequities in society can be addressed through legal and political action.[8]

The Second Wave of Feminism Is More Theoretical

A second, explanatory wave of feminism arose in the 1960s and in many ways still continues. The second wave of feminism was more speculative and is notable for its attempt to construct a theory of women, which would facilitate the development of feminist ethics and other branches of feminist thought.[9] This endeavour has been called essentialism.

The second wave also explored the inequalities in the social and psychological roles assigned to women. Two of the preliminary texts that explore these issues are Simone de Beauvoir's *Le Deuxième Sexe* (1949)[10] and Betty Friedan's *The Feminine Mystique* (1963),[11] which argue that our idea of a woman is a social construction. This construction has been internalized by women and leads them to seek fulfillment in a manner that has failed to fulfill their needs.

There are a number of different theoretical positions in second-wave feminism.[12] In a book entitled *In a Different Voice: Psychological Theory and Women's Development* (1982), Carol Gilligan has argued that women have an ethic of care. Men, on the other hand, have an ethic of rights, which is based on the concept of justice and finds expression in the legal order.[13] Furthermore, the male perspective finds expression in liberal theories like utilitarianism, which fail to capture the reality of women's experience.

Gilligan's theory crosses a number of disciplinary boundaries and is legal only incidentally. It nevertheless sets out competing theories of morality and sees the idea of rights as predominantly patriarchal. Gilligan argues that women look at the connections between people rather than recognized individuals in isolation from each other. Women respond to needs, rather than rights, and are motivated to prevent harm, rather than redress it. The law does not accommodate the feminine view, which has been relegated to the domestic arena, outside the ordinary reach of the law.

Annette Baier has taken a similar position and argues that a convincing ethical theory must include the insights of both genders.[14] Baier rejects the detached, patriarchal perspective of the liberal tradition and argues that ethics must include an account of our attachment to other people. Nel Noddings also sets out an ethic of care based on relationships, arguing that a feminine approach is preferable.[15] These authors see the abstract, atomistic conception of the individual in the common law as inherently male.

Matsuda Argues that Individuals Must Always Be Seen in Context

The second wave of feminism contains a number of identifiable themes. One of these themes is that the concept of justice enshrined in the law leaves out too much. The predominant view, outside liberal feminism, has been that the liberal notion of individual equality is a male reduction that fails to capture the experience of women and minorities. The second wave literature has been described as an "attack on liberal approaches to law and feminism and the associated conceptions of objectivity, universality, gender neutrality, and privacy."[16]

This sort of "attack" is typified by Mari Matsuda's critique of John Rawls' theory of justice. Rawls asks us to imagine the kind of political system a group of hypothetical individuals would choose behind the veil of ignorance. Matsuda objects that individual people always exist in social, political, and cultural circumstances, which will inevitably enter into their views. These circumstances include their relations to other people. It is therefore of no assistance to ask what people would think, abstractly, if they existed outside such a context.[17]

Matsuda argues that the liberal and analytic traditions have neglected the experience of women. As a result, these traditions favour logic and a narrow rationality over intuition, emotion, and the experience of those without wealth and power. This leads into a superficial philosophical idealism: ideas are valued over people and their "felt" experiences. Like other feminists, she looks for the discrepancies between these ideas and the reality of women's lives. The formal proposition that there should be equal pay for work of equal value, for example, is undermined by the reality that male occupations are of higher value than female occupations. It is the subjective experience of the unequal distribution of power and wealth in society, rather than some abstract idea of equality, that matters.

Matsuda also rejects liberal theory on the basis that it treats individuals as if they are disconnected from each other. As a result, their general well-being depends on the satisfaction of their exclusive interests, which may not include a regard for other people. This view subscribes to the common good only when it serves an individual's isolated self-interest. Legally, it fails to calculate the loss suffered by those who lose their relationships with other people.

MacKinnon Argues that Law Is Politics

There is also a substantive theme in the second-wave literature. This theme is prominent in the work of Catharine MacKinnon, who has argued that legal theory needs to deal directly with the imbalance of power behind the abstractions that populate the law. Like Matsuda, she criticizes the formalism in the common law, which hides the inequalities in the distribution of power and wealth in society and portrays the results in individual cases as a matter of logical necessity.

Like the critical theorists, MacKinnon implicitly adopts a political conception of law. She also subscribes to the idea that there is a second front in politics, which manifests itself in the judicial process. The substance of the law, MacKinnon writes, is "politics."[18] It follows that judges and legal commentators should acknowledge the political nature of their role and bring the political conflicts under the surface of the law to the forefront of the discussion. The process of adjudication should focus on the external consequences of the process of the adjudication, as it is experienced by those who are affected by its results.

MacKinnon's argument calls for a normative realism in legal practice, one that adopts a critical stance toward the legal abstractions used in the courtroom. The problem is that there is plenty of room for disagreement as to the "substance" of abstractions like freedom of speech, which is highly rhetorical in MacKinnon's formulation, and not amenable to proof. Nor is it clear that an adjudicative forum is the proper place to resolve highly contentious policy positions, which are tinged with ideology.

The substantive view comes to the fore in the context of MacKinnon's provocative position on pornography and the nature of the sexual relations between men and women.[19] MacKinnon argues that we should acknowledge that men and women have fundamentally different views of pornography. It follows that the substantive sources of both views need to be investigated by the courts and brought into the legal analysis.[20]

The Third Wave Has a Postmodern Side

The references to "third-wave" feminism in the literature are easily overstated, since the term does not suggest that the work of second-wave feminism has come to an end.[21] The suggestion is merely that there has been a discernible reaction, in feminist circles, to the positions adopted by theorists in the second wave.[22] The third wave of feminism has also been described as post-feminism, though this term describes a more general reaction against feminist theory, which suggests that feminism has done its necessary work.[23]

It is nevertheless clear that the third wave rejects the essentialist project, which tries to identify the properties or characteristics that give women their identity as women. There has been a general rejection of the idea that the gender and identity of women has a definite metaphysical or biological basis. These developments gave rise first to anti-essentialism and later "anti-anti-essentialism," which was based on the realization that the initial rejection of essentialism removed the fundamental justification for feminist theory in the first place. There is also a view in the third-wave literature that earlier attempts at definition favoured the experiences of some women over others. One of the early figures in this development is bell hooks. In *Ain't I a Woman: Black Women and Feminism*,[24] hooks argues that middle-class white feminists have failed to address the relationship between race, class, and gender.

Other feminists have also raised the question of who has the authority to speak for women on moral issues. Carolyn Pedwell suggests, for example, that there is a racial and cultural filter in the literature that portrays cosmetic surgery in a neutral and more positive manner than it portrays cultural practices like female circumcision.[25] Indeed, multicultural feminists have argued that Western attitudes toward female "cutting" often serve to assert the "positional superiority" of Western moral values and perpetrate a neocolonial "othering" of African women.[26]

As Margaret Anderson writes, in the fourth reading, similar concerns have also found expression in an interest in the de-construction of gender and the popular representation of women.[27] The feminist discussion of these issues takes us into postmodernism and a highly abstract analysis of race, class, and personal identity. The idea that human reality is socially constructed has opened up alternative approaches to the earlier essentialist project, such as feminist genealogy.[28]

Feminist Theory Focusses On Transformation and Oppression

There is an element of revolution in feminist theory, which is fundamentally polemical. This element surfaces in the personal tone of much of the feminist literature, which distinguishes it from most academic work. In part, this tone comes from the idea of "consciousness-raising," which holds that our subjective experience of injustice and inequity should provide the foundation of the legal discussion. Personal narratives have political significance.

Ann Scales, for example, extends MacKinnon's substantive analysis to more foundational issues like domination and oppression.[29] Scales discounts the "objective" claims of the legal inquiry. She critiques realism, as well as positivism, on the basis that it did not go far enough in analyzing the political nature of the law. Scales argues that liberal theory rests on an abstract assumption of equality, which can only redress the differences between equally situated individuals. This restriction favours the existing distribution of power in society and makes it impossible to address the structural inequalities in the social and political order.

Scales further argues that the claim to objectivity is false and advocates an approach that is "result-oriented" and "coherent" with our experience of life. Again, she follows MacKinnon in endorsing an "inequality approach" that focusses on whether the law contributes to the deep inequalities in the distribution of power in society. The issue in dealing with discrimination, for example, is whether the challenged policy contributes to the subordination of women or other minorities. The traditional legal analysis hides this question.

Philosophically, the focus of feminist theory seems to have shifted to broader issues of domination, oppression, and subordination.[30] In *Feminist Theory: From Margin to Center*, for example, bell hooks argues that the "white-supremacist capitalist patriarchy" is corrupt, and that it is simply not possible to achieve equality in the existing legal and political system.[31] Feminism must therefore adopt a transformative character.

There are two projects in transformative feminism. The first is a descriptive project: it is simply to develop a legal theory that describes the law accurately, that is to say, in a manner that captures the experience of law by those who are oppressed and without power.[32] The second project is normative: it is to formulate a jurisprudence that sets out in some detail what the law should be.[33] In many ways, at least, this project is part of a general response to the failure of domestic systems of law and politics to solve outstanding social, environmental, and economic issues.

Postmodernism has opened up the normative project to alternative approaches to the study of law, such as feminist genealogy, discourse analysis, and social constructionist theory.[34] Discourse analysis has been used by feminists to unveil the epistemological assumptions behind a given text. It has also been used to investigate the way that the linguistic elements of the legal discourse maintain the distribution of power and authority in society.[35]

A significant part of the feminist literature rejects theory, in favour of "direct action," and puts experience ahead of the philosophical enterprise. Since theory cannot capture the reality of women in a social context, there must be room for poetry and other forms of narrative in feminist theory.[36] This suggestion raises issues with regard to the limits of philosophy and more conventional academic enterprises.

The Major Criticism of the Alternative Literature Is that It Reduces Law to Politics

From a historical perspective, the major criticism of feminist and critical theory is probably that it sees the law as a second front in politics.[37] This leads to a case-by-case, "results-oriented" jurisprudence that reduces the legal system to a forum in which competing political interests struggle for predominance. This inevitably politicizes the process of appointing judges and promotes an unruly political dynamic that can easily overtake the entire system. These kinds of developments naturally affect the attitudes of judges and legitimize the role of political considerations in the decision-making process.

The failure of the critical and feminist literature to recognize the independence and neutrality of the legal system is evident in its neglect of the legal concept of legitimacy. The political concept of law naturally bases the legitimacy of the law on a political footing. This position differs from the common law position, however, which has always held that the legitimacy of legal decisions derives from the consistent application of rules and principles.[38] The historical idea is clearly that the courts are there to settle disputes between different members of society, on the basis of principles and values that have been accepted by the parties on both sides of a dispute. It is this consensual feature that guarantees the legal and political neutrality of judicial decisions and gives them inherent authority.

Many contemporary theorists also overlook the place of fact-finding in the judicial task. This is significant because it provides a tested foundation for legal decisions. The trial process accordingly takes place within the parameters established by the facts. This provides a source of grounding in evidence, from both sides, which is often missing from the academic exercise. There is far less speculation, and far less opinion, in the caselaw than the contemporary theoretical work acknowledges. The bulk of the caselaw proceeds on the basis of a general consensus as to the applicable law, which reduces the role of politics in the system.

The Alternative Literature Has an Uncritical Side

From a more contemporary perspective, however, the most significant criticism of the critical and feminist literature is probably that it has failed to turn its critical lens on itself. There is an ideological cast to much of the alternative literature, which often suggests that the common law has privileged a set of liberal beliefs that protect the social and economic distribution of power in society. It might easily be asked, however, whether critical studies and feminist theories privilege another set of beliefs, which merely provide an alternative set of assumptions and place them above examination.

There is a corresponding lack of introspection in the alternative literature, which raises its own challenge in terms of deconstruction. If the authenticity of feminist theory rests on its reliance on personal narrative, for example, it does not seem possible to inquire into its validity without examining the psychological and sociological considerations behind it. There are larger issues here, moreover, that apply to all academic work. If judicial decisions are open to questions of institutional partiality and self-interest, why should academic work be immune from such an inquiry? It is doubtful whether it is possible to deconstruct power without deconstructing the deconstruction.

The Alternative Literature Is Ahistorical

There is also a problem with the fact that most of the critical and feminist literature is ahistorical. Jeanne Schroeder has complained, for example, that contemporary feminist theories rest on a "sense of self" that does not "take into account the very different selves experienced by people living in other cultures and other historical periods."[39] Although most of the contemporary philosophical literature fails in the same way, that is because it relies so heavily on the analytic tradition, which assumes that the operation of reason and logic is sufficient to determine the validity of philosophical arguments. In both cases, however, it is a mistake to think that the law and legal theory can be understood without some appreciation of the social, cultural, and political circumstances in which it arises.

There are many examples. The current theoretical literature oversimplifies the history of the law, which originally gave legal personality to the family rather than the individual. Thus the legal restrictions that prohibited women from inheriting the family's property also applied to most of the males in the family. The purpose of these restrictions was to prevent the dissipation of the family property. It is also clear that custom saw this kind of ownership more in the nature of a trust than anything else. It is an "act of cultural hubris," to use a phrase from Schroeder, to assume that the unusually acute notions of the individual and property that we currently hold enjoy universal status.

Notes

1. See Thomas C. Heller, for example, "Structuralism and Critique", *Stanford Law Review* 36 (Jan. 1984): 127–98. This paper was presented as part of the Critical Legal Studies Symposium mentioned in the reading from Kelman.

2. The idea that these antinomies have some larger ontological status can be traced to Karl Marx and Georg Wilhelm Frederick Hegel.

3. Edmund Husserl (1859–1938), a mathematician who turned to philosophy, founded the discipline of phenomenology. Husserl believed that subjective experience has a logical structure, which can be scientifically studied. For a brief introduction to the school as it applies to law, see the entry "phenomenology of law" in vol. 1 of Christopher Berry Gray, ed., *Philosophy of Law: An Encyclopedia* (New York: Garland, 1999).

4. See the additional online reading from Kennedy's *Legal Reasoning: Collected Essays* (Aurora, CO: Davies Group, 2008).

5. See the additional online reading from White's *Heracles' Bow: Essays on the Rhetoric and Poetics of Law* (Madison: University of Wisconsin, 1985).

6. There are many "feminisms." One example is ecofeminism. See Heather Eaton and Lois Ann Lorentzen, eds., *Ecofeminism and Globalization: Exploring Culture, Context, and Religion* (Lanham, MD: Rowman & Littlefield, 2003), which deals with "the empirical, the conceptual (cultural/symbolic), and the epistemological" claim, in philosophy and in theology, that women are connected more intimately to nature than men are.

7. See Maggie Humm, *The Dictionary of Feminist Theory*, 2nd ed. (Columbus: Ohio State University, 1995), p. 251.

8. This is exemplified by *Edwards v. A.G. of Canada*, which was discussed in Chapter 8.

9. See Catharine MacKinnon, for example, *Feminism Unmodified: Discourses on Life and Law* (Cambridge, MA: Harvard University, 1987).

10. Simone de Beauvoir, *Le Deuxième Sexe* (Paris: Gallimard, 1949); translated as *The Second Sex* in 1953. A translation is available at www.marxists.org/reference/subject/ethics/de-beauvoir/2nd-sex/index.htm.

11. Betty Friedan, *The Feminine Mystique* (New York: Norton, 1963). Chapter 1 is available at www.h-net.org/~hst203/documents/friedan1.html. Also see Evelyn Reed, "A Study of *The Feminine Mystique*," *International Socialist Review*, 25, no. 1 (Winter 1964): 24–7, available at www.marxists.org/archive/reed-evelyn/1964/friedan-review.htm.

12. See the table in Ann Oakley, ed., *Subject Women* (New York: Pantheon, 1981), pp. 335–8, that sets out a schematic list of tendencies in the women's liberation movement. This table provides a convenient comparison of different positions in the earlier feminist literature.

13. See Carol Gilligan, *In a Different Voice: Psychological Theory and Women's Development* (Cambridge, MA: Harvard University, 1982).

14. See Annette C. Baier, "What Do Women Want in a Moral Theory?" and "The Need for More than Justice," in *Moral Prejudices*, as cited in the suggestions for further reading, pp. 1–17 and 18–32.

15. See Nel Noddings, *Caring: A Feminine Approach to Ethics and Moral Education* (Berkeley: University of California, 1984).

16. This phrase is from Carole Pateman, in "Sex and Power," a review essay on Catharine MacKinnon's *Feminism Unmodified*, in *Ethics* 100, no. 2 (Jan. 1990): 398–407, at p. 398, where she writes that MacKinnon "launches a vigorous attack on liberal approaches to law and feminism and the associated conceptions of objectivity, universality, gender neutrality, and privacy; and presents some firm views on epistemology and the character of feminist theory."

17. Feminist theory has neglected the fact that the historical common law, and its "case-by-case" approach, is notable primarily for its empirical grounding. This explains both Oliver Wendell Holmes' comment that the life of the common law has been "experience" and Roscoe Pound's criticism of "a jurisprudence of conceptions."

18. Catharine MacKinnon, "Introduction: Realizing Law," in *Women's Lives, Men's Laws* (Cambridge, MA: Harvard University, 2000). An excerpt from this introduction is given in the additional online readings listed in the Appendix.

19. See Catharine MacKinnon, *Only Words* (Cambridge, MA: Harvard University, 1993). But her position is inherently controversial. See Ronald Dworkin's review of *Only Words*, "Women and Pornography," in the *New York Review of Books* (21 October 1993), and the rather heated exchange of letters between MacKinnon and Dworkin in "Pornography: An Exchange," *New York Review of Books* (3 March 1994).

20. MacKinnon makes a similar argument in political theory. See *Toward a Feminist Theory of the State* (Cambridge, MA: Harvard University, 1989), where she discusses feminism, Marxism, and the liberal state.

21. The term "third wave" was apparently first used by Rebecca Walker in an article entitled "Becoming the Third Wave," published in *Ms. Magazine* 12, no. 2 (2002): 86–8.

22. See Melody Berger, ed., for example, *We Don't Need another Wave* (Emeryville, CA: Seal, 2006).

23. For a helpful discussion of these terms, see the "riposte" ("Postfeminism vs. the Third Wave") to "Introduction: Waves," by Alison Piepmeier, dated 17 March 2006, at www.electronicbookreview.com/thread/writingpostfeminism/reconfiguredrip2. And see the additional online reading from Margaret Thornton's "'Post-Feminism' in the Legal Academy?," *Feminist Review* 95 (2010): 92–98, in which Thornton argues that post-feminism has merely allowed the "market" to re-entrench "conventional notions of gender."

24. bell hooks, *Ain't I a Woman: Black Women and Feminism*, as cited in the suggestions for further reading.

25. Carolyn Pedwell, "Theorizing 'African' Female Genital Cutting and 'Western' Body Modifications: A Critique of the Continuum and Analogue Approaches," *Feminist Review* 86 (2007): 45–66, at p. 61: "In a historical context in which African women's bodies have been routinely fetishized, pathologized and violated by Westerners, interventions in discourses relating to FGC [Female Genital Cutting] by feminists speaking from Western locations have been perceived by many indigenous African women as ethnocentric and imperialist." Pedwell's account raises legitimate questions, but it is also highly analytic and often loses itself in abstractions.

26. See Máire Ní Mhórdha, "Female Genital Cutting: Traditional Practice or Human Rights Violation? An Exploration of Interpretations of FGC and Its Implications for Development in Africa", *Participatory Development Working Papers* (January 2007). Available at http://asiapacific.anu.edu.au/maapd/papers.

27. See Carrie Hamilton, for example, "The Gender Politics of Political Violence: Women Armed Activists in ETA," *Feminist Review* 86 (2007): 132–48, which studies the popular representation of women in political violence and terrorism. And see Marysia Zalewski, "'I Don't Even Know What Gender Is': A Discussion of the Connections between Gender, Gender Mainstreaming, and Feminist Theory," *Review of International Studies* 36 (2010): 3–27.

28. See Alison Stone, "Essentialism and Anti-essentialism in Feminist Philosophy," *Journal of Moral Philosophy* 1, no. 2 (2004): 135–53.

29. Ann Scales, *Legal Feminism: Activism, Lawyering, and Legal Theory* (New York: New York University, 2006).

30. bell hooks, *Feminist Theory: From Margin to Center* (Boston, MA: South End, 1984). The title refers to the attempt to see the margin and the centre (i.e., the whole) of things, simultaneously.

31. ibid.

32. This is an important trend in the wider literature, but it seems particularly important in the feminist discussion of terrorism. See Menna Khalil, for example, "Guantanamo Detainees: Invisible Subjects, Legal Objects," *Anthropology News* (December 2010), p. 26. And see the excerpt from Margaret Denike in the additional online readings for Chapter 19 listed in the Appendix.

33. The word "jurisprudence" is used very loosely in the feminist literature. But see Patricia Smith, *Feminist Jurisprudence* (New York: Oxford University, 1993).

34. See Allison Stone, for example, "Towards a Genealogical Feminism: A Reading of Judith Butler's Political Thought," *Contemporary Political Theory* 4, no. 1 (2005): 4–24.

35. See Michelle M. Lazar, ed., *Feminist Critical Discourse Analysis: Gender, Power, and Ideology in Discourse*, as cited in the suggestions for further reading.

36. See Kelly Zen-Yie Tsai, "Bonus Track: Real Women I Know," in "Spokenwordlife: A Transcontinental Catalog in Multiple Movements," as cited in the suggestions for further reading.

37. The conservative view is certainly that this has merely helped to dismantle the authority on which the legitimacy of the law rests.

38. Thus Roscoe Pound wrote, in *Justice According to Law* (New Haven, CT: Yale University, 1951), at p. 89, that the strength of judicial reasoning lies in the persistence of this dynamic, which upholds the law "against excitement and clamour." The United States Supreme Court distinguishes between the legal and political concepts of legitimacy in *Planned Parenthood of Southeastern Pa. v. Casey* (1992), 505 U.S. 833, and states, at 866, that "the Court's legitimacy depends on making legally principled decisions."

39. Jeanne L. Schroeder, "Feminism Historicized: Medieval Misogynist Stereotypes in Contemporary Feminist Jurisprudence," *Iowa Law Review* 75 (1989–90): 1135–217, at p. 1137.

40. See the additional online reading from White's *Heracles' Bow*, op. cit.

41. See the additional online reading from Kennedy's *Legal Reasoning*, op. cit.

42. See the additional online reading from Thornton's "'Post-feminism' in the Legal Academy?," op. cit.

Study Questions

1. Do you agree with Kelman's argument that liberalism is "beset" by "irreducible, irremediable, irresolvable" contradictions? Why, why not?

2. Why are "determiniles" significant in CLS? What do they measure?

3. Suppose that you are a second-wave feminist. What is wrong with liberal theory? How does the idea of context come into this?

4. What is essentialism?

5. Feminists often say that the personal is political. How does this come into their analysis of law?

6. James Boyd White has suggested that the law has become a rational machine that can be used to implement virtually any set of policies. This, he says, "has led to a kind of substantive neutrality or emptiness that makes it natural once again to see a connection between modern law and ancient rhetoric."[40] Do you agree? Why, why not? Is the word "emptiness" worrying?

7. Duncan Kennedy has argued that the phenomenological "work" of legal interpretation is missing from the legal positivist account of judicial decision-making.[41] What is he referring to?

8. Margaret Thornton has argued that post-feminism is really a rejection of feminism.[42] Do you agree?

Further Reading

Annette C. Baier, *Moral Prejudices* (Cambridge, MA: Harvard University, 1994).

James Boyle, ed., *Critical Legal Studies* (New York: New York University, 1994).

Virginia Held, "Moral Prejudices: Essays on Ethics," *Philosophy and Phenomenological Research* 57, no. 3 (September 1997): 703–7.

bell hooks, *Ain't I a Woman: Black Women and Feminism* (Boston, MA: South End, 1981).

Michelle M. Lazar, ed., *Feminist Critical Discourse Analysis: Gender, Power, and Ideology in Discourse* (New York: Palgrave Macmillan, 2005).

"Postmodernism and Law: A Symposium," *University of Colorado Law Review* 62 (1991): 439–636. See the foreword by Pierre Schlag and papers by Jennifer Wicke, David Kennedy, Mary Joe Frug, James Boyle, Richard Thomas, and Dale Jamieson.

Kelly Zen-Yie Tsai, "Bonus Track: Real Women I Know," in "Spokenwordlife: A Transcontinental Catalog in Multiple Movements," in *We Don't Need Another Wave*, ed. Melody Berger (Emeryville, CA: Seal, 2006), pp. 277–82.

Part II | *Jurisprudence, Applied Philosophy, and Contemporary Developments*

Part II moves from a historical survey of the major themes in philosophy of law and legal theory to a survey of the common law jurisprudence. There is considerable confusion about the subject matter of jurisprudence, and in spite of the efforts of authors like William Salmond and Roscoe Pound, the concept remains relatively muddy. The initial difficulty is that the fields of philosophy of law and jurisprudence now overlap, and the word "jurisprudence" has acquired so many meanings over the last hundred years that it has become inherently vague.

Some of the confusion in the concept can be traced to the use of the term "analytical jurisprudence" to describe the conventional approach to the study of law, which separates the substantive and procedural aspects in the law schools. This approach comes out of legal positivism but can be traced further back philosophically, to the kind of rational inquiry that we find in the work of figures like Kant. The complaint from more critical theorists is that analytical jurisprudence treats the law as a technical science and focusses on the meaning of terms and the logical structure of the law. This technical focus neglects substantive inquiries and narrows the field of jurisprudence.

It is important to make a clear distinction between jurisprudence and the ordinary discipline of law. This distinction is complicated in the common law by the fact that the practice of law, by its very nature, frequently crosses over into jurisprudence. The best that we can say in the context of the common law tradition is that the field of jurisprudence includes the science of legal decision-making, the study of the conceptual framework of the law, and the study of the general principles that have provided the foundations of the caselaw. Since these principles have been set out in the caselaw, however, the word is also used to refer to the general body of decisions in a particular area. Thus we speak of the "constitutional jurisprudence" or the "criminal jurisprudence."

The More Accurate Way to Explain the Term "Jurisprudence" Is to Review the Tasks Assigned to the Judiciary

The philosophical attempt to define the word "jurisprudence" has been inconclusive, however. The more accurate way to explain the meaning of the word "jurisprudence," at least in the common law tradition, is to review the different tasks assigned to the judiciary in rendering their decisions. It is possible to discern at least three judicial tasks that can be distinguished from each other.

The First Judicial Task Is Adjudicative

The first judicial task is adjudicative. The primary responsibility of trial judges is to decide the specific disputes that come before them. The initial step in this process is to "find" the facts of the case. Judges then consult statutes and caselaw to "find" the law that applies to the facts before them and then apply that law to the facts. This logical process produces the decision in the case. The common law judge's primary responsibility is to reach the right decision in the case before the court. This task takes precedence over the other aspects of the judge's role.

The Second Judicial Task Is to Develop the Jurisprudence

The second judicial task is to develop the jurisprudence. This task consists of setting out the fundamental framework of the law and developing the rules and tests that are needed to perform the first judicial task. Although this exercise has moral and social underpinnings, and takes the law into policy issues, it also has a mechanical side. The ultimate purpose of the exercise in jurisprudence is to create the logical machinery that produces the decision in specific cases.

The jurisprudential inquiry is fundamentally theoretical, and it is general rather than particular. The common law jurisprudence has been described as a loosely fitting set of clothes: there is considerable room for movement in it. It has also been said that the common law—and therefore the jurisprudence—follows the facts. This is because the common law jurisprudence has been developed on a case-by-case basis, in answer to the questions raised by the facts in specific cases. The jurisprudential task is therefore subordinated to the needs of adjudication.

The task of developing the jurisprudence is nevertheless an inevitable part of the judicial role in the common law tradition. Although individual trial judges may develop a reputation for their skill in developing the jurisprudence, this task is usually assigned to the appellate courts. It is the appellate courts that have the responsibility for maintaining the integrity of the legal framework in which legal decisions are made and correcting any errors of law in the decisions of the trial courts.

The Third Judicial Task Is Constitutional

The third task is to decide any constitutional issues that arise in a case. This task requires that judges decide many issues regarding private rights and the powers of the executive and administrative branches of government. It is the special responsibility of the judiciary to determine where the limits of political government lie. Such decisions raise many issues regarding the relationship between the legal and political orders. The jurisprudential and the constitutional tasks naturally overlap, and the prominence of a written constitution in Canada and in the United States has encouraged the development of a more active jurisprudence.

The Common Law Jurisprudence Is the Product of a Process of Discovery

The character of the common law derives from the fact that the judiciary have the principal role in developing the jurisprudence. They do so, moreover, by a process of discovery, which "finds" the relevant law in practice and precedent. This process has its roots in tribal practice and came into the common law because the royal judges (the common law judges) were expected to decide cases in accordance with local customs. This convention required that judges investigate the customary law and consider the general principles on which it rests.

The Common Law Jurisprudence Has an Empirical Character

The civil law system provided the model for the legal systems in continental Europe. This model made its way into New France, and the civil law of Quebec, which is based on the *Code Civile* and the *Code de Procédure*. Most of the legal systems in the world are modelled on the civil system of law.

The civil law system is based on the idea that the law has a rational framework, which exists in some abstract sense, outside any investigation into the facts of a case. This idea is Cartesian and implicitly awards the rational framework of the law a more ontological status. The civil system holds that the law is the product of an abstract rational enterprise, which finds expression in written codes. These codes provide a set of categories for the analysis of human events and determine, *a priori*, what the legal consequences of an act will be. In the civil law system, the essential responsibility of a judge is to find the precise provision that the case falls under in the relevant *Code* and apply it. The foundations of the common law, on the other hand, can be found in the facts of individual cases. The epistemology of the common law has its roots in materialism, rather than idealism, and is celebrated for its empirical character. This empirical character places the highest value on human experience. Since a judge deduces the relevant principles of jurisprudence from the decisions made in similar cases, the general outlines of the common law are inherently vague. This lack of specificity has its advantages. Although the common law suffers from a certain degree of improvisation, it is a supple system of law, with remarkable flexibility.

The Individual Chapters in Part II Review the Major Aspects of the Caselaw

The chapters in Part II review the elements in the jurisprudence that give the different areas of the common law their fundamental structure. Since it is difficult to understand the development of the jurisprudence outside its historical context, these chapters involve the same genealogical approach adopted in Part I. Although the review of the jurisprudence is far from comprehensive, it is enough to give the reader a good grasp of the fundamental framework of the common law. The different chapters also consider a number of moral and practical issues that arise in applying abstract concepts to the situations that actually give rise to litigation.

Chapters 14 and 15 deal with the private law, the law of the persons, which covers the legal relations between private persons. These chapters set out the fundamental legal framework of the civil law. This part of the law is the oldest part of the common law, which governs the formal relations between the members of society who have legal persons. It is our membership in society that gives us legal persons, which possesses rights and liabilities.

The focus then turns to the public law. Chapter 16 reviews the development of the criminal law. The criminal law is the most prominent branch of the public law and is more accurately seen as penal law, which prescribes punishments. The criminal law has political origins, however, and is associated with the development of the state and central government. This development resulted in the designation of certain forms of conduct as wrongs against the King, who had charge of the public interest. Chapter 17 deals more specifically with punishment.

Chapter 18 deals with the other major branch of the public law, and the third judicial task, which is constitutional. It is this aspect of the judicial role that has attracted the most attention in contemporary legal theory, probably because the liberal literature places a premium on our personal freedoms. Many of the issues that arise in this context concern the scope of the criminal law. Although it leaves out many issues, it is frequently said that the constitutional law governs the relations between government and persons.

The last chapter deals with current issues in the jurisprudence. The chapter focusses on the slow emergence of a global system of justice. This system of justice is predicated on the introduction of a binding legal regime in the international arena, which places the state and political forms of government under legal constraints. There is no doubt that the formulation of a compulsory law in the international realm represents the most significant theoretical development in the contemporary law, which has begun to restore the historical ascendancy of the law over the political order.

Further Reading

William S. Holdsworth, *A History of English Law*, 16 vols. (London and Methuen: Sweet and Maxwell, 1966).

S.F.C. Milsom, *Historical Foundations of the Common Law*, 2nd ed. (London: Butterworths, 1981).

George Whitecross Paton, *A Text-Book of Jurisprudence* (Oxford: Clarendon, 1946). Available at http:// heinonline.org/.

Roscoe Pound, *Jurisprudence*. 5 vols. (St. Paul, MN: West Pub. Co., 1959). Available at http://heinonline.org/.

John William Salmond, *Jurisprudence*, 7th ed. (London: Sweet and Maxwell, 1924). Available at http:// heinonline.org/.

14 Private Law: The Civil Law Is Based on the Rights of the Person

Readings

- Adapted from "The Legal Concept of the Person: A Relational Account," by Paul Groarke
- From "Human Rights: Legitimizing a Recent Concept," by Elaine Pagels
- From "What Is Private Property?," by Jeremy Waldron

Review

- Review the reading from *Commentaries on the Laws of England*, by William Blackstone, given in Chapter 4, on pp. 77–79.
- Review the reading from *Edwards v. A.G. of Canada*, [1930] A.C. 124 (P.C.), given in Chapter 8, on pp. 179–182.

Legal rights have extended, historically, only to individuals who have been recognized as members of society. These individuals have legal "persons." Common law lawyers refer to the law that governs the formal relations between persons as the "civil law." Blackstone bases this part of the law on the rights of the person. This notion of a right needs to be distinguished from the notion that makes its way into ethical and political debates. The following chapter reviews the origins of our legal rights, the legal concept of the person, and the concept of private property.

⚹ Readings ⚹

Adapted from Paul Groarke, "The Legal Concept of the Person: A Relational Account," *The Heythrop Journal* 51, no. 1 (March 2010): 298–313.

The right to address a legal body and claim a legal remedy is called standing. This right has been restricted, historically, to individuals who have a legal person. The history of the law is accordingly a history of persons.

Any survey of the caselaw quickly establishes that the legal person is a fictional entity, to which the law assigns rights and obligations. As Westel Willoughby wrote, in 1924, "the legal personality of the so-called natural person is as artificial as the personality of a corporation":

> In both cases the character or attribute of personality is but a creation of the jurist's mind,—a mere conception which he finds it useful to employ in order to give logical coherence to his thought.[1]

The legal person merely functions as a placeholder—much like a checker in a game of checkers—in the scheme of formal relations that make up the law. It does not exist outside our relations with other persons.

As a simple historical matter, however, the derivation of the rights of the person lies in our membership in human society rather than our status as human beings. This explains the real significance of documents like the *Universal Declaration of Human Rights* and the *International Covenant on Civil and Political Rights*, which implicitly recognize that every independent human being is a member of society.[2] From the perspective of the legal person, these documents accordingly grant everyone the standing needed to pursue a legal remedy. It follows that it is our membership in human society, rather than some set of free-standing rights, that has become inalienable.

The Word "Person" Originally Referred to a Mask

Thomas Gilby sets out the etymology of the word "person" in a book on Thomas Aquinas:

> The term *persona* originally meant the part a man played on the stage, the face, or mask, he showed the world, the figure he cut, the personage in which he appeared: thus Sabellius said that the Person of the Father was the Son in that he was born of Mary, and the Holy Ghost in that he sanctifies us. Afterwards, it acquired a legal sense and indicated free status, the man *sui juris et non alieni* [i.e., who has the capacity, unlike the foreigner, to make legal decisions] or of official standing, thus the *persona publica*.[3]

The idea is that a member of society has a public or official identity, which performs his social role.

There is a grammatical confusion in both the law and the academic literature, and it is quite incorrect, theoretically, to describe a man or woman, for example, as a "person." The correct statement is that a man or a woman has a legal person. Conceptually, it is this person—rather than the individual behind it—that has legal relations with other persons.

The Legal Concept of the Legal Person Was Developed in the Context of Ownership

The common law concept of the person seems to have evolved more specifically in the context of ownership. The second edition of *Jowitt's Dictionary of English Law* puts the matter in this way:

> In jurisprudence, a person is . . . capable of having rights and of being liable to duties, while a thing is the subject of rights and duties.[4]

There have been cases that seem to escape such a simple classification. One example is human slaves, which seem to have been endowed with a legal person for some purposes and seen as "things" for others.[5]

The Common Law Has Traditionally Considered Animals Things

The case of animals, which have generally been classified as property in the common law, provides one example of this distinction. Animals are things and do not have a legal person. It follows that an animal has no standing in the courts. As a result, animals have enjoyed rights only indirectly, by virtue of the owner's rights. There is nevertheless a history of statutory protection, which confers at least some of the benefits of human society on animals.[6]

The standard doctrine does not explain the earlier history of the law. As Paul Schiff Berman writes,

> Records indicate that trials of animals took place throughout Europe and elsewhere from the ninth through the nineteenth centuries. Individual animals were tried (usually for killing human beings) in secular courts according to common law precedents dating back to the Book of Exodus.[7]

These examples are anomalous. There is nevertheless an idea in these cases that an animal may participate enough in the moral and religious aspects of social life to acquire an *ad hoc* legal person in an appropriate case. This acknowledges that an animal may be a member of society, whose relations with the other members of society can be subjected to legal scrutiny.

Gary L. Francione traces the idea that animals are property to the ethical position adopted by Western philosophers. René Descartes argued that our moral obligations do not extend to animals, who are nothing more than "machines." Emmanuel Kant argued that "animals are merely a means to human ends."[8] Sue Donaldson and Will Kymlicka have written that many of the arguments in the current debate about animal rights "are eerily similar to arguments about human slavery."[9] This tends to overlook some of the practical problems that arise in this context, and the question whether animals have the intellectual and linguistic resources to participate fully in the trial process.

The emerging view is that persons who have the custody of a "companion animal" should be seen as guardians rather than simple owners.[10] The usual analogy is with children, who have a legal person, albeit one with a very restricted legal capacity in civil matters. There are many ways, however, in which mature animals exercise a much higher degree of autonomy than a child and are therefore in a better position to make decisions.

A Human Being Acquires a Legal Person When It Acquires Social Rights and Duties

The idea of human rights is at least potentially misleading. The history of the law makes it clear that a human being acquires a legal person only when it acquires social rights and duties. This is evident in the sixth edition of Bouvier's *Law Dictionary*, published in 1856, which states that a human being is a man, whether he is a member of society or not. A person, on the other hand, "is a man considered according to the rank he holds in society, with all the rights that this entitles him, and all the duties it imposes."[11] The rights that a human being with a legal person enjoys accordingly derive from his membership in human society rather than his existence as a natural individual.

Thus the Foetus Does Not Have a Legal Person

This is illustrated by the caselaw on the foetus. In *Tremblay v. Daigle* [1989] 2 S.C.R. 530, for example, the father of an unborn child attempted to file a suit on its behalf, in order to prevent the mother from seeking an abortion. The Supreme Court of Canada held that the foetus cannot be described as a juridical person under the law and legally remains a part of its mother.[12]

The court in *Daigle* commented on the difference between the legal, philosophical, and scientific understandings of a person. Scientific arguments, for example, are not determinative:

> The task of properly classifying a foetus in law and in science are different pursuits. Ascribing personhood to a foetus in law is a fundamentally normative task. It results in the recognition of rights and duties—a matter which falls outside the concerns of scientific classification.[13]

The legal inquiry raises social and practical concerns that do not arise in the metaphysical or scientific inquiry.[14] There are many complexities. It is possible to file a suit on behalf of a child, for example, for injuries that it sustained while *en ventre sa mère*.[15] These are injuries that it suffered before it became a person. The response to any logical objection is apparently that it is the child, rather than the foetus, who enjoys these rights, and only after its birth.

The Legal Person Extends Beyond the Physical Limits of the Individual

The social character of the legal concept of the person expresses itself in its immaterial aspects. In *Johnson v. Bradstreet Co.*, 13 S.E. 250 (1889; S.C.Ga.), for example, a court held that libel was properly characterized as an injury to the person. At 251, the court wrote:

> Person is a broad term, and legally includes, not only the physical body and members, but also every bodily sense and personal attribute, among which is the reputation a man has acquired. Reputation is a sort of right to enjoy the good opinion of others, and is capable of growth and real existence, as an arm or leg.

The court went on to hold that the legal person survives the death of the individual. An estate is therefore entitled to sue someone who libels the deceased for injury to his person.[16]

The legal person may also include other physical people. The law of Texas, for example, considers an assault against an individual's spouse or child an offence against his person.[17] These kinds of examples demonstrate that the legal person is a conceptual entity, governed by social considerations, which may or may not coincide with the physical individual.

"Artificial" Entities May Have Legal Persons

Nor is there anything in the legal concept of the person that restricts it to natural beings. The law recognizes artificial persons like corporations or estates, which attract a wide range of rights and duties. Canon 113 of the *Code of Canon Law*, for example, states that the Catholic Church and the Apostolic See "have the status of a moral person by divine disposition."[18]

In *Wilmot v. London Road Car Co.*, [1908–10] All E.R. Rep. 908, Sir Herbert Cozens-Hardy M.R.[19] cited Coke's *Institutes* as authority for the proposition that the word "person" extends to any identity that possesses the capacity to own and transfer property. Fletcher Moulton L.J. took note of the role played by limited companies in business affairs:

> the gradual change in the organisation of societies which has been going on for the last century whereby more and more of the business of the country is done by corporations and less and less by private individuals, has brought with it an increased tendency to use the word person as including all those who can perform the duties of persons with regard to property.[20]

The law essentially assumes that there is an individual behind the person, who has the volitional capacity to make decisions.

The Government Has a Legal Person

The later common law traditionally held that the sovereign is the source of the law, and therefore beyond its reach. This rule has seen considerable erosion over time, however. In *Stanley v. Schwalby* (1893), 147 U.S. 508, for example, the United States Supreme Court held that the word "person" in a statute of limitations included the United States, "as a body politic and corporate."

Many of the technical issues that arise in this context relate to the construction of statutes. In *Vermont Agency of Natural Resources v. United States* (2000), 529 U.S. 765, for example, the same court held that the term "person" in the *False Claims Act* included states, in spite of the presumption against such a reading. This is explained by public policy considerations. Judges are obliged to consult the purpose of legislation in interpreting its provisions. A Canadian court has held, on a similar basis, that a government and the citizens they represent qualify as a "person" under the *Canadian Bill of Rights*. The right to a fair hearing in any litigation accordingly extends to government parties.[21]

Notes

1. Westel W. Willoughby, *The Fundamental Concepts of Public Law* (Macmillan: New York, 1924), p. 34.

2. There are similar developments in other areas. This is apparent in documents like the *Universal Declaration of Human Responsibilities* and the work of Hans Küng and others in compiling the *Declarations of the Religions for a Global Ethic*. See the websites of the Center for Global Ethics (http://globalethic.org) and the InterAction Council at (www.interactioncouncil.org).

3. Thomas Gilby, *The Political Thought of Thomas Aquinas* (Chicago: University of Chicago, 1958), p. 238.

4. William Allen Jowitt, Clifford Walsh, and John McDonald Burke, *Jowitt's Dictionary of English Law*, 2nd ed. (London: Sweet & Maxwell, 1977)

5. So that Willoughby declares, op. cit., at p. 33, that a legal person may "be treated as a thing when brought into relation to other legal persons. For example, a slave so far as he is treated as the property of his master, or a serf, so far as he is bound to serve his superior, is viewed as a thing." And see Bouvier's *A Law Dictionary*, as cited *infra*, which states that slaves "are sometimes ranked not with persons but with things."

6. This is true, even for a cat who talks: *Miles v. City Council of Augusta*, (1983) 710 F. 2d 1542 (11th Cir.), at note 5: "This court will not hear a claim that Blackie's right to free speech has been infringed. First, although Blackie arguably possesses a very unusual ability, he cannot be considered a 'person' and is therefore not protected by the Bill of Rights."

7. Paul Schiff Berman, "An Observation and a Strange but True 'Tale': What Might the Historical Trials of Animals Tell Us about the Transformative Potential of Law in American Culture?," *Hastings Law Journal* 52 (November 2000): 123–78, at p. 127. And see E.P. Evans, *The Criminal Prosecution and Capital Punishment of Animals* (New York: E.P. Dutton, 1906), which lists over two hundred cases of animal trials between 824 and 1906.

8. See Gary L. Francione, "Animals—Property or Persons?," in *Animal Rights: Current Debates and New Direction*, ed. Cass R. Sunstein and Martha C. Nussbaum (Oxford: Oxford University, 2004), pp. 108–42.

9. Sue Donaldson and Will Kymlicka, "The Moral Ark," *Queen's Quarterly* 114, no. 2 (Summer 2007): 187–205, at p. 190.

10. See Susan Hankin, "Not a Living Room Sofa: Changing the Legal Status of Companion Animals," *Rutgers Journal of Law & Public Policy* 4, no. 2 (Winter 2007): 314–410, at pp. 371–5. And see the decision in *Vallance v. Naaykens*, 2001 BCSC 656 (CanLII), where a contract for the sale of a dog characterized the sale as an "adoption."

11. John Bouvier, *A Law Dictionary*, rev. 6th ed. (1856). Available at www.constitution.org/bouv/bouvier.htm.

12. This explains why the offence of procuring a miscarriage has not been considered homicide. See *R. v. Sullivan* (1988), 65 C.R. (3d) 256 (B.C.C.A.), for example, which dealt with whether a midwife who delivered a stillborn child could be convicted of criminal negligence causing the death of a person. The view was apparently different in the early Middle Ages.

13. *Tremblay v. Daigle* [1989] 2 S.C.R. 530, pp. 552–3.

14. See *Winnipeg Child and Family Services v. D.F.G.* [1997] 3 S.C.R. 925, where the same court observed that the position in the common law and civil law traditions is the same.

15. A child may sue its mother in negligence for the injuries that it suffered in a motor vehicle accident during her pregnancy. Though the majority of the Supreme Court of Canada recently disagreed in *Dobson (Litigation Guardian of) v. Dobson* [1999] 2 S.C.R. 753.

16. Though this has been changed by legislation in many jurisdictions.

17. The *Texas Penal Code* states that assault can be committed by "intentionally, knowingly, or recklessly causing bodily injury to another, including the person's spouse." See *Beltran v. City of El Paso*, 2004 U.S. App. LEXIS 7234 (Fifth Cir.).

18. E. Caparros, M. Theriault, and J. Thorn, *Code of Canon Law Annotated: Latin-English edition of the* Code of Canon Law *and English-language translation of the 5th Spanish-language edition of the commentary* (Montreal: Wilson & Lafleur, 1993).

19. Master of the Rolls.

20.   *Wilmot v. London Road Car Co.*, [1908–10] All E.R. Rep. 908, p. 913.

21.   To hold otherwise would make a "mockery" of the system of justice. See *Government of the Northwest Territories v. Public Service Alliance of Canada and Canadian Human Rights Commission*, [2001] 3 FC 566 (F.C.A.) at para. 55.

From Elaine Pagels, "Human Rights: Legitimizing a Recent Concept," *Annals of the American Academy of Political and Social Science* 442 (March 1979): 57–62.

Advocates of human rights policy claim not only that there are human rights but also that these rights have universal applicability. What—if anything—justifies this claim? . . .

[Consider] Condorcet's[1] observation that "the notion of human rights was absent from the legal conceptions of the Romans and Greeks; this seems to hold equally of the Jewish, Chinese, and all other ancient civilizations that have since come to light." . . . Much more common and far more universal, in historical and geographical terms, is the opposite idea: that society confers upon its members whatever rights, privileges, or exemptions they enjoy. According to this pattern, ultimate value derives from the social order. . . .

Some have suggested that the idea of human rights can be traced to the ancient code of Hammurabi which ensures, for example, certain legal protections against mutilation and torture. But they fail to acknowledge that these exemptions applied only to aristocrats: lower class people and slaves had no such exemptions. The structure of the Hammurabi code indicates that these "rights," such as they were, derived entirely from society. . . .

In Rome . . . [o]nly Roman citizens, a small percentage of the population, had specific rights, and these were minimal indeed: a citizen could not be tortured or condemned without a trial; if condemned to death, the citizen had the privilege of being beheaded, rather than tortured to death in the public arena, as noncitizens were. Again, this legal system is based on the premise that rights are conferred—or withheld—by the state.

The pattern is not just ancient history: it was also the dominant form of political theory in Christian Europe since the fourth century . . . [and] has prevailed in nonwestern countries as well. Among the tribes of Australia, Africa, North and South America, tribal hierarchy and tribal custom are understood to be sanctioned by the divine order or nature. They allow no recourse for the individual—or individual "rights"—outside of the tribal structure.

A similar pattern has prevailed for centuries in Hindu societies of India, Cambodia, Nepal, and in Pakistan. . . . The caste system, endorsed as the reflection of that order, fixed the ranks of society into the three upper classes, defined by their privileges; the fourth class consisted of people who maintained minimal rights; and below these were the "untouchables," who remained outside of society and outside any system of rights. . . .

To this list we might add Marxist societies, which invert the religious pattern and claim that the social order reflects inviolable natural laws, analogous to the laws of biology and physics. Here again, value resides in the social order. It makes no sense, in this context, to speak of individual rights prior to participation in society. . . .

Note

1.   Editor's note: The Marquis de Condorcet (1743–1794), also known as Nicolas de Condorcet, was a French "humanist" and political theorist who played a major role in the French Revolution. He has been seen by later authors as a champion of natural rights.

From Jeremy Waldron, "What Is Private Property?," *Oxford Journal of Legal Studies* 5, no. 3 (Winter 1985): 313–49.

Private Property Is Made Up of Bundles of Rights

Why has private property been thought indefinable? Consider the relation between a person (call her Susan) and an object—say, a motor car—generally taken to be *her* private property. The layman thinks of this as a two-place relation of *ownership* between a person and a thing: Susan owns that Porsche.

But the lawyer tells us that legal relations cannot exist between people and Porsches, because Porsches cannot have rights or duties or be bound by or recognize rules. The legal relation involved must be a relation between *persons*—between Susan and her neighbours, say, or Susan and the police, or Susan and everyone else. But when we ask what this relation is, we find that the answer is not at all simple.

With regard to Susan's Porsche, there are all sorts of legal relations between Susan and other people. Susan has a legal liberty to use it [the car] in certain ways; for example, she owes no duty to anyone to refrain from putting her houseplants in it. But that is true only of *some* of the ways that the car could (physically) be used. She is not at liberty to drive it on the footpath or to drive it anywhere at a speed faster than 70 MPH. Indeed, she is not at liberty to drive it at all without a licence from the authorities.

As well as her liberties, Susan also has certain rights. She has what Hohfeld[1] called a "claim-right" against everyone else—her neighbours, her friends, the local car thief, everyone in the community—that they should not use her Porsche without her permission. But Susan also owes certain duties to other people in relation to the vehicle. She must keep it in good order and see that it does not become a nuisance to her neighbours. She is liable to pay damages if it rolls into her neighbour's fence. These rights, liberties, and duties are the basic stuff of ownership.

But legal relations can be changed, and, certainly in our society, if Susan owns the Porsche, then *she* is in a position to change them. She has the power to sell it or give it to somebody else, in which case all the legal relations change . . . But she may also, in certain circumstances, have her own legal position altered in relation to the Porsche: she is liable to have the car seized in execution of a judgement summons for debt. And so on. . . .

Private property, then, is . . . not a simple relationship at all. It involves a complex bundle of relations, which differ considerably in their character and effect. If that were all, there would be no problem of definition: private property would be a bundle of rights, but if it remained constant for all or most of the cases that we want to describe as private property, the bundle as a whole could be defined in terms of its contents. But, of course, it does not remain constant, and that is where the difficulties begin.

Each of the legal relations involved in Susan's ownership of the Porsche is not only distinct, but in principle separable, from each of the others. It is possible, for example, that someone has a liberty to use an automobile without having any of the other rights or powers which Susan has. Because they are distinct and separable, the component relations may be taken apart and reconstituted in different combinations, so that we may get smaller bundles of the rights that were involved originally in this large bundle we called ownership. . . .

Salmond Argued That We Own Rights Rather Than Property

[W]e should consider Salmond's[2] well-known insistence that it is improper to talk about the ownership of things and that we ought to talk about the ownership of *rights* instead. Salmond's argument seems to be based on considerations of consistency: it is inconsistent to talk sometimes of owning rights and at other times of owning things.[3] . . . There is some merit in this. . . .

[But a] better approach is the following. To say that a person *owns X* is to say that he is vested by the law with certain rights in respect of *X*. He does not own the rights, rather he *has* them, and because he has them he owns the object in question. . . .

The Concept of Property Is Based on the Right of Allocation

Private Property Belongs to Some Individual

The organizing idea of a private property system is that, in principle, each resource *belongs* to some individual.[4] At its simplest and most abstract, the idea can be explained in the following way. Imagine that the material resources available for use in a society have been divided into discrete parcels (call each parcel an *object*), and that each object has the name of an individual member of the society attached to it. . . .

In a private property system, a rule is laid down that, in the case of each object, the individual person whose name is attached to that object is to determine [i.e., allocate] how the object shall be used and by whom. His decision is to be upheld by the society as final. . . .

Collective Property Belongs to Society as a Whole

In a system of collective property, the problem of allocation is solved by the application of a social rule that access to and the use of material resources in particular cases are to be determined by reference to the collective interests of society as a whole. If there is any question about how or by whom resources like land, industrial plant, housing, and so on are to be used, then those questions are to be resolved by favouring the use which is most conducive to the collective social interest. . . .

Common Property Is Available to Everyone

In a system of common property, rules governing access to and control of material resources are organized on the basis that *each* resource is in principle available for the use of *every* member alike. . . . Our familiarity with this idea . . . stems . . . from our familiarity with the way in which the allocation of certain resources are handled in almost all societies: parks and national reserves are the best example. . . .

The Legal Categories of Property Are More Complex

As categories of social, economic, or political science, it is clear that these ideas of a private property system, a collective property system, and a common property system are very much "ideal typic" categories. It is clear also that, to quote [Max] Weber, "none of these ideal types . . . is usually to be found in historical cases in 'pure' form." In Britain, for example, some industries (like British Leyland) are collectively owned, while others (like Times Newspapers) are privately owned. In the Soviet Union, the most recent constitution makes explicit provision for the private ownership of houses and smallholdings, even while it insists that the land and basic means of production are the property of the state. . . .

This means that our ideal types of property system are somewhat difficult to apply in the real world. We can identify . . . [a number of difficulties here. One is that no] society, whatever its ideological predilections, can avoid the fact that some resources are more amenable to some types of property rule than others. In the case of sunlight and air, for example, it seems hard to envisage anything like private property. Common property here seems the "obvious" solution: people simply make use of these resources as and when they want to. For other resources, like clothes, toothbrushes, and food for the table, it is hard to see how they could be regulated except on a private property basis. Finally there are resources like highways and artillery pieces, over which most societies have found it necessary to exercise collective control. . . .

Even in the face of these and other complications, I think it is still possible to say, of most actual societies, whether their property system is one of common, collective, or private property. Partly this is a matter of the society's self-understanding. In Britain, despite considerable industrial nationalization, there remains a feeling that property rules are still organized primarily around the idea of private ownership. In the Soviet Union, by contrast, . . . the official ideology and self-understanding of the society points firmly towards state or collective property as the dominant property idea. . . .

Notes

1.   Editor's note: Wesley Newcomb Hohfeld (1879–1918), the author of *Fundamental Legal Conceptions, as Applied in Judicial Reasoning and Other Legal Essays*, ed. Walter Wheeler Cook (New Haven, CT: Yale University, 1919), which Waldron subsequently cites.

2.   Editor's note: John William Salmond (1862–1924) was an influential professor of law and judge whose work in legal theory included *Essays in Jurisprudence and Legal History* (1891), *The First Principles of Jurisprudence* (1893), and *Jurisprudence, or the Theory of the Law* (1902), published under the titles *Jurisprudence* and *Salmond on Jurisprudence* in later editions.

3.   Waldron's note: [John W. Salmond] *Salmond on Jurisprudence*, 7th edn (London: Sweet and Maxwell, 1924), 279.

4.   Editor's note: i.e., some person—some individual who has a legal person.

✷ Discussion ✦

The branch of the common law that deals with the relations between private persons is called the civil law. It is the civil law that establishes the private rights and duties that connect individual persons to each other. In order to understand the civil law, we accordingly need to understand what a "person" is, in law, and then investigate the rights and duties that attach to persons.

The word "person" originally referred to the mask or face worn by the performers in a play. Legally, it came to signify the public face of someone who is performing some official role. We still distinguish between a judge, for example, who is acting in an official capacity and the judge's private person. This separation of private and public identities is essential in a legal context: legal rights and duties vest in the person, who is obliged to perform the individual's legal duties. Over time, the word "person" acquired a second, opposing sense. The second sense of the word, which derives from the theological inquiry into the person of Christ, refers to the private, innermost identity of the individual, which exists privately. This is now the predominant association of the word, which comes into play when we speak of the "personal" choices in our lives.

The legal person is associated with the public use of the term. In many ways, the word "persona" now seems more fitting in this context, since the legal person is a distinct personality, which can be separated from the physical individual who possesses it. This is often lost, in the modern use of the term. It is usually said, for example, that *Edwards v. A.G. of Canada*, which was discussed in Chapter 8, recognized that women are persons. This recognition is at least grammatically misleading, given the dual meaning of "person," and merely reflects the fact that the law sees only the legal person, and not the individual behind that person.

The Legal Person Functions like a Placeholder in a Game

It is difficult to understand what the legal person is, however, without a basic idea of the mechanics of the legal system. However serious its consequences, the civil law can be thought of, mechanically, as a kind of game, with predetermined outcomes. It is the law that provides the rules of the game and determines the consequences that flow from the moves taken by the players. Like other games, moreover, the law creates its own reality, separate from the reality in which the players live.

This analogy helps to clarify the role played by the legal person in the legal system. If the law is a game, with defined moves, it is evident that each of the players in the game needs a marker or a placeholder. The legal person provides a placeholder for the individual players in the game and identifies each individual's location vis-à-vis the other players. In a more complex game, the placeholder may take the form of a figure or a character that represents a player in the game. The role assigned to different figures or characters may differ, and it is tempting to see the law as a virtual reality that populates the legal representation of society with legal persons.

The analogy with a game is also helpful because the civil law, like a game, carves out an area of decision-making that can be separated from the rest of our lives. This area of decision-making is governed by legal rules, which provide a conceptual framework in which we can enter into relations with other people. The distinguishing feature of these relations, unlike other moral and social relations, is that they are recognized and enforced by the courts. For the purposes of legal analysis, these relations exist conceptually, like the relations between figures or characters in a game.

The analogy with a game explains some of the features of the legal person. Like a placeholder or a character in a game, the legal person has its own existence and can be separated from the individual whom it represents. In itself, then, the person is a legal and social fiction, which exists abstractly, as and where it is needed, for the purpose of determining legal rights and duties. The legal person accordingly continues to exist, for example, after the death of the physical individual who possesses the person.

The Law Allows the Legal Person to Collect Perquisites

The law endows the legal person with attributes, in much the same way that a game might endow a figure or character with specific abilities or powers. These attributes allow the legal person to collect certain perquisites, much like the perquisites that individual players might collect in playing a game. It is the placeholder, however, rather than the player, that has the right to exercise these perquisites. In much the same way, the legal perquisites collected by an individual recognized by the law attach to the legal person rather than the individual who possesses the person. As a result, these perquisites have been seen literally as limbs or growths that are physically attached to the legal person by a legal ligament.

There are many examples. The common law holds that an individual's reputation is like a living thing that attaches to the legal person. An injury to an individual's reputation is accordingly a personal injury, like a wound or a physical injury, which harms the person. The historical rights of the person included the right to enjoy one's marriage without interference from other persons. This right gave rise to common law torts like "alienation of affection" and "criminal conversation," which protected the relationship between spouses. The historical rationale was nevertheless that the marriage and its comforts had become part of the legal person. The loss of these comforts accordingly gave rise to a legal action for injury to the person of the plaintiff.

The Attributes of the Legal Person Give Rise to Rights and Duties

The analogy of the game also explains the mechanics of a lawsuit. From the perspective of litigation, rights that provide the basis of the civil law. The legal person has legal duties, in addition, and acquires liabilities. In most cases, at least, rights and liabilities are the inverse of each other, since it is one person's right that gives rise to another person's liability.

An Individual without a Legal Person Has No Legal Rights

The important point in the context of theory is that legal rights and duties are attached to legal persons rather than the individuals who possess those persons. It follows that an individual without a legal person has no "standing" in court and exists quite literally outside the law. Such individuals may have moral and even social rights, but they have no legal rights and cannot assert their rights in a court.

The analogy of a game helps to explain such circumstances. In order to play in a game, an individual must have a placeholder that can take an active part in the game and collect the perquisites that it awards. From an internal perspective in the game, it is the place-holders or the characters, rather than the players, that participate in the game and enjoy its fortunes and vicissitudes. An individual without a legal person is in the same position as an individual without a placeholder or a character and stands outside the game.

The issue of standing historically refers to the right of an individual to appear before the court and request a remedy. This right belongs to the legal person. Thus, Blackstone writes that a man who enters a monastery—and renounces his civil rights and duties—is considered dead in the civil law. He cannot sue under a contract and he cannot be sued. His estate passes to his heirs at the time he enters holy orders in the same way that it would if he had physically died. It is not the monk who dies, of course, but his legal person, and with his legal person, his legal rights and duties. This does not mean that the monk has no private life or, more importantly, no social life; it is rather that he lives these lives outside the law.

An Individual Must Be a Member of Society to Qualify for a Legal Person

It follows that the first question that we need to ask in studying the civil law is relatively simple: who has a legal person? The answer to such a question is pivotal, since it will determine who has legal rights. The common law leaves the question to be decided by individual judges, on a case-by-case basis. This approach requires that a judge consider the exigencies before the court before making a decision.

There are nevertheless a number of conditions that determine whether an individual qualifies for a legal person. Since the law regulates our social relations, the underlying issue is whether society recognizes that the individual is a member of society. There are logical reasons behind this requirement, since the historical position has always been that the law is there to regulate the relations within society. It is evident, historically, that people in earlier times placed enormous significance on their membership in society, precisely because the benefit and protection of the law extended only to the members of society.

This understanding can be traced back to our tribal ancestors and manifested itself most dramatically in the institution of outlawry, which made its way into the common law. Like the monk, the outlaw was no longer a member of civil society and had no legal person. The difference is that the monk was a member of a religious society and had the identity and legal status that went with it. The outlaw lived in the legal wilderness, outside the law and human society altogether, at the mercy of chance. It has been said that the killing of an outlaw was a justifiable homicide, but the more accurate view is that the law did not take notice of the death, since the outlaw had no legal person.

An Individual Must Also Have an Official or Formal Role in Society

The caselaw suggests that the fact that individuals are members of society, however, may not be enough in itself to give them legal persons. It is only the members of society who have the capacity to enter into formal relationships who have legal persons. This is a matter full of degrees and gradations. A child, for example, does not possess a legal person in many areas of the civil law. A child therefore cannot enter into an autonomous contract or insist on its performance. The word "formal" in this context refers to those members of society who have something akin to an official status and can make decisions that are recognizably public. It is impossible to say what this consists of with any certainty, however, and the question whether an individual is a formal member of society can be answered only in the context of the precise circumstances of each case. It nevertheless appears that this idea, historically, comes from the fact that it was the representatives of families rather than individuals who possessed a legal person, owned property, and conducted public business. The question of standing that naturally arose in such a situation was accordingly whether an individual had the capacity to enter into agreements that bound the family.[1]

An Individual Must Also Have the Capacity to Make Binding Decisions

It follows from this formal requirement that the notion of an individual in the law has never been restricted to a discrete human individual. In point of fact, it is the individualism in modern society and the willingness of contemporary courts to invest discrete individuals with legal persons that is historically significant. This can be seen in the analogy of a game: there is no obvious reason that a group of people cannot be given a placeholder in a game and play alongside individuals who have obtained placeholders of their own.

The fundamental historical issue in deciding whether an individual or collective entity has a legal person has very little to do with its inherent individuality. The idea that an "artificial" identity like a university, a business corporation, or an estate has a legal personality is based on the recognition that such entities can enter into contracts and other binding obligations. The caselaw frequently refers to the "directing mind" or "will" of the corporation.

The judicial answer to the question whether a particular individual, group, or organization has a legal person accordingly depends on whether the party has the capacity to make independent, binding decisions and enter into legal obligations. This capacity has traditionally been determined by consulting the ordinary practices in society. If a putative person regularly enters into commercial agreements, for example, or takes on binding obligations, the courts will generally recognize that the individual has a legal person and can enter into relations with other legal persons.

The Judicial View as to Who Has a Legal Person Is Constantly Evolving

The social views that the judiciary consult in determining whether an individual has a legal person have developed over time. As a result, it is evident that courts are more willing to recognize that an entity has a legal person today than they were in the past. This development reflects the atomism in the liberal tradition, which accords metaphysical status to the discrete existence of individuals. It also reflects the contemporary tendency to use the courts for the purpose of enforcing moral claims that have historically stood outside the common law.[2] The common law traditionally left the issue whether a shop owner would accept a particular person as a customer, for example, in the moral realm and did not enter into questions such as discrimination.

This moral agenda can be seen in the case of animals, whose status in the common law is clearly under reconsideration. Although there is a long history of protecting animals in the statutory law, the common law courts have traditionally held that animals do not possess a legal person. As a result, animals cannot own property or inherit. There are signs, however, that the common law courts have begun to look more favourably on the idea that an animal is a legal person. There is now a movement to give companion animals a status similar to that of human beings—and at least the beginning of a legal person—for the purpose of enjoying a trust or life estate.[3]

The same issue has arisen in the civil system of law. In 2008, an Austrian group applied for a declaration that a chimpanzee, named in court documents as "Matthew Hiasl Pan," had a legal person and was therefore entitled to the appointment of a trustee. This request was made primarily so that he could legally own property.[4] The literature has ignored the problem of liability, however, and if an animal has a legal person, it logically has legal duties. It may therefore be sued for breaching such duties and held liable for its actions. This issue was at least canvassed in *Dye v. Wargo*, 253 F.3d 296 (7th Cir. 2001), where an individual named a police dog as a defendant in a suit for contravention of his constitutional rights.

The historical position in the common law with regard to animals is directly related to the question of standing. The common law position did not mean that animals were not entitled to care, consideration, and the benefit of property, or even that animals have no moral or social rights. It meant that animals have no standing in a court and cannot seek a legal remedy—either in their own capacity or through an intermediary—to enforce such rights. There is no doubt that some of this thinking is based on the idea that an animal could not, in the legal phrase, "instruct counsel" and express itself intelligently in the courts.

It is nevertheless evident that this view is changing. Any issues of communication in a court are clearly a matter of degree: there is no reason that a human representative cannot understand and convey the fundamental wishes of an animal to a legal tribunal. The emerging view, moreover, is that animals enjoy some of the most fundamental rights of the human person, such as the right to life.[5] The most challenging legal issues regarding animals may lie in the right to liberty.

The Civil Law Gives the Legal Person the Freedom to Enter into Binding Relationships

The civil law in the common law system can be seen as a set of rules and principles that governs the relations between legal persons. It does not govern these relations directly but provides sanctions if the individuals in these relations fail to honour them. The civil law accordingly functions in many ways like a set of moral and legal regulations and sets the parameters in which legal decisions may be made. These regulations generally leave it to individuals to determine the substantive content of their relations, though they contain a general prohibition against illegal behaviour.

The character of the civil law is at least implicitly contractual. From a functional perspective, the legal rights and duties of the legal person connect that person to other legal persons in the matrix of legal obligations that make up the legal system. These obligations are mandatory: they create binding duties and reciprocal rights. It is the consistent interpretation of these obligations, moreover, under the doctrine of *stare decisis*, that maintains the cohesiveness and integrity of the legal system.

The matrix of legal obligations that makes up the civil law is not capable of precise definition, since the individuals who have legal persons are free to make their own decisions within the framework provided by the law. This is, again, like a game: the players may make any move they like, within the rules of the game. Indeed, the purpose of the game, as Hart suggested, it to allow the players to make personal choices and exercise their will freely.

This focus on personal autonomy also introduces an important premise into the civil law, which is that it is not the business of judges to make decisions for those who come before the courts. It is for the individuals and parties to determine what constitutes a fair price or a reasonable contract. It is for the woman making a will to decide which of her children should receive the largest part of her estate.

The Civil Law Holds that Legal Rights and Duties Are Binding

The civil law governs the relations between legal persons by recognizing that certain obligations are legally binding. Although there are moral and sociological reasons for recognizing only certain obligations, those reasons exist outside the legal system. The common law courts merely follow society in recognizing that some obligations are binding and accordingly give rise to legal rights and duties. This conclusion is a matter of precedent, deductive reasoning, and the general social mores in society. The refusal of the courts to recognize a contract with a minor, for example, is based on the social view that children cannot appreciate the significance of such an agreement.

A Civil Law in the Common Law System Is Adversarial

From a historical perspective, it is the coercive powers of the courts that give our legal obligations their compulsory character. The common law courts have always had their own sources of authority, outside the statutory law, in custom and precedent. As we have seen, these sources of authority predate the idea of the political contract and the origins of central government. It is true that these customary sources of authority were later subordinated to the legislature, at least in the theory of the common law. This shift did not change the nature of the legal process, however, or the fundamental role of the courts in deciding individual disputes.

The role of the common law courts is more in the nature of an intervenor than anything else. From a procedural perspective, the plaintiff is appealing to the court to step into a private dispute between the plaintiff and the defendants. This form of appeal is an ancient feature of the legal system. The civil judge in Roman law was an intermediary, albeit an intermediary invested with the coercive powers of the state, who was asked to decide a private dispute. A civil case is called a lawsuit because the plaintiff is a suitor who appeals to the court for its assistance. The plaintiff is asking the judge to order the defendants to fulfill their obligations to the plaintiff.

The rights that the courts enforce are already in existence, at least from a conceptual perspective, and a judge is merely deciding whether the plaintiff is entitled to a remedy. The idea that there is a simple demarcation between legal rights and other rights is fallacious, and the substantive issue in a court is whether the law recognizes the right that the plaintiff is claiming. This decision is inevitably made on a case-by-case basis, after a dispute has arisen. The general role of the courts in the common law system has always been retrospective, and a trial judge is inevitably determining what law applies to past events.

The common law is an adversarial system. The plaintiff has entered into a contest with the defendants and "wins" or "loses" the case. The competitive aspects of the common law system reflect the origins of the trial process in practices like trial by combat. These origins help to explain the role of a judge in the common law, which differs from the role of a judge in the civil system. A common law judge is a referee and umpire who decides the procedural issues that arise between the parties, as well as someone who decides upon a verdict. It is only after the parties have "closed" their cases that the judge takes on a substantive role, and determines the facts of the case, in order to decide whether the plaintiff has won the case.

The mechanics of a civil suit reflect the adversarial nature of the common law process. The plaintiff asserts his rights. These rights are expressed in the form of a "pleading" like a statement of claim, which essentially states that the defendants had an obligation to the plaintiff, which gave rise to legal duties. The defendants failed to fulfill some such duty, as a result of which the plaintiff suffered some loss or harm, which requires redress. The duty might be as simple as the duty to provide the services or merchandise set out in a contract. The defendant responds by filing a pleading like a statement of defence, which responds to the statement of claim, usually by denying some essential averment. A defendant might plead, for example, that the contract was never signed and that the duties did not arise, or were waived, or annulled. A judge in the common law is not an investigator, and it is the plaintiff and the defendant who own the case and frame the issues. As a result, the common law tends to examine disputes from the perspective of the successful party.

Historically, a Legal Right Was a Prerogative Awarded by Society

The civil prerogatives of the legal person consist primarily of rights. The rest of the chapter accordingly examines the legal concept of rights and distinguishes it from natural rights, as well as the nature and origin of property rights.

The historical origins of the word "right" are related to the idea that public officials have a public person, which enjoys the rights and duties associated with that role. As we have seen, this provides the origins of the legal concept of the legal person. In its earlier use, a right was a social prerogative awarded by society, which attached to a person's official rank. As Elaine Pagels writes, even a punishment was a "right" in this analysis. The idea of rights nevertheless began to change over time. This shift is apparent in Blackstone's *Commentaries*, which reflects the philosophical developments of the seventeenth and eighteenth centuries rather than legal practice. In some ways, at least, Blackstone speaks of our legal rights as if they are natural rights, which derive from our existence as human individuals, independently of our membership in society. This misrepresents the historical idea of legal rights, which attach only to those individuals who have legal persons.

The actual derivation of the word "right" in legal usage is relatively obscure, since the law was originally based on duties. The entries in the *Oxford English Dictionary* suggest that the legal notion of rights developed out of the more general use of the word "right" to indicate that something is in accordance with law or morality.[6]

The word was also used, however, to describe the act of setting something right or straight. The legal use of the term "right" probably derives from the latter meaning of the word. This is because the civil law is based on private wrongs. The plaintiff is accordingly asking the court to correct the wrong and set it right. The prominence of rights in the civil law can be attributed to the fact that the person asserting the "right" is the principal actor in the process and carries the action forward. The primary question before the court is nevertheless whether the defendants have wronged the plaintiff, and failed in some duty to the plaintiff.

Legal Rights Need to Be Distinguished from Natural Rights

The historical idea of legal rights differs markedly from the idea of natural rights, which has received so much attention in the political and philosophical literature. It is the idea of natural rights that finds its way into the *Universal Declaration of Human Rights* and gives rise to the concept of human rights. The same idea now provides the philosophical foundations of the individual rights found in the *Canadian Charter of Rights and Freedoms* and the constitutional law.

The increasing prominence of natural rights in the contemporary law has made it increasingly difficult to separate the moral and legal meanings of the word "right." We now say that a person has a "right" rhetorically, in an ethical context, in order to assert that a particular claim is morally justified. In the civil law, however, the word "right" simply refers to the fact that a person who has been wronged is entitled to go before a court and request a legal remedy.

Legal Rights Derive from Society

The legal application of the concept of natural rights outside the constitutional law is confusing and interferes with the technical analysis of legal rights. Since it is the members of society who have legal persons, it makes no sense, historically, to say that an individual who is not a member of society has legal rights. The historical idea of legal rights was firmly based on the idea that the law—that is, the law recognized and enforced by the courts—is there to govern the relations between the members of society. The law accordingly does not exist outside of the society to which it applies. The historical solution to the injustice caused by the fact that certain individuals do not have legal rights has simply been to extend the membership in society to such individuals and grant them a legal person.

The philosophical view that the law is there to regulate the relations between the members of society found expression in the ideas of the political contract and legal positivism, which hold that there is no government—or law—in the state of nature. The idea of natural rights, on the other hand, seems to hold that there are legal rights outside society, in the state of nature. From the perspective of legal positivism, this is tantamount to saying that there are compulsory rights, enforced by government, in the realm where no government exists. The contradiction in such an assertion undoubtedly explains Jeremy Bentham's famous comment that the idea of natural rights is "nonsense on stilts."

The argument in natural law theory is more complicated, since the natural law provided the basis for the theory of natural rights. Even if the natural law creates rights, however, those rights become legal rights only after they have been filtered through the judicial system. Historically, the fact that made a right a "legal" right was the fact that the courts *recognized* the binding nature of the duties underlying the right. This decision was originally based on custom, which provided the source of the common law, but the larger appeal was to the substantive consensus in society. It follows that natural law theory does not, in itself, deny that the content of our legal rights derives from our membership in society.

The same kind of argument has been made, on a more conceptual level, by communitarians. Jean Bethke Elshtain, for example, has suggested that the problem with the contemporary understanding of rights is that it sees rights as the possessions of a freestanding individual.[7] This view is an ontological mistake: the rights of the person have their provenance in our membership in some form of community and do not exist outside our connections with other people. As a result, there is always a social context that must be considered in deciding the nature and extent of our rights.

From a foundational perspective, legal rights preserve the dignity of the individual person in its relations with other people. This is a social concept of dignity, which entails the freedom to make binding decisions and enter into formal relations with other people. This freedom provides the legal person with the capacity that it needs to enjoy the formal rights and perquisites that go with its membership in some form of community. It also guarantees a kind of mutual respect and legal reciprocity in our legal relations, which are premised on the idea that the parties to a contract, for example, are autonomous and substantively equal.

Waldron Argues that Private Property Consists of a Bundle of Rights

The reading from Waldron investigates the concepts of ownership and private property. These are political and philosophical terms rather than legal terms. Although John William Salmond, an influential figure in the common law jurisprudence, uses the term "ownership" in a legal context, the word is too general to be of much assistance in the courts.[8] The problem, as the reading from Waldron illustrates, is that it is a relatively empty concept, which fails to catch many of the legal reservations that come with owning property.

Waldron seems to struggle with the fact that legal rights are subject to endless qualification. The central proposition in the statement that Susan "owns" a car, for example, is probably that she has an exclusive right to possess the car. In spite of this, most people, at least, would have no difficulty saying that someone who purchases a car under a conditional sales agreement owns the car, even though the seller can repossess it if the owner fails to make the payments. Nor does it matter that the city has the right to take possession of the car if the owner parks it in the wrong place, and the right to hold it until the owner pays the cost of towing and storage.

The common law divides the rights of ownership into the ownership of land, or real property—thus the term "real estate"—and the ownership of chattels, or movables, the latter being specific articles that can be freely transferred and disposed of, at least in theory. A physical object that is "fixed" to land is called a fixture and is considered part of the land; indeed, strictly speaking, a house is a fixture in the common law, and it is the land that is transferred by an agreement for sale. This rule may apply to items such as unharvested crops, which have their roots embedded in the soil. A person who buys a piece of land with unharvested crops has accordingly bought the crops.

The Legal Right to Property Is Relative to Other Persons

The other major problem with the statement that someone "owns" something is that legal rights, as Waldron suggests, govern the relations between persons rather than the relations between persons and things. The role of a civil court is to resolve a dispute between a plaintiff and the defendants and provide a remedy if the defendants have failed to fulfill some duty.

A plaintiff in a lawsuit is merely asserting that he has a right to a thing, relative to someone else, which entitles him to the use or possession of property. This assertion is based on the general duty of other persons to respect such a right and is not a metaphysical claim. The relative nature of the legal concept of ownership may explain why Salmond, a celebrated judge, insisted that we own rights rather than things.[9]

It is difficult to conceive of a human society in which there is no concept of property. There may well be some special relation between an individual and the thing owned, and it is an interesting question, morally and philosophically, how such a relation exists. The courts do not decide abstract questions, however, and the statement that someone "owns" a particular thing means very little, outside the precise facts of a case.

The fundamental question in legal theory is more restricted: what is it, we need to ask, that gives us the legal right to own something? The obvious legal answer is the same for property rights as it is for other rights. It is society that guarantees our legal claims to property and distributes legal rights and duties among the members of society. The policy assumption, at least, is that the legal rules in the caselaw serve the public interest, even when they favour the individual person. The more difficult question is whether this policy assumption is justified.

De Laveleye Traces the Origins of Property to Occupancy, Labour, the Social Contract, Law and Government, Necessity, and Our Natural Rights

Émile Louis Victor de Laveleye, who was famous for his investigation into the origins of "primitive property," listed six major theories that explain the origins of the legal ownership of real property.[10] The distinguishing feature of the right to private property, he asserts, is not the right to use and possess a specific parcel of land; it is the right to prevent other people from using that land. He accordingly concludes that it is the exclusive nature of private property that needs to be justified. Any theory of private property must provide a convincing rationale for the restrictions on the use of the property by other people.

De Laveleye tests each of the theories in the historical literature. The first theory is based on simple possession. The idea of possession includes the occupancy, for example, of empty land. De Laveleye argues that the theory of occupancy fails, however, since we have no historical memory of empty lands. Hunters and gatherers had their recognized territory, and land has always been occupied, in one fashion or another. There is a good argument, moreover, that the idea that the land in places like North America and Australia was empty was merely a pretext that justified European encroachment on these lands.

The second theory is based on labour and holds that we own the fruits of our toil. The underlying idea appears to be that individuals own what they create. A farmer, for example, is entitled to the possession of the farm that he creates, as well as the vegetables he grows, by dint of his own hard work. The theories of occupancy and labour are joined together by John Locke, whose theory of property was used to justify the appropriation of land by settlers in the "new" world, who took the position that the land was not in use.[11]

The third theory bases private rights to land on the idea of the social contract, while the fourth theory bases these rights on the existence of positive law and government. These ideas have been put forward by a wide range of authors, from Maximilien Robespierre (one of the foremost figures in the French Revolution) to Jeremy Bentham. The problem with the third theory is that there is no historical evidence that human individuals ever entered into such a contract. It will be clear to any lawyer that the problem with the argument from law and government is that the law only provides the legal guarantees that protect the ownership of property. It does not explain how ownership arose in the first place.

The fifth theory that de Laveleye summarizes is based on physical and economic necessity: we simply need certain things in order to survive and accordingly have the right to own them. The sixth theory, which is related to the fifth, extends the notion of natural rights to the right of property. This argument is based on the natural law, and the idea that God or the divine order has ultimately given us the right to take what we rationally need, in order to survive and flourish.

De Laveleye argues that the problem with these theories, like the other theories, is that they do not explain the exclusive aspects of private property. There may be an argument that we are all entitled to take what we need from nature or the resources held in common: but this does not establish why we are entitled to prevent other people from taking it as well. None of the theories of the origins of private property explain why we are allowed to take more than we need or transfer our private interest to other people, who can then exclude other people from the enjoyment of the property.

The Modern System of Private Property Can Be Traced to the Increasing Prominence of the Individual

Jeremy Waldron suggests that the legal and political system in Western democracies is based on the concept of private property. This suggestion seems reasonably accurate, but it neglects the historical evolution of the system. As de Laveleye writes, the institution of private property as we know it, which permits the "full ownership" of private lands, is a relatively recent invention. The important point is that the historical source of our conception of private property can be traced to the increasing prominence of the individual in the common law.

The outlines of the early evolution of property are a matter of conjecture. In the beginning, however, it seems that land was used rather than owned. There were no borders in the modern sense, since there were no states. It was nevertheless recognized that a people's use and occupation of land gave them rights to that land. In some sense, at least, we can say that land was collectively owned. This sense of ownership eventually gave rise to the development of the concept of property in the civil law, which gave members of society rights vis-à-vis each other and permitted families the private use of lands.[12]

All of this is very approximate. The main lines in the development of the legal concept of property are nonetheless apparent. As de Laveleye argues, it is the development of the notion of exclusiveness that seems to be crucial. The increasing individualism in society also seems significant, and it found expression in the recognition that it is discrete human beings who possess a legal person. This goes against the earlier view that individuals obtain their rights from their membership in the family.

These two factors contributed to a range of social, industrial, and political developments that facilitated the accumulation of private property. It is evident, moreover, that the civil law provided the mechanism that consolidated the economic disparities that resulted from such developments. As we have seen, this led to a constitutional struggle in the United States and provided much of the impetus for the development of legal realism and critical theory. It is an interesting question whether it is possible to redesign this body of law in a way that resolves the competition between private and public interests more equitably.

Historically, Land Was Held in Common, Then Enclosed

The idea that the underlying title to land was vested in the community was replaced, with considerable social strife, by the idea of private ownership. The historical process by which the use of common land was restricted in England is usually referred to as "enclosure" (originally spelled "inclosure"), a term that refers to the erection of fences or other barriers to prevent others from using land. The process of enclosure was highly disputed and led to riots and even revolution.[13] By the eighteenth century, Parliament had passed "Inclosure Acts" to alienate land that had historically been held in common.

It has been argued that the process of enclosure reflected the decreasing authority of the King and the Star Chamber, which permitted local aristocracies and wealthy landowners to seize community land. There is a rival view in the Marxist literature, however, that holds that the wealthy controlled the political process and made use of the forces of the state for their own benefit.[14] The argument against this view, at least in the neoliberal and contractarian literature, is that the historical "commons" was morally and economically unsustainable.[15] These are matters, however, for a study of society and politics.[16]

The more interesting aspect of this process from the perspective of legal theory is that it reflects a profound sociological and psychological change in society, as a result of which individuals no longer identify themselves primarily as members of a family or a community. This process of transformation is ongoing, though there are areas of the world where the sociology behind the traditional law and tribal systems remains strong. Indeed, recent patterns of immigration have brought the sensibilities behind the traditional and modern legal views into conflict with each other. The most troubling example is probably the return of honour killing, which is carried out to cleanse a family's shame. This kind of practice reflects a more general sensibility, which places the perceived interests of the family above the interests of its individual members. It remains to be seen if the inherent conflict between these competing views can be reconciled.

Notes

1. Marriage, for example, was originally seen as a contract between two families, rather than the husband and the wife.

2. See Lawrence M. Friedman, "Is There a Modern Legal Culture?," *Ratio Juris* 7, no. 2 (July 1994): 117–131, which discusses the change in popular attitudes toward the law and the courts. Legislatures have also entered into moral territory, however, in passing legislation that requires judges to enter into an examination of moral issues. See Pauline Ridge, for example, "Moral Duty, Religious Faith and the Regulation of Testation," *University of New South Wales Law Journal* 28, no. 3 (2005): 720–739, which considers Australian legislation that allows a judge to override a deceased's wishes if those wishes do not conform to the generally prevailing moral standards in society.

3. See the summary of recent developments in Suzette Daniels, for example, "Honorary Trusts," in "An Introduction to Pet in Wills and Pet Euthanasia," available at www.animallaw.info/articles/arusdanielssuzette2004.htm. And see Susan Hankin's "Not a Living Room Sofa: Changing the Legal Status of Companion Animals," as cited in the suggestions for further reading, at pp. 359ff. and 363.

4. It seems relatively easy to imagine situations in which an animal has a moral right to something and at least "morally" owns it.

5. See Sue Donaldson and Will Kymlicka, for example, "The Moral Ark," *Queen's Quarterly* 114, no. 2 (Summer 2007): 187–205. And see Cass R. Sunstein & Martha C. Nussbaum, eds., *Animal Rights: Current Debates and New Directions* (Oxford: Oxford University, 2004).

6. See the discussion in Louis Groarke, *Moral Reasoning: Rediscovering the Ethical Tradition* (Toronto: Oxford University, 2011), p. 401ff.

7. Jean Bethke Elshtain, "The Dignity of the Human Person and the Idea of Human Rights: Four Inquiries," *Journal of Law & Religion* 14 (1999–2000): 53–65, at pp. 63 and 57.

8. See John W. Salmond, *Jurisprudence*, 7th ed. (London: Stevens and Haynes, 1913).

9. See Chapter 12, "Ownership," in Salmond, ibid., at p. 220: "That which a man owns is in all cases a right. When, as is often the case, we speak of the ownership of a material object, this is merely a convenient figure of speech. To own a piece of land means in truth to own a particular kind of right in the land, namely, the fee simple of it. . . . Every right is owned; and nothing can be owned except a right. Every man is the owner of the rights which are his."

10. Émile Louis Victor de Laveleye, "The Theory of Property," as cited in the suggestions for further reading.

11. See the additional online reading from Locke's *Two Treatises of Government* (1691).

12. The classical sources on the history of property are probably Henry Sumner Maine and de Laveleye. See Émile de Laveleye, *Primitive Property*, trans. by G.R.L. Marriott (London: Macmillan, 1878). Available at http://heinonline.org. For a modern discussion of the theory of property in the common law, see Robert P. Burns, "Blackstone's Theory of the Absolute Rights of Property," *University of Cincinnati Law Review* 54 (1985–6): 67–86.

13. See J.A. Yelling, *Common Field and Enclosure in England, 1450–1850*, for example, (Hamden, CT: Archon Books, 1977).

14. There is a wide-ranging historical literature on the subject of the enclosures. See, for example, Leigh Shaw-Taylor, "Parliamentary Enclosure and the Emergence of an English Agricultural Proletariat," *Journal of Economic History* 61 (2001): 640–62. But also see G.E. Mingay, *Parliamentary Enclosure in England: An Introduction to Its Causes, Incidence and Impact 1750–1850* (London: Longman, 1997) and J.M. Neeson, *Commoners: Common Right, Enclosure and Social Change in England 1700–1820* (Cambridge, MA: Cambridge University, 1993).

15. This has been called the "tragedy of the commons" in the neoliberal literature. The term was popularized by Garrett Hardin, in "The Tragedy of the Commons," *Science* 162, no. 3859 (December 1968): 1243–8, available at www.sciencemag.org. Hardin argues that the right of all herdsmen to graze their cattle on the land designated as a "commons" is unsustainable because it is in the interest of each herdsman to graze

as many cattle as possible on the land. Eventually the land will be over-grazed, and everyone will suffer the consequences.

16. For a discussion of the major theories of property, from a more political perspective, see Stephen R. Munzer, *A Theory of Property* (Cambridge, MA: Cambridge University, 1991).

Study Questions

1. The meaning of the word "person" has changed over time. The most accurate statement is that we *have* legal persons. What is it, then, that gives us a legal person?

2. Why are the courts reluctant to give the foetus a legal person?

3. Do you think that animals should be given legal persons? Do you think animals should be able to inherit? Why, why not?

4. How has the law protected animals, historically, if they are nothing more than property?

5. How does the historical concept of rights differ from the concept of natural rights, which gave rise to the idea of human rights?

6. Do you agree with Salmond's position, which is explained in the excerpt by Waldron? Do we own things, or rights?

Further Reading

Émile Louis Victor de Laveleye, "The Theory of Property," in *The Rational Basis of Legal Institutions* (New York: Macmillan, 1923), pp. 167–84.

Richard Epstein, *Takings: Private Property and the Power of Eminent Domain* (Cambridge, MA: Harvard University, 1985).

Gary L. Francione, "Animals—Property or Persons?," in *Animal Rights: Current Debates and New Direction*, ed. Cass R. Sunstein and Martha C. Nussbaum (Oxford: Oxford University, 2004), pp. 108–42.

Susan Hankin, "Not a Living Room Sofa: Changing the Legal Status of Companion Animals," *Rutgers Journal of Law & Public Policy* 4, no. 2 (Winter 2007): 314–410.

Georg Wilhelm Friedrich Hegel, "First Part: Abstract Right," in *Philosophy of Right* (Oxford: Oxford University, [1822] 1967).

Frederick Pollock, *A First Book of Jurisprudence for Students* (London: Macmillan, 1896). Available at http://heinonline.org. In particular, see chapters 3, 5, 6, and 7.

Vallance v. Naaykens, 2001 BCSC 656 (CanLII).

15 Private Law: Liability Is Based on Legal Duties and the Principle of Cause

Readings

- From *The Common Law*, by Oliver Wendell Holmes
- Digest of *Jordan House Ltd. v. Menow*, [1974] S.C.R. 239
- From *Principles of Contract at Law and in Equity*, by Frederick Pollock

The idea of legal liability appears to have developed out of the interplay of three factors. The first is the principle of causation. The second is the attachment of liability, originally to those objects that cause us harm, and later to the persons who possess them. The third and relatively erratic factor is the concept of a private wrong, which is far less significant than the caselaw would suggest. Historically, civil liability arises out of the breach of a recognized legal duty. These sorts of duties are generally found in contracts, torts, and the principles of restitution. There are additional sources of positive duties in statute law and general public policy.

✠ Readings ✠

From Oliver Wendell Holmes, *The Common Law* (Boston: Little, Brown, and Company, 1881).

Early Forms of Liability

Plutarch, in his *Solon*, tells us that a dog that had bitten a man was to be delivered up bound to a log four cubits long. Plato made elaborate provisions in his Laws for many such cases. If a slave killed a man, he was to be given up to the relatives of the deceased.... If a beast killed a man, it was to be slain and cast beyond the borders. If an inanimate thing caused death, it was to be cast beyond the borders in like manner, and expiation was to be made.

  Nor was all this an ideal creation of merely imagined law, for it was said in one of the speeches of Æschines, that "we banish beyond our borders stocks and stones and steel, voiceless and mindless things, if they chance to kill a man; and if a man commits suicide, bury the hand that struck the blow afar from its body." . . .

In the Roman law we find the similar principles of the *noxæ deditio* gradually leading to further results. The Twelve Tables (451 BC) provided that, if an animal had done damage, either the animal was to be surrendered or the damage paid for. We learn from Gaius that the same rule was applied to the torts of children or slaves, and there is some trace of it with regard to inanimate things. . . .

The action was not based . . . on the fault of the parent or owner. If it had been, it would always have been brought against the person who had control of the slave or animal at the time it did the harm complained of, and who, if anyone, was to blame for not preventing the injury. So far from this being the course, the person to be sued was the owner at the time of suing. The action followed the guilty thing into whosoever hands it came. . . .

All this shows very clearly that the liability of the owner was merely a way of getting at the slave or animal which was the immediate cause of offence. . . . The liability of the owner was simply a liability of the offending thing. In the primitive customs of Greece it was enforced by a judicial process expressly directed against the object, animate or inanimate. . . .

Another peculiarity to be noticed is that the liability seems to have been regarded as attached to the body doing the damage, in an almost physical sense. . . . This line of thought . . . would perhaps explain the well-known law of the Twelve Tables as to insolvent debtors. According to that law, if a man was indebted to several creditors and insolvent, after certain formalities they might cut up his body and divide it among them. If there was a single creditor, he might put his debtor to death or sell him as a slave. If no other right were given but to reduce a debtor to slavery, the law might be taken to look only to compensation. . . . But the right to put to death looks like vengeance, and the division of the body shows that the debt was conceived very literally to inhere in or bind the body with a *vinculum juris* [a binding legal obligation that constrained the body physically, as an iron fetter or chain would]. . . .

[S]o far as I am able to trace the order of development in the customs of the German tribes, it seems to have been entirely similar to that which we have already followed. . . . Alfred's laws (AD 871–901) have a like provision as to cattle. "If a neat wound a man, let the neat be delivered up or compounded for." . . . In 1333 it was stated for law, that, "if my dog kills your sheep, and I, freshly after the fact, tender you the dog, you are without recovery against me." . . .

Deodands

As long ago as Bracton,[1] in [a] case [where] a man was slain, the coroner was to value the object causing the death, and that was to be forfeited as deodand *"pro rege"* [for the King].[2] It was to be given to God, that is to say to the Church, for the King, to be expended for the good of his soul. . . . The King . . . supplanted the family in the claim on the guilty thing, and the Church supplanted him. . . .

If a man fell from a tree, the tree was deodand. If he drowned in a well, the well was to be filled up. . . . [I]t has been repeated from Queen Elizabeth's time to within one hundred years, that if my horse strikes a man, and afterwards I sell my horse, and after that the man dies, the horse shall be forfeited. Hence it is, that, in all indictments for homicide, until very lately it has been necessary to state the instrument causing the death and its value, as that the stroke was given by a certain penknife, value sixpence, so as to secure the forfeiture. It is said that a steam engine has been forfeited in this way. . . .

In the early books which have just been referred to, and long afterwards, the fact of motion is adverted to as of much importance. A maxim of Henry Spigurnel, a judge in the time of Edward I, is reported, that "where a man is killed by a cart, or by the fall of a house, or in other like manner, and the thing in motion is the cause of the death, it shall be deodand." . . .

Ships

[T]he reader sees how motion gives life to the object forfeited. The most striking example of this sort is a ship. And accordingly the old books say that, if a man falls from a ship and is drowned, the motion of the ship must be taken to cause the death, and the ship is forfeited. . . .

A ship is the most living of inanimate things. . . . It is only by supposing the ship to have been treated as if endowed with personality, that the arbitrary seeming peculiarities of the maritime law can be made intelligible, and on that supposition they at once become consistent and logical.[3] . . .

The following is a passage from a judgement by Chief Justice Marshall, which is quoted with approval by Judge Story in giving the opinion of the Supreme Court of the United States:

> This is not a proceeding against the owner; it is a proceeding against the vessel for an offence committed by the vessel. . . . It is true that inanimate matter can commit no offence. But this body is animated and put in action by the crew, who are guided by the master. The vessel acts and speaks by the master. She reports herself by the master. . . .

And again Judge Story quotes from another case: "The thing is here primarily considered as the offender, or rather the offence is primarily attached to the thing."

Notes

1. Editor's note: English jurist Henry of Bracton (d. 1268).
2. Editor's note: The *Oxford English Dictionary* defines "deodand" as: "a personal chattel which, having been the immediate occasion of the death of a human being, was given to God as an expiatory offering, i.e. forfeited to the Crown to be applied to pious uses, e.g. to be distributed in alms. (Abolished in 1846.)"
3. Editor's note: Holmes further notes that in a collision between ships, it is the ship—and not the owner—that is legally responsible for the collision.

Digest of the Decision of Bora Laskin. For the Supreme Court of Canada in *Jordan House Ltd. v. Menow*, [1974] S.C.R. 239.

Supreme Court of Canada

Jordan House Limited (Defendant) Appellant;

and

John James Menow (Plaintiff)

Present: Martland, Judson, Ritchie, Spence and Laskin J.J.

The judgement of Martland, Spence, and Laskin J.J. was delivered by

LASKIN J.—

The hotel premises front is on Highway No. 8, a much-travelled two-lane highway running east and west between Hamilton and Niagara Falls, Ontario. Menow was a frequent patron of the hotel's beverage room and was well known to the owner-operator of the hotel, one Fernick. Menow had a tendency to drink to excess and then to act recklessly, although ordinarily he was courteous and mannerly. The hotel management and the beverage room employees knew of his propensities, and, indeed, about a year before the events out of which this case arose he had been barred from the hotel for a period of time because he annoyed other customers.

On January 18, 1968, Fernick came on duty at about 7 p.m. and saw that the plaintiff was then sober. He was served with beer from time to time, and there is a finding that towards 10 p.m. Fernick was aware that Menow was drinking to excess and that he had become intoxicated, the hotel having sold beer to Menow past the point of visible or apparent intoxication. At about 10 p.m. or 10.15 p.m. Menow was seen wandering around to other tables in the beverage room and consequently was ejected from the hotel by its employees.

The evidence shows that he was put out on a dark and rainy night and that he was wearing dark clothes not readily visible to motorists. It appears that Menow, when he was outside the hotel, was picked up by an unknown third person and taken part of the way home. It was while continuing in an easterly direction that Menow was struck by an oncoming vehicle.

On the foregoing facts, Haines J. found that the hotel owed and was in breach of a common law duty of care to Menow. The duty of care was first put on two grounds, each related but in different ways, to certain statutes. Adverting to s.53(3) of *The Liquor Licence Act*, R.S.O. 1960, c.218, and to s.81 of *The Liquor Control Act*, R.S.O. 1960, c.217, Haines J. held that in contravening those provisions the hotel was in breach of a common law duty to Menow not to serve him intoxicating drink when he was visibly intoxicated.

Although in the view of the trial judge, s.53(4) and (6) of *The Liquor Licence Act* imposes a duty on a licensed hotel operator to eject an intoxicated patron and empowers his forcible removal if he refuses to leave on request, he held that this authority is qualified by a duty not to subject that patron to danger of personal injury, foreseeable as a result of eviction. In the present case Haines J. accordingly found that the hotel was vicariously liable for the actions of its employees, who were in breach of a common law duty of care not to eject Menow when they knew or ought to have known that he would thereby be placed in a position of danger to his personal safety.[1]

Negligence Is Based on a Duty of Care

The common law assesses liability for negligence on the basis of breach of a duty of care arising from a foreseeable and unreasonable risk of harm to one person created by the act or omission of another. Since liability is predicated upon fault, the guiding principle assumes a nexus or relationship between the injured person and the injuring person which makes it reasonable to conclude that the latter owes a duty to the former not to expose him to an unreasonable risk of harm. Moreover, in considering whether the risk of injury to which a person may be exposed is one that he should not reasonably have to run, it is relevant to relate the probability and the gravity of injury to the burden that would be imposed upon the prospective defendant in taking avoiding measures.

The hotel, however, was not in the position of persons in general. It was in an invitor–invitee relationship with Menow as one of its patrons, and it was aware, through its employees, of his intoxicated condition, a condition which, on the findings of the trial judge, it fed in violation of applicable liquor licence and liquor control legislation. There was a probable risk of personal injury to Menow if he was turned out of the hotel to proceed on foot on a much-travelled highway passing in front of the hotel.

Therefore there is, in my opinion, nothing unreasonable in calling upon the hotel in such circumstances to take care to see that Menow is not exposed to injury because of his intoxication. A call to the police or a call to his employer immediately come to mind as easily available preventive measures; or a taxi-cab could be summoned to take him home, or arrangements made to this end with another patron able and willing to do so. The operator had in other instances provided rides. He also had spare rooms at the time, into one of which Menow could have been put.

Given the relationship between Menow and the hotel, the proper conclusion is that the hotel came under a duty to Menow to see that he got home safely by taking him under its charge or putting him under the charge of a responsible person, or to see that he was not turned out alone until he was in a reasonably fit condition to look after himself. There was, in this case, a breach of this duty for which the hotel must respond according to the degree of fault found against it. The harm that ensued was that which was reasonably foreseeable by reason of what the hotel did (in turning Menow out), and failed to do (in not taking preventive measures).

The imposition of liability upon the hotel in the circumstances that I have recounted has roots in an earlier decision of the Court. The affinity of *Dunn v. Dominion Atlantic*

Railway Co. (1920), 60 S.C.R. 310, with the present case is sufficiently shown by the following three sentences from the reasons of Anglin J., who allowed the appeal of the administrator of the estate of a deceased passenger, who was killed by a passing train when put off at a closed and unlighted station in a drunken condition:

> The right of removal of a disorderly passenger which is conferred on the conductor (under a railway bylaw) is not absolute. It must be exercised reasonably. He cannot under it justify putting a passenger off the train under such circumstances that, as a direct consequence, he is exposed to danger of losing his life or of serious personal injury.

I do not regard the *Dunn* case as turning on the fact that the defendant was a common carrier, any more than I regard it as relevant here whether or not the defendant hotel was under innkeeper's liability in respect of the operation of its beverage room.

The Plaintiff Did Not Assume the Risk but Was Contributorily Negligent

Counsel for the appellant did not argue on causation, but did contend that any duty that the hotel might have had evaporated because of voluntary assumption of risk. The argument is untenable, whether put on the basis of Menow's self-intoxication or on the basis of the situation that faced him when he was put out of the hotel. In his condition, as found by the trial judge, it is impossible to say that he both appreciated the risk of injury and impliedly agreed to bear the legal consequences. However, the trial judge did find Menow contributorily negligent in becoming intoxicated, adverting in this connection to s.80(2) of *The Liquor Control Act* which enjoins any person against being in an intoxicated condition in a public place. This finding has not been attacked.

I would dismiss the appeal with costs.

RITCHIE J.—

I agree with my brother Laskin that this appeal should be dismissed. For my part, however, the circumstances giving rise to the appellant's liability were that the innkeeper and his staff, who were well aware of the respondent's propensity for irresponsible behaviour under the influence of drink, assisted or at least permitted him to consume a quantity of beer which they should have known might well result in his being incapable of taking care of himself when exposed to the hazards of traffic. Their knowledge of the respondent's somewhat limited capacity for consuming alcoholic stimulants without becoming befuddled and sometimes obstreperous, seized them with a duty to be careful not to serve him with repeated drinks after the effects of what he had already consumed should have been obvious.

In my view it was a breach of this duty which gave rise to liability in the present case.

Note

1. Editor's note: The doctrine of vicarious liability holds that an employer is liable for the acts performed by its employees in the course of their employment.

From Frederick Pollock, et al., *Principles of Contract at Law and in Equity: A Treatise on the General Principles Concerning the Validity of Agreements in the Law of England and America*, 3rd American ed. (New York: Baker, Voorhis, and Company, 1906).

Agreement, Proposal, and Acceptance

[T]he most popular description of a contract that can be given is also the most exact one, namely that it is a promise or set of promises which the law will enforce. The specific mark of contract is the creation of a right, not to a thing, but to another man's conduct in the future. He who has given the promise is bound to him who accepts it, not merely because he had or expressed a certain intention, but because he so expressed himself as to entitle the other party to rely on his acting in a certain way. . . .

Definitions

A series of statements in the form of definitions . . . may help to clear the way.

1. Contract. Every agreement and promise enforceable by law is a contract.
2. Agreement. An agreement is an act in the law whereby two or more persons declare their consent as to any act or thing to be done or forborne by some or one of those persons for the use of the others or other of them.
3. Expression of consent. Such declaration may take place by
    a. the concurrence of the parties in a spoken or written form of words as expressing their common intention, or
    b. an offer made by some or one of them, and accepted by the others or other of them.
4. Promise and offer. The declaration of any party to an agreement, so far as it relates to anything to be done or forborne on his part, is called a promise. The expression of a person's willingness to become, according to the terms expressed, a party to an agreement, is called an offer or proposal. An offer may become a promise by acceptance, but is not a promise unless and until it is accepted. . . .

The Agreement Must Possess a Legal Character

The first and most essential element of an agreement is the consent of the parties. There must be the meeting of two minds in one and the same intention. But in order that their consent may make an agreement of which the law can take notice, other conditions must be fulfilled. The agreement must be . . . concerned with duties and rights which can be dealt with by a court of justice. . . . An appointment between two friends to go out for a walk or to read a book together is not an agreement in the legal sense: for it is not meant to produce, nor does it produce, any new legal duty or right. . . .

The Agreement Must Create a Legal Obligation

By obligation we mean the relation that exists between two persons of whom one has a private and peculiar right . . . to control the other's actions by calling upon him to do or forbear some particular thing. . . .

This Usually Requires a Proposal and Acceptance

It is possible . . . to analyze and define agreement as constituted in every case by the acceptance of a proposal. . . . And it is appropriate to most of the contracts which occur in daily life, buying and selling, letting and hiring, in short all transactions which involve striking a bargain. One party proposes his terms; the other accepts, rejects, or meets them with a counter-proposal: and thus they go on till there is a final refusal and breaking off, or till one of them names terms which the other can accept as they stand. . . .

It [nevertheless] seems overstrained to apply this analysis to a case in which the consent of the parties is declared in a set form, as where they both execute a deed or sign a written agreement. . . . Take the common case of [the terms of] a lease. . . . Shall we say that he who accepts them first thereby proposes them to the other? And what if they accept at the same moment?[1] The case of competitors in a race who, by accepting rules laid down by the managing committee, become bound to one another to observe those rules, is even stronger. . . .

A Promise under Seal Does Not Require Proof of an Agreement

Where the promise is embodied in a deed [and therefore under seal], there is an apparent anomaly; for the deed is irrevocable and binding on the promisor from the moment of its execution by him, even before any acceptance by the promisee. . . . As a matter of history, the very object of the Anglo-Norman writing under seal was to dispense with any other kind of proof, and to substitute the authenticated will of the parties themselves for an appeal to the hazards of oath, ordeal, or judicial combat. . . .

A Contract Must Have Consideration

In our law we require, for the validity of an informal contract, not merely agreement or deliberate intention, but bargain; a gratuitous promise is not enforceable unless included in the higher obligation of a deed [i.e., unless it is under seal]. The rules as to proposal and acceptance cannot be fully understood without bearing this in mind. . . .

[C]onsideration [may be described] as an act or forbearance, or the promise thereof, which is offered by one party to an agreement, and accepted by the other, as an inducement to that other's act or promise. . . .

Unlawful Agreements

We have . . . in the main three sorts of agreements which are unlawful and void, according as the matter or purpose of them is:

1. contrary to positive law
2. contrary to positive morality recognized as such by law
3. contrary to the common weal as tending
   a. to the prejudice of the State in external relations
   b. to the prejudice of the State in internal relations
   c. to improper or excessive interference with the lawful actions of individual citizens. . . .

Agreement to Commit Offence, Void

The simplest case is an agreement to commit a crime or indictable offence: "If one bind himself to kill a man, burn a house, maintain a suit, or the like, it is void." With one or two exceptions on which it is needless to dwell, obviously criminal agreements do not occur in our own time and . . . no attempt is made to enforce them. In the eighteenth century a bill was filed on the Equity side of the Exchequer by a highwayman against his fellow for a partnership account. The bill was reported to the Court both scandalous and impertinent, and the plaintiff's solicitors were fined and his counsel ordered to pay costs. . . .

Agreement Is Also Void When Its Ulterior Object Is an Offence

Moreover a contract may be illegal because an offence is contemplated as its ulterior result, or because it invites to the commission of crime. For example, an agreement to pay money to A's executors if A commits suicide would be void; and although there is nothing unlawful in printing, no right of action can arise for work done in printing a criminal libel. . . .

Agreement For Civil Wrong to Third Persons Is Void

Again an agreement will generally be illegal . . . if it contemplates any civil injury to third persons. Thus an agreement to divide the profits of a fraudulent scheme, or to carry out some object in itself not unlawful by means of an apparent trespass, breach of contract, or breach of trust is unlawful and void. . . .

Note

1. Editor's note: In most cases, at least, the case of a lease presents no difficulty, since it is the landlord who drafts the lease, and who therefore makes the offer.

✣ Discussion ✦

The following chapter reviews the concept of civil liability, which holds that legal persons are responsible for the wrongs suffered by other people. The term "wrong" in this context originally referred to the idea that the plaintiff in a civil suit has suffered a harm or loss that he should not have suffered. The significance of the word has shifted over time and now suggests that the defendant has done something morally wrong. Although there is a residue of moral fault in the concept of civil liability, to avoid confusion, it is best to distinguish legal wrongs from moral wrongs. The central question in deciding liability is whether the plaintiff deserves to be compensated, rather than whether the defendant has done something wrong.

The question of compensation brings a significant policy component into the caselaw and raises complicated logical and ethical issues with regard to the extent of our responsibilities to other people. Many of these issues require the exercise of judgement, which provides the philosophical core of this body of law. Who is responsible, for example, if a thirteen-year-old boy hits a homerun and "beans" a passerby—who steps back into the roadway and causes an accident? Is the boy liable? Are his parents liable? Is the league? What about the passerby, who should not have stepped into the traffic?

The Principle of Liability in the Early Law Was Simple Cause

The historical development of civil liability is easy to trace. The most significant feature of the early civil law, from a modern perspective, is that it was not based on blame or moral fault. Frances Bowes Sayre writes:

> The so-called *Leges Henrici Primi*, compiled about the year 1118, containing a jumble of mixed rules from many sources but seeking to state a body of true English law that was neither Roman nor canon law, contains several survivals of this same rough and ready justice. "If some one in the sport of archery or other form of exercise kill another with a missile or by some such accident, let him repay; for the law is that he who commits evil unknowingly must pay for it knowingly."[1]

This concept of liability is usually referred to as strict liability and does not require proof of moral blame. The idea of blameworthiness came in only later, through the influence of the canon law.

The principle of liability in the early law was simple cause. It was the thing that caused the wrong that was legally responsible for the harm it had caused. This principle applied literally to animate and inanimate objects, as well as to people. The conception of "wrong" in the earliest law was metaphysical rather than moral, and it expressed itself in the belief that something must be done to remove the cause of the disruption in the proper order of things. This concept of liability was connected with expiation, which is often explained as atonement. The usual form of expiation was to present the person who had been wronged with the thing that had caused the wrong. The idea was that this would pacify the person who had been wronged and restore the natural relations between things.

A Few Authors Have Challenged This Position, but Unsuccessfully

There are authors who take a different position. Alan Calnan argues, in response to Oliver Wendell Holmes, that torts have always been based on the idea that the defendant's actions were morally blameworthy.[2] Calnan has joined others, such as Percy Winfield, in arguing that the idea of strict liability is a mistaken gloss placed on inconclusive early sources.[3]

Calnan has examined actions of trespass in the early common law, which provided the original cause of action in cases of personal injury.

> No matter how "trespass" was defined, the underlying question in all medieval tort cases was always the same: did the facts reveal a wrong worthy of redress?[4]

This provided the basis for the development of the law of torts, which deals explicitly with legal wrongs.

Calnan's example does not resolve the question. If the plaintiff loses an eye as a result of the defendant's actions, on the original understanding in the law, he has been wronged. This is true, regardless of whether the defendant did something morally wrong or not. The original view in the common law changed, under the influence of Christianity and the canon law, which held that the defendant was liable because he had done something morally blameworthy. As Victor Windeyer writes:

> The Anglo-Saxons probably did not, in general, hold men liable as wrongdoers unless they had, to use Maitland's phrase, done some "distinct voluntary act" which contributed to the happening of the injury complained of. But they, not infrequently, held them liable in cases in which modern law would certainly say they had acted without any negligence and without any intent to do harm.[5]

If a man's weapon inadvertently injured another person, if his bull gored someone, if his dog bit, he was liable.[6]

The fundamental issue in this early scheme of liability was simple cause. It was still necessary to show that the defendant had acted in some sense and caused the harm. This stipulation leaves open a defence in cases where a defendant has not done anything. A man who has acted involuntarily, for example, and fallen into someone because a ruffian in the crowd has pushed him has not "caused" the resulting harm and cannot be held liable under such a scheme.

It Is Simple Cause that Explains the Liability of Objects in the Early Law

It is the principle of simple cause that explains the treatment of objects in the early law. Holmes writes that civil liability in earliest times was attached to the weapon or object that injured the victim, rather than the person who owned it. Indeed, there was a court in Athens, the Prytaneion, that tried animals and inanimate objects. A sword or spear that had caused a death was destroyed or cast out of the city. This practice was a form of banishment.[7]

It seems clear that the ancient law did not make a hard conceptual distinction between human persons and things. In many cases, at least, the person who injured or killed another person was treated essentially as an object. In the earliest times, Holmes suggests, a son who had killed someone else must be surrendered to the family that had suffered the loss, who could do what they like with him. This practice provided a significant part of the motivation for the development of compensation, which entered the law at a later stage, an alternative to the surrender of the object that had caused the harm.

The *Vinculum Juris* and the Practice of Deodands Show that Liability Was Believed to Exist Physically

The idea that liability attached physically to the offending thing carried over into the written law. The Roman law, for example, held that liability attaches to the person by a *vinculum juris*, a legal fetter or tie. Holmes writes that this fetter was "conceived very literally to inhere in or bind the body."[8] Thus, Holmes writes, the creditors could demand that the body of an insolvent debtor be divided up and distributed among them to satisfy the debts.

The physical idea of liability was also preserved in the common law practice of deodands. Victor Windeyer writes that this practice was a holdover from much earlier times:

> The name deodand [from *Deo*, "God"] tells us that the forfeited article was given to God, according to [John] Cowel "for the pacification of His wrath." We know that during the Middle Ages the value of the deodand was often used for masses for the dead man's soul, and after the Reformation usually given to some charity. But deodands were probably a survival from superstitious times before Christianity. Originally, apparently, the kinsmen of the dead man received the deodand, perhaps as compensation for their loss, but more probably because it was itself an unclean and guilty thing which they must destroy.[9]

It was the invention of steam engines that led to the abolition of deodands in 1846. Parliament appears to have taken the view that it was unreasonable to expect defendants to absorb the cost of surrendering such expensive machines.[10]

The desire to destroy an offending thing found its way into other practices. During the Middle Ages, for example, the corpses of individuals who were found to be vampires or witches were burned. Although we tend to see this destruction as a kind of punishment, burning was seen as a way of physically destroying the offending thing.

These kinds of practices clearly satisfy a human feeling that objects physically associated with evil events are malign. Although we tend to attribute this to psychological sources, the original idea was metaphysical and continues to surface in modern times. Most of us, at least, would not choose to live in a house where a gruesome murder was committed. When a young man was beheaded on a bus in Manitoba in 2008, his family was outraged that the bus was put back into service.[11]

There Are Remnants of the Idea of Physical Liability in the Law of Dangerous Animals and Product Law

There are remnants of this idea in a few exceptional cases in which a plaintiff is entitled to sue the thing that causes a wrong rather than its owner. A fighting dog, for example, is an inherently dangerous object, and it can be sued, in its own right, independently of its owner. This is in spite of the fact that the dog is property in the common law and has no legal person.[12]

These kinds of cases seem to take us back to the beginning of civil compensation. The BBC reported in 2008 that a bear was convicted and held liable for the theft of honey in Macedonia. The state was ordered to pay for the damage, apparently because the bear belonged to a protected species. It is interesting that this case recreates the historical dynamic that gave rise to the civil law, which permitted a defendant to provide compensation in lieu of surrendering the offending thing.

There are also traces of physical liability in product law, which is generally regulated by statute. Goods may be seized by inspectors or customs officials because they make extravagant or misleading claims. In such a case, which is *in rem*—against the whole world rather than against a particular defendant—the products may be sued. In *U.S. v. an Undetermined Number of Cases, etc.* (1964) 338 F. 2d 157, for example, crates containing bottles of cider vinegar and honey, along with books, were named as defendants.The government in *U.S. v. an Undetermined Number of Cases* argued that the books constituted a prohibited form of labelling, which made a misleading claim that the vinegar and honey would cure certain ills.[13] It is interesting, philosophically, that the case treats the crates, bottles, and books as a single object for the purposes of legal analysis. Although the government suggested that the seller of the goods had done something illicit, its argument was not based on the misconduct of the seller. The position of the government was simply that the close physical proximity of the products to each other had caused a misrepresentation. They were therefore liable.

The Civil Law Was Based on the Transfer of Liability from Things to Persons

The civil law governs the relations between persons. The emergence of this body of law was accordingly based on the transfer of liability from the object that had caused the wrong to persons. A civil suit was between persons, who shared rights and duties. Liability was still based on cause, but the principle of cause relocated itself in the notion that it was the defendant's failure in his duty to the plaintiff that had caused the wrong suffered by the plaintiff. The idea of awarding monetary damages was already present in the customary law, which contained an extensive tariff of payments for injuries that had been inflicted on others. This scheme of payments functioned in many ways like a kind of insurance scheme, which was there to provide compensation to those who had suffered a wrong. The amount of compensation was based on the social rank of the individual who had been harmed.

The distinction that we now make between the civil and the criminal law is a later development. Henry Sumner Maine writes that "the penal law" of ancient communities is the law of torts. If we open the *Commentaries* of Gaius, for example, we find that offences:

> which we are accustomed to regard exclusively as crimes are exclusively treated as torts, and not theft only, but assault and violent robbery, are associated by the jurisconsult with trespass, libel, and slander. All alike gave rise to an obligation of *vinculum juris*, and were all requited by a payment of money.[14]

The purpose of the payment was to placate the victim and restore the relations between the members of society.

The division of the common law into the civil and criminal law was based on a division of liability between private and public wrongs. The parties in a civil suit are private persons, who are usually called the plaintiff and the defendant. The word "plaintiff" refers to someone who complains, which explains why the plaintiff is sometimes called the "complainant." These terms draw attention to the nature of the judicial process, which was based historically on the idea that the courts have inherent authority over the parties.[15] This authority gives the courts the discretion to step into private disputes at the request of the parties and order a remedy.

The civil process is a contest between private parties, then, who have "conduct" of the case. It is the parties who decide what claims, arguments, and evidence will be heard by the court. The interests of the competing parties are equal, unlike in the criminal process, and the standard of proof is "on a balance of probabilities."[16] The plaintiff must prove that the case set out in the statement of claim is more probable than not. The evidence must be clear and convincing.

The Transfer of Liability to Persons Brought Fault into the Analysis

The civil law has historically provided remedies like monetary damages and "specific performance" (which requires a defendant to fulfill a contract) for breaches in the duties between persons. The theory of liability behind this law is that the defendant's breach of duty caused the plaintiff's harm. Historically, this theory took shape under the influence of the canon law, which introduced the notion of moral blame into the analysis. This development eventually moved the notion of "wrong" from the harm suffered by the plaintiff to the defendant's breach of duty.

The fundamental moral conception in the canon law, which came into the civil and the criminal law, was the conception of sin. This conception brought in a new idea of wrong, based on the moral responsibilities of the defendant, which infiltrated and then overwhelmed the thinking in the earlier law. There are many reasons for this change in thinking: it is nevertheless evident that it was part of the slow development of a less fatalistic view of human life and an increasing emphasis on the role of individuals in what occurs.

These philosophical changes brought a new standard of liability into the legal process, which was based on moral fault. This standard slowly relocated the source of civil liability in the exercise of volition, without displacing the principle of cause. The larger dynamic behind this new theory of liability held that the wrongs we suffer are caused by the immoral acts of others. The implications of such a dynamic are far-reaching, since it suggests, psychologically, that someone must be blamed for the harm we suffer.

The Principle of Simple Cause Has Nevertheless Been Preserved in Cases of Strict Liability

We have already seen that the original principle of cause has been preserved in cases of strict liability, like those involving dangerous goods, which do not require proof of moral fault. William Prosser has also argued that the so-called "warranties" in the sale of food and drink, which are usually traced to a fictional contract, are actually a holdover from the earlier law.[17] The remarkable persistence of simple cause as the deciding factor in determining civil liability in some areas of the law suggests that concepts like "responsibility" are often a moral gloss on a more basic legal analysis. This reflects the problematic nature of the newer theory of liability, which at least implicitly treats liability as a kind of penalty for immoral conduct rather than a means of compensation.

It is not clear that the introduction of the principle of fault in the civil law served the public policy behind the law. Although the new theory of liability inevitably favoured defendants, there are competing tensions in the modern common law that have never been resolved. Many authors have suggested that the principle of simple cause provides a more rational basis for the distribution of losses than does the principle of blame, which brings an uneven and relatively subjective standard into the law. The increasing reliance on no-fault insurance schemes to deal with automobile accidents illustrates that the use of blame to determine liability presents problems.

This preference for simple cause in assigning civil liability is evident in other systems of law. In 1940, for example, F.H. Lawson wrote that, in France,

> The more advanced modern jurists have built . . . an objective theory of responsibility, according to which anyone who makes use of anything is liable for the damage caused by it unless he can show that the damage was due to the fault of the victim, or to *cas fortuit* or *force majeure*, terms which are roughly equivalent to inevitable accident and act of God.[18]

It is interesting that this "objective theory" merely returns us to the ancient view, which gave rise to liability in the first place.

The Duties in the Civil Law Are Based on Social Norms

We have already seen that civil liability is based on two factors. The first is that the defendant has breached a duty to the plaintiff. The second is that the defendant's breach of duty caused the plaintiff harm.

The existence of such duties is determined by social norms, which reflect the customary origins of the common law. In *Palsgraf v. Long Island Railroad Co.* (1928), 248 N.Y. 339, Chief Justice Cardozo wrote that the issue in deciding liability is whether the defendant has satisfied "the norm of conduct, the customary standard to which behavior must conform."[19] There is significant room for movement in such a standard, which could conceivably vary across jurisdictions, in accordance with differences in the social customs in different societies.

The Principal Sources of Duties Are Found in Contracts, Torts, and Equity

The duties in the civil law may derive from various sources. It has sometimes been said that our civil law recognizes those duties that arise from contracts, torts, and restitution, which is a remedy in equity.[20] There are additional sources of duty in statute law and general public policy, which may limit the actions of private persons.[21] This is a relatively arbitrary scheme, however, and fails to acknowledge that the duties recognized by the common law arise principally out of the facts presented by specific cases. This is compounded by the development of the early caselaw, which was based on specific causes of action that developed independently of each other and often overlap. As a result, the line between different causes of action is often blurred and the courts have considerable freedom in which to develop new duties.

The duties that arise in torts are general duties, which are owed to other persons generally rather than to a specific person. These general duties contrast with the duties that arise from contract, which are specific to the parties who have entered into the contract. Although the law regards the breach of a legal duty as a civil wrong, the term "wrong" in this context is substantially diluted and indicates primarily that the wronged person has a right to a legal remedy. This legal usage is apparent in the law of "unjust enrichment," which requires that a person who receives a gratuitous benefit pay for it. There is no need to establish a moral wrong in such a case.

Liability in Contracts Is Based on Promises

Christopher Columbus Langdell argued that the law of contracts has developed on a logical, case-by-case basis. This method of developing the caselaw has reduced the role of judicial discretion and public policy in the law of contracts. There is nevertheless an argument that

Langdell's systematic account of the law of contracts is illusory. Grant Gilmore has argued that the law of contracts is composed of a relatively hazardous collection of cases that simply tells us what agreements the common law courts have found binding.[22]

Gilmore's argument does not change the fundamental mechanics of this body of law. The essential allegation in contracts is that the defendant has breached a specific, contractual duty to the plaintiff. These duties arise out of an exchange of promises, which together form an agreement. The promises are binding because each of the persons making a promise has received consideration for the promise. In practical terms, this is much like saying that the promisor (the person who makes the promise) has been paid for it.

There is no agreement without consent, which gives rise to a *consensus ad idem* (a meeting of minds), under which the agreement crystallizes in a binding contract. This consent must be full, not partial. The failure of a medical clinic, for example, to inform a patient of possible side effects may vitiate the contract and the patient's obligation to pay for the service.

An Impossible Contract Is Not Binding

There are many interesting logical issues related to liability under contract law. The law recognizes that some contracts are void *ab initio* (and do not come into existence) because they cannot be performed. The parties to a contract cannot agree to an impossibility. Pollock gives the example of a thing "contrary to the course of nature, *quod natura fieri non concedit*," such as an agreement "to make a river run uphill."[23] There are other examples, such as a contract for the private sale of a navy ship (which is publicly owned), or a contract for the sale of the British crown jewels.

It is only "objective" and not "subjective" impossibility that bars redress, however. This stipulation means that

> an absolute contract to load a full cargo of guano at a certain island was not discharged by there not being enough guano there to make a cargo: and where a charter-party required a ship to be loaded with usual despatch, it was held to be no answer to an action for delay in loading that a frost had stopped the navigation of the canal by which the cargo would [normally] have been brought.[24]

The policy behind such a position is significant: it is the defendant who must bear such risks and protect himself from the normal exigencies of his trade or business.

Liability in Torts Is Based on Fault

The law of torts is based on general duties. The breach of these duties constitutes a civil wrong, an observation that explains the use of the word "tort," which comes from the Latin and French and literally means "wrong." There is a long list of tortious wrongs, which include assault and battery, false imprisonment, trespass, conversion (by which a person "converts" another person's property to his own use), defamation, fraud, nuisance, and civil conspiracy.

The notion of "wrong" in torts has distinct moral overtones. Some of this is a reflection of the subject matter of the various torts, but some of it is a reflection of the replacement of the principle of simple cause with the principle of moral fault. This moral view has been buttressed more recently by the liberal analysis of torts in the theoretical literature, which brings in the concepts of freedom, equality, and choice to explain the role of fault in this body of law. The law of torts, David Owen writes, is "based upon the equal abstract right of every person to pursue his own interests without undue interference from others."[25] The analytical and utilitarian tendencies in the academic discussion are reflected in its use of economic methods to measure loss.

The liberal formulation is nevertheless problematic. The legal foundation of torts does not lie in freedom. It lies in duty, and in the obligation of persons to take care in their dealings with other persons. The historical purpose of the law of torts was to provide a remedy for those members of society who have been harmed by the actions of other members of society. The rationale behind this development was conservative and reciprocal: the fundamental purpose of the civil law was to discourage individual persons from seeking their own remedies.[26] The law was developed to assuage the wrongs suffered by plaintiffs rather than to maximize the freedom of defendants.

There Are Competing Instincts in Negligence

The liberal position nevertheless helps to explain the origins of the law of negligence. Charles Gregory writes that the move from strict liability to negligence was based on the idea that new enterprises should be allowed to develop without the additional burden of paying for damages caused inadvertently, without fault.[27] This idea was complemented by the development of a philosophical and psychological view that legal liability must be justified. There is a modern feeling, at least, that defendants should not be held responsible unless they have done something wrong.

There are competing instincts in the law. Negligence has also been used to extend liability beyond the "intentional" torts. This development is usually traced to *Donoghue v. Stevenson*, [1932] A.C. 562, where the plaintiff discovered the decomposed remains of a snail in a bottle of ginger beer. The House of Lords extended the liability for negligence to harm that was reasonably foreseeable.[28] The excerpt from Justice Laskin's judgement in *Jordan House Ltd. v. Menow* also extends liability, on the basis that a defendant may voluntarily assume a duty to another person through its own conduct.

The theory of negligence set out in *Donoghue v. Stevenson* is based on a "duty of care." William Prosser tells us that this duty requires the defendant "to conform to a certain standard of conduct, for the protection of others against unreasonable risks."[29] The relevant standard of conduct is based on the "reasonable man," who exercises the care and diligence of an ordinary but prudent member of the public. This was famously described by Lord Justice Greer, in *Hall v. Brooklands Auto-Racing Club* (1933) 1 K.B. 205, as the standard of conduct of "the man on the Clapham omnibus."

Cook v. Lewis: **The Standard of Liability in Torts Takes the Mechanisms of the Legal Process into Account**

The standard of liability in torts takes the mechanisms of the legal process into account. The decisions in the common law provide a record of a contest between a particular plaintiff and defendant, which can be decided only on the basis of the evidence before the court. As a result, any decision on liability by a judge is a relative matter, which reflects the exigencies of each case. A finding that the defendants' negligence caused the harm suffered by the plaintiff merely means that, in all the circumstances of the case, the defendant should bear the cost of the harm suffered by the plaintiff.

The instrumental nature of the common law is illustrated by *Cook v. Lewis*, [1951] S.C.R. 830, where two hunters fired their guns "almost simultaneously." Although one of the shots apparently struck the plaintiff in the face, it was not possible to tell which of the defendants had fired the shot. The jury dismissed the case on the basis that the plaintiff had not proven which of the two defendants had caused the injuries.

The Supreme Court of Canada sent the case back for a new trial. Justice Rand held that the judge and jury at trial had failed to take the "auxiliary mechanisms" of the law into account. If the jury found that Cook and Akenhead were negligent, he ruled, the plaintiff had proved its case and the burden of proof would shift to the defendants. It was then for each of the defendants to prove that the other defendant had injured the plaintiff. If they failed to do so, they would have to share the liability equally, in spite of the fact that the evidence was inconclusive as to who fired the guilty shot.

The decision of the Supreme Court of Canada is clearly based on the firm belief that the purpose of the principle of cause is to determine who should pay for the harm suffered by the plaintiff. This can be compared to the task of a criminal court, which is there specifically to deal with immoral conduct and could not have convicted the defendants on the ordinary criminal standard. The policy issue before the court in *Cook v. Lewis* was merely whether the plaintiff should be compensated, and if the evidence established that both of the defendants had committed a tortious wrong, why should they escape liability? The facts of the case suggest that the defendants were trying to escape their liabilities on a technical matter of proof.

Marconato and Marconato v. Franklin: **The Thin Skull Rule Reflects the Concern with Compensation**

The fact that the historical sources of the civil law lie in the need to compensate those who have suffered "wrongs," rather than moral blame, is still reflected in the thin skull rule. This rule holds that the defendant is liable for the full extent of the plaintiff's injuries, even if the injuries are unexpectedly severe as a result of the plaintiff's prior condition. Thus, the defendant cannot complain that the plaintiff has an "eggshell" skull, for example, and escape the resulting costs.

In *Marconato and Marconato v. Franklin* [1974] B.C.J. No. 704, Mrs. Marconato was driving a car that was hit by the defendant's car. She suffered a "moderate cervical strain."

She and her husband subsequently sued for general and special damages. General damages cover non-pecuniary losses, such as pain, suffering, and the loss of enjoyment of life. Special damages cover ascertainable pecuniary losses, such as the cost of a visit to a physiotherapist or a taxi fare.

The only issue at trial was whether the husband was entitled to general damages for the loss of "consortium." Mrs. Marconato had suffered a personality change after the accident and had become morose and uncommunicative. The marriage had lost its "togetherness" as a result. This result was unexpected:

> The consequences for Mrs. Marconato could no more be foreseen than it could be foreseen by a tortfeasor that his victim was thin skulled and that a minor blow to the head would cause very serious injury. It is implicit, however, in the principle that a wrongdoer takes his victim as he finds him, that he takes his victim with all the victim's peculiar susceptibilities and vulnerabilities.[30]

It follows that the defendant was liable for "all the consequences" of the negligence, including the loss of consortium.

The usual rationale for the thin skull rule is that it is preferable to place the burden for the loss on the tortfeasor, who has done something wrong.[31] This is a modern explanation, however, and the original reasoning in the common law was rather that the misfortune should not have befallen the plaintiff, who must be compensated. The historical view rests on simple cause and merely holds that the burden of fate falls logically on the person who causes the harm to the victim. This was clearly to prevent retaliation and preserve the relations between the members of society.

The Doctrine of Contributory Negligence Focusses on Fault

There are competing legal doctrines, such as contributory negligence, that restrict damages. The term "contributory negligence" has two meanings, however. H.L.A. Hart and Tony Honoré use it to describe a specific act of negligence on the part of the plaintiff that forms a necessary part of the chain of events that caused the harm.[32] An example might be the act of a driver who lets his car drift carelessly into the path of a vehicle that is negligently overtaking him. The English common law has historically treated such an act as a *novus actus interveniens*, a new and intervening act, which causes the resulting harm. It accordingly prevents the plaintiff from recovering damages from the defendant.

The second use of the term "contributory negligence" refers to an act of the plaintiff, separate from the events that led to the harm, that increases the magnitude of the harm that the plaintiff has suffered. The simplest example is probably the failure of a passenger in a motor vehicle to use a seat belt, which reduces the quantum of damages in many jurisdictions.[33] It has been held that the thin skull rule does not apply in such cases because the plaintiff had a duty to wear a seat belt.[34]

There are two ways of explaining such a ruling. The first is that the plaintiff's duty offsets the defendant's duty and reduces the fault that attaches to the defendant. The plaintiff is also to blame, and a competing duty cannot be classified as a pre-existing condition.[35] It could also be argued that the defendant has only "caused" the harm that would have resulted if the plaintiff had been wearing a seat belt. Since the courts seem to be penalizing passengers who do not wear seat belts, however, the motivating factor appears to be fault.

Norberg v. Wynrib: *Equity Is Based on Fiduciary Duties*

The duties in the civil law often overlap. This is apparent in *Norberg v. Wynrib* [1992] 2 S.C.R. 226, where the plaintiff became addicted to pain killers. Her doctor subsequently provided her with drugs in return for emotional and sexual favours. The Supreme Court of Canada held that the relationship between the doctor and his patient had many of the elements of contract.[36] It also gave rise to "a duty of care," however, which would provide the necessary foundation for an action in torts. There was nevertheless no liability in contracts, or torts, since the plaintiff had agreed to the arrangement and there was no obvious source of negligence.[37]

Justices McLachlin and L'Heureux-Dubé nevertheless held that there was a third source of liability in equity, which includes the law of trusts and recognizes fiduciary relationships:

> In negligence and contract the parties are taken to be independent and equal actors, concerned primarily with their own self-interest. . . . The essence of a fiduciary relationship, by contrast, is that one party exercises power on behalf of another and pledges himself or herself to act in the best interests of the other.

A fiduciary relationship is built upon trust, like the relationship between a parent and a child or a teacher and a student.

Justices McLachlin and L'Heureux-Dubé held that the relationship between a doctor and a patient is a fiduciary relationship. Thus,

> a physician takes the power which a patient normally has over her body, and which she cedes to him for the purposes of treatment. The physician is pledged by the nature of his calling to use the power the patient cedes him exclusively for her benefit. If he breaks that pledge, he is liable.

A doctor is not entitled to sacrifice a patient's interests merely because the patient is prepared to allow the doctor do so.

Madam Justice McLachlin also suggests that gender comes into the analysis. In her view, the case provides a casebook example of a male doctor exploiting a female patient.

The evidence is clear that Ms. Norberg found the sexual contact degrading and dehumanizing. She avoided it for as long as she could, leaving Dr. Wynrib's care when he first suggested it. When desperation drove her back, she submitted only when her addiction rendered it absolutely necessary.

These comments appear to excuse the conduct of the plaintiff. This is highly disputable: neither party had acted admirably, and the plaintiff acknowledged that she had played on the respondent's loneliness in order to obtain her prescriptions.

Cause Is Still the Principal Underlying Factor in Deciding Civil Liability

The principal underlying issue in deciding civil liability remains cause. The principle of cause changed over time, however, as the moral concerns that entered the civil law migrated to the analysis of cause. Although it is difficult to gauge how far the early common law might have traced cause in determining liability, the principle of simple cause is an objective principle, which does not rest on the perception of the defendant. The question whether the harm caused by a defendant's negligent act was reasonably foreseeable, on the other hand, suggests that the defendant has not caused any harm that he was unable to foresee.

This change in the principle of cause raises a philosophical question: what do we mean when we say that the defendant's breach of duty to the plaintiff "caused" the harm or loss that the plaintiff suffered? One answer to this question is primarily negative: it cannot be said that the defendant's action has legally caused the harm unless it is a *sine qua non*. It must also be a precipitating factor, which actually gave rise to the discrete chain of events that led to the harm. In *Athey v. Leonati*, [1996] 3 S.C.R. 458, the Supreme Court of Canada accordingly held that cause has been established if the harm would not have occurred "but for" the actions of the defendant; in such circumstances, the defendant is liable.

Collingwood Distinguishes between Cause and Necessary Conditions

The test set out by the Supreme Court of Canada seems insufficient, however. There are many conditions precedent, without which an accident could not happen, that are not considered the "cause" of an event. Many events are at least temporally necessary, if the defendant's actions are going to cause the plaintiff harm. Are we going to say, for example, that my parents' decision to immigrate to Canada "caused" my car collision in Calgary, since the accident would not have occurred if we had stayed in England?

It is widely recognized that an action becomes the direct cause of harm only if it takes place in a particular context. John Stuart Mill, for example, took the position that the whole set of conditions that lead to an event constitutes the cause of the event. It is arbitrary, in Mill's view, to settle upon one of these conditions as the "true cause" of the event.

R.G. Collingwood argued, against Mill, that we need to distinguish between the "cause" of an event and the necessary conditions that allow the cause to take effect. He gives the example of books that go mouldy: "damp will not cause books to go mouldy unless there are mouldy spores about."[38] The "damp" is not a cause: it is one of the necessary conditions, without which the cause cannot trigger the consequences that concern us.

As H.L.A. Hart and A.M. Honoré write, in *Causation in the Law*, Collingwood "treats the question 'What is the cause of an event?' as if it was always equivalent to 'How can we produce or prevent this?'"[39] We use the word "cause," however, in many circumstances where we are unable to produce or prevent an event from occurring. The fact that we cannot prevent cancer, for example, does not stop us from speaking of the "cause" of cancer.

The more fundamental argument in *Causation in the Law* is that the principle of cause is open to ordinary analysis, outside the law. "Causal judgements," they write,

> are not specifically legal. They appeal to a notion which is part of everyday life and which ordinary people, including jurymen, can handle with a minimum of guidance. There is no gain, and much danger, in seeking to assimilate them to policy judgments which are specifically legal, whether they concern particular rules of law or represent aims of the legal system as a whole.[40]

The use of ordinary judgement allows us to distinguish between "causes" in the true sense and "mere conditions."[41]

The legal analysis of cause traces the logical pedigree of the events that culminated in the wrong suffered by the plaintiff. The law attaches liability to the defendant's breach of a legal duty if the breach constitutes the starting point of the series of events that causes the plaintiff harm. To be the cause, this breach must disrupt the natural succession of events and circumstances, forcing events to branch out in a new and unanticipated direction. On this understanding of cause, alone, each breach of a legal duty that gives rise to a new branch in this succession of events arguably gives rise to a new cause of action.

The Law Restricts Civil Liability to Proximate Cause

There is also the issue of remoteness. The civil law sees the events that logically give rise to the plaintiff's harm as a chain of causes. The defendant is liable only for acts that occur in close causal proximity to the event that causes the harm or loss. The difficulty in determining whether the defendant's actions are a proximate cause of the plaintiff's damages is illustrated by Mr. Justice Andrews' dissenting decision in the case of *Palsgraf v. Long Island Railroad Co., supra.* Justice Andrews asks us to consider the following facts:

> A chauffeur negligently collides with another car which is filled with dynamite, although he could not know it. An explosion follows. A, walking on the sidewalk nearby, is killed. B, sitting in a window of a building opposite, is cut by flying

glass. C, likewise sitting in a window a block away, is similarly injured. And a further illustration. A nursemaid, ten blocks away, startled by the noise, involuntarily drops a baby from her arms to the walk.[42]

This may be a false dilemma, since the obvious argument is that it is the driver of the second car who is negligent, in loading his vehicle with dynamite. Indeed, the act of loading the car with dynamite appears to be the proximate cause of most—if not all—of the resulting damage.

It is nevertheless a matter of judgement whether a proximate link exists between the chauffeur's actions and the harm suffered by each of the other individuals. As we have seen, the standard used by the courts in deciding such issues is whether the harm was reasonably foreseeable. Thus, Justice Andrews writes,

> C may not recover while A may. As to B it is a question for court or jury. We will all agree that the baby might not. Because, we are again told, the chauffeur had no reason to believe his conduct involved any risk of injuring either C or the baby.

It follows that foresight is one of the ingredients of proximate cause, which is not decided on a simple temporal or physical basis.

Justice Andrews' comments insert a subjective qualifier into the legal analysis of cause. The chauffeur's understanding is relevant to the determination whether the accident caused the injury to B and C. This illustrates the nature of the legal principle of cause, which is there to apportion rights and duties between the persons in society. It is notable that the issue of blame clearly filters into the assessment of cause and brings a policy component directly into the law. The standard of liability in negligence, reasonable foreseeability, is a moral tool that is used to determine whether the imperatives in a particular case are sufficient to trigger a duty:

> All we mean by the word "proximate" is that because of convenience, of public policy, of a rough sense of justice, the law arbitrarily declines to trace a series of events beyond a certain point. This is not logic, it is practical politics.

This reference to a "rough sense of justice" and "practical politics" demonstrates how the introduction of moral considerations into the analysis of cause often brings a political element into the caselaw.[43]

There is no doubt that some of the confusions and inconsistencies in the caselaw can be traced to differences in the political views of individual judges.[44] It is also clear that defendants may have benefitted from the political views of judges who felt that it was in the public interest to restrict the extent of liability in the civil law. Some of these restrictions are a product of industrial and technological advances, which have created potential liabilities (in the case, for example, of atomic energy) that were inconceivable in the past.[45] There are practical limits on the ability of any party to pay damages.

The Assessment of Probabilities in Damages Has Diluted the Principle of Cause

These kinds of issues arise in many contexts. The principle of cause has been diluted by the introduction of "risk analysis" into the assessment of damages, a development that can be traced to the influence of economics on the contemporary caselaw. Recently, the common law courts have begun to allow recovery on the basis of probabilities, such as the probability of cancer occurring rather than its actual occurrence.[46]

This new development goes against the traditional proposition, based on *restitutio in integrum*, which holds that the defendant must compensate the victim for the whole of the loss that the defendant has caused. The real effect of this risk-based approach is to widen the scope of the law and allow recovery in cases on the margins of liability. At the same time, it seems like a weak compromise that muddies the law and leaves plaintiffs with a fraction of the compensation that they need to recover their loss.

The Doctrines of Inevitable Accident and Act of God Are Based on Cause

The confusion that entered the law when the moral concept of fault entered into the analysis of cause is evident in doctrines like inevitable accident (sometimes called "unavoidable accident") and act of God. These doctrines hold that a defendant is not liable for circumstances that could not have been reasonably prevented. The usual example is the case of a defendant who has his first epileptic seizure while driving a motor vehicle.[47] If the driver has no way of knowing that the attack will occur, it could not have been foreseen, and the driver cannot be held liable in negligence.

The caselaw is misleading, however, since it suggests that the defendant in such a case is free of liability because he has done nothing wrong. The real issue, however, lies in cause. Either the defendant's act was involuntary, in which case there is no breach of a legal duty, or the seizure constituted a *novus actus intervenus*, and the defendant was a passive participant in what occurred. In either case, it cannot be said that the defendant's breach of a legal duty caused the harm.

Notes

1. Frances Bowes Sayre, "Mens Rea," *Harvard Law Review* 45 (1931–2): 974–1026, at p. 978.
2. See Alan Calnan, *A Revisionist History of Tort Law*, as cited in the suggestions for further reading, at p. 31: "The flaws in Holmes' historiography were fundamental and far-reaching." Calnan argues that Holmes used his historical research to justify his own theory of the development of torts.
3. Percy H. Winfield, "The Myth of Absolute Liability," *Law Quarterly Review* 42 (1926): 37–51.
4. Calnan, op. cit., p. 291.
5. W.J.V. Windeyer, "The Mental Elements of Tort and Crime," in *Lectures on Legal History*, 2nd ed. (Sydney: Law Book Company of Australasia, 1957), at p. 22.

6.   Though of course there were complications, and a trespasser, for example, was lucky to get off so lightly.

7.   This is not to suggest that a murderer escaped liability because his weapon, for example, was liable.

8.   Oliver Wendell Holmes, *The Common Law*, as cited in the readings, p. 14. Available at http://heinonline.org.

9.   W.J.V. Windeyer, *Lectures on Legal History*, op. cit., p. 21.

10. For a discussion of the resurgence in the use of deodands in the nineteenth century, and their eventual abolition, see Elisabeth Cawthon, "New Life for the Deodand: Coroners' Inquests and Occupational Deaths in England, 1830–46," *The American Journal of Legal History* 33, no. 2 (April 1989): 137–47.

11. See the story from the *Canadian Press*: Chinta Puxley, "Victim's Family Outraged Greyhound Bus Where Man Beheaded Still on the Road" (4 June 2009), available, for example, at www.freerepublic.com/focus/f-news/2264861/posts. And see Paul Groarke, "We Have to Realize that Something Wrong Has Happened," *Daily Gleaner* (25 June 2009).

12. Thus, in *U.S.A. v. Approximately 54 Pit Bulldogs* (Dist. Ct. of Eastern Virginia, Civil Action No.: 3.07CV397, 2007), the authorities obtained an order against the dogs belonging to Michael Vick, a quarterback in the National Football League.

13. The full style of cause of the cases is: *U.S. v. an Undetermined Number of Cases, Each Case Containing 24 Bottles of an Article Labeled in Part: (Bottle) "Sterling Vinegar and Honey Aged in Wood Cider Blended with Finest Honey Contents 1 Pint Product of Sterling Cider Co., Inc., Sterling, Mass." and an Undetermined Number of Copies of the Books Entitled "Folk Medicine" and "Arthritis and Folk Medicine," both by D.C. Jarvis, Balanced Foods, Inc., Claimant-Appellant* (1964) 338 F. 2d 157. Available at http://federal-circuits.vlex.com/vid/vinegar-cider-pint-arthritis-37626478.

14. Henry Sumner Maine, "Early History of Delict and Crime," in *Ancient Law: Its Connection with the Early History of Society and Its Relation to Modern Ideas* (London: J. Murray, 1920), p. 392ff. Available at http://heinonline.org.

15. The plaintiff is sometimes described as the claimant, complainant, or petitioner; the defendant is sometimes described as the respondent.

16. It is often said that the standard of proof in a civil case is "on a preponderance of evidence." This is misleading, since the sufficiency of the evidence may still be an issue, even if the plaintiff leads more evidence than the defendant.

17. See the additional online reading from Prosser's "The Assault upon the Citadel" (1960).

18. F.H. Lawson, "Notes on the History of Tort in the Civil Law," *Journal of Comparative Legislation and International Law*, 3rd series, 22, no. 4 (1940): 136–65, at p. 150. Available at www.jstor.org.

19. Available at www.courts.state.ny.us.

20. See David G. Owen, ed., *Philosophical Foundations of Tort Law* (Oxford: Clarendon, 1995) and D.J. Ibbetson, *A Historical Introduction to the Law of Obligations*, as cited in the suggestions for further reading. Though it should be noted that the term "obligations" is rarely used in legal practice.

21. In *In Re Estate of Charles Millar, Deceased*, [1938] S.C.R. 1, for example, the court considered whether public policy prevented the deceased from leaving the residue of his estate "to the mother who has since my death given birth in Toronto to the greatest number of children as shown by the registrations under the Vital Statistics Act."

22. See Grant Gilmore, *The Death of Contract*, as cited in the suggestions for further reading.

23. Pollock, *Principles of Contract at Law and in Equity*, as cited in the readings, p. 398.

24. ibid., p. 527.

25. David G. Owen, "Philosophical Foundations of Fault in Tort Law," in *Philosophical Foundations of Tort Law*, op. cit., p. 207.

26. See William Holdsworth, *History of English Law*, vol. 3 (London: Sweet & Maxwell, 1955), p. 278: "The first business of the law, and more especially of the law of crime and tort, is to suppress self-help."

27. Charles O. Gregory, "Trespass to Negligence to Absolute Liability," as cited in the suggestions for further reading.

28. The doctrine of "reasonable foreseeability" was discussed at length in *Overseas Tankship (UK) Ltd. v. Morts Dock & Engineering Company Ltd* [1961] U.K.P.C. 1 (18 January 1961), [1995] 2 All E.R. 736, a case commonly known as "Wagon Mound (No. 1)," which is available at www.bailii.org.

29. William L. Prosser, "The Assault upon the Citadel," as cited in the suggestions for further reading.

30. *Marconato and Marconato v. Franklin* [1974] B.C.J. No. 704, p. 47.

31. The courts are aware that the general use of insurance policies makes the kind of inequities that might arise in such a circumstance less onerous than they might appear.

32. H.L.A. Hart and Tony Honoré, *Causation in the Law*, as cited infra.

33. The failure to wear a seat belt is an omission. Omissions may be acts in law, however. A person who refuses to step off a set of train tracks at the sight of an oncoming train has acted and "caused" his own injuries.

34. The use of a seat belt is required by statute in most jurisdictions.

35. Compare *Jordan House Ltd. v. Menow*, as cited in the readings, where the plaintiff had allegedly breached his own duty under the *Liquor Control Act*. It is worth asking in which sense, and in what way, the plaintiff had been contributorily negligent?

36. This is one of the reasons that the courts place so much emphasis on consent in a medical context, since consent is an essential part of the consensus *ad idem* that creates a binding agreement.

37. It is not clear that the court is correct in this ruling. There is plenty of room for an argument that a doctor who feeds a patient's addiction is negligent.

38. See R.G. Collingwood, "On the So-Called Idea of Causation," *Proceedings of the Aristotelian Society*, n.s. 38 (1937–1938): 85–112, at pp. 89–91.

39. H.L.A. Hart and Tony Honoré, *Causation in the Law*, 2nd ed. (Oxford: Clarendon, [1959] 1985), p. 33. This seems to offer the most extensive examination of the legal theory of cause in the contemporary literature.

40. ibid., p. iv.

41. See Peter Lipton, "Causation Outside the Law," in *Jurisprudence: Cambridge Essays*, ed. Hyman Gross and Ross Harrison (Oxford: Clarendon, 1992), pp. 127–48. Available at www.hps.cam.ac.uk/people/lipton/causation_outside_the_law.pdf.

42. *Palsgraf v. Long Island Railroad Co.*, op. cit.

43. See Hart and Honoré, op. cit., at pp. 304–7, where they make a distinction between physical and economic harm and suggest that the courts are reluctant to provide compensation for economic harm because that would interfere with the individual freedoms of defendants.

44. See Charles O. Gregory's comment, for example, in "Trespass to Negligence to Absolute Liability," op. cit., at p. 359, that the law of torts is a "mass of contradictions."

45. This has led to statutory restrictions on liability, which raise moral and political issues of their own. Should enterprises that cannot meet their potential liabilities be allowed to conduct their affairs outside the normal constraints of the civil law?

46. See, for example, Glen O. Robinson, "Probabilistic Causation and Compensation for Tortious Risk," *Journal of Legal Studies* 14 (December 1985): 779–98, at p. 789ff. And see the discussion, for example, in *Laferrière v. Lawson*, [1991] 1 S.C.R. 541.

47. See the cases discussed in Robert D. Kligman, "Inevitable Accident and the Infirm Driver: What You Do Know Can Kill You," *Advocates' Quarterly* 8 (1987): 311–19. Available at http://heinonline.org.

Study Questions

1. Why did earlier peoples believe that civil liability was attached to the object that caused a personal harm?

2. What is the basis of liability in torts?

3. What is the basis of liability in contracts?

4.   What is the basis of liability in equity?

5.   What role do moral values and social policy play in torts, contracts, and equity?

6.   Imagine that you are driving down the freeway, daydreaming, and hit another car. The force of the collision drives the second car into a third car. Imagine that the resulting collision drives the third car into a fourth car, and so on, indefinitely. Where does your liability stop? At the twelfth car? At the twenty-third car? Explain.

7.   What was Collingwood's criticism of the idea of cause?

Further Reading

Alan Calnan, *A Revisionist History of Tort Law: From Holmesian Realism to Neoclassical Rationalism* (Durham, NC: Carolina Academic, 2005).

Donoghue v. Stevenson, [1932] A.C. 562. Available at www.bailii.org. The seminal case in the law of negligence.

Grant Gilmore, *The Death of Contract*, 2nd ed., ed. K.L. Collins (Columbus: Ohio State University [1974] 1995).

Charles O. Gregory, "Trespass to Negligence to Absolute Liability," *Virginia Law Review* 37, no. 3 (1951): 359–97. Available at http://heinonline.org.

D.J. Ibbetson, *A Historical Introduction to the Law of Obligations* (Oxford: Oxford University, 1999).

Frederic William Maitland, "The Origin of Equity," in *Equity: Also the Forms of Action at Common Law—Two Courses of Lectures by F.W. Maitland*, ed. A.H. Chaytor and W.J. Whittaker (Cambridge, MA: Cambridge University, 1929). Available at http://heinonline.org.

Richard A. Posner, *Economic Analysis of Law*, 8th ed. (New York: Aspen Publishers, 2010). See Part II, in particular, which includes a discussion of property, contracts, torts, and the evolution of the common law.

William L. Prosser, "The Assault upon the Citadel (Strict Liability to the Consumer)," *Yale Law Journal* 69, no. 7 (1960): 1099–148. Available at http://heinonline.org.

16 Public Law: A Crime Is a Public Wrong

Readings

- From *Lectures on Legal History*, by W.J.V. Windeyer
- From "*Mens Rea*," by Frances Bowes Sayre
- From "The Enforcement of Morals," by Sir Patrick Devlin
- From *Law, Liberty, and Morality*, by H.L.A. Hart

The criminal law is based on two fundamental concepts. The first is the idea of a public wrong, which came out of the idea of the King's peace and the pleas of the Crown. The second is the concept of *mens rea*, which brought a moral component into the criminal law. The moral character of the criminal law remains its distinguishing feature: a crime requires a vicious act of will. Yet this requirement has become problematic in the case of some offences, because there is far less agreement in contemporary society than there was in the past as to what constitutes an immoral act. Some of the uncertainty that this has created has to be attributed historically to the use of the criminal law to enforce matters of private morality. These issues were debated by H.L.A. Hart and Patrick Devlin, a judge, who argued that society has the prerogative to punish individuals for moral offences.

⊰ Readings ⊱

From W.J.V. Windeyer, *Lectures on Legal History*, 2nd ed. (Sydney: Law Book Company of Australasia, 1957).[1]

The Origins of the Criminal Law Lie in the King's Peace[2]

The history of the development of criminal law is the history of the King's peace. . . . But the King's peace was not the only peace which existed in the land. There was the peace of fairs and markets, the peace of Church buildings, the peace of the moots, protected by a law of Alfred which forbade fighting at meetings. In every Hundred and Shire there was also an indefinite peace of the community. And most important of all, every freeman had his peace, or *mund*, in his own household. . . . By their oldest customary law, the English regarded as a wrongdoer the man who broke the peace of a household. To strike a man in another's house was not merely a wrong to the injured man. It was a wrong to the householder, for it had disturbed his peace. . . .

The King's peace was probably at first only the peace of his household. It existed in the neighbourhood where he was resident for the time being. It existed over a more wide-spread area at particular times, such as at the coronation, at Christmas, and at Easter. It could be conferred by him on his servants and attendants. It was extended by degrees to travelers on the King's highways. . . .

The gradual extension of the King's peace, till it comprehended his whole kingdom and all his subjects and was always in existence, was the beginning of modern criminal law. But this extension had not proceeded far before the Norman Conquest and was not completed until long afterwards. Until the reign of Richard I, the King's peace died with the King and did not begin again until it was proclaimed and made effective by his successor. . . .

Another element in Anglo-Saxon law, which was of great importance in the progress towards a distinct criminal law, was the law of *wite* as distinct from *wer* [the payment of blood money].[3] Compensation to the injured man, or the kindred of the man who was slain, was not, in every case, a sufficient atonement. From very early days another payment called *wite* had to be made for serious wrongs. This was not paid as compensation for the injury; it was more in the nature of a fine. It was payable not to the injured party or his representative, but to the King, or, perhaps in early times, to the community.

There were also some offences of peculiar gravity which were *boteless* or *bootless*. That is to say, no *bot* [a payment of compensation] could be given for them. They were not reparable; and for them punishment was inflicted. As time went on, the number of these offences became greater; and they came to be regarded as offensive to the King and punishable by him. . . .

The usual penalties for a *bootless* offence were either death, which was the common fate of a thief caught in the act and of other serious offenders, reduction to slavery, outlawry, or mutilation. The last seems to have been sometimes based on a savage attempt to make the punishment fit the crime; for example, a thief, long suspected but, until the last, never caught, might have a hand or foot cut off; a false coiner's hand would be cut off and fastened up over the mint; and adulterers, those guilty of rape, and public slanderers were liable to horrible mutilations, the last often having their tongues cut out. In practice these brutalities may have been somewhat mitigated by the power which the King had, in some cases, to allow heavy fines instead of mutilation. . . .

[During the twelfth century, other] wrongs became crimes, subjects for the King's justice, punishable by death or maiming. Some became punishable by discretionary money penalties, known as amercements, instead of by the old fixed *wites*. . . .

The Criminal Law Was Part of the Pleas of the Crown

The distinction between what we now call tort and what we now call crime was still undeveloped. . . . What we call criminal law was then, and for centuries later, comprehended under the term *pleas of the Crown*, as distinct from *common pleas*, which were civil actions. The gravest offences among the pleas of the Crown became known as *felonies*. This group included homicide, mayhem, wounding, false imprisonment, arson, robbery, rape, burglary, and larceny. . . . A convicted felon suffered death or mutilation and his lands became disinherited and escheated to his lord. A fugitive felon was liable to be outlawed. . . .

Today we divide crimes into treason, felonies, and misdemeanours. But the mediaeval lawyers did not use the last word nor recognize this classification. All wrongs of violence were for them breaches of the King's peace. As such, they were pleas of the Crown, technically known as *trespasses vi et armies*. For laymen, the word "trespass" today often means only an unlawful entry on the land of another. For modem lawyers, it means any actionable wrong to the person or property of another. For mediaeval lawyers, it meant simply a wrongful act, or, in a narrower sense, a wrongful act not amounting to a felony. . . .

Notes

1. Editor's note: Sir William John Victor Windeyer (1900–1987) was a professor of law and a judge, on both the High Court of Australia and the Privy Council.
2. Editor's note: Windeyer is following the lead of Frederick Pollock, in "The King's Peace in the Middle Ages," *Harvard Law Review* 13 (1899–1900): 177–90. Windeyer's account of the King's peace has attracted attention in the field of victimology, which traces the criminal law to the state's assertion of a monopoly on the right to prosecute offenders. See "The Historical Role of the Victim in Criminal Law," in Lynne N. Henderson, "The Wrongs of Victim's Rights," *Stanford Law Review* 37, no. 4 (April 1985): 937–1021, at pp. 938–42.
3. Editor's note: The Old English word "*wergild*" refers literally to a "man payment," which attached a fixed price to an individual's life on the basis of his social rank.

From Frances Bowes Sayre, "*Mens Rea*," *Harvard Law Review* 45 (1931–2): 974–1026.

"There can be no crime, large or small, without an evil mind," says Bishop. "It is therefore a principle of our legal system, as probably it is of every other, that the essence of an offence is the wrongful intent, without which it cannot exist."[1] . . .

The Early Law Did Not Require a Criminal Intent

From such records as remain some of our ablest legal students have concluded that primitive English law started from a basis bordering on absolute liability. The law, which was seeking to supplant the blood feud by inducing the victim or his kin to accept money payments in place of taking violent revenge, seemed to concentrate its gaze rather upon the outraged victims or would-be avengers who must be brought under control than upon the actual blameworthiness of the accused. . . .

"Whoever shall have killed a man," runs the old Westgothic Law, "whether he committed the homicide intending to or not intending to (*volens aut nolens*),. . . let him be handed over into the *potestas* [power or authority] of the parents or next of kin of the deceased." . . .

In early times, with the exception of killings under the King's warrant or in the pursuit of justice, which had always been justifiable, . . . [a] killer seems to have been held liable for every death which he caused, whether intentionally or accidentally.

The Beginnings of *Mens Rea* Can Be Found in Bracton

By the end of the twelfth century two influences were making themselves strongly felt. One was the Roman law which, resuscitated in the universities in the eleventh and twelfth centuries, was sweeping over Europe with new power. . . . This . . . study of law necessitated fresh examination of underlying legal concepts; and the Roman law conceptions of *dolus* and *culpa* required careful consideration of the mental element in crime.[2]

A second influence, even more powerful, was the canon law, whose insistence upon moral guilt emphasized still further the mental element in crime. In the determination of sin the mental element must be scrutinized quite as closely as the physical act. "Whosoever looketh on a woman to lust after her hath committed adultery with her already in his heart," said Christ; and following this teaching the penitential books naturally made the measure of penance for various sins very largely dependent upon the state of mind.

There was constant interaction and reaction between church and state law. It was the priests of the church who conducted the trials by ordeal and monks or priests who were the educators of the day. Small wonder then that our earliest reference to *mens rea* in an English law book is a scrap copied in from the teachings of the church. The book of *Leges* [laws] of Henry I . . . in discussing perjury recites that *reum non facit nisi mens rea* [there is no guilt unless there is a guilty mind].[3]

Bracton,[4] whose book, written in the middle of the thirteenth century, powerfully influenced the later shaping of the common law, was strongly tinged with the canonists' ideas. . . . [H]e says,

> we must consider with what mind (*animo*) or with what intent (*voluntate*) a thing is done, in fact or in judgement, in order that it may be determined accordingly what action should follow and what punishment. For take away the will and every act will be indifferent, because your state of mind gives meaning to your act, and a crime is not committed unless the intent to injure (*nocendi voluntas*) intervene, nor is a theft committed except with the intent to steal.

Further along, speaking of homicide by misadventure, after giving various examples . . . Bracton says that he who kills by misadventure

> but without an intent to kill, ought to be acquitted, because a crime is not committed unless the intent to injure (*voluntas nocendi*) intervene. . . . And this is in accordance with what might be said of the infant or the madman, since the

innocence of design protects the one and the lack of reason in committing the act excuses the other. . . .

After Bracton, *Mens Rea* Becomes a Requirement of the Criminal Law

Henceforth the criminal law . . . begins to insist upon a *mens rea* as an essential of criminality. . . . The formula found in the *Leges* of Henry I that *"reum non facit nisi mens rea"* [there is no guilt unless there is a guilty mind] was seized upon and used as a convenient label for the newer ideas, finally to evolve in Coke's *Third Institute* as *"actus non facit reum nisi mens sit rea"* [the act does not make one guilty unless the mind is also guilty]. . . . The transition from the more primitive concept of liability was all the easier because . . . most of the thirteenth century felonies from their very nature already involved an intentional element. Robbery and rape necessitate a design; they cannot possibly be committed through mischance. . . .

We can trace the changed attitude in new generalizations concerning the necessity of an evil intent which . . . make their appearance as settled doctrines in the writings of Coke and Hale during the seventeenth century. . . . During the centuries following Bracton's day this growing consciousness of a blameworthy mind or felonious intent as the basis of criminality is sometimes seized upon to mark the line of increasing differentiation between the crime and the tort, for the allowance of damages continued to be in the main independent of considerations of moral blameworthiness.

Notes

1. Editor's note: The reference is to American lawyer Joel Prentiss Bishop (1814–1901). Sayre footnotes the source of the quote as Bishop's *Criminal Law*, 9th ed. (1930), section 287, and includes a passage from John William Salmond's *Jurisprudence*, 3rd ed. (1930): "There are two conditions to be fulfilled before penal responsibility can rightly be imposed. . . . [One] is the doing of some act by the person to be held liable. . . . [The other] is the *mens rea* or guilty mind with which the act is done. . . before the law can justly punish the act, an inquiry must be made into the mental attitude of the doer."

2. Editor's note: Although the distinction between these terms is a matter of judgement and inherently imprecise, the term *"dolus"* applies to acts characterized by some form of malice or more explicit intention; *"culpa"* is often translated as "fault," and may include negligence.

3. Sayre's note: *Leges Henrici Primi*, c. 5, Section 28. As has been pointed out this goes back to St. Augustine, who in a sermon on James 5:12 ("swear not neither by heaven neither by the earth, neither by any other oath") declared that if a man believing that no rain fell in a certain spot, nevertheless for self-interest testifies that it did rain there, even though in fact it did rain he is a perjurer in the eyes of God.

4. Editor's note: Henry of Bracton was a judge of Court of King's Bench from 1247–50 and again from 1253–57. As noted in Chapter 4, he was famous as the author and editor of *On the Laws and Customs of England*, which ostensibly surveyed the whole of English law.

From Sir Patrick Devlin, "The Enforcement of Morals," in *Proceedings of the British Academy* (London: Oxford University, 1959), pp. 129–51.

The *Report of the Committee on Homosexual Offences and Prostitution*, generally known as the *Wolfenden Report*,[1] . . . sets out clearly and carefully what in relation to its subjects it considers the function of the law to be. . . . Early in the *Report* the Committee puts forward:

> Our own formulation of the function of the criminal law so far as it concerns the subjects of this enquiry. In this field, its function, as we see it, is to preserve public order and decency, to protect the citizen from what is offensive or injurious, and to provide sufficient safeguards against [the] exploitation and corruption of others. . . .
>
> It is not, in our view, the function of the law to intervene in the private lives of citizens, or to seek to enforce any particular pattern of behaviour, further than is necessary to carry out the purposes we have outlined. . . . there must remain a realm of private morality and immorality which is, in brief and crude terms, not the law's business. . . .

History of the Criminal Law

It is true that for many centuries the criminal law was much concerned with keeping the peace and little, if at all, with sexual morals. But it would be wrong to infer from that that it had no moral content. . . . The criminal law of England has from the very first concerned itself with moral principles. A simple way of testing this point is to consider the attitude which the criminal law adopts towards consent.

Subject to certain exceptions inherent in the nature of particular crimes, the criminal law has never permitted consent of the victim to be used as a defence. In rape, for example, consent negatives an essential element. But consent of the victim is no defence to a charge of murder. It is not a defence to any form of assault that the victim thought his punishment well deserved and submitted to it.[2] . . . The reason why a man may not consent to the commission of an offence against himself beforehand or forgive it afterwards is because it is an offence against society. . . .

Euthanasia or the killing of another at his own request, suicide, attempted suicide and suicide pacts, duelling, abortion, incest between brother and sister, are all acts which can be done in private and without offence to others and need not involve the corruption or exploitation of others. Many people think that the law on some of these subjects is in need of reform, but no one hitherto has gone so far as to suggest that they should all be left outside the criminal law as matters of private morality. . . .

We Need to Answer Three Questions

1. Does Society Have the Right to Pass Judgement on Matters of Morals?

What makes a society of any sort is community of ideas, not only political ideas but also ideas about the way its members should behave and govern their lives; these latter ideas are its morals. Every society has a moral structure as well as a political one. . . . Take, for example, the institution of marriage. Whether a man should be allowed to take more than one wife is something about which every society has to make up its mind one way or the other. In England we believe in the Christian idea of marriage and therefore adopt monogamy as a moral principle.

Consequently the Christian institution of marriage has become the basis of family life and so part of the structure of our society. . . . [I]t remains there because it is built into the house in which we live and could not be removed without bringing it down. The great majority of those who live in this country accept it because it is the Christian idea of marriage and for them the only true one. But a non-Christian is bound by it, not because it is part of Christianity but because, rightly or wrongly, it has been adopted by the society in which he lives. . . .

I return to the statement that I have already made, that society means a community of ideas; without shared ideas on politics, morals, and ethics no society can exist. . . .

2. If Society Has the Right to Pass Judgement, Does It Have the Right to Use the Weapon of the Law to Enforce Its Judgement?

[I]f society has the right to make a judgement and has it on the basis that a recognized morality is as necessary to society as, say, a recognized government, then society may use the law to preserve morality in the same way as it uses it to safeguard anything else that is essential to its existence. If therefore the first proposition is securely established with all its implications, prima facie society has the right to legislate against immorality as such.

The Wolfenden Report, notwithstanding that it seems to admit the right of society to condemn homosexuality and prostitution as immoral, requires special circumstances to be shown to justify the intervention of the law. I think that this is wrong in principle. . . .

Here again I think that the political parallel is legitimate. The law of treason is directed against aiding the King's enemies and against sedition from within. The justification for this is that established government is necessary for the existence of society and therefore its safety against violent overthrow must be secured. But an established morality is as necessary as good government to the welfare of society. Societies disintegrate from within more frequently than they are broken up by external pressures. There is disintegration when no common morality is observed and history shows that the loosening of moral bonds is often the first stage of disintegration, so that society is justified in taking the same steps to preserve its moral code as it does to preserve its government and other essential institutions. The suppression of vice is as much the law's business as the suppression of subversive activities. . . .

You may argue that if a man's sins affect only himself it cannot be the concern of society. If he chooses to get drunk every night in the privacy of his own home, is anyone except himself the worse for it? But suppose a quarter or a half of the population got drunk every night, what sort of society would it be? You cannot set a theoretical limit to the number of people who can get drunk before society is entitled to legislate against drunkenness. . . .

3. If Society Has the Right to Use the Weapon of the Law, When Should It Make Use of It?

In what circumstances the State should exercise its power is the third of the interrogatories I have framed. But before I get to it I must raise a point which might have been brought up in any one of the three. How are the moral judgements of society to be ascertained? . . . It is surely not enough that they should be reached by the opinion of the majority; it would be too much to require the individual assent of every citizen. English law has evolved and regularly uses a standard which does not depend on the counting of the heads. It is that of the reasonable man. He is not to be confused with the rational man. He is not expected to reason about anything and his judgement may be largely a matter of feeling. It is the viewpoint of the man in the street—or to use an archaism familiar to all lawyers—the man in the Clapham omnibus. . . .

For my purpose I should like to call him the man in the jury box, for the moral judgement of society must be something about which any twelve men or women drawn at random might after discussion be expected to be unanimous. This was the standard the judges applied in the days before Parliament was as active as it is now and when they laid down rules of public policy. They did not think of themselves as making law but simply as stating principles which every right-minded person would accept as valid. It is what [Frederick] Pollock called "practical morality," which is based not on theological or philosophical foundations but "in the mass of continuous experience half-consciously or unconsciously accumulated and embodied in the morality of common sense." . . .

Any immorality is capable of affecting society injuriously and in effect to a greater or lesser extent it usually does; this is what gives the law its locus standi. It cannot be shut out. But—and this brings me to the third question—the individual has a locus standi too; he cannot be expected to surrender to the judgement of society the whole conduct of his life. It is the old and familiar question of striking a balance between the rights and interests of society and those of the individual. . . .

To take a very down-to-earth example, let me consider the right of the individual whose house adjoins the highway to have access to it; that means in these days the right to have vehicles stationary in the highway. . . . There are many cases in which the courts have had to balance the private right of access against the public right to use the highway without obstruction. It cannot be done by carving up the highway into public and private areas. It is done by recognizing that . . . the rights of each must be curtailed so as to ensure as far as possible that the essential needs of each are safeguarded. . . .

This then is how I believe my third interrogatory should be answered—not by the formulation of hard and fast rules, but by a judgement in each case taking into account the sort of factors I have been mentioning. . . . The boundary between the criminal law and the moral law is fixed by balancing in the case of each particular crime the pros and cons of legal enforcement in accordance with the sort of considerations I have been outlining. . . .

Notes

1. Editor's note: The government of the United Kingdom established the Committee on Homosexual Offences and Prostitution in 1954. The Committee became known as the Wolfenden Committee, after its chairman, Sir John Wolfenden (1906–1985), and published its report in 1957. The report recommended that "homosexual behaviour between consenting adults in private should no longer be a criminal offence" and held, more broadly, that it is not the function of the criminal law "to intervene in the private life of citizens, or to seek to enforce any particular pattern of behaviour." On 16 September 1957, *Time Magazine* reported: "The recommendation on adult (over 21) homosexuality touched off the most violent reaction." "Bad, retrograde and utterly to be condemned," snapped Lord Beaverbrook's *Evening Standard*. "Freeing adult males from any penalties could only succeed in intensifying and multiplying this form of depravity." Lord Rothermere's *Daily Mail* agreed: "Great nations have fallen and empires decayed because corruption became socially acceptable." The full text of the report is available at http://nationalarchives.gov.uk.
2. Editor's note: This point seems debatable, particularly in the context of assault, which, in Canada, certainly requires a lack of consent; but the same is true in the case of fraud and theft, which naturally rest on the fact that the owner of the property did not consent to the taking.

From H.L.A. Hart, *Law, Liberty, and Morality* (Stanford, CA: Stanford University, 1963).

Much dissatisfaction has for long been felt in England with the criminal law relating to both prostitution and homosexuality, and in 1954 the committee well known as the Wolfenden Committee was appointed to consider the state of the law. This committee reported in September 1957 and recommended certain changes in the law on both topics. As to homosexuality they recommended by a majority of 12 to 1 that homosexual practices between consenting adults in private should no longer be a crime; as to prostitution they unanimously recommended that, though it should not itself be made illegal, legislation should be passed "to drive it off the streets" on the ground that public soliciting was an offensive nuisance to ordinary citizens. . . .

The Wolfenden Committee Has Adopted a Position Similar to that of John Stuart Mill

What concerns us here is less the fate of the Wolfenden Committee's recommendations than the principles by which these were supported. These are strikingly similar to those expounded by Mill in his essay *On Liberty*.[1] . . . Mill's principles are still very much alive in the criticism of law, whatever their theoretical deficiencies may be. But twice in one hundred years they have been challenged by two masters of the Common Law.

The first of these was the great Victorian judge and historian of the Criminal Law, James Fitzjames Stephen. His criticism of Mill is to be found in the sombre and impressive book *Liberty, Equality, Fraternity*, which he wrote as a direct reply to Mill's essay "On Liberty." . . . Stephen thought . . . that the law might justifiably enforce morality as such or, as he said, that the law should be "a persecution of the grosser forms of vice." Nearly a century later . . . Lord Devlin, now a member of the House of Lords and a most distinguished writer on the criminal law, in his essay on "The Enforcement of Morals" . . . argued . . . that "the suppression of vice is as much the law's business as the suppression of subversive activities.". . . [He further argues] that it is permissible for any society to take the steps needed to preserve its own existence as an organized society, and he thinks that immorality—even private sexual immorality—may, like treason, be something which jeopardizes a society's existence. . . .

[One] feature of our question worth attention is simply that it is a question of justifications. In asking it we are committed at least to the general critical principle that the use of legal coercion by any society calls for justification as something *prima facie* objectionable to be tolerated only for the sake of some countervailing good. . . .

It is salutary to inquire precisely what it is that is *prima facie* objectionable in the legal enforcement of morality; for the idea of legal enforcement is in fact less simple than is often assumed. It has two different but related aspects. One is the actual punishment of the offender. This characteristically involves depriving him of liberty of movement or of property or of association with family or friends, or the infliction upon him of physical pain or even death. All these are things which are assumed to be wrong to inflict on others without special justification. . . .

The second aspect of legal enforcement bears on those who may never offend against the law, but are coerced into obedience by the threat of legal punishment. . . . Such restrictions, it is to be noted, may be thought of as calling for justification for several quite distinct reasons. The unimpeded exercise by individuals of free choice may be held a value in itself with which it is *prima facie* wrong to interfere; or it may be thought valuable because it enables individuals to experiment—even with living—and to discover things valuable both to themselves and to others.

But interference with individual liberty may be thought an evil requiring justification for simpler, utilitarian reasons; for it is itself the infliction of a special form of suffering—often very acute—on those whose desires are frustrated by the fear of punishment. This is of particular importance in the case of laws enforcing a sexual morality. They may create misery of a quite special degree. . . . Unlike sexual impulses, the impulse to steal or to wound or even kill is not, except in a minority of mentally abnormal cases, a recurrent and insistent part of daily life. Resistance to the temptation to commit these crimes is not often, as the suppression of sexual impulses generally is, something which affects the development or balance of the individual's emotional life, happiness, and personality.

The Distinction between Paternalism and Legal Moralism

Lord Devlin . . . points out that, subject to certain exceptions such as rape, the criminal law has never admitted the consent of the victim as a defence. It is not a defence to a charge of murder or a deliberate assault, and this is why euthanasia or mercy killing terminating a man's life at his own request is still murder. . . . [H]e asserts of the rule under discussion, "There is only one explanation," and this is that "there are certain standards of behaviour or moral principles which society requires to be observed." . . . But Lord Devlin's statement that "there is only one explanation" is simply not true. The rules excluding the victim's consent as a defence to charges of murder or assault may perfectly well be explained as a piece of paternalism, designed to protect individuals against themselves. . . .

But paternalism . . . is a perfectly coherent policy. Indeed, it seems very strange in mid-twentieth century to insist upon this, for the wane of *laissez faire* since Mill's day is one of the commonplaces of social history, and instances of paternalism now abound in our law, criminal and civil. The supply of drugs or narcotics, even to adults, except under medical prescription is punishable by the criminal law, and it would seem very dogmatic to say of the law creating this offence that "there is only one explanation," namely, that the law was concerned not with the protection of the would-be purchasers against themselves, but only with the punishment of the seller for his immorality. . . .

The neglect of the distinction between paternalism and what I have termed legal moralism is important as a form of a more general error. It is too often assumed that if a law is not designed to protect one man from another its only rationale can be that it is designed to punish moral wickedness or, in Lord Devlin's words, "to enforce a moral principle." Thus it is often urged that statutes punishing cruelty to animals can only be explained in that way. But it is certainly intelligible . . . to say that the law is here concerned with the suffering . . . of animals, rather than with the immorality of torturing them.

The Moral Gradation of Punishment

I now turn back to a very different and perhaps more illuminating error made by Stephen, in his effort to show that the criminal law not only should be but actually was a "persecution of the grosser forms of vice" . . . His argument is simply this. When the question is how severely an offender should be punished, an estimate of the degree of moral wickedness involved in the crime is always relevant. . . .

But from this fact Stephen, like many others, inferred too much. He claimed that if we attach importance to the principle that the moral difference between offences should be reflected in the gradation of legal punishments, this showed that the *object* of such punishment was not merely to prevent acts "dangerous to society" but "to be a persecution of the grosser forms of vice." . . .

Surely this argument is a *non sequitur* generated by Stephen's failure to see that the questions "What sort of conduct may justifiably be punished?" and "How severely should we punish different offenses?" are distinct and independent questions. There are many reasons why we might wish the legal gradation of the seriousness of crimes, expressed in its scale of punishments, not to conflict with common estimates of their comparative wickedness. One reason is that such a conflict is undesirable on simple utilitarian grounds: it might either confuse moral judgements or bring the law into disrepute, or both. Another reason is that principles of justice or fairness between different offenders require morally distinguishable offences to be treated differently and morally similar offences to be treated alike. . . .

There Is a Moderate and an Extreme Thesis

When we turn from these examples which are certainly disputable to the positive grounds held to justify the legal enforcement of morality it is important to distinguish a moderate and an extreme thesis. . . . Lord Devlin seems to me to maintain, for most of his essay, the moderate thesis and Stephen the extreme one.

According to the moderate thesis, a shared morality is the cement of society; without it there would be aggregates of individuals but no society. . . . [W]e must not view conduct in isolation from its effect on moral code: if we remember this, we can see that one who is "no menace to others" nonetheless may by his immoral conduct "threaten one of the great moral principles" on which society is based. In this sense the breach of moral principle is an offence "against society as a whole" and society may use the law to preserve its morality as it uses it to safeguard anything else essential to its existence. . . .

By contrast, the extreme thesis does not look upon a shared morality as of merely instrumental value analogous to ordered government, and it does not justify the punishment of immorality as a step taken, like the punishment of treason, to preserve society from dissolution or collapse. Instead, the enforcement of morality is regarded as a thing of value, even if immoral acts harm no one directly, or indirectly by weakening the moral cement of society. . . .

Lord Devlin appears to defend the moderate thesis. . . . [Yet] apart from one vague reference to "history" showing that "the loosening of moral bonds is often the first stage of disintegration," no evidence is produced [by Devlin] to show that deviation from accepted sexual morality, even by adults in private, is something which, like treason, threatens the existence of society. No reputable historian has maintained this thesis, and there is indeed much evidence against it. As a proposition of fact it is entitled to no more respect than the Emperor Justinian's statement that homosexuality was the cause of earthquakes.

Note

1.   Editor's note: John Stuart Mill, *On Liberty* (London: Longman, Roberts, & Gree Co., 1959), which has been published in many later editions. Hart is referring to Mill's famous *dictum* that "the only purpose for which power can rightfully be exercised over any member of a civilized community" is to prevent harm to others.

⇥ Discussion ⇤

The following chapter reviews the development of the criminal law. The most fundamental issue that arises in this context is simple enough. What is it that makes murder or theft, for example, a "crime"? The answer to this question must take account of the fact that the criminal law came out of the moral customs of the people. A criminal offence is primarily a moral wrong. This fact was eventually enshrined in the idea that proof of a criminal offence requires blameworthiness. A satisfactory answer to the definitional question must also recognize, however, that the criminal law is a product of the state. Historically, the criminal law was used to justify and consolidate the increasing power of the state. Criminologists usually refer to this as "social control."

The Criminal Law Has Its Roots in the King's Peace

The roots of the criminal law can be found in the King's peace. In the customary law, before the advent of the common law, every household had its peace. A person who violated this peace had wronged the household. The King had a larger peace, which moved with him, his servants, and his officials and protected everything that appertained to his household. After the Norman Conquest in 1066, the King's peace was extended to "the King's highway" and protected anyone who travelled upon it. This protection was slowly extended, until it encompassed the entire realm and covered the public at large. Anyone who violated the King's peace had wronged the King.

The extension of the King's peace to the entire realm was part of a determined effort to assert the supremacy of the central government. This effort met with considerable opposition. England had been divided into a variety of kingdoms before the Norman Conquest, and government was overwhelmingly local. As James Fitzjames Stephen wrote, it was only "after a long series of struggles that the King became 'the source of justice, the lord and patron of his people, the owner of the public lands.'"[1]

The substantive sources of the criminal law, however, can be found in the moral customs of the people. The common law judges relied on the customary law in determining what constituted a wrong. This law existed long before there was a centralized system or Parliament and political government. In point of fact, it was the customary law that gave the new machinery of justice its legitimacy.

The Idea of a Crime Comes from Felonies

It was the establishment of royal courts with exclusive jurisdiction over felonies that gave rise to the criminal law.[2] By the end of the twelfth century, the King's court, originally the *Curia Regis* but later the Court of King's Bench, had already divided the country into judicial districts. This division led to the establishment of regular assizes, during which the judges of the Court of King's Bench would summon juries and hear the most serious criminal cases. The fundamentals of the tribal law had survived in the "hundreds courts," and in the shire or county courts, which handled local matters. There were also feudal courts, however, and ecclesiastical courts, which were seen by the Church and local "magnates" as important sources of revenue.

The ascendancy of the royal courts in the criminal arena was assured by the *Assize of Clarendon*, in 1166, when Henry II created a grand-jury system. The *Assize* decreed that the royal justices inquire of twelve lawful men in each township, under oath, if there were robbers, murderers, or thieves in the vicinity.[3] This removed the jurisdiction of the local and the ecclesiastical courts to try felonies.[4]

A crime, historically, is a felony. The concept of a felony came out of the Norman tradition in France, which reserved the name "felony" for the worst offences. The word itself comes from the Latin *felo*—meaning fierce, vicious, base—and refers to grievous wrongs, like murder and robbery. These wrongs were thought to betray offenders' feudal obligations to their lord. By the twelfth century, felonies were widely seen as wrongs against the King. They were therefore tried in the King's court.

From a historical perspective, Henry II's decree looks like a shrewd political compromise, which guaranteed the authority of the royal courts, even as it gave the local community the primary responsibility for convictions. The grand jury was a familiar institution in England, as it had been used since the time of the *Domesday Book* to settle legal questions concerning land. It was also part of the legal tradition in the Danelaw, that part of England that the Vikings had settled, and had subsequently entered the Anglo-Saxon legal system.[5]

These developments eventually gave rise to a rough division between felonies (now known as indictable offences in England and Canada) and misdemeanours (summary conviction offences), which were dealt with by local authorities. The appointment of justices of the peace by the King, who could try minor offences, further eroded the authority of the indigenous courts and increased the power of the King.

The Criminal Law Came Out of the Pleas of the Crown

The division of the common law into the civil law and the criminal law was based on the parties to the suit. A matter brought by a private person was called a "common plea" and had to be tried in the Court of Common Pleas. A matter brought by the King or his representative was a "plea of the Crown" and had to be tried in the Court of King's Bench. There has never been a clean dividing line between the subject matter of civil and criminal cases, and many crimes, such as assault and fraud, provide causes of action in torts.

The pleas of the Crown gave the Court of King's Bench authority over any matter that concerned the King. This authority was an ancient prerogative of kings, in England and elsewhere, and was known as the "pleas of the sword" in Normandy, a reference to the right of a king or a lord to use force in defence of his interests.[6] The difference in the case of the Norman kings was that they claimed all of England. It was the fact that their courts exercised authority over the entire country that laid the foundations for the common law.

The Pleas of the Crown Were One of the Primary Sources of Revenue for the Emerging State

Pollock and Maitland describe the list of the pleas of the Crown under William the Conqueror and the Norman kings who succeeded him as "long, disorderly, elastic."[7] These pleas simply dealt with any matter that engaged the King's interests. William Holdsworth accordingly writes that the pleas of the Crown had no substantive foundation and included a wide variety of actions concerning the proprietary rights of the Crown and the behaviour of public officials, as well as crimes. As a result, it has never been entirely clear which of the pleas of the Crown constituted crimes.[8]

Fiscal realities played a prominent role in these developments. Although the substantive sources of the criminal law lie firmly in moral customs, it is evident that the major reason for including felonies in the pleas of the Crown was that they gave rise to fines and forfeitures. The King therefore had a financial interest in having offences characterized as felonies.[9] Many authors have argued that the major impetus behind the creation of the royal courts and the rise of the criminal law was to obtain revenue for the growing bureaucracy of the state.[10]

Trial by Ordeal Was Replaced by an Evidentiary Process

The purpose of Henry II's grand juries was to determine who should be charged with a criminal offence. The accused person was originally tried by ordeal. The ordeal usually consisted of holding a heated iron bar, sprinkled with holy water, for nine paces or being bound and submerged in cold water. If pus formed in the accused's hand, or he floated on the water, it was a sign of God's disfavour, and he was found guilty.[11] This practice ended when Pope Innocent III prohibited the clergy from participating in trial by ordeal in 1215. Over time, the ordeal was replaced by "petty" (from *petit*, meaning little) juries, who slowly took on the role of determining guilt. There were many objections to the new system, which left people at the mercy of their neighbours.[12]

The evidentiary process developed slowly. At the beginning, jurors made their decisions on the basis of their personal knowledge of the case before them. Although witnesses could be brought before the court, Albert Thomas Carter writes that the jurors "were at liberty to make what inquiries they chose."[13] It was a long time "before it was thought necessary to produce evidence to support a prosecution, and longer still before the prisoner was allowed any evidence at all."

The Jurisdiction of the New Process Was Disputed

These early juries did not, however, enjoy any inherent authority over the accused. The accused was accordingly required to submit to the jurisdiction of the court. Under the first *Statute of Westminster*, passed in 1275, persons who refused a jury trial were to be placed in a prison and starved until they submitted to the jurisdiction of the court. Later this regimen became the direful *peine forte et dure* ("hard and forceful punishment"), under which persons who "stood mute" and refused to attorn to the jurisdiction of the courts were crushed by large stones until they entered a plea or suffocated.

The brutality of these measures is a testament to the rapacity of the new apparatus of the state, whose primary interest lay in the fact that felons forfeited their estates to the Crown. Accused persons who refused to enter a plea would die; but their estates remained intact and passed to their heirs. Sociologically, this looks like a conflict between the older family ties that provided the basis of the tribes and clans and the coercive powers of the emerging state.

The significant observation in legal theory is that the King and the state had the power to seize and hold accused individuals, and even to (passively) kill them, but no authority to subject them to the trial process. The royal judges would not proceed without the consent of the accused. This need for consent bears testament to the fact that the King's court had no legal authority over the accused, in spite of the raw physical powers of the King.

A Crime Is a Public Wrong

Historically, then, a crime was a breach of the King's peace; long after the King's peace became the public peace, every crime was called a "breach of the peace," a phrase that explains why accused person is released on the condition that he "keep the peace and be of good behavior." Although the roots of the criminal law lie in moral custom and the idea that the accused has committed a moral wrong, the criminal law also rests on an underlying claim that the accused has somehow harmed the public interest. A crime is accordingly a public wrong. Indeed, it is the allegation that the public interest has been harmed that justifies the intervention of the state. The exact nature of the harm that a crime envisages varies from offence to offence but clearly includes public safety and the general health of the public.

The Criminal Law Rests on an Assumption that the Accused Committed a Voluntary Act

A conviction for a criminal offence rests on three fundamental facts. The first is that the accused has acted voluntarily. This fact is presumed. A person who establishes that he has acted involuntarily cannot be convicted of a criminal offence. The rationale behind this comes from an earlier time, when wrongs like murder and theft were treated as civil matters. As we saw in the preceding chapter, the principle of liability in this body of law was simple cause. Persons who had acted involuntarily were not liable in this body of law because they had not caused the wrong suffered by the victim.

An Accused Who Establishes Automatism Cannot Be Convicted

The common law includes voluntariness in the *actus reus* of an offence and holds that an accused who acts involuntarily has not legally acted. In law, then, such a person has not committed the "guilty act" that makes up the crime. This line of reasoning has given rise to the so-called "defence" of automatism, under which accused individuals who act in an automatic, "robotic" state—through no fault of their own—cannot be convicted.

Automatism is nevertheless a preliminary issue rather than a defence, and it merely determines whether a court can proceed to consider the case on its merits. The bulk of the caselaw the accused must establish involuntariness, on a balance of probabilities.[14] Voluntariness goes to the capacity of the accused, rather than guilt, and can be distinguished from related defences, like duress and necessity, which raise a different kind of issue.

The caselaw usually divides automatism into "insane" and "non-insane" automatism.[15] The issue in the case of insane automatism is not the mental disorder, however, but the absence of a volitional act, which renders any further analysis of the case unnecessary. There are many other cases, such as involuntary intoxication, in which someone has put drugs or alcohol into the accused's drink. The issue has also been raised in cases of senility, sleepwalking, an epileptic seizure, or a toxic reaction.[16]

Logically, automatism has the same origins as civil doctrines like act of God and inevitable accident. The idea is essentially that some intervening or external event has occurred, as a result of which it cannot be said that the accused caused the prohibited wrong. The intervening event may be physical or psychological, but it is the fact that the accused was in an automatic state, through no fault of his own, that is pivotal. The issues that arise in this context raise the kind of philosophical issues that John Locke raised in *An Essay on Human Understanding*: when can we say that the accused person is the same person who committed an immoral act?[17]

A Voluntary Omission Is an Act for the Purposes of the Criminal Law

The concept of an act in the criminal law, as in the civil law, includes a voluntary omission. Someone who wilfully or recklessly omits to perform a legal duty, such as the provision of the necessaries of life, has committed a criminal act. Historically, the blameworthy act that the criminal law condemns is the "act" of volition rather than the *actus reus* of the offence. As a result, the issue in the case of criminal omissions is not whether the accused has "acted" in some overt physical sense. It is whether the omission was "advertent," in the language of the common law, and therefore volitional. The presumption that an accused's acts are volitional appears to hold, in such circumstances.

The Question in a Criminal Trial Is Whether the Accused Is Guilty

The criminal process focusses on culpability, or guilt, rather than liability. The accused's culpability for a criminal offence is based on the breach of a public duty. This duty was originally a duty to the King. The issue, in historical terms, is whether the accused breached the peace. The Crown must prove the second and third facts that must be established in order to secure a conviction for a criminal offence. The second fact is that the physical circumstances that make up the crime occurred. These circumstances originally constituted the entire crime and arguably still do, since they contain the public wrong that the criminal law prohibits. The third fact is that the accused possessed the *mens rea* of the offence.

The focus of the criminal process on the personal culpability of the accused has left us with an unduly restricted idea of a criminal offence that leaves out many of the physical circumstances that constitute part of a crime. We accordingly say that the accused "committed" an offence. This statement is misleading, from a theoretical perspective, since the elements of an offence extend well beyond the actions of the accused. The prosecution in a case of "causing a disturbance," for example, must prove that someone was disturbed. This is an external fact, which nevertheless forms a necessary part of the offence.

From a theoretical perspective, it seems more accurate to say that a crime is a prohibited happening or event. The accused's act certainly provides the most conspicuous part of such an event, but it may not be sufficient, on its own, to establish the commission of the crime. The legal definitions of many criminal offences refer to the consequences of the accused's actions. An accused cannot be convicted of criminal negligence causing death, for example, unless someone has died. This is a fact that must be proven by the prosecution.

The Crown Must Prove the Physical Circumstances of the Offence, which Include the Actus Reus

A crime, then, can be seen simply as a prohibited set of circumstances that breaches the public peace. The culpability of the accused for a crime requires proof that the accused committed an *actus reus*, a guilty act, which is included in the physical circumstances of the offence. It is usually said that the elements of the offence must be proven beyond a reasonable doubt. This requirement is easily misunderstood, however, and many offences merely require proof of physical circumstances.

The crime of possessing stolen property illustrates how little is required to prove the *actus reus* of the offence. All the prosecution must prove, on such a charge, is that the accused was in possession of the stolen property. This is a state or condition, rather than an act, and there is no guilty act in the normal sense of the word. The theoretical explanation is presumable that the active or advertent possession of the property constitutes a legal act, or that it is not possible to possess stolen property without "doing" something with the property, which provides the necessary act. As a matter of common sense, it is irrelevant what the precise act that may be.

The criminal law defines the *actus reus* of an offence in general terms. The *actus reus* of theft is not the taking itself, but the act of depriving a person of the enjoyment of his property. This act can take many forms. The *actus reus* of an offence may also include elements of physical cause or contemplate a specific transaction. In order to be convicted of murder, a person must "cause" the death of a human being. In order to be convicted of criminal negligence, a person must "cause" death or bodily harm to another person.[18]

Some of the issues that arise in this context resemble the kinds of issues that regularly arise in the civil courts. No one, historically, could be charged with "culpable homicide" unless the relevant death occurred within "one year and one day" from the time of the accused's actions.[19] As the annotation under the relevant section in *Tremeear's Criminal Code* puts it,

. . . codifies the arbitrary common law rule which rested in the difficulty of tracing the causative link when a substantial period intervened between the infliction of the injury and [the victim's] death.[20]

This example brings a doctrine like proximate cause into the criminal law.

The *Actus Reus* of an Offence May Include Omissions

The *actus reus* of an offence may also consist of the failure to fulfill a specific legal duty. The failure to safeguard an excavation or an "opening in ice" is an offence under the *Criminal Code of Canada*.[21] So is the failure to provide the necessaries of life to one's spouse or children.[22] It is not clear, however, that the *actus reus* of such offences is supplied by the failure to act rather than the positive actions of the accused, whatever they were, in a set of circumstances that gave rise to a public duty to do something else.

There are also charges, like criminal negligence, that rest on the failure to perform the same kind of general duties that give rise to liability in the civil law. The criminal law distinguishes between advertent omissions, which are voluntary and therefore culpable, and inadvertent omissions, which are not. The real objection to the inclusion of such offences in the criminal law is that the culpability for such offences often seems to rest on the fact that the accused caused death or injury rather than a positive act. Historically, this seems to take us into the civil law and a diluted notion of blame.

The Crown Must Also Prove Mens Rea, *which Contains the Mental Elements of the Offence*

An accused's culpability for a criminal offence rests on moral blameworthiness. This has historically required proof of *mens rea*, or guilty mind, which refers to the essential mental elements of crime. The concept of *mens rea* comes from the canon law and the notion of sin. It is this element in a criminal offence that justifies punishment, which provides the distinctive feature of the criminal law.

The canon law has traditionally held that a person has not sinned unless he consciously—not wilfully but consciously, knowingly—committed the offence.[23] Consciousness—the accused's awareness of the identity of the offence—became a technical requirement of the canon law, however, in the context of perjury. This requirement was introduced because the canon law held that it is not enough to prove that the accused had sworn to something that was untrue; it must be proved that he had intended to say something that was untrue.

Historically, the common law described *mens rea* as "malice aforethought." This phrase brings a strong moral component into the criminal law, not because the accused chose to act (a question that goes to voluntariness), but because the accused intended to commit a prohibited act.[24] The philosophical assumption behind *mens rea* is that the accused knowingly intended to commit an act that society prohibits. The assumption behind the element of *mens rea* is accordingly that the accused intended to commit a specific act that the members of society consider wrong. It is *mens rea* that accordingly establishes the viciousness of the culpable act.[25]

It Is the Accused's Intention to Commit the *Actus Reus* that Matters

The predominant element in *mens rea* is intention. The *mens rea* of theft is the intention to deprive someone of his property. *Mens rea* may also include other elements, however, such as wilfulness or recklessness. In Canada, for example, it is an offence to "wilfully" promote "hatred against any identifiable group".[26]

Mens rea does not require any proof that the accused intended to do something wrong.[27] That requirement would make it impossible to convict an accused for disobeying a law with which he disagrees. The Crown is required only to prove that the accused intended to commit the *actus reus* of the offence. It is not the intention to commit the crime of theft but the intention to commit the act that constitutes theft that is decisive.

It is the accused's knowledge that he possessed a switchblade, for example, that constitutes the *mens rea* of possessing a prohibited weapon (to wit, one switchblade), and he is not entitled to an acquittal merely because he did not know that a switchblade is prohibited. As the Alberta Court of Appeal held in *R. v. Baxter* (1982), 6 C.C.C. (3d) 447, the belief that it is lawful to possess a certain weapon is a mistake of law, not fact, and provides no defence. The position in the law is that an ordinary person knows he should not be carrying a switchblade.

The reality in a courtroom is that the mental state of the accused is usually inferred from the witnesses' description of the relevant physical events, since it is impossible to see into the mind of the accused. The *mens rea* of possession of stolen property, for example, is normally proven by the simple fact that he possessed it, in circumstances that give rise to such an inference. There is a legal presumption that a person intends the natural consequences of his acts.

The Ambit of *Mens Rea* Is Extended by Doctrines Like Transferred Intent

There are many complexities in the law of *mens rea*. The criminal courts have now recognized, for example, that there are objective forms of *mens rea*. There are also a number of historical doctrines that extended the ambit of *mens rea*, in order to prevent a blameworthy accused from escaping punishment. The doctrine of transferred intent, for example, holds that an accused's intention to kill a particular person, such as his employer, is transferred to anyone else that he might kill in trying to do so. If John shoots at Borden, for example, and shoots wide, so that Reginald is killed, John is guilty of the murder of Reginald. Similarly, in Canada, a person who kills someone else while trying to commit suicide is guilty of murder by virtue of the doctrine of "transferred intent," whereby the intention to kill oneself is transferred to the forbidden event, the killing of another person.[28]

There is also a doctrine of constructive murder in the common law, which "constructs" the offence of murder in cases where the accused did not possess a specific intention to kill. In *R. v. Desmond, Barrett and Others* (1868), 11 Cox C.C. 146, for example, the accused used dynamite to try and free his associates from prison.[29] When the explosion killed people living nearby, the court held that the necessary intention to kill was present, on the basis that he could foresee the possibility that his actions would cause someone's death. This interpretation was sufficient to convert the offence into murder. This raises constitutional issues, since it permits the court to enter a conviction on the basis of foresight, rather than intention, and arguably introduces a civil standard of liability into the criminal law.

There are also psychological complexities. It is possible to do something intentionally without wanting—and therefore without legally intending—to do so. In *R. v. Steane*, [1947] K.B. 997, the English Court of Criminal Appeal overturned the accused's conviction for "assisting the enemy," in spite of the fact that he intentionally made propaganda broadcasts for the Nazi state. His defence was that he was essentially forced to give the broadcasts and did not intend to assist the enemy.

The More Serious Criminal Offences Require Proof of a General and a Specific Intention

The more serious criminal offences usually require a specific and a general intention. The *mens rea* of assault, for example, consists only of a general intention: the intention to apply force. Assault causing bodily harm, however, also requires proof of a specific intention: the intention to cause bodily harm. An accused who is charged with assault causing bodily harm, and possesses only the general intention to apply force, can be convicted of the "lesser included" offence of assault.

Murder requires proof of an intention to kill, which is a specific intention. If an accused charged with murder killed another person unintentionally—without the intent to kill a human person—the Crown has not proven the *mens rea* for murder and the accused must be acquitted. If the accused committed an unlawful act, however, he may still be convicted of the "included" offence of manslaughter, which does not require an intent to kill.[30] First degree murder requires proof an additional mental element—the murder must be "planned and deliberate"—and the question whether the accused possesses the necessary *mens rea* can be relatively complicated.[31]

Voluntary Intoxication Is Not a Defence

There is no defence of intoxication. *Archbold*, one of the leading authorities on the English criminal law, states that self-induced drunkenness may impair an accused's ability "to foresee or measure the consequences of his actions," his "power to judge between right and wrong," and "his power of self-control."[32] None of these factors will provide a defence.

The judge or jury trying a case is nevertheless obliged to consider all of the evidence relating to the mental state of the accused in determining whether the accused possessed the *mens rea* of an offence. The accused might have been angry or clinically depressed or sick or intoxicated. All of this evidence must be taken into account in determining whether the accused possessed the required intention. Evidence of drunkenness may accordingly raise a doubt that the accused possessed a specific intention; short of establishing insanity or automatism, however, it will not negate a general intention.

The Common Law Presumes that the Accused Is Sane

There is a presumption in the common law that everyone is sane. If it is established, how-ever, that the accused was unable to form the *mens rea* of the offence, as a result of a mental disorder, the accused is not "criminally responsible." The law of insanity, or mental disor-der, comes from the *M'Naughten* rules.[33]

There are two distinct rules. The first rule holds that the accused must have been able to appreciate the "nature and quality" of his actions. This means that the accused was capable of knowing what he was doing and could discern that it had moral significance. The second rule holds that the accused must have been capable of knowing that his actions were wrong. This refers to the fact that the actions are wrong according to the moral and legal standards generally accepted in society.[34]

The Crown Must Prove both the Actus Reus *and* Mens Rea

The Crown must prove both the *actus reus* and *mens rea*. Historically, the criminal law has declined to convict an accused for evil thoughts alone, on the basis that punishment cannot be justified without a physical act. As a result, the charge of conspiracy has always had a disreputable place in the criminal law, since it requires minimal evidence of *actus reus*. Similar issues arise in the context of attempted offences. The *mens rea* for criminal negligence and many crimes of omission also seems minimal.

An Absolute and Strict Liability Offence Does Not Require Proof of *Mens Rea*

The criminal courts also deal with summary conviction offences, or misdemeanours, which historically came under the jurisdiction of local courts. These offences now include many regulatory offences, relating to matters like workplace safety, hunting and fishing, and pub-lic health. These "public welfare" offences are distinguishable from true criminal offences.

As the Supreme Court of Canada discusses in *R. v. Sault Ste. Marie* [1978] 2 S.C.R. 1299, the idea of a "public welfare" offence was developed by the courts in the nineteenth century to simplify prosecutions for offences relating to industrial or commercial activities. This was done because it is inherently difficult to prove that a corporation possessed the *mens rea* of an offence. As a result of the new development, the Crown was required only to prove *actus reus*.

The court in *Sault Ste. Marie* divides public welfare offences into "absolute liability" and "strict liability" offences. Absolute liability offences are often called "regulatory offences" and are based on a certain "standard of care" rather than moral fault.[35] There are relatively few absolute liability offences in the caselaw, though it has been suggested that offences relating to vehicle safety come within this category of offences.[36] One example is failing to stop for a red light.[37] The courts take the position that the intentions of the accused are irrelevant in such cases. Strict liability offences are quasi-criminal and have a more pro-nounced moral element. An example might be driving a motor vehicle well over the speed limit, which has been classified as "stunting."[38]

The prosecution's only obligation in the case of absolute and strict liability offences is to prove the *actus reus* of the offence. In the case of strict liability offences, however, the accused is entitled to an acquittal if he can establish that he exercised "due diligence," on a balance of probabilities.[39] The Canadian courts have held that the factor that determines whether an offence is a true criminal offence—and requires proof of *mens rea*—is whether a conviction jeopardizes the liberty of the subject. This raises an issue of punishment.[40]

Legal Defences Are Usually Described as Justifications or Excuses

It is usually said that defences can be described as justifications or excuses. The justifications include self-defence and compulsion.[41] The usual form of compulsion is necessity, which clearly applies if a person breaks into a home in the middle of winter in order to avoid freezing to death. Excuses are more esoteric, ranging from defences like accident or mistake of fact (in which the accused believed in a set of facts that would render his actions lawful) to insanity and involuntary intoxication.

This kind of classification seems illusory, however, and merely leads us into distracting moral debates about the kind of conduct that can be justified. The better way of looking at defences is probably to recognize that every defence negates some element in the case put forward by the Crown. Defences like necessity (and duress, which is usually classified as an excuse) appear to go to the voluntariness of the accused's act.[42]

This is a more accurate way of looking at defences because it recognizes that the burden of proof in a criminal case always remains on the Crown. Any successful defence will raise a doubt as to some element in the case put forward by the prosecution. The issue at the end of every case is accordingly the same: it is simply whether the prosecution has proved the elements of the offence beyond a reasonable doubt. Any list of common law defences merely provides an index to the caselaw and helps the lawyers to locate helpful precedents. The primary virtue of the common law in this context is that it is open-ended and leaves room for constant adjustment and readjustment in the context of specific cases.

Hart and Devlin Debate the Role of Morality in the Criminal Law

The debate between H.L.A. Hart and Patrick Devlin, a well-known judge, focussed on the role of morality in the criminal law. This sort of issue raises questions about the role of judges in the system, since the criminal law in England is the product of judicial decisions rather than statute law. The standard critique of the common law in this regard is that judges have no right to impose their moral views on society.

Devlin's response to such critiques was that judges have traditionally relied on the moral consensus in society, rather than their own views, in deciding what constitutes a crime. Even if the legislature is given the responsibility to enact the criminal law, the law must ultimately be applied and interpreted in accordance with a broad ethical consensus in society. There is no doubt that this process of interpretation has become more and more difficult, as a result of the increasing diversity in contemporary Western society. This diversity is partly the result of religious and cultural changes in society, but it is also the result of the liberal views that have taken hold of the popular imagination. These views place the highest value on individual choice in moral issues.

Devlin Argues that the Criminal Law Maintains Moral Norms

Devlin's view of the criminal law enlarges the idea of the peace on which the criminal law was based. There is no distinction, he argues, between the public and private spheres in matters of crime. Take the example of cruelty to animals. How is it relevant, he asks, whether the cruelty takes place in public or in private? This kind of argument is based, however, on the assumption that the state has a monopoly in moral matters and misses the historical issue, which is whether it is the state, the family, the church, or the local community that should deal with private moral matters.

Devlin implicitly follows the lead of sociologists in suggesting that the purpose of the criminal law is to maintain moral norms:

> No society can do without intolerance, indignation, and disgust; they are the forces behind the moral law, and indeed it can be argued that if they or something like them are not present the feelings of society cannot be weighty enough to deprive the individual of freedom of choice.[43]

The troubling issue is whether a political entity like the state needs indignation and the animosity toward wrong-doers to sustain itself.

One of Hart's main criticisms of Devlin's position is that there is no evidence that moral deviations undermine the bonds that hold a society together. Yet Hart fails to recognize the work of Émile Durkheim and many social scientists who have suggested that the maintenance of norms is essential in maintaining a cohesive society. The commentary in the social sciences takes the discussion in another direction, however, and raises questions with regard to the use of the law for the purposes of social control. The real beneficiary of such a process, in the context of criminal law, is the state rather than society, and the deeper question is whether the use of the criminal law to consolidate the power and control of the political apparatus of the state can be justified.

Devlin's Argument Rests on the Assumption that Individuals Are Obliged to Respect the Moral Consensus in Society

There are a number of possible responses to the positions that Hart and Devlin adopted. There are certainly criminal offences that deal with conduct that is considered morally acceptable by large segments of the population. Prostitution, polygamy, and minor drug offences may be among them. It is interesting that Devlin falls back on the example of polygamy, in order to justify the criminal law, since the provisions of the *Criminal Code of Canada* that deal with polygamy have now been questioned.

Some of this reflects changes in popular attitudes. Much of it, however, reflects the historical replacement of the earlier common law, which was made up of caselaw and based on moral custom, with statute law, which has frequently been used for the purposes of social control. Most of the criminal law is composed of older offences—assault, robbery, murder, and dishonesty offences—that were universally condemned. It seems clear that the machinery of the state made ample use of the moral legitimacy that the prosecution of these offences provided, in justifying the extension of its executive and administrative powers.

In any event, the fundamental assumption in Devlin's argument is not that criminal offences are necessarily and inherently wrong. It is that society sees them as wrong. This assumption is reflected in the requirement of *mens rea*, which requires only proof that the accused is aware of the moral consensus in society and contravened it. This also provides the essential justification for punishment. The inquiry in a criminal court is never a simple ethical inquiry into the question whether the acts of the accused are moral or immoral.

The more challenging issues arise when the criminal law does not reflect prevailing norms; but this is precisely where the moral jurisdiction of the judiciary comes into play most forcefully. Hart seems to neglect the role of the courts in making sure that the laws passed by political institutions are in keeping with the moral customs of the people.

Hart's View Comes to the Fore in R. v. Brown

The moral issues discussed by Hart and Devlin came to a head in the case of *R. v. Brown* [1993] 2 All E.R. 75 (House of Lords), where the appellants had been convicted of assault causing bodily harm and wounding.[44] The crux of the case lies in the common law definition of assault. There must generally be an application of force, or touching, without the consent of the person who was touched.[45]

The headnote of the *R. v. Brown* recites the facts as follows:

> The appellants belonged to a group of sado-masochistic homosexuals who over a 10-year period from 1978 willingly participated in the commission of acts of violence against each other, including genital torture, for the sexual pleasure which it engendered in the giving and receiving of pain.

The argument was that the alleged victims consented to the application of force. There was therefore no assault.

The level of violence was disturbing:

> The charges against the appellants were based on genital torture and violence to the buttocks, anus, penis, testicles and nipples. The victims were degraded and humiliated, sometimes beaten, sometimes wounded with instruments and sometimes branded. Bloodletting and the smearing of human blood produced excitement. . . . Cruelty to human beings was on occasions supplemented by cruelty to animals in the form of bestiality.

The question that the case raises in jurisprudence is whether the judges were entitled to nullify whatever consent was given on the basis of public policy.

The majority in the House of Lords dismissed the appeals. Lord Templeman wrote:

> Society is entitled and bound to protect itself against a cult of violence. Pleasure derived from the infliction of pain is an evil thing. Cruelty is uncivilised.

Lord Mustill dissented, without endorsing the conduct of the accused:

> Nor in the least do I suggest that ethical pronouncements are meaningless, that there is no difference between right and wrong, that sadism is praiseworthy, or that new opinions on sexual morality are necessarily superior to the old. . . . What I do say is that these are questions of private morality; that the standards by which they fall to be judged are not those of the criminal law; and that if these standards are to be upheld the individual must enforce them upon himself according to his own moral standards.

Lord Mustill clearly borrows the language of the *Wolfenden Report*, which is mentioned in the reading from Hart, and which recommended that matters of private morality—like prostitution and homosexuality—should be removed from the criminal law.

Can an Individual Consent to Bodily Harm?

The issues that arose in *R. v. Brown* pose additional difficulties in Canada, since assault is explicitly defined in the *Criminal Code of Canada* as the application of force without the consent of the victim.[46] This has modified the common law. In spite of this, some Canadian courts have held—really in defiance of the *Code*—that an accused cannot consent to bodily harm. The theoretical issue is accordingly whether judges have the moral and constitutional authority to intervene—and negate the consent of the parties—on the basis of public policy.[47]

Notes

1. James Fitzjames Stephen, *A History of the Criminal Law of England* (London: Macmillan, 1883), p. 67. Stephen is quoting William Stubbs, *A Constitutional History of England in Its Origin and Development*, vol. 1 (Oxford: Clarendon, 1880), at p. 207.
2. The most authoritative source on the history of the criminal law in England, which recounts these developments in considerable detail, is James Fitzjames Stephen's *History of the Criminal Law of England* (London: MacMillan and Co., 1883). Available at http://heinonline.org. Excerpts from this work are listed in the Appendix.
3. The use of the oath is significant: the word "jury" comes from the Latin "*juro*," which means to "swear or take an oath."
4. See Howard Goldstein, *Grand Jury Practice* (New York: Law Journal, 1998), s. 2.02.

5.   The jury system was probably known to the Normans (literally, the "Northmen"), who came over with the Conquest, since they were of Viking stock. The conception of "law" (a Norse word) was central to the traditions of the Norse, who had a reputation for litigation and a history of using juries, with as many as 36 members.

6.   See volume 1 of James Fitzjames Stephen, *History of the Criminal Law of England*, op. cit., at p. 85, where he quotes "Mr. Stubbs": "the King specifies the pleas of criminal justice which he retains for his own administration and profit; such a list is given in the laws of Canute; breach of the King's protection, house-breaking, assault, neglect of the 'fyrd' (military service), and outlawry. These were the original pleas of the Crown and were decided by the King's officers in the local courts." The quote is from William Stubbs, *A Constitutional History of England*, op. cit., at p. 187.

7.   See Pollock and Maitland, vol. 2 of *The History of the English Law Before the Time of Edward I*, as cited in the suggestions for further reading, p. 109.

8.   See William Holdsworth, vol. 2 of *A History Of English Law*, 4th ed. (London: Methuen, 1936).

9.   These interests led to technical disputes. There was a controversy, for example, as to whether certain offences should be classified as felonies or treasons. This was based on the fact that the land of the felon was forfeited to his lord; that of a traitor, to the King. See Windeyer, *Lectures on Legal History*, as cited in the readings, p. 64.

10. See, for example, Nicholas Adam Curott and Edward Peter Stringham, "The Rise of Government Law Enforcement in England," as cited in the suggestions for further reading. This work provides a libertarian account of such a development.

11. The real force of these legal processes lay in the tribal idea that there is no dividing line between the material and supernatural worlds. The early Christian view was that both God and the devil were participants in natural events.

12. It is clear that one of the motivations in introducing the new system of trial was that it ensured convictions. The ordeal was far more forgiving. See Margaret H. Kerr, Richard D. Forsyth, and Michael J. Plyley, "Cold Water and Hot Iron: Trial by Ordeal in England," *Journal of Interdisciplinary History* 22, no. 4 (Spring 1992): 573–95.

13. See "Criminal Trials and the Criminal Jury," Chapter 22 of Albert Thomas Carter, *A History of English Legal Institutions* (London: Butterworth, 1902), pp. 199–212, at p. 210. Available at http://heinonline.org.

14. There is some disagreement in the caselaw. See the decision of Bastarache J. in *R. v. Stone*, [1999] 2 S.C.R. 290, at para. 171 and following, and see the convenient list of legal points in *R. v. White*, 2000 NFCA 63, at para. 16.

15. Non-insane automatism has been mythologized as "temporary insanity."

16. See the notorious case of *R. v. Parks*, [1992] 2 S.C.R. 871, in which the accused was acquitted because he was sleepwalking at the time of the alleged murders.

17. John Locke, "On Identity and Diversity," in Chapter XXVII, Book II, of *An Essay Concerning Human Understanding* (1689), which is available in many editions, both in print and online.

18. These examples are taken from sections 229, 220, and 221 of the *Criminal Code of Canada*, R.S.C. 1985.

19. ibid., s. 227, which has now been repealed. This repeal raises legal, ethical, and philosophical issues of its own.

20. David Watt and Michelle K. Fuerst, eds., *Tremeear's Criminal Code* (Toronto: Carswell, 2002).

21. *Criminal Code of Canada*, s. 263.

22. ibid., s. 215.

23. *Mens rea* apparently became a part of the canon law on the basis that immoral thoughts were sufficient in themselves to attract punishment. The common law rejects such an idea.

24. Other bodies of law developed in the same manner. See Hermann Mannheim, for example, Part I of "*Mens Rea* in German and English Criminal Law," *Journal of Comparative Legislation and International*

Law, 3rd ser., 17, no. 1 (1935): pp. 82–101, at p. 83, where he writes that the criminal law in Germany progressed from "the principle of responsibility for the mere result (*Erfolghaftung*) to the principle of the guilty mind (*Schuldhaftung*)."

25. Although *mens rea* is a criminal concept, intentional torts like fraud and civil conspiracy raise similar issues. The proof of malice, in slander, for example, requires proof of a mental element, but on a lesser standard and in a weakened form.

26. *Criminal Code of Canada*, s. 319(2).

27. See Pollock and Maitland, op. cit., at 469.

28. See s. 229(b) of the *Criminal Code of Canada*.

29. This case is mentioned by H.L.A. Hart in *Punishment and Responsibility* (New York: Oxford University, 1968), p. 199ff., at footnote 1.

30. This requirement should not be construed too literally. The intention to kill in the criminal law naturally includes recklessness.

31. See s. 231(2) of the *Criminal Code of Canada*.

32. John Frederick Archbold and P.J. Richardson, *Archbold: Criminal Pleading, Evidence and Practice* (London, England: Sweet & Maxwell, 1999), in s. 42.

33. These rules were formulated in *M'Naughten's Case* (1843) 10 C. & F. 200, a famous English case. A transcript of the trial is available at www.oldbaileyonline.org.

34. For a Canadian example, see the discussion in *R. v. Ratti*, [1991] 1 S.C.R. 68.

35. Although the courts have applied this rationale to both absolute liability and strict liability offences, it clearly falters in the latter case.

36. In *R. v. Kanda*, 2008 ONCA 22 (CanLII), at para. 24, the Ontario Court of Appeal gives the following example of an absolute liability offence: "84.1(1) Where a wheel becomes detached from a commercial motor vehicle, or from a vehicle being drawn by a commercial motor vehicle, while the commercial motor vehicle is on a highway, the operator of the commercial motor vehicle and the owner of the vehicle from which the wheel became detached are guilty of an offence."

37. See *R. v. Kurtzman* (1991), 4 O.R. (3d) 417, 50 O.A.C. 20 (O.C.A.).

38. See *R. v. Aftab*, 2009 ONCJ 153 (CanLII), at para. 10, and *R. v. Brown*, 2009 ONCJ 6 (CanLII). These cases note that speeding has previously been considered an absolute liability offence.

39. The idea, again, is to establish that the accused exercised the expected standard of care. It is clear, however, that a conviction for a strict liability offence—pollution is an obvious example—usually has moral connotations.

40. See *Re B.C. Motor Vehicle Act*, [1985] 2 S.C.R. 486.

41. See Warren Brookbanks, for example, "Compulsion and Self-Defence," *Victoria University Wellington Law Review* 20 (1990): 95–116. Available at http://heinonline.org.

42. The real anomaly here is that an accused advancing a defence needs only to raise a reasonable doubt, whereas an accused who argues that his or her actions were involuntary must establish the involuntariness on a balance of probabilities.

43. Devlin, "The Enforcement of Morals," as cited in the readings, pp. 143–4.

44. The decisions in the case are available at www.cirp.org/library/legal/UKlaw/rvbrown1993.

45. There is some discussion in *R. v. Brown* as to whether the lack of consent is a necessary element of the offence. In Canada, and in many jurisdictions, the prosecution must prove that the victim did not consent to the application of force.

46. See s. 265(1)(a) of the *Criminal Code of Canada*.

47. See *R. v. Carriere*, [1987] A.J. No. 105 (Alta. C.A.), a digest of which is listed in the Appendix. Although the court in *Carriere* does not discuss the question, it was argued in *Carriere* that the Crown charged the accused with the wrong offence. There is a charge of "unlawfully causing bodily harm" in the *Criminal Code of Canada*, and the "knife fight" in question could be characterized as a "duel," or disturbing the

peace; none of these offences require proof of a lack of consent. The difficulty for the court in such a situation is that that the accused could not be convicted of these offences without an amendment to the charge.

Study Questions

1. What is the fundamental difference between a tort and a crime?

2. What is the fundamental difference between modern societies and earlier societies that existed without a criminal law?

3. Why were crimes historically considered breaches of the peace? Whose peace did they breach?

4. What was a felony? Why were juries brought into the trial process for felonies?

5. What three facts must be established in order to convict an accused of a criminal offence? Which facts must be proved?

6. When, in Devlin's view, must the law intervene in matters of morals?

7. Do you agree with Devlin, who was a conservative, or Hart, who takes a liberal position? Why?

8. Why do Hart's arguments against Devlin seem particularly compelling in the context of sexual norms and deviations from those norms?

9. Do you agree with the decision of the House of Lords in *R. v. Brown*? Why, why not?

Further Reading

Leigh Bienen, "Homicide in Chicago 1870–1930" (Northwestern University School of Law, 2008). Available at http://homicide.northwestern.edu.

Nicholas Adam Curott and Edward Peter Stringham, "The Rise of Government Law Enforcement in England," in *The Pursuit of Justice: Law and Economics of Legal Institutions*, ed. Edward J. Lopez (New York: Palgrave Macmillan, 2010). Available at http://ssrn.com.

Julius Goebel Jr., *Felony and Misdemeanor: A Study in the History of English Criminal Procedure* (New York: Commonwealth Fund, 1937).

Colin Howard and Brent Fisse, *Criminal Law*, 5th ed. (North Ryde, Au.: Law Book, 1990).

Stewart Macaulay, "Crime and Custom in Business Society," *Journal of Law and Society* 22, no. 2 (June 1995): 248–58. Available at www.law.wisc.edu/facstaff/macaulay/papers/crime_custom.pdf.

Henry Sumner Maine, "Early History of Delict and Crime," in *Ancient Law—Its Connection with the Early History of Society and Its Relation to Modern Ideas* (London: J. Murray, 1920).

Frederick Pollock, "The King's Peace in the Middle Ages," *Harvard Law Review* 13 (1899–1900): 177–90. Available at http://heinonline.org.

Frederick Pollock and Frederic William Maitland, "Crime and Tort," in vol. 2 of *The History of the English Law before the Time of Edward I*, 2nd ed. (Cambridge: Cambridge University, 1898), pp. 448–557. Available at http://heinonline.org.

R. v. Parks, [1992] 2 S.C.R. 871. This case discusses automatism and somnambulism.

James Fitzjames Stephen, *A General View of the Criminal Law of England*, 2nd ed. (London: Macmillan, 1890), at p. 80. Available at http://heinonline.org.

17 Public Law: Punishment and Sentencing

Readings

- Leviticus 24:13–22
- Deuteronomy 19:16–21
- Qur'an 5:45
- From *An Essay on Crimes and Punishments*, by Cesare Beccaria
- Digest of *R. v. J.J.*, 2004 NLCA 81

The historical function of the criminal law was to punish wrongdoers. The following chapter accordingly reviews the history of formal punishments, which were exacted by a recognized legal authority. These punishments have their deepest roots in the tribal law and the *lex talionis*, which still finds expression in religious tomes like the Bible and the Qur'an. The remedies in this body of law were based on cosmological concerns and a desire for expiation, rather than punishment in the modern sense. The purpose of the early legal law was to restore the relations between the wrongdoer and the person who was wronged.

The formal punishments in the common law derive from the notion of sin, which relocated the principle of cause in the physical body and personal will of the offender. The Christian idea that individual sinners must suffer was used to justify the harsh punishments in the criminal law, which were originally a personal matter between the King and the offender, but were soon after used to consolidate the power of the emerging state. Many criminologists and social scientists have argued that the real purpose of these punishments was political: they provided a means of social control, which enforced social norms and gave the political order control of the populace. The original idea of punishment, now known as retribution, has been displaced by the principle of deterrence in the modern law; this principle was introduced by Cesare Beccaria in his *Essay on Crimes and Punishments*, and it came into the common law tradition through the work of Jeremy Bentham and the utilitarians.

The chapter also considers the legal issues raised by the death penalty and includes a digest of an appellate review of a decision by a sentencing circle, which takes us back to the tribal origins of the law.

⚜ Readings ⚜

Leviticus 24:13–23, in *The New Jerusalem Bible* (Garden City, NY: Doubleday, 1985). Available at www.catholic.org/bible.

Yahweh spoke to Moses and said:

"Take the man who pronounced the curse outside the camp. All those who heard him must then lay their hands on his head, and the whole community must then stone him.

Then say to the Israelites: 'Anyone who curses his god will bear the consequences of his sin, and anyone who blasphemes the name of Yahweh will be put to death; the whole community will stone him; be he alien or native-born, if he blasphemes the Name, he will be put to death. Anyone who strikes down any other human being will be put to death. Anyone who strikes down an animal will make restitution for it: a life for a life.

Anyone who injures a neighbour shall receive the same in return, broken limb for broken limb, eye for eye, tooth for tooth. As the injury inflicted, so will be the injury suffered. Whoever strikes down an animal will make restitution for it, and whoever strikes down a human being will be put to death.

The sentence you pass will be the same, whether on native-born or on alien; for I am Yahweh your God.'"

Moses having told the Israelites this, they took the man who had pronounced the curse out of the camp and stoned him. And so the Israelites carried out Yahweh's order to Moses.

Deuteronomy 19:16–21, in *The Holy Bible, New International Version* ([1973] 2011). Available at www.biblegateway.com.

Witnesses

If a malicious witness takes the stand to accuse someone of a crime, the two people involved in the dispute must stand in the presence of the LORD before the priests and the judges who are in office at the time. The judges must make a thorough investigation, and if the witness proves to be a liar, giving false testimony against a fellow Israelite, then do to the false witness as that witness intended to do to the other party. You must purge the evil from among you.

The rest of the people will hear of this and be afraid, and never again will such an evil thing be done among you. Show no pity: life for life, eye for eye, tooth for tooth, hand for hand, foot for foot.

Qur'an 5:45, in *The Meaning of the Glorious Qur'an*, trans. Marmaduke Mohammad Pickthall (New York: Knopf, 1930). Available at www.sacred-texts.com/isl.

And We prescribed for them therein: The life for the life, and the eye for the eye, and the nose for the nose, and the ear for the ear, and the tooth for the tooth, and for wounds retaliation. But whoso forgoeth it (in the way of charity) it shall be expiation for him.[1]

Note

1.   Editor's note: The Qur'an refers to the teachings of the Torah, the five books of Moses, in the previous verse. It is accordingly restating (and mitigating) the position found in the early books of the Bible.

From Cesare Beccaria, *An Essay on Crimes and Punishments*, new ed. (Albany: W.C. Little, 1872.)

Of the Advantage of Immediate Punishment

In general, as I have before observed, *The degree of the punishment, and the consequences of a crime, ought to be so contrived, as to have the greatest possible effect on others, with the least possible pain to the delinquent.* If there be any society in which this is not a fundamental principle, it is an unlawful society; for mankind, by their union, originally intended to subject themselves to the least evils possible.

An immediate punishment is more useful; because the smaller the interval of time between the punishment and the crime, the stronger and more lasting will be the association of the two ideas of *Crime* and *Punishment*: so that they may be considered, one as the cause, and the other as the unavoidable and necessary effect. . . .

It is, then, of the greatest importance, that the punishment should succeed the crime, as immediately as possible, if we intend, that, in the rude minds of the multitude, the seducing picture of the advantage arising from the crime, should instantly awake the attendant idea of punishment. Delaying the punishment serves only to separate these two ideas; and thus affects the minds of the spectators rather as being a terrible sight than the necessary consequence of a crime; the horror of which should contribute to heighten the idea of the punishment.

There is another excellent method of strengthening this important connection between the ideas of crime and punishment; that is, to make the punishment as analogous as possible to the nature of the crime; in order that the punishment may lead the mind to consider the crime in a different point of view, from that in which it was placed by the flattering idea of promised advantages. . . .

Of the Mildness of Punishments

If punishments be very severe, men are naturally led to the perpetration of other crimes, to avoid the punishment due to the first. The countries and times most notorious for severity of punishments, were always those in which the most bloody and inhuman actions and the most atrocious crimes were committed; for the hand of the legislator and the assassin were directed by the same spirit of ferocity: which on the throne, dictated laws of iron to slaves and savages, and in private instigated the subject to sacrifice one tyrant, to make room for another.

In proportion as punishments become more cruel, the minds of men, as a fluid rises to the same height with that which surrounds it, grow hardened and insensible. . . . That a punishment may produce the effect required, it is sufficient that the *evil* it occasions should exceed the *good* expected from the crime; including in the calculation the certainty of the punishment, and the privation of the expected advantage. All severity beyond this is superfluous, and therefore tyrannical. . . .

Of the Punishment of Death

The useless profusion of punishments, which has never made men better, induces me to inquire, whether the punishment of *death* be really just or useful in a well-governed state? What *right*, I ask, have men to cut the throats of their fellow-creatures? Certainly not that on which the sovereignty and laws are founded.

The laws . . . represent the general will, which is [only] the aggregate of that of each individual. Did anyone ever give to others the right of taking away his life? . . . If it were so, how shall it be reconciled to the maxim which tells us, that a man has no right to kill himself? Which he certainly must have, if he could give it away to another. But the punishment of death is not authorized by any right; for I have demonstrated that no such right exists. It is therefore a war of a whole nation against a citizen, whose destruction they consider as necessary or useful to the general good. . . .

The death of a citizen cannot be necessary but in one case. When, though deprived of his liberty, he has such power and connections as may endanger the security of the nation; when his existence may produce a dangerous revolution in the established form of government. But even in this case, it can only be necessary when a nation is on the verge of recovering or losing its liberty; or in times of absolute anarchy, when the disorders themselves hold the place of laws. . . .

It is not the intenseness of the pain that has the greatest effect on the mind, but its continuance; for our sensibility is more easily and more powerfully affected by weak, but by repeated impressions, than by a violent but momentary impulse. The power of habit is universal over every sensible being. As it is by that we learn to speak, to walk, and to satisfy our necessities, so the ideas of morality are stamped on our minds by repeated impressions. The death of a criminal is a terrible but momentary spectacle, and therefore a less efficacious method of deterring others, than the continued example of a man deprived of his liberty, condemned as a beast of burden, to repair, by his labour, the injury he has done to society. *If I commit such a crime*, says the spectator to himself, *I shall be reduced to that miserable condition for the rest of my life. . . .*

A punishment, to be just, should have only that degree of severity which is sufficient to deter others. Now there is no man, who, upon the least reflection, would put in competition the total and perpetual loss of his liberty, with the greatest advantages he could possibly obtain in consequence of a crime. Perpetual slavery, then, has in it all that is necessary to deter the most hardened and determined, as much as the punishment of death. I say, it has more. There are many who can look upon death with intrepidity and firmness; some through fanaticism, and others through vanity, which attends us even to the grave; others from a desperate resolution, either to get rid of their misery, or cease to live: but fanaticism and vanity forsake the criminal in slavery, in chains and fetters, in an iron cage; and despair seems rather the beginning than the end of their misery. . . .

I shall be told, that perpetual slavery is as painful a punishment as death, and therefore as cruel. I answer, that if all the miserable moments in the life of a slave were collected into one point, it would be a more cruel punishment than any other; but these are scattered through his whole life, whilst the pain of death exerts all its force in a moment. There is also another advantage in the punishment of slavery, which is, that it is more terrible to the spectator than to the sufferer himself; for the spectator considers the sum of all his wretched moments, whilst the sufferer, by the misery of the present, is prevented from thinking of the future. . . .

The punishment of death is pernicious to society, from the example of barbarity it affords. . . . Is it not absurd, that the laws, which detect and punish homicide, should, in order to prevent murder, publicly commit murder themselves? . . . What must men think, when they see wise magistrates and grave ministers of justice, with indifference and tranquillity, dragging a criminal to death, and whilst a wretch trembles with agony, expecting the fatal stroke, the judge, who has condemned him, with the coldest insensibility, and perhaps with no small gratification from the exercise of his authority, quits his tribunal to enjoy the comforts and pleasures of life? They will say, "Ah! those cruel formalities of justice are a cloak to tyranny, they are a secret language, a solemn veil, intended to conceal the sword by which we are sacrificed to the insatiable idol of despotism. Murder, which they would represent to us as an horrible crime, we see practiced by them without repugnance or remorse. Let us follow their example. . . ."

Digest of *R. v. J.J.*, 2004 NLCA 81 (CanLII).

J.J., an Innu living in Labrador, was convicted of assaulting A.M.P. by forcing a beer bottle into her vagina while she was sleeping. This was the seventeenth assault by J.J. against A.M.P.; J.J. had also been convicted of various other assaults against women. At the time of the offence he was on probation arising from an earlier assault on A.M.P.

The judge convened a sentencing circle; it recommended a two year conditional sentence. The judge gave effect to this recommendation. The Crown appeals the sentence on the grounds that the judge committed errors in principle and that the sentence is demonstrably unfit, having regard to denunciation and deterrence. The Crown is seeking a term of imprisonment.

I will address when, in general, a sentencing circle should be used and how the results of a sentencing circle should be utilized; I will then deal with the sentencing circle in this case.

When Should a Sentencing Circle Be Used?

I find the case law from Saskatchewan persuasive as to when a sentencing circle should be used. I would adopt the Saskatchewan Court of Appeal decisions in *R. v. Morin* 1995 CanLII 3999 (SKA) and *R. v. Taylor* 1997 CanLII 9813 (SK CA). In light of these decisions, I would note five general factors to be considered in deciding whether or not to use a sentencing circle:

1. the willingness and suitability of the convicted person;
2. the willingness of the victim (freely given);
3. the willingness of a suitable community to participate in the circle and in implementing its recommendations;
4. whether the offence, in all the circumstances, is one that requires a term of imprisonment; and
5. such other relevant factors as may appear important to the trial judge, in the context of the case.

How Should the Results of a Sentencing Circle Be Used?

In addressing fitness of sentence, the Court in *R. v. Morin* commented on the treatment to be given to sentencing circle recommendations. Justice Sherstobitoff, writing for the majority, stated at para. 19:

> Since there is no provision in the *Criminal Code* for the use of sentencing circles, it is implicit in their use, and recognized by all of the judgments mentioned above, that when sentencing circles are used, the power and duty to impose a fit sentence remains vested exclusively in the trial judge. If a sentencing circle is used, and it

recommends a sentence which is not a fit sentence, the judge is duty bound to ignore the recommendation to the extent that it varies from what is a fit sentence.

Justice Sherstobitoff then commented on the purpose of sentencing circles, commencing at para. 26:

> The question, then, is to what extent can the sentencing judge make meaningful use of the recommendations of sentencing circles?
>
> The very purpose of sentencing circles seems to be to fashion sentences that will differ in some mix or measure from those which the courts have up to now imposed in order to take into account aboriginal culture and traditions, and in order to permit and to take into account direct community participation in both the imposition and administration of the sentence. It also seems implicit in all discussions of sentencing circles that they will in many cases, if not most of them, recommend sentences imposing lesser terms of incarceration than would have been imposed by a judge alone and to substitute alternative sanctions, usually involving the community in the administration of those sanctions.

The case must be one in which a court is justified in taking a calculated risk and departing from the usual range of sentencing. As to the fitness of sentence imposed on Mr. Morin, Justice Sherstobitoff made the following comments, commencing at para. 33:

> The sentence imposed on Mr. Morin . . . falls well below the bottom of the range for the offence of robbery with violence by a person with a record of violent offences. In this case, the judge said he would have, but for the sentencing circle, considered the appropriate sentence to be four years' imprisonment, but would have reduced it to three years because Mr. Morin had spent 226 days in remand awaiting trial. . . . This Court has repeatedly said that three years imprisonment is the starting point for sentences for the robbery of convenience stores, gas bars, and like commercial enterprises.

The Court doubted the sincerity of Mr. Morin's wish to take the necessary steps to rehabilitate himself and questioned the efficacy of a sentence of electronic monitoring and probation for a man with a record of breaching these kinds of conditions. The Court of Appeal accordingly sentenced Mr. Morin to 15 months in prison (in addition to the time already served on remand), followed by probation.

Turning to the sentence imposed in this case, it is clear that the sentencing judge considered the aboriginal identity of the offender and sought to give effect to his understanding of traditional aboriginal justice. However, in so doing, the sentencing judge lost sight of the court's overriding duty to impose a sentence which, given the particular facts of the offence, the offender, the victim, and the community, is fit in the circumstances.

In *R. v. Taylor, supra*, the accused, a 28 year old aboriginal man, was convicted of three counts of assault against his estranged partner, including sexual assault. A sentencing circle was held and the circle recommended that the offender be banished for one year to a remote island. The trial judge took into account that Mr. Turner had spent nine months in jail on remand, together with six months in isolation; he sentenced the offender to a further 90 days imprisonment and three years' probation. The probation order required the accused to spend a further six months in isolation.

Chief Justice Bayda, writing for the majority, noted that Mr. Taylor's sentence had three general components, imprisonment, banishment, and probation; imprisonment was primarily retributive in nature; banishment was primarily restorative in nature, in that it had as its central feature an imperative for self-discipline, self-treatment, introspection, self-examination of one's goals, and other means of self-improvement; probation was primarily restorative in nature.

Chief Justice Bayda stated, in paras. 84–6:

> In arriving at his decision the [trial] judge exercised a discretion to adopt almost in their entirety the recommendations made by the circle participants. Those participants—in excess of twenty—represented the community that produced the offender, the community that was willing to support him in his quest to restore himself, and the community into which he was expected to reintegrate and continue to live. The recommendations took two sessions of informal discussions lasting in excess of a day and one half at which all aspects of the sentence including restorative and retributive measures were thoroughly examined. Important as well was the circumstance of the victim's eventual willing participation and her concurrence in the recommendations. . . .
>
> That, of course, does not end the matter. It is still necessary to determine whether in the context of his primary decision the judge properly applied the correct body of principles to arrive at his sentence.

Chief Justice Bayda stated that the sufficiency of denunciation must be assessed primarily from the perspective of the community most affected by the sentence. The community, via the sentencing circle, had created the sentence and circle participants were clear that they did not see the banishment component as "letting off" Mr. Taylor. If banishment or isolation was considered by community members to be more or less equivalent to imprisonment, then, the Chief Justice determined, Mr. Taylor must be deemed to have served approximately two years in prison. Two years served is roughly equivalent to a sentence of four years, given the probability of early release and parole. The circle participants were aware of this.

Chief Justice Bayda found that the sentence being broadly equivalent to a sentence of four years imprisonment would not be out of the range of sentences normally imposed in circumstances similar to those in the case. For the trial judge to vary the sentence from the norm to accommodate that "mix of accepted sentencing goals" fashioned by the "particular community" is not a breach of the principle of parity as it has been refined and enunciated in the caselaw. In the result, the sentence imposed by the trial judge, based in large measure on the results of the sentencing circle, was upheld.

The Sentencing Circle in the Present Case

On June 17, 2003, a sentencing circle was held in the present case. The next day in court, counsel made submissions to the trial judge. Crown counsel sought a term of imprisonment. On June 30, the trial judge rendered his decision; it gave effect to the recommendations of the sentencing circle and imposed a conditional sentence of two years less a day.

Did the trial judge deal with the issue of whether or not to use a sentencing circle properly? In my view, he did not. I would be less concerned if the offence here were of a nature—e.g. a series of thefts without violence—where public safety was not significantly threatened. That was not the case. (As A.M.P. said in her Victim Impact Statement: "I have fear for my life—almost every day.")

Disposition

Ordinarily, I would now consider whether the sentence was demonstrably unfit and, if so, what should a fit sentence be, in light of the circumstances. However, I will not do this. This is one of those cases where, with the passage of time and developments that have occurred since the offence, it is in the interests of justice to leave the sentence (flawed as it is) in place to run its course.

J.J. has stopped drinking. He has not re-offended. He is taking care of his children. He appears to have turned around his life. For this Court to impose a sentence of imprisonment might well jeopardize this. I am obliged to accept the reality of the existing circumstances and accordingly this appeal to impose a term of imprisonment must be denied.

✦ Discussion ✦

The modern idea of punishment was a product of two developments. The first is the introduction of the Christian notion of sin, which replaced the older tribal beliefs. The second is the emergence of the state, which used the criminal law to justify the increasing authority of the central government.

The Primary Motive Behind the Tribal Law Was Reconciliation

The fundamental purpose of the earliest law was to protect the integrity of the tribal structure, which was based on the relationship between family units. As a result, the tribal law emphasized reconciliation and social harmony. Although the elements that came to the fore in the later development of the law must have been present, one way or another, issues like retribution were dealt with privately. There was no formal mechanism like the criminal law in early societies to adjudicate moral wrongs and prescribe punishments. The origins of formal punishment can nevertheless be found in the tribal idea that things that threaten the tribe must be removed.

The Tribal Law Found Expression in the Lex Talionis

The early law made its way into the Old Testament and other sources as the *lex talionis*, which we know as "an eye for an eye, a tooth for a tooth." This law has been misinterpreted in modern times, probably because we live under a system of central government that prohibits the private use of force. This was not the case in early societies, which left it to families to deal with wrongs to the family. This often led to the excessive use of force, and feuds, which threatened the unity of the tribe.

The purpose of the *lex talionis* was accordingly to prevent feuds, by regulating the relations between families and placing limits on the private use of force. Families were allowed to retaliate for a wrong, but within strict limits, and were not allowed to use greater force than the force that had been used against them. The purpose of the *lex talionis* was accordingly to bring conflicts to a close: the wronged family was not entitled to retaliate any further once the original wrong had been redressed. The law prevented the counter-retaliation produced by the use of excessive force and restored the neutrality in the relations between different families.

The same kind of reasoning lies behind the biblical rule that false witnesses be put to death. The problem with false evidence, from a social perspective, is that it stirs up feelings of indignation and resentment, which lead to uncontrollable violence. The passage from *Deuteronomy* makes it clear that the purpose of such a rule was to prevent discord within the tribe.

The *Lex Talionis* Had Its Roots in Cosmology Rather Than Punishment

The literature on punishment often suggests that the *lex talionis* was based on retribution. This is a modern interpretation, which relies on a different sense of the word "retribution." Victims who seek retribution in the modern sense are seeking some form of vengeance: they want those who have hurt them to suffer. This is not the fundamental impetus behind the *lex talionis*, which has cosmological origins.

The legal mechanics of the early law are based on the idea that there is a natural law. The *lex talionis* was based on the idea that the social, physical, and spiritual worlds all existed together in early pre-scientific societies, and a violation of the law in any of these areas might disrupt the relations within the natural order. There was a general belief that such a disruption inevitably led to calamity. There is a sense in which the early view extends our social relations beyond human interactions into the physical and spiritual worlds, which exist far more comfortably and companionably in the entire scheme of the cosmos.

The original purpose of legal redress was accordingly to restore the natural and legal relations between existing things and avert the misfortune that would otherwise follow their disruption. However vague the contents of this early cosmology may seem to the modern mind, the legal mechanics of such a system are clear. In order to maintain the proper functioning of the cosmos, the relations between different parts of the system had to be constantly balanced. This balancing extended to the relations within the tribe, which were based on the reciprocity in the relations between families and clans. From the perspective of the early law, the relationship between two families was not a single relationship. Each family had a relationship with the other, and if one family wronged the other, the two relationships diverged. The resulting disparity must accordingly be redressed. The *lex talionis* was designed to address such disparities. An act of retaliation in such a scheme was not retribution in the modern sense, but a kind of cancelling, which removed the inequality in the relations between the relevant parties. The purpose of such an act was to restore the natural relationship between them.[1]

Although the cosmological views behind the *lex talionis* was not based on revenge, there is a sense in which they required the use of force. This is because the original wrong had to be annulled, and a violent wrong called for a violent reversal. The problem from a modern perspective was not that individuals were permitted to inflict an equivalent harm on the wrongdoer—it was that they were obliged to do so.

The rigour in such a system was furnished by the fatalism that existed in early societies. The idea that changed the general underpinnings of the law and ushered in the criminal law was the belief that the events in human society are determined by our moral choices. Individual fault was not a significant consideration in the early law. As a result, the law did not permit excuses. Acts that violated the natural and cosmological order had to be rectified.

The concept of honour comes into this as well, but it is clear that men who restored their family's honour by killing or wounding someone in another family were not acting merely out of emotion. They were acting out of a legal and moral sense of duty. This is still the case with so-called "honour killings," which have re-emerged in Western society, as a result of changing patterns of immigration.[2] These killings are difficult to control, precisely because the individuals who commit them feel morally compelled to carry them out, in order to remove some sense of family shame.

The Purpose of the Early Legal Remedies Was Expiation

The beginning of the process that gave rise to the criminal law can be found in the desire for expiation, or atonement. The legal mechanics of such an idea rested on the existence of a relationship that created binding obligations. It was the wrongdoer's failure to honour such obligations that gave rise to the "wrong" that provided the basis of a recognizable legal process. The legal and formal feature of the process was that a priest—or some other legal authority—must have had the power to order some form of atonement. The historical literature tells us that the purpose of atonement was to pacify the party—the god, the spirit, the person, even the object—that had been wronged. This restored the natural order of things and allowed the parties to resume their relations.

The idea of atonement was particularly significant in the Hebrew tradition, which entered the common law through the general conversion to Christianity. The key to this tradition lies in the personal relationship between Yahweh and his chosen people. If the people honoured other gods, and offended Yahweh, misfortune would befall them. He must therefore be pacified. This need to pacify Yahweh still provides the theological explanation of the crucifixion of Jesus.

The idea of pacification was part of the framework in which the early law existed. Although the endorsement of mercy in the Qur'an mitigates the severity of the *lex talionis*, it does so only on the basis that the victim has first been pacified and the proper relations between the offender and victim have been restored. The same desire for pacification can be found in the penalties in the Greek and Roman laws, which were higher if the offender had aroused the victim's wrath. The original idea behind the criminal law was that the King had been offended and must therefore be appeased.

The development of the early law was based on the replacement of the general idea of expiation with a distinct legal remedy, which determined what constituted an appropriate form of redress. The usual remedy was based on the idea that the cause of the wrong must be identified and removed. This was true, first for the civil law, and later for the criminal law. The differences in these two branches of the common law appeared later.

The usual legal remedy was to give up the offending thing. This was accomplished by surrendering an object or animal to the victim, in the case of a private wrong, or by casting it out of the city, in the case of a public wrong. The penalties for public wrongs were a collective act, a kind of symbolic banishment that purged society of something unclean. The same thinking applied to objects and people. The idea that an offending thing must be cast into the wilderness, outside society and outside the protections of the law, clearly explains the institution of outlawry.[3]

This idea made its way into formal punishments such as hanging or burning, which provided a way of removing the physical cause of a wrong. It also explains the medieval practices described by E.P. Evans, which now seem bizarre:

> Even the dead, who should have been hanged, but escaped their due punishment, could not rest in their graves until the corpse had suffered the proper legal penalty at the hands of the public executioner. Their restless ghosts wandered about as vampires or other malicious spooks until their crimes had been expiated by digging up their bodies and suspending them from the gallows.[4]

Bodies were hung until they fell apart. This was a matter of physically removing the thing that had caused a wrong from society.

Superstition and spiritual beliefs naturally entered into these practices. But the legal explanation is cause. The reason that a stake was driven through a vampire's heart was that it kept the vampire in the ground and stopped it from leaving the grave. The staking was a kind of constructive banishment, which prevented the offending creature from mixing with members of society. The bodies of werewolves and vampires that continued to haunt the community were dug out of the grave and burned. The destruction of the physical body erased the cause of the wrong.

The desire for expiation carried over into the formal punishments in the criminal law, which were based on the idea that wrongdoers must be hurt. This requirement that the offender suffer seems to be the distinguishing idea in punishment. The ethical justification of punishment can be traced to the Christian notion of sin, which located the source of a criminal wrong in the will of the wrongdoer.[5] This relocated the cause of a criminal wrong in the individual who committed the offence. It also brought in the biblical idea that sinners must be punished.

The objective of legal redress, however, remained the same in the early criminal law. The governing idea was that the physical cause of the wrong must be removed. The idea that the cause of the wrong was located physically in the individual who committed the wrong accordingly provided the rationale for many of the more brutal punishments in the common law, which often consisted of removing the offending part of the body. A thief would have his hand cut off; a sexual offender might be castrated. Such punishments were adaptations of the earlier idea of expiation, now internalized within the body of the offender, which held that the thing that caused a wrong must be literally cast out.

The theological underpinnings of these punishments can be found in the Gospel of Mark, Chapter 9, where Jesus instructs his disciples:

> 43. And if thy hand offend thee, cut it off: it is better for thee to enter into life maimed, than having two hands to go into hell, into the fire that never shall be quenched. . . .

> 47. And if thine eye offend thee, pluck it out: it is better for thee to enter into the kingdom of God with one eye, than having two eyes to be cast into hell fire.[6]

These passages were construed literally in the early criminal law.

Whatever the motive behind public punishments, it is clear that enforcement was possible only because the populace had accepted that the wrongdoer must suffer. It is also clear that Christian concepts like purgatory promoted the view that sinners benefitted from their punishment. The justification for the removal of an offending eye or limb on the new understanding was that it saved the wrongdoer.[7] The purpose of punishment was accordingly ethical and religious: it was now a social duty that society owed the victim, the community, and, indeed, the offender. There is still a strong feeling in society that wrongdoers must be punished, and for their own good. Historically, the state took on the role of a guarantor in such a scheme and provided the services that the system required.

One of the Purposes of the State Was Punishment

The rise of the criminal law in England can be traced to the new-found power of the central government, which asserted increasing control over the country. The central assumption in the political theory behind this development is that there is a sovereign power, vested in the executive branch of government, that exercises legitimate authority over private persons. This authority finds its natural expression in the right to go to war and the right to punish malefactors.

Henry Sumner Maine, a famous legal historian, wrote that there are four stages in the development of any criminal law. The first is the conscious development of a concept of crime. This concept is built upon the idea of the state: "the conception of Crime, as distinguished from that of Wrong or Tort, and from that of Sin, involves the idea of injury to the State or collective community." This conception of crime gives rise to the idea of punishment. "Each indictment," Maine writes, "becomes a bill of pains and penalties."[8] The other stages in the development of the criminal law concern the creation of occasional and then permanent courts. It is the necessity of punishment, however, that justifies these institutional developments.

Hobbes Awards the Right of Punishment to the King

The state's right to punish is a product of the evolution of the King's peace. In *Leviathan*, published in 1651, Thomas Hobbes states that the "first and Fundamentall Law of nature" is "to seek Peace, and follow it."[9] This fundamental law requires a "coercive power," however, vested in the sovereign, and ultimately the nation-state, which will take us out of the condition of war that characterizes the state of nature. The significance of Hobbes' position is that the emerging state, on this explanation, finds its justification in the use of force to compel individuals to follow the law.

Historically, the argument in *Leviathan* looks like an apologetic, since it is clearly designed to justify the power of the central government. It is simply wrong to suggest that people lived in the state of nature, however, prior to the emergence of the state. It was the rule of law that guaranteed stability and order in England before William the Conqueror laid the foundations for modern government. Earlier kings had no power to change the customary law and were merely seen as custodians of the legal order.

Hobbes' theory of the state neglects the historical realities in these developments. The idea that it is necessary to punish bad people was significant because it served the interests of those in power and provided the King and the apparatus of the state with a *raison d'être*: the prosecution and punishment of criminal offenders. Although the substance of the criminal law came from the customary law and the ecclesiastical tradition, the historical record makes it clear that the idea of a crime—a public wrong—was used primarily to justify the increasing authority of the central government.[10]

Criminologists Have Argued that the Purpose of Punishment Was Social Control

There is considerable support for the idea that the criminal law and formal punishment provided a convenient rational for the power of the state in the social sciences. Many criminologists have taken the position that the real purpose of the criminal law is to maintain social control.[11] Émile Durkheim, for example, suggested that crime is a sign of a healthy society, since it establishes norms.[12] The maintenance of these norms serves the interests of those who benefit from the current distribution of power in society.

Michel Foucault has argued that the idea of "the criminal" was used to justify the introduction of police in the eighteenth century:

> What makes the presence and control of the police tolerable for the population, if not fear of the criminal? This institution of the police, which is so recent and so oppressive, is only justified by that fear. If we accept the presence in our midst of these uniformed men, who have exclusive right to carry arms, who demand our papers, who come and prowl on our doorsteps, how would any of this be possible if there were no criminals?[13]

Hobbes' suggestion that a strong state was needed to deal with crime is essentially a projection. It was the state that needed the phenomena of crime to justify its increasing control.

There are counter-arguments. The conventional historical explanation is that police were introduced because it became impossible to control criminal activity in large metropolitan areas. There is also the fact that the foundations of the criminal law and its punishments lie firmly in moral custom, and there is historical evidence, at least, that the extension of the King's peace gave ordinary people a sense of security. The real intellectual change, however, was in the conceptual transfer of the consequences of wrongdoing from the natural order to the social and political order. Early peoples believed that the disruption of the natural order would have consequences for the wrongdoer; this changed in the new scheme of wrongs, which replaced the machinery of the natural world with the formal punishments prescribed by the criminal law.

The Main Function of the Criminal Law Was to Prescribe Punishments

The motivations behind the earliest common law punishments were mixed. There was a strong desire in the bureaucracy to consolidate the authority of the state. One of the major objects of punishment in the early common law was simply to provide revenue for the central government. The criminal courts also had a normative role, however, and assisted in the creation and maintenance of social norms. The criminal law also had a moral purpose:

sinners must be punished. Indeed, the different purposes of the criminal law all seem to converge in the formal process of prescribing punishments. Politically, the maiming of offenders continually reminded the population of the terrifying power of the King.

It Is the Prospect of Punishment that Explains the Procedural Protections in the Criminal Law

It is the prospect of punishment that explains the distinctive character of the criminal law, which presents the contest between the state and the individual in its starkest terms. The historical issue on punishment was whether the accused would be stripped of his liberty. This liberty is the relative liberty enjoyed by the members of society, which was guaranteed by the customary law. This guarantee still finds an echo in the protections that the criminal law extends to the accused person, which are ultimately based on the idea that punishment is an extraordinary measure, and must therefore be justified. These protections include the strict interpretation of criminal statutes, the rigorous application of exclusionary rules of evidence, and the narrow definition of specific crimes, all of which protect the liberty of the subject.

The significance of this relative liberty also surfaces in William Blackstone's famous statement "that it is better that ten guilty persons escape, than that one innocent suffer."[14] The criminal law in the common law system is designed to protect the liberty of the accused, however, rather than to vindicate his innocence. It is the accused's interest in liberty that provides the real explanation of the principle of culpability in the criminal law, which is based on moral blameworthiness. The fundamental idea in the criminal law is that the accused cannot be stripped of this liberty—and subjected to formal punishment—without moral justification.

The same concerns also explain the standard of proof in a criminal case, which requires that the prosecution prove all of the elements of the offence "beyond a reasonable doubt." This burden of proof is usually described as "moral certainty: a jury must be morally certain that the accused committed the offence before it enters a conviction. This standard was nevertheless brought into the law to reassure anxious jurors, who were reluctant to convict accused persons of capital offences. This reluctance was based on religious grounds, since the conviction of an innocent person was considered a mortal sin and carried damnation with it.[15]

The Early Punishments in the Criminal Law Had Their Origins in Outlawry

The formal punishments in the criminal law came from the customary law, which gave those who had been wronged the right to use force against the wrongdoer. Frederick Pollock and Frederic William Maitland accordingly write that a breach of the King's peace "made the wrongdoer the King's enemy."[16] The wrongdoer had put himself in a condition of war with the King, who had a right to retaliate. As a result, the penalties awarded by the early Norman kings were seen as a private matter between the King and the wrongdoer.

This position is reflected in the idiosyncratic nature of the first criminal punishments:

> The Conqueror would have no one hanged; emasculation and exoculation were to serve instead. Henry I would now take money and now refuse it. He would reintroduce the practice of hanging thieves taken in the act. Loss of hand and foot became fashionable under Henry II; but we are told of him that he hanged homicides and exiled traitors.[17]

It took a long time for the King's interests to merge with the public interest.

The important remark from the perspective of theory is that the King's right to punish did not come from the status or position of the King. It came from the status of the offender, who became an outlaw on conviction. This meant that he was no longer considered a member of society and was not entitled to the protections of the law. He had been expelled from society, into a conceptual wilderness, and legally did not exist.

The offender's loss of his legal status meant that the King could do what he wanted with the offender. Pollock and Maitland cite evidence in the German source that

> many of the pure punishments, the "afflictive" punishments, have their root in outlawry. They are mitigations of that comprehensive penalty. The outlaw forfeits all, life and limb, lands and goods. This, as law and kingship grow stronger, puts the fate of many criminals into the King's hands. The King may take life and choose the kind of death, or he may be content with a limb; he can insist on banishment or abjuration of his realm or a forfeiture of chattels.[18]

A felon surrendered his "life or member" to the King. He lost his land and goods, which went to the King or his lord.[19]

These punishments were based on the outlaw's loss of the relative liberty enjoyed by the members of society. This was a legal and a positive liberty, which was made up in good measure of the duties owed to the accused by other members of society. These duties naturally went beyond any list of prerogatives, but they included the duty to respect the integrity of the accused's body and the accused's enjoyment of property, along with the relative freedoms and amenities that provided individual persons with the peace and security that was needed to pursue their happiness within the framework of the law. The liberty that the accused enjoyed accordingly came with rights, which he lost on conviction. There was accordingly nothing to protect him from the depredations of the King and the state.

A convicted felon is most accurately seen as a wild animal, who had no protections in the law. The historical record makes it clear that the bureaucracy of the state took full advantage of his perilous position. The idea of fines[20] came from amercements, under which the King in his "mercy" released an offender from imprisonment, forfeiture, or physical punishment in return for the payment of a specified sum. This was a lucrative practice, like the confiscation of property, and often struck ordinary people as an official form of theft.

The Judiciary Developed a Tariff of Punishments

The punishments in the criminal law were standardized in the thirteenth century, when royal judges began to exercise their own discretion in sentencing. The severity of the punishment for different offences was based on the relative depravity of different offences.[21] This assessment of the value of different wrongs created a tariff system of sentencing, which is still with us. The judicial estimate of the moral wrong attached to different offences has nevertheless fluctuated over time, as social attitudes change.

From the perspective of punishment, the sentencing process is best seen as an exercise in taxonomy, or classification. There are two stages in this exercise. In the first stage, judges must decide whether to convict the accused. In order to make such a decision, they must first divide the human acts that come before the courts into various classes and categories of wrong. They do this by consulting the existing law, defining specific offences, and determining whether the facts in the specific cases that come before them comport with the definition of a particular offence. This collective process groups similar acts together and determines their general location on a sliding scale of depravity.

The second and more active stage of the process takes place in sentencing. In this stage of the exercise, a judge must determine the blameworthiness of the offender before the court. In order to do so, the judge must weigh a variety of factors, which determine the gravity of the crime in relation to other crimes in the same category of offence. This requires a similar measurement, on a second sliding scale, to determine more exactly where the crime sits in the full range of criminal offences and accordingly determines the appropriate sentence.

Sentencing in the Modern Law Has at Least Four Major Aims

The idea of punishment is still present in the law of sentencing, though other theories have now intruded on it. The general literature identifies at least four major aims in sentencing: 1) retribution; 2) deterrence; 3) rehabilitation; and 4) the restoration of the community. Although deterrence has become the major consideration in the courts, judges routinely consider all of these factors in sentencing offenders.

The First Aim Is Punishment, which Is Now Called "Retribution"

The historical goal of punishment in the criminal law was to hurt the offender. This goal has usually been called "retribution" in the theoretical literature and remains a fundamental consideration in sentencing. Retribution in the modern sense goes beyond the *lex talionis*, both because the primary purpose of such an exercise is to make the offender suffer, and because retribution is based on a desire for vindication. The offender must demonstrably lose the contest, in order to right the balance between the offender and the victim.[22]

There have been many attempts to explain retribution.[23] Westel Willoughby (1867–1945), a lawyer and political scientist, argued that the purpose of retribution goes beyond "revenge." Thus, he writes, Georg Wilhelm Friedrich Hegel justifies "the deliberate infliction of suffering upon a wrongdoer," but only for the purpose of "awakening" the offender "to a true comprehension of the nature of his deed."[24]

Jean Hampton has argued in a similar vein that retribution seeks to demonstrate that the offender's act was wrong. Hampton's argument is based on Kantian principles, which hold that individuals have equal value.[25] The offender has denied this equality by using another human being for personal ends. An obvious example might be sexual assault: the offender has used the victim for personal gratification, without regard for the victim's wishes.

On Hampton's view, retribution is not so much the infliction of pain as the infliction of a "defeat":

> A false moral claim has been made. Moral reality has been denied. The retributivist demands that the false claim be corrected. The wrongdoer must be humbled to show that he isn't the lord of the victim. If I cause the wrongdoer to suffer in proportion to my suffering at his hands, his elevation over me is denied, and [moral] reality is reaffirmed. The purported master is mastered by me in turn, and in this way I show that he is my peer.[26]

This argument has some force, though the idea that "the defeat of the wrongdoer at the hand of the victim" proves his equality seems strained.

Punishment Also Finds Expression in the Denunciatory Aspects of Sentencing

The desire to punish an offender also finds expression in the denunciatory aspects of sentencing. Although there is an educational element in this part of sentencing, it is the public expression of disapprobation, indignation, or, indeed, outrage that seems primary. In *R. v. J.J.*, for example, the judicial denunciation of the offender's acts plays a major role in sentencing. It is clear that the judiciary, at least, believes that one of the purposes of sentencing is to publically declare that criminal acts are morally wrong and require punishment.

Historically, denunciation seems to be rooted in the idea of pacification, which played such an important part in the early law. Denunciation requires that the sentence be severe enough to publicly recognize the extent of the offender's wrong. This publicly condemns such acts: the Court of Appeal in *R. v. J.J.* expressed concern that the sentence recommended by the sentencing circle did not express the requisite degree of alarm at the offender's conduct. The denunciatory aspects of sentencing called for a term of imprisonment.

The Second and Major Aim of Sentencing Is Deterrence

The major consideration in the modern law of sentencing, however, is deterrence. The principle of deterrence is a product, philosophically, of utilitarianism, which replaces the idea of punishment with the idea that the offender's behaviour must be corrected. The primary aim of sentencing on this theory is to deter the offender from committing another offence. This aim is related to the idea of rehabilitation, though traditionally utilitarians are more concerned with public welfare than the psychological reform of the offender. As long as offenders do not harm other people, they are entitled to the same freedoms as other people. Michel Foucault has nevertheless criticized the behavioural approach as a coercive attempt to control the individual and maintain social conformity.[27]

The First Systematic Treatment of Deterrence Can Be Found in Beccaria's *Crimes and Punishments*

Beccaria's contribution to philosophy is usually neglected. This seems surprising, since Bentham acknowledged that the principle of utility came from Beccaria's *Crimes and Punishments*.[28] Yet Beccaria is widely recognized, in spite of this general neglect, as the first author who set out the basic principles of deterrence in a systematic way.

The fundamentals of Beccaria's theory are unabashedly liberal: the state obtains its authority from the consent of individual people, who have agreed to the political contract. Individual people are self-interested and want to avoid pain and suffering. They have accordingly entered society, as the Grotian tradition holds, in order to avoid the unhappiness of life in the state of nature.

Beccaria nevertheless reasons that individuals will want to maintain the maximum freedom possible, in order to satisfy their personal desires and seek their own happiness, unfettered by the restraints imposed upon them by other people. They have accordingly agreed only to give up that minimal amount of freedom that is necessary to obtain the protection of human society. It follows that the government has been given the authority to punish people only when it is necessary to do so, and only to the extent that it is needed to prevent individuals from breaking the essential rules of society.

Beccaria's theory also sets out a number of technical stipulations. It is only actions, for example, and not thoughts, that determine whether punishment is appropriate. This is because the "one true measure of criminality is the damage done to the nation." Beccaria acknowledges the historical significance of banishment, which he describes as a social death. He conceives of imprisonment as a kind of banishment, since it excludes offenders from the company of other people.

The Significance of Deterrence in the Common Law Is Attributable to the Utilitarians

Despite the importance of Beccaria's *Crimes and Punishments*, the significance of deterrence in the common law tradition is attributable to the influence of Jeremy Bentham and the utilitarians. This philosophical tradition extends as far as H.L.A. Hart, who set out a theory of criminal responsibility that combines elements of retribution and utility.[29]

The utilitarians believed that individuals commit crimes because it is in their rational self-interest to do so. The objective of sentencing is accordingly to create a situation in which it is in the offender's self-interest to obey the law. This objective is generally accomplished by punishment, which is meant to dissuade the offender from re-offending.

The utilitarian view of sentencing is based on the idea that pain and suffering is an evil and should therefore be minimized.[30] The offender should suffer only to the extent necessary to change his behaviour. This position goes against the idea in the earlier law that the offender must suffer. The utilitarian view contains elements of the moral idea of wrong that came into the criminal law from the canon law, since it sees the decision to commit a crime as a personal choice but replaces the moral underpinnings of the criminal law with social and political criteria.

The primary justification for criminal sanctions in utilitarianism is clearly that it protects the safety and security of the public. Bentham argues that it accomplishes this end in two ways:

1. it deters other members of the public from acting in the same way as the offender, and
2. it reforms the behaviour of the offender.

The word "reform" nevertheless has a rather narrow meaning here, since Bentham was not concerned with the private life of the offender.

The Courts Distinguish between General Deterrence and Specific Deterrence

The criminal courts have distinguished between general deterrence and specific deterrence. General deterrence refers to the effect that a sentence has in discouraging the public at large from committing the kinds of offences committed by the offender. Specific deterrence refers to the effect of the sentence in discouraging the specific offender before the court from committing another offence.

The broader justification for sentencing in utilitarianism has to be that it serves the greater happiness. This position is problematic, philosophically, since it suggests that offenders should be punished when it serves the larger interests of society. This suggestion seems to justify the use of criminal sanctions for the purposes of social control. It also goes against the common law, however, and the prevailing views in society, which still hold that offenders are liable to punishment because they are morally blameworthy. The utilitarian position also contravenes the Kantian rule that individual persons must not be treated as a means to an end.

Bentham Had a Practical and Technical Interest in Sentencing

Bentham had a developed interest in penology and a model prison, the Panopticon (the "see-everywhere"), which gave a prison "keeper" the ability to watch inmates without being observed. The idea behind such a design is that it creates a state of persistent and potential watchfulness that induces inmates to act as if they are being watched at all times. This is sufficient, in Bentham's estimation, to correct their behaviour. Michel Foucault has discussed the Panopticon in *Discipline and Punish* and argues that it captures the self-conscious sense of being watched that characterizes the modern era.[31]

Bentham discussed the technicalities of sentencing. In the *Principles of Morals and Legislation*, he sets out twelve rules governing the proportion of punishments to offences. Some of these rules may seem surprising, such as Rule 8, which suggests that punishment should be increased in accordance with the length of time that has elapsed since the commission of the crime. The reasoning behind this suggestion is that the lapse of time makes it proportionately more difficult to change the offender's behaviour.

Bentham also provided an inventory of different punishments and drafted a "Specimen of a Penal Code," which sets out the aggravations that would justify an increase in punishment.[32] Although this inventory shows insight, Bentham's penchant for making lists and classifications has an eccentric cast. He includes the offender's "violation" of the victim's sleep, for example, as a significant aggravating factor.

The problem with Bentham's work lies in its abstraction, which shows little knowledge of the practical realities of the criminal process. In point of fact, the speculative nature of Bentham's work is singularly out of keeping with the common law tradition, which is based on the decisions reached in specific cases rather than the rational adumbration of a logical system. Bentham does not seem to have appreciated that any list of sentencing factors will be incomplete.

The Third Aim Is the Reform and Rehabilitation of Offenders

The third aim of sentencing is to rehabilitate the offender. This aim has been referred to as the "reformatory" aspect of sentencing and has a place in the communitarian tradition, since the idea of rehabilitation is ultimately to return offenders to their place in the community. As a general rule, however, rehabilitation enters the sentencing process only in mitigation, on the basis that deterrence cannot succeed unless the offender has been rehabilitated.

There is both a personal and a social side to rehabilitation. The personal side, which focusses on the reform of the specific offender, naturally brings subjective and psychological issues into the courtroom. There is real doubt as to how far the courts can go, ethically, in ordering that offenders receive treatment.[33] C.S. Lewis argues against a therapeutic approach to sentencing in "The Humanitarian Theory of Punishment," where he argues that crime should not be seen as a "disease" and left to experts, who cure the offender.[34] The attempt to change offenders, psychologically, clearly goes against the liberal view that the legal process should not interfere with the private choices of individual persons.

The Fourth Aim Is to Restore Offenders to Their Place in the Community

The fourth aim of sentencing is to restore the offender's status as a full member of the community. This aim is usually called "restorative justice" and takes us back to the beginnings of the criminal justice system.[35] The essential premise of such a theory is that offenders have, by virtue of their actions, severed their relations with other persons and lost their place in the community.

The purpose of sentencing in restorative justice is to repair the relationship between the offender and other people, in order to restore the offender to his or her rightful place in society. One of the limits on the theory of restorative justice is that it cannot deal with those situations where an individual's serial behaviour, for example, makes him dangerously antisocial. There are clearly individuals who simply cannot be "restored" to a meaningful place in society. It follows that restorative justice has serious limits and can be applied only in appropriate cases.

It has been said that the goal of restorative justice is, in one word, community. As Lode Walgrave argues, there is a simplistic assumption that communities "are good *per se*."[36] This assumption is philosophically questionable: there are many communities, Walgrave argues, that function as "pockets of intolerance and prejudice" or operate with their own set of norms, in opposition to the norms that prevail in the larger society.[37]

One of the Features of Restorative Justice Is Victim–Offender Reconciliation

One of the more prominent features of restorative justice is victim–offender reconciliation, which has been used most frequently in the context of young offenders.[38] In this kind of formal reconciliation process, an offender meets the individuals victimized by the offence. This encounter gives victims the opportunity to explain the impact of the offence on their lives. It also gives offenders the opportunity to explain their motivations, express remorse, and find ways to repair the harm to the victims. The reconciliation that this encounter provides helps to restore the offender to the community. This process is arguably more in the nature of reparation, however, which historically came within the ambit of the civil law.

The Courts Have Also Used Sentencing Circles

The communitarian nature of restorative justice manifests itself in the participation of the community in the sentencing process. This has come to the fore in the use of sentencing circles in Aboriginal communities. Although the legal responsibility to determine the appropriate sentence remains with the presiding judge, sentencing circles give the community the opportunity to reach a consensus as to the way in which an offender should be re-integrated in the community.

In *R. v. W.B.T.*, [1997] CanLII 9813 (SKCA), for example, a sentencing circle recommended that the offender be banished to a remote island in northern Saskatchewan.[39] The accused was accordingly sentenced to a term of probation, with a number of specific conditions, which instructed him to live on a remote island, cut wood for the winter, build a cabin according to the plans drawn up by the Justice Committee of the tribe, dig a pit and build an outhouse, put in a vegetable garden, and refrain from the use of alcohol and non-prescription drugs.

The purpose of the banishment was to isolate the offender, until he was ready to return to the community. The probation order placed him under supervision and provided for his eventual re-integration into the community. The sentencing circle expressed the view that the banishment and the accompanying provisions were in the interests of the community as well as the offender and would ensure the safety of everyone when he returned.

The decision in *R. v. J.J.* illustrates the conflicting considerations that arise in the contemporary use of sentencing circles. Some of this conflict reflects the conflict between two systems of law. The indigenous practices that express themselves in sentencing circles are based on the tribal law, which predates the common law. The purpose of this law is to maintain relations within the tribe and minimize further conflict. This is fundamentally different from the purpose of the criminal law, which focusses on punishment and deterrence. It is notable that the mechanisms of the tribal law operate internally and psychologically, without the external pressures and "coercive power" that we associate with the state. One of the practical reasons that sentencing circles tend to place such a premium on reconciliation and avoid punitive sanctions—which are often counter-productive and provoke hostility—is that the members of such small communities must live in close proximity to each other for their entire lives.

The Most Prominent Ingredient in Sentencing Is Judicial Discretion

The most prominent ingredient in sentencing is judicial discretion. This discretion allows a judge to tailor a sentence to the specific offender before the court. This tailoring is done by applying the sentencing principles commonly recognized in the caselaw. A number of these principles have been codified in section 718 of the *Criminal Code of Canada*:

> 718. The fundamental purpose of sentencing is to contribute, along with crime prevention initiatives, to respect for the law and the maintenance of a just, peaceful and safe society by imposing just sanctions that have one or more of the following objectives:
> a. to denounce unlawful conduct;
> b. to deter the offender and other persons from committing offences;
> c. to separate offenders from society, where necessary;
> d. to assist in rehabilitating offenders;
> e. to provide reparations for harm done to victims or to the community; and
> f. to promote a sense of responsibility in offenders, and acknowledgment of the harm done to victims and to the community.[40]

The *Criminal Code* also lists aggravating factors, such as the fact that an offence was committed for the benefit of a criminal organization.

This is a relatively *ad hoc* list of principles, however, which does not provide a rigorous conceptual regime for sentencing. This approach is in keeping with the common law, which has not, historically, placed restrictions on the factors that may be considered in sentencing. Here again the significance of judicial discretion is clear. It does not seem possible to envisage every set of circumstances that may come before the courts, much less classify them, and there seems to be little substitute for legal and moral experience in determining what constitutes an appropriate sentence in particular cases.

The common law includes many additional factors, such as breach of trust. If an employee stole from an employer, or a teacher abused a student, or a doctor sexually assaulted a patient, the starting point of the sentence will probably be imprisonment. Motive may also come into play, and a judge may take the reasons for the offence into account in determining the appropriate sentence.[41]

A major public policy issue has arisen out of the political complaint that judges are too lenient in sentencing. This complaint has led many legislatures, particularly in the United States, to pass "sentencing guidelines," which fix the sentences for particular offences within a very narrow range. In Canada, there have been amendments to the *Criminal Code* that prescribe minimum or mandatory sentences, and that require judges to issue ancillary orders or additional and consecutive sentences.

The purpose of these legislative initiatives is to limit the discretion of the sentencing judge. The major criticism of such policies is simple enough. The reality is that politicians have little or no knowledge of the precise circumstances of the cases that come before the courts; they are therefore not in a position to judge what is appropriate in a specific case. They are also relatively uninformed as to the relative gravity of different offences and the complexities that enter into the general operation of the criminal justice system.

The Discretionary Element in Sentencing Allows the Standards in Sentencing to Evolve

The discretionary element in sentencing affects the sentencing process in a number of ways. Since judges have different personalities and backgrounds, they may have different views as to the appropriate sentence for a particular offence. This may naturally give rise to discrepancies in the decisions of different judges. The law deals with these irregularities through the appellate process, which gives courts of appeal the final say in the process.

There are larger historical issues, however. Since the moral standards in society are constantly evolving, the moral views of the judiciary are always shifting. As a result, the appropriate range of sentences for a given offence is constantly changing. This range is also affected by developments in policy and the social sciences. The discretionary aspects of sentencing accordingly allow sentencing standards to change, over time, as public attitudes change.

It Was the Judiciary Who Stopped the Practice of Whipping

The discretionary aspects of sentencing explain many changes in the law. Whipping, for example, was a routine form of punishment in England and was a part of prison life in Canada until the 1960s. The consolidation of the *Criminal Code of Canada* in 1953 retained whipping for acts of indecency and rape, carnal knowledge of a girl under 14 years of age, and robbery. Section 148 read:

148. Every male person who assaults another person with intent to commit buggery or who indecently assaults another male person is guilty of an indictable offence and is liable to imprisonment for ten years and to be whipped.

Sexual offences were singled out for such a punishment.
The 1953 *Code* specified:

641. (1) Where a person is liable to be sentenced to be whipped, the court may sentence him to be whipped on one, two or three occasions within the limits of the prison in which he is confined.

The sentencing judge was to specify the number of strokes "to be administered on each occasion." The instrument to be used was a "cat-o'-nine tails," unless the judge specified some other instrument.

These provisions were not repealed until 1972, long after the judiciary had become uncomfortable with whipping and stopped the practice. Although two courts ordered whipping in the early sixties, the punishment was overturned on appeal in both cases.[42] The strap and the paddle continued to be used as a disciplinary tool in prisons and reformatories after it had gone out of use in sentencing. Many prison wardens took the position that it was an indispensable part of the prison regimen.[43]

It Was the United States Supreme Court that Overruled the Death Penalty

The death penalty also raises issues with regard to the discretion of judges in sentencing criminal offenders. Although the majority of voters in many American states support the death penalty, it is clear that attitudes toward the penalty have changed substantially in recent times. Some of this is a reflection of a philosophical shift in our attitude toward death. This is evident in the position adopted in 1868 by John Stuart Mill, who supported the death penalty in a speech to the British Parliament, on the basis that life imprisonment is a punishment much worse than death.[44] This view has apparently reversed itself and is now regarded as unacceptable in most countries.

The views of the judiciary on the death penalty have also changed over time. This is evident in the decision of the United States Supreme Court in *Furman v. Georgia* (1972), 408 U.S. 238, which held that the death penalty constituted "cruel and unusual" punishment under the United States constitution.[45] The bench of judges in *Furman* recognized that the law of sentencing reflects the fact that the moral views in society are constantly evolving. It follows that a sentence that was believed to be fair or just in the past may now be considered cruel.

The argument that succeeded in *Furman*, however, was not that the infliction of the death penalty was cruel and unusual in itself. Although the petitioners made such an argument, they also argued that the death penalty was applied arbitrarily and discriminated against minorities. The latter assertion was based on statistical evidence that it was black men, convicted by white juries, who were usually sentenced to death.

Justice Douglas held that this evidence of discrimination was sufficient to render the death penalty "cruel and unusual":

> The words "cruel and unusual" certainly include penalties that are barbaric. But the words, at least when read in light of the English proscription against selective and irregular use of penalties, suggest that it is "cruel and unusual" to apply the death penalty—or any other penalty—selectively to minorities whose numbers are few, who are outcasts of society, and who are unpopular, but whom society is willing to see suffer though it would not countenance general application of the same penalty across the board.

Justice Douglas also held that the death penalty is in and of itself a cruel form of punishment.

The majority in *Furman* found that the selective application of the death penalty—which was compared to being struck by lightning—was cruel and unusual. It was therefore unconstitutional, though it could conceivably be reintroduced, on a more representative basis. The minority in the case held that the judiciary did not have the discretion to decide whether specific punishments are morally permissible. Chief Justice Burger wrote:

> For this reason, early commentators suggested that the "cruel and unusual punishments" clause was an unnecessary constitutional provision. As acknowledged in the principal brief for petitioners, . . . punishments such as branding and the cutting off of ears, which were commonplace at the time of the adoption of the Constitution, passed from the penal scene without judicial intervention because they became basically offensive to the people, and the legislatures responded to this sentiment.[46]

The moral evaluation of the punishments in the criminal law must be left to the legislature. The dissenting judges in *Furman*—those who upheld the death penalty—found that the majority had imposed their personal views on the rest of society. Their actions in doing so intruded into an area of decision-making reserved for the legislature: it is "the legislative judgment" that "is presumed to embody the basic standards of decency prevailing in the society."[47] The case naturally raises many issues: for one thing, the dissenting judges neglect the differences between the ordinary law and the constitutional law. This is significant because the constitutional law is based on a moral consensus in society rather than the views of the majority. This does not decide the constitutional issue by itself; it nevertheless means that it is not enough to consult the views of the majority and leave out the views of the minority. Nor is there any guarantee that a measure passed by the legislature is supported by the majority of the populace rather than a majority of legislators. Since it is judges who must send an offender to death, it stands to reason that judges are more sensitive to the issue than is the public at large.

The Judiciary Has Also Increased the Sentences for Environmental Offences

The prominence of judicial discretion in sentencing also allows judges to increase the tariff of sentences for particular offences. In *R. v. United Keno Hill Mines Ltd.*, [1980] Y.J. No. 10, for example, Chief Justice Stewart wrote that environmental offences were considered relatively minor offences until the 1960s. The government and prosecution saw criminal charges as a convenient threat, which could be used "to coerce offenders to institute pollution abatement programs." There has been a new recognition, since then, that pollution is a crime, as it may result in death or staggering environmental degradation.

The Chief Justice held, essentially, that a framework of sentencing is needed that recognizes the seriousness of these offences. This framework must recognize the nature and vulnerability of the environment and should not look on the environment as a mere object. It is accordingly more fitting to conceive of environmental offences as a kind of assault. This assault, moreover, is a fundamental breach of trust. A sentencing court must therefore consider the particular victim—certain ecological areas may be more sensitive than others—and the extent of the injury that it has suffered. If the environment has suffered irreparable injuries, the penalties must be severe.

The court then listed six considerations that might affect the sentence awarded in a specific case. These considerations are:

a.   the degree of deliberation in the actions before the court, which goes to the criminality of the accused's conduct;
b.   the extent of a company's attempt to comply with government regulations;
c.   evidence of real remorse;
d.   the circumstances of the corporation in question, since any fine or penalty must be sufficient to deter it from reoffending, but (in most cases at least) not so great as to bankrupt the company;
e.   the profits realized from the offences; and
f.   the criminal record, if any, of the offending company.

The court also suggested that individual decision-makers who are responsible for any decision to violate the law should be held personally responsible for the crime.

The decision of the court with regard to the personal culpability of corporate officers rests on the principle of deterrence. The reality is that executives are the only individuals in a position to stop a company from harming the environment:

> After a few corporate presidents are prosecuted, it is likely senior executives will make it their business to know what all subordinates are doing and effective policies and checks against illegal activities will be implemented.

Corporate executives should not be shielded from the punishments in the criminal law because the company carried out the crime.

The court's concern with the culpability of individual executives also reflects a more general recognition that everyone is equal before the law. In a study of corporate criminal responsibility, the Law Reform Commission of Canada argued that a lenient attitude toward the criminal conduct of corporate officials fostered a lack of respect for the law and the legal system:

> If criminal law is to be a respected force in society, it is important that these acts not be treated more leniently than antisocial acts in the streets. To ignore, for example, evidence of fraud or corruption in corporations, to ignore deliberate or even careless action that threatens to destroy order within the economy, can create the dangerous impression that people in groups controlling economic power are beyond the law.[48]

These observations raise issues that go far beyond environmental offences, at a time when it has become clear that individuals in high places have not been prosecuted to the full extent of the law.

Notes

1.   There is still a sense in which legal systems seem to follow such a logic, but it is buried well beneath the surface of the law.

2.   There is a relatively new literature on the crime of honour killing, which has become a trenchant issue in most Western countries. For a brief but informative review of the issue, see Ursula Smartt, "Honour Killings," *Justice of the Peace* (7 and 14 January 2006), pp. 4–7. Available at www.ursulasmartt.com/pdf/JustPeace%5B1%5D.HonourKillings.9.1.06.pdf. And see Phyllis Chesler, "Worldwide Trends in Honor Killings," *Middle East Quarterly* 17, no. 2 (Spring 2010): 3–11.

3.   The Hebrew practice of letting a "scape-goat" loose in the desert on Yom Kippur, the Day of Atonement, is critical in the intellectual history of these ideas.

4.   E.P. Evans, *The Criminal Prosecution and Capital Punishment of Animals*, as cited in the suggestions for further reading, p. 195. There are bizarre examples. In 896, the body of Pope Formosus was exhumed, provided with a lawyer, and tried of usurping the papal dignity. He was subsequently convicted and "condemned to deposition" (putrefaction); his body was thrown into the Tiber as "a pestilential thing." See Evans, at p. 198ff. The bodies of Oliver Cromwell and John Bradshaw, who both played a role in the execution of Charles I, were dug up in 1661 and symbolically executed in the manner required for traitors.

5.   The concepts of wrong in the early civil law and the criminal law are distinguishable. The first refers us to the wrong suffered by the plaintiff; the second, to the wrong committed by the accused.

6.   King James Bible, Mark 9:43 and 47. And see Matthew 18:8: "Wherefore if thy hand or thy foot offend thee, cut them off, and cast them from thee: it is better for thee to enter into life halt or maimed, rather than having two hands or two feet to be cast into everlasting fire." Available at http://kingjbible.com.

7.   The same kind of rationale lies behind the institution of torture. The torturer had an ethical and religious defence: the person who confessed was saved.

8.   These comments are made in the context of Roman law. See Henry Sumner Maine, *Ancient Law—Its Connection with the Early History of Society and Its Relation to Modern Ideas* (London: J. Murray, 1920), at p. 392ff. Available at http://heinonline.org.

9.   Thomas Hobbes, *Leviathan, or the Matter, Forme and Power of a Commonwealth, Ecclesiasticall and Civill*, ed. Richard Tuck (Cambridge: Cambridge University, 1991).

10. See Julius Goebel Jr., *Felony and Misdemeanor: A Study in the History of English Criminal Procedure* (New York: Commonwealth Fund, 1937).

11. This is not a new idea and appears in the work of Han Fei Zi, a Chinese philosopher in the third century BCE.

12. See Émile Durkheim, for example, *The Rules of Sociological Method*, ed. George E.G. Catlin, trans. Sarah A. Solovay and John H. Mueller (New York: The Free Press, [1895] 1938).

13. "Prison Talk: An Interview with Michel Foucault," as cited in the suggestions for further reading, at p. 47.

14. William Blackstone, *Commentaries on the Laws of England*, in 4 vols. (Buffalo, NY: William S. Hein, [1765–9] 1992), p. 352. Available at http://heinonline.org.

15. See James Q. Whitman, *The Origins of Reasonable Doubt: Theological Roots of the Criminal Trial* (New Haven, CT: Yale University, 2008).

16. Frederick Pollock and Frederic William Maitland, "Crime and Tort," Chapter VIII in vol. 2 of *The History of English Law before the Time of Edward I*, 2nd ed. (Cambridge: Cambridge University, 1898), at p. 45. Available at http://heinonline.org.

17. ibid.

18. ibid., at p. 461.

19. See K.J. Kesselring, "Felony Forfeiture in England, c. 1170–1870," as cited in the suggestions for further reading, at p. 204: "By the time of the classic legal treatise known as *Glanvill*, written c. 1187–89, the standard formula noted earlier prevailed: from traitors, all lands and chattels to the King, and from felons, all chattels to the King and all lands to the lord after the King's year and a day. Both *Magna Carta* and the *Prerogativa Regis* repeated and enshrined this rule."

20. The word "fine" has a number of meanings, historically, and may refer to the payment of a sum in return for some right bestowed by the King, a sum paid to avoid imprisonment, or an amount fixed by statute.

21. There are antecedents in the relative value of different sins in the Catholic tradition.

22. This is an essential aspect of the common law tradition, which still operates on the idea that someone has "won" the case.

23. See Richard Posner, for example, "Retribution and Related Concepts of Punishment," *The Journal of Legal Studies* 9, no. 1 (January 1980), pp. 71–92. Available at www.jstor.org. C.S. Lewis advocates a moral theory of punishment, with retributive elements, in "The Humanitarian Theory of Punishment," which is cited *infra*. And see, more generally, Ted Honderich, *Punishment: The Supposed Justifications*, 2nd ed. (New York: Brace & World, 1989).

24. Westel W. Willoughby, "A Survey of Ethical Theories of Punishment," in *Rational Basis of Legal Institutions*, various authors (New York: Macmillan, 1923), pp. 555–71, at p. 566.

25. Jean Hampton, "A New Theory of Retribution," as cited in the suggestions for further reading.

26. ibid., at p. 398.

27. See Michel Foucault's *Surveiller et Punir: Naissance de la Prison* (Paris: Gallimard, 1975); translated as *Discipline and Punish: The Birth of the Prison* by Alan Sheridan (New York: Pantheon, 1977).

28. There are many editions of Beccaria's famous work. One is *On Crimes and Punishments*, 5th ed., trans. Graeme R. Newman and Pietro Marongiu (New Brunswick: Transaction, 2009).

29. See H.L.A. Hart, *Punishment and Responsibility: Essays in the Philosophy of Law* (Oxford: Oxford University, 1968).

30. Bentham's haphazard views on punishment are widely scattered through his work, much of which was unpublished. Two books, *The Rationale of Reward* (1825) and *The Rationale of Punishment* (1830), were based on *Théorie des Peines et des Récompenses*, which was edited and published by Étienne Dumont in 1811, and which contains enough interpolations to make any account of Bentham's views problematic. For a convenient introduction to Bentham's theory of punishment, see Hugo Bedau, "Bentham's Theory of Punishment: Origin and Content," as cited in the suggestions for further reading.

31. Foucault discusses the Panopticon in his highly celebrated work *Discipline and Punish: The Birth of the Prison*, which is cited in note 27. Foucault argues that the operative factor in imprisonment is the inmate's

psychological assumption that he is being watched. He accordingly corrects his behaviour to satisfy his keeper. It is being watched, Foucault argues, that characterizes the modern era in punishment.

32. John Bowring, ed., *The Works of Jeremy Bentham*, vol. 1 (Edinburgh: William Tait, 1843), at pp. 16–165.

33. A medical example that has arisen recently is chemical castration, which has been made compulsory in some states and a condition of parole in others.

34. See C.S. Lewis, "The Humanitarian Theory of Punishment," in *God in the Dock: Essays on Theology and Ethics*, ed. Walter Hooper (Grand Rapids: Eerdmans, 1970), pp. 287–300.

35. For a general resource on the theory and practice of restorative justice, see Centre for Justice and Reconciliation, *Restorative Justice Online* (2011). Available at www.restorativejustice.org. Also see Elmar G.M. Weitekamp and Hans-Jürgen Kerner, eds., *Restorative Justice: Theoretical Foundations* (Cullompton, UK: Willan, 2002).

36. Lode Walgrave, "From Community to Dominion: In Search of Social Values for Restorative Justice," in Elmar G.M. Weitekamp and Hans-Jürgen Kerner, eds., ibid., pp. 71–89.

37. "Differential association" is one of the more common explanations of crime offered by criminologists, particularly in the case of young offenders.

38. The *Youth Criminal Justice Act*, S.C. 2002 c. 1 contains a number of informative provisions dealing with the sentencing of young offenders. See s. 3 ("Declaration of Principle"), s. 6 ("Warnings, Cautions and Referrals"), and s. 38 ("Sentencing: Purposes and Principles"). Available at www.canlii.org.

39. And see, generally, *R. v. Craft*, 2006 YKTC 19, which discusses the use of a sentencing circle in the context of a conviction for impaired driving. "*R. v. T.D.P.*: A Young Offender, His Sentencing Circle and the *Y.C.J.A.*," *Saskatchewan Law Review* 68 (2005): 455–74 comments on the use of a sentencing circle in the instance of young offender. Also see P. Dawn Mills, "The Myth of Swan: The Case of *Regina v. Taylor*," *Canadian Journal of Native Studies* XVIII, no. 2 (1998): 255–70.

40. Section 38(2) of the *Youth Criminal Justice Act*, S.C. 2002 c. 1, contains a similar set of principles, which emphasizes the re-integration of young offenders into society.

41. There is an example of a sentencing decision for murder listed in the Appendix.

42. See *R. v. Woods* (1961), 130 C.C.C. 181 (N.B.S.C. App. Div.) and *R. v. Dupont* (1962), 133 C.C.C. 33, 39 W.W.R. 217, 38 C.R. 162 (B.C.C.A.).

43. For a convenient account of corporal punishment in the Canadian system, see www.corpun.com/rules. htm. It was apparently common to perform half of the punishment (e.g., 10 of 20 strokes), with the remaining half held in reserve. If the inmate behaved, he escaped the remaining half.

44. See the appendix to John Stuart Mill, *Utilitarianism and the 1868 Speech on Capital Punishment*, ed. George Sher (Indianapolis: Hackett, 2001), pp. 65–71, at p. 66: "What comparison can there really be, in point of severity, between consigning a man to the short pang of a rapid death, and immuring him in a living tomb, there to linger out what may be a long life in the hardest and most monotonous toil, without any of its alleviations or rewards—debarred from all pleasant sights and sounds, and cut off from all earthly hope, except a slight mitigation of bodily restraint, or a small improvement of diet?"

45. Audio recordings of the arguments of counsel in the case are available at www.oyez.org.

46. The Chief Justice continued: "Judicial findings of impermissible cruelty have been limited, for the most part, to offensive punishments devised without specific authority by prison officials, not by legislatures."

47. It is interesting that the dissenting judges in *Furman* cite the decisions of Oliver Wendell Holmes, who held that the Supreme Court should exercise restraint in the face of progressive legislation. The argument on the death penalty is that judges should exercise a similar restraint in the face of legislation that many would consider reactionary.

48. Law Reform Commission of Canada, "Criminal Responsibility for Group Action" (Working Paper 16, 1976), at p. 65.

Study Questions

1. What are the cosmological views behind the *lex talionis*?

2. Where did the idea that an offender must suffer come from? Why did people believe that the punishments in the criminal law were good for the offender?

3. Why was outlawry so significant in the development of the formal punishments in the criminal law?

4. Do you agree with the court's decision in *R. v. J.J.*? What was the goal of sentencing in the case?

5. Should sentencing circles be restricted to Aboriginal offenders? Why, why not?

6. Do Cesare Beccaria and Jeremy Bentham believe in punishment? Is punishment a necessary part of deterrence and correction?

7. Why did the United States Supreme Court conclude that capital punishment is "cruel and unusual" in *Furman v. Georgia*?

8. Is it possible to imagine a situation in which punishments that were considered cruel and unusual in the past are no longer considered "cruel and unusual"? (This would mean that unconstitutional punishments could conceivably become constitutional.)

Further Reading

Hugo Bedau, "Bentham's Theory of Punishment: Origin and Content," *Journal of Bentham Studies* 7 (2004). Available at www.ucl.ac.uk/silva/Bentham-Project/journals/journal_of_bentham_studies.

Centre for Justice and Reconciliation, *Restorative Justice Online* (2011). Available at www.restorativejustice.org.

E.P. Evans, *The Criminal Prosecution and Capital Punishment of Animals* (New York: E.P. Dutton, 1906).

C. Farrell, *World Corporal Punishment Research* (2001). Available at www.corpun.com/rules.htm.

Michel Foucault, "Prison Talk: An Interview with Michel Foucault," in *Power/Knowledge: Selected Interviews and Other Writings 1972–1977*, ed. Colin Gordon, trans. Colin Gordon, Leo Marshall, John Mepham, and Kate Sober (New York: Pantheon, 1980).

Jean Hampton, "A New Theory of Retribution," in *Liability and Responsibility: Essays in Law and Morals*, ed. R.G. Frey and Christopher W. Morris (New York: Cambridge University, 1991), pp. 377–414.

Thomas Hobbes, *Hobbes's Leviathan Reprinted from the Edition of 1651 with an Essay by the Late W.G. Pogson Smith* (Oxford: Clarendon, 1909). Available at http://oll.libertyfund.org.

K.J. Kesselring, "Felony Forfeiture in England, c. 1170–1870," *The Journal of Legal History* 30, no. 3 (2009): 2010–226.

Terance D. Miethe and Hong Lu, *Punishment: A Comparative Historical Perspective* (Cambridge: Cambridge University, 2005).

"Purpose and Principles of Sentencing," s. 718 of the *Criminal Code of Canada*, R.S.C. 1985, c. C-46. Available at www.canlii.org.

18

Public Law: The Constitutional Law Places Legal Limits on the Institution of Political Government

Readings

- From "Tribal Philosophies and the *Canadian Charter of Rights and Freedoms*," by Menno Boldt and J. Anthony Long
- From the *Canadian Charter of Rights and Freedoms*
- Digest of *R. v. Stillman*, [1997] S.C.J. 34
- Digest of *R. v. Zundel*, [1992] S.C.J. 75

The origins of the constitutional law lie in the tribal and customary law. This law provided a cosmological source of order in early societies, so much so that it could be said that tribes were governed by law rather than politics. The constitutional law was a much later development, which came out of the *Magna Carta* and the idea that the customary law placed legal limits on the power of central government. As Menno Boldt and Anthony Long write, the emergence of the state brought in a new principle of organization in society, which eventually gave rise to the idea that the law is a product of the exercise of the sovereign power and "made" by Parliament. This idea placed the political order above the legal order and gave it ascendancy. However, the deficiencies in the new theory led to the development of a distinct body of supreme law, above the political order and the ordinary law, that placed legal limits on the law-making powers of the state. This development crystallized in the written constitutions that provided the statutory basis for the creation of Canada and the United States.

The most contentious legal issues in contemporary times have arisen in the constitutional law. Although there is nothing in principle that prevents the protection of group rights in a written constitution, the constitutional law focusses on the rights of the individual, which been most heavily litigated in the criminal law. The digests of the decisions of the Supreme Court of Canada in *R. v. Stillman* and *R. v. Zundel* illustrate the way in which the procedural and substantive guarantees in the *Charter of Rights and Freedoms* operate in the legal process. The adversarial way in which these guarantees operate derives directly from the common law, which has always seen the criminal process as a contest between the controlling interests of the state and the liberties of the person. The limits on political government in the *Charter* protect minorities from the views of the majority and raise controversial moral questions with regard to issues like abortion, pornography, and euthanasia.

❖ Readings ❖

From Menno Boldt and J. Anthony Long, "Tribal Philosophies and the *Canadian Charter of Rights and Freedoms*," *Ethnic and Racial Studies* 7, no. 4 (1984): 478–93.

Two Theories of Man and Society

In the western-liberal tradition the dominant conception of society is that of an aggregate of individuals, each with their own self-interest. The state is a product of collective agreement, an emanation from the individual will, created to perform functions necessary for the common good. As such, the state is an artificial creation, not based in any "natural order." Individuals within the state place themselves under common political authority and agree to a common political obligation to the state. The *individual* is believed to be morally prior to any *group* and, in relation to the state, individuals are viewed as acting for themselves, not as members of any collectivity.

The generic individualism of liberal political theory is illustrated by the political philosophies of [Jean-Jacques] Rousseau, [Thomas] Hobbes, [John] Locke, [John Stuart], Mill, and others. For example, Rousseau believed in the individual who is born free even though everywhere being in chains. The chains Rousseau referred to were created by the social group which superimposed itself on the individual. Hobbes conceived of society as reducible to individual wills in possession of certain natural and inalienable rights. An underlying premise for both Rousseau and Hobbes was that individual self-interest ought to take pre-eminence over group rights and claims. . . .

North American Indians had a very different conception of man and society. Society was conceived of as cosmocentric rather than homocentric. Robert Vachon (1982: 7)[1] states that their reference point was not the individual but the "whole" which is the cosmic order. Their conception of the individual was one of subordination to the whole. This conception was derived from their experience of the interrelatedness of all life (human, animal, plants, and things), and the need for harmony amongst all parts. The whole and the parts can survive only if each part fulfills its role. In the cosmocentric perspective animals, plants, and things were regarded as having souls or spirits and were dealt with as "persons" who had human qualities of thinking, feeling, and understanding, and who had volitional capacities as well (Hallowell).[2] Social interaction occurred between human beings and other-than-human "persons" involving reciprocal relations and mutual obligations. . . . In such a society there is no concept of inherent individual claims to inalienable rights.

In the Hobbesian political philosophy the exercise of authority was deemed necessary to protect society against rampant individual self-interest. But, in tribal society individual self-interest was viewed as inextricably intertwined with tribal survival. That is, the general good and the individual good were virtually identical (Mohawk Nation, 1977; Ortiz, 1979).[3] Hence, the social relations which give rise to individuality did not exist. . . .

Social Structure and Human Rights

The western-liberal doctrine of human rights grew out of the European experience of feudalism and the associated belief in the inherent inequality of men. Concern with constitutionally guaranteed individual rights was, in part, a reaction to centralization of power. It reflected the need, in western societies, to protect the individual against the powers of the state, and various forms of personal authority. The doctrine of individual rights gained additional relevance in western societies because individual initiative and competition were deemed essential for economic development. The capitalist market economy thrived on competitive individualism. Thus, the doctrine of autonomous individualism served both as stimulus and justification for the idea of individual rights in western societies. The modern western capitalist polity and economy produces a society in which the individual is in need of protection against forces that threaten to overwhelm him. In this context individualized rights have emerged as a response to existing objective conditions.

North American Indian tribes, by contrast, did not have the experience of feudalism. Moreover, unlike European states, the foundation of their social order was not based on hierarchical power wielded by a centralized political authority. Power and authority could not be claimed by, or delegated to, any individual or subset of the tribe; it was vested only in the tribe as a whole. . . .

By unreservedly accepting customary authority as their legitimate guide in living and working together Indians were freed from the need for coercive personal power, hierarchical authority relationships, and a separate ruling entity to maintain order. Because there was no state and no rulers, individuals had no need for protection from the authority of others.

Custom not only offered a well elaborated system of individual duties and responsibilities but was designed to protect human dignity. . . . Dignity was protected by a system of unwritten, positively-stated, mutual duties, rather than negatively-stated, individual, legal rights. Other than one's obligation to impersonal custom, the individual was unrestrained in his autonomy and freedom. Anything not proscribed by custom was "permitted." Because custom represented sacred and ultimate wisdom it was not construed as an infringement or threat to individual autonomy or freedom. . . .

[T]raditionally Indian communities engaged in an extensive consultation process in the selection of their leaders, and all decisions affecting the group required a consensus by members. However, under the democratic representative electoral system imposed upon them by the Canadian government, leaders are generally elected by a minority of members, and the associated organization of delegated authority and hierarchical structures has relegated most members of the Indian community to the periphery of the decision-making process. . .

The *Charter* and Tribal Traditions

Native Indian leaders hold that the *Canadian Charter of Rights and Freedoms* . . . threatens the destruction of their cosmocentric philosophy, their spiritual unity, and the customary precepts of their tribal society. In their brief to the Parliamentary Subcommittee on Indian Women and the Indian Act, the Assembly of First Nations gave clear expression to their concern over the impact of the *Charter*'s philosophy of individualism on their traditional way of life.

> As Indian people we cannot afford to have individual rights override collective rights. Our societies have never been structured in that way, unlike yours, and that is where the clash comes. . . . If you isolate the individual rights from the collective rights, then you are heading down another path that is even more discriminatory. . . .[4]

Indian leaders have identified several potentially critical consequences should the *Charter* apply to them. They fear that disgruntled members of their communities will exploit the *Charter*'s provisions to their individual advantage, thereby undermining existing group norms. They believe that a series of judicial decisions in favour of individual rights *versus* group rights will result in a "snowballing" of individualism. . . .

Furthermore, the *Charter* requires that Indian government be based on a western-liberal democratic theory of individualism (one man, one vote), delegated authority, hierarchical structures, and so on. These provisions will not allow Indians to develop a social organization and government built on their traditional values. . . .

Although Indians want constitutional protection from abuse by the larger society they believe their security lies in laws protecting their collective rights, not individual rights. They want to be protected as a group, not as individuals, from state violation of their human dignity and freedom. They do not reject individualized conceptions of human rights on principle. . . . But, they do assert that the doctrine of individualism and inherent inalienable rights, on which the *Charter* rests, is not part of their cultural heritage, serves no positive purpose for them, and threatens their integrity and survival as a unique people. By imposing highly individualistic conceptions of civil and political rights upon them the Canadian government will destroy their collective community. . . .

Collective Rights

Since the time of Hobbes and Locke political theorists have tended to conceive of rights in terms of individuals in relation to the state. Recently, however, Vernon Van Dyke (1974, 1980, 1982)[5] has advocated a more complex paradigm in which rights for groups . . . would be recognized on the grounds that human needs exist at various levels and that the existence of needs, whether at the level of the individual, or the level of the community, implies a right to meet such needs. Van Dyke holds that most discriminatory practices are directed against individuals because of their membership in groups. . . . This, he proposes, implies a right by the group to address such anti-group sanctions. . . .

Advocates of liberal democratic doctrine oppose the recognition of group rights because they believe that group rights have a negative impact on individual rights; that group rights are likely to prevail at the expense of individual rights. The Canadian Human Rights Commission takes the position that, while individual and collective rights can coexist, individual rights must have priority over group rights.

> You cannot swallow up the rights of individuals in order to protect the collectivity. . . . The fundamental principle has to be that you cannot have group rights if you do not have individual rights; that is the foundation of everything. . . .

Tension and conflict between group rights and individual rights are bound to occur when the criteria for each are developed in isolation from the other. . . .

Although United Nations' declarations and covenants on human rights uniformly emphasize individual protection, the principle that certain collectivities have a right to preserve their culture and to survive as groups also appears in various contexts.

Notes

1. Editor's note: The reference is to Robert Vachon, "Univers Juridique Autochtone Traditionnel Contemporain et Lute pour les Droits Autochtones," *Interculture* 15, no. 2–3 (1982): 2–19.
2. Editor's note: The reference is to Irving Hallowell, "Ojibwa World View," an "unpublished, undated paper".
3. Editor's note: The references are to Mohawk Nation, *A Basic Call to Consciousness: The Hau de no saw nee Address to the Western World* (Mohawk Nation, NY: Akwesasne, 1977) and Alfonso Ortiz, "Summary," in W.R. Swagerty, ed., *Indian Sovereignty: Proceedings of the 2nd Annual Conference on Problems and Issues Concerning American Indians Today* (Chicago, IL: Newberry Library, 1979).
4. Editor's note: The reference is to Assembly of First Nations, *Memorandum Concerning the Rights of the First Nations of Canada and the Canadian Constitution* (Ottawa, ON, 16 June 1982; Ottawa), pp. 17–18.
5. Editor's note: The references are to Vernon Van Dyke, "Human Rights and the Rights of Groups," *American Journal of Political Science* 18, no. 4 (1974): 725–42; "The Cultural Rights of Peoples," *Universal Human Rights* 2, no. 2 (1980): 1–21; and "Collective Entities and Moral Rights: Problems in Liberal Democratic Thought," *The Journal of Politics* 44, no. 1 (1982): 21–40.

From the *Canadian Charter of Rights and Freedoms*, Part I of the *Constitution Act, 1982*. Available at http:// laws-lois.justice.gc.ca/eng/Const/Const_index.html.

Guarantee of Rights and Freedoms

1. The *Canadian Charter of Rights and Freedoms* guarantees the rights and freedoms set out in it subject only to such reasonable limits prescribed by law as can be demonstrably justified in a free and democratic society.

Fundamental Freedoms

2. Everyone has the following fundamental freedoms:
    a. freedom of conscience and religion;
    b. freedom of thought, belief, opinion, and expression, including freedom of the press and other media of communication;
    c. freedom of peaceful assembly; and
    d. freedom of association. . . .

Legal Rights

7. Everyone has the right to life, liberty, and security of the person and the right not to be deprived thereof except in accordance with the principles of fundamental justice.

8. Everyone has the right to be secure against unreasonable search or seizure. . . .

10. Everyone has the right on arrest or detention . . .
    a. to be informed promptly of the reasons therefor;
    b. to retain and instruct counsel without delay and to be informed of that right; and
    c. to have the validity of the detention determined by way of *habeas corpus* and to be released if the detention is not lawful.

11. Any person charged with an offence has the right . . .
    a. to be informed without reasonable delay of the specific offence;
    b. to be tried within a reasonable time;
    c. not to be compelled to be a witness in proceedings against that person in respect of the offence;
    d. to be presumed innocent until proven guilty according to law in a fair and public hearing by an independent and impartial tribunal;
    e. not to be denied reasonable bail without just cause;
    f. except in the case of an offence under military law tried before a military tribunal, to the benefit of trial by jury where the maximum punishment for the offence is imprisonment for five years or a more severe punishment. . . .

Treatment or Punishment

12. Everyone has the right not to be subjected to any cruel and unusual treatment or punishment.

Equality Rights

15. (1) Every individual is equal before and under the law and has the right to the equal protection and equal benefit of the law without discrimination and, in particular, without discrimination based on race, national or ethnic origin, colour, religion, sex, age, or mental or physical disability.

Enforcement

24. (1) Anyone whose rights or freedoms, as guaranteed by this *Charter*, have been infringed or denied may apply to a court of competent jurisdiction to obtain such remedy as the court considers appropriate and just in the circumstances.

(2) Where, in proceedings under subsection (1), a court concludes that evidence was obtained in a manner that infringed or denied any rights or freedoms guaranteed by this *Charter*, the evidence shall be excluded if it is established that, having regard to all the circumstances, the admission of it in the proceedings would bring the administration of justice into disrepute.

Digest of *R. v. Stillman*, [1997] S.C.J. 34. Disclosure.

William Wayne Dale Stillman was arrested in 1991 for first degree murder. He was 17 years old at the time and the last person seen with the victim, a teenage girl. After his arrest, Stillman was allowed to meet with his lawyers, who gave the police a letter stating that he had been advised not to provide any bodily samples, including hair and teeth imprints. The letter also stated: "He is not to talk to you at all without one of the undersigned being present."

In spite of the letter, the police took scalp samples from Stillman, under the "threat of force," and instructed him to pull out samples of his pubic hair. Plasticine impressions of his teeth were taken. A police officer then interviewed Stillman for an hour, and Stillman sobbed throughout the interview. He was then escorted to the washroom, where he used a tissue to blow his nose. After he threw the tissue in a wastebasket, it was seized by the police for the purpose of identifying his DNA.

The samples, impressions, and seizures were tendered as evidence at Stillman's trial. The defence objected, on the basis that his rights had been violated under the *Canadian Charter of Rights and Freedoms*. The trial judge concluded that the hair samples and teeth impressions had been obtained in violation of s. 8 of the *Charter of Rights*, which gives everyone security against unreasonable search and seizure. They were nevertheless admissible, since their admission into evidence would not bring the administration of justice into disrepute under s. 24. The judge also held that the tissue and mucus had not been obtained in violation of the *Charter*. All of the seizures were accordingly entered into evidence.

The majority in the Supreme Court of Canada allowed Stillman's appeal from conviction and ordered a new trial. The court held that the hair samples and teeth impressions had been obtained in violation of s. 7 and s. 8 of the *Charter*. The police had breached Stillman's right to "security of the person" in a manner that was inconsistent with the principles of fundamental justice in s. 7. Their actions had invaded his privacy and breached the sanctity of his body, which is essential to the maintenance of human dignity.

The search for evidence on the accused's body, without the consent of the accused or some legal authority, violates s. 7 if it intrudes upon an individual's body in more than a minimal fashion. The seizure of the tissue and mucus violated s. 8, since Stillman's lawyers had made it clear that he was not consenting to its seizure. The court nevertheless found that the police may seize such items, if the accused has abandoned them and given up his "privacy interest" in them.

The majority held that evidence that is seized in violation of the *Charter* must be excluded at trial under s. 24(2) if it renders the trial unfair. If an accused is compelled to provide the evidence, and thereby incriminate himself, it is "conscriptive." Conscriptive evidence will normally render a trial unfair. It should not be excluded, however, unless the violation of the *Charter* was a serious violation, which would undermine the confidence of the public in the administration of justice. If the Crown can demonstrate on a balance of probabilities that the evidence could have been obtained by some non-conscriptive means, it may be admitted.

The hair samples and teeth impressions must be classified as conscriptive evidence. The court concluded, moreover, that the actions of the police in seizing this evidence constituted a serious and deliberate violation of the *Charter*. The evidence must therefore be excluded. The tissue and mucus was admissible. Although the police had disregarded the letter from Stillman's lawyers, the violation was not serious, since it did not interfere with his bodily integrity or undermine his dignity.

Digest of *R. v. Zundel*, [1992] S.C.J. 75.

Ernst Zundel was charged with "spreading false news" contrary to section 181 of the *Criminal Code of Canada*, which states:

> Every one who wilfully publishes a statement, tale or news that he knows is false and that causes or is likely to cause injury or mischief to a public interest is guilty of an indictable offence and liable to imprisonment for a term not exceeding two years.

Zundel was charged under s. 181 for publishing a pamphlet entitled "Did Six Million Really Die?" Zundel had contributed a preface and an afterword to the pamphlet, which had previously been published in the United States and England. The authors disputed the assertion that six million Jews were killed before and during World War II, and argued that the Holocaust was a myth perpetrated by a worldwide Jewish conspiracy.

The majority in the Supreme Court of Canada held that s. 181 violates the guarantee of freedom of expression in s. 2(b) of the *Canadian Charter of Rights and Freedoms*. Since s. 2(b) protects unpopular and offensive views, the content of the communication is irrelevant. The purpose of the guarantee is to permit free expression. This freedom promotes the discovery of the truth, participation in political and social discourse, and self-fulfilment. Section 2(b) specifically protects beliefs that the majority in society regards as wrong or false.

Since s. 181 may subject a person to a criminal conviction and potential imprisonment for the publication of words, it restricts freedom of expression and places limits on the guarantee in s. 2(b). The question in the case is accordingly whether s. 181 can be justified as a "reasonable limit" under s. 1 of the *Charter*. This depends upon the objective of the provision. In order to ascertain that objective, the court must look at the intention of Parliament when the provision was enacted.

Section 181 dates from the *Statute of Westminster* in 1275. It was introduced in order to prevent the deliberate spread of slanderous statements against the nobles of the realm. This was considered necessary to preserve political harmony in the state. To suggest that the objective of s. 181 is to combat hate propaganda or racism is to go beyond its history and its wording.

The fact that the section has rarely been used despite its long history supports the view that it is not essential to the maintenance of a free and democratic society. The section does not have an objective of sufficient importance to justify overriding the right of free expression and cannot be upheld under s. 1 of the *Charter*. It is notable that other provisions, such as s. 319(2) of the *Criminal Code*, deal with hate propaganda more fairly and more effectively.

☙ Discussion ❧

The constitutional law is made up of the part of the common law that places limits on the powers of the state. These limits have their own abstract character: if the ordinary law places limits on our conduct, the constitutional law places limits on those limits; it is composed of "meta-limits," which restrict the power of government to make and enforce laws. The substantive content of these limits is open to adjustment, in accordance with prevailing views. The constitutional law prevents the legislature from passing laws, for example, that curtail fundamental rights and freedoms. There are currently arguments before the courts that the laws against polygamy, assisted suicide, and nudity in public all contravene the *Canadian Charter of Rights and Freedoms* and are therefore unconstitutional. These arguments reflect the increasing diversity in Western society, which expresses itself in the idea that the majority has no right to impose its moral views on individuals and minorities.

The Constitutional Law Has Its Roots in the Tribal Law and the Customary Law

William Holdsworth wrote that the "chief characteristic" of the English constitution can be found in "the supremacy of law."[1] This idea has its origins in the early tribal law, which was based on custom, independently of any political power. At the beginning, it is clear, a King had no authority to change the customary law.

The law took precedence. P.D. King writes that the Visigoth kings, for example, who rose to power after the fall of the Roman Empire, claimed the divine right to rule. This claim did not mean the King could do whatever he wanted, however: "the lofty pre-eminence of the monarch, serene and glorious, involved no justification of arbitrariness in his rule." God had given the King his realm "for the prevention and correction" of sin, and "for the benefit of those over whom he reigned."[2] The power that the King enjoyed came with conditions.

It was accordingly the divine right of kings that provided the historical kernel of the constitutional law. As Alan Calnan writes,

> The King's fate often depended on his commitment to justice and his fidelity to customary law. The common convictions of the community held even higher authority than the King. In fact, customary law was viewed as a kind of natural law which embodied the community's sense of equity and reasonableness.[3]

The ascendancy of this law was not open to question.

The Magna Carta *Asserted the Supremacy of the Law over the King*

The development of the constitutional law in England can be traced to the struggle of the Norman kings to form a central government. The reaction of the local barons was to reassert the authority of the customary law over the King and the apparatus of his government. This reaction led to the signing of the *Charter of Liberties* (1100) and the *Magna Carta* (1215), under which Henry I and King John were forced to acknowledge the supremacy of the customary law.

The contest between these forces was a product of the depredations of the central government. The barons complained that the King had used the amercements and forfeitures in the criminal law to confiscate the property of their families.[4] In article 39 of the *Magna Carta*, they accordingly forced King John to agree that

> No freeman shall be taken or imprisoned or disseised or exiled or in any way destroyed, nor will we go upon him nor send upon him, except by the lawful judgment of his peers or [and] by the law of the land.

This requirement explains the antecedents, at least, of *habeus corpus*, under which judges had the authority to order that the King's officials deliver "the body" of the prisoner and demonstrate that the imprisonment was lawful.[5]

The idea of liberty to which the *Magna Carta* refers—later the sacred liberty of the subject—is a relative and a positive liberty. The *Magna Carta* guarantees the rights enjoyed by the members of society, who are free to pursue their lives within the safety and protection of the law, without interference from the King and the central government. This idea of liberty lies at the heart of the right to "life, liberty and security of the person" guaranteed by section 7 of the *Canadian Charter of Rights and Freedoms*.[6]

The Constitutional Law Was a Reaction to the Idea of Parliamentary Supremacy

The constitutional law that we are familiar with arose much later, however, after the emergence of the central government had raised the King and Parliament above the ordinary law. This shift gave the political order ascendancy over the legal order and gave rise to the doctrine of parliamentary supremacy, which is also known as "parliamentary sovereignty."[7] The historical English doctrine, which is found in William Blackstone, transfers the ascendancy—and supremacy—of the customary law to the political order. This transfer of authority to the political system was accomplished by slowly relocating the sources of the law in Parliament.

The mechanics of such a development are interesting. We tend to think that the law is binding because it is passed by Parliament. Historically, however, it was the other way around. It was Parliament that borrowed the authority of the customary law, in order to cement its own claim to political power. Thus, when the House of Commons passed and re-passed the *Magna Carta*, it was implicitly suggesting that it had the authority to pass binding laws.[8]

All of this is bound up in the emergence of the modern state. The development that marked the creation of the state was the appropriation of the law-making power by the political institutions of a central government. This move maintained the rule of law, which had existed under the customary law, but gave the political order ascendancy over the ordinary law. The idea that the law was supreme was nonetheless revived in the development of the constitutional law and the idea, much later, of a written constitution.

Holdsworth writes that Henry of Bracton believed that the law "should bind all within the realm—King and subject alike."[9] Edward Coke, citing Bracton, takes the same position in *Prohibitions del Roy, in* 1658: *Quod Rex non debet esse sub homine, sed sub Deo & Lege*—the King should not be under any man, but is under God and law.[10] This idea was displaced by the doctrine of parliamentary supremacy but eventually resurfaced in the idea that there is a body of law that governs the exercise of the sovereign power.

The Transfer of Ascendancy to Parliament Was Justified on a Democratic Basis

The modern justification for the transfer of legal authority to Parliament is that Parliament is a democratic institution. This argument features prominently in the work of Jeremy Bentham, who argued against the common law because it gives the judiciary the authority to decide the law for the rest of society. Bentham misrepresents the common law, however, which was based on custom and the moral consensus in society rather than the personal views of the judiciary.

The rise of Parliament created problems of its own. The reality is that the democratic system replaced the social, cultural, and religious consensus behind the customary law with the principle of majority rule. This principle is the real innovation in the development of the political institutions of government, which led to the increasing centralization of power in the state. The rise of democratic institutions also created a political class, which often served the interests of the wealthy and powerful rather than the public. The deeper problem, however, is that the introduction of democratic institutions increased the divisions in society by creating discernible minorities, who had no voice in government. The competition that this produced reinvigorated the idea that the political order—and implicitly the majority—must be subject to legal and constitutional limits.

The Theory of Constitutionalism Traces the Powers of Government to a Written Constitution

The emergence of the modern state was pivotal in these developments. The modern theory of the state in Western democratic tradition is based on "constitutionalism," which is sometimes described as "liberal constitutionalism."[11] Constitutionalism maintains that the power of the state and the political institutions within the state must be legally limited. This theory has often been justified on the basis that governments hold power on the terms and conditions set by the people under the political contract. These terms are ideally set out in a written constitution. The legal sources of the constitutional law in the common law tradition are much deeper, however, and lie in the traditional resistance to central government.

The advantage of a written constitution is naturally that it clarifies the principles that have been enshrined in the constitutional law. The constitutional law also contains concepts like the rule of law, however, and the maxim that whatever is not prohibited is permitted.[12] The legal adage that "a man's home is his castle," which restricts the legal authority of the police, also has constitutional significance.

A written constitution nevertheless contains a convenient set of verbal formulas, which determine whether the provisions of ordinary statutes fall within the constitutional powers of the legislature. From a procedural perspective, these provisions function much like the precepts of the Christian natural law, which invalidate those positive laws that conflict with them. This similarity is apparent in the language of written constitutions, which is general, inclusive, and full of moral implications.

The effectiveness of a written constitution rests on our ability to distinguish between ordinary and constitutional statutes. This task can present difficulties: the *Canadian Bill of Rights*, S.C. 1960, c. 44, for example, was an ordinary statute and was not accorded the status that it needed to comfortably override more recent legislation until after the proclamation of the *Charter of Rights*. The Canadian courts have now characterized ordinary statutes that deal with fundamental matters like human rights as "quasi-constitutional."[13] These statutes generally take precedence over other statutes.[14]

One of the Purposes of a Written Constitution Is to Distribute the Sovereign Power

The fundamental purpose of a written constitution is to limit the institution of political government by placing limits on the exercise of the sovereign power. In federal systems, like Canada and the United States, one of the ways that this is accomplished is by dividing the sovereign power between different levels of government. One of the purposes of the

Canadian and American constitutions is accordingly to distribute the sovereign power and create the institutional framework under which the country is governed. This framework includes restrictions on the number and distribution of representatives or senators, the dates of elections, the admission of new provinces, and the physical location of seats of government.

In Canada, the *British North America Act, 1867* divided the powers of government between the federal and provincial governments.[15] Section 91, for example, states that the government of Canada has exclusive jurisdiction to pass criminal law. Section 92 gives the provinces exclusive jurisdiction over property and civil rights. As a general rule, legislation that intrudes into the jurisdiction of another level of government is *ultra vires*—that is to say, beyond the powers and therefore outside the jurisdiction of the relevant government.

The conventional formulation of this rule is found in the *Margarine Reference*, where the Supreme Court of Canada and the Judicial Committee of the Privy Council considered the validity of the federal *Dairy Industry Act*.[16] Section 5(a) of that Act, which was there to protect dairy farmers, made the sale of margarine manufactured "from any fat other than that of milk or cream" an offence under the criminal law power. Both courts rejected the argument that the federal government had the competence to enact such a provision.

At the Supreme Court, Justice Rand held that a valid criminal law provision must serve a public purpose such as public peace, order, security, health, or morality, and cannot be used for economic regulation.[17] The Judicial Committee of the Privy Council agreed and struck down the legislation on the basis that it was "in pith and substance" related to property and civil rights, since it restricted the rights of individuals to participate in local trade.[18]

The *Secession Reference* Recognizes the Supremacy of the Rule of Law

The more recent caselaw has recognized the supremacy of the rule of law and placed the political order and the sovereign power under legal constraints. In *Reference re Secession of Quebec*, [1998] 2 S.C.R. 217, the Supreme Court of Canada held that our system of government is based on both the rule of law and constitutionalism. It follows that "the law is supreme over the acts of both government and private persons." Neither the executive nor the legislative branch of government may "transgress" the provisions of the constitution: "indeed, their sole claim to exercise lawful authority rests in the powers allocated to them under the Constitution, and can come from no other source."

The Supreme Court also held that the principles on which the *Constitution* is based rank higher than its specific provisions. It is notable that the Canadian position is different from the American position, in this regard, which is sometimes referred to as "popular sovereignty" or "the sovereignty of the people." The American position clearly holds that the people are above the constitution and therefore supreme.[19] There is a corresponding theoretical argument that the people hold the "constituent power" of the state, which brings the state and the sovereign power into being.[20] If this argument means that a democratic majority holds the sovereign power, however, it simply reasserts the ascendancy of the political order.

The Constitutional Law Also Places Limits on the Legislative Power

The constitutional law also regulates the relations between government and the individuals and groups who are governed by placing substantive limits on the law-making power of the state. The most conspicuous part of the contemporary constitutional law lies in the rights of the individual. These rights were originally called natural rights because they accrue to us as natural beings and cannot be removed by society. They are therefore inalienable. Most of the natural rights that we are familiar with were originally set out in explicit terms in the *Déclaration des Droits de l'Homme et du Citoyen* (the *Declaration of the Rights of Man and the Citizen*) of 1789, during the French Revolution. It was this set of rights that came into the common law tradition when the *Bill of Rights* was entrenched in the American constitution in 1791.

The usual formulation of natural rights in modern constitutions suggests that these rights exist, morally and legally, outside the legislative guarantees that give them force. There are traces of this idea in the criminal law. The defence of necessity, for example, holds that the accused's right to preserve himself takes precedence over his ordinary legal obligations. This line of reasoning recognizes the broad constitutional character of our rights.[21]

The idea of natural rights still provides the focus of the constitutional law, though many of these rights are now referred to legally as the rights of the individual. This terminology brings in the idea of human rights, since the word "individual" in law refers to human persons.[22] At the same time, the constitutional law is always evolving, and it is conceivable that animals will be awarded such rights in the future. In point of fact, the historical rationale behind the idea of constitutional rights is that the members of society are entitled to the protection of the law. If animals are considered to be members of society, it follows that they are entitled to some degree of protection.

The use of the term "rights" in the constitutional law has legal rather than ethical origins and refers to the legal prerogatives of someone who is owed a duty. It is the existence of duties that explains the attraction of the concept of rights, which lies in the fact that they oblige other people to do things for us. Rhetorically, the peremptory nature of a right converts a claim into a demand. In the case of the constitutional law, moreover, it is the state that owes the individual the relevant duty.

The Contemporary Understanding of These Rights Is Found in the Liberal Tradition

The contemporary understanding of our individual rights comes out of the liberal tradition and the work of John Stuart Mill. In his most famous work, *On Liberty*, which was published in 1859, Mill argues that the centralization of power in the state has created a kind of tyranny over the individual.[23] This is true, whether the state is run by a monarchy or by democratic institutions.

"The limitation, therefore," Mill writes, "of the power of government over individuals loses none of its importance when the holders of power are regularly accountable to the community." The interests of the majority and the individual often diverge in a democratic society. The individual must therefore be protected from the tyranny of "prevailing opinion and feeling," which imposes the "ideas and practices" of the majority on the rest of society.

Mill accordingly tries to locate the philosophical limits of the "power which can be legitimately exercised by society over the individual." He finds these limits in the concept of "liberty," which historically limited the power of the King. Although Mill does not appear to realize that the origins of such a concept can be found in the customary law, he recognizes that the concept gives rise to freedoms that have constitutional implications. This concept gives rise to freedoms that look, at least, like constitutional rights. Such freedoms include the freedom of conscience and expression, the freedom of "tastes and pursuits," and the freedom to associate with other individuals.

Mill Holds that the State Can Intervene Only in the Instance of Harm

Mill argues that the concept of liberty governs the relationship between the individual and the state. The "sole end," he writes,

> for which mankind are warranted, individually or collectively, in interfering with the liberty of action of any of their number, is self-protection. That the only purpose for which power can be rightfully exercised over any member of a civilized community, against his will, is to prevent harm to others.

This principle places conceptual limits on the legal limits that the state can legitimately place on our freedoms. Although Mill's theory is a political rather than a legal theory, these meta-limits provide the general ethical framework in which most contemporary theorists analyze our constitutional rights.

Mill rejects the notion of a social contract. He nevertheless argues that rights and freedoms are reciprocal, and individual persons are obliged to "observe a certain line of conduct" toward other people in return for society's protection of their liberties.[24] We are accordingly obliged to respect the rights of other people, and to share the burdens of society. Neither obligation extends into the realm of private conduct, however, and the way we live our individual lives—how we eat, for example—is outside the scope of public legislation.

Mill sets out the liberal position, which often fails to distinguish between society and the state. This is significant because it was historically society that placed limits on the exercise of the sovereign power. The historical position can nevertheless be read into the liberal argument that the state is entitled to exercise control over our actions only when those actions have a demonstrable effect on others. It follows that

> no person ought to be punished simply for being drunk; but a soldier or policeman should be punished for being drunk on duty. Whenever, in short, there is a definite

damage, or a definite risk of damage, either to an individual or to the public, the case is taken out of the province of liberty and placed in that of morality or law.

This kind of principle has clearly made its way into section 1 of the *Charter of Rights and Freedoms*, which states that legislative limits on our conduct must be "demonstrably justified in a free and democratic society."

There are problems with the liberal analysis, however, which is too vague to be of much assistance in many cases. The reality is that the exercise of private rights—like the right to consume liquor or smoke cigarettes—may affect the distribution of public benefits in society. If nothing else, the medicare system must bear the cost of treating someone who has developed lung cancer after years of smoking cigarettes. The constitutional question is accordingly more nuanced, and the issue is, rather, at what point is the impact on other people sufficient to justify some form of intervention?

Mill's Argument Is Based on a Distinction between the Private Sphere and the Public Sphere

After setting out the harm principle, Mill goes on to argue that the sphere of private action is "the appropriate region of human liberty." We are entitled to act as we wish in our private lives. This idea is based on an exaggerated distinction, however, between the private and public spheres, which suggests that there is an unregulated private sphere in which we enjoy complete freedom. This is not the historical idea behind the constitutional law, which rests on a relative notion of liberty that comes with duties to the other members of society.

Like many liberals, Mill defines liberty in abstract terms, outside any moral or social context. This approach reflects the liberal view that individual rights are free-standing rights, which attach to the natural individual rather than the members of society. They accordingly precede our membership in society and set the terms on which we enter into relations with other people. This idea runs into difficulties in a legal context, since the law implicitly assumes that it is society that gives us the rights and liberties recognized by the law. There is a philosophical sense in which legal remedies have their provenance in society: the only quality or property that gives our constitutional rights legal force is that judges feel obliged to recognize them. It is this line of reasoning that explains why Jeremy Bentham, in spite of his liberal views, dismissed the idea of "natural and imprescriptible rights" as "nonsense on stilts" and "anti-legal rights."[25]

The historical purpose behind the law that gave rise to the constitutional law is not to free us from the constraints of society.[26] It is to guarantee our membership in society. The issue of liberty arises in the constitutional law, not because the law has oppressed us in our personal lives, but because the King has done so. This new form of law is a reaction to the introduction of the state and a new form of government, based on the political contract. The freedom that the *Magna Carta* asserts is freedom from central government.

The difficulty with the liberal idea of a private sphere is easily illustrated. We might understandably say, for example, that the state has no right to regulate sexual intercourse, since intercourse is a private matter. But of course intercourse with children is prohibited and the criminal law forbids intercourse without consent. The statement that sexual intercourse is a private matter is simply too crude to catch the legal issues that arise in such a context.

The difficulty does not stop there. If we say that we have an undefined "right" to enjoy sexual intercourse—and surely we do—we cannot determine the legal and constitutional extent of such a right in the common law without examining the facts in specific cases. The liberal position nevertheless instinctively recognizes the distinction between the ethical and legal limits on our conduct. From a legal and constitutional perspective, it is the consequences of our conduct on other people that is pivotal. This can be illustrated as follows: a married man, for example, may have unprotected intercourse with an extramarital partner who is infected with HIV. The problem from a legal and a constitutional perspective is that he may infect his spouse. His wife may give birth to an infected child. These are social rather than moral factors, which determine whether the state may constitutionally limit his right to engage in intercourse.

There Is Also a Distinction between Positive and Negative Rights in the Liberal Literature

The liberal literature also distinguishes between "positive" and "negative" rights.[27] A negative right obliges other people to refrain from doing anything that would interfere with the exercise of an individual right. A positive right obliges other people to do something that would facilitate the exercise of such a right. The right to some form of welfare or social assistance is usually cited as an example of a positive right, though this example usually does not arise in a constitutional context. There is certainly room for argument that Canadians have a positive right to the provision of medical services under s. 7 of the *Charter of Rights and Freedoms*, which guarantees "security of the person." This guarantee presumably includes a right to an abortion.[28]

The distinction between negative and positive rights often breaks down, however. It might be argued, for example, that a neo-Nazi group has the same right as other groups to march peaceably through the streets. This is a negative right, but it raises positive obligations: if the neo-Nazi group has a right to protest, this merely raises a second question. Does the municipality, for example, have an obligation to provide a police escort, in order to prevent protestors who oppose the march from interfering with the marchers' freedom of expression?

The *Canadian Charter of Rights and Freedoms* Introduces a Normative Standard into the Constitutional Law

The *Canadian Charter of Rights and Freedoms* guarantees individual rights. Brian Dickson, one of Canada's chief justices, wrote that the political impetus behind the *Charter of Rights* came from the increasing recognition of human rights in the international law.

This recognition is evident in international agreements like the *International Covenant on Economic, Social and Cultural Rights* and the *International Covenant on Civil and Political Rights*.[29]

Dickson writes that the *Charter of Rights and Freedoms*, like the American *Bill of Rights*, introduces a normative standard into the constitutional law. As a result, judges are required to consider what the law "should" be in deciding constitutional cases. This brings moral considerations directly into the constitutional law. The Canadian judiciary is now obliged to consult moral principles and the substantive consensus in society in deciding the constitutional validity of particular laws. The *Charter* has accordingly given the Supreme Court and the judiciary moral supervision of the statutory law. It is important to add that this does not give the courts any legislative authority.

The Rights of the Individual in the Constitutional Law Are Based on the Dignity of the Person

The concept of individual rights enshrined in the contemporary constitutional law is based on the dignity of the individual human person. This concept provides the philosophical foundation for the analysis of some of the parallel provisions in the American and Canadian constitutions. This kind of analysis is particularly important in the context of the right not to be subjected to cruel and unusual punishment.

The significance of the concept of dignity in deciding the issues that arise under such a provision is probably best illustrated by *Furman v. Georgia, supra*, where Justice Brennan held that the Eighth Amendment to the Constitution of the United States

> prohibits the infliction of uncivilized and inhuman punishments. The State, even as it punishes, must treat its members with respect for their intrinsic worth as human beings. A punishment is "cruel and unusual," therefore, if it does not comport with human dignity.[30]

The word "dignity" refers to the fact that an individual is entitled to the esteem and respect of other people. *Furman* holds that an offender remains a member of society and is still entitled to its protections. An offender is not an outlaw.

Boldt and Long Argue that the Constitutional Law Should Also Recognize the Dignity of the Group

The *Charter of Rights and Freedoms* and the Canadian constitution guarantee group rights, such as the right to denominational schools, and language rights.[31] Such guarantees raise familiar questions in Quebec, where individual store owners have claimed the right to use whatever language they wish on their store signs. Do the collective rights of francophones, who wish to preserve their language, annul the owners' exercise of their individual rights? The communitarian answer to this question is apparently "yes"; the liberal answer is apparently "no".

As Menno Boldt and Anthony Long suggest, however, the rights and freedoms in the *Charter* are generally designed to protect the individual from the encroachments of the state. These safeguards make little sense in a tribal context, however, since tribes are governed by consensus. The tribal law is based on moral custom and operates on the basis that individuals have internalized the law. There is accordingly no need for the coercive mechanisms that we associate with the state.

Boldt and Long go further, however, and argue that the *Charter* undermines traditional forms of Aboriginal government. This is because tribes function on the basis of consensus, rather than the democratic principle. The idea that the members of the First Nations require constitutional rights that protect the individual from the majority, moreover, is a European interpolation that interferes with the dynamics of the tribe. Boldt and Long argue that the solution to such a problem lies in the constitutional recognition of group rights, which enshrine the dignity of tribes and other groups.

The Constitutional Law Nevertheless Focusses on Individual Rights

The focus of the *Charter* jurisprudence nevertheless lies in the area of individual rights and freedoms. The prominence of these rights in the criminal law reflects the adversarial nature of the trial process in the common law and the fact that a criminal trial is a contest between the individual and the state. This system of trial exists in sharp contrast to the inquisitorial process that exists in France and other countries with a civil system of law.

Stephan Landsman has written that the adversarial process has three fundamental characteristics. The first characteristic is that the decision-maker occupies a neutral, passive role in the process. The second is that the parties should choose and present the evidence. The third is that the introduction of evidence is governed by a "highly structured forensic procedure." Out of "the sharp clash of proofs presented by adversaries," the truth—and if not the truth, the right result—will ultimately emerge.[32]

The judge in the common law system is a referee or an umpire, as well as a judge, whose responsibility in the evidentiary process is to see that the parties present their evidence in accordance with the established rules. This has many constitutional overtones: if the conduct of the police in obtaining evidence undermines the confidence of the public in the administration of justice, for example, the evidence may be excluded under section 24 of the *Charter*. Since the rules of the criminal process govern the conduct of the Crown and the state, they have always had a distinctly constitutional flavour.[33]

The character of the constitutional law in the common law tradition reflects the adversarial nature of the common law process. One of the constant criticisms of the common law trial process is that it is highly competitive. This magnifies the disputatious nature of the process and introduces many complications. Criminal trials in the common law are beset with procedural wrangles, which prolong the legal process far beyond its natural duration. Landsman writes that this focus on competition increases the importance of ethical rules in the process, which favours the development of a "win-at-any-cost attitude."

The Adversarial Nature of the Constitutional Law Comes to the Fore in Criminal Cases like Zundel *and* Stillman

The adversarial nature of the constitutional law comes to the fore in the criminal law. Much of this has to do with the procedural history of the common law, which always saw a trial as a kind of contest. The nature of this contest cannot be fully understood without some appreciation of the highly decentralized form of government that existed in England before the Conquest, and the widespread resistance to the central government. Although the English kings eventually gained firm control of the country, largely through the use of force and the legal system, they remained adversaries who constantly fought to restrict the freedoms of the people.

The common law trial process has always borne the features of a battle. The role of the judge is merely to require that the parties follow the rules of the fight. This idea was heightened in the criminal law by the fact that the King is seeking to potentially deprive individuals of their fundamental liberty. There is no doubt that our constitutional rights and the procedural requirements of the criminal law have merely replaced the weapons that were originally used in trial by combat.

The digests of the *Zundel* and the *Stillman* cases speak to the history of this law. The crime of "spreading false news," under which Zundel was charged, is the product of an England that was still highly decentralized and run largely by barons, powerful land-owners, who were wont to defend their reputations by force of arms. The purpose of making the act of spreading false news an offence was to preserve the peace among equals, under a weak central government. The constitutional issue in the case concerns the liberty of expression, which guarantees the right of everyone to speak freely. The limitation that section 181 places on freedom of expression cannot be justified in a society where the historical threat to the public peace no longer exists.

The roots of the decision in *R. v. Stillman*, as well as the roots of the right against unreasonable search and seizure, can be found in the right against self-incrimination. This right is another legal manifestation of the inviolability of individual members of society, who were legally entitled to enjoy their liberties, without physical interference from the King or his officials. The King's exercise of power over the individual person is exceptional and must always be justified.

The Civil System of Law Is Inquisitorial and Does Not Recognize These Constitutional Rights

The nature of these constitutional rights can best be understood by comparing the common law and civil law systems. The trial process in the civil system of law is inquisitorial, rather than adversarial, and does not recognize the same constitutional rights that the common law system recognizes. In the civil law system, it is the judge, rather than the parties, who owns the process and determines the parameters of the inquiry. It is the judge who asks the questions of the witnesses. There are few of the procedural and evidentiary battles that characterize trials in North America, and the length of trials is much shorter. This brevity saves the resources of the system of justice.

It is often said that the civil system is more efficient than the common law. This probably reflects the different purposes of the trial process in the two systems: the civil trial is often described as an inquiry, rather than a competition between the state and individual persons, and the purpose of the criminal trial in the civil system is simply to determine the truth. Although the criminal trial in the common law can also be described as a search for the truth, the historical focus of the common law process is liberty and punishment. As a result, the concern with fairness and due process that characterizes the common law is not a major factor in the civil process. At the same time, the judiciary in the civil system has a policing role and functions in many ways as part of the bureaucracy of the state.

The Differences between the Common Law and the Civil Law System Can Be Seen in the Right to Silence

The right to silence—which is now seen primarily as an extension of the right against self-incrimination—provides a good illustration of the differences between the approach to criminal prosecutions in the common law system and that in the civil system of law.[34] There is no right to silence in the civil system, and criminal trials usually begin by taking a statement from the accused.[35]

The constitutional origins of the right to silence are relatively recent. The accused was originally not allowed to testify. This practice was based on the firm belief, as John Henry Wigmore puts it, that the evidence of the accused could not be trusted, since it was in the interests of a guilty person to lie.[36] The same prohibition was accordingly extended to individuals who had a pecuniary interest in the outcome of the litigation.

There are many critics of the right to silence. K. Van Dijkhorst, a South African judge, suggests that the adversarial idea behind such a right merely damages the system:

> Society does not see a duel with a criminal. It does not wish to give him a fair chance to escape like the fox in order to make the hunt more interesting. . . . It is normal for a child who has stolen a cookie to be questioned by his parent on its disappearance. It would be absurd if the child's defence is that he may not be questioned and in any event cannot be expected to reply as this might incriminate him. Yet when he has stolen a bicycle this is the accepted situation vis-à-vis police and court, entrenched in our Constitution.[37]

The problem with this analysis is that the state is not in the position of a parent. The common law has historically regarded the intrusion of the forces of the state into private affairs with suspicion. The constitutional law rejects the idea that individuals have any obligation to co-operate with their prosecutors.

The criticism of the common law process nevertheless goes very deep. Barton Ingraham, an American lawyer writes that the rules of evidence in an adversarial system of justice are a perfect tool for keeping the facts out of sight and out of the courtroom so that the jury is not fully acquainted with all the facts in the case. For these reasons, it would be a marvel, indeed, if the adversarial system produced a better system of justice than a more inquisitorial one.[38]

The trial procedure in the American system, Ingraham argues, has become a game rather than a process "specifically designed to get at the truth." As a result, he argues, it is "virtually impossible" to achieve justice in "America's present-day adversary system."

Notes

1. Sir William Holdsworth, *A History of English Law*, 4th ed., vol. 2 (London: Methuen, 1936), 195ff.
2. See P.D. King, *Law and Society in the Visigoth Kingdom* (Cambridge: Cambridge University, 1972), at p. 26ff.
3. Alan Calnan, *A Revisionist History of Tort Law: From Holmesian Realism to Neoclassical Rationalism* (Durham, NC: Carolina Academic, 2005) at p. 94.
4. See article 20, for example, of the *Magna Carta*. For the text of the *Magna Carta* and a technical commentary, see *Magna Carta: A Commentary on the Great Charter of King John*, with a "historical" introduction by William Sharp McKechnie (Glasgow: Maclehose, 1914). And see Ellis Sandoz, ed., *The Roots of Liberty: Magna Carta, Ancient Constitution, and the Anglo-American Tradition of Rule of Law* (Indianapolis: Liberty Fund, 2008). Both texts are available at http://oll.libertyfund.org.
5. Although *habeus corpus* was originally a private and a local remedy and seems to have been used to ensure the safekeeping of a prisoner in gaol (jail), it was later used to secure the release of those who had been wrongly imprisoned by the King or his agents. McKechnie and Sandoz, ibid., address the technical niceties of the writ.
6. See the excerpt from *Re B.C. Motor Vehicle Act*, [1985] 2 S.C.R. 486 listed in the Appendix.
7. The use of the term "parliamentary supremacy" is a reflection of the increasing power of Parliament vis-à-vis the King. The English theory is that the King or Queen holds the sovereign power, which gives the state the power to pass laws, but can exercise the sovereign power only in accordance with the wishes of Parliament. There is accordingly a constitutional convention that the sovereign will consent to whatever laws Parliament in its wisdom decides to pass. A statute nevertheless does not become law until the King or Queen has consented to it.
8. Edward Coke asserted in Parliament in 1621 that the *Magna Carta* had been "confirmed" by Parliament 32 times. See Steve Sheppard, ed., *The Selected Writings of Edward Coke*, vol. 3 (Indianapolis: Liberty Fund, 2003), p. 1211.
9. Holdsworth, op cit.
10. See Joyce Lee Malcolm, ed., *The Struggle for Sovereignty: Seventeenth-Century English Political Tracts*, vol. 1 (Indianapolis: Liberty Fund, 1999). Available at http://oll.libertyfund.org. Also note that this maxim remains a fundamental part of the active law. See *State of Haryana and Others vs Bhajan Lal and Others*, Civil Appeal No. 5412 of 1990, a decision of the Indian Supreme Court, available at www.lawyersclubindia.com.
11. The term "liberal" refers to the fact that the constitution protects individuals and minorities.
12. See John Laws, for example, "The Rule of Reason—An International Heritage," in Mads Tønnesson Andenæs and Duncan Fairgrieve, eds., *Judicial Review in International Perspective* (Hague: Kluwer Law, 2000), pp. 247–59, at p. 256.
13. An example is the *Canadian Human Rights Act*, R.S.C. 1985, c. H-6, which deals with discrimination and the communication of hate messages. See, for example, the remark of Justice Binnie in *Canada (House of Commons) v. Vaid*, 2005 S.C.C. 30, [2005] 1 S.C.R. 667, at para. 81: "As stated earlier, the *Canadian*

Human Rights Act is a quasi-constitutional document and we should affirm that any exemption from its provisions must be clearly stated."

14. In the case of ordinary legislation, it is normally assumed as a matter of statutory construction that Parliament intended that the later legislation take precedence.

15. The current version of this statute is referred to as *The Constitution Act*, 1867 (UK), 30 & 31 Victoria, c. 3, and is available at http://canlii.org.

16. See *Reference re Validity of Section 5(a) Dairy Industry Act*, [1949] S.C.R. 1.

17. See the decision, at p. 50: "Is the prohibition then enacted with a view to a public purpose which can support it as being in relation to criminal law? Public peace, order, security, health, morality: these are the ordinary though not exclusive ends served by that law, but they do not appear to be the object of the parliamentary action here."

18. See *Canadian Federation of Agriculture v. Attorney General for Quebec*, [1951] A.C. 179 (P.C.).

19. The matter is complex, but the general idea of popular sovereignty is reflected in the preamble to the American constitution, which reads: "We the People of the United States, in Order to form a more perfect Union, establish Justice, insure domestic Tranquility, provide for the common defence, promote the general Welfare, and secure the Blessings of Liberty to ourselves and our Posterity, do ordain and establish this Constitution for the United States of America." See *Afroyim v. Rusk* (1967), 387 U.S. 253, for example, at 257, where the United States Supreme Court considered whether the government can take away a citizen's citizenship: "In our country the people are sovereign and the Government cannot sever its relationship to the people by taking away their citizenship."

20. The concept of the "constituent power," or "*pouvoir constituant*," acquired particular importance in the work of Carl Schmitt, the most renowned legal theorist of the Nazi era. See Renato Cristi, for example, "Carl Schmitt on Sovereignty and Constituent Power," *Canadian Journal of Law & Jurisprudence* 10 (1997): 189–201.

21. See *Perka v. the Queen*, [1984] 2 S.C.R. 232. The defence of necessity can also be explained under the natural law, since the pre-eminent duty under the natural law is to preserve oneself. The right to preserve oneself in the theory of natural rights is based on the fact that we have a duty to do so under the natural law.

22. See *Christian Labour Association v. B.C. Transportation Financing Authority*, 2000 BCSC 727 (CanLII), where the court held that a union is not an "individual" and therefore does not enjoy freedom of association under s. 2(d) of the *Charter*. The courts have also held that s. 7 of the *Charter*, which guarantees "everyone" life, liberty, and security of the person, does not extend to corporations. See *Dywidag Systems International, Canada Ltd. v. Zutphen Brothers Construction Ltd.*, [1990] 1 S.C.R. 705, which affirms *Irwin Toy Ltd. v. Quebec (Attorney General)*, [1989] 1 S.C.R. 927.

23. John Stuart Mill, *On Liberty and the Subjection of Women* (New York: Henry Holt and Co., 1879), p. 145. Available at http://oll.libertyfund.org.

24. This shows the historical transformation of the concept of law, which was originally seen as an independent check on those with political authority. Mill implicitly places this check under political rather than legal regulation.

25. Jeremy Bentham, *Anarchical Fallacies Being an Examination of the Declarations of Rights Issued During the French Revolution*, as cited in the suggestions for further reading.

26. The paradox may be that liberalism has apparently removed many of the social and moral constraints on the individual, without in any way dismantling the increasing levels of social control that gave rise to the demand for individual freedoms and rights in the first place.

27. This distinction is usually traced to Isaiah Berlin's argument that there is a positive and a negative concept of liberty. See Isaiah Berlin, "Two Concepts of Liberty," in *Four Essays on Liberty* (London: Oxford University, 2002). Originally published in 1969.

28. See *R. v. Morgentaler*, [1988] 1 S.C.R. 30.

29. Brian Dickson, "The Canadian Charter of Rights and Freedoms: Context and Evolution," as cited in the suggestions for further reading.

30. *Furman v. Georgia* (1972), ibid., at 277. Available at www.law.cornell.edu.

31. See s. 19(1) of the *Charter*, for example: "Either English or French may be used by any person in, or in any pleading in or process issuing from, any court established by Parliament." And see s. 23(2): "Citizens of Canada of whom any child has received or is receiving primary or secondary school instruction in English or French in Canada, have the right to have all their children receive primary and secondary school instruction in the same language."

32. See Stephan Landsman, "A Brief Survey of the Development of the Adversary System," as cited in the suggestions for further reading.

33. The *Criminal Code of Canada* contains a common law right to make "full answer and defence," which clearly has constitutional overtones.

34. There are at least two issues here. One is whether the accused has the right to remain silent. Another is whether the accused's silence is incriminating. In *R. v. Noble*, [1997] 1 S.C.R. 874, Sopinka J. held that it is always necessary to keep the burden of proof in a criminal case on the Crown. This prohibits a judge or jury from relying on the failure of an accused to testify as evidence that determines guilt. The decision in *Noble* is available at www.canlii.org.

35. See Van Dijkhorst's brief assessment of the French system, in "The Right to Silence," as cited *infra*, at pp. 37–8. There are nevertheless signs that accused persons in the civil system have begun to assert the constitutional rights recognized in the common law.

36. See John Henry Wigmore, "Testimonial Qualifications: Emotional Capacity; Interest as a Testimonial Disqualification," in *A Treatise on the Anglo-American System of Evidence in Trials at Common Law Including the Statutes and Judicial Decisions of All Jurisdictions of the United States and Canada*, 2nd ed., 5 vols. (Boston: Little, Brown, 1923), sections 575–87, at section 576, p. 996. "Total exclusion from the stand," Wigmore writes, "is the proper safeguard against a false decision, whenever the persons offered are of a class specially likely to speak falsely." Yet Jeremy Bentham, for example, argues that the exclusion is of no assistance to the innocent, since they must logically testify, in order to put their position forward. See Jeremy Bentham, "Examination of Another Case of Vexation: Self-Inculpation," Chapter XI of his *Treatise on Judicial Evidence*. Extracted from the Manuscripts of Jeremy Bentham by M. Dumont. (London: J.W. Paget, 1825), 240–5, at p. 241. Both sources are available at http://heinonline.org.

37. K. Van Dijkhorst, "The Right to Silence: Is the Game Worth the Candle?," *South African Law Journal* 118 (2001): 26–58, at p. 30. Dijkhorst recommends the "abolition" of the right to silence in South Africa and quotes John William Salmond, at p. 31, as authority that "the compulsory examination of the accused is an essential feature of sound criminal procedure." Available at http://heinonline.org.

38. Barton L. Ingraham, "The Right of Silence, the Presumption of Innocence, the Burden of Proof, and a Modest Proposal: A Reply to O'Reilly," as cited in the suggestions for further reading.

Study Questions

1. Do you agree that the constitutional law takes us back to the early common law? Why, why not? Section 52 of the *Canadian Charter of Rights and Freedoms* says that the *Charter* is the "supreme law" of Canada. What does this say about the relationship between the legal order and the political order in Canada?

2. Why do Menno Boldt and Anthony Long argue that the guarantees in the *Charter of Rights* will undermine tribal government? What do they propose as a solution?

3. What were the facts in *R. v. Stillman*? Why did the Supreme Court hold that section 7 of the *Charter* had been violated?

4. What offence was Ernst Zundel charged with in *R. v. Zundel*? Why was it unconstitutional?

5. Do you believe in the right against self-incrimination? Should there be a constitutional right to silence?

6. Do you think the adversarial nature of the common law tradition is problematic? Do you prefer the approach followed by the common law or the civil system toward criminal trials? Why? (You may want to consider I.P. Callison's discussion of the civil system of law in the additional online readings listed in the Appendix.)

Further Reading

Raoul Berger, *Government by Judiciary: The Transformation of the Fourteenth Amendment*, 2nd ed. (Indianapolis: Liberty Fund, 1997). Available at http://oll.libertyfund.org.

Brian Dickson, "The Canadian Charter of Rights and Freedoms: Context and Evolution," in *The Canadian Charter of Rights and Freedom*, 3rd ed., ed. Gérald A. Beaudoin and Errol Mendes (Scarborough, ON: Carswell, 1996), pp. 1–19.

A.R.N. Cross, "The Right to Silence and the Presumption of Innocence—Sacred Cows or Safeguards of Liberty?," *Journal of the Society of Public Teachers of Law* 11 (1970).

Richard H. Field, "The Right to Silence: A Rejoinder to Professor Cross," *Journal of the Society of Public Teachers of Law*, n.s., 11 (December 1970): 66–75 and 76–80. Available at http://heinonline.org.

Barton L. Ingraham, "The Right of Silence, the Presumption of Innocence, the Burden of Proof, and a Modest Proposal: A Reply to O'Reilly," *Journal of Criminal Law & Criminology* 86, no. 2 (1995–6): 559–95.

Stephan Landsman, "A Brief Survey of the Development of the Adversary System," *Ohio State Law Journal*, 44 (1983): 712–39.

Gregory O'Reilly, "England Limits the Right to Silence and Moves towards an Inquisitorial System of Justice," *Journal of Criminal Law & Criminology* 85, no. 2 (1994): 402–52.

R. v. Khawaja, 2010 O.N.C.A. 862. The digest of this case is included in the additional online readings for Chapter 19.

Ellis Sandoz, ed., *The Roots of Liberty: Magna Carta, Ancient Constitution, and the Anglo-American Tradition of Rule of Law* (Indianapolis: Liberty Fund, 2008). Available at http://oll.libertyfund.org.

19 Globalization: The International Law and the Doctrine of Sovereignty Are Changing

Readings

- "A Primer on the Application of the International Law in Canada," by Paul Groarke
- From *Questioning Sovereignty: Law, State, and Nation in the European Commonwealth,* by Neil MacCormick

The current international system is based on the idea that states are sovereign. The theory behind the system accordingly holds that the obligations of states in the international realm are based on agreement and consent, rather than law. This position has recently been questioned because it does not provide a satisfactory means for dealing with states that oppress individuals or minorities. It also fails to provide a binding mechanism for dealing with broader international problems, such as climate change, that extend beyond the boundaries of individual states. As a result, the historical doctrine of sovereignty is slowly being replaced with a doctrine of limited or legitimate sovereignty, which places legal restrictions on the exercise of the sovereign power. There are corresponding changes in the law of states. The most significant change is the emergence of a compulsory body of law in the international arena, which has historically been seen as a political realm that exists outside the law. This new law has two possible sources: one is a substantive source, which is found in the customary sources of the law; the other is a political source, which must be located in some form of government. There is a consensus that states are bound by the customary law known as the *jus cogens*, which guarantees the rights of individuals and minorities.

⋈ Readings ⋈

Paul Groarke, "A Primer on the Application of the International Law in Canada" (2004, 2008). Adapted from a paper delivered at a conference of the Canadian Human Rights Tribunal.

The Classical View

Louis-Philippe Pigeon sets out the classical view on the application of the international law in a domestic forum in his admirable book, *Drafting and Interpreting Legislation*:

> British theory, to which we subscribe, holds that treaties do not of themselves make law. In the United States, once a treaty is ratified by the Senate, it becomes the supreme law of the land, but this is not so in Canada, or in England. . . . If a treaty is to have force of law, a statute must be passed promulgating that treaty as law, or amending the law as a result of the treaty. Otherwise, the courts cannot apply the treaty. They can apply the law only, and the treaty has no force of law unless this is provided for by legislation.[1]

This process of domestic adoption is called incorporation. Although the principle of incorporation still ostensibly governs the domestic application of international law, it is plain that it no longer holds the force that it once possessed.

There Are Three Principles of Application

It seems fair to say that the operation of international conventions in Canadian courts and tribunals is currently governed by three principles. The first holds that international law binds Canadian courts only after it has been incorporated into Canadian law. This principle derives from the classical view. The courts have enlarged its operation by allowing incorporation by specific statutes, through the general provisions of the *Charter*, and by necessary implication.

The second principle originally functioned as a corollary of the first. It holds that international conventions that have not been incorporated into Canadian law may nevertheless provide a helpful aid in statutory interpretation. Thus, Pigeon states that there is a presumption that legislators have not contravened them "when enacting subsequent legislation, unless the intent to do so is clearly expressed: see *Salomon v. Commissioners of Customs*, [1967] 2 Q.B. 116 (C.A.); *The Atlantic Star*, [1974] A.C. 436 at 455 9 (H.L.)." This principle remains good law, though it has been eclipsed by more recent developments.

The third principle is still contentious. It holds that domestic courts and tribunals are obliged to take some international conventions into account in their deliberations. This goes beyond the idea that governments should respect international law and recognizes the legal authority of the global system of justice. The best example of this development is probably the law of human rights, which is now routinely held to constitute an obligatory part of the customary international law.

Ratification, Implementation, and Transformation

The first principle requires that international law be incorporated into the domestic law. There are two procedural issues that arise in this context. The first is whether the convention in question has been signed and ratified. The second is implementation. This process has been described by Ruth Sullivan in *Driedger on the Construction of Statutes*:

Under Canadian law, international conventions do not automatically become a part of the domestic law of Canada. When Canada becomes a signatory to a convention that obliges it to make expenditure or to alter existing law in any way, the appropriate implementing legislation must be enacted by the legislature with jurisdiction over the relevant matters. This legislature decides the extent to which and the manner in which Canada's obligations will be carried out and in light of its decisions enacts appropriate implementing legislation.[2]

The reality is that this practice has slowly withered, probably because it has become impracticable. There are many conventions that are at best implemented by implication.

It is the older caselaw that focusses on issues of implementation. In *Francis v. The Queen*, [1956] S.C.R. 618, Justice Rand stated that Canada's obligations under international treaties take effect only when the obligation has been legislatively "transformed." This term encompasses a range of possibilities, from partial to full incorporation. The idea of transformation is based on the traditional doctrine that the power to make law lies in the domestic political arena, where it is held by the legislative branch of government. The courts accordingly must follow the dictates of the legislature in a democratic state, rather than the community of states.

This ignores the problem of majoritarianism. There is nevertheless little doubt that the domestic will must prevail in a case where the legislature has clearly indicated its intention to depart from the strictures of international law. As P.A. Côté puts it, in *The Interpretation of Legislation in Canada*:

> A statute is not void or inoperative simply because it violates international obligations or convention. . . . the courts cannot refuse to apply an enactment simply because it contradicts a treaty or a rule of international law.[3]

In spite of this, there are many signs that the second and third principles have rendered the process of transformation obsolete.

Interpretation

The second principle holds, in contradistinction to the first, that the domestic law should be interpreted in accordance with Canada's international obligations. As Justice McNair states, in *International Fund for Animal Welfare Inc. v. Canada*, [1987] 1 F.C. 244, at 131: "The rule is well established that an enactment should be interpreted, as far as practicable and its language admits, in conformity with the rules of international law."

Ruth Sullivan writes that there are two sides to this "presumption":

> First, the legislature is presumed to comply with the obligations owed by Canada as a signatory of international instruments and more generally as a member of

the international community. In choosing among possible interpretations, therefore, the courts avoid interpretations that would put Canada in breach of any of its international obligations. Second, the legislature is presumed to respect the values and principles enshrined in international law, both customary and conventional. These constitute a part of the legal context in which legislation is enacted and read. In so far as possible, therefore, interpretations that reflect these values and principles are preferred.[4]

Côté tells us that there has been a "burgeoning" of cases using international law as a guide to interpretation. This is, he writes, "another indication of the globalization of legal relationships which characterizes our era."[5]

There is nothing, however, in the rule of interpretation that affects the primacy of domestic law. Canadian legislatures may choose to depart from international law or the principles behind it in the pursuit of some domestic goal. In the case of an open conflict, it is the domestic legislation that prevails. The trend in the jurisprudence is nevertheless to treat the international law with increasing if rather unpredictable deference. It is of note in this context that the second branch of the principle is now of general application. Thus, in *National Corn Growers Assn. v. Canada (Import Tribunal)*, [1990] 2 S.C.R. 1324, at 174, the Supreme Court of Canada held: "The Court of Appeal's suggestion that recourse to an international treaty is only available where the provision of domestic legislation is ambiguous on its face is to be rejected."

There are a number of significant decisions, such as *United States v. Burns*, [2001] 1 S.C.R. 283, that demonstrate the willingness of the courts to make use of the international law in determining the substantive content of the *Charter of Rights*. The court in *Burns* held that the government was obliged to obtain assurances that the two accused would not be executed before extraditing them to the United States. The court relied extensively on international instruments such as the *Convention on the Rights of the Child*, the *International Covenant on Civil and Political Rights with Optional Protocol*, and the *Protocol to the American Convention on Human Rights to Abolish the Death Penalty*, 29 I.L.M. 1447. It is significant that the court also took guidance from a number of treaties that do not apply to Canada.

The reliance on international conventions in establishing the aims and significance of domestic human rights legislation seems uncontroversial. In *Bailey v. M.N.R.* (1980), 1 C.H.R.R. D/193, at 11847, for example, an early human rights tribunal held: "Resort can be had to international law and the international obligations assumed by Canada, in interpreting the meaning of the *Canadian Human Rights Act*." The Tribunal then consulted the language of the optional protocol to the *International Covenant on Civil and Political Rights*.[6]

The more difficult issues lie in those cases where there are competing considerations. International conventions are replete with general principles, which are easily cited as authority for conflicting propositions. It would seem difficult for a domestic court to navigate its way through these kinds of issues without consulting the jurisprudence that determines when these principles come into play. This is a potentially more significant development, which would bring foreign law before courts and tribunals.

Human Rights

It is the third principle, however, that seems most significant from a theoretical perspective. It implicitly holds that the fundamental international law has a status akin to that of the constitutional law. The most compelling example is the rights of the person, usually described as human rights. The International Court of Justice and other legal bodies have held that states cannot derogate from human rights instruments. It is routinely asserted that states are bound by the *jus cogens* and the customary international law. There is now a general recognition that states that have obligations *erga omnes* (i.e., toward all) under international customary law.[7]

From a historical perspective, these are all radical developments, which go against the traditional doctrine of state sovereignty. Some of the comments in the literature can undoubtedly be discounted as exaggerations. Many political scientists and sociologists have long argued that the norms that exist in the international arena have been applied in an extremely selective manner. It would be naive to ignore the fact that "human rights," for example, have often been used to further a Western political agenda in the international arena.

The status of the fundamental law is nevertheless changing. There is a general consensus, for example, that international human rights instruments are now compulsory. It follows— as a positive theoretical matter—that states are bound by legal constraints. Although the contents of this body of law have yet to be delineated with any exactitude, it is clear that it contains those rights that guarantee bodily integrity and the most basic human needs. This includes international conventions dealing with torture, genocide, and racial discrimination, and may include a right to food.[8] There are separate but related issues that arise in the environmental arena, which cannot be regulated without a compulsory international law.

The process by which this change has occurred has been incremental. As early as the *Reference Re Public Service Employee Relations Act*, [1987] 1 S.C.R. 313, at 350, Dickson, C.J.C. held that "the norms of international law" provide "a relevant and persuasive source for interpretation of the provisions of the *Charter*." This comment can be extended to the law of human rights in general. The more dramatic development, however, as a result of this process of "persuasion," is that the fundamental law has begun to infiltrate the body of constitutional principle on which the courts rely in interpreting ordinary legislation.

This is clearly part of a global process under which the systems of national or municipal law have begun to merge in some larger body of general law. The most notorious decision in this area is *Baker v. Canada (Minister of Citizenship and Immigration)*, [1999] 2 S.C.R. 817, where the appellant had applied to the Minister of Citizenship and Immigration for a statutory exemption from the requirement that she make her application for permanent residence from outside Canada on "humanitarian and compassionate" grounds.[9] The application was made on the basis that the failure to grant the exemption would have an adverse effect on her Canadian-born children, since it would result in her deportation.

The appellant sought a review of the Minister's denial of the application in the Federal Court on the basis of Article 3(1) of the *Convention on the Rights of the Child* Can. T.S. 1992 No. 3, which states:

Article 3

1. In all actions concerning children, whether undertaken by public or private social welfare institutions, courts of law, administrative authorities or legislative bodies, the best interests of the child shall be a primary consideration.

The Federal Court rejected the application on the basis that *Convention on the Rights of the Child* was not a part of the domestic law of Canada.

The majority in the Supreme Court agreed that the *Convention* had not been implemented and was therefore not a part of the domestic law. In spite of this, it upheld the appeal on the basis that the "values reflected in international human rights law" must be taken into account in interpreting the statute. The "interests, needs and rights" of children were "central" in determining whether the Minister of Citizenship and Immigration had exercised his power reasonably.

There are many problems with the decision, which seems to introduce a new substantive requirement into the domestic law. The idea that the rights of children and their parents can simply be collapsed into each other also seems highly problematic. Although Justice Cory dissented, it was only on the basis that the decision would allow the executive branch of government to change the domestic law without the approval of the legislative branch. This seems to miss the obvious issue, which is not whether the executive has bound the state without legislative intervention, but whether the judiciary has done so.

Notes

1. Louis-Philippe Pigeon, *Drafting and Interpreting Legislation* (Toronto: Carswell, 1988).
2. R. Sullivan, *Driedger on the Construction of Statutes*, 3rd ed. (Toronto: Butterworths, 1994), p. 330.
3. P.A. Côté, *The Interpretation of Legislation in Canada*, 4th ed. (Toronto: Carswell, 2000), pp. 367f.
4. Sullivan, op. cit., p. 330.
5. Côté, op. cit., p. 369.
6. Also see *Nealy v. Johnston* (1989), 10 C.H.H.R. D/6450 (C.H.R.T.), and *Saskatchewan Human Rights Commission v. Waldo* (1984), 5 C.H.R.R. D/2074 (Sask. Bd. of Inquiry), where the Board held: "At all three levels of the law—at the provincial in the Code, at the national in the Charter, and at the international in the International Covenant on Civil and Political Rights, the Board is bound by legislation which promotes both the freedom of expression and egalitarian rights such as those prohibiting discrimination on the basis of sex." The use of the word "bound" is provocative.
7. Maurizio Ragazzi, *The Concept of International Obligations Erga Omnes*, Oxford Monographs in International Law (Oxford: Oxford University, 1997; 2000).
8. See, for example, Marco Borghi and Letizia Postiglione Blommestein, eds, *For an Effective Right to Adequate Food: Proceedings of the International Seminar on "The Right to Food: A Right for Peace and Development in the Twenty-First Century"* (Switzerland: Fribourg University, 2002).

9.   See section 114(2) of the *Immigration Act*, R.S.C., 1985, c. I-2: "The Governor in Council may, by regula-
     tion, authorize the Minister to exempt any person from any regulation made under subsection (1) . . .
     where the Minister is satisfied that the person should be exempted from that regulation . . . owing to the
     existence of compassionate or humanitarian considerations."

From Neil MacCormick, *Questioning Sovereignty: Law, State, and Nation in the European Commonwealth* (Oxford: Oxford University, 1999).

The Traditional Concept of Sovereignty Gives the Political Order Precedence

Sovereign power is, then, territorial in character, and is power not subject to limitation by higher or coordinate power. It is material to consider which of the two species identified, political or legal sovereignty, has priority. Is ultimate political power a precondition of ultimate legal authority, or vice versa? The tradition of Hobbes, carried on by Austin, reconceptualized in the Germanic tradition by Carl Schmitt, unhesitatingly ascribes primacy to the political. However it comes about that one person or group is habitually obeyed by others, thereby acquiring the power to enforce physical sanctions over any recalcitrant elements, the person or persons who hold this position are able to issue commands to others within their society, and those commands are laws. . . .

Law is then dependent on political sovereignty. Only a sovereign person or group, absolutely sovereign at home, independent of any purported external power, can be an authentic source of law. In Schmitt's version, the key to the ultimate basis of law lies in the question who can exercise effective power on behalf of a whole community in states of emergency or "states of exception" when ordinary legal provisions break down or prove inadequate.[1]

Persuasive and illuminating though such accounts may be for some types of politico-legal order, they have been found wanting in respect of those situations in which there is a standing constitutional tradition. Under such a tradition, the powers of state are effectively divided according to a constitutional scheme that is respected in the practical conduct of affairs. There is then a difficulty in identifying any sovereign being or sovereign entity holding power without any legal limitation. Confronted with the example of federal states, Austin in particular was driven back to analyzing such cases, in particular the USA, in terms of the sovereignty of the people. . . .

A Law-State or *Rechtsstaat*, However, Is Not Subordinated to a Political Sovereign outside or above the Law

For the case of the *Rechtsstaat*, law has to be explained in terms that do not presuppose the prior existence of an absolute political sovereignty. I am happy to suggest such terms. Law, as stated above, is an institutional system of rules or norms involving both duties which are required of legal subjects and powers vested in legal institutions holding legislative, executive, or judicial power.

Legal systems so understood do not only and do not necessarily exist in states. There are non-state systems of law, such as for example Canon law, public international law, the specialist international law represented by the *European Convention on Human Rights*, and the law of the European Union, and other less presently relevant forms of law as well. But the point of the *Rechtsstaat* is that it is a state which has law, and in which law regulates and restricts the conduct of political officials as well as citizens, presupposing no monolithic political sovereign power outside or above the law. . . .

This seems to show that sovereignty is neither necessary to the existence of law and state nor even desirable. A well-ordered Law-State or *Rechtsstaat* is not subordinated to any political sovereign outside or above the law, nor is it necessarily constructed around some constitutional organ which enjoys sovereignty conferred by law. Certainly, the classical theory of the British constitution ascribed sovereignty to the monarch in Parliament, or, more summarily, to Parliament itself. This was held to be a doctrine of the common law, and to be advantageous as a legal dispensation on the ground that it secured the political sovereignty of the electorate. But such supreme legal power ascribed to a single organ is not necessary even in a unitary state, and is incompatible with the very frame of government of a federal state.

Nevertheless, before dismissing sovereignty out of hand, we need to reflect on a further distinction, that between internal and external sovereignty. As was stated above, sovereignty is power not subject to limitation by higher or coordinate power, held independently over some territory. It is clear that this could apply in two different ways. If we look at a state in terms of its internal ordering, we may ask whether there is any person who enjoys power without higher power internally to the state. Either in the political or in the legal sense, we may discover that all power holders are subject to some legal or some political checks or controls. In that case, there is no single sovereign internal to the state, neither a legal nor a political sovereign.

On the other hand, we might survey the same state from the outside, considering its relations with other states and international or religious or commercial organizations. We might conclude that in this perspective a state, whatever its internal distribution of legal or political power, is a "sovereign state" in the sense that the totality of legal or political powers exercised within it is in fact subject to no higher power exercised from without.

What we shall therefore call "external sovereignty" characterizes a state which is not subject to superior political power or legal authority in respect of its territory. Politically, this enables us to distinguish a fully or substantially independent state from a mere satellite or client state which, even if legally independent, has no effective independent power of decision. In a legal sense, external sovereignty is the authority granted by international law to each state to exercise legal control over its own territory without deference to any claim of legal superiority made by another state or organization. This is coupled with the right under international law to be free from the exercise of military power or political interference by other states. . . .

These distinctions make it possible to account for the concept of "divided sovereignty," which some theorists, such as Austin and Schmitt, have taken to be a contradiction in terms. They were anxious to argue that nothing which has supreme power can coexist with a rival supreme power in any stable way within a single legal or political order. . . .

Nevertheless, the distinction of external and internal sovereignty shows that even a strict definition of sovereignty permits a sense of divided or limited sovereignty. The point is this. A state that is sovereign in the external sense may have a constitution under which no full sovereign power is possessed by any organ of state. . . .

Each such organ is effectively limited by checks and controls exercised by another. Where that is so, and where constitutional stability has engendered a political system in which the limits laid down in the constitution are well respected, we can predict that there will be no internal political sovereign. Yet externally, the state may be as sovereign as it is possible to imagine. The United States, Canada, Australia, and Switzerland, all provide rather good examples of this. . . .

The European Community Provides an Illustration of This Principle

The next point is to discuss the relevance of contemporary developments to these concepts. I particularly wish to consider their relevance and usefulness in the context of the developing European Union. . . .

[S]ince at least 1964, it has been the doctrine of the European Court of Justice that the Community (as it now is) constitutes a new legal order, neither a subordinate part of the laws of the member states nor simply a sub-system of International law. . . . There are now long-established Community organs for law-making, for executive action, and for judicial law-application. . . .

[T]he criteria for recognition of the validity of Community legal provisions are now internal to this legal system. The system has acquired what Niklas Luhmann or Günther Teubner would characterize as self-referentiality. As a system, it differentiates itself from other systems by whose distinct criteria of validity Community legal provisions are also valid and applicable. This is the case within the legal orders of member states, each of whose organs acknowledge Community provisions as valid and applicable in relevant situations, in a manner coordinated with, and justifiable by, reference to the member state's own internal criteria of validity. . . .

The application and enforcement of rights and obligations under Community law remain, to a considerable extent, matters for implementation by the authorities of member states, though remedies can now be awarded against states by the European Court to compensate for damages arising from state action found to have been in breach of Community obligations. . . . So far as concerns the validity of national legislation, legislators within state systems are now limited by the requirement to avoid conflict with valid Community law. Community decisions of various kinds can change law within state systems regardless of the operation of the normal internal legislative process. . . .

[I]t is clear that absolute or unitary sovereignty is entirely absent from the legal and political setting of the European Community. Neither politically nor legally is any member state in possession of ultimate power over its own internal affairs. . . . Legally, community legislation binds member states and overrides internal state-law within the respective criteria of validity. So the states are no longer fully sovereign states externally, nor can any of their internal organs be considered to enjoy present internal sovereignty under law. . . .

Note

1.   Editor's note: MacCormick cites this as C. Schmitt, "*Was bedeutet der Streit um den Rechtsstaat?*," *ZStW* 95 (1935), 189. As a theorist, Schmitt has often been seen as an apologist for the Third Reich.

✥ Discussion ✥

The State System Is Based on the Removal of the Moral Authority Provided by the Church

The modern state system is based on the Peace of Westphalia. The theoretical idea behind the state system is that nation-states exist in a state of nature. This idea was a product of the Protestant Reformation, which removed the moral authority of the Church over kings and rules. This was a crucial development, since it left states with the prerogative to govern themselves. The move away from a single source of moral authority (which had expressed itself historically in the divine right of kings) was part of a larger trend that left the natural law open to interpretation. Many Protestant theologians, emphasizing the essential depravity of human nature, disputed the very existence of a natural law. It was accordingly for individual states and rulers to decide the substantive issues that arise within the borders of the state as they saw fit.

Grotius' Theory Was Influential because It Promoted the Idea that States Are Sovereign

The theory behind the international law in the Westphalian system is usually traced to Hugo Grotius, whose work clearly met the needs of the emerging system.[1] The idea that states are sovereign favoured the development of an international law based on both the contracts between individual states and the customs of the larger community of states. Although Grotius believed that states are subject to moral rules in the state of nature, there is no central mechanism in his theory to determine whether the natural law has been violated. It is for individual states to interpret and apply the natural law for themselves.

Although many scholars resist the analogy, Grotius' theory inevitably fosters the idea that states can be seen as individual persons, who exist in the state of nature, subject only to the natural law and their own ability to assert their will on other states.[2] The self-interest in Grotius' conception of natural rights, which was discussed in Chapter 3, is easily translated to states, and the general consensus is that individual states act in accordance with their own self-interest.[3]

The Peace of Westphalia Gave Rise to the Principle of Non-intervention

The Peace of Westphalia recognized that nations had a political right of self-determination and replaced the old idea that the law took precedence over the political order with a new idea, which gave the political order ascendancy. This idea is based on the political contract and holds that law is a product of civil government and the coercive powers of the states. It is the person or persons who hold the sovereign power who make law. Since there is no government and no sovereign power in the international realm, there is no law in the strict sense of the word. There are customs, but one of the fundamental problems with the positivist conception of law is that it is based on the threat of force, and without a coercive power in the international realm, these customs must be regarded as moral prescriptions rather than law.

The Westphalian system parcels out the world among states. Historically, it was the state's control of a particular territory that gave it jurisdiction over the events that occurred in that territory. The Westphalian system is based on the idea that this control is exclusive: there is no international government, there are no overlapping jurisdictions, and states are legally autonomous and self-regulating. As a result, the central principle in the Westphalian system is that states are not entitled to intervene in the internal affairs of other states. This principle is usually referred to as the principle of non-intervention.

There are many criticisms of such a principle. The historical application of the principle of non-intervention has been extremely selective. The principle has not prevented powerful states from intervening in the affairs of other states. It has merely obliged them to do so clandestinely. This explains the remarkable lack of transparency in international relations. Another criticism is that the principle leaves the internal victims of an oppressive or illegitimate state without any form of relief in the international system.[4]

The reality is that the international order is regulated by politics rather than law. This fact has fostered a strong spirit of realism in political theory, which suggests that the behaviour of states in the international realm is ultimately determined by power and self-interest. As a result, it has been suggested that the fundamental principles of international law merely provide a convenient justification, when it is needed, for the actions of powerful states. This idea has led Stephen Krasner, for one, to describe the international state system as "organized hypocrisy."[5]

The International Law Is Based on Agreement

The Westphalian theory of sovereignty regards individual states as equal, independent members of the international community. This development gave states the freedom that Grotius attributed to individuals in the state of nature and left them in a position to contract as they wished with one another. As a result, the major source of the so-called "international law" became treaties. This "law" is based on the agreement and consent of the contracting states rather than prescriptive law. The conception of law behind the Westphalian system is elective rather than compulsory. There is a philosophical question whether this conception of law is properly described as "law."

Historically, the international law has dealt solely with the relations between sovereign states. The idea that the agreements and conventions that govern these relations constitute a form of law is problematic, however, since the doctrine of sovereignty raises states above the law. Even the use of the word "govern" is problematic in this context. As a result, it is often said that the so-called international law is made up of convention rather than law.[6] These conventions express norms, which describe the way that states customarily behave or should behave, rather than a set of compulsory prescriptions. The international law is not enforceable by the courts in the usual sense, and the prevailing view is that international courts and tribunals have the jurisdiction to decide issues between states only because the states in question have accepted their jurisdiction. The characteristic obtuseness of the reasoning employed by international courts can be attributed to the linguistic manoeuvring that is necessary to preserve the intellectual appearance that states are sovereign and cannot be compelled to act against their will.

The Historical International Law Is Made Up of the Law of Treaties and the Customary International Law

The historical international law is composed of the law of treaties and the customary international law. The idea behind the customary international law is that certain customs and practices have been accepted as "law" by the community of states; over time, these customs and practices have accordingly acquired the force of law. The fundamental argument in theoretical terms is that political conventions may crystallize into law. The principles of diplomatic immunity, which have now been formalized in the *Vienna Convention on Diplomatic Relations* (April 1961), have often been cited as examples of customary law. The conventional view is that the international customary law is based on the consent of states. Aside from the uncertainty of the customary international law, the major difficulty with this body of law is that the institutional machinery for the enforcement of such law is extremely weak.

There are other forms of customary law. Although the *jus cogens* is usually included in the customary international law, and is a customary species of law, it is not based on the consent of states. The *jus cogens* is accordingly distinct, and aligned with the customary law that originally gave rise to the common law, which was based on moral custom. This older form of law was substantive and implicitly constitutional, like the natural law, and placed limits on the actions of those in positions of political power. The *jus cogens* is based on a conception of law that is different from the customary international law and forms part of a new, compulsory law of states. This new law of states requires its own discussion.

The bulk of the historical international law is composed of treaty law.[7] The international treaty system has many deficiencies, however. Like statute law, the written law that finds its way into treaties is incomplete and does not provide the general framework needed for a viable legal system. There are many procedural and substantive gaps in the treaty scheme, which has historically found itself at the mercy of the political forces in the state system. International courts have accordingly been forced to find other sources of law, in judicial practice and the work of scholars, who are sometimes described as "publicists" in the jargon of the international law.

The more important observation is that the force of treaties is relative and inconsistent. Treaties that have been followed for relatively long periods of time are more likely to be followed in the future. The only issue, however, is that in theory, treaties come into effect only when they have been signed and ratified, and they apply only to those states that have ratified them. Many of the most significant treaty documents—such as the *Kyoto Protocol to the United Nations Framework Convention on Climate Change* (December 1997)—have not been ratified by a sufficient number of states to solve the problems they were intended to address.

The internal state process of ratifying international agreements has presented its own problems, since governments may sign treaties without sufficient legislative support to ratify them. The politics within a state may change, and localized political forces may contest the ratification process for their own political purposes. The many gaps and exceptions in the international treaty system have made it difficult to develop consistent regulatory regimes in the international realm. This fundamental problem is evident in the case of whaling, which cannot be successfully regulated unless all of the world's whaling states agree to the regulatory regime.

The Historical International Law Is a Voluntary System of Law

The historical doctrine of state sovereignty has made it difficult to regulate the behaviour of states in the international realm. There are nevertheless institutional mechanisms in the international arena that provide at least some supervision of states. These mechanisms are primarily political, however, and implicitly informal, since their efficacy rests ultimately on the agreement of states rather than the rigorous application of legal principle.

The international community has relied increasingly on the resolutions of the United Nations Security Council to regulate the behaviour of illegitimate states. These resolutions are *ad hoc* and particular; they do not possess the general character that John Austin, for example, attributed to laws. Since the Security Council has never functioned as a legislative chamber, these resolutions are more in the nature of policy resolutions or moral opinions, which express the consensus among the most powerful states.

The legal obligation of individual states to follow the Security Council's resolutions is unclear. The assertion that a breach of a Security Council resolution is a breach of international law means very little and simply provides a legal justification, in advance, for the actions that individual states may take to enforce such resolutions. These responses are not like the actions that a state might take to enforce the ruling of a court or other judicial organ. The Security Council has a political rather than a judicial function, and there is nothing in its makeup that prevents it from breaching generally accepted legal principles. The legality of the actions taken by independent states to enforce its resolutions is always open to question. Some of the Security Council resolutions authorizing the use of military force by states, for example, appear to contravene the principle of non-intervention.

The confusing status of Security Council resolutions reflects the rather idiosyncratic use of the word "law" in the international order. From a theoretical perspective, sovereign states exist in a realm in which obligations are voluntary and political rather than legal. Although the international order is changing, the Security Council does not enjoy any legal jurisdiction over other states, which are legally free to decide whether they accept such resolutions. It is rather that other states may suffer political consequences if they fail to follow such resolutions. The use of the Security Council reflects the prevalence of power in the international order, which has given the most powerful states a privileged position in the international law. This privileged position is evident in the veto enjoyed by the permanent members of the Security Council.

These political observations highlight the fact that the state system, at its roots, is a voluntary system of law. This means that states and the political actors within states are ultimately governed by political rather than legal constraints. Although these constraints place significant limits on the actions of some individual states, they have little impact on the actions of states that are powerful enough to resist the political pressures placed upon them by other states. There is also the problem of obdurate or recalcitrant states, which refuse to accede to the legitimate demands of the international community.

The use of political mechanisms like the Security Council to regulate the behaviour of states reflects the fact that the mechanisms in the international system, like the treaty system, are based on the idea that states exist in a political realm, outside the reach of the compulsory law. This idea is problematic, since there is little evidence to suggest that the kind of political sanctions that are available in the system are sufficient to solve the problem of oppression.[8] There is certainly no legal mechanism in the system to order that states comply with their commitments under the international law or face the kind of enforcement measures routinely ordered by domestic courts. The reality is that international instruments like the *Universal Declaration of Human Rights* are statements of principle rather than enforceable statutory instruments. This aspect of the system seems to deprive the protections in such a document of the essential character of legal rights, which obtain their status from the fact that they are enforced by the courts.

The Doctrine of Sovereignty Is Changing

There are many indications that the traditional doctrine of state sovereignty is changing. There are at least two aspects to this development. The first is that the theoretical litera- ture now recognizes that there are sources of law outside the state.[9] There is an increasing recognition that many international agencies, for example, perform a regulatory and even legislative function, which gives their decisions the force of law. Many sources of custom and convention have also been given legal force, simply on the basis that it is not possible to conduct business in the international realm without a legal framework in which busi- ness can be carried on.[10] This kind of framework can be seen in the relatively informal development of the law of sports and the legal regulation of the Internet.[11]

The second aspect is the emergence of a compulsory law of states. This is not inter- national law in the traditional sense, which is binding only because individual states have agreed to it. The new law of states implicitly adopts the position that there is a higher source of binding law, above and outside the state, which requires that states conduct themselves in accordance with universal moral and legal principles. This new law is not elective; it is compulsory.

The Jus Cogens *Is a Compulsory Customary Law*

There are many reasons that the Westphalian division of the world into autonomous states, which exist in isolation from each other, has become increasingly artificial. The many failures in the existing system, the violence of illegitimate or oppressive states, and the habitual reliance on war to resolve disputes in the international arena have led many theorists to postulate that states and political leaders must be subjected to the constraints of law. This explains the recent recognition that there is a *jus cogens*, a "compelling law" in the international sphere, which places moral limits on the actions of sovereign states.

The introduction of this new law of states has been halting. The decisions in the inter- national jurisprudence state that the *jus cogens* is made up of "peremptory norms," rather than laws, which rest on the moral consensus in human society. The use of such a nomen- clature simply masks the fact that states are bound by the *jus cogens*, which takes preced- ence over the political order, and perpetrates the Westphalian fiction that states exist above the law. In point of fact, the *jus cogens* simply revives the historical ascendancy of the cus- tomary law, which gave rise to the common law, and originally placed moral limits on the exercise of political power. There is now a general agreement that the *jus cogens* takes pre- cedence over the ordinary international law and voids any treaty that contravenes its tenets.

The recent literature has heralded the formal recognition of the *jus cogens* but left its contents a matter of dispute. Anthony D'Amato suggests that the "long bull market in *jus cogens* stock began when Professor Grigory Tunkin proclaimed in 1974 that the Brezhnev doctrine is a norm of *jus cogens*."[12] This Russian doctrine held that socialist states were entitled to intervene in the affairs of other socialist states when socialism was threatened. Tunkin's proclamation was followed by the decision of the International Court of Justice in the *Nicaragua* case, in 1986, where the court ruled that the international prohibition on the use of force was "a conspicuous example of a rule of international law having the character of *jus cogens*."[13]

D'Amato continues:

> Demonstrating slightly greater restraint than the judges were the *rapporteurs* of the *Third Restatement of the Foreign Relations Law of the United States* [702 (1987)], who conceded that "not all human rights norms are peremptory norms (*jus cogens*), but those in clauses (a) to (f) of this section are, and an international agreement that violates them is void."[14]

The clauses in question contain prohibitions against genocide, slavery, murder or disappearance, torture, "prolonged arbitrary detention," and systematic racial discrimination. The exact content of the *jus cogens* is difficult to gauge; the international law now recognizes, however, that the substantive consensus in the customary law places legal limits on states and the state system.

A State Cannot Derogate from Human Rights

The existing commentary agrees on two fundamental points. There is general agreement that the *jus cogens* prohibits the unwarranted and illegal use of force by states. There is a similar agreement that it includes protections for human rights. Indeed, the language of inalienable rights has permeated the international law through a plethora of declarations, charters, and conventions, such as the *Universal Declaration of Human Rights* (December 1948), the *European Convention on Human Rights* (November 1950), and the *International Covenant on Civil and Political Rights* (December 1966).[15] States are obliged to respect the rights guaranteed by these conventions.

The international law has its own way of stating such a proposition. The caselaw routinely proclaims that states cannot derogate—diminish or take away—from treaties that guarantee our fundamental human rights. This is merely a way of saying—in the rather arcane language of the Westphalian system—that the provisions of the treaties and conventions that guarantee fundamental human rights are compulsory. As a result, there is no longer any legal requirement that states ratify and adopt such agreements, which are binding, with or without the consent of states. This position has many constitutional implications, since it follows that the *jus cogens* places limits on the exercise of political power within the state. It also has meta-constitutional implications, however, since in theory it nullifies the legal effect of any constitutional provision that conflicts with it, at least in the international realm.

The practical significance of these rights has yet to be determined. Although this body of law has clear constitutional implications, and raises doubts about the validity of domestic laws that contravene these guarantees, the legal system in the international realm does not have the institutional resources to deal with such issues. The European Court of Human Rights is probably the best example of an international tribunal, which exercises the kind of supervening jurisdiction that this body of law contemplates. As this point, it has generally been left to domestic courts to decide the significance of the *jus cogens* within the state. Domestic courts have been willing to incorporate this body of principle into the domestic law only as an interpretive aid, however, which assists the judiciary in interpreting and applying the ordinary law. It is nevertheless clear that the rhetorical development of the *jus cogens* has elevated the fundamental rights of the person above the prerogatives of the state.

There Are Also Obligations, *Erga Omnes*

The new law of states also contains the principle of *erga omnes*, which holds that some violations of the norms of international law are so significant that they impose positive obligations on states. Thus, it is not simply that *jus cogens* forbids genocide or racial discrimination. The principle of *erga omnes* holds that states are positively obliged to take action to prevent genocide and rectify racial discrimination.[16] This obligation is significant because in many cases—the case of apartheid in South Africa is commonly cited—it seems to require that states at least implicitly intervene in the internal affairs of other states.

There Is Now a Transnational and an International Criminal Law

There is now an international criminal law, which extends the application of the international law to individuals. This is a new development, since the fundamental basis of a court's jurisdiction in the criminal law is territoriality, which gives the courts in the state where a crime occurs jurisdiction over the offence.[17] Although there are historical qualifications on the principle, they have little bearing on the fundamental doctrine that the state's control of its territory gives it the ultimate authority in determining criminal liability.[18]

The Fundamental Idea Behind the Criminal Law Is that Society Has Been Wronged

There were good reasons for the historical position, both from the perspective of the evaluation of evidence and from the broader theoretical perspective that a crime has traditionally been considered a wrong against society. It is naive and unrealistic to think that a jury in Thailand is in a good position to determine whether a witness's account of an event that occurred in the Northwest Territories in December is credible. It has also been left, historically, to the people in a particular society to determine whether the accused's acts constitute a moral wrong and a crime. Polygamy may be an offence in one country and society, but not in another.

It is true that certain kinds of conduct are considered wrong in most societies. Murder may be a universal wrong: it is nevertheless a wrong against the state, and the society within the state, which has been wronged by the actions of the person who commits a crime. The jurisdiction of the state to prosecute an accused for a criminal offence, historically, came from the fact that the public has been wronged.

The major advantage of the historical system was that the criminal jurisdiction of states was exclusive. This exclusive authority gave the system a simple logical foundation and made it relatively easy to determine which state had jurisdiction over an offence.[19] There was no room in the historical system for international offences.

The Domestic Criminal Law Now Contains Extra-territorial Offences

The theory of the criminal law has been complicated, however, by the increasing introduction of extra-territorial offences. These offences give a state the authority to try its own nationals, or the citizens of other states, for crimes committed entirely outside its territory. The list of extra-territorial offences ranges from sexual assault to terrorism and torture.[20]

The rationale that is usually advanced for prosecuting extra-territorial offences is moral. Bad people must be punished. States have accordingly assumed the jurisdiction to try individuals, for example, in cases where there is no realistic prospect of prosecution in the state where the offence occurred.[21] The moral justification for prosecuting individuals is often overstated, however, and masks the political side of these developments. The political reality is that the assertion of extra-territorial jurisdiction by individual states in recent years constitutes a clear attempt to assert the authority of the state beyond its historical limits.[22] Since the principle of double jeopardy prohibits multiple prosecutions for the same offence, these extra-territorial claims potentially take the right to decide whether to prosecute the accused out of the hands of the state where the offence occurred.[23]

The Fundamental Idea Behind the International Criminal Law Is that Humanity Has Been Wronged

The argument for an international criminal law comes out of the concept of "crimes against humanity," which was introduced at the Nuremberg trials after the Second World War.[24] This concept implicitly distinguishes between ordinary criminal offences, which have wronged a particular society, and extraordinary criminal offences, which have wronged all of humanity. They accordingly "shock the conscience of mankind." Beth Van Schaack and Ron Slye make a distinction, in this context, between "atrocity crimes," like genocide and crimes against humanity, and military crimes, which are committed in armed conflict.[25]

The United Nations Security Council has created international criminal tribunals to deal with atrocities, crimes against humanity, and war crimes in Rwanda, the "former Yugoslavia," Cambodia, Sierra Leone, and Lebanon. There are a number of arguments behind the creation of these tribunals. In some instances, there is a legitimate argument that these kinds of offences cannot be adjudicated properly in the states where they have occurred; in other instances, the argument is that the states where these offences occur have a moral duty to prosecute the individuals who commit them, and that the international community must step in where they have failed to do so. The reality, however, is that the Security Council's actions have been *ad hoc* and impromptu, and the organization of the Council, which gives its permanent members a veto, has granted the most powerful states complete immunity from prosecution.

There are other kinds of cases that should arguably be prosecuted in an international court. In some cases, for example, public sentiment may make it impossible to give an accused a fair trial in a particular state. There are also cases in which an offence may occur in many countries, simultaneously, through the use of an international medium like the Internet. These are subsidiary issues, however, which need to be addressed within the context of a larger theory. At this point, there is no principled, systematic division of domestic and international offences, and the role of international criminal courts is in pressing need of clarification.

The international law has yet to settle when the international process should take precedence over the ordinary criminal process. The Special Tribunal for Lebanon, which was created to investigate and prosecute those responsible for the murder of Rafic Hariri, the former prime minister of Lebanon, provides a case in point. It is plain that the murder of a political figure comes within the normal competence of domestic courts. The defence in the case has argued that the characterization of Hariri's murder as an international act of terrorism constitutes political interference in the internal affairs of Lebanon.[26]

The Inconsistency of the International Law Is Illustrated by the Principle of Humanitarian Intervention

The theoretical deficiencies of the international law lie primarily in the fact that the system lacks any principle of consistency. The resulting lack of order in the system has left the international law at the mercy of the changing political winds that regularly buffet the world.

The selective nature of the system is illustrated by the principle of humanitarian intervention. This principle has been traced to Grotius' idea that states function as individuals in the state of nature and, as a result, have "the natural right to punish violators of the laws of nature."[27] The problem is that this kind of principle has been used by powerful states to justify their interventions in the internal affairs of other states.

The fundamental legal difficulty with humanitarian intervention is accordingly that it is selective. States inevitably consult their own self-interest in deciding whether to intervene in a humanitarian crisis and may intervene in one instance and not in another, in spite of the fact that the exigencies in the second instance are equally compelling. This approach inevitably suggests that some atrocities require a response, while others do not. The failure to adopt a principled legal approach to these matters is illustrated by the Security Council's referral of the "violent repression of civilian demonstrators" in Libya to the International Criminal Court in 2011 (Security Council Resolution #1970), a resolution that ignored the fact that many of the members of the Security Council have themselves rejected the jurisdiction of the court.

There Are Two Possible Sources of a Compulsory Law of States

There are two possible sources of a compulsory law of states. The first is positivist and lies in some form of political government; the second lies in customary law. The political source of a compulsory law of states would require a political contract, between states or peoples, or between all people. This kind of contract could take many forms but would create a sovereign power in the international realm, over the state, with the authority to pass binding laws.[28]

The creation of a sovereign power in the international realm could usher in world government. It seems clear that any attempt to create such a government could succeed only as a federation that preserves many of the sovereign powers of legitimate states. There are good reasons, moreover, to fear the consolidation of power that such a form of government would entail, since it would create an enormous capacity for the abuse of power. It is impossible, as a consequence, to conceive of world government without strict constitutional protections for individuals and groups. It nevertheless seems clear that the legal systems of the world are slowly merging, and there is room for an incremental customary tradition—like the common law—that slowly synthesizes the competing legal systems.

The legal source of a compulsory law of states lies in the recognition that there is a binding customary law. This idea has already found expression in the *jus cogens*, which holds that the legal order has ascendancy and takes precedence over the political order. A system based on a superior customary law would not prevent the development of legislative institutions in the international realm, but it would subject legislation—like other forms of positive law—to the moral consensus on which the law is based. This kind of global constitutionalism would naturally increase the authority of the judiciary in the international realm. Such a system would take us back to the customary law and the recognition that the law exists independently of political power and the political apparatus of government.

MacCormick Argues that Sovereignty Should Be Divided

In *Questioning Sovereignty*, Neil MacCormick argues that the chief shortcoming of the modern theory of the state is that it subordinates the legal order to the political order. The *Rechtsstaat*—the law-state—that MacCormick proposes to deal with this shortcoming places legal limits on those who hold the sovereign power. The idea of such a state is based on the constitutional tradition, which divides the powers of government between different levels and branches of government. As a result, there is no "person or group" who has complete control of the sovereign power.[29]

This Division of Sovereignty Is Illustrated by the European Union

MacCormick argues that the European Union provides a successful model of divided sovereignty, which places legal checks on the political sovereignty of individual states. The European system of government is innovative because it is made up of sovereign states that are nevertheless subject to the law of the European community. The most striking feature of the European Union in this regard is that it contains an administrative bureaucracy and its own system of justice, but it does not have political government.[30] The union functions more as a consortium of states—sometimes called a "polity"—rather than a state of its own. The prerogatives of government remain firmly in the hands of individual states. The political question is whether the European system of regulation might provide a model for the development of similar consortiums in other regions of the world.

It is not clear that the division of sovereignty is the crucial consideration here, however. The significant development is rather that the absence of the political apparatus of government has implicitly elevated the courts of the European Union above the member states. The guarantees found in the *European Convention on Human Rights* (November 1950), for example, supersede the legislative, executive, and legal powers of the member states. The *Convention* creates a Court of Human Rights, with the authority to order states to comply with the terms of the *Convention*. This system provides a source of law and a legal venue, outside the state, that places limits on political actors within the state.

There are allied developments, outside the state, that have contributed to the idea that the law exists independently of the exercise of political power. As Marc Hertogh argues, the positivist idea that the state has a monopoly on the making of laws cannot explain the developments in the global arena.[31] There are many international associations—such as the associations that regulate sports—that have begun to create specialized bodies of law in the international realm, independently of the state.

The Recognition that There Is a Compulsory Law of States Has Raised Many Practical Issues

The recognition of a new compulsory law of states has raised many practical and institutional issues. For one thing, it is not possible to place meaningful legal limits on the political prerogatives of the state without the establishment of an independent legal system in the international arena. The challenges in creating such a system are daunting.

It is evident from the decisions of the International Court of Justice that the partiality that has characterized the politics within the United Nations has regularly made its way into international legal organs. One of the deepest problems in this arena is the appointment of the judiciary, who often function more as arbitrators or state representatives than as independent judicial actors. This problem is a reflection of the concentration of power in the state system, which remains firmly in the hands of political actors, who feel compelled to serve the interest of the states they represent.

The most pivotal issue that arises in this context, however, concerns the psychological failure of states to recognize that their obligation to follow the substantive law takes precedence over their perceived self-interests. This attitude seems to have positivist origins, in the Hobbesian view that the binding force of the law comes from the existence of a central coercive authority, which has the power to punish those who disobey the law. The problem is that the positivist view fosters the idea that states have no real obligation to obey the international law, since there is no central authority with the power to punish them if they fail to do so. This view has clearly been internalized by states and their political leaders, who have yet to recognize the compulsory nature of their legal obligations in the international realm. Since the resulting legal vacuum must be filled—that is the nature of vacuums—it may be inevitable that political power and the threat of force has come in to fill it.

The Traditional Doctrine of Sovereignty Is Being Replaced with a Doctrine of Legitimate Sovereignty

The reality is that the traditional doctrine of state sovereignty has begun to unravel. The *jus cogens* and the international criminal law are only part of such a development. It has also become apparent that issues such as the rising of the sea and the extinction of species need to be dealt with on a global basis. This realization has led to the development of a new and more conditional theory of sovereignty, which is contingent on the legitimacy of the state and its actions.[32]

The principle of legitimacy holds that a state's title to the sovereign power is subject to legal conditions. A state that oppresses its people is illegitimate and therefore loses its legal claim—its title—to the prerogatives of government. The argument from legitimacy is most compelling in dire moral circumstances and places moral limits on the political sovereignty of the state.

The Supreme Court of Canada Has Held that Political Events like Secession Are Subject to Legal Constraints

The idea that the sovereign status of the state comes with conditions finds support in the decision of the Supreme Court of Canada in the *Secession Reference*, [1998] 2 S.C.R. 217, where the court ruled that Quebec could legally secede only if certain conditions were met. The Supreme Court based its ruling on the fundamental principles underlying the constitution, such as the principle that minorities must be protected, rather than the written terms of the constitution. The decision recognizes that any written document is based on assumptions and premises that we implicitly consult in interpreting it. It is not possible to interpret a constitution without drawing on fundamental legal principles that exist outside it and inform us how to apply its provisions. This is also necessary to deal with situations in which the provisions of a constitution are conflicting.

The *Secession Reference* is important because it places legal constraints on political actors, who hold power only on the basis that their actions in the political realm are legally legitimate. The decision holds that there is an extra-constitutional law, which governs the constitution much as the constitution governs the ordinary law. Since the constitution logically exists above the state and limits the sovereign power, this extra-constitutional law is presumably situated in a realm of binding international law. This body of meta-constitutional law invalidates the illegitimate actions of those who hold the sovereign power.

The Challenges to the State Order Have Manifested Themselves in the Problem of Terrorism

The doctrine of state sovereignty seems to have taken on a new kind of urgency in recent years. This is because there is a new volatility in the state system. The roots of the volatility are open to discussion. The Internet and other electronic developments seem to have changed the essential sociology that gave rise to the national identities that have maintained the integrity and cohesiveness of individual states. At the same time, however, ethnic and religious rivalries have resurfaced, with a new intensity, and challenged the state system and the distribution of power within it. This shift has occurred at a time, however, when the raw destructive power consolidated in the state has reached unimaginable proportions.

One of the disturbing political developments in our time is the rise of terrorism. This rise has happened on two fronts: one is within the state; the other exists in the international arena. We can refer to these different kinds of terrorism as internal and external. Internally, terrorists have targeted states and governments who refuse to recognize the claims of minorities. This has been true of the Tamils in Sri Lanka, the Chechens in Russia, and the tribal people in Assam. More recently, however, terrorists have participated in an external struggle between different states and societies. Thus, Islamic militants reserve the right to strike at civilian and industrial targets in the United States and other Western states.

The development of terrorism as an accepted form of political action among certain groups threatens the legal and political orders inside and outside the state. Terrorism is alarming legally because terrorists display a complete disregard for the moral and legal limits that have been customarily placed on our conduct. It is also alarming, however, because the more recent response of states, as Margaret Denike has written, is to classify terrorism as a kind of war, to which states must respond with a war of their own.[33] This response is significant from a theoretical perspective because war takes place in the political realm in which states exist, outside the ordinary reach of the law.

Internal Terrorism Is Usually an Attack on the Legitimacy of the State

Although terrorism is notoriously difficult to define,[34] the consensus is that that terrorism is fundamentally political. Victoria Held, for example, has described terrorism as "political violence." This is apparent in the fact that terrorism is often justified or disregarded once the political aims of the terrorist group have been met.[35] The internal forms of terrorism clearly question the legitimacy of the prevailing political order.[36]

It seems clear that terrorism is usually an attempt, as Held suggests, to change the political *status quo* by terrifying the populace.[37] The exceptional cases do not remove the reality that terrorists are usually motivated by the belief that the state has oppressed a minority and is therefore illegitimate.[38] The academic literature has suggested that terrorism is a response to "persecution."[39]

The issue in legal theory is that terrorism is political violence, unrestrained by law. In that sense, at least, all forms of terrorism resemble war. The theoretical source of such violence is not hard to find. Like revolution, terrorism is a kind of repudiation, by which individuals or groups violently reject the existing political order. On the positivist model, this constitutes a rejection of the political contract, which in positivist theory returns us to the state of nature. The usual justification for internal terrorism lies in the right of revolution in the work of liberal philosophers like John Locke, and the larger right of self-defence, which gives individuals and groups the right of self-preservation.[40]

Internal Terrorism Often Reflects the Failure of the State and the State System to Provide a Remedy for Oppression

To all appearances, at least, terrorism is a product of the majoritarian bias of democratic theory, which in principle gives the majority within the state control of the apparatus of the state.[41] This includes control of the police and the military. Terrorism is often a product of the fact that there is no real remedy available to a minority in the face of systematic oppression by the state. The terrorist argument is that the state and the political structure within the state is illegitimate as a consequence and must be changed, if necessary by attacking the civilian population, which ultimately has the power to change the political system.

The significant observation in a theoretical context is that there is currently no effective legal mechanism, inside or outside the state, to deal with the allegations of illegitimacy at the root of the terrorism that occurs within the state. The absence of such a mechanism is one of the facts that produce terrorism. There is no disputing the fact that there are illegitimate states, which have oppressed minorities, who have an ethical and political right to seek changes in the political system within the state. The legal solution to terrorism, in many cases, is to provide a legal forum in which the claim of oppression can be tested without violence to the public. Such a process might naturally result in a legal finding that the claim of oppression cannot be substantiated in law.

The Threat of External Terrorism Has Been Used to Justify the Increasing Concentration of Power in the State

The air of crisis created by external forms of terrorism has been used by Western governments to reinforce the power and authority of the state. Many commentators have argued that the spectre of the terrorist has been used to justify the increasing militarism of Western states, the passage of repressive legislation, and the suspension of human rights.[42] Victor V. Ramraj, Michael Hor, and Kent Roach have argued that terrorist offences have been portrayed as "new super-criminal offences."[43] This has been used to consolidate social control and increase power of the apparatus of the state.

There are naturally commentators on the other side, who argue that the magnitude of the threat posed by external terrorism justifies a corresponding increase in the security measures adopted by the police and other agencies to protect the safety of the public. The major issue that external terrorism raises in legal theory, however, is whether the actions undertaken by the state in the political realm, outside the reach of the courts and the legal system, can be justified. The fundamental question is whether the political restraints on state actors can ever be sufficient to guarantee the fairness, justice, and indeed morality of their actions.[44]

The use of a rhetorical "declaration of war" against terrorists implicitly places the conflict between the state and terrorism in the abstract political realm where sovereign states exist. This idea frees both sides from ordinary legal constraints and gives free rein to the unruly political forces that exist in such a realm. Thus, the terrorists' use of indiscriminate violence—like the state's use of "extraordinary rendition," offshore detention centres, and, recently, drones—takes place outside the rule of law.[45] In such a conflict, there are only the politics that motivate the various actors, and the naked use of power.

Notes

1. Grotius is naturally a single thinker, in a long line of historical figures, who dealt with these issues. See Benedict Kingsbury and Benjamin Straumann, "The State of Nature and Commercial Sociability in Early Modern International Legal Thought," *Grotiana* 31 (2010): 22–43, who discuss this historical background and describe Grotius' concept of the natural law, at p. 31, as "a theory of ethics couched in legal terms."

2. See the quotation from Kingsbury and Straumann, ibid., at p. 36.

3. An analogy might be made between states and business corporations in this context.

4. Nor is there any obvious means to correct the artificial delineation of borders. Since the delineation of borders may decide whether a particular group will constitute a majority or a minority within a state, and contemporary systems of government favour majorities, this has led to fierce conflicts within the state.

5. See Stephen D. Krasner, *Sovereignty: Organized Hypocrisy* (Princeton, NJ: Princeton University, 1999), which provides a realist account of the state system and suggests that the reigning principle in the international arena is power.

6. This concept of "convention" has a constitutional dimension. See the discussion of constitutional convention in *Re: Resolution to Amend the Constitution*, [1981] 1 S.C.R. 753, and the passage at p. 853, where Chief Justice Laskin writes: "The observance of constitutional conventions depends upon the acceptance of the obligation of conformance by the actors deemed to be bound thereby. When this consideration is insufficient to compel observance no court may enforce the convention by legal action. The sanction for non-observance of a convention is political in that disregard of a convention may lead to political defeat, to loss of office, or to other political consequences, but it will not engage the attention of the courts which are limited to matters of law alone."

7. The United Nations Treaty Collection is available at treaties.un.org/Home.aspx.

8. See Eric Neumayer, "Do International Human Rights Treaties Improve Respect for Human Rights?," *Journal of Conflict Resolution* 49 (2005): 925–53. And see Emilie M. Hafner-Burton and Kiyoteru Tsutsui, "Justice Lost! The Failure of International Human Rights Law to Matter Where Needed Most," *Journal of Peace Research* 44 (2007): 407–25.

9. See Marc Hertogh, "What Is Non-state Law? Mapping the Other Hemisphere of the Legal World" (July 2007). Available at http://ssrn.com. And see Gunther Teubner, ed., for example, *Global Law without a State* (Aldershot, Hants: Ashgate/Dartmouth, 1997).

10. This is in keeping with the practice of the civil courts in the common law tradition, which have recognized that the customs within an industry have legal force. See *Canadian Pacific Hotels Ltd. v. Bank of Montreal*, [1987] 1 S.C.R. 711, for example, where Le Dain J. holds that terms may be implied in a contract on the basis of custom or usage.

11. See T. Schultz, "The Lex Sportiva Turns Up at the Turin Olympics: Supremacy of Non-state Law and Strange Loops," as cited in the suggestions for further reading. And see J.R. Nafziger, "International Sports Law as a Process for Resolving Disputes," *International and Comparative Law Quarterly* 45 (1996): 130–49. Also see D.R. Johnson and D. Post, "Law and Borders: The Rise of Law in Cyberspace," *Stanford Law Review* 5, no. 48 (1996): 1367–402.

12. Anthony D'Amato, "It's a Bird, It's a Plane, It's *Jus Cogens*!," *Connecticut Journal of International Law* 6, no. 1 (1991). Available at http://anthonydamato.law.northwestern.edu/Papers-1/A914.html.

13. See *Military and Paramilitary Activities in and against Nicaragua (Nicaragua v. United States of America), Merits* as cited in the suggestions for further reading, at para. 190, where the court quotes the International Law Commission's statement that the prohibition on the use of force in article 2(4) of the *United Nations Charter* "constitutes a conspicuous example of a rule in international law having the character of *jus cogens*."

14. The same *Restatement* agrees that "the principles of the United Nations *Charter* prohibiting the use of force have the character of *jus cogens*."

15. There are many other conventions that contain similar guarantees, such as the *American Convention on Human Rights for the Americas* (November 1969), and the *Convention on the Rights of Persons with Disabilities* (December 2006). For a convenient repository of declarations and conventions passed by the United Nations General Assembly, see www.un.org/documents/instruments/docs_en.asp.

16. See Maurizio Ragazzi, *The Concept of International Obligations Erga Omnes* (Oxford: Clarendon, 1997).

17. The general rule is that some part of the offence must have occurred within the territory of the state. See H. G. Hanbury, "The Territorial Limits of Criminal Jurisdiction," *Transactions of the Grotius Society* 37 (1951): 171–84. And see Mika Hayashi, "Objective Territorial Principle or Effects Doctrine? Jurisdiction and Cyberspace," *International Law* 6 (2006): 285–302, which suggests that the principle of territoriality has been affirmed in the caselaw dealing with the Internet.

18. As Hanbury recognizes, ibid, in note 19, the principle of extra-territoriality gives the courts within a state jurisdiction over cases where the results (or "effects") of the offence occur within the territory of the state. The consequences of an offence are generally part of the *actus reus*, however, so this means that part of the offence occurred within the state. Someone who is poisoned in Africa and dies of the poisoning in Canada has not been murdered until he dies—in Canada.

19. Although there were exceptions in the case of criminal enterprises that crossed borders, as a general rule the accused could be tried only in one place.

20. Beth Van Schaack and Ron Slye have described the emergence of these extra-territorial offences as a body of "transnational criminal law." See Beth Van Schaack and Ron Slye, "Defining International Criminal Law," as cited in the suggestions for further reading.

21. In a parallel development, plaintiffs have been permitted to sue individuals for the commission of crimes in jurisdictions where domestic authorities have chosen not to prosecute. An example is *Filártiga v. Peña-Irala*, 630 F.2d 876 (2d Cir. 1980), in which the United States Court of Appeals held that the American courts could grant a remedy against a Paraguayan citizen in the United States, for his actions in torturing another Paraguayan in Paraguay.

22. The trial of Manuel Noriega, the former leader of Panama, may provide the most conspicuous example of such a development. See *United States v. Noriega*, 746 F. Supp. 1506 [S.D. Fla. 1990]. Available at http://caselaw.findlaw.com/us-11th-circuit/1089768.html.

23. This has led to allegations, for example, that the United States has chosen to "immunize" its forces from prosecution abroad by including international war crimes and torture within the scope of its own criminal law.

24. See Jordan J. Paust, Telford Taylor, M. Cherif Bassiouni, "Forty Years after the Nuremberg and Tokyo Tribunals: The Impact of the War Crimes Trials on International and National Law," *American Society of International Law Proceedings* 80 (1986): 56–64, and Henry T. King Jr., "The Legacy of Nuremberg," *Case Western Reserve Journal of International Law* 34 (2002): 335–56, which provide the factual and the public policy context in which the trials took place.

25. Beth Van Schaack and Ron Slye, "Defining International Criminal Law," as cited in the suggestions for further reading.

26. See the website of the Special Tribunal for Lebanon, at www.stl-tsl.org.

27. See Kingsbury and Straumann, op. cit., at p. 32, where they note that Grotius adopts "a permissive attitude to what is now called humanitarian intervention": "Any violation of the natural law and the rights it gives rise to triggers the right to punish, a right parasitic upon the existence of a strong normative framework. For Grotius, the parallel between individuals and states is complete: polities have the same set of rights and duties in the state of nature as individuals, including the natural right to punish violators of the laws of nature."

28. This would extend such a law to other entities, like corporations, which obtain their legal personality from the state.

29. This can be problematic. If the chief advantage of legal positivism—as H.L.A. Hart suggests—is that it allows us to identify valid laws, there are advantages to the traditional state system.

30. The European Union has a parliamentary assembly, but it is an intentionally weak legislative chamber and does not exercise the powers of a traditional legislative body. See Kristin Archick, "The European Parliament," *Congressional Research Service* reports (updated 2006), available at www.au.af.mil/au/awc/awcgate/crs/rs21998.pdf.

31. See the additional online reading from Hertogh's "What Is Non-state Law? Mapping the Other Hemisphere of the Legal World," *supra*.

32. See the discussion of legitimacy in Paul Groarke, *Dividing the State: Legitimacy, Secession and the Doctrine of Oppression*, as cited in the suggestions for further reading.

33. See Margaret Denike, "The Human Rights of Others: Sovereignty, Legitimacy, and 'Just Causes' for the 'War on Terror,'" *Hypatia* 24, no. 2 (2008): 95–121. An excerpt from this work is included in the additional online readings for this chapter listed in the Appendix.

34. The Supreme Court of Canada considered the meaning of the word "terrorism" in *Suresh v. Canada (Minister of Citizenship and Immigration)*, 2002 S.C.C. 1, [2002] 1 S.C.R. 3, at paras. 93–8. Although the court recognized that the word is polemical, it concluded that "terrorism," in s. 19 of the *Immigration Act*, R.S.C. 1985, c. I-2, includes "any act intended to cause death or bodily injury to a civilian or to any other person not taking an active part in the hostilities in a situation of armed conflict, when the purpose of such act, by its very nature or context, is to intimidate a population, or to compel a government or an international organization to do or abstain from doing any act." This interpretation of the word is instructive but not definitive, since the interpretation of the words in statutes changes in accordance with the circumstances in which the word is used.

35. See Victoria Held, "Terrorism and War," *The Journal of Ethics* 8 (2004):59–75, at p. 63.

36. See Martha Crenshaw, for example, "The Causes of Terrorism," *Comparative Politics*, 13, no. 4 (July 1981): 379–99, at p. 385, where she suggests that terrorism occurs when terrorists perceive that a political regime "has forfeited its status as the standard of legitimacy."

37. See Held, op. cit. And see Held, *How Terrorism Is Wrong: Morality and Political Violence* (Oxford: Oxford University, 2008).

38. While many authors have argued that states have practiced terrorism, these arguments seem to collapse "terrorism" into the simple use of terror. There is a moral argument here. It is clearly wrong to condemn the use of terror by separatists without condemning the state's use of terror to maintain itself. This moral equivalency should not be allowed to obscure the generally recognized meaning of the term, however.

39. See Johnny Ryan, for example, "Four P-Words of Militant Islamist Radicalization and Recruitment: Persecution, Precedent, Piety, and Perseverance," *Studies in Conflict & Terrorism* 7, no. 3 (November 2007): 985–1011.

40. The right of revolution is usually traced to Locke's *Second Treatise of Civil Government*. See John Locke, *Two Treatises of Government*, ed. Thomas Hollis (London: A. Millar et al., 1764), available at http://oll.libertyfund.org.

41. This is not a question of simple numbers. There may be within the state a "constructive" majority, which exercises the powers of a majority for economic or other reasons.

42. See Denike, op. cit., at p. 109: "Typical of the discourses of terrorism is the story that it poses a threat so serious and so exceptional that neither domestic nor international law is adequate to define or contain it, and existing legal processes are insufficient to address it. . . . This casting of terrorism, which both relies on and reinforces mythic stereotypes of its perpetrators, victims and vanquishers, has been mobilized to justify sweeping legal reforms that expand the scope and control of executive power and its judicial mechanisms at the expense of marginalized groups." For an example of a case in this area, see *Canada (Public Safety and Emergency Preparedness) v. Agraira*, 2011 FCA 103 (CanLII), which deals with "'a foreign national' who was found to be inadmissible to Canada on security grounds."

43. See the Introduction to Victor V. Ramraj, Michael Hor, and Kent Roach, eds., *Global Antiterrorism Law and Policy* (Cambridge: Cambridge University, 2005), at p. 3.

44. See Don E. Scheid, for example, "Indefinite Detention of Mega-terrorists in the War on Terror," *Criminal Justice Ethics* 29, no. 1 (April 2010): 1–28. And see Emanuel Gross, "Self-Defense against Terrorism—What Does It Mean? The Israeli Perspective," *Journal of Military Ethics* 1, no. 2 (2002): 91–108, which argues that the policy of "preventive action" adopted by Israel is legally and morally legitimate.

45. See the discussion of "targeted killing" in Steven R. Ratner, "Predator and Prey: Seizing and Killing Suspected Terrorists Abroad," *The Journal of Political Philosophy* 15, no. 3 (2007): 251–75.

Study Questions

1. Explain the process by which international treaties have traditionally been included in the domestic law. What is ratification? Implementation?

2. If states are sovereign in the international law, how can they be regulated? How does the current system of international relations deal with the problem of oppressive and illegitimate states?

3. What do we mean when we say that the international law is normative? Why does state practice play such an important role in the international order?

4. What does the decision of the Supreme Court of Canada in the *Secession Reference* tell us about the relationship between the legal and political orders? Which order should take precedence, in your opinion? Why?

5. What are obligations *erga omnes*? What do these obligations tell us about the changing nature of the international law?

6. Margaret Denike argues that humanitarian intervention has merely allowed Western states to assert their supremacy over other states. Do you agree? Why, why not? (See the additional online reading from Denike's "The Human Rights of Others: Sovereignty, Legitimacy, and 'Just Causes' for the 'War on Terror.'")

7. If you are a committed legal positivist, but firmly believe that we need an international criminal law, you probably believe in world government. Why?

Further Reading

P. Schiff Berman, "Global Legal Pluralism," *Southern California Law Review* 80 (2007): 1155. Available at http://papers.ssrn.com.

Jutta Brunnée and Stephen J. Toope, "A Hesitant Embrace: The Application of International Law by Canadian Courts," *Canadian Yearbook of International Law* 40 (2002): 3.

Paul Groarke, *Dividing the State: Legitimacy, Secession and the Doctrine of Oppression* (Aldershot, Hants: Ashgate, 2004).

Legality of Use of Force (Serbia and Montenegro v. Belgium), 1999 I.C.J. Rep. 124, available at www.icj-cij.org.

Military and Paramilitary Activities in and against Nicaragua (Nicaragua v. United States of America), Merits, 1986 I.C.J. Rep. 14. Available at www.icj-cij.org, though the case itself appears in the list of cases for 1984.

The *Peace Palace Library* has an extensive library of papers and other resources dealing with all aspects of international law and policy. Available at www.peacepalacelibrary.nl.

Maurizio Ragazzi, *The Concept of International Obligations Erga Omnes*, Oxford Monographs in International Law (Oxford: Oxford University, 1997, 2000).

Reference re Secession of Quebec, [1998] 2 S.C.R. 217.

Thomas Schultz, "The Lex Sportiva Turns Up at the Turin Olympics: Supremacy of Non-state Law and Strange Loops," *JusLetter* (April 2006). Available at http://ssrn.com.

Beth Van Schaack and Ron Slye, "Defining International Criminal Law," Santa Clara University Legal Studies Research Paper no. 07-32 (August 2007). Available at http://ssrn.com.

Appendix

Guide to The Additional Online Readings

The following pages list the additional online readings for each chapter. These readings are available at the following site: www.oupcanada.com/LegalTheories.

Chapter 1

Tribes and the Origins of Law

1. From Leopold Pospíšil, *Anthropology of Law: A Comparative Theory* (New York: Harper and Row, 1971).
2. From E. Adamson Hoebel, *The Law of Primitive Man: A Study in Comparative Legal Dynamics* (Cambridge, MA: Harvard University, 1954).
3. From Tom Porter, "Traditions of the Constitution of the Six Nations," in *Pathways to Self-Determination: Canadian Indians and the Canadian State*, ed. Leroy Little Bear, Menno Boldt, and J. Anthony Long (Toronto: University of Toronto, 1984), pp. 14–21.
4. From Sir Francis Palgrave, *The Rise and Progress of the English Commonwealth, Anglo-Saxon Period: Part II, Proofs and Illustrations*, vol. 7 of *The Collected Historical Works of Sir Francis Palgrave*, ed. R.H. Inglis Palgrave (Cambridge: Cambridge University, 1921).

Chapter 2

The Christian Tradition

1. From John Finnis, *Aquinas: Moral, Political, and Legal Theory* (Oxford: Oxford University, 1998).

Chapter 3

The Shift to Natural Rights and the Political Contract

1. From Hugo Grotius, *De Jure Praedae Commentarius* [*Commentary on the Law of Prize and Booty*], vol. 1, trans. Gladys L. Williams and Walter H. Zeydel (Oxford: Clarendon, [1604] 1950).
2. From Samuel Pufendorf, *Elementorum Jurisprudentiae Universalis Libri Duo* [*The Elements of Universal Jurisprudence*], vol. 2, trans. William Abbott Oldfather (Oxford: Clarendon, [1672] 1931).

Chapter 4

Early Scientism: Law Is the Science of Judges and Places Limits on the King

1. From Frederick Pollock, *A First Book of Jurisprudence for Students of the Common Law* (London: Macmillan, 1896).
2. From William Blackstone, *Commentaries on the Laws of England*, facsimile ed., in 4 vols. (Buffalo, NY: William S. Hein, [1765–9] 1992).

Chapter 5

Law Is a Product of Utility or Pure Reason

1. From Jeremy Bentham, *Of Laws in General*, ed. H.L.A. Hart, in *The Collected Works of Jeremy Bentham*, gen. ed. H. Burns (London: Athlone, 1970).
2. From Roscoe Pound, *Justice According to Law* (New Haven, CT: Yale University, 1951).

Chapter 6

Legal Positivism: The Political Order Takes Precedence

1. From John Austin, *The Province of Jurisprudence Determined* (London: John Murray, 1832).
2. From Jean-Jacques Rousseau, "The Social Contract," in *The Social Contract and the First and Second Discourses*, trans. Susan Dunn (New Haven: Yale University, 2002).

Chapter 7

Modern Scientism: Formalism, Legal Skepticism, and Pragmatism

1. From Christopher Columbus Langdell, "Harvard Celebration Speech," *Law Review Quarterly* 9 (1887): 123–5.
2. From Roscoe Pound, "Mechanical Jurisprudence," *Columbia Law Review* 8 (1908): 605–23.

Chapter 8

Constitutionalism: Legal Skepticism and the Doctrine of the Living Tree

1. From *Adkins v. Children's Hospital* (1923), 261 U.S. 525.

Chapter 9

Legal Realism Adopts an External Perspective

1. From Roscoe Pound, "The Call for a Realist Jurisprudence," *Harvard Law Review* 44 (1931): 697–711.
2. From Karl Llewellyn, "Some Realism about Realism—Responding to Dean Pound," *Harvard Law Review* 44 (1931): 1222–56.
3. From Jerome Frank, *Law and the Modern Mind* (London: Stevens & Sons, [1930] 1949).

Chapter 10

Later Positivism: The Law Derives Its Authority from the State

1. From Lon L. Fuller, "Positivism and Fidelity to Law—A Reply to Professor Hart," *Harvard Law Review* 71, no. 4 (1957): 63–72.

Chapter 11

The Hart–Fuller Debate and the Procedural Account of the Natural Law

1. Section 15 of the *Criminal Code*, S.C. 1953-54, C-51.
2. From *Martin's Annual Criminal Code 1955*, in *Martin's Online Criminal Code*. Available at http://clb5. canadalawbook.ca/martins_online.
3. From Lon L. Fuller, "Positivism and Fidelity to Law—A Reply to Professor Hart," *Harvard Law Review* 71, no. 4 (1957): 630–72.

Chapter 12

Contemporary Liberal Theory: Dworkin's Critique of Hart's Positivism

1. From Ronald Dworkin, *Law's Empire* (Cambridge, MA: Belknap, 1986).

Chapter 13

The New Realism: Critical Legal Studies, Feminism, and Postmodernism

1. From James Boyd White, *Heracles' Bow: Essays on the Rhetoric and Poetics of the Law* (Madison: University of Wisconsin, 1985).
2. From Duncan Kennedy, "A Left Phenomenological Alternative to the Hart/Kelsen Theory of Legal Interpretation," in *Legal Reasoning: Collected Essays* (Aurora, CO: Davies Group, 2008).
3. From Catharine MacKinnon, *Women's Lives, Men's Laws* (Cambridge: Belknap, 2002).
4. From Margaret Thornton, "'Post-feminism' in the Legal Academy?," *Feminist Review* 95 (2010): 92–8.

Chapter 14

The Private Law: The Civil Law Is Based on the Rights of the Person

1. From Christopher D. Stone, "Should Trees Have Standing?—Toward Legal Rights for Natural Objects," *Southern California Law Review* 45 (1972): 450–501.
2. From John Locke, "Of Property," in *Economic Writing and Two Treatises of Government*, vol. 4 of *The Works of John Locke in Nine Volumes*, 12th ed. (London: Rivington, [1691] 1824).

Chapter 15

Private Law: Liability Is Based on Legal Duties and the Principle of Cause

1. William L. Prosser, "The Assault upon the Citadel (Strict Liability to the Consumer)," *Yale Law Journal* 69, no. 7 (1960): 1099–148.

Chapter 16

Public Law: A Crime Is a Public Wrong

1. From James Fitzjames Stephen, *A History of the Criminal Law of England* (London: Macmillan, 1883).
2. From *Re B.C. Motor Vehicle Act*, [1985] 2 S.C.R. 486.
3. Digest of *R. v. Carriere* [1987] ABCA 39.

Chapter 17

Public Law: Punishment and Sentencing

1. From *Furman v. Georgia* (1972), 408 U.S. 238.
2. Digest of *R. v. Coutu*, [2006] MJ No. 272.
3. From Jarich Oosten and Frédéric Laugrand, "*Qaujimajatuqangit* and Social Problems in Modern Inuit Society: An Elders Workshop on *Angakkuuniq*," *Études/Inuit/Studies* 26, no. 1 (2002): 17–44.

Chapter 18

Public Law: The Constitutional Law Places Legal Limits on the Institution of Political Government

1. From Alexander Hamilton, Paper No. 78, "A View of the Constitution of the Judicial Department in Relation to the Tenure of Good Behaviour," in Alexander Hamilton, James Madison, and John Jay, *The Federalist, on the New Constitution*, vol. 2 (New York: George F. Hopkins, 1802), pp. 209–18.
2. From I.P. Callison, *Courts of Injustice* (New York: Twayne, 1956).

Chapter 19

Globalization: The International Law and the Doctrine of Sovereignty Are Changing

1. From Marc Hertogh, "What Is Non-state Law? Mapping the Other Hemisphere of the Legal World?" (July 2007). Available at SSRN: http://ssrn.com/abstract=1008451.
2. From Margaret Denike, "The Human Rights of Others: Sovereignty, Legitimacy, and 'Just Causes' for the 'War on Terror,'" *Hypatia* 24, no. 2 (2008): 95–121.
3. Digest of the Constitutional Ruling in *R. v. Khawaja*, 2010 ONCA 862.
4. From Alan Brudner, "Excusing Necessity and Terror: What Criminal Law Can Teach Constitutional Law," *Criminal Law and Philosophy* 3 (2009): 147–66.

Glossary

ab initio From the beginning; from first principles.

actus reus The guilty act, which constitutes the major component of a crime. It is comprised of all of the physical circumstances that must be present in order to establish a crime. The word "act" is a misnomer here, and the *actus reus* refers rather to the breach of the public peace that gives rise to liability and includes facts (such as the death of a homicide victim) outside the acts of the accused.

ad hoc Created, often out of necessity, for a specific purpose.

alienation of affection A tort, a civil wrong generally brought by a deserted spouse against a third party who is responsible for the departure of the deserting spouse.

amercement A financial penalty, originally issued by the King in place of a demand for the body of the prisoner.

antinomies Logical opposites, which contradict each other and are therefore incompatible.

a posteriori After; usually a reference to something that can only exist after some experience, such as knowledge acquired *a posteriori*.

appellant The party that appeals the decision of a trial court to a court of appeal, or the decision of a court of appeal to a supreme court (or other higher court).

a priori Before; something that precedes experience, such as *a priori* knowledge, which we can deduce by logical analysis, independently of our experience. The natural law arguably exists *a priori* to the circumstances to which it applies. Something that is deduced *a priori* is deduced from first principles rather than experience.

assize A sitting or session of a superior court, historically the King's court, which was required to travel to the place where it sat, usually seasonally; the term now is used more frequently in the case of courts of appeal, which sit only during prescribed periods.

ataraxia A state of suspended belief in which we achieve tranquility; attainment of this state is the object of skepticism.

boteless *Bote* referred to the payment of a stipulated sum for a wrong done to someone. A *boteless* crime was a crime that could not be requited by the payment of a financial penalty and therefore required some physical punishment.

caselaw Law that has been formulated by the outcome of former cases.

chattels A movable article of personal property.

coercive Having the power to require compliance.

communitarian Someone who argues that individuals can be understood only in terms of their relationship to other people.

conditions precedent Conditions that must be in place before an event can occur.

consensus ad idem A meeting of the minds, which occurs when the parties to a contract join in the same interpretation of the essential terms of the contract.

consequentialism The view that the consequences of an action determine its morality.

constitutionalism The ideology that holds that the government should have designated limitations in its influence, and its authority comes from adhering these limitations.

contra Against.

cosmocentric Regarding humans as a part of, but not the central element or priority of, the universe.

Court of Chancery In England, the court of equity rather than common law; the Court of Chancery and the Court of King's Bench, a common law court, were rivals in jurisdiction and power.

criminal conversation   A tort, a civil wrong.

culpability   Guilt, blameworthiness.

de facto   True in fact; a stipulation, rule, or condition that exists in fact, rather than by force of law; a *de facto* law is a law that is enforced, whether it is valid or not.

de jure   True in law: a stipulation, rule, or condition that exists by operation of law, rather than mere politics or physical force.

denunciation   Public condemnation of a wrong.

descriptive   That which describes or sets out the factual circumstances of a given system or legal event.

desideratum   Something required; one of Lon Fuller's eight requirements of a valid legal system.

deterrence   The idea that the punishment for an offence should be used to prevent or discourage people from committing it.

dogma   A set of beliefs that is held to be established beyond dispute and not subject to revision.

ecclesiastical courts   Courts with jurisdiction in spiritual or religious matters, which applied Church law, known as canon law.

en ventre sa mère   Legally, a child in its mother's womb; a child rather than a foetus because it potentially has rights of its own; a child injured *en ventre sa mère* can sue for damages in spite of the fact it has no legal person.

epistemology   The theory of knowledge; hence *epistemological*, relating in some way to the subject of knowledge.

equity   A flexible body of law and legal remedies based on conscience and general principles of justice rather than strict legal rules. Equity developed separately from the common law, in order to meet its deficiencies; equity was a product of the discretionary power of the King to right the wrongs suffered by his subjects and was originally invoked as an exercise of his political rather than legal authority.

erga omnes   Rights or obligations that are owed to all persons.

exoculation   The punishment of ripping out the eyes of an offender.

expiation   Atonement, by which an offender, his kin, or community annul the original wrong.

ex post facto   After the fact; an *ex post facto* law is a law that has been passed or proclaimed after the events to which it is intended to apply. Such laws are inherently unfair, since they did not exist when the events occurred, and people cannot be expected to conform their conduct to non-existent laws.

external point of view   A view external to an individual and to which the individual may not subscribe. Such a view determines whether a given norm, rule, or law is binding on the individual.

fallibilism   The belief that what we know is always incomplete or insufficient, and subject to correction; this belief may technically give rise to a question whether we "know" anything.

felony   An offence that must be tried in the King's court; a true criminal offence, as opposed to a misdemeanour or a summary conviction offence, which historically must be tried by a jury; in Canada, an indictable offence.

formalism   The belief that the law can be logically and rationally deduced from the existing body of legal rules and principles, as it is expressed in the existing caselaw.

grand unified theory of law   The idea that the law forms a single coherent whole; an idea that suggests that different laws are inherently consistent.

grundnorm   Kelsen's basic norm, from which all legal norms are derived.

habeas corpus   Literally, "have the body"; a historical legal action through which a court orders the authority holding a prisoner to deliver the body of the prisoner to the court, so that the court can determine whether the prisoner has been lawfully held.

hard legal positivism   The positivism of figures like John Austin and Jeremy Bentham, who held that law derives its authority solely from its political warrant, irrespective of its morality.

harm principle   The principle, usually attributed to John Stuart Mill in *On Liberty*, that we have the freedom to pursue our own happiness, as long as we do not harm other people.

Hegelian   In accordance with the views of Georg Wilhelm Friedrich Hegel, who believed in a kind of idealism, a wholism, that held that being is single and whole, and that it develops in a pre-determined manner, independently of the actions of individual actors; in philosophy of law and jurisprudence, Hegel's thought reinforced the Kantian idea that the law is a logical product of a rationally developing system rather than the product of, for example, experience.

heterogeneous   Varied.

homocentric   A cosmological view that sees humankind as the centre of the universe.

hundreds and **hundreds courts**   Hundreds were rough administrative units, of a local nature, in early England; in theory each hundred consisted of ten tythings, a group of ten families, and exercised the powers of local government, which included legal, political, and police functions.

internal point of view   The view to which an individual or group subscribes, in a personal and psychological capacity, particularly in deciding whether a given norm, rule, or law is obligatory.

international law   Historically, the "international law" has been viewed as convention, which creates norms, rather than law; the international law is theoretically binding on sovereign states because they have chosen to follow it.

interpolation   The insertion of words or meaning, usually by inference, that clarifies or narrows the meaning of legislation or a piece of writing.

Jim Crow laws   Laws that excluded black people; there were many municipal laws, for example, that required that "coloured" people leave the town before nightfall.

judicial behaviouralism   The idea that the decisions made by judges are determined by social conditioning and reflect judges' ethnic, political, and economic backgrounds.

jus cogens   That part of the law known (*cogens*) to all, in every society; in the international law,

fundamental principles (or the set of those principles) that have been accepted as binding by the international community (in the language of the international law, "from which no derogation is permitted").

knowledge   Usually described, in epistemology and philosophy, as "justified true belief," which requires certainty and distinguishes knowledge from opinion or belief; the usual issue in the epistemological literature is whether we can "know" anything.

legal person   See **person**.

legal positivism   Generally, the theory that the law derives its validity from political sources; legal positivism thus rejects the idea, in the natural law, that the law derives its validity from moral sources.

legal realism   The theory that judicial decisions can ultimately be traced to the political views, social background, or psychological makeup of judges, rather than to the operation of precedents or logic; there is an argument in later realism, related to sociology of law, that the law is ultimately an expression of power and reflects the interests of those who possess it.

lex talionis   The law of retaliation, which prevailed among tribes and required a tooth for a tooth, an eye for an eye, etc.

magistrates   Judges or judicial officers who deal with matters of a local nature and enjoy only those powers delegated to them by statute; they accordingly do not enjoy the inherent authority of a superior court.

Magna Carta   The "Great Charter"; the English charter, written in 1215, that became the basis for English rights.

majoritarianism   A traditional political-philosophy that asserts that a certain majority within the population is entitled to a certain degree of priority in society and has the right to make decisions that affect the society as a whole.

malefactor   Wrongdoer; the person who has committed a particular wrong.

mens rea   "Guilty mind"; the intention to commit the *actus reus*. The concept of *mens rea* overlaps with the question of moral responsibility but is in fact distinct. Although there is an implication that the *mens rea* includes some awareness that the *actus reus* is considered wrong in society, this is not the focus of *mens rea*, which concerned itself historically with the question whether the offender intended to do the particular act in question.

metaphysics   The study of being *qua* being; the attempt to understand the fundamental structure and patterns of existence.

mistake of fact   A criminal defence, in which the accused allegedly believed a set of facts that, had they been true, would have made his or her unlawful actions lawful.

mudrum   The customary offence from which the crime of murder derives. It is significant because the concern was with the means by which the person was killed, such as poisoning.

nadir   The lowest point of something; as opposed to its zenith, or highest point.

natural law   The law accessible to everyone, through the exercise of the faculty of reason and the pursuit of the natural inclinations of the human person.

natural rights   Rights that derive from our natural existence as physical individuals; these rights are inherent and "inalienable" they cannot be separated from the individual who possesses them.

negative rights   In the liberal literature, a negative right is a right that creates a duty that other people refrain from interfering in our actions; freedom of expression, for example, may give rise to a negative right, which prevents the government from inhibiting or restricting an individual's expression.

non sequitur   Something that "does not follow"; a statement or a conclusion that does not follow logically or rationally from what has been said.

norm   From the Greek *nomos*, which referred to custom; an accepted way of behaving; expected conduct.

normative   Concerning what should or ought to be, rather than what is; as opposed to descriptive.

novus actus interveniens   A new intervening act; generally used in the context of causation.

obdurate   Hard, resistant; a person who stubbornly refuses to change his or her opinion or course of action.

ontological   What really is.

ontology   The study of being and the nature of being.

oppression   Persecution of an identified person or group, usually a minority, by those who hold power.

paternalism   The belief that the state, for example, has the right and indeed the obligation to make decisions for individuals in certain situations, in order to protect individuals from harm or to promote their interests. This position is problematic in the liberal literature because it interferes with negative liberty.

Peace of Westphalia   The European treaties that ended the Hundred Years War and established the current state system. This system is based on the idea of state sovereignty and the principle of non-intervention, which holds that states are not entitled to interfere in each other's internal affairs.

peine forte et dure   The use of stones or other heavy weights to force a person to attorn (transfer oneself over) to the jurisdiction of the King's court. Individuals generally refused to attorn to the court's jurisdiction because the King had the right to confiscate the property of a convicted person.

perjury   The offence of lying under oath.

person, legal person   An entity that is conceptually separate from the physical person and to which legal rights and duties attach. An individual without a legal person has no standing in a court and cannot seek legal relief.

petty jury   A jury of 12, used to try criminal cases, from the French *petit*, meaning "small," in order to distinguish it from a *grand* (large) jury, which has commonly been used to determine whether charges should be laid.

phenomenology   The study of consciousness and conscious experience.

phenomenology of law A school of philosophy that examines the nature and structure of legal experience and the way in which that experience is formulated. This school holds that there is nothing behind experience (such as some external physical reality) that explains it.

pleas of the Crown In law, a plea or action on behalf of the King or Queen against a subject or other person, which must be tried in the King's court; since the public interest vested in the King or Queen, such pleas included criminal actions and other actions between the people and a person.

political sovereignty Political (as opposed to legal) supremacy; the political capacity of being independent and capable of making autonomous decisions.

positive rights In the liberal literature, a positive right is a right that creates a positive duty to intervene or take action, like a right to medical treatment, which requires that government or other persons take some positive action to provide an individual with the necessary treatment.

precedents Previous legal decisions, which are in theory binding on the judges who decide subsequent cases.

prima facie On the face of it; used to describe something sufficient to prove a case, if it is not contested.

promulgated Proclaimed; published; made public; known.

property That which can be owned; in the common law, "real property" refers to land, and the ownership of land includes those things that are affixed to it, such as a house or a building.

Protestant Reformation A religious and theological development led by Martin Luther, among others, that protested many of the theological doctrines and also the central authority of the Catholic Church. One of the central themes in this protest was that everyone can access and interpret scriptures, an idea that promoted a notion of equality that is central to the modern experience; it also promoted the idea that the individual is independent and sovereign.

question of fact A question that requires some examination and evaluation of the evidence; in ordinary circumstances, questions of fact must generally be decided by the judge who has heard the evidence.

question of law A legal question, in distinction to a question of fact, which provides the essential basis of an appeal; the trial judge must have "erred" in law, though it is now possible to appeal a verdict on a question of mixed fact and law.

quo warranto On what authority; by what warrant?

R. An abbreviation for *Rex* or *Regina*, used in the style of cause of criminal matters, which are between the King or the Queen and the accused.

ratio decidendi The reason for the decision.

repudiation An act of rejection, by which a party refuses to perform its obligations under a contract and accordingly rejects it.

restitutio in integrum Restoration to the original condition; the principal doctrine in damages, which holds that the defendant must restore the plaintiff in whole—i.e., to the position that the plaintiff was in before the harm or loss.

restorative justice A theory of justice, usually applied in the criminal courts, that holds that the purpose of sentencing or punishment is to restore the offender's membership in the community.

retribution Punishment of a wrongdoer that is morally necessary and rightfully makes him or her suffer; the right of a victim to demand such a punishment or exact it, as compensation for the wrong.

retroactive law A law that applies to past events.

rule of recognition Hart's axiomatic rule, which allows us to determine whether any given rule is a law.

scientism The idea that law (or morality) is subject to rational discovery through a process of systematic inquiry and deduction; behind this is an idea that knowledge is the product of rational inquiry.

self-incrimination   The provision of evidence against oneself, which raises an inference of guilt or liability.

self-reference   The condition in which something refers merely to itself; a definition that refers only to the thing that it defines is logically incoherent and unintelligible.

sentencing circle   An Aboriginal form of restorative justice, based on consensus, under which the wrongdoer, the victim, and members of the community agree upon what sentence is appropriate. The legal responsibility to decide what sentence will be imposed nevertheless remains with the sentencing judge.

sine qua non   Literally translated, "without which not"; used to describe an act or occurrence that is absolutely essential in a given context.

skepticism   The view that nothing can be known; we have only opinion and belief, which is never certain.

sovereignty   The authority or power to make autonomous decisions.

stare decisis   Stand by the decision; the principle under which a judge must follow past rulings when deciding on a case.

state   A political association of people or peoples, with a discrete government, that is institutionally autonomous and recognized as such by other states.

state of nature   The philosophical idea—which is prominent in Thomas Hobbes, but is historically dubious—that people lived in a condition without law before the advent central government. This idea was later transferred to the international law, which has historically held that sovereign states exist in the state of nature, outside the reach of law.

substantive   Relating to the content of the law, the part of the law that gives it its meaning; often used to distinguish "substantive" law from "procedural" law.

superior court   A court with the jurisdiction to hear any matter or cause that arises within its jurisdiction; sometimes called a "high" or "higher" court.

tort   That part of the civil law that deals with private wrongs. A cause of action in torts is based on the plaintiff's claim that the defendant breached a civil duty to the plaintiff. Historically, the idea of a crime developed from torts, and it is based on the accusation that the accused breached a duty owed to society and therefore committed a public wrong.

ultra vires   Literally "beyond the powers," meaning it does not require legal authorities.

utility   Usefulness, the measure in utilitarianism of the ethical and social value of something, based on its contribution to the greatest happiness of the greatest number.

voluntary   Chosen, deliberate; brought about by an act of the will. Aristotle suggests that it is the voluntary nature of an immoral act that makes it immoral. Historically, legal liability did not attach to an involuntary act.

wer (**wergild**)   Blood money; the stipulated value of a certain person in the tribal and customary law.

Index

Credits

Chapter 1

Frederick Pollock, *A First Book Of Jurisprudence For Students Of The Common Law*. London; New York: Macmillan, 1896. [Extract from pp. 15, 24, 27–28, 29].

Jarich Oosten, Frédéric Laugrand; 'Qaujimajatuqangit and social problems in modern Inuit society. An elders workshop on angakkuuniq', *Études/Inuit/Studies*, 2002, 26(1): 17–44. [Extract from pp. 20–22, 26, 31–32].

Edward S. Curtis, 'The Apache', in Vol. I of *The North American Indian: Being A Series Of Volumes Picturing And Describing The Indians Of The United States And Alaska*. Edited by Frederick Webb Hodge. (New York: Johnson Reprint Corporation; 1970; orig. published by Curtis in 1907), pp. 3–52.

Frederic Seebohm, *Tribal Custom In Anglo-Saxon Law: Being An Essay Supplemental To (1) ' The English Village Community'; (2) ' The Tribal System In Wales'* (New York: Longmans, Green; 1911).

K. N. Llewelyn And E. Adamson Hoebel, *The Cheyenne Way: Conflict And Case Law In Primitive Jurisprudence*. Norman: University Of Oklahoma, 1941.

E. Adamson Hoebel, Reprinted by permission of the publisher from "The Eskimo: Rudimentary Law in a Primitive Anarchy," in *The Law of Primitive Man: A Study in Comparative Legal Dynamics* by E. Adamson Hoebel, pp. 73–74, 76–77, Cambridge, Mass.: Harvard University Press, Copyright © 1954 by the President and Fellows of Harvard College. Copyright © renewed 1982 by Edward Adamson Hoebel.

Chapter 2

The Summa Theologica of St. Thomas Aquinas. Second and Revised Edition, 1920. Literally translated by Fathers of the English Dominican Province. Online Edition © 2006 by Kevin Knight http://www.newadvent.org/summa/2090.htm.

Chapter 3

Hugo Grotius. *De Iure Praedae Commentarius* (Commentary On The Law Of Prize And Booty), vol I, trans. by Gladys L. Williams with the collaboration of Walter H. Zeydel, and with a

Preface by George A. Finch. Oxford and London: Clarendon Press, Geoffrey Cumberlege; 1950. [Extract from pp. 8–13, 18–20, 22–23, 26–28.] By permission of Oxford University Press.

Samuel Pufendorf. *Elementorum Jurisprdentia Universalis Libri Duo*, Vol. II, trans. William Abbott Oldfather, with an intro. by Hans Wehberg (trans. by Edwin H. Zeydel). Oxford & London: Clarendon Press, Humphrey Milford; 1931. [Extract from pp. 58–60, 147–150, 155–162, 165].

Chapter 4

Dr. Bonham's Case. Sir Edward Coke. *The Selected Writings and Speeches of Sir Edward Coke*, ed. Steve Sheppard. Indianapolis: Liberty Fund, 2003. Vol. 1 of 3. Chapter: I: Reports. First Published in the Reports, volume 8, page 113 b.

Decision in Case 1070, the City of London against Wood (1701), 88 Eng. Rep. 1592. Sourced from HeinOnline. [Extract from pp. 1592, 1594, 1596, 1602.].

COMMENTARIES ON THE LAWS OF ENGLAND 1765–1769 Facsimile edition, in 4 volumes by William Blackstone (1992) 833 words from pp. 120–121, 125, 130–131, 134, 136–139. By permission of Oxford University Press.

*William Marbury v. James Madison, Secretary Of State Of The United State*s (1803), 5 U.S. 137.

Chapter 5

Jeremy Bentham. *Of Laws in General*, edited by H.L.A. Hart (London: University of London, Athlone; 1970). Part of H. Burns, Gen. ed., The Collected Works Of Jeremy Bentham.

Immanuel Kant. *The Philosophy Of Law: An Exposition Of The Fundamental Principles Of Jurisprudence As The Science Of Right* [1796]. Translated by William. Hastie (Edinburgh: Clark, 1887). [Extract from pp. 14–18, 20–22, 109–111].

Chapter 6

John Austin, *The Province of Jurisprudence Determined*. (London: J. Murray, 1832) [Extract from pp. 1–13, 15–17, 27–29, 136–139, 199–201, 207–208, 210, 213–214].

Thomas Hill Green, *Lectures on the Principles of Political Obligation*. With a preface by Bernard Bosanquet and an Introduction by Lord Lindsay of Birker (London: Longmans, Green; 1941) Reprinted from Vol. II of R.L. Nettleship, ed., Works of Thomas Hill Green (London: Longmans, Green; 1906).

Albert Venn Dicey, *Introduction to the Study of the Law of the Constitution*, 6th ed. (London and New York: Macmillan, 1902; originally published in 1885). [Extract from pp. 37–38, 41–45, 69–71].

Chapter 7

Christopher Columbus Langdell, *A Selection of Cases on the Law of Contracts. With References and Citations*. (Boston: Little, Brown; 1871) [Extract from pp. v–vii].

Oliver Wendell Holmes, *Book Notice: A Selection of Cases on the Law of Contracts, with a Summary of the Topics covered by the Cases*. (by C.C. Langdell. Boston: Little, Brown, & Co. 1879; two vols.), in *The American Law Review*, also indexed as the United States Law Review (1880) 14, 233–235. [Extract from pp. 233–234].

Roscoe Pound, 'Mechanical Jurisprudence' *Columbia Law Review* (1908) 8; 605–623. [Extract from pp. 605–615, 620–622].

Chapter 8

Albert Venn Dicey, *Introduction to the Study of the Law of the Constitution*, 6th ed. (London and New York: Macmillan, 1902; originally published in 1885). [Extract from pp. 134–141...].

Oliver Wendell Holmes, Jr., 'The Path of the Law', *Harvard Law Review*, (1896–1897) 10; 8, 457–478. [Extract from pp. 457, 459–462, 464–471, 474–475].

John Sankey Re: Meaning of the Word 'Persons' in Section 24 of the *British North America Act*, 1867 (1929) *Edwards v. A.G. of Canada*, [1930] A.C. 124 (P.C.) [Extract from pp. 1–3, 7–12, 14].

Chapter 9

Karl N. Llewellyn , 'A Realistic Jurisprudence—the Next Step', *Columbia Law Review* (Apr. 1930) Vol. 30, No. 4, pp. 431–465. [Extract from pp. 447–449, 464–465].

Jerome Frank, *Law and the Modern Mind* (London: Stevens & Sons; 1930, 1949; sixth printing) (from pp. 32–7, 100–14).

Chapter 10

Hans Kelsen, *Pure Theory of Law*, trans. Max Knight (Berkeley: University of California; 1967). A Translation of the 2nd Edition of *Reine Rechtslehre* (Vienna: Verlag Franz Deuticke; 1960)

697–711. (reading from pp. 105, 193–5).

The Concept of Law, 2E by H. L. A. Hart edited by Penelope A. Bulloch & Joseph Raz (1994) 3. By permission of Oxford University Press.

H.L.A. Hart, 'Positivism and the Separation of Law and Morals', *Harvard Law Review* (1957) 71; 593–629. (Reading from pp. 607–611, 613, 615.) (quote from p. 608).

Chapter 11

Lon L. Fuller, *The Morality of Law* (New Haven And London: Yale University, 1964). (reading: pp. 41, 46, 49, 51, 53–4, 63–7, 69, 71–2, 79–82, 95–100) (quotes from pp. 41, 38, and 97).

H.L.A. Hart, 'Positivism and the Separation of Law and Morals', *Harvard Law Review* (1957) 71; 593–629. [Extract from pp. 615–619].

Lon L. Fuller, 'Positivism and Fidelity to Law—A Reply to Professor Hart, *Harvard Law Review* (1957) 71, no. 4; 630–672. [Extract from pp. 650–655, 660.] (extract from p. 641).

Chapter 12

Ronald Dworkin, 'The Model of Rules', *University of Chicago Law Review* 35 (1967–1968), 14–47. [Extract from pp. 17–18, 22–33, 35–39.] (quote from p. 41).

The Concept of Law, 2e by H. L. A. Hart edited by Penelope A. Bulloch & Joseph Raz (1994) 3. By permission of Oxford University Press.

Chapter 13

Mark Kelman, Reprinted by permission of the publisher from *A Guide to Critical Legal Studies* by Mark Kelman, pp. 1–6, Cambridge, Mass.: Harvard University Press, Copyright © 1987 by the Fellows of Harvard College.

Mark Tushnet, 'Critical Legal Studies: A Political History', *Yale Law Journal*, (Mar., 1991) 100; 5, 1515–1544. (Reading from pp. 1516–18, 1523–8, 1530, 1538–40).

Mari J. Matsuda, "Liberal Jurisprudence And Abstracted Visions Of Human Nature: A Feminist Critique Of Rawls' *Theory Of Justice*", *New Mexico Law Review* 613 (1986) 16, 613–630. [Extract from pp. 615–621, 624–628].

Andersen, Margaret L., *Thinking About Women: Sociological Perspectives on Sex and Gender*, 4th Edition, © 1997, pp. 370–380. Reprinted by permission of Pearson Education, Inc., Upper Saddle River, NJ.

Chapter 14

Paul Groarke, Excerpt from 'The Legal Concept of the Person: A Relational Account.' *The Heythrop Journal* (March, 2010) 51: 2; 298–313.

Elaine Pagels, 'The Historical Origins of Rights' 'Human Rights: Legitimizing a Recent Concept.' *Annals of the American Academy of Political and Social Science* (March, 1979) 442; The Human Dimension of Foreign Policy: An American Perspective, 57–62. [Extract from pp. 58–59.

Jeremy Waldron, 'What Is Private Property?' *Oxford Journal of Legal Studies* (Winter, 1985) 5: 3; 313–349. [Extract from pp. 314–315, 326–329, 331–333].

Chapter 15

Oliver Wendell Holmes, Jr. 'The Liability of Things', From *The Common Law* (1881). [Extract from pp. 7–11, 14, 18–19, 22, 24–27, 29].

Digest of the Decision of Bora Laskin. For the Supreme Court of Canada in *Jordan House Ltd. v. Menow*, [1974] S.C.R. 239; 1973 CanLII 16 (S.C.C.). [Extract from pp. 241–244, 247–251].

Frederick Pollock, et al., *Principles Of Contract At Law And In Equity: A Treatise On The General Principles Concerning The Validity Of Agreements In The Law Of England And America.* 3rd American ed.; compiled from the 7th English ed, "Wall's Pollock on Contracts", with annotations and additions by Gustavus II. Wald and Samuel Williston. [Rpt. Littleton, Colorado: Rothman & Co., 1988] New York: Baker, Voorhis, 1906. [Extract from pp. 1–9, 373–4, 376]. (quote from p. 527).

W. J. V. Windeyer, "The Mental Elements of Tort and Crime", in *Lectures On Legal History* (2d), (Sydney, Aus.: Law Book Company Of Australasia, 1957) at pp. 21, 22 [Extracts from pp. 22, 21].

Chapter 16

W.J.V. Windeyer. *Lectures On Legal History.* 2nd ed. Sydney, Aus.: Law Book Company Of Australasia, 1957. [Extract from pp. 19–21, 63–64].

Frances Bowes Sayre. "Mens Rea." *Harvard Law Review* (1931–1932) 45; 974–1026.

Sir Patrick Devlin. 'The Enforcement of Morals'. (The 1959 Maccabaean Lecture In Jurisprudence).

Proceedings Of The British Academy (1959) XlV; 129–151. [Extract from pp. 129–130, 133–142, 148.] (quote from pp. 143–4).

H.L.A. Hart. *Law, Liberty And Morality. The Harry Camp Lectures.* Stanford, Ca.: Stanford University, 1963. [Extract from pp. 13, 16, 19–22, 30–37, 48–50].

Chapter 17

Excerpt from *The New Jerusalem Bible*, copyright © 1966, 1985 by Darton, Longman, & Todd, Ltd and Doubleday, a division of Random House, Inc. Reprinted by permission.

Deuteronomy 19:16–21, in *The Holy Bible*, New International Version ([1973] 2011). Available at www.biblegateway.com.

Qur'an 5:45, in *The Meaning of the Glorious Qur'an*, trans. Marmaduke Mohammad Pickthall (New York: Knopf, 1930). Available at www.sacred-texts.com/isl.

Cesare Beccaria. *An Essay on Crimes and Punishments with a Commentary by M. de Voltaire.* New ed., corrected. Albany: W.C. Little, 1872. [Extract from pp. 74–76, 94–95, 97–102, 104–106].

Restorative Justice and Sentencing Circles: Digest of *R. v. J.J.*, 2004 NLCA 81.

Chapter 18

Menno Boldt and J. Anthony Long. "Tribal Philosophies And The Canadian Charter Of Rights And Freedoms." Ethnic and Racial Studies (1984) 7: 4; 478–49.

Excerpts from the *Canadian Charter Of Rights And Freedoms*, being Part I Of *The Constitution Act*, 1982. [Extract from sections 1, 2, 7, 8, 10, 11, 12, 15, and 24].

R. v. Stillman [1997] 1 S.C.R. 607, No. 34. Disclosure.

R. v. Zundel, [1992] 2 S.C.R. 731.

Chapter 19

Paul Groarke, 'A Primer on the Application of the International Law in Canada' (2004, 2008).

R. Sullivan, *Driedger on the Construction of Statutes*, 3e. (Toronto: Butterworths, 1994), p. 330.

MacCormick, Neil, "Sovereignty: Myth and Reality" in Scottish Affairs, no. 11, Spring 1995, 1–13. Used by permission of the publisher.